# Racism, Colonialism, and Indigeneity in Canada

## A READER

Edited by **Martin J. Cannon** | **Lina Sunseri**   SECOND EDITION

**OXFORD**
UNIVERSITY PRESS

# OXFORD
## UNIVERSITY PRESS

Oxford University Press is a department of the University of Oxford.
It furthers the University's objective of excellence in research, scholarship,
and education by publishing worldwide. Oxford is a registered trade mark of
Oxford University Press in the UK and in certain other countries.

Published in Canada by
Oxford University Press
8 Sampson Mews, Suite 204,
Don Mills, Ontario M3C 0H5 Canada

www.oupcanada.com

**Library and Archives Canada Cataloguing in Publication**

Racism, colonialism, and indigeneity in Canada : a reader / edited by
Martin J. Cannon & Lina Sunseri.—Second edition.

Includes bibliographical references.
ISBN 978-0-19-902051-5 (softcover)

1. Native peoples—Colonization—Canada.   2. Native peoples—Canada—
Social conditions.   3. Native peoples—Canada—Government relations.
4. Indians, Treatment of—Canada.   5. Racism—Canada.   6. Canada—Race
relations.   I. Cannon, Martin John, 1969-, editor   II. Sunseri, Lina, editor

E78.C2R32 2017        305.897'071        C2017-902563-5

Cover and interior design: Sherill Chapman

Oxford University Press is committed to our environment.
This book is printed on Forest Stewardship Council® certified paper
and comes from responsible sources.

MIX
Paper from
responsible sources
FSC
www.fsc.org   FSC® C004071

Printed and bound in Canada
2  3  4 — 21  20  19  18

# Contents

# Foreword

## Indigeneity and the Politics of Nations: Racism, Colonialism, Citizenship, and Sovereignty

*Jodi A. Byrd*

Second editions of books are propitious occasions that call us to pause and reflect upon the temporal junctures and crossings that have brought words and ideas forward from then to now. They offer opportunities to revise and reframe, reconsider, or perhaps just state once more and again, the threads of continuity that ultimately serve to shape a conversation, inform a study, or even build a field. Over the past five years, Indigenous studies has gained immense ground in North America and across the other Anglophone Settler colonies in Australia and New Zealand. At once geopolitically specific and theoretically expansive, the continued circulation of indigeneity as a critical concept within academic disciplines and activist movements reflects deeper continuities of Indigenous presences and knowledges that have survived centuries of invasions, dispossessions, removals, and devastating losses. As the recent #IdleNoMore movement and the Standing Rock Sioux #NoDAPL protests demonstrate, Indigenous Peoples and communities continue to be at the forefront of struggles for justice, fighting against the extractive logics of tar sands, hydroelectric damming, and pipelines that imperil the fragile balance between humans and all other life and affect how we relate to one another on the lands we cohabitate. As corporations risk turning water into fire and setting the planet to burn in the pursuit of accumulation, Indigenous communities across North America continue to defend their lands through assertions of the sovereign responsibilities of relationalities, treaties, and government-to-government negotiations and diplomacies.

Yet, as much as Indigenous Peoples continue to resist and struggle toward decolonial futures, settlement in North America continues to entrench itself through the shifting terrains of liberal and neoconservative regimes in a push–pull of dominance that prioritizes profit through the gendered and racial violences of colonial capitalism. Understanding that entrenchment is a daunting task, one that in many ways draws us from the brutal and embodied specificities of militarized police violence affecting individuals to the larger scales of occupations, land seizures, pipelines, drones, walled borders, and the barrage of rocks and bombs killing thousands. We are witnessing a doubling-down of State-sanctioned violence targeting black, trans, queer, Indigenous, Muslim, immigrant, and women's bodies. At the same time, social media documents for us a daily barrage of racial aggressions aimed at already embattled groups as white masculinity in particular asserts the primacy of its own precarity and insists that the cornerstones of its cultural heritage are under egregious assault. State institutions meanwhile assert civility as the foundational principle of inclusivity to test the limits of legality to unhire minorities, dismantle programs, and curb political activism and mobilizations against oppression. Violence is becoming spectacularized, and then quickly normalized as entirely appropriate and proportionate when targeted against individuals, groups, and peoples already constructed as irrational, uncivil, hostile, criminal, and inhuman. Inequality and precarity are, by their very nature, the domain of nation-state politics, and sovereignty and borders are both sites of endangerment and violation as well as signs of protection and safety from harm. Within the dialectics of biopolitical power, life, death, property, and the assertion of self are all accomplished within and through the realms of sovereignty.

One of the major contributions that Indigenous studies has made to such conversations is the attention scholars in the field continue to give to the ways that law and sovereignty define, construct, and enact themselves through the logics of colonialism whether it is in the policing the boundaries between civilization and savagery that produce Indianness as a sign of difference or through the seizure of territoriality at the limits of legality and through the force of law *making* that is built on the ruptures and innovations of procedures and precedents enacted to codify possession and dispossession—of land, of status, of language, culture, and identity. Always pushing for the horizon through discovery and the justice of rationality, Settler nation-states assert their authority by denying the rights and existence of anything standing before them. Indigenous intellectualism represents a return push toward righting relationships and affirming presence, and it is a vital counter to the death-dealing regimes of Settler politics. Despite being absolutely necessary and foundational to producing knowledge about the past and present, however, Indigenous studies in academia remains fragile at best, and easily violable through appropriation and ventriloquism, orientalism and citational practices that amplify only a few select voices, and the machinations of institutional administrators seeking to curtail academic freedom, faculty governance, and critical thinking more broadly.

That is why a book such as Martin Cannon and Lina Sunseri's *Racism, Colonialism, and Indigeneity: A Reader* is so important in establishing the rigorous methodological stakes for the research Indigenous scholars undertake in academic institutions. Since it was first published, this book has helped cohere the shape of Indigenous studies in Canada by drawing together an array of Indigenous scholars to provide thorough documentation of the cultural, historical, and political contexts facing Indigenous Peoples and their communities in North America. With expansive interdisciplinarity, this collection encourages us to trace, understand, and confront how racism and colonialism produce dominant stereotypes of Indianness that underscore the specific laws and policies impacting Indigenous Peoples with careful precision. At the same time, the scholarship included here signals the strength and vitality of Indigenous research methodologies and scholarship in offering strategies not just for survival but for decolonial reconfigurations of treaty relationships that move beyond Settler gestures of recognition or reconciliation. In evoking a range of Indigenous traditions, stories, and philosophies, the case studies, pedagogies, and critical reflections included throughout offer a multiplicity of theoretical perspectives on Settler colonialism and indigeneity. Finally and most significantly, Cannon and Sunseri invite readers—whether newcomers to or experts in the field—to participate in the shared responsibilities that the imbricated, intersectional, and gendered histories of racism and colonialism necessitate for each of us living on Indigenous lands.

As each of these essays thoughtfully and carefully demonstrate, Indigenous Peoples have borne the brunt of historical violations and harms within and beyond the legalities of Settler States, and that is because sexual assault, educational disparities, violence, imprisonment, and trauma go hand in hand with colonization, genocide, theft of lands, and the loss of languages and cultures. The quotidian and structural inequalities to which Indigenous Peoples, and Indigenous women and children in particular, are exposed are extreme, pernicious, and unrelenting. However, as Sarah Deer points out, naming such statistics an epidemic already serves the State when it even bothers to record and report the data at all. Epidemic is a word that connotes outbreak, pandemic, problem, or impurity. It catastrophizes, but it also delimits temporality. Epidemic is a word that, according to Deer, "deflects responsibility because it fails to acknowledge the agency of perpetrators and those who allow the problem to continue. The word also utterly fails to account for the crisis's roots in history and law. . . . rape is a fundamental result of colonialism, a history of violence reaching back centuries. An epidemic is a contagious disease; rape is a crime against humanity" (Deer, 2015: x). By all measures, asymmetrical violation and harm are always demonstrated to have disproportionately impacted Indigenous communities at rates higher than any other population in North America.

Such statistical data and metrics, however, often serve as a basis for the well-known story that even Settler institutions like to tell themselves about history—overwhelmed Indigenous Peoples lamentably succumbed to the inevitable impact of diseases, technological advances, alcohol, and the sheer number of newcomers. It is the regrettable tragedy of democracy, an unfortunate, blameless, and unavoidable cost that had to be paid to bring society to the contemporary fulfillment of its promised freedoms and equalities. Existing on, but not using the land efficiently, Indians and their land required improvement to meet the needs and standards of civilized society. One of the core tenets underlying Indigenous theorizations is the necessity of spatializing and reorienting antiracist, decolonial, and queer struggles against State-sanctioned violence through an attentiveness to the very land upon which those oppressions occur. It is a theoretical move done at risk of erasure because it is a move always made within the context of an ongoing colonialism that denies its own existence through the enactment and acknowledgment of violence. The colonization of Indigenous lands in Settler States is accomplished precisely through the inequalities that stem from the historical and ongoing structures of enforced and indentured labour; criminalization of borders; illegalization of bodies and populations; and surveillance of thought, speech, and actions within a deepening entrenchment of anti-intellectualism and culturally produced ignorance.

While Indigenous Peoples understand the quotidian meanings of colonialism through the embodied and felt historical experiences of violence, Settlers and non-natives living on Indigenous lands have an obligation to apprehend their place in Settler colonialism as well. Certainly, the structures of settlement were enacted to benefit Settlers; what is more pernicious is how those structures, once in place, are then operationalized to dispossess everyone whether they are Indigenous, Settler, or arrivants. The Indigenous scholars that Martin Cannon and Lina Sunseri bring together in this collection provide insights into how racism and colonialism are imbricated systems of dispossession, but more, they provide tools to disrupt the precarities that threaten us all and provide strategies for alternative futures that draw on Indigenous philosophies grounded in land, kinship, stories, and traditions.

# All Our Relations: Acknowledgements

This anthology of writings stems from conversations we have had about them as scholarly works, and in general, since meeting each other as graduate students at York University in the mid-1990s. Faced with the formidable responsibility of teaching courses concerning social justice, Indigenous peoples, and racism, we have incorporated these writings in our classes and discussions, and we have spoken about them with friends, family, colleagues, students, and, sometimes, the authors themselves. In each case, we feel they contain instructive insights, indispensable to those wishing to explore and combat racism and colonialism in Canada.

As colleagues and friends, we share much in common as Indigenous peoples. We are both Haudenosaunee—our fathers English and Italian respectively. We also share in our experience of post-secondary education wherein, as students of the Sociology of Race and Ethnic Relations, it seemed at times that racism and colonialism—and its impact on Indigenous peoples—did not fare centrally enough. The inspiration for this book thus emerged, at least in part, out of our undergraduate frustrations. We hope this anthology—and pedagogical components—will work toward fostering change within the academy, and for younger generations of Indigenous and non-Indigenous peoples.

There are many people to be acknowledged for the realization of this book. We especially wish to extend our gratitude to Oxford University Press for their diligence and enthusiasm at every stage of the publication process. Nancy Reilly, Jennifer Mueller, Jodi Lewchuk, Jennifer Wallace, and Jessie Coffey helped us to realize the first edition of *Racism, Colonialism, and Indigeneity in Canada*. We wish to thank Ian Gibson and Darcey Pepper for helping us to realize the second edition of this book.

A number of colleagues and friends have supported and challenged us over the years and also need to be acknowledged. We are grateful to Trish Monture (Mohawk), Celia Haig-Brown, Bonita Lawrence (Miqmaw), Taiaiake Alfred (Mohawk), Beverley Jacobs (Mohawk), and Susan Dion (Lenape). Martin wishes to acknowledge colleagues, including Verna St Denis (University of Saskatchewan), Sherene Razack and Rinaldo Walcott (OISE/University of Toronto). Lina wishes to acknowledge her colleagues at Brescia, Western University, in particular Lisa Jakubowski. While we are both responsible for the articles, openers, and pedagogical material we have included in this book, these individuals have in some way supported us and shaped our ideas and thinking.

We wish to acknowledge students who have assisted us in realizing this second edition, including Sam Spady and Alice Meyers, both of whom provided research assistance. Martin also wishes to thank Leslie Thielen Wilson and Susanne Waldorf.

We also thank friends and family for loving and supporting us over the many years. Martin wishes to thank his parents and immediate and extended family. Lina wishes to thank her parents and immediate and extended family.

But most importantly, we want to give our thanks to the Creator, Sky Woman, and All Our Relations for nurturing us and providing us with daily gifts.

# Not Disappearing
## An Introduction to the Text

Our second edition of *Racism, Colonialism, and Indigeneity in Canada* follows on the heels of several significant developments and events in Canada. Since 2011, following from the publication of our first edition, the Idle No More movement that began in 2012–2013 galvanized the Canadian public by drawing attention to Settler colonial laws and policies that negatively impact the lives of Indigenous peoples. We witnessed as part of this movement, a refusal on behalf of the State to negotiate with Chief Teresa Spence. Until only recently, it was the same State that refused to address through an inquiry the violence directed toward women and also two spirited peoples. And in 2015, Canada's Truth and Reconciliation Commission (TRC) released its final report listing 94 "calls to action" necessary to repair the harm imposed by Indian Residential Schools (IRS).

The violence enacted on Indigenous communities via IRS is far from being a matter of the historical past. In fact, Cindy Blackstock (2007) has argued that IRS, while they may have closed their doors, have morphed into child welfare practices. Canadian courts have agreed with Blackstock, and the Canadian human rights tribunal, in issuing a recent judgment that argues Canada discriminates against children on reserves, especially because "on-reserve child welfare receives up to 38% less funding than elsewhere." Combined, these issues point to a set of critical issues in need of reconciliation in Canada; notably, the need to acknowledge that Settler colonialism is what Patrick Wolfe (2006) has referred to as a "structure" and not "event" that remains in place today; and also, the need for a set of theoretical perspectives written by Indigenous scholars in particular that address the past and present history of Settler colonial wrongdoing.

The range of theoretical perspectives written by and about Indigenous North Americans on race and Settler colonialism is vast in scope. This book could not possibly capture all of these voices. Instead, we seek to provide an initial overview of perspectives, as well as some of the issues, themes, and concerns that have been raised when it comes to addressing matters of Settler colonialism and Indigeneity. Some of these perspectives draw attention to the structural and interpersonal impacts of racism on the lives of our peoples and nations. Others draw attention to the obligations of Indigenous peoples and Settler colonialists where understanding, acknowledging, and taking responsibility for systemic colonial injustices is concerned. We would like to suggest that early nation-to-nation agreements represent an important set of organizing principles where realizing the shared responsibility to address colonial injustice is concerned, and toward a renewal and rejuvenation of Settler–Indigenous relations.

Turtle Island is a word that is commonly used by Indigenous peoples to refer to North America. For Haudenosaunee[1] (sometimes called the Six Nations or Iroquois) our story of creation describes how this land came to be. Our elders tell us that before this earth was created, there was only water and water beings. There also existed the sky world and sky beings. One day, Sky Woman fell from this world and brought with her the medicines: the corn, squash, beans, tobacco, and strawberries that sustain us. The water beings laid Sky Woman and her medicines upon a turtle's back and Mother Earth was created. This version of the creation story, albeit shortened for our purposes here, has been told in slightly different ways. Our elders have kept these teachings alive, even when forbidden by racist, colonial, and genocidal legislation (Posluns, 2007) and we give Yawa:ko (thanks) for their ongoing resistance.

We take the maintenance of our traditional stories seriously. We are also concerned with the memory of historic treaties made on a nation-to-nation basis between our ancestors and the newcomers to Turtle Island. We believe these agreements hold original instructions and are key to showing how Indigenous and non-Indigenous peoples alike might address colonial injustice and racism. The Two-Row Wampum or Guswentah in particular is an agreement that is familiar to us as Haudenosaunee scholars. A historic wampum—a beaded belt embroidered from fresh water shells—serves to formalize or "certify" original nation-to-nation agreements. Wampum are of great significance to our ancestors because they function to formalize agreements and, as Patricia Monture-Angus (1999: 36–7) has explained, were neither easily forgotten nor destroyed.

The Two-Row Wampum dates to 1613 and is represented on a beaded belt which contains two purple beaded lines against a white backdrop. As Williams and Nelson (1995: 3) have described, "The two row wampum . . . symbolizes the river of life on which the Crown's sailing ship and the Haudenosaunee canoe both travel." The three white rows are recognized as symbolizing an everlasting "peace, friendship, and respect between the two nations" (quoted in Johnston, 1986: 32; also see Monture-Angus, 1999: 37). Peace, friendship, and respect—as represented by the three white rows—embody the basis upon which we are "bounded together" and also interdependent (Mackey, 2016: 135; see also Hill, 2008: 30 and Turner, 2006: 45). The metaphor of the European vessel and Confederacy canoe functions to characterize two distinct jurisdictions which were ordained in 1664 to co-exist independently (Borrows, 1997: 164–5). Originally exchanged with Dutch traders, and subsequently the British Crown, the Two-Row Wampum belt speaks of separate jurisdictions. As Johnston (1986: 11) writes:

> The two were to co-exist as independent entities, each respecting the autonomy of the other. The two rows of purple wampum, representing the two governments, run parallel, never crossing. The two vessels travel together, as allies, but neither nation tries to steer the other's vessel. In the relationship envisioned by the Two Row Wampum, neither government has the authority to legislate for the other.

In the twenty-first century, the Two-Row Wampum continues to be of tremendous significance. For the Six Nations Confederacy, the Guswentah establishes an historic relationship with the British Crown as an independent nation and also as allies. Moreover, the Two-Row Wampum embodies the principle of separate jurisdictions. This is something that other Indigenous scholars on Turtle Island have highlighted in their work. For example, Lynn Gehl (2014) reminds all Canadians that the original spirit of the Royal Proclamation of 1763 and the 1764 Treaty at Niagara were both intended to enable Algonquin Anishinaabeg to live as sovereign nations practising mino-pimadiziwin (the good life). Leanne Simpson (2008, and in this volume) also talks about the treaties made among ourselves as nations, including Gdoo-naaganinaa, our Dish With One Spoon, intended to provide Haudenosaunee and Anishinabe with a means of realizing separate jurisdictions within a shared territory. From this perspective, racism and Settler colonialism—in seeking as they do to disrupt and restrict the lives of Indigenous peoples ranging from issues of land administration to the ability for us to determine our own peoples—constitutes a British "foot" in the Haudenosaunee canoe.

Although we use racism here to mean a violation of original principles set out in original nation-to-nation agreements, racism has been and can be defined academically in several different ways. Henry and Tator (2006: 5) define racism as a set of "assumptions, attitudes, beliefs, and behaviours of individuals as well as to the institutional policies, process, and practices that flow from those understandings." Combined, racism refers to societal disadvantages experienced by a people or group. Racism can be further divided into the forms it takes in society, including individual, systemic, and structural racism (ibid., 350–2).

Individual racism stems from an individual's conscious and/or personal prejudice (ibid., 350). It refers to outward and overt attitudes of intolerance or bigotry. Systemic racism refers to policies and practices that result in the exclusion of individuals, or that work to effect considerable disadvantages on a specific group. Systemic racism can be both institutional and structural; the former referring to "racial discrimination that derives from individuals carrying out the dictates of others who are prejudiced or of a prejudiced society" (ibid., 352). Lastly, structural racism refers to inequalities that are "rooted in the system-wide operation of a society" (ibid., 352). They refer to practices that "exclude substantial numbers . . . of particular groups from significant participation in major social institutions" (ibid., 352).

Racism is not always obvious, overt, or even impolite. Indeed, Henry and Tator have focused on racism as it is effected in liberal and democratic societies like Canada. They define racism as essentially "democratic," describing it as "any set of justificatory arguments and mechanisms that permit individuals to maintain racist beliefs while championing democratic values" (ibid., 19). It is through 12 popular discourses that racism is structured and effected, including the discourse of denial, political correctness, colour-blindness, equal opportunity, blaming the victim, white victimization, reverse racism, binary polarization, moral panic, multiculturalism, liberal tolerance, and the discourse of national identity (for a detailed discussion, see Henry and Tator, 2006).

We take these academic definitions of racism seriously, but as discussed, we argue that within an Indigenous context racist ideologies and practices violate ancient principles set out in the Two-Row Wampum among other original agreements made between Indigenous and Settler populations. The treaties and original principles between Indigenous and newcomer populations have not been fully respected but the spirit of this relationship—however wounded it has become—cannot be so easily broken. Indeed, it is our objective to first revisit the original principles and to remind all future generations, Indigenous or otherwise, of its terms.

Each author in this collection is re-telling the story of "settlement" (read colonization) through Indigenous eyes, hearts, minds, and souls and in the process has never forgotten, metaphorically speaking, that historic treaty principles were originally meant to guide us in our relationship with one another. The one party has always acted accordingly with respect to original principles and intention of the original agreements, and throughout the centuries has reminded the colonizer to keep its foot out of its canoe; in short to respect the autonomy of Indigenous peoples as we have respected Settler colonists. The voices in this collection will vary somewhat because of the multiplicity of our experiences, but we feel that we share in common a commitment to restore the original balance upon which the two entities ought to be travelling. We believe that in order to restore balance, each side needs to follow treaty principles and to know of the historical forces that upset them and brought about much disruption on Turtle Island. Once that happens, then healing can begin and a new peaceful and just journey re-taken.

The word "Haudenosaunee," or People of the Longhouse, is one that we use to describe our individual sense of identity and well-being. And while we might be just as comfortable with using words like "Ukwehuwé" (the Original People), "Onyota'a:ka" (People of the Standing Stone), or even "Six Nations," we resist the concept of "Indian" to describe our collective identity. Naming is a powerful act of self-determination; in naming ourselves Haudenosaunee we are explicitly connecting ourselves to the League of the Six Nations, (re)claiming our connections with the past, present, and future peoples who make up that League wherever they or their spirits might reside in Turtle Island.

We are bound together as Haudenosaunee through kinship and clan affiliation and have an interdependent responsibility that therefore guides our every thought and act. As Monture (2008: 156) writes:

> [O]ne must understand something of the person's tribal tradition as this grounds who they are, as well as the symbols and styles they will use. . . . my name grounds me in the gift of words Creator gave me. It is both identity and direction. It is strength and responsibility. It is this location, as Mohawk citizen and woman, which guides the way I see the patterns that in turn ground my understanding of who I am and what I know.

Both of us are positioned as Ukwehuwé, Onyota'a:ka, and Turtle Clan. Not all Haudenosaunee are Longhouse or possess traditional names. "Yeliwi:saks" is the spiritual name belonging to Lina assigned to her by her clan mother which translates as "She Is Gathering Stories/Knowledge." Through the naming, she carries the responsibility of gathering stories and sharing the power of these words with others. Naming ourselves Onyota'a:ka is a powerful act of decolonization as it (re)juvenates our national identity, and tells the rest of the world that we were and are nations and are calling on others to see and treat us as such. The history of governing ourselves dates back many centuries before the arrival of ha dih nyoh (white settler).

This book stems in part from our individual and collective sense of resistance to the term "Indian," as it is one that embodies the historic and contemporary violation of Guswentah among other original agreements made between Settler and Indigenous populations, and the autonomous right of Indigenous nations to determine their own citizenry. "Indian" embodies the very first act of colonial injustice and we believe that neither decolonization nor self-determination can be realized unless we challenge this history that institutionalized Indianness. We agree with other Ukwehuwé scholars in seeing the act of self-determination to begin first with the Self (Monture, 1999). We also agree with Indigenous scholars who speak of their own nationhood and resist foreign impositions that require the terms "Aboriginal," "First Nations," and "Indian" to be used when describing Indigenous people (Alfred, 2005). We must begin to (re)identify ourselves as Indigenous nations based on our own individual peoplehood and kinship organization (Andersen, 2014, and in this volume).

Indigenous peoples became Indians under a legal classification that did not distinguish between their linguistic and cultural differences or between the multiplicity of Indigenous nations at the time. People became Indians so that the state could delimit the occupation of lands to Indians alone. It was through these sorting out of lands that the concretization of race as a social construct took place in Canada. Prior to colonization, Indigenous peoples defined themselves as distinct nations with their own socio-economic and political systems. Under Settler colonialism, the Canadian State treated all Indigenous nations as one "Indian race"; their oneness constructed by virtue of otherness. This process coincided with the conceptualization of Turtle Island as "terra nullius," a land imagined as empty and unoccupied. Property was therefore equated with whiteness (Harris, 1993); a process that allowed the colonizer to dispossess Indigenous nations of their lands.

Another motive for instituting the *Indian Act* was to protect Indians from outside land encroachments (Tobias, 1983). Early Indian policies sought to encourage the gradual civilization of the Indians through enfranchisement (ibid., 42). Enfranchisement aimed to assimilate the Indians of Canada. The premise of the legislation was simple: upon meeting certain criteria, men who were literate, free of debt, and of good moral character could (along with their "dependents") give up legal *Indian Act* status and become ordinary Canadians with all the according rights and privileges (ibid., 42) The title and premise of enfranchisement law reveals its racist underpinnings: one could not be a "civilized person" without giving up their Indian status. This is how racial categories were institutionalized. The first group to be racialized in Canada were the Indigenous peoples.

The *Indian Act* held the potential to reorganize Haudenosaunee kinship structures, in particular because they were both matrilocal and matrilineal prior to contact. Kinship structures were based on the clan system, where descent was passed through the women's line. This stood in opposition to the patrilineal registration criteria of the *Indian Act*. If one considers that in Canada, and in most of Europe, women were not considered persons but merely the property of men, the *Indian Act* clearly devalued females and the powers they enjoyed in some Indigenous nations. The process of establishing the category "Indian" was therefore also informed by patriarchal understandings. What this history suggests to us is that the colonial enterprise of racism is inseparable from (hetero)sexism and patriarchy as this has been argued by many Indigenous scholars (see Anderson, 2000; Cannon, forthcoming; Green, 2007; Lawrence, 2004; Monture, 1995; Smith, 2005, 2006; Sunseri, 2000, 2011).

Patriarchy has been defined as:

> [H]ierarchical relations between men and women, manifested in familial and social structures alike, in a descending order from an authoritarian—if oftentimes benevolent—male head, to male dominance in personal, political, cultural and social life, and to patriarchal families where the law of the father prevails. (Code, 2000: 378)

Patriarchy invaded our nations, transforming what was largely egalitarianism into an imbalanced set of gender relations. Jacobs (2014) defines patriarchy as none other than an attack on Indigenous womanhood following from colonization that has enabled a continued violence to be enacted on the bodies of Indigenous women. In this book, we wish to investigate these and other ideological transformations of race and gender, as well as the interlocking ways in which patriarchal notions were reaffirmed through Indian policy and other broader sets of social relations.

The *Indian Act* entrenches a set of legalized parameters involving lands. As Satzewich and Wotherspoon (1993) have pointed out, the *Indian Act* provided for the appropriation of Indigenous territories and the accumulation of capital. "The land was acquired [through] the forcible and relentless dispossession of Indigenous peoples, the theft of their territories, and the implementation of legislation and policies designed to affect their total disappearance as peoples" (Lawrence, 2002: 23). As such, "any theorizing of race must go beyond simple cultural politics [and] acknowledge the centrality of broader political and economic developments" (Anderson quoted in Wallis and Fleras, 2009: xv). The history of capitalist relations is therefore inseparable from the emergence of race as a social construct in North America. Having said that, Canada has tried to erase its historical record. It is through storytelling that we might hope to reveal and redress the hidden dimensions of political economy. As Monture (2008: 156) notes, storytelling traditions are very common in our Indigenous nations, and "through our stories we learn who we are. These stories teach about identity and responsibility." Through the stories we gather by writers in this book, we openly name the *Indian Act* and all other socio-political structures imposed by the Canadian State as imperialist projects.

The *Indian Act* imposed an "elected" band council system of governance upon Indigenous nations. These councils were empowered to make by-laws and, upon approval of the Superintendent of Indian Affairs, to deal with all other concerns. An elective system of governance remained a choice for Indigenous nations in Canada until an amendment in 1895. After this time, the government delegated itself the authority to depose both chiefs and councillors of bands not following an elected system (Tobias, 1983: 46–7; *Indian Act* [S.C. 1895, c.35, s.3] reprinted in Venne, 1981: 141). It is important to acknowledge that the *Indian Act* represented an imposition to already established, hereditary forms of government. We see this as a blatant act of colonialism. In seeking to replace traditional governance with an elective model, the belief in European political superiority and higher civilization became institutionalized. These ways of thinking are not confined to the past: an example of ongoing beliefs about European superiority takes place whenever the contributions of Indigenous peoples are said to have offered nothing to the building of North American civilization (*The Globe & Mail*, 24 October 2008).

We want to suggest that the *Indian Act* and other policies represent the very first instance of racialized thinking and institutionalized racism in Canada. We also want to examine how an Indian/white colour line is established and constructed under Settler colonialism. The processes that continue today to uphold, maintain, and reproduce a set of racialized ways of thinking were put into place over 150 years ago. By Settler colonialism, we are referring to the process whereby Indigenous peoples were dispossessed of their lands through a series of genocidal acts, including the imposition of racial hierarchy through Indian status distinctions. Whiteness itself became constructed as the superior racial category and consequently white supremacy has become legitimatized and normalized (Razack, 2002).

The category of Indian is by no means a neutral one. It is a category established by Europeans to refer to Indigenous difference. These distinctions are inherent to processes of racialization and Settler colonialism. Kauanui (2008: 194) has written of the way in which taxonomies of race and blood quantum thinking are tied to theft of lands and the legal extinguishment of Indigenous peoples (see also Palmater, 2011). The legal extinguishment of Indians continues today in Canada as shown in the recent *McIvor* case (Cannon, 2014). Lina Sunseri (2011: 83) writes of the link between racialization and Settler colonialism as follows:

> The process whereby social relations between people became structured by attributing significant meaning to human biological and physical characteristics is referred to as racialization. This process helped to categorize colonized peoples as "races" that were "naturally different" from the colonizers. Of course, this categorization was never neutral but was closely linked to the formation of the unequal social and economic power relations inherent to colonialism.

The construction of Indigenous difference takes place through processes of racialization and additional sets of discursive practices. Edward Said (1978) referred to an "Orientalist" discourse, a Western construction of the Orient seen as essentially "different" and inferior to the "West." When Indians are represented as the Other in their own lands, they are seen in contrast to the colonizer. Within the binary framework of Self and Other, the outcomes provide for injustice. Indigenous peoples are pathologized as genetically inferior and deviant, while the Western Self becomes the progressive, modern, and civilized subject (Sunseri, 2007). It also provides the ideological justification for the ongoing dispossession of lands, the accompanying attack on sovereignty, and the maintenance of cultural imperialism required for the furthering of capitalist exploitation.

Issues of race are not easily introduced into conversations about the self-determination of Indigenous peoples. Indeed, as Rob Porter (1999: 158), a Seneca scholar, suggests, transforming conceptions of separate political status into matters of race works ultimately to erode the status of Indigenous peoples as citizens of separate sovereigns. He writes:

> Even though Indigenous society is rooted in a sovereignty separate and apart from American sovereignty, Indians today appear to be suggesting that they should be treated in the same way as such racial minority groups as African Americans and Asian Americans.... While it certainly is the case that Indians have long been thought to be of a different "race," protestations solely along racial lines can only serve to undermine the perception that Indian nations have a political existence separate and apart from that of the United States. (ibid., 154)

It is incumbent upon us as Ukwehuwé to think seriously about the issues raised by Porter. In contemplating our own Haudenosaunee existence, we acknowledge that original nation-to-nation agreements were made at the time of contact with Settler colonists, including Guswentah or Two-Row Wampum. These wampum do not make reference to Ukwehuwé as races of people, but rather sovereign nations whose inherent rights were granted by the Creator, or as Augie Fleras has put it, nations who "share the sovereignty of Canada through multiple and overlapping jurisdictions" (2009: 78). We also feel that before a timeless and unbroken assertion of sovereignty can be fully realized, it will be necessary to acknowledge that colonial injustice, racism, and sexism are inextricably linked, historically, and even still today.

To begin to think about the interconnections we are describing, it is important to revisit Canada's *Indian Act*, and more specifically, Indian status distinctions. The *Indian Act* exemplifies the institutionalized racism and patriarchy that has characterized colonial dominance. Indian status is the process whereby Indigenous nations became Indians for state administrative purposes. It refers to a set of practices, beliefs, and ways of thinking that made—and continue to make—Indianness compulsory. In order to restore our status as Indigenous nations, indeed as separate political entities, it will be important to think about these historic processes, and as the Cree leader Phil Fontaine has put it, "to move citizenship to the jurisdiction where it properly belongs and that is with First Nations governments." In this book, we want to suggest that asserting our political status as Indigenous nations is impossible without challenging histories of racialization.

We are not suggesting that the *Indian Act* is everything when it comes to determining Indigenous identities. Indeed, many Ukwehuwé prefer to talk of identity and citizenship—as we have in this Introduction—in nation-specific terms. But even as we assert our nation-based identities—indeed even as we know who it is that we are—the *Indian Act* continues to make possible the ongoing *involuntary enfranchisement* of our people. Involuntary enfranchisement takes place in Canada whenever a status Indian (registered under S. 6(2) of the *Indian Act*) marries and has children with a non-Indian person (Cannon, 2008: 15). This act of exogamous, "out-marriage" is by no means a neutral one because under current provisions it works to disenfranchise the grandchildren of women who married non-Indians before 1985. These individuals are a new class of "involuntarily enfranchised" Indians—their loss of legal entitlements is brought on by their parent's choice to marry non-Indians (ibid.).

Under amendments to the *Indian Act* in 1985, people were registered under one of seven different sections of the *Indian Act*. The major difference was between sections 6(1) and 6(2). S. 6(1) Indians passed on Indian status to offspring; s. 6(2) Indians passed on status to offspring only if married to an Indian (Magnet, 2003: 55). This matter of discrimination was raised at both the Superior Court and Court of Appeal levels in British Columbia in what is known as the *McIvor* case. It has been found that S. 6, in the conferring of Indian status, discriminates between the descendants of Indian men and women who married non-Indians because it is women's children who are registered under S. 6(2). The justices have all agreed unanimously: the treatment for Indian women and their children who claim Indian descent through them is unequal to that afforded to Indian men and their descendants (*McIvor v. Canada, Registrar, Indian and Northern Affairs*, 2007 BCSC 827 at 236). In recognizing that the grandchildren of *Indian women* were being treated differently than the grandchildren of *Indian men*, the *McIvor* case set the way for changes to federal Indian policy. It is now possible for the grandchildren of Indian women to be federally recognized as Indians (Cannon, 2014).

The history of S 6(2) of the *Indian Act* shows how pervasive the impact of sexism has been on the lives of Indigenous peoples. Of course sexism is not the only issue involved. Race and racism can also be used to describe historic injustices imposed by the *Indian Act*. The process whereby Indigenous nations became status Indians for state administrative purposes involves deeply racialized thinking. The issue itself is one that even our courts have been unable to address and acknowledge, even in progressive BC Court of Appeal judgments like the *McIvor* case. The case itself shows how intractable the institutionalized racism that characterizes the colonial present has become. The category "Indian" literally disappears below the surface of progressive politics and the law. Furthermore, in order to resist the category, we must appropriate and affirm its use. Bonita Lawrence describes the paradox we are highlighting. As she writes: "Legal categories . . . shape peoples' lives. They set the terms that individuals and communities must utilize even in resisting these categories" (2004: 230).

We concur with Robert Porter that being awarded racial minority status cannot be understood as the central issue facing Indigenous peoples today. Having said that, we feel it is important to raise as a matter of political scrutiny and critical reflection the process through which we became racialized as Indians in Canada. This thinking does not start with adopting racial minority status but in revisiting Indianness itself. If the very first act of historical and colonial injustice involved the re-naming of our diverse nations, then the urgency of dismantling racialized regimes cannot be underestimated or denied. If it is true that histories of racialization have made racism so intractable, so institutionalized, then we cannot be truly free of colonial domination if the racism directed at our nations remains intact.

In saying that we are nations and citizens of Indigenous nations, we are not only opposing the *Indian Act* and other racialized processes, we are also opposing an identity-making process that was—and is still today—key to the building of Canada as a nation (Thobani, 2007). We also want to encourage and further current discussions about the way in which non-white Settler populations are invited into racialized, nation state, and border imperialist ways of thinking about citizenship and belonging (Wallia, 2013; Sehdev, 2011; Phung, 2011; Madden, 2009; Lawrence and Amadahy, 2009). In that sense, this book is as much about white supremacy as it is about race, Settler colonialism, and Indigeneity. By refusing the category "Indian," we are asking all Canadians to think about how identity legislation plays a part in creating colonial settlements, and indeed lands for the taking. We are saying that our territories extend far beyond the identity classification schemes used to define them as "reserve-based lands." We want white and non-white Settler populations to think of themselves in relationship to Indigenous nations and not just the Canadian nation-state (Palmater, 2011; Thobani, 2007). We are asserting our political status as separate political entities, but we are simultaneously challenging the racialization and sexism that comprises Settler colonialism.

In contemplating the current Canadian political landscape, including developments related to Idle No More and TRC "calls to action," it will be necessary to address the matter of colonial reparations including a return to original treaty and nation-to-nation principles. Both in general and in light of recent developments we want readers of the second edition to consider the following: What sort of relationship do people want or see themselves as having with Indigenous nations? How are Canadians complicit in ongoing Settler colonialism? What is the responsibility of all Canadians to address historic wrongs? What sorts of symbolic and material work goes into the dispossession of lands, including the urban spaces we occupy and have always occupied? In addition to providing an overview of the writings of Indigenous peoples on and about race and Settler colonialism, it is our hope that this book will engage readers in anticolonial dialogue and action.

## Organization of the Book

As surely as racism is not disappearing in North America, neither are Indigenous peoples. We offer only a glimpse of the work that is being done to understand the interconnections between race, racialization, racism, sexism, and colonialism over the past centuries. In outlining the resistance to these systems of inequality, the book draws from multiple theoretical frameworks and crosses disciplinary boundaries. This is inevitable, if not desirable: many standpoints, views, identities, and backgrounds make up Indigenous knowledge and scholarship, and our experience is shaped by where we are located within communities, the academy, and mainstream society. These differences are sources of strength because the authors in this collection offer their own gifts, their own ways of knowing and being Indigenous on Turtle Island. Each is focused on specific themes, issues, and questions that offer a unique set of perspectives about race, racism, sexism, colonialism, and decolonization.

We open the book with a review of some central theoretical foundations. How are we to explain what has occurred, and continues to occur, to Indigenous people across this land? In Chapter 1, Taiaiake Alfred tackles this question by suggesting that "we need to understand clearly who and what constitutes our enemy," and the "imperial arrogance, the institutional and attitudinal expressions of the prejudicial biases inherent in European and Euro-American cultures." His chapter provides readers with a look at who/what this enemy is and how, through its own arrogance, it has actively participated in the imperialist and colonialist processes that have sought to dispossess Onkwehonwe from territorial, political, and cultural autonomy.

In Chapter 2, Leanne Simpson provides a context for understanding how it is that relations of "peace, mutual respect and mutual benefit" between nations (Settler and Indigenous) might be rejuvenated in accordance with traditional principles contained in early diplomatic and treaty relationships. She reminds us, as does Alfred, that we ought to look inward and at ancient principles rather than the status quo or Eurocentric worldviews where "resurgence, re-creation, and decolonizing" relationships is concerned.

Part Two of this book consists of two chapters outlining the history of nation-building in Canada and the construction of a racialized Indian Other. In Chapter 3, Deborah Doxtator shows how the idea of Indian was created using labels such as ferocious, drunkards, and primitive, and through stereotypical symbols like tepees, totem poles, and face paint. These symbols persist in the colonial imagination and have little to do with the actual people of the past or present. Doxtator shows how "Indians" have been portrayed in history textbooks: either as tools, as threats, as allies; nevertheless always secondary to the official heroes and builders of the nation. Colonialism is hardly ever taken up seriously in history textbooks; instead it is conceptualized as "settlement," as something that "just happened." In this way, we concur with Doxtator: the mythology of the "two founding nations" and the disappearing Indian endures within the minds of most Canadians. It is no wonder Indigenous youth feel alienated by the educational system. How are they able to see themselves reflected in textbooks if the history of their ancestors is not honestly represented?

Thomas King picks up on this review by Doxtator in Chapter 4. He is concerned with the Indian that exists in the Settler imagination. The imaginary itself requires that Indigenous peoples always be disappearing in order to make possible, among other things, the recovery and recuperation of Settler sovereignty and lands dispossession. Much has been invested in a representation of Indigenous peoples, from popular culture to theatrics, in order to rid the state of "the inconvenient Indian."

Part Three of the book looks at how Indigenous territories and notions of peoplehood have been shaped by Settler colonialism. In Chapter 5, Bonita Lawrence challenges the dominant historical narratives of Canada and rewrites them from an Indigenous perspective. She examines the impact of racism and colonialism on Indigenous lands and communities in what is now called Eastern Canada. Although we cannot homogenize Indigenous experiences with colonialism, there are similar patterns that link them. In Chapter 6, Chris Andersen addresses the matter of nationhood, in particular state-based and European models that do little to centre matters of relationality and kinship organization. He emphasizes the importance of peoplehood, a concept that exists well beyond racialized categories imposed by the state, as well as some of the theoretical literature involving nationhood.

Racism and colonialism have had a profound influence on Indigenous identities. How we see ourselves, how others perceive us, how we treat each other, and how we treat those outside of our groups is all shaped by racializing colonial discourses. These discourses have very little to do with traditional ways of being and governing ourselves. In Chapter 7, Martin Cannon illuminates how Canadian courts perceive of us and work to re-establish and further entrench the category Indian in turn failing to address nation based definitions of identity and belonging. Courts in particular perpetuate a Eurocentric fiction that separates "woman" from "Indian" such that the colonizing and historically racialized process whereby Indigenous women became Indians is left unaddressed. The effect has not only been to recuperate

Settler sovereignty and theft of lands, it also disavows traditional ways of thinking about gender, identity, and belonging.

In Chapter 8, Chris Finley provides an overview of efforts being put into place by GLBTQ2 peoples to realize sexuality and erotic expression. She is less concerned with courts of law, and the vested ways in which they seek to impose heteronormative and Eurocentric ways of thinking about gender and sexuality than she is with matters of resurgence and re-vitalization. Her work nuances the ways in which heteropatriarchy is being contested, and opens "sex positive and queer friendly discussions of sexuality in Native communities and Native Studies."

Part Five addresses issues of gender violence affecting Indigenous women, by examining the interconnection between Settler colonialism, racism, sexism, and patriarchy. Undoubt-edly centuries of devaluation of Indigenous peoples in general, and of women in particular, has led to an attack on egalitarian gender relations, and an epidemic of gendered violence, as the reported Missing and Murdered Indigenous Women (MMIW) cases illustrate.

Fay Blaney, in Chapter 9, describes the work that the Aboriginal Women's Action Net-work (AWAN) has done since 1995 to raise awareness of the sexism and violence directed against Indigenous women, and to bring justice and social change for Indigenous women. She provides examples of the resistance and challenges AWAN has met in their work, from police institutions, media, and some Indigenous organizations. These events, however, did not stop AWAN from ensuring that women escaping from discrimination and violence had a place to go to for support and aid in their demand for justice. This chapter illustrates that Indigenous women, despite the many forms of oppression, discrimination, and violence, are resilient, strong, and can work collaboratively for transformative change.

In Chapter 10, Anita Olsen Harper highlights the Sisters in Spirit Campaign to bring awareness of the Missing and Murdered Indigenous Women cases of Canada. In her chap-ter, she shows how through colonialism, Indigenous women began to be treated as inferior to men, lost their traditional powers in their nations, and faced multiple forms of oppres-sion. Mainstream media, police, and the Canadian State, she further argues, have largely ignored the alarming high numbers of MMIW. Hence, justice has failed Indigenous women. However, through efforts by Indigenous communities, supportive allies, and increased awareness of the MMIW issue, she is hopeful that a future positive engagement with relevant government and non-government sources could lead to an end to this epidemic gendered sexual violence.

Part Six addresses issues of belonging, displacement, and the dismantling of traditional family life. The Sixties Scoop and transracial adoption have demonstrably impacted on tradi-tional family relations. Many children were taken away from their biological families because they were deemed unfit to parent. In Chapter 11, Shandra Spears explores her own personal narrative, looking at the impact these policies had on children who later grew up discon-nected from their birth families and communities. These are traumatic experiences that were part of a genocidal attempt by the state to get rid of the "Indian problem." By appropriating these children and placing them into white families and communities, it was thought that Indians would just disappear.

Lynn Gehl in Chapter 12 addresses the matter of unstated paternity, an issue that has impacted profoundly Indigenous families, identity, and belonging. The *Indian Act* currently perpetuates patriarchal understandings by instituting the imperative that women state the paternity of children at the time of registration. She argues that the "negative presumption of unstated paternity"—the idea that one's father is not an Indian—has resulted in the displacement of numerous children from Indigenous nations.

Part Seven of the book explores Indigenous rights, citizenship, and nationalism through Indigenous perspectives. In Chapter 13, Bonita Lawrence examines contemporary self-government and comprehensive claims policy negotiations. She convincingly argues that these negotiations are still constraining Indigenous peoples, as the Canadian government ultimately still holds more power in the process, thereby limiting Indigenous rights of sovereignty, and often further reducing Indigenous lands. The current negotiations processes do not, then, correspond to the original principles of a nation-to-nation relationship between Indigenous nations and Canada.

In Chapter 14, Audra Simpson shows how Indigenous rights to self-determination are tied to sovereignty over matters of membership to Indigenous nations. Focusing on her own Kahnawake Mohawk Nation, she explores the complexities and contentions surrounding discourses and practices of citizenship. In her chapter, she covers traditional criteria of membership, the impact of the *Indian Act* on "band" membership rules, the contentious "blood quantum" rule, as well as the various lived experiences of citizenship that do exist in her community. All of these contemporary forms of citizenship, Simpson reminds us, are linked to colonialism, and are issues that the nation must confront as it proceeds to decolonize itself.

Part Eight of the book addresses Indigenous education from a perspective that centres critically anticolonial and reform-based efforts that forgo a culturalist line. In light of calls by Canada's Truth and Reconciliation Commission and the Canadian Association of Deans of Education to have all Canadians take responsibility for colonial injustices, we highlight authors who ask in particular how Settler populations might work to create programmatic and pedagogical initiatives and efforts aimed at Settler decolonizing, colonial reparations, and relationships rejuvenation.

Verna St Denis, a Cree/Métis scholar, revisits the usage of culture theory in Indigenous education and questions, in Chapter 15, the extent to which studying culture can disrupt unequal power relations that exist between Indigenous and Settler Canadians. She argues that the current focus on cultural difference and incommensurability does little to displace the unequal power relations that have arisen in Settler colonial society. This prevents all students—both Settler and Indigenous—from thinking critically about colonial realities and the strategies that might be used to repair them.

In Chapter 16, Martin Cannon is concerned with the building, maintenance, and rejuvenation of Settler–Indigenous relationships and learning. He asks how it is possible to engage learners, especially white Settler, migrant, and migrant Indigenous populations to think about Settler colonialism and white supremacy. He asks how teacher education might be invigorated and transformed at this critical moment in time so that all Canadians are better able to consider, name, know about, and challenge an investment in colonial dominance and complicity.

Part Nine of the book covers issues of violence and criminality as experienced by Indigenous peoples. In Chapter 17, Joyce Green starts with a critical overview of the freezing death of Neil Stonechild and the public and legal responses to it. Green links systemic and institutional racism and demands that Canadian society take racism in all its existing forms before social cohesion can take place. Only then, can justice be delivered to the family of Neil Stonechild and others who froze to death—as well as those facing similar abuses and violence at the hands of the police.

In Chapter 18, Patricia Monture-Okanee and Mary Ellen Turpel offer an Indigenous perspective on criminal justice. They do so by deconstructing concepts embedded in the Canadian criminal justice system: justice, equal access to justice, equitable treatment, and respect. They also examine concepts such as alternative justice, a parallel justice system, and a separate justice system. They suggest that criminal justice be looked at in a holistic manner: its institutions, norms, and how these have treated Indigenous people. For justice to be truly served, it is necessary to acknowledge and respect Indigenous difference as well as their separate political status.

In Part Ten we link poverty with colonial histories of dispossession that left many nations and communities in the economic margins of one of the wealthiest countries in the world. In Chapter 19, Pam Palmater discusses the Idle No More Movement that began in the fall of 2012, and took Canadians by surprise. This movement was initiated by four women who intended to make Canadians more aware of the negative impacts that Bill C-45 would have on our environment, and in particular on Indigenous territories and peoples. As Palmater covers in the chapter, Idle No More was also effective in bringing awareness of the ongoing poor socio-economic conditions affecting Indigenous nations due to centuries of colonialism. Idle No More has been a call for action to all Canadians to work together to end colonialism and improve the socio-economic conditions under which Indigenous communities are currently living.

Cindy Baskin, in Chapter 20, shows how the current homelessness of Indigenous youth in cities is linked to colonialism, in particular child welfare policies. She focuses on policy-based and systemic barriers that have contributed to the marginalization of Indigenous peoples and families. She concludes by making some proposals for positive change for Indigenous youth and the general Indigenous population.

In Part 11, we explore problems involving racism and colonialism in Canada's health care system. We draw attention, in particular, to authors who are concerned with anticolonial approaches to health care services delivery. In Chapter 21, Simon Brascoupé and Catherine Waters point to a New Zealand–based scholarship concerning cultural safety, in turn showing a series of analytical gaps in the Canadian literature. As they suggest, cultural safety is useful in prompting critical questions about cultural difference, wellness, and the material and symbolic perception of Indigenous deficit and inferiority.

Janet Smylie and Billy Allan, in Chapter 22, call on culturally sensitive health care practitioners to address racism more purposefully by addressing and reconciling the scholarly epidemiological research illuminating the colonial determinants of health. They draw attention to health and wellness outcomes that are impacted by issues of poverty, environmental racism, and displacement brought on by Settler colonialism. They call on health care practitioners to research, understand, become activist minded about, and indeed remedy the factors producing disparate and negative health indicators.

We conclude the second edition of *Racism, Indigeneity, and Colonization in Canada* with Part Twelve: Resistance. As the chapters in this part demonstrate, Indigenous peoples have never been "idle" in their efforts to resist colonial injustices. Rather, we have always lived accordingly to the principles of our traditional teachings and of the treaties entered with Settler Canadians.

In Chapter 23, Leanne Simpson discusses how the decision to fast by Chief Theresa Spence of Attawapiskat at the height of the Idle No More Movement in 2012–2013 was a significant political act of resistance and self-determination. When Chief Spence decided to enact the Indigenous tradition of fasting, she intended to remind all that her own people in Attawapiskat, as in many other Indigenous communities, had been "fasting"—meaning that they have endured centuries of colonial injustices. This act of resistance by Chief Spence, as well as the broader Idle No More movement, is a reminder to all Canadians that colonialism is still alive and hurting us all, and we each one of us, Indigenous and non-Indigenous, are responsible to change the current conditions and decolonize ourselves and the land.

In the final chapter of the book, Jeff Corntassel and Cheryl Bryce point out that Indigenous acts of self-determination are simply Indigenous ways of acting responsibly to their lands, peoples, and all creations. Whenever Indigenous peoples are resisting to colonial destructive policies and practices, they are revitalizing and protecting their Indigenous territories and ways of being. In so doing, they are maintaining a holistic relationship with all Creation, despite the barriers imposed on them by the colonial Canadian government or capitalist projects that threaten their territories. As these last two chapters of the book show, Indigenous people have always resisted racism and Settler colonialism; indeed have never been idle.

The intent of this book is to examine the interplay of racism and colonial forces and how these have shaped the lives of Indigenous peoples and their relations with Settler colonialists. Our aim is to provide insight into what can be done to address historic wrongdoings and envision a different path, one where the founding principles of the Two-Row Wampum are re-established.

## Notes

1. The word "Haudenosaunee," meaning "People of the Longhouse" (a reference to the distinctive houses in which our ancestors once resided), may differ depending on the Six Nations person or community to whom one is speaking. For example, Taiaiake Alfred refers to his people (the people of Kahnawake Mohawk Nation) as "Rotinohshonni" (1995: 38; 1999: xi). Doxtator (1996) chose the word "Rotinonhsyonni." We use the word "Haudenosaunee" as it is one that is familiar to us, and also one that has been used by the Six Nations people in political dealings with the Canadian state (see Haudenosaunee Confederacy, 1983). Several words used henceforth in this book, including the words "Ukwehuwé" (the Original People) and "Onyota'a:ka" (People of the Standing Stone), are in Oneida (the language of both of our Indigenous ancestors), and we are grateful for the advice that has been provided to us in this regard by several Oneida speakers.

# PART ONE

❖

# Theoretical Foundations

## Editor Introduction

We introduce the second edition of *Racism, Colonialism, and Indigeneity in Canada* with a set of two theoretical perspectives offered by Indigenous scholars on matters of colonial dominance, racism, and Indigenous resurgence. The articles we have selected provide a way of thinking about racism as a continually evolving and post-colonizing process that is informed by—and indeed inseparable from—early colonial precedents. We highlight an Indigenous perspective concerning precolonial political diplomacy which explores the meaning of treaty and an unbroken assertion of sovereignty. The readings provide a glimpse of the kinds of assumptions and understandings that are, in some cases, negated by some of academic scholarship, contemporary knowledge production, racism, the colonial politics of recognition, as well as cultures of redress and reconciliation.

According to Alfred, racism cannot be reduced to individuals alone. Indeed, the enemy is not even the "white man" in racial terms. Instead, racism is a way of thinking with an imperialist's mindset. Combating racism must therefore employ institutional analyses centred on its ideological basis and underpinnings. It is "the belief in the superiority and universality of Euro-American culture" that requires our unwavering attention and scrutiny. As Leanne Simpson points out, we need to ask critical questions about sovereignty and nationhood, including how it is that we related to each other and Indigenous and Settler peoples in what is now called Canada and in the original, first historic instance. We must revisit and ask critical questions about taken-for-granted practices that foreclose historic questions about Settler colonialism in Canada, such as capitalism, democracy, and individual rights. These practices embody apparatuses of power now firmly entrenched into Settler colonial consciousness.

Imperialist ways of thinking are not easily dismantled. This is because they are continually enabled through social and political processes that fashion the Indian as Other within the racialized colonial imaginary. Indigenous nations continue to be consumed under the category "Aboriginal" or even "Indian"—a process that is exemplary of the material and ideological violence that erases colonial histories of dispossession, nation-to-nation agreements, and the diversity that exists among us as Ukwehuwé. This way of thinking also eclipses the individual specificity of language, worldviews, and political culture of the original First Nations people, including the Nishnaabeg diplomacy described by Leanne Simpson. "Aboriginalism," writes Alfred, expunges histories of dominance aimed at Indigenous peoples. Furthermore, it predetermines a set of social and political outcomes (see Coulthard, 2014).

The reparation of colonial and racialized injustices will remain complicated so long as they are shaped by Eurocentric principles. Before Indigenous peoples can take their rightful place as partners in the founding of what is now called Canada—and before any real change can be realized in the areas of law, politics, and economics—the meaning of justice itself must be entirely reconceptualized. Colonial reparations must also be seen as a responsibility—not a gift—of white Settler society. It will be necessary to decolonize our own ways of thinking as Indigenous peoples; that is, to think outside of the racialized categories and taken-for-granted processes that have been made available to use by the colonizer.

Meaningful change also requires that we think about knowledge production. Whose knowledge is valued and with what set of consequences? How have Indigenous knowledges been defined, addressed, incorporated, or assumed out of existence in courts, curricula, and other sites of power? What knowledges inform and structure legal and political outcomes? For Leanne Simpson, we need to be vigilant in asking these sorts of questions, starting not with the political status quo established by governments and Settler colonists, but rather relationally, and with respect granted toward the stories told by our own people and nations when it comes to visioning "peace, mutual respect, and mutual benefit." We share in Simpson's perspective along with other Indigenous scholars who suggest that the political landscape of Canada be transformed into one that fosters public education and Settler literacy about Indigenous peoples, treaty-making, and political traditions.

Amid calls for an anticolonial and decolonizing pedagogy, and also an approach to public education that centres Indigenous histories and Settler colonialism, the articles we have selected address two major areas of theorization. First, both articles discern a colonial politics of recognition that has been shaped by unchecked State racialization practices and that treat all Indigenous peoples as if we were the same in law—as Indians and/or "Aboriginals"—despite the grassroots community we continue to share and maintain with each other as nations, and with Settlers, as well as the subtle nuances that exist between us as nations with respect to sovereignty and governance (see also Andersen, this volume). We continue to exercise our sovereignty as Indigenous peoples and nations (Simpson, 2014; Sunseri, 2011). We acknowledge territoriality and all our relations.

The articles we have selected also affirm that nation-to-nation agreements were bilateral at the time of colonial contact in what is now Canada, and that it is both the Crown's and Government of Canada's responsibility to sort out where it is that Settler Canadians fit in relation to existing treaty and nation-to-nation agreements (Borrows, 1997). Leanne Simpson highlights the relationship we are in with each other, respectively, as Indigenous peoples and as Indigenous people and Settlers. There is a need to provide for Settler–Indigenous relationships building and rejuvenation in Canada. Allegiances between Settler and migrant peoples are not always "in contract" with Canada, but rather and also with Indigenous peoples. These ways of thinking about contact must flourish and will require constitutional amendments, especially where the idea of "Indian" is concerned, and also, where it is that Settler Canadians fit with respect to Settler–Indigenous wrongs and also Settler relations and responsibility.

Indeed, the literature suggests that there is a conversation to be had in Canada, a renewal of dialogue, especially where Settler–Indigenous relations are concerned. Simon (2013: 136) wrote of the interpersonal and intercultural dimensions of Settler–Indigenous relationships in Canada, calling on "non-Indigenous peoples" to sort out where they "fit in relation to Aboriginal peoples" (see also Cannon, this volume). Thobani (2007) nuanced the ways in which people of colour, as Settlers, are invited to participate in multiculturalism, envisioning a relationship with Canada alone and not with Indigenous nations (see also Wallia, 2013). Lawrence and Amadahy (2009: 126) have also written: "black people without known Indigenous heritage . . . may have little allegiance to the Canadian Settler State but have no option for their survival but to fight for increasing power within it."

The literature suggests that non-white Settlers do not share the same relationship to white supremacy, Canadian Settler colonialism, and also to Indigenous peoples (Phung, 2011; Sehdev, 2011).

The articles we have selected focus on Indigenous peoples getting to know each other, our representation and demographics, the nature of our social conditions under Settler colonialism, and how it is that a dialogue between Settler and Indigenous peoples might best be rejuvenated. What we are suggesting in this book is to look inward at Settler culture, and the history of Settler colonialism, and to think about how we might begin to rebuild Settler–Indigenous relations beyond constructions of the other. We are also asking that our respective nationhood be given consideration, and also, where it is that all Settlers fit in relation to this history. The matter of relationships building and rejuvenation is especially relevant in light of recent developments concerning Canada's public apology and the Truth and Reconciliation Commission (TRC).

The TRC has suggested that emphasis be placed on reparations and renewal, especially where Settler–Indigenous relationships and the rejuvenation of original nation-to-nation principles is concerned. The second edition of *Racism, Colonialism, and Indigeneity in Canada*—like the first edition, and also following from TRC recommendations—is focused on inviting a new and historically informed dialogue concerning histories of Settler colonialism and reparations. We recognize the importance of Settler and Indigenous dialogue—a reconfiguration of relationships in what is now called Canada—about Settler-Indigenous relations and the history of Settler colonialism. The readings convey a relational sovereignty and set of anticolonial principles that need to inform and indeed shape next steps in a post-apology and post-TRC Canada.

# CHAPTER 1

# Colonial Stains on Our Existence

*Taiaiake Alfred*

I f Onkwehonwe movements are to force Settler societies to transcend colonialism, we need to understand clearly who and what constitutes our enemy. The "problem" or "challenge" we face has been explained in many ways, but to move our discussion forward I will state it in a blunt and

forcefully true way: the problem we face is Euro-american arrogance, the institutional and attitudinal expressions of the prejudicial biases inherent in European and Euroamerican cultures. This is not the abstract concept it may appear to be on first reading; it is the fundamental source of stress, discord, and injustice and capitalizes on the ubiquitous nature of imperialism and the threat it presents. The challenge we face is made up of specific patterns of behaviour among Settlers and our own people: choices made to support mentalities that developed in serving the colonization of our lands as well as the unrestrained greed and selfishness of mainstream society. We must add to this the superficial monotheistic justifications for the unnatural and misunderstood place and purpose of human beings in the world, an emphatic refusal to look inward, and an aggressive denial of the value of nature. . . .

So, in the framework of this struggle, what kinds of people make up Settler societies today? From the position of a movement for change, it is very important to distinguish between the various elements of the Settler population and to develop appropriate strategies of contention for each of the adversaries and enemies. There are those whom Albert Memmi called the "colonizers who refuse" to accept their position and role in the unjust state, usually left-wing intellectuals (Memmi, 1991: 43).[1] These are people whose indignation at the theoretical injustices of imperialism as an historical process (usually thought of as happening in foreign countries rather than their own beloved backyards) is not accompanied by action. They may be progressive politically, but they usually hold a strong attachment to the colonial state and to their own privileges within Settler society. They are effectively silenced by being caught in the squeeze between their intellectual deconstructions of power and their moral cowardice when it comes to doing something about injustice in a real sense. The colonizers who refuse to acknowledge their privilege and inheritance of wrongs are practising another form of selfishness and hypocrisy—they claim the right and privilege of indignation and the power to judge those cruder colonizers among them and attempt to use this rhetorical posture to release themselves of their own responsibility for the colonial enterprise, both historically and in the way it has affected their own lives, their families' privileges, and their communities' formation. These people are paralyzed by fear. Their guilt renders them useless to our struggle and paradoxically makes them one of the strongest blocs of hard-core conservatism in Settler society. Put so eloquently by the African-American writer Audre Lorde, "guilt

is just another name for impotence, for defensiveness destructive of communication, it becomes a device to protect ignorance . . . the ultimate protection for changelessness" (Lorde, 1984).

Another arm of the colonial body is the colonizer who accepts his or her role, who has internalized colonial myths, mainly racist histories, notions of white superiority, and the lie of progress (or the immigrants' hope that material accumulation and expansion of wealth is indeed the formula for happiness, acceptability by the white man, and legitimacy as citizens). This posture is simple enough to understand and hardly needs further elaboration, except to acknowledge that the majority of the Settler population is in this category, an indication of the vastness of the challenge ahead of us. . . .

Onkwehonwe rights and freedoms are always falsely identified in the mass media and public commentary (which are tacitly supported by the government) as the instruments by which Settlers are victimized. Recognizing and respecting Onkwehonwe rights is played off against white people's property values and their personal and emotional security, which are all at base an assertion of convenience and entitlement to continue in the benefit of crimes by earlier generations without recompense to the actual people who suffered in the relationship. The convenience of this assertion as justification for the unwillingness of the white population to take serious stands against injustice should not be lost on anyone; the pronouncement that Onkwehonwe rights harm white people is simply not true and cannot be supported with evidence. It is nothing but a Rhodesian projection of white power onto a framework of potential Onkwehonwe achievement and re-empowerment.

These false decolonization processes also demand clear demarcations of the territorial bounds of the concept of Onkwehonwe nationhood. This may not sound like such a problem at first glance, but it is, in fact, a conscious tactic designed to ensure the failure of meaningful negotiations. The demand for territorial clarity and non-overlapping negotiations on land issues is predicated on an acceptance of the Euroamerican way of viewing land, demarking and dividing the land and environment and relationships between peoples on the basis of European-derived notions of property, ownership, and jurisdiction (Seed, 1995).

These are the fundamentals of Euroamerican arrogance projected onto the politics of decolonization. This is what Memmi's disease of the European looks like to us today. Is there a cure? Is there a way to break the grip of this powerful sickness in the hearts and minds of Settler society?

These questions are of enormous significance. How do we make their history and their country mean something different to people who feel entitled to the symbolic and real monopoly they enjoy on the social dynamics of our relationship and on the cultural landscape?[2] It seems that if we are to move beyond the charitable racism of current policies or paternalist progressivism of liberal reconciliation models, justice must become a *duty* of, not a *gift* from, the Settler.[3] And for this to happen, Settler society must be forced into a reckoning with its past, its present, its future, and itself. White people who are not yet decolonized must come to admit they were and are wrong. They must admit that Onkwehonwe have rights that are collective and inherent to their indigeneity and that are autonomous from the Settler society—rights to land, to culture, and to community. The Settlers' inability to comprehend justice for Onkwehonwe from within their own cultural frame is simple. Why are the Settlers' supposed gifts and concessions, stingy and reluctant though they are, toward Onkwehonwe not seen as duties? Because that would mean the Settlers must admit that they were and are wrong and would imply a set of rights for Onkwehonwe.

## The Other Side of Fear

The colonial relationship is a dynamic one of arrogance, complacency, and complicity. Aboriginalist complicity with the injustice and Onkwehonwe complacency toward our rights and freedoms enable this arrogance. Euroamerican pretensions are empowered and emboldened by the unwillingness of Onkwehonwe to defend the truth and by people's participation in the white man's lies. As Onkwehonwe who are committed to the Original Teachings, there is not supposed to be any space between the principles we hold and the practice of our lives. This is the very meaning of integrity: having the mental toughness and emotional strength to stand up for what we believe is right. The challenge is to master, not conquer, fear and to engage in the constant fight to resist both the corrupting effects of the financial, sensual, and psychological weapons used by the colonial authorities to undermine Onkwehonwe people and the corrosive effect on the Onkwehonwe mind and soul of Euroamerican culture and society. The question here is a real and immediate one for Onkwehonwe who enter the struggle actively: How do we deal with the psychological and physical battle fatigue which, in most cases, leads to eventual despair and defeatism? . . .

Five hundred years of physical and psychological warfare have created a colonial culture of fear among both subdued and dominant peoples. We have emerged out of a shameful past, a history of racial and religious hatreds, of extreme violence, and of profound injustice. It is impossible to even acknowledge it truthfully. Colonial culture, for both the victims and the perpetrators, is fundamentally a denial of the past and of its moral implications. It is an aversion to the truth about who we really are and where it is that we come from. More than the moneyed privilege of the newcomers, more than the chaotic disadvantage of the original peoples, this is what we have inherited from our colonial past: relationships founded on hatred and violence and a culture founded on lies to assuage the guilt or shame of it all. We are afraid of our memories, afraid of what we have become, afraid of each other, and afraid for the future. Fear is the foundation of the way we are in the world and the way we think about the future. It is normal, and we have grown used to it.

All of what we know as government and law is founded on these fears. The powerful in our society manage the words we hear and the images we see to ensure that we remain afraid. Although the past and its implications are self-evident, we are complicit in their denial because it is too painful or arduous or costly to imagine an existence unbound from the lies. Emotionally and psychologically, we are attached to this mythology of colonialism because it explains the Euroamerican conquest and normalizes it in our lives. The perpetrators know that it is wrong to steal a country and so deny it is a crime; the victims know that it is shameful to accept defeat lying down. Yet, complacency rules over both because the thought of what might come out of transcending the lies is too . . . fearsome.

Lying complacent in a narrow conception of the past and nearly paralyzed by fear in a constrained vision of the future, both the colonized and colonizers have been forced to accept and live with a state of unfreedom. This is the most profound meaning of colonialism's modern turn. Of course, this is made possible because the vast lie has been embedded in every aspect of our lives for so long as memory, as identity, and as political and economic relations of domination and exploitation.

What kind of culture has been produced by this denial of truth and wearing down of authenticity—of rooted, healthy, and meaningful ways of life—in the service of political and economic power? This question must be asked not only of the subdued but of the dominant as well. Colonialism is a total relationship of power, and it has shaped the existence, not only of those who have lost, but also those who have profited. . . .

## Spaces We Occupy

In many countries, the term "aboriginal" is seen as an inoffensive and innocuous substitute for more caustic words like "Indian," or "Native." Unpacked as a social, political, and intellectual construction, however, it is a highly offensive word. It reflects the prevailing colonial mentality in its redefinition of Onkwehonwe away from our original languages,[4] because it fashions "the people" as a symbol and concept constructed on, and totally amenable to, colonialism. Being aboriginal, once the implications are fully understood, is repugnant to anyone

who desires to preserve Onkwehonwe ways of life. The ideas that Onkwehonwe will be inevitably integrated wholly into the Settler society (meaning that their autonomous existences will be terminated actively or voluntarily) and that their governments and lands will be subsumed within the colonial state have become the accepted ideological frame of Settler society, state governments, and many Onkwehonwe themselves. It is the lens through which they view the problem of colonial injustice. Aboriginalism is the new paradigm. But what is it, exactly?

Aboriginalism is assimilation's end-game, the terminological and psychic displacement of authentic indigenous identities, beliefs, and behaviours with one designed by Indian Department bureaucrats, government lawyers, and judges to complete the imperial objective of exterminating Onkwehonwe presences from the social and political landscape. It is the final stage of the annihilation of an independent existence for the original peoples, a cultural and political-economic process of state-sponsored identity invention to dispossess and assimilate the remnants of the Onkwehonwe who are still tied to this land and to indigenous ways of life.

Aboriginalism is the ideology of the Onkwehonwe surrender to the social and mental pathologies that have come to define colonized indigenous existences and the inauthentic, disconnected lives too many of our people find themselves leading. It is the latest version of the many ideologies of conquest that have been used to justify assaults on our peoples' rights and freedoms. The Settlers have been very successful, through education and religion, in turning Onkwehonwe against one another and creating a segment of people in our communities who will collaborate with government to do the work formerly assigned to colonial agents. But beyond this obvious complicity, there is also the widespread descent into defeatism among many of our people. In fact, the real effect of this widespread defeatism—social suffering by Onkwehonwe—is the most visible feature of our communities to the outside world. Aboriginalism obscures everything that is historically true and meaningful about Onkwehonwe—our origins, languages, and names; our land, our heritage, and our rights—and puts in their place views of history and of ourselves and our futures that are nothing more than the self-justifying myths and fantasies of the Settler. Onkwehonwe, Anishnaabe, and Dene are denied their full and rooted meaning, and our people are made to become aboriginal; in the process real and meaningful connections to our pasts, our rights, and our strength are severed. This is the genocidal function of Aboriginalism, the prettied-up face of neo-colonialism that is dispassionately integrated into the media, government, and academic discourses as integration, development, and, sometimes more honestly, as assimilation. It is the attempt to destroy authentic existences and replace them with ways of life and self-definitions that best serve Euroamerican wants, needs, and beliefs. . . .

Aboriginalism is a sickness, an aspiration to assimilation, expanded into a wholesale cultural project and political agenda. It is a false consciousness, a thorough and perpetual embedding of colonial identities. Within this inauthentic consciousness are non-contentious cooperative identities, institutions, and strategies for interacting with the colonizer. The lost people who accept the aboriginal status created for them by the colonizer can assume various postures; lacking an identity rooted in an Onkwehonwe culture, they find it necessary to select identities and cultural choices from the menu presented to them by the Settler society and the machinery of the state. The most pronounced and obvious of these are the "victims of history," who seek only to *recover* from the past and live in peace with the Settlers, and the "aboriginal litigants," who pray with their white brothers and sisters to a Christian god and strive before white judges for *reconciliation* between Settler and Onkwehonwe. Both the victim and litigant reflect the essential colonial process of civilizing the Onkwehonwe, making us into citizens of the conquering states, so that instead of fighting for ourselves and what is right, we seek a *resolution* that is acceptable to and non-disruptive for the state and society we have come to embrace and identify with.

This is the basic vocabulary of aboriginalism as a political ideology: recovery, reconciliation, and resolution. To this I may also add *resistance*, because, even though it is outwardly hostile to the "enemy," constructing one's identity and life strictly in opposition to the colonizer is another form of white-man worship. All of these are false representations of the Onkwehonwe heritage of struggle. All of them, from the soft and passive legalist to the hard-core guerrilla fighter, demand on the part of Onkwehonwe an abandonment of our rooted identities and the adoption of one that is consistent with a submissive culture or a foreign culture. To fight against genocide, we are told to arm ourselves and take vengeance upon the white man. To fight against economic oppression, we are told to become capitalists and to live for money. To fight against unfair laws, we are told to become lawyers and change the system from within. None of these paths is our own! And none of them are capable of liberating us from colonialism with our Onkwehonwe spirits and identities intact. They demand that we surrender our true selves to become what it is we are fighting against, so that we may better it or defeat it. . . .

Meaningful change, the transcendence of colonialism, and the restoration of Onkwehonwe strength and freedom can only be achieved through the resurgence of an Onkwehonwe *spirit* and *consciousness* directed into *contention* with the very foundations of colonialism. Onkwehonwe do need to challenge the continuing hateful conquest of our peoples, but not with a misguided rage channelled through the futile delusions of money, institutional power, or vengeful violence. Seriously, what is the best hope these can offer us? Social order and cultural stasis enshrined in law; mass conversion to the white man's religion of consumerism; or killing a few whites. None of these reflect the ideals of peace, respect, harmony, and coexistence that are the heart of Onkwehonwe philosophies. We are taught to confront hate with the force of love and to struggle to live in the face of ever-present death and the bringers of it. But we must do it *our* way, or risk being transformed by the fight into that (and those) which we are struggling against. . . .

In contrast to this internalist approach—which we could summarize as an acceptance of assimilation with demands for mediation of its effects *within* the state—a more rooted indigenous peoples' movement has been emerging globally over the last 30 years as a movement *against* the state and *for* the re-emergence of Onkwehonwe existences as cultural and political entities unto themselves. Onkwehonwe are in relationships with Settlers, but are not subsumed within the state and are not drawn into its modern liberal ideology of selfish individualism and unrestrained consumption. Central to this, and in stark opposition to the reformist internalist aboriginal approaches, has been indigenous peoples' direct contention with capitalism. Especially in Ecuador and Bolivia, and with the Zapatista movement in Mexico (Selverston-Scher, 2001; Brysk, 2000; Holloway and Peláez, 1998), Onkwehonwe have acted on their realization that capitalist economics and liberal delusions of progress are not opportunities for indigenous peoples' gain, but the very engines of colonial aggression and injustice towards their peoples. The goals of this globalized indigenous movement have been developed to reflect the people's sensitive understanding of the political economy of neo-colonialism: the recognition of Onkwehonwe national existences along with collective rights of self-determination; respect for Onkwehonwe connections to their lands and the rights that flow from those connections; and the preservation and revitalization of indigenous cultures, especially languages, religions, and forms of governance.[5]

These indigenous movements are truly movements against what the dominant societies see as modernity. They share the notion of a balanced existence tied in meaningful ways to their heritage and the belief in the necessity of actively defending their existence. For Onkwehonwe, their politics is the carrying-out of the right and responsibility to be different from mainstream society. This is indeed the fight of all Onkwehonwe who remain true to the spirit of their ancestors: it is a fight for independence and for connection to one's heritage. . . .

In my mind, *regeneration* is the direct application of the principle of acting against our ingrained and oppressive fears. Imagine if regeneration of ourselves and our nations took the place of the goal of "recovery" (so individualizing and terminal and so much a part of the industry built up around residential school and substance abuse healing among our peoples). Think of the freedom inherent in embracing the struggle to transcend what has been done to us rather than the effort to gain compensation for the crimes or to placate feelings and sensibilities.

*Restitution*, which is the application of the principles of clarity and honesty to politics, would take the place of the goal of "reconciliation," which is promoted so vehemently by liberal thinkers and church groups, but which is fatally flawed because it depends on the false notion of a moral equivalency between Onkwehonwe and Settlers and on a basic acceptance of colonial institutions and relationships. Reconciliation gives Onkwehonwe a place inside of Settler society with no requirement for Settlers to forego any of their ill-gotten gains personally or collectively. Restitution, as the alternative antidote and perspective, is based on the proven notion that real peace-making requires making amends for harm done before any of the other steps to restore the fabric of a relationship can be taken. Restitution is, in fact, the precondition for any form of true reconciliation to take place (Redekop, 2003).

*Resurgence*, which applies the principle of courageous action against injustice, could replace the notion of seeking "resolution" to the colonial problem. Certainty and finality of land settlements are the objective in the Settler society's courts and are promoted through state-sponsored negotiation processes to achieve order in the relationship, order which ratifies colonial institutions and facilitates the perpetuation of the original injustice, from which comes their very existence. Resurgence is acting beyond resistance. It is what resistance always hopes to become: from a rooted position of strength, resistance defeats the temptation to stand down, to take what is offered by the state in exchange for being pacified. In rejecting the temptation to join the Settlers and their state, seeking instead to confront Settler society in a struggle to force an end to the imperial reality and to lay down the preconditions for a peaceful coexistence, we would choose to use contention as a means of widespread enlightenment and societal change. . . .

Reconciliation itself needs to be intellectually and politically deconstructed as the orienting goal of the Onkwehonwe struggle. How do we break the hold of this emasculating concept? The logic of reconciliation as justice is clear: without massive restitution, including land, financial transfers, and other forms of assistance to compensate for past harms and continuing injustices committed against our peoples, reconciliation would permanently enshrine colonial injustices and is itself a further injustice. This much is clear in our Onkwehonwe frame of understanding. But what about other people's understandings of the nature of the problem we are facing? The nearly complete ignorance of the Settler society about the true facts of their people's relationship with Onkwehonwe and their wilful denial of historical reality detract from any possibility of meaningful discussion on true reconciliation. Limited to a discussion of history that includes only the last five or ten years, the corporate media and general public focus on the billions of dollars handed out to the Onkwehonwe per year from federal treasuries and spent inefficiently. The complex story of what went on in the past and the tangled complexities of the past's impact on the present and future of our relationships are reduced to questions of "entitlements," "rights," and "good governance" within the already established structures of the state. Consider the effect of lengthening our view and extending society's view. Considering 100 or 300 years of interactions, it would become clear, even to the Settlers, that the real problem facing their country is that two nations are fighting over questions of conquest and survival, of empire or genocide, and moral claims to be just societies. Considering the long view and true facts, the Indian Problem becomes a question of the struggle for right and wrong, for justice in its most basic form. Something was stolen, lies were told, and they've never been made right. That, I believe, is the crux of the problem. We must shift away from the pacifying

discourse and reframe people's perception of the problem so that it is not a question of how to reconcile with colonialism that faces us. Instead, we must think of restitution as the first step towards creating justice and a moral society out of the immoral racism that is the foundation and core of all colonial countries. What was stolen must be given back, amends must be made for the crimes that were committed, from which all Settlers, old families and recent immigrants alike, have gained their existences as citizens of these colonial countries. . . .

Even the act of proposing a shift to this kind of discussion is a radical challenge to the reconciling negotiations that try to fit Onkwehonwe into the colonial legacy rather than to confront and defeat it. When I speak of restitution, I am speaking of restoring ourselves as peoples, our spiritual power, dignity, and the economic bases for our autonomy. . . .

Recasting the Onkwehonwe struggle as one of seeking restitution as the precondition to reconciliation is not extremist or irrational. Restitution, as a broad goal, involves demanding the return of what was stolen, accepting reparations (either land, material, or monetary recompense) for what cannot be returned, and forging a new socio-political relationship based on the Settler state's admission of wrongdoing and acceptance of the responsibility and obligation to engage Onkwehonwe peoples in a restitution-reconciliation peace-building process. . . .

Unprejudiced logics of decolonization point . . . to the need to create coexistence among autonomous political communities. Eventual peaceful coexistence demands a decolonization process in which Onkwehonwe will be extricated from, not further entrenched within, the values, cultures, and practices of liberal democracy. If the goals of decolonization are justice and peace, then the process to achieve these goals must reflect a basic covenant on the part of both Onkwehonwe and Settlers to honour each others' existences. This honouring cannot happen when one partner in the relationship is asked to sacrifice their heritage and identity in exchange for peace. This is why the only possibility of a just relationship between Onkwehonwe and the Settler society is the conception of a nation-to-nation partnership between peoples, the kind of relationship reflected in the original treaties of peace and friendship consecrated between indigenous peoples and the newcomers when white people first started arriving in our territories. And the only way to remove ourselves from the injustice of the present relationship is to begin to implement a process of resurgence-apology-restitution and seek to restore the pre-colonial relationship of sharing and cooperation among diverse peoples. . . .

Just as Onkwehonwe have commonality in our basic demands, responses to those demands have been the same across borders among the (so-called) progressive Settler states, those with significant indigenous populations and that seek an accord with those peoples. These state governments have refused territorial concessions to halt or redress patterns of colonial occupation; they insist that all resource development be jointly administered; they defend the legal and constitutional supremacy of the colonial state and insist on a subordinate governmental status for Onkwehonwe nations; and they insist on rights equivalency among Settler populations and Onkwehonwe, even in those territories recognized as Onkwehonwe homelands and in settlement lands within the indigenous nations' recognized spheres of governmental authority. From Nunavut in the Arctic to Tierra del Fuego and across the Pacific Ocean to Aotearoa, there is consistency in this pattern of demand and response.

The intransigence of Settler states has resulted in further degradations of Onkwehonwe lives and sparked serious violent conflicts in all countries with significant Onkwehonwe presence, ranging from the overt violent racism in Australian society, to the intractable and costly legal disputes over land title in Canada, to the armed insurgencies and violent repression common in Latin American countries. Unfortunately for Onkwehonwe, the intransigence of the Settler has been a profitable strategy, as Onkwehonwe groups have found it extremely difficult to continue to push for their demands in the face of the multiple strategies of delay, distraction, and containment employed by state governments. . . .

In the face of this intransigence, this generation of Onkwehonwe have some serious choices to make. Depending on whether we confront the challenge before us or not, there are a number of possible scenarios that may play out for our people. Our societies may collapse, and our next generations will die of self-destruction because of our decision to allow things to continue the way they are going. We may choose to retreat from the challenge in front of us, to become stagnant and passive, and to rely upon bureaucracy and technology for solutions to our problems, giving the Settlers even more control over our lives. Or, we can choose to fight for our existence as Onkwehonwe and our inherent rights and freedoms; we can embrace our challenges and engage our predicament.[6] . . .

Cycles of oppression are being repeated through generations in Onkwehonwe communities. Colonial economic relations are reflected in the political and legal structures of contemporary Onkwehonwe societies, and they result in Onkwehonwe having to adapt culturally to this reality and to individuals reacting in particularly destructive and unhealthy (but completely comprehensible) ways. These social and health problems seem to be so vexing to governments; large amounts of money have been allocated to implement government-run organizations and policies geared towards alleviating these problems in both the United States and Canada, for example, but they have had only limited positive effect on the health status of our communities. But these problems are not really mysterious nor are they unsolvable. The social and health problems besetting Onkwehonwe are the logical result of a situation wherein people respond or adapt to unresolved colonial injustices. People in indigenous communities develop complexes of behaviour and mental attitudes that reflect their colonial situation and out flow unhealthy and destructive behaviours. It is a very simple problem to understand when we consider the whole context of the situation and all of the factors involved (Chandler and Lalonde, 1998). . . .

## Notes

1. A notable and honourable exception from Memmi's own time is Jean-Paul Sartre.
2. For more on the urgency of redefining the colonial reality, see Memmi, *The Colonizer and the Colonized*, 103.
3. For more on this point see Richard Day, "Who is This 'We' That Gives the Gift? Native American Political Theory and 'the Western Tradition,'" *Critical Horizons 2*, 2 (2001): 173–201.
4. I will remind the reader here that I am using the word "Onkwehonwe" because I am Kanien'kehaka, and that in

rejecting the white man's word, in this act of linguistic resurgence. I am not meaning to obscure or discourage the use of *Anishnaabe, Dene, Dakelh*, or any of the other authentic words for the people in indigenous languages.

5. For further discussion of the globalized indigenous movements' structure and goals, see Brysk, *From Tribal Village to Global Village*, 59.
6. These scenarios for the future draw on Duane Elgin, *Voluntary Simplicity*, rev. ed. (New York, NY: William Morrow, 1993), 179–91.

## References

Brysk, Allison. 2000. *From Tribal Village to Global Village: Indian Rights and International Relations in Latin America*. Stanford, CA: Stanford University Press.

Chandler, Michael J., and Christopher Lalonde. 1998. "Cultural Continuity as a Hedge against Suicide in Canada's First Nations," *Transcultural Psychiatry* 35: 191–219.

Holloway, John, and Eloina Peláez. 2000. *Zapatista!* London, UK: Pluto Press.

Kaplan, Robert D. 2001. "Looking the World in the Eye," *The Atlantic* December: 68–82.

Lorde, Audre. 1984. "The Uses of Anger," *Sister Outsider*. Freedom, CA: Crossing Press.

Memmi, Albert. 1991. *The Colonizer and the Colonized*. Boston, MA: Beacon Press.

Redekop, Vern. 2003. *From Violence to Blessing: How an Understanding of Deep-Rooted Conflicts Can Open Paths to Reconciliation*. Montréal: Novalis.

Seed, Patricia. 1995. *Ceremonies of Possession in Europe's Conquest of the New World*. Cambridge, UK: Cambridge University Press.

Selverston-Scher, Melina. 2001. *Ethnopolitics in Ecuador: Indigenous Rights and the Strengthening of Democracy*. Miami, FL: North-South Center Press.

## CHAPTER 2

# Looking after Gdoo-naaganinaa
## Precolonial Nishnaabeg Diplomatic and Treaty Relationships

*Leanne Simpson*

It has long been known that Indigenous nations had their own processes for making and maintaining peaceful diplomatic relationships, such as Gdoo-naaganinaa,[1] with other Indigenous nations prior to colonization.[2] These "treaty processes" were grounded in the worldviews, language,

knowledge systems, and political cultures of the nations involved, and they were governed by the common Indigenous ethics of justice, peace, respect, reciprocity, and accountability. Indigenous peoples understood these agreements in terms of relationship, and renewal processes were paramount in maintaining these international agreements. They also viewed treaties in terms of both rights and responsibilities, and they took their

From *Wicazo Sa Review* 23, 2 (2008): 29–42. Reprinted with permission from the University of Minnesota Press.

responsibilities in maintaining treaty relations seriously. Although these agreements were political in nature, viewed through the lens of Indigenous worldviews, values, and traditional political cultures, one can begin to appreciate that these agreements were also sacred, made in the presence of the spiritual world and solemnized in ceremony. . . .

Harold Johnson, a Cree, explains traditional Cree conceptualizations of treaty relationships in his territory, Kiciwamanawak, in terms of relations and relationships. He writes that when the colonizers first came to his territory, Cree law applied, the foundation of which rests in the "maintenance of harmonious relations." He sees the treaty as an adoption ceremony, where the Cree adopted the settlers as family and took them in as relatives, inviting them to live in Kiciwamanawak and live by the laws of the Cree. . . .[3]

For the past decade, I have been interested in understanding how my ancestors, the Mississauga of the Nishnaabeg Nation,[4] understood and lived up to their responsibilities to the land, their families, their clans, and their nation and with neighboring nations. Through years of learning from our elders and Nishnaabeg knowledge keepers, spending time on the land, and interpreting the academic literature through an Nishnaabeg lens, I have come to understand Nishnaabeg conceptualizations of treaties and treaty relationships . . . and these conceptualizations exist in stark contrast to the Eurocanadian view of treaties entrenched in the colonial legal system, the historical record, and often the contemporary academy.

In Canada, many Indigenous scholars have argued that the "Canadian state's political relationship with Aboriginal Peoples should be renewed with respect to the early treaties."[5] Although this is an important decolonizing strategy, the fact remains that Canadian politicians and scholars, as well as Canadians in general, have a poor understanding of Indigenous treaty-making traditions, Indigenous political traditions, and Indigenous cultures in general. For many, the idea that Indigenous nations had their own precolonial diplomatic relations and political cultures exists in sharp contrast to the racist stereotype of "savages

wandering around in the bush" still prominent in mainstream Canadian culture.[6] For others, it is difficult to understand that although both Indigenous and European nations engaged in treaty making before contact with each other, the traditions, beliefs, and worldviews that defined concepts such as "treaties" were extremely different. This misunderstanding is further confounded by the fact that as time passed, the colonizers' view of treaties was entrenched in the Eurocanadian legal system and the academy, and that there are few written records of treaty agreements made in the early colonial period where Indigenous perspectives were most influential. Destabilizing and decolonizing the concept of "treaty" then becomes paramount to appreciate what our ancestors intended to happen when those very first agreements and relationships were established, and to explore the relevance of Indigenous views of "treaty" and "treaty relationships" in contemporary times.

The purpose of this paper is to begin to articulate Nishnaabeg cultural perspectives on our relationships within our territory, whether those relationships were with the land, with the animal nations that form the basis of our clan system, or with neighbouring Indigenous nations and confederacies. . . . I begin by discussing cultural contexts within which Nishnaabeg people maintained and nurtured relationships within their territory. I then discuss two examples of treaty relationships with the nonhuman world, concluding with a discussion of precolonial international treaty relationships with the Dakota Nation and the Haudenosaunee Confederacy. Although these perspectives are not new or unique to Nishnaabeg knowledge holders and our elders, they exist in contrast to mainstream academic literature regarding treaties.

## Bimaadiziwin: Relationships as the Context for Nishnaabeg Treaty Making

Our ancestors knew that maintaining good relationships as individuals, in families, in clans, and in our nation and with other Indigenous nations and confederacies was the basis for lasting peace . . . Bimaadiziwin or "living the good life . . ."[7] is a way of ensuring human beings live in balance with the natural world, their family, their clan, and their nation and it is carried out through the Seven Grandfather teachings, embedded in the social and political structures of the Nishnaabeg. . . .

At the individual level, Nishnaabeg culture allowed for strong individual autonomy and freedom, while at the same time the needs of the collective were paramount. There was a belief that good governance and political relationships begin with individuals and how they relate to each other in families.

Haudenosaunee academic Trish Monture explains a similar concept among the Haudenosaunee:

> As I have come to understand it, self-determination begins with looking at yourself and your family and deciding if and when you are living responsibly. Self-determination is principally, that is first and foremost, about relationships. Communities cannot be self-governing unless members of those communities are well and living in a responsible way.[8]

In a real sense for the Nishnaabeg, relating to one's immediate family, the land, the members of their clan, and their relations in the nonhuman world in a good way was the foundation of good governance in a collective sense. Promoting Bimaadiziwin in the affairs of the nations begins with practicing Bimaadiziwin in one's everyday life. . . .

## Nishnaabeg Doodem

Traditional Nishnaabeg political culture was based on our clan system. . . . Clans connected families to particular animal nations and territories, where relationships with those animal nations were formalized, ritualized, and nurtured.[9] Clan members held and continue to hold specific responsibilities in terms of taking care of a particular part of the territory, and specific clans hold

particular responsibilities related to governance.[10] Individual clans had responsibilities to a particular geographic region of the territory, and their relationship with that region was a source of knowledge, spirituality, and sustenance. They also were required to maintain and nurture a special relationship with their clan animal. . . .

## Treaty Making with Animal Nations

In many instances, clan leaders negotiated particular agreements with animal nations or clans to promote Bimaadiziwin and balance with the region. In Mississauga territory,[11] for example, the people of the fish clans, who are the intellectuals of the nation, met with the fish nations[12] twice a year for thousands of years at Mnjikanming,[13] the small narrows between Lake Simcoe and Lake Couchiching. The fish nations and the fish clans gathered to talk, to tend to their treaty relationships, and to renew life just as the Gizhe-mnido[14] had instructed them. These were important gatherings because the fish nations sustained the Nishnaabeg Nation during times when other sources of food were scarce . . . Nishnaabeg people . . . only took as much as they needed and never wasted. . . .

. . . Nishnaabeg scholar John Borrows retells one of our sacred stories in *Recovering Canada: The Resurgence of Indigenous Law*[15] and further illustrates the importance of these diplomatic agreements between human and animal nations. In a time long ago, all of the deer, moose, and caribou suddenly disappeared from the Nishnaabeg territory. When the people went looking for them, they discovered the animals had been captured by the crows. After some negotiation, the people learned that the crows were not holding the moose, deer, and caribou against their will. The animals had willingly left the territory because the Nishnaabeg were no longer respecting them. The Nishnaabeg had been wasting their meat and not treating their bodies with the proper reverence. The animals knew that the people could not live without them, and when the animal nations met in council, the chief deer outlined how the Nishnaabeg nation could make amends:

> Honour and respect our lives and our beings, in life and in death. Cease doing what offends our spirits. Do not waste our flesh. Preserve fields and forests for our homes. To show your commitment to these things and as a remembrance of the anguish you have brought upon us, always leave tobacco leaf from where you take us. Gifts are important to build our relationship once again.[16]

The Nishnaabeg agreed and the animals returned to their territory. Contemporary Nishnaabeg hunters still go through the many rituals outlined that day when they kill a deer or moose, a process that honors the relationships our people have with these animals and the agreement our ancestors made with the Hoof Clan to maintain the good life. Judy DaSilva, Nishnaabeg-kwe[17] from Asubpeechoseewagong Netum Anishinaabek (Grassy Narrows) in northwest Ontario explains how these teachings are still relevant in her community today:

> When a hunter kills a moose, there is a certain part of the moose that the hunter takes off, and leaves in the forest, and with that the hunter will say a few words to thank the moose for providing food for his family. . . . My brother said our grandmother told him that you do not get an animal because you are a good hunter, but because the animal feels sorry for you and gives himself to you to feed your family. This is why when our people hunt, these thoughts are ingrained in their minds and their hearts and they have great respect for the animals they get.[18]

According to Nishnaabeg traditions, it is my understanding that our relationship with the moose nation, the deer nation, and the caribou nation is a treaty relationship like any other, and all the parties involved have both rights and responsibilities in terms of maintaining the agreement and the relationship between our nations. . . . [T]reaties are about maintaining peace through

healthy collective relationships . . . and there are two common terms in the language that refer to agreements made between two nations: "Chi-debahk-(in)-Nee-Gay-Win," which refers to an open agreement with matters to be added to it, and "Bug-in-Ee-Gay," which relates to "letting it go."[19] It is my understanding that "Chi-debahk-(in)-Nee-Gay-Win" is not meant to be interpreted as an unfinished agreement, rather it is an agreement that is an ongoing reciprocal and dynamic relationship to be nurtured, maintained, and respected. Treaties made by the Nishnaabeg with colonial powers in Canada as late as the Robinson–Huron Treaty of 1850, according to the oral tradition of the Nishnaabeg, was to be "added to."[20] This type of agreement was absolutely necessary in negotiations between nations with different languages and in the times before the written word, but it should not be viewed as an archaic or obsolete form of political culture. Oral agreements based on relationship, negotiation, and understanding required plenty of maintenance and nurturing to ensure lasting peace. That maintenance required commitment and hard work, but also encouraged understanding another point of view and when done correctly can bring about a lasting peace for all involved.

# Nishnaabeg International Diplomacy

. . . The ethics of respect and reciprocity were reflected in international Nishnaabeg diplomatic relations through the process known as "waiting in the woods" or "waiting at the woods' edge." Omàmìwinini[21] scholar Paula Sherman explains: "[I]t would have been expected that upon leaving one's own territory to cross into someone else's territory, that an individual or a group would build a fire to announce that they were 'waiting in the woods.'"[22]

An Omàmìwinini delegation would have been sent out with a string of white wampum to welcome them to Omàmìwinini territory. Omàmìwinini would have prepared a feast for them, and gifts would have been exchanged. . . . Visitors to one's territory were to be treated with the utmost respect to promote peaceful diplomatic relations between nations. These relations were also formalized in treaties, and the following section discusses two examples of precolonial Nishnaabeg treaties with neighboring nations.

## Our Drum and Our Dish: Treaty Making with Other Indigenous Nations

The Nishnaabeg Nation, in addition to living up to their treaty relationships with the nonhuman world, also made political agreements with their neighbouring nations. . . .

Gdoo-naaganinaa acknowledged that both the Nishnaabeg and the Haudenosaunee were eating out of the same dish through shared hunting territory and the ecological connections between their territories.[23] The dish represented the shared territory, although it is important to remember that sharing territory for hunting did not involve interfering with one another's sovereignty as nations. It represented harmony and interconnection, as both parties were to be responsible for taking care of the dish. . . . The Nishnaabeg Nation and the confederacy related to each other through the practice of Gdoo-naaganinaa, it was not just simply agreed upon, but practiced as part of the diplomatic relations between the Nishnaabeg Nation and the confederacy. All of the nations involved had particular responsibilities to live up to in order to enjoy the rights of the agreement. . . .

Nishnaabeg environmental ethics[24] dictated that individuals could only take as much as they needed, that they must share everything following Nishnaabeg redistribution of wealth customs, and no part of the animal could be wasted. . . . Nishnaabeg custom required decision makers to consider the impact of their decisions on all the plant and animal nations, in addition to the next seven generations of Nishnaabeg.

The Haudenosaunee refer to the treaty as the "Dish with One Spoon" and there is an associated wampum belt. . . .[25] [I]n the Haudenosaunee version there is one spoon not only to reinforce the idea of sharing and responsibility, but also to promote peace. There are no knives allowed around the dish so that no one gets hurt.[26] Again, Haudenosaunee people understood the treaty as a relationship with both rights and responsibilities. Haudenosaunee land ethics also ensured the health of the shared territory for generations to come.[27]

## Our Dish in Contemporary Times

At no time did the Haudenosaunee assume that their participation in the Dish with One Spoon treaty meant that they could fully colonize Nishnaabeg territory or assimilate Nishnaabeg people into Haudenosaunee culture. At no time did the Haudenosaunee assume that the Nishnaabeg intended to give up their sovereignty, independence, or nationhood. Both political entities assumed that they would share the territory, that they would both take care of their shared hunting grounds, and that they would remain separate, sovereign, self-determining, and independent nations. Similarly, the Nishnaabeg did not feel the need to "ask" or "negotiate" with the Haudenosaunee Confederacy for the "right" to "self-government. . . ." [B]oth parties knew they had a shared responsibility to take care of the territory, following their own culturally based environmental ethics to ensure that the plant and animal nations they were so dependent on them carried on in a healthy state in perpetuity. Both parties knew that they had to follow their own cultural protocols for renewing the relationship on a regular basis to promote peace, goodwill, and friendship among the Nishnaabeg and the Haudenosaunee. Both parties knew they had to follow the original instructions passed down to them from their ancestors if peace was to be maintained.

Although Gdoo-naaganinaa is a living treaty with the Haudenosaunee, the Nishnaabeg understanding of it can give us great insight into Nishnaabeg traditions governing treaty making and their expectations in their early interactions with settler governments. . . . They expected Gdoo-naaganinaa would be taken care of so that their way of life could continue for the generations to come. They expected respect for their government, their sovereignty, and their nation. They expected a relationship of peace, mutual respect, and mutual benefit, and these were the same expectations the Nishnaabeg carried with them into the colonial period. . . .

Too often in contemporary times we are presented with a worldview that renders us incapable of visioning any alternatives to our present situation and relationship with colonial governments and settler states. Indigenist thinkers compel us to return to our own knowledge systems to find answers. For the Nishnaabeg people, Gdoo-naaganinaa does just that. It gives us an ancient template for realizing separate jurisdictions within a shared territory. It outlines the "rights" and "responsibilities" of both parties in the ongoing relationship, and it clearly demonstrates that our ancestors did not intend for our nations to be subsumed by the British crown or the Canadian state when they negotiated those original treaties. It is time to decolonize our relationships with our neighboring nations, and it is time to decolonize our relationship with the Canadian state.

# Notes

1. Gdoo-naaganinaa means "Our Dish" and refers to a pre-colonial treaty between the Nishnaabeg and the Haudenosaunee Confederacy. This is the inclusive form, as opposed to the ndoo-naaganinaa "our dish (but not yours)." Gdoo-naaganinaa is a symbol of our shared ecology and territory in southern Ontario.

2. For a more complete discussion see the *Final Report of the Royal Commission on Aboriginal Peoples*, vol. 1 (Ottawa, Ontario: Minister of Supply and Services, 1996), http://www.ainc-inac. gc.ca/ch/rcap/sg/sg11_e.html#36.

3. Harold Johnson, *Two Families: Treaties and Government* (Saskatoon, Saskatchewan: Purich Publishing, 2007), 27.

4. Dale Turner, *This Is Not a Peace Pipe: Towards a Critical Indigenous Philosophy* (Toronto, Ontario: University of Toronto Press, 2006), 8. This concept is known as treaty federalism in Canada.

5. Turner, *This Is Not a Peace Pipe*, 3–38, and for a broader discussion on this imagery in Canadian culture generally see Daniel Frances, *The Imaginary Indian: The Image of the Indian in Canadian Culture* (Vancouver, British Columbia: Arsenal Pulp Press, 1992).

6. Lester-Irabinna Rigney, "Internationalization of an Indigenous Anticolonial Cultural Critique of Research Methodologies: A Guide to Indigenist Research Methodology and Its Principles," *Wicazo Sa Review* 14, no. 2 (Fall 1999): 109–22; Linda Tuhiwai Smith, *Decolonizing Methodologies: Research and Indigenous Peoples* (London: Zed Books, 1999); Kiera Ladner, "When Buffalo Speaks: Creating an AlterNative Understanding of Traditional Blackfoot Governance" (PhD dissertation, Department of Political Science, Carleton University, 2001), 37–38.

7. Ladner, "When Buffalo Speaks," 69–70.

8. These are known to the Nishnaabeg as the Seven Grandfather teachings, see Eddie Benton Banai, *The Mishomis Book* (Hayward, Wis.: Red School House Publishing, 1988), 64.

9. This has somewhat changed in contemporary times. While many elders and knowledge holders acknowledge that there was/is a distinct territoriality to the clan system, with specific clans holding responsibilities to particular areas as also evidenced by Darlene Johnson ("Connecting People to Place: Great Lakes Aboriginal History in Cultural Context," report prepared for the Ipperwash Inquiry, 2004, http://www.ipperwashinquiry.ca/transcripts/pdf/P1_Tab_1.pdf) in the Eurocanadian historical record, there are now often many different clans present (and many people who do not know their clan affiliation at all) in a single reserve community. This is in part a result of the original colonial construction of our communities.

10. Located in the southeastern portion of Nishnaabeg territory.

11. To Western scientists different species of fish gather at this location in the spring and fall to migrate and spawn. To the Nishnaabeg, these are not just "species of fish," they are nations within their own right, with political structures unto their own. This reflects a different conceptualization of "nationalism" similar to the conceptualizations in Ladner's *Women and Blackfoot Nationalism*. To be clear, fish clans represent the Nishnaabeg people, fish nations are the actual species of fish.

12. Mnjikanming is located near Orillia, Ontario, Canada, and has a series of ancient fish weirs reminding us of this relationship.

13. Creator.

14. John Borrows, *Recovering Canada: The Resurgence of Indigenous Law* (Toronto, Ontario: University of Toronto Press, 2002), 16–20.

15. Ibid., 19. Borrows notes that there are many slightly different versions of this story in print and in our oral traditions.

16. Nishnaabeg women.

17. Interviewed for another project by Leanne Simpson, 31 March 2003. Judy DaSilva is a traditional knowledge holder and environmental activist.

18. James Morrison, *The Robinson Treaties of 1850: A Case Study*, prepared for the Royal Commission on Aboriginal Peoples (Ottawa, Ontario: Minister of Supply and Services, 1994). (Research reports from the Royal Commission on Aboriginal Peoples are available in digital form on "For Seven Generations: An Informational Legacy of the Royal Commission on Aboriginal Peoples [RCAP] CD-ROM," Libraxus.)

19. Ibid.

20. This is how Algonquin people are known in their language.

21. Paula Sherman, "Indawendiwin: Spiritual Ecology as the Foundation of Omàmìwinini Relations." (PhD dissertation, Department of Indigenous Studies, Trent University, 2007), 207.

22. Ibid.

23. For a complete discussion see Leanne Simpson, "Traditional Ecological Knowledge: Insights, Issues and Implications." PhD dissertation, University of Manitoba, 1999.

24. The dish wampum belt is currently housed at the Royal Ontario Museum. For a Nishnaabeg historical telling of the meaning of the wampum belt see D. Johnson, "Connecting People to Place."

25. The purpose of this paper is to focus on discussing Nishnaabeg pre-colonial treaty-making processes. For discussions of the treaty from a Haudenosaunee perspective see Barbara Gray's "The Effects of the Fur Trade on Peace: A Haudenosaunee Woman's Perspective," in *Aboriginal People and the Fur Trade: Proceedings of the 8th North American Fur Trade Conferences*, Louise Johnson, ed. (Akwesasne, Mohawk Territory: Dollco Printing, 2001), n.p.; J.A. Gibson, "Concerning the League: The Iroquois League Tradition as Dictated in Onondaga," H. Woodbury, R. Henry, and H. Webster, eds, *Algonquian and Iroquoian Linguistics Memoir* 9 (1991); A.C. Parker, *Parker on the Iroquois: Iroquois Uses of Maize and Other Food Plants: The Code of Handsome Lake, the Seneca Prophet: The Constitution of the Five Nations* (New York: State University of New York, 1992).

26. For a complete discussion of Haudenosaunee land ethics see Susan Hill, "The Clay We Are Made of: An Examination of Haudenosaunee Land Tenure on the Grand River Territory" (PhD dissertation, Department of Indigenous Studies, Trent University, 2006); Susan Hill, "Traveling Down the River of Life Together in Peace and Friendship, Forever: Haudenosaunee Land Ethics and Treaty Agreements as the Basis for Restructuring the Relationship with the British Crown," Leanne Simpson, ed., *Lighting the Eighth Fire: The Liberation, Resurgence and Protection of Indigenous Nations* (Winnipeg, Manitoba: Arbeiter Ring, forthcoming).

27. Banai, *Mishomis Book*, 90–95.

# PART ONE

## Additional Readings

Alfred, Taiaiake (Gerald). *Peace, Power, Righteousness: An Indigenous Manifesto*. Toronto: Oxford University Press, 1999.

Ashok, Mathur, Jonathan Dewar, and Mike DeGagné, eds. *Cultivating Canada: Reconciliation through the Lens of Cultural Diversity*. Ottawa: Aboriginal Healing Foundation Research Series, 2011.

Monture, Patricia. *Thunder in My Soul: A Mohawk Woman Speaks*. Halifax: Fernwood Publishing, 1995.

——. *Journeying Forward: Dreaming First Nations Independence*. Halifax: Fernwood Publishing, 1999.

Neves, Stephanie Nohelani, Andrea Smith, and Michelle H. Raheja. *Native Studies Keywords*. Tuscan: The University of Arizona Press, 2015.

Simpson, Audra, and Andrea Smith. *Theorizing Native Studies*. Durham, NC: Duke University Press, 2014.

Vowell, Chelsea. *Indigenous Writes: A Guide to First Nations, Métis & Inuit Issues in Canada*. Winnipeg: Highwater Press, 2016.

## Relevant Websites

**CBC 8th Fire: Aboriginal Peoples, Canada & the Way Forward**

http://www.cbc.ca/8thfire/2011/11/tv-series-8th-fire.html

*Drawing on extended interviews and media footage, this CBC-produced four-part documentary series provides an in-depth look at the legacy of Settler colonialism in Canada calling on Settler and Indigenous peoples to reconcile historic pasts and build harmonious futures.*

**Ogimaa Mikana: Reclaiming/Renaming**

http://ogimaamikana.tumblr.com/

*This website documents an aesthetic endeavour to name, re-map, and re-assert an Indigenous presence in what is now called Toronto and the Province of Ontario.*

**Tribal Nations Maps**

http://www.tribalnationsmaps.com

*This website outlines the work of Aaron Carapella (Cherokee) who has created maps (available for purchase) illustrating the original territories and names of the Indigenous peoples of North America.*

**Royal Commission on Aboriginal Peoples (All Volumes)**

http://www.collectionscnada.gc.ca/webarchives/200711150553257/

http://www.ainc-inac.gc.ca/ch/rcap/sg/sgmm_e.html

*The Royal Commission on Aboriginal Peoples (RCAP) was released in 1996 and consists of five volumes. While not an exhaustive source, it offers a great deal of information and history of the Indigenous peoples of Canada and their relationships with the Canadian State.*

# Films

*The Grandfather of All Treaties.* Dir. Candace Maracle. Vtape, 2015.
*The Re-naming of PKOLS.* Dir. Steven Davies. Steven Davies, 2015.
*The Disappearing Indian.* Dir. Grant McLean. National Film Board of Canada, 1995.

*The Other Side of the Ledger: An Indian View of the Hudson's Bay Company.* Dir. Willie Dunn and Martin De Falco. National Film Board of Canada, 1972.
*You Are on Indian Land.* Dir. Mort Ransen. National Film Board of Canada, 1969.

# Key Terms

Aboriginalism
Colonialism
Gdoo-naaganinaa
Resurgence

Racism
Ukwehuwé
White Settler society

# Discussion Questions

1.  What is meant by "Aboriginalism"? How does it structure and disregard the aspirations of Indigenous nations? How does it embody the history of Settler colonialism?
2.  How does Leanne Betasamosake Simpson define Gdoo-naaganinaa? What is the significance of the "Dish with One Spoon" where political diplomacy and decolonizing relationships are concerned?

3.  What are the similarities and differences between the following terms: anticolonialism, post-colonializing, and neocolonialism?
4.  What is the role of fear, according to Taiaiake Alfred, where maintaining colonial relationships and ideology is concerned? What would it take to move toward colonial reparations beyond fear?

# Activities

Take 10–20 minutes to reflect on what you have been taught about Indigenous and Canadian histories. Discuss your individual reflections as a class. What kinds of patterns and differences emerge? How do these lessons make you feel? How have they impacted on the way you think of yourself and the land on which you live?

Read Audra Simpson's article "Subjects of Sovereignty: Indigeneity, The Revenue Rule, and the Juridics of Failed Consent" and organize a class discussion about Mort Ransen's film

*You Are on Indian Land.* According to Simpson, what is it that makes "savagery and lawlessness" possible in "the public mind" and how is this represented in the film? What does it mean to describe Canadian law as a "failed episode of consent" and how is this embodied in the "Settler anxiety" depicted in the film?

Watch the 1955 National Film Board production *The Disappearing Indian* (written and directed by Grant McLean). What colonial tropes, Eurocentric knowledge, and assumptions are present in this film?

# PART TWO

❖

# Nation-Building and the Deeply Racialized Other

## Editor Introduction

In his book *Everything You Know about Indians Is Wrong*, Comanche curator Paul Chaat Smith asks Americans to think *seriously* about the representation of Indigenous peoples in the historic colonial imaginary. His concern is with romanticism, or the depiction of Indigenous peoples based on myths, stereotypes, and oversimplification. Romanticism has long constituted a distinct form of racism aimed at Indigenous peoples. As Chaat Smith writes, it is "a specialized vocabulary created by Euros for Indians" ensuring in turn "a status as strange, primitive and exotic" (2009: 17). In this chapter, we provide a set of two articles written by Indigenous scholars on matters of race and representation.

Mohawk scholar Deborah Doxtator raises the idea of Indianness. In her view, the concept cannot be considered without addressing historic acts of racism and Settler colonial injustice. Indianness is required in order to construct Indigenous peoples as different and Other. In the minds of white Settler colonists, Indians are everything that civilization is not. They live in a world of long ago. They refuse to adopt modern conveniences. Their deficits enable and effect histories of dispossession. Defined as just so many teepees, headdresses, and totem poles, Indianness makes possible what Smith (2006: 68) referred to as a pillar in the logic of genocide: the idea that Indigenous peoples must always be disappearing.

Histories of genocide are made possible through rigid assertions of difference between "real Indians" and Others. Without the difference produced through myths and stereotypes about "authentic'" or "real Indians," there can be nothing gained (or lost) by Indigenous peoples. They cannot move past the primitivism that defines their culture, or become civilized, for that matter. Resistance is paradoxical. The refusal to perform Indianness only reaffirms the idea that they have all but disappeared. Romanticism makes possible the ongoing dispossession of Indigenous peoples. So long as Indians are incapable of being themselves, rendered invisible, or no longer living, the act of land appropriation ensues.

Romanticism makes possible a caricature of Indigenous identities. It forecloses the breadth of Indigenous identities that exist and are possible in modern contexts. As Chaat Smith writes, "silence about our own complicated histories supports the colonizer's idea that the only real Indians are full blooded, from a reservation, speak their language, and practice the religion of their ancestors" (2009: 26). How do we explain this need for authenticity? What are modern practices of difference making, where are they located, and how do they operate in the contemporary world? These are just some of questions being asked by Indigenous scholars about colonial representations of Indianness.

The politics of representation is just as much tied to whiteness as it is to Indianness. In saying this, we are not suggesting that Indigenous peoples abandon the work that is done in communities in order to focus on non-Indian issues. Rather, we want to take seriously the meaning of Indianness in the mind of the colonizer. If the privilege of whiteness is to pass invisibly as the norm, then the time has come to expose the difference that Indianness makes. As Carol Schick and Cree/Métis scholar Verna St Denis wrote: "addressing racism means more than examining the experience of those who experience racism" (2005: 299). Challenging racism also involves exposing the ways that "white men name and mark Others, thereby naming and marking themselves" (ibid.)

Naming and marking Others as different does not only involve racist beliefs about the inherent superiority and inferiority of individuals. Historically, the process of difference making was gendered—often involving sexist and demeaning assumptions about Indigenous women. This was especially true of early colonialism in what is now Canada. As Cree scholar Winona Stevenson wrote, stereotypes about Indigenous women were often used to create boundaries between Indigenous and white Settler populations (1999). Many of these understandings served to justify early colonial dominance and policies of exclusion.

Representations of Indianness are central to the construction of white Settler identities. The colonizer imagines himself as civilized, but only insofar as he establishes himself in contrast with the mythical construction of savagism. The ideal woman construct discussed by Stevenson is inseparable from this process of upholding the binary between civility and savagism. She suggests that missionary accounts are rife with examples of "exploited, overworked drudges, abused, misused, [and] dirty" (1999: 58). Put simply, the pinnacle of European womanhood would likely never have been accomplished without colonial representations of Indigenous womanhood.

In order to justify the appropriation of Indian lands, the colonizer has always to prove the inferiority of Indigenous peoples. The rationale for these kinds of dispossession found their early ideological basis in colonial representations of Indianness and savagery. As Stevenson (1999: 64) who quotes the work of Sarah Carter (1997) shows "expounding the righteous triumph of civilization over savagery" required "proving the inferiority of the Indian." These understandings enabled the transfer of Indian lands into the colonizers' hands, gave way to the statutory subjugation of Indigenous women, and have stood the test of time into the twenty-first century (Cannon, 2014). As Razack (2002) points out in her discussion of the murder of Pamela George, representations of Indian womanhood in particular work still today to construct bodies that are violable with impunity.

The challenge we face as Indigenous peoples today is very much dependent on the ability to claim a more vibrant and dynamic representation of our peoples. As Thomas King suggests, the mission in particular remains complicated by practices that reproduce the "Dead Indian," which he defines as "the stereotypes and clichés that North America has conjured up out of experience and out of its collective imaginings and fears." It is this precise colonial imaginary that works to disappear both "Live" and "Legal" Indians—Indians who are required to "get out of the way" in order for the "counterfeit" to ensue. The conundrum, as King suggests, is even further complicated by a tendency on behalf of a Settler State to rid itself of the "Indian problem" and to recuperate its own Settler sovereignty at every turn.

Like Doxtator, Chaat Smith, and many other Indigenous artists and critical thinkers, Thomas King focuses on the task of reinventing ourselves as "Indians," and in the face of popular and scholarly representations that have relegated us to past domains. There is another story to be told in his estimation. They tell the story of contemporary Indians, including traditional symbols and meanings resituated in the present (Simpson, 1998: 52). They force us to "reflect on what . . . things meant, and what they now mean" (ibid., 52–3). The task of reinvention will remain as much urgent as it is difficult into the future. As Chaat Smith suggests, it will "require invention, not rewriting" (2009: 52). It may even require "a final break with a form that was never about us in the first place" (ibid.).

CHAPTER 3

# "The Idea of Indianness" and Once Upon a Time
## The Role of Indians in History

*Deborah Doxtator*

Just a little more than a hundred years ago school texts were describing Indians as being "ferocious and quarrelsome," "great gluttons" and "great drunkards" (Miles, 1870: xxii). How have attitudes towards Indian people changed? Do people still carry in their minds the idea, even if it goes unsaid, that Indian culture is "primitive" and incapable of survival in a twentieth-century environment? Are some people still looking for the disappearing Indian? What does "Indian" mean?

Teepees, headdresses, totem poles, birch bark canoes, face paint, fringes, buckskin, and tomahawks—when anyone sees images, drawings, or paintings of these things they immediately think of "*Indians*." They are symbols of "Indianness" that have become immediately recognizable to the public. To take it one step further, they are the symbols that the public uses in its definition of what an Indian is. To the average person, Indians, *real* Indians, in their purest form of "Indianness," live in a world of long ago where there are no high-rises, no

snowmobiles, no colour television. They live in the woods or in places that are unknown called "Indian Reserves." The Indians that people know best are the ones they have read about in adventure stories as a child, cut out and pasted in school projects, read about in the newspaper. They may have "played Indian" as a game, or dressed up as an Indian for Halloween. To many people "Indians" are not real, any more than Bugs Bunny, Marilyn Monroe, or Anne of Green Gables are real to them. So it is not surprising that when they do meet Indian people they have some very strange ideas about how "Indians" behave, live, and speak.

In their excitement at meeting this celebrity, this "Indian," people sometimes say foolish things, that if they thought about it, they would never ask anyone: "Is that your own hair?," "What is the significance of that design, is it sacred?," "Say something in *Indian*." Other Indian people have been asked whether or not their blood is red, or if feathers once grew out of their heads.

It is very difficult to discuss "Indianness" with any measure of neutrality. The emotions and experience of both parties in the relationship between "Indians" and "Whites" has been such that there is no easy way to discuss the facts. It is impossible

---

In Deborah Doxtator, *Fluffs and Feathers: An Exhibit on the Symbols of Indianness: A Resource Guide* (Brantford: Woodland Cultural Centre), 199. Reprinted with permission.

to discuss the concept of "Indianness" without addressing racism and the injustices that have occurred. It is impossible to talk about "Indianness" without facing the uncomfortable reality of the dispossession of one people by another. . . .

"Indian" has meant so many things, both good and bad: from an idealized all-spiritual, environmentalist, to a "primitive" down-trodden welfare case. These popular images of "Indians" have very little to do with actual people. Instead they reflect the ideas that one culture has manufactured about another people. These images influence the concept of "Indianness" held by many people.

Definitions of "Indianness" have changed a little over the past four hundred years. In the seventeenth century, there were debates concerning whether or not Indians were animals or human beings. In the twentieth century, the debate about Indians has shifted to whether or not "Indians" are competent human beings, capable of running their own affairs. For decades, Indian children grew up being told that their culture was inferior, their religion was wrong, and their language useless.

The concept of "The Indian" as primitive, undeveloped, and inferior has a long history, that extends back into the sixteenth century (Dickason, 1984: 35). Ever since the two races first met, non-Indians have been trying to teach, convert, "improve" or otherwise change Indian peoples. The idea has persisted that, somehow, Indians are really just undeveloped human beings in desperate need of training in the proper way to live and make a living.

Academic disciplines still have great difficulty accepting Indian art, history, literature, music, and technology as art, history, literature, music, and technology without first placing it in an anthropological context. Museums continue to foster the view of Indians as "pre-historic." They have special galleries that focus on presenting something called "Native Culture" in ways that are perceived inappropriate for "Canadian culture." It is not particularly unusual for museums such as the National Museum of Civilization to display human remains from a native culture which have included skeletal remains in their archaeological exhibits. It is

seen as being comparable to scientific displays of the skeleton of "Early Man." But it is not likely that the bones of Laura Secord will be installed in any museum exhibit in the near future. Indians, like the "Iron-Age" man, are seen as being separated from modern technological society by the fact that their technology, or rather perceived lack of it, makes them "primitives" or "wild-men," ancient ancestors that just don't exist anymore.

It has been difficult for industrial Canadian society to accept that non-industrial cultures are still viable. To Canadian society, Indian cultures are based firmly in the past, and Western culture has a tradition of repudiating the past as out-of-date and irrelevant to the present. Since the sixteenth century, "Indians" have been seen as representing an earlier, less civilized version of Europeans. They have, in the minds of Europeans and Canadians, come to symbolize human beings at an earlier, less complex stage of development.

This has meant that images of "Indians" created by Western society have emphasized their perception of Indian inferiority. In the nineteenth and early twentieth centuries "Indian" culture was either denounced as immoral or seen as having degenerated from a higher form of culture. To those who were inclined to see the world as a struggle between good and bad, God and the Devil, Indians were "pagans," devil worshippers. To those who accepted Darwin's theories of evolution, Indians were seen as halfway between men and beasts, simple people who needed to be eventually "raised" to the level of Western civilization through education and training. To those who saw the world in terms of a "golden past" against which everything in the present could never measure up, "Indians were simply no longer what they used to be" (Barbeau, 1923). No matter what the approach, all of these views concluded that Indian societies were ultimately inferior to Western societies.

Every culture creates images of how it sees itself and the rest of the world. Incidental to these images of self-definition are definitions of the "other." Canadian society through control over such tools as advertising, literature, history, and the entertainment media has the power to create images of other peoples and these images often operate as a form of social control. For example, images in the media of women as incompetent, physically inferior, and scatter-brained have justified why women should not hold executive positions in Canadian business. Racial stereotypes in television situation-comedies have justified why it is all right to deny other racial groups access to power and financial rewards. Indians as part of a different racial group have been subject to this type of "control" but also to a unique form of physiological warfare. Minority groups often endure discrimination but they never experience situations in which the discriminating group usurps their identity. The image of the "romantic Indian princess" was created for the benefit and imagination of Euro-Canadian, not for the benefit of Indian people. It uses symbols derived from Indian cultures and changes them so that they better suit the needs of Canadian society. Through use of the romantic images of "Indian princesses" and "Indian chiefs" non-Indian people can become "noble Indians" in their own minds. . . .

## Once Upon a Time: The Role of Indians in History

In disposition the Savages were fierce, cruel and cunning. They seldom forgave an affront. They used to SCALP the enemies whom they had killed, and to torment those whom they had taken alive. . . . However, as the Indians were so cruel and bloodthirsty, we cannot but lament and condemn the practice of using their services in warfare. Those who used them were often unable to manage them. (Miles, 1870)

Eighteen days after setting out Davis handed over his charges to the personnel at Fort Battleford—from outside the buildings. Realizing from personal experience the effect of such close contact with over a thousand Indians, the personnel there suggested that before presenting his dispatches it might be well for Davis to strip to the skin, burn his clothing and take a bath. (Robins, 1948)

Interpretations of history can best be understood as a series of stories or myths. My generation grew up with the story of how North America was "discovered" by Christopher Columbus and of how civilization was "started" by the French. There were lots of statements in the textbooks about "virgin land," "uninhabited territories." Then suddenly into the picture came the Indians. Sometimes they were portrayed as tools, sometimes as threats, sometimes as allies. Indians were incidental because the story was not about them. They were just there—in the way.

I remember learning about Cartier, about Frontenac, about Brock, and feeling disappointed that the Indians always lost. When we studied the fur trade, the Indians were always doing foolish things, giving up all their valuable fur resources worth thousands of dollars for a few pots and pans, selling huge tracts of land for a handful of shiny beads. I didn't want to accept it, but there it was in print, in the textbook that never lied.

It wasn't until I went to University that I understood that what I had read, studied, and reiterated in my test answers was a type of story. It was somebody else's story about how Canada was settled, and it functioned as a justification and explanation for "the way things happened." This fall I discovered that the story still functions in this way. One of my tutorial students remarked to me that he felt it was unfair to blame the Canadian government for the reserve system and broken treaties because it was unintentional that the treaty promises were not kept, that no one had planned that the Cree in Saskatchewan would starve, that it "just happened."

The Canadian history textbook was sprinkled with references to the clash between "primitive and civilized societies." It stated that "despite their nomadic habits and their mixed blood the Métis were not savages," but "unsophisticated peoples." Métis people had "primitive nationalism"; Crees didn't advance to the battle, they "prowled" around neighbourhoods frightening townspeople. Riel himself was said to be filled with "primitive aggressiveness and hostility" (Francis et al., 1986). In the bulk of the reading, Indians still were in the periphery of the story, their part was still that of the obstacle, and source of conflict.

Historically, these stories about Indians being "primitive," violent, and generally incompetent at self-government justified two elements of Canadian Indian policy: non-Indian land settlement and non-Indian control over Indians. For example, it was easy for nineteenth and often twentieth century analysts to justify why Indians no longer should control the land. They simply didn't know how to use it "properly." They built no roads, no fences, raised no cattle, they were not "improving" the land with European technology. Regulations were passed in the Canadian Parliament to control Indians—where they could live, how they were governed, how they should make their living. In the years following the second Riel Rebellion, Indians in the west were not allowed to leave their reserves without the permission of the Indian agent. The government decided who was an Indian and who was not. During the nineteenth century, no other group in Canada was as closely regulated and controlled.

Why were Indian people so closely watched and regulated? Why has this regulation seemed understandable to the public? Why does the phrase "wild Indians" make the public feel uneasy if not frightened? Conflict between Indians fighting for their land and settlers fighting to take the land happened in the relatively recent past, only a hundred years ago. Or it may be as some have argued, that Indians have always been viewed by historians and other scholars as being a submerged, frighteningly violent part of the Euro-North American psyche (Fielder, 1968).

Indians have always been viewed by Euro-North Americans in comparison with themselves. In the seventeenth century, Europeans believed that all of mankind was descended from Adam, the first man. Europeans also believed in a hierarchy of mankind. At the top of the hierarchy of societies, not surprisingly, were Europeans, and under them in development and "civilization" were all of the other peoples who were not Europeans.

From the beginning, Europeans had tried to set Indians into this order of peoples. The earliest perceptions of Indians were that they were more like the ancient Romans or Biblical Israelites than they were

like Europeans. Lafitau, an early French "Indian" scholar went to great pains to demonstrate the similarity of North American customs and language to classical models. Early engravings of Indians often present them in poses and clothing that suggests a connection with ancient Greece or Rome. . . .

This tradition of presenting Indian individuals as classical figures has continued well into the twentieth century in the form of heraldry on coats of arms of Canadian cities (City of Toronto, City of Brantford), provinces (Newfoundland, Nova Scotia), and historical cultural organizations (Ontario Historical Society).

In establishing the hierarchy of societies, the major criteria for classification was industrial technology and material wealth—two accomplishments of which Europeans were very proud. When this criteria was applied to Indians, most Europeans came to the conclusion that "Indians" were also "savages." They lacked all the things that were necessary to be accepted as "civilized" and as Europeans. They had no printing presses, no books, no wine, no factories, no European style government, no Christianity, no guns, and "no polite conversations" (Dickason, 1984: 52). The associations of Indians with the European tradition of the "primitive" half-animal "wild man" were so strong that Indians were often depicted with long flowing beards and body hair even though explorers repeatedly remarked upon the fact that surprisingly, Indians were not very hairy and did not have beards.

To Cartier on the Gaspe coast in 1534, there was no doubt that the occupants of the new land were to be considered "wild" men:

> This people may well be called savage; for they are the sorriest folk there can be in the world and the whole lot of them had not anything above the value of five sous, their canoes and fishing nets excepted. . . . They have no other dwelling but their canoes which they turn upside down and sleep on the ground underneath. They eat their meat almost raw, only warming it a little on the coals and the same with their fish. (Hoffman, 1961: 135)

Described as being without houses, possessions, and comforts, the Indian nonetheless attracted some interest from those Europeans who were interested in changing materialistic European society. Like unfallen man, Adam, the Indians appeared to be very generous with their possessions and as some saw them, completely, "without evil and without guile" (Berkhofer, 1979: 11). This idyllic "Adam" side to the "savage" "uncivilized" man was used to great effect by those who were dissatisfied with society and sought to reform it. They presented "Indians" in ways that directly criticized European society.

Peter Martyr's sixteenth century history of the conquest of the "New World" contrasted the "crafty deceitful" Europeans with the "Indians" who lived instead in a world of innocence, liberty, and ease uncorrupted by civilized ideas of property, greed, and luxury (Crane, 1952: 4). In Montaigne's "On Cannibals," Brazilian people were used to criticize French poverty and social inequality. He contrasted the aboriginal practices of cannibalism with the common European practice of torture and concluded "better to eat your dead enemy as do the Amerindians than to eat a man alive in the manner of the Europeans" (Dickason, 1984: 56). Similarly the women of France were chastened for their lack of affection for their children, scarcely waiting "the birth of their children to put them out to nursemaids," unlike "savage women" who breast-fed their own children with no ill physical effects (Jaenan, 1976: 33).

By the seventeenth century, Europeans had certain fixed ideas about what an Indian was supposed to look like. The "official costume" of Indians in European art was a feather skirt and upright head-dress occasionally with some feathers at the wrists and ankles (Chiapelli, 1976: 504). The physical remoteness of Indians to Europeans made it possible to create representations of abstract "Indians" that bore no resemblance to reality. In a sixteenth century illustration depicting Amerigo Vespucci awakening "America" from the sleep in her hammock, America is represented as being a nude Indian woman. She is surrounded by European-looking animals in a forest scene; a spear is propped against a tree. These abstract depictions of Indians created a visual symbolic language that was immediately recognizable as "Indianness"; nudity, feathers, headdresses, bows and arrows. It was upon this system of symbols that nineteenth and twentieth century symbolic language about "Indianness" was elaborated and developed.

Whenever Canadian and American society has found itself in competition with Indians over land and resources, the images generated about Indians by the non-Indian public are predictably negative. They are designed to create feelings of hate and anger. The newspaper engravings of the late nineteenth century provide ample examples of images of hate. "The Sentinel's Evening Visitors," depicting Indian women waiting to get a drink of the guard's whiskey, possibly in exchange for certain services, and the sketch entitled "Indian Loafers" both from Canadian newspapers, illustrate the feeling of disgust that the public was expected to share with the artist. Depictions of leering crazed Indians threatening women and children, riding demented through their camps crying for scalps, making off with stock animals and anything else that was portable, were common in newspapers of the 1870, and 1880s such as *The Graphic* and *The Illustrated War News*.

The pictorial story in these same newspapers of the Canadian and American participants in the wars with the Indians are strikingly heroic. Although an Indian may be depicted as scowling, demented, savage beyond all reason, the settler or the soldier is neat, calm, and in control. Although threatened, they appear as though they will never be defeated. This sense of the superiority, of "British cheer and pluck" in the Battle of Batoche was reflected in the newspaper coverage of the victory for the Canadian forces:

The charge started at high noon by routing them out of the advanced pits. At 3:30 p.m. the enemy were totally routed, many having been killed and wounded, many more were prisoners in our hands and others had fled and were hiding in the surrounding bushes. Col. Williams said simply: "Men will you follow me?" The answer was drowned in a roar of cheering such as I never heard before. Over the bluff we went, yelling like mad. The Indians fired one volley and ran. Neither the Indians nor halfbreeds stood their ground. (*Winnipeg Free Press*, 13 May 1910)

## References

Barbeau, Marus. 1923. *Indian Days in the Canadian Rockies*. Toronto: MacMillan.

Berkhofer, Robert. 1979. *The White Man's Indian*. New York: Vintage Books.

Chiapelli, Fred. 1976. *First Images of America*, Vol. 1. Berkeley: University of California.

Crane, Fred. 1952. "The Noble Savage in America 1815–1860." Unpublished PhD Thesis, Yale University.

Dickason, Olive. 1984. *Myth of the Savage*. Calgary: University of Alberta Press.

Fielder, Leslie. 1968. *The Return of the Vanishing American*. Toronto: Stern and Day.

Francis, Douglas, et al., eds. 1986. *Readings in Canadian History: Post Confederation* (pp. 63–127). Toronto: Holt Rinehart and Winston of Canada, Ltd.

Hoffman, Bernard. 1961. *Cabot to Cartier*. Toronto: University of Toronto Press.

Jaenen, C.J. 1976. *Friend and Foe*. New York: Columbia University Press.

Miles, Henry. 1870. *The Child's History of Canada: For the Use of the Elementary Schools and of the Young Reader*. Montreal: Dawson Brothers.

Robins, John D., ed. 1948. "West by North" in *A Pocketful of Canada*, written for the Canadian Council of Education for Citizenship. Toronto: Collins.

*Winnipeg Free Press*. 1910. Friday, 13 May. Souvenir Reprint, Glenbow Archives.

## CHAPTER 4

# Too Heavy to Lift

*Thomas King*

*Few looking at photos of mixed-bloods would be likely to say, "But they don't look like Irishmen."*

—Louis Owens, *I Hear the Train*

Indians come in all sorts of social and historical configurations. North American popular culture is littered with savage, noble, and dying Indians, while in real life we have Dead Indians, Live Indians, and Legal Indians.

Dead Indians are, sometimes, just that. Dead Indians. But the Dead Indians I'm talking about are not the deceased sort. Nor are they all that inconvenient. They are the stereotypes and clichés that North America has conjured up out of

In *The Inconvenient Indian: A Curious Account of Native People in North America*. (Toronto: Doubleday Canada, 2012), 53–76. Excerpted from *The Inconvenient Indian* by Thomas King. Copyright © 2012 Thomas King. Reprinted by permission of Anchor Canada/Doubleday Canada, a division of Penguin Random House Canada Limited.

experience and out of its collective imaginings and fears. North America has had a long association with Native people, but despite the history that the two groups have shared, North America no longer *sees* Indians. What it sees are war bonnets, beaded shirts, fringed deerskin dresses, loincloths, headbands, feathered lances, tomahawks, moccasins, face paint, and bone chokers. These bits of cultural debris—authentic and constructed—are what literary theorists like to call "signifiers," signs that create a "simulacrum," which Jean Baudrillard, the French sociologist and postmodern theorist, succinctly explained as something that "is never that which conceals the truth—it is the truth which conceals that there is none."

. . . For those of us who are not French theorists but who know the difference between a motor home and a single-wide trailer, a simulacrum is something that represents something that never existed. Or, in other words, the only truth of the thing is the lie itself. . . .

You can find Dead Indians everywhere. Rodeos, powwows, movies, television commercials. . . .

I probably sound testy, and I suppose part of me is. But I shouldn't be. After all, Dead Indians are the only antiquity that North America has. Europe has Greece and Rome. China has the powerful dynasties. Russia has the Cossacks. South and Central America have the Aztecs, the Incas, and the Maya.

North America has Dead Indians.

This is why Littlefeather didn't show up in a Dior gown, and why West and Campbell and Fontaine didn't arrive at their respective events in Brioni suits, Canali dress shirts, Zegni ties, and Salvatore Ferragamo shoes. Whatever cultural significance they may have for Native peoples, full feather headdresses and beaded buckskins are, first and foremost, White North America's signifiers of Indian authenticity. Their visual value at ceremonies in Los Angeles or Ottawa is—as the credit card people say—priceless. . . .

On the other hand, if you like the West and are the outdoors type, you can run out to Wyoming and pedal your bicycle over Dead Indian Pass, spend the evening at Dead Indian campground, and in the morning cycle across Dead Indian Meadows on your way to Dead Indian Peak. If you happen to be in California, you can hike Dead Indian Canyon. And if you're an angler, you can fish Dead Indian Creek in Oregon or Dead Indian Lake in Oklahoma, though the U.S. Board on Geographic Names recently voted to rename it Dead Warrior Lake.

Sometimes you can only watch and marvel at the ways in which the Dead Indian has been turned into products: Red Chief Sugar, Calumet Baking Soda, the Atlanta Braves, Big Chief Jerky, Grey Owl Wild Rice, Red Man Tobacco, the Chicago Blackhawks, Mutual of Omaha, Winnebago Motor Homes, Big Chief Tablet, Indian motorcycles, the Washington Redskins, American Spirit Cigarettes, Jeep Cherokee, the Cleveland Indians, and Tomahawk missiles. . . .

One of my favourite Dead Indian products is Land O' Lakes butter, which features an Indian Maiden in a buckskin dress on her knees holding a box of butter at bosom level. The wag who designed the box arranged it so that if you fold the box in a certain way, the Indian woman winds up *au naturel,* sporting naked breasts. Such a clever fellow. . . .

All of this pales by comparison with the contemporary entrepreneurs who have made a bull-market business out of Dead Indian culture and spirituality. . . . Folks such as Lynn Andrews, Mary Summer Rains, Jamie Samms, Don Le Vie, Jr., and Mary Elizabeth Marlow, just to mention some of the more prominent New Age spiritual CEOs, have manufactured fictional Dead Indian entities—Agnes Whistling Elk, Ruby Plenty Chiefs, No Eyes, Iron Thunderhorse, Barking Tree, and Max the crystal skull—who supposedly taught them the secrets of Native spirituality. They have created Dead Indian narratives that are an impossible mix of Taoism, Buddhism, Druidism, science fiction, and general nonsense, tied together with Dead Indian ceremony and sinew to give their product provenance and validity, along with a patina of exoticism. . . .

From the frequency with which Dead Indians appear in advertising, in the names of businesses, as icons for sports teams, as marketing devices for everything from cleaning products to underwear, and as stalking goats for New Age spiritual flimflam, you might think that Native people were a significant target for sales. We're not, of course. We don't buy this crap. At least not enough to support such a bustling market. But there's really no need to ask whom Dead Indians are aimed at, is there?

All of which brings us to Live Indians.

Among the many new things that Europeans had to deal with upon their arrival in the North American wilderness were Live Indians. Live Indians, from an Old World point of view, were an intriguing, perplexing, and annoying part of life in the New World. . . .

[T]he death of the Indian was a working part of North American mythology. This dying was not the fault of non-Natives. The demise of Indians was seen as a tenet of natural law, which favoured the strong and eliminated the weak.

George Catlin, who travelled around North America in the 1830s painting Live Indians, said of the tribes he visited that, "in a few years, perhaps, they will have entirely disappeared from the face of the earth, and all that will be remembered of them will be that they existed and were numbered among the barbarous tribes that once inhabited this vast Continent. . . ." The American newspaperman Horace Greeley, on a trip west in 1859, was not quite as kind as Catlin… "The Indians are children . . .", "These people must die out—there is no help for them. . . ."

Problem was, Live Indians didn't die out. They were supposed to, but they didn't. Since North America already had the Dead Indian, Live Indians were neither needed nor wanted. They were irrelevant, and as the nineteenth century rolled into the twentieth century, Live Indians were forgotten, safely stored away on reservations and reserves or scattered in the rural backwaters and cityscapes of Canada and the United States. Out of Sight, out of mind. Out of mind, out of Sight.

All Native people living in North America today are Live Indians. Vine Deloria, the Lakota scholar and writer, didn't use the term "Live Indians" when he wrote his famous 1969 manifesto *Custer Died for Your Sins*. Instead, he talked about Native people being "transparent." "Our foremost plight," said Deloria, "is our transparency. People can tell just by looking at us what we want, what should be done to help us, how we feel, and what a 'real' Indian is really like." Deloria might as well have said that Indians are invisible. North Americans certainly *see* contemporary Native people. They just don't *see* us as Indians.

When I was kicking around San Francisco, there was an Aboriginal photographer, a Mandan from the Fort Berthold reservation in South Dakota named Zig Jackson, who had a wonderful wit. For one of his photographic series, "Entering Zig's Indian Reservation," he took photographs of himself in a feathered headdress wandering the streets of San Francisco, riding cable cars and buses, looking in store windows. What he was after and what he was able to catch were the apprehensive and delighted reactions of non-Natives as they came face to face with their Dead Indian come to life.

Carlisle Indian Industrial School, an early residential school, took photographs of Indians when they first came to that institution and then photographed them after they had been "cleaned up," so that the world could see the civilizing effects of Christianity and education on Indians. Not to be outdone, the Mormon Church, or the Church of Jesus Christ of Latter-Day Saints (LDS), has for years maintained an impressive collection of photographs of Indian children, taken when the children were first brought into the church's Home Placement Program. This was a program in place from 1947 to 1996, through which Native families were encouraged to send their kids off-reservation to live with Mormon families, the expectation being that these children would have a greater chance at Success if they were raised and educated in White society. The purpose of the photographs was to track the change in the children's skin colour, from dark to light, from savagism to civilization. . . .

When I lived in Salt Lake City, I was privileged to see some of the Church's Polaroids. Frankly, I couldn't see much of a difference between the "before" and "after" shots, but then I wasn't looking at the photographs through the lens of scripture.

In the late 1970s, I went to Acoma Pueblo and took the tour of the old village up on the mesa. One of the adobe houses had a television antenna fixed to the roof. . . . One of the women in the group, a woman in her late thirties from Ohio, was annoyed by the presence of the television set. This was supposed to be an authentic Indian village, she complained to the rest of the group. Real Indians, she told us, didn't have televisions. . . .

In order to maintain the cult and sanctity of the Dead Indian, North America has decided that Live Indians living today cannot be genuine Indians. This sentiment is a curious reworking of one of the cornerstones of Christianity, the idea of innocence and original sin. Dead Indians are Garden of Eden-variety Indians. Pure, Noble, Innocent. Perfectly authentic. Jean-Jacques Rousseau Indians. Not a feather out of place. Live Indians are fallen Indians, modern, contemporary copies, not authentic Indians at all, Indians by biological association only.

Many Native people have tried to counter this authenticity twaddle by insisting on tribal names—Blackfoot, Navajo, Mohawk, Seminole, Hoopa, Chickasaw, Mandan, Tuscarora, Pima, Omaha, Cree, Haida, Salish, Lakota, Mi'kmaq, Ho-Chunk—and while this is an excellent idea, it has been too much for North America to manage. As with the Dead Indian, North America has, for a very long time now, insisted on a collective noun for Live Indians—Indians, Aboriginals, First Nations, Natives, First Peoples—even though there are over 600 recognized nations in Canada and over 550 recognized nations in the United States....

Dead Indians. Live Indians. You would think that these two Indians would be akin to matter and anti-matter, that it would be impossible for both of them to occupy the same space, but each year Live Indians and Dead Indians come together at powwows and ceremonies and art markets from Alberta to Arizona, Oklahoma to Ontario, the Northwest Territories to New Mexico. At the same time, with remarkable frequency, Live Indians cum Dead Indians show up at major North American social, artistic, and governmental events and galas to pose for the cameras and to gather up any political advantage that might be available....

For Native people, the distinction between Dead Indians and Live Indians is almost impossible to maintain. But North America doesn't have this problem. All it has to do is hold the two Indians up to the light. Dead Indians are dignified, noble, silent, suitably garbed. And dead. Live Indians are invisible, unruly, disappointing. And breathing. One is a romantic reminder of a heroic but fictional past. The other is simply an unpleasant, contemporary surprise....

Let's be clear, Live Indians dance at powwows. And when we dance, when we sing at the drum, when we perform ceremonies, we are not doing it for North America's entertainment. Where North America sees Dead Indians come to life, we see our families and our relations. We do these things to remind ourselves who we are, to remind ourselves where we come from, and to remind ourselves of our relationship with the earth. Mostly, though, we do these things because we enjoy them. And because they are important.

I know that this sort of rhetoric—"our relationship with the earth"—sounds worn out and corny, but that's not the fault of Native people. Phrases such as "Mother Earth," "in harmony with nature," and "seven generations" have been kidnapped by White North America and stripped of their power. Today, Mother Earth is a Canadian alternative rock band, a Memphis Slim song, an alternative-living magazine; and a short story by Isaac Asimov.... "Harmony with Nature" is a hypnosis session that you can download for only $12.95 and which will "gently guide you into a rapturous sense of connection to the whole of natural creation...."

There's a "Seven Generations" company out of Burlington, Vermont, that sells "naturally safe and effective household products," while an outfit called "Hellfish Family" will sell you a T-shirt that has a crucifixion scene on the back with "Seven Generations" at the top and "You Are Not My Christ" at the bottom for $12.95....

Dead Indians. Live Indians. In the end, it is an impossible tangle. Thank goodness there are Legal Indians.

Legal Indians are considerably more straightforward. Legal Indians are Live Indians, because only Live Indians can be Legal Indians, but not all Live Indians are Legal Indians.

Is that clear?

Legal Indians are those Indians who are recognized as being Indians by the Canadian and U.S. governments. Government Indians, if you like. In Canada, Legal Indians are officially known as "Status Indians," Indians who are registered with the federal government as Indians under the terms of the Indian Act.

According to the 2006 census, Canada had a population of about 565,000 Status Indians.... In the United States, federal "recognition," the American version of "Status," is granted to tribes rather than individuals, and in 2009, the government's Federal Register recognized some 564 tribes whose enrolled members were eligible for federal assistance....

As I said, these numbers will never be accurate. But if they are close, it means that only about 40 percent of Live Indians in North America are Legal Indians. A few more than one in three. This is important because the only Indians that the governments of Canada and the United States have any interest in are the Legal ones.

"Interest," though, is probably is too positive a term, for while North America loves the Dead Indian and ignores the Live Indian, North America *hates* the Legal Indian. Savagely. The Legal Indian was one of those errors in judgment that North America made and has been trying to correct for the last 150 years. . . .

[B]ecause of the treaties, Legal Indians are entitled to certain rights and privileges . . . —with the exception of certain First Nations bands in British Columbia and some executive order reservations in the States—Legal Indians are the only Indians who are eligible to receive them.

A great many people in North America believe that Canada and the United States, in a moment of inexplicable generosity, gave treaty rights to Native people as a gift. Of course, anyone familiar with the history of Indians in North America knows that Native people paid for every treaty right, and in some cases, paid more than once. The idea that either country gave First Nations something for free is horseshit.

Sorry. I should have been polite and said "anyone familiar with Native history knows that this is in error" or "knows that this is untrue," but . . ., as Sherman Alexie (Spokane-Coeur d'Alene) reminds us in his poem "How to Write the Great American Indian Novel," "real" Indians come from a horse culture.

In Canada, Legal Indians are defined by the Indian Act, a series of pronouncements and regulations, rights and prohibitions, originally struck in 1876, which has wound its snaky way along to the present day. The act itself does more than just define Legal Indians. It has been the main mechanism for controlling the lives and destinies of Legal Indians in Canada, and throughout the life of the act, amendments have been made to the original document to fine-tune this control. . . .

A 1905 amendment allowed the removal of Aboriginal people from reserves that were too close to White towns of more than 8,000 residents. . . .

Until at least 1968, Legal Indians could be "enfranchised," which simply meant that the government could take Status away from a Legal Indian,

with or without consent, and replace it with Canadian citizenship. Technically, enfranchisement was proffered as a positive, entailing, among other benefits, the right to vote and drink. All you had to do was give up being a Legal Indian and become . . . well, that was the question, wasn't it. Legal Indian women could be "enfranchised" if they married non-Native or non-Status men. If Legal Indians voted in a federal election, they would be "enfranchised." Get a university degree and you were automatically "enfranchised." If you served in the military, you were "enfranchised." If you were a clergyman or a lawyer, you were "enfranchised. . . ."

In the United States, Legal Indians are enrolled members of tribes that are federally recognized. That's the general rule. However, tribes control how their membership rolls are created and maintained, and eligibility for membership varies from nation to nation. Most base their membership on blood quantum. If you have enough Native blood in you, then you are eligible for enrollment, and, once enrolled, are a Legal Indian.

In Canada, loss of Status has been an individual matter, one Legal Indian at a time. A rather slow process. In the United States, where things reportedly move faster, the government, particularly in the 1950s, set about "enfranchising" entire tribes en masse. They started with the Menominee in Wisconsin and the Klamath in Oregon and, in the space of about ten years, they removed another 107 tribes from the federal registry. . . .

In 1969, the Canadian government tried to pull a homegrown Termination Act—the 1969 White Paper—out of its Parliamentary canal. In that year, Prime Minister Pierre Trudeau blithely intimated that there was no such thing as Indian entitlement to land or Native rights and suggested that it was in the best interests of First Nations people to give up their reserves and assimilate into Canadian society. The reaction was immediate and fierce. Almost every Indian organization came out against the plan. Whatever the problems were with the Indian Act and with the Department of Indian Affairs, Native people were sure that giving up their land and their treaty rights was not the answer. . . .

All North America dreams about is the Dead Indian. There's a good reason, of course. The Dead

Indian is what North America wants to be. Which probably explains the creation and proliferation of Indian hobbyist clubs, social organizations that have sprung up in North America and around the world as well, where non-Indians can spend their leisure time and weekends pretending to be Dead Indians.

There are Indian clubs in Florida, Texas, California, Washington, Oregon, Idaho, New Mexico, and Arizona . . . , in Italy, in France, in Poland, in Hungary, and in most of the other eastern European and Scandinavian countries. . . .

I haven't found any clubs in Canada yet, but would guess there must be a couple hidden away here and there . . . while Woodcraft Indians and the Scouts made use of what they saw as Indian content in their structures and performances, neither was an "Indian club."

Indian clubs are magnets for non-Natives who want to transform themselves, just for a day or two, into Dead Indians. Folks who attend go to dance and sing and participate in pipe ceremonies and sweats. . . .

The one thing that you can say about Indian hobbyists is that they take their fantasies seriously. Still, all of this dress-up, roleplaying silliness has as much to do with Indians as an Eskimo Pie has to do with the Inuit.

The irony is that these clubs and the sentiments they espouse would be better served if Live Indians and Legal Indians somehow disappeared, got out of the way. After all, there's nothing worse than having the original available when you're trying to sell the counterfeit.

Live Indians. Legal Indians.

If you listen carefully, you can almost hear North America cry out, in homage to Henry II and his feud with Thomas à Becket, "Who will rid me of these meddlesome Indians?"

And, as luck would have it, Canada and the United States are working on a solution.

# PART TWO

## Additional Readings

Misko-Kìsikàwihkwè (Acoose, Janice). *Iskwewak Kah'Ki Yaw Ni Wahkomakanak: Neither Indian Princesses nor Easy Squaws*, 2nd Edition. Toronto: Women's Press, 2016.

Chaat Smith, Paul. *Everything You Know about Indians Is Wrong*. Minneapolis, MN: University of Minnesota Press, 2009.

Deloria, Philip J. *Indians in Unexpected Places*. Lawrence, KS: University Press of Kansas, 2004.

Duffek, Karen, and Tania Willard, eds. *Lawrence Paul Yuxweluptun: Unceded Territories*. Vancouver: The Museum of Anthropology at UBC Press, 2016.

Francis, Daniel. *The Imaginary Indian: The Image of the Indian in Canadian Culture*. Arsenal Pulp Press, 1992.

L'Hirondelle Hill, Gabrielle, and Sophie McCall, eds. *The Land We Are: Artists and Writers Unsettle the Politics of Reconciliation*. Winnipeg: Arbiter Ring Press, 2015.

Marubbio, M. Elise, and Eric L. Buffalohead. *Native Americans on Film: Conversations, Teaching, and Theory*. Baltimore, MD: The University of Press of Kentucky, 2013.

Singer, Beverly R. *Wiping the War Paint off the Lens: Native American Film and Video*. Minneapolis, MN: University of Minnesota Press, 2001.

## Relevant Websites

**Zig Jackson Photography**

http://www.risingbuffaloarts.com

*Rising Buffalo (Zig Jackson) is a photographer of mixed Mandan, Hidatsa, and Arikara ancestry whose award-winning art and* *portraiture explores issues of cultural identity, representation, and appropriation across spaces marked as white/urban and Indian/reserve.*

**Kent Monkman**

http://www.kentmonkman.com

*Kent Monkman (Cree) is a multidisciplinary artist whose numerous films, paintings, installations, portraits, and performances explore issues of race and representation, Settler colonialism, gender identity, sexuality, and queer presence, often through a performance moniker, Miss Chief Eagle Testickle.*

## The National Museum of the American Indian

http://www.nmai.si.edu

*The National Museum of the American Indian is "the sixteenth museum of the Smithsonian Institution. It is the first national museum dedicated to the preservation, study, and exhibition of the life, languages, literature, history, and arts of Native Americans. Established by an act of Congress in 1989 (amendment in 1996), the museum works in collaboration with the Native peoples of the Western Hemisphere to protect and foster their cultures by reaffirming traditions and beliefs, encouraging contemporary artistic expression, and empowering the Indian voice."*

## Jeff Thomas

http://jeff-thomas.ca

*Haudenosaunee artist, photographer, and curator Jeff Thomas explores the presence of Indigenous peoples in urban and contemporary spaces, the silences produced by photographic histories—including those produced by Edward S. Curtis—and seeks to engage both Indigenous and Settler populations in critical conversations about Indianness and the colonial imaginary.*

# Films

*Aboriginality.* Dir. Dominique Keller and Tom Jackson. National Film Board of Canada, 2008.

*Casualties of Modernity.* Dir. Kent Monkman. Vtape, 2015.

*Couple in the Cage: A Guatinaui Odyssey.* Dir. Coco Fusco and Paula Heredia. Third World Newsreel, 1993.

*Reel Injun.* Dir. Neil Diamond. National Film Board of Canada, 2009.

*Shooting Indians: A Journey with Jeffrey Thomas, A Film by Ali Kazimi.* Dir. Ali Kazimi. Peripheral Visions Film and Video Inc., 1997.

# Key Terms

Authenticity
Colonial imaginary
Dead Indians
The Other

Representation
Romanticism
Stereotype

# Discussion Questions

1. What does Thomas King mean by "Dead Indians"? How do we explain the fascination historically with "Dead Indians"? Where do "Dead Indians" stand in relation to "Live Indians" and "Legal Indians"?

2. How do images of "Indians" created by Settler societies work to perpetuate racism and lands dispossession? How do they work to enable and benefit Settler colonialism? What are the implications of the "Noble Savage" or renderings of Indigenous peoples as a "disappearing race"?

3. How do we explain the need for certainty about Indian difference? Where are these practices located and how do they operate in the contemporary world? What kinds of material consequences does keeping the racialized Other firmly intact have in legitimating and perpetuating Canadian Settler colonialism?

4. If Settler populations are complicit in producing colonial representations of Indianness, then what is the way forward in terms of provoking a more critical consciousness to disrupt them? What sorts of Settler consciousness are possible and/or already being realized?

# Activities

Identify different representations of "Indians" in popular culture (e.g., Disney films, children's literature, "Cowboy and Indian" figurines, Halloween costumes, etc.). For whom and what do these representations serve?

Locate some local, provincial, state, or national sports teams that have "Indian" names or mascots. How are these altogether common and racist practices allowable? What does their persistence suggest?

How have representations of "Indians" been handled by regional media in your area over the last five years? How are the individuals and stories being portrayed? If you were to rework these representations differently, how would you do it and why?

# PART THREE

❖

# Race, Territoriality, and Peoplehood

## Editor Introduction

The idea of North America as a once vast open wilderness, historically unoccupied and empty prior to the arrival of first white Settlers is a powerful myth informing much of Canadian and American history. The early and sometimes forcible displacement of Indigenous peoples and territories rests on this fiction, furthered by an assumption that racism does not define the colonial past. "In order for Canada to have a viable national identity," writes Miqmaw scholar Bonita Lawrence, "the historical record of how the land was acquired must be erased." In this chapter, we provide a set of two theoretical perspectives contesting this erasure, the future of nationhood shaped by territorial displacement, and also, a scholarship that defines the rewriting of lands in solely racialized terms.

The displacement of Indigenous peoples has a long history. The history varies regionally, but in many cases, though certainly not all, it involved the movement of people from traditional territories to lands created for them by the colonizer. From the mid-1800s, it was effected through colonial policy aimed at putting some Indigenous peoples on Indian reserves—originally meant to protect us and thought to provide us with the Eurocentric education and instruction necessary for our assimilation into an emerging capitalist economy. The idea was that reserves and other rural, remote, and economically marginalized lands were the only appropriate place for us as Indians. These and other kinds of symbolic violence persist even today.

Today, many Indigenous peoples live in cities. In 2001, only slightly more than half of the registered Indian population lived on reserves in Canada. The statistic is revealing of a choice by at least some Indigenous peoples to reject the economic marginalization of reserve life and move into urban contexts. Social scientists have spent countless hours documenting the experience of "Aboriginal peoples in cities." Much of this literature has focused on the cultural incommensurability of Indians and urban ways of life, including the social problems plaguing Indigenous populations when they arrive in cities. These analyses offer little, if any, insight into difference-making practices that have long characterized Settler colonialism.

In order to mark spaces as urban, Indigenous bodies are regulated. Historically, this took place through policy, including the reserve and pass system. Indians belonged on reserves and required the approval of Indian agents to leave them. Today, the policing of Indigenous bodies is as symbolic as it is material. It is accomplished through the invisibility of countless urban Indigenous peoples thought assimilated, or who, as the Cree politician Ovide Mercredi once put it, "blend effortlessly into the multicultural framework of Canadian society." It is also accomplished through over-policing, racial profiling, and police brutality, as evidenced in Cree scholar Tasha Hubbard's 2004 film *Two Worlds Colliding* about the freezing deaths of Indigenous men in Saskatoon, Saskatchewan.

The challenge we face as urban Indigenous peoples is as much a problem of poverty, inadequate housing, and ineffectual services delivery as it is a problem of exclusion and recognition. Indigeneity and urbanity are by no means incompatible to one another, nor do they stand in a dichotomous, either/or relation. The assumption is that we do not belong in cities. This prevents us from seeing that many of us as Indigenous peoples—the authors included— have lived in urban locations for generations. It negates the reality that many Canadian cities are situated on or near traditional Indigenous territories. It defies the historical reality that not all Indigenous peoples were placed on reserves. It prevents us from acknowledging exclusionary practices and from understanding the work that goes into providing the ongoing ideological justification for the displacement of our peoples.

The racism effected through difference-making and other spatial practices has not been experienced uniformly among all Indigenous peoples. For some Indigenous women, racism and sexism intersected to separate them from communities and to erode their rights and influence within communities. In Canada, the requirement that all women lose status as Indians—and therefore all birthrights and entitlements—upon marriage to non-Indian men contributed to their relocation to cities until the 1985 *Indian Act* amendments. Others came to cities because of federal and provincial/territorial laws that fell short of addressing the distribution of matrimonial real property upon dissolution of marriage (Bastien, 2008; Montour, 1987). This matter was not addressed by Canada until 2009. Canada did not remove blatant sexism in the *Indian Act* until 2010 under its *Gender Equity in Indian Registration Act* (see Part Four, this volume).

The re-writing of lands involved highly racialized ways of thinking employed by the State to define some Indigenous peoples as Indians and others as not. The effect was to leave some people without federal recognition, or to displace and remove them from the land altogether. Of course, the history of Indigenous peoples in Settler colonial Canada, as Chris Andersen (2014: 204) writes, "is not only irreducible to its relationship to Indianness but also obscured." He points to the danger of charting Indigenous landscapes and identities in solely racialized terms, such that these approaches "beggar the kinds of deep analysis that would accord Métis peoplehood an autonomous footing linked but in no way reducible to . . . Indianness" (ibid.). The sorting of lands may have been effected in part by Indianness in Canada, but the racialization of Indigenous peoples cannot be understood as a uniform process that legislatively impacted on "Métis," "half-breed," and "mixed-blood" peoples in the same ways.

Indigenous peoples find their ethnogenesis not in histories of racialization, but in a distinct constellation of land-based, historical, and pre-colonial relationships. Indeed, by working to complicate a "Métis as mixed" train of logic, Andersen (Chapter 4, this volume) favours a "people-to-people" based way of thinking about identity, nationhood, and events at once tied to and embodied in the land. He centres a detailed analysis of lands, the political economy surrounding them, and the events connecting people to lands, an approach at times lacking in scholarship, seeking to link histories of Settler colonialism, racialization, and lands dispossession. The process through which Indigenous peoples were impacted by Settler colonialism, accommodated, and in turn challenged colonial power requires greater historical understanding and appreciation. These sorts of understandings cannot happen without a more anticolonial and nuanced recounting of lands.

Bonita Lawrence provides another such way of recounting histories of Settler colonialism and lands, particularly as this relates to both land theft and dispossession. In Chapter 5, she rewrites histories of the land, challenging the normative and Eurocentric frameworks that have defined much of academic scholarship. As she suggests, some historians have written of dispossession in ways that prevent us from understanding the perspectives of Indigenous peoples experiencing and challenging its authority. Her chapter aims to "decolonize the history of Eastern Canada," dismantling in turn a number of myths that are crucial to Canadian nation-building, including the idea that Settler colonialism was a benign process, innocent of racism, genocide, and legislative hegemony.

## CHAPTER 5

# Rewriting Histories of the Land
## Colonization and Indigenous Resistance in Eastern Canada

*Bonita Lawrence*

---

*The claim to a national culture in the past does not only rehabilitate that nation and serve as a justification for the hope of a future national culture. In the sphere of socioaffective equilibrium, it is responsible for an important change in the native. Perhaps we have not sufficiently demonstrated that colonialism is not simply content to impose its rule upon the present and future of a dominated country. Colonialism is not merely satisfied with holding a people in its grip and emptying the native's brain of all form and content. By a kind of perverse logic, it turns to the past of an oppressed people, and distorts, disfigures, and destroys it.*

—Frantz Fanon, *The Wretched of the Earth*

Canadian national identity is deeply rooted in the notion of Canada as a vast northern wilderness, the possession of which makes Canadians unique and "pure" of character. Because of this, and in order for Canada to have a viable national identity, the histories of Indigenous nations,[1] in all their diversity and longevity, must be erased. Furthermore, in order to maintain Canadians' self-image as a fundamentally "decent" people innocent of any wrongdoing, the historical record of how the land was acquired—the forcible and relentless dispossession of Indigenous peoples, the theft of their territories, and the implementation

of legislation and policies designed to effect their total disappearance as peoples—must also be erased. It has therefore been crucial that the survivors of this process be silenced—that Native people be deliberately denied a voice within national discourses (LaRocque, 1993).

A crucial part of the silencing of Indigenous voices is the demand that Indigenous scholars attempting to write about their histories conform to academic discourses that have already staked a claim to expertise about our pasts—notably anthropology and history. For many Aboriginal scholars from Eastern Canada who seek information about the past, exploring the "seminal" works of contemporary non-Native "experts" is an exercise in alienation. It is impossible for Native people to see themselves in the unknown and

---

In Sherene Razack, ed., *Race, Space and the Law: Unmapping a White Settler Society* (Toronto: Between the Lines Press, 2002), 21–46. Used with permission of the publisher.

unknowable shadowy figures portrayed on the peripheries of the white settlements of colonial Nova Scotia, New France, and Upper Canada, whose lives are deduced solely through archaeological evidence or the journals of those who sought to conquer, convert, defraud, or in any other way prosper off them. This results in the depiction of ancestors who resemble "stick figures"; noble savages, proud or wily, inevitably primitive. For the most part, Indigenous scholars engaged in academic writing about the past certainly have little interest in making the premises of such works central to their own writing—and yet the academic canon demands that they build their work on the back of these "authoritative" sources. We should be clear that contemporary white historians have often argued in defence of Aboriginal peoples, seeking to challenge the minor roles that Native people have traditionally been consigned in the (discursively created) "historical record." What is never envisioned, however, is that Indigenous communities should be seen as final arbiters of their own histories.

What is the cost for Native peoples, when these academic disciplines "own" our pasts? First of all, colonization is normalized. "Native history" becomes accounts of specific intervals of "contact," accounts which neutralize processes of genocide, which never mention racism, and which do not take as part of their purview the devastating and ongoing implications of the policies and processes that are so neutrally described. A second problem, which primarily affects Aboriginal peoples in Eastern Canada, is the longevity of colonization and the fact that some Indigenous peoples are considered by non-Native academics to be virtually extinct, to exist only in the pages of historical texts. In such a context, the living descendants of the Aboriginal peoples of Eastern Canada are all too seldom viewed as those who should play central roles in any writing about the histories of their ancestors.

Most important, however, is the power that is lost when non-Native "experts" define Indigenous peoples' pasts—the power that inheres when oppressed peoples choose the tools that they need

to help them understand themselves and their histories:

> The development of theories by Indigenous scholars which attempt to explain our existence in contemporary society (as opposed to the "traditional" society constructed under modernism) has only just begun. Not all these theories claim to be derived from some "pure" sense of what it means to be Indigenous, nor do they claim to be theories which have been developed in a vacuum separated from any association with civil and human rights movements, other nationalist struggles, or other theoretical approaches. What is claimed, however, is that new ways of theorizing by Indigenous scholars are grounded in a real sense of, and sensitivity towards, what it means to be an Indigenous person. . . . Contained within this imperative is a sense of being able to determine priorities, to bring to the centre those issues of our own choosing, and to discuss them amongst ourselves. (Smith, 1999: 38)

For Indigenous peoples, telling our histories involves recovering our own stories of the past and asserting the epistemological foundations that inform our stories of the past. It also involves documenting processes of colonization from the perspectives of those who experienced it. As a result, this chapter, as an attempt to decolonize the history of Eastern Canada, focuses on Indigenous communities' stories of land theft and dispossession, as well as the resistance that these communities manifested towards colonization. It relies primarily on the endeavours of Indigenous elders and scholars who are researching community histories to shape its parameters. Knowledge-carriers such as Donald Marshall Senior and Indigenous scholars who carry out research on behalf of Indigenous communities such as Daniel Paul, Sakej Henderson, and Georges Sioui are my primary sources. For broader overviews of the colonization process, I draw on the works of Aboriginal historians such as Olivia Dickason and Winona Stevenson. In some instances, I rely on non-Native scholars who have consulted Native elders, such as Peter Schmalz, or who have conducted research specifically *for* Indigenous communities involved in resisting colonization (where those communities retain control over ownership of the knowledge and how it is to be used), such as James Morrison. In instances where no other information is available, the detailed work of non-Native scholars such as Bruce Trigger and J.R. Miller is used to make connections between different events and to document regional processes. The issues at hand are whether the scholar in question is Indigenous and the extent to which the scholar documents the perspectives of Indigenous communities about their own pasts.

As history is currently written, from outside Indigenous perspectives, we cannot see colonization *as* colonization. We cannot grasp the overall picture of a focused, concerted process of invasion and land theft. Winona Stevenson has summarized how the "big picture" looks to Aboriginal peoples: "Mercantilists wanted our furs, missionaries wanted our souls, colonial governments, and later, Canada, wanted our lands" (Stevenson, 1999: 49). And yet, this complex rendition of a global geopolitical process can obscure how these histories come together in the experiences of different Indigenous nations "on the ground." It also obscures the *processes* that enabled colonizers to acquire the land, and the *policies* that were put into place to control the peoples displaced from the land. As a decolonization history, the perspectives informing this work highlight Aboriginal communities' experiences of these colonial processes, while challenging a number of the myths that are crucial to Canadian nation-building, such as the notion that the colonization process was benign and through which Canada maintains its posture of being "innocent" of racism and genocide. Other myths about Native savagery and the benefits of European technologies are challenged by Native communities' accounts of their own histories and are explored below.

# Mercantile Colonialism: Trade and Warfare

The French and early British trade regimes in Canada did not feature the relentless slaughter and enslavement of Indigenous peoples that marked the Spanish conquest of much of "Latin" America. Nor did they possess the implacable determination to obtain Indigenous land for settlement, by any means necessary, that marked much of the British colonial period in New England. Thus the interval of mercantile colonialism in Canada has been portrayed as relatively innocuous. And yet, northeastern North America was invaded by hundreds of trade ships of different European nations engaged in a massive competition for markets; an invasion instrumental in destabilizing existing intertribal political alliances in eastern North America. It is impossible, for example, to discount the central role that competition for markets played in the large-scale intertribal warfare that appears to have developed, relatively anomalously, throughout the sixteenth, seventeenth, and eighteenth centuries in much of eastern Canada and northeastern United States. Oral history and archeological evidence demonstrate that these wars were unique in the history of these Indigenous nations.

It is important to take into consideration the extent to which the new commodities offered by the Europeans gave obvious material advantages to those nations who successfully controlled different trade routes. Inevitably, however, as communities became reliant on trade to obtain many of the necessities of life, access to trade routes became not only desirable but actually necessary for survival (particular as diseases began to decimate populations, as the animal life was affected, and as missionaries began to make inroads on traditional practices).[2] These pressures resulted in such extreme levels of competition between Indigenous nations that an escalation into continuous warfare was almost inevitable. . . .

Warfare and trade among Indigenous nations profoundly changed the ecology of the land and way of life for nations of many regions. Yet these should not be seen as evidence of Indigenous savagery or of a breakdown of Indigenous values;[3] rather, these profound changes, in part, resulted from the severe pressures caused by the intense competition of European powers during mercantile colonialism to depopulate entire regions of all fur-bearing animals.

# Disease and Christianization in the Huron-Wendat Nation

Although French colonial policies focused primarily on the fur trade, under the terms of the Doctrine of Discovery, the monopolies they granted to different individuals in different regions included the mandatory presence of Christian missionaries.[4] The missionaries relied on trade wars (and the epidemics frequently preceding or accompanying them) to harvest converts from Indigenous populations physically devastated by mass death. Nowhere is this more obvious than among the Huron-Wendat people.

The Wendat, whom the Jesuits labelled "Huron," were the five confederated nations of the territory known as Wendake (now the Penetanguishene Peninsula jutting into Georgian Bay). It was made up of twenty-five towns, with a population that peaked at thirty thousand in the fifteenth century (Sioui, 1999: 84–5). The Wendat relied both on agriculture and fishing, and until extensive contact with French traders began in 1609, they enjoyed remarkable health and an abundance of food.

Georges Sioui suggests that Wendat communities first came into contact with disease through the French, who were dealing with large groupings of Wendat living together as agricultural people. It was not until 1634, however, when the Jesuits, who had visited in 1626, returned to set up a mission that the Wendat encountered a continuous wave of epidemics, which culminated in the virulent smallpox epidemic of 1640 that cut their population in half (Trigger, 1994: 51). So many elders and youths died in the epidemics that the Wendat began to experience serious problems in maintaining their traditional livelihoods and grew extremely dependent on French trade for survival. The epidemics also had a catastrophic effect on the Wendat worldview. The psychological shock of such an extreme loss of life was experienced as sorcery, as the introduction of a malevolent power into the Wendat universe (Sioui, 1999: 86).

It was into this weakened population that the Jesuits managed to insinuate themselves, using their influence in France to have French traders withdrawn and replaced by Jesuit lay employees.

The Jesuits sought to impress the Huron with their technological superiority and allowed their traders to sell certain goods, particularly guns, only to Christian converts (Trigger, 1994: 54). As the number of Christian converts grew in response to such virtual blackmail, the Jesuits gradually obtained enough power in the communities to forbid the practising of Wendat spiritual rituals. . . .

Many lost their tribal status in Kansas, but a small group of Wyandot acquired a reserve in northeastern Oklahoma where they continue to live today. A small number of Wendat remained in Ontario and maintained two reserves in the Windsor region. In the early nineteenth century, both reserves were ceded and sold by the Crown. A small acreage remained and was occupied by a group known as the Anderdon band. This band, consisting of the remaining forty-one Wendat families in Ontario, were enfranchised under the *Indian Act* in 1881, at which point they officially ceased to exist as "Indians." Their land base was divided up into individual allotments. Despite the loss of a collective land base and "Indian" status, the descendants of the forty-one families in Windsor still consider themselves Wendat (Trigger, 1994: 55–61). . . .

The catastrophic changes that the Huron-Wendat have undergone are perhaps less important than the fact that they have survived as a people, and that their worldview has changed but remains fundamentally Wendat. These myths of savagery and of a "loss of culture" form an essential part of contemporary settler ideology—a justification for the denial of restitution for colonization, the backlash against Aboriginal harvesting rights, and policies of repression against Native communities. Through exploring Huron-Wendat history informed by their own realities, a culture regarded as "dead" by the mainstream speaks to us about its contemporary world.

## The Mi'kmaq: Diplomacy and Armed Resistance

Not all nations faced the Wendat experience of Christianization. The Mi'kmaq nation was perhaps unique in the way it used Christianity as a source of resistance to colonization in the earliest years of contact with Europeans.

Mi'kmaki, "the land of friendship," covers present-day Newfoundland, St-Pierre and Mique-lon, Nova Scotia, New Brunswick, the Magdalen Islands, and the Gaspé Peninsula. It is the territory of the Mi'kmaq, which means "the allied people." The Mi'kmaq nation became centralized during a fourteenth-century war with the Iroquois Confederacy. Since then it has been led by the Sante Mawiomi, the Grand Council, and has been divided into seven regions, each with its Sakamaws or chiefs. It is part of the Wabanaki Confederacy, which includes the Mi'kmaq, the Abenakis in Quebec, the Maliseets in western New Brunswick, and the Passamaquoddies and Penobscots in New England (Richardson, 1989: 78). . . .

The Mi'kmaq people were the first Native people in North America to encounter Europeans, and were aware of the political implications of contact. The French entered their territory in earnest in the sixteenth century and had set up small maritime colonies by the early seventeenth century. Knowledge of the genocide of Indigenous peoples in the Caribbean and Mexico by the Spanish . . . reached the Mi'kmaq by the mid-sixteenth century. In response to this information, and to the spread of disease that increased with greater contact, the Mi'kmaq avoided the French coastal settlements and consolidated their relationships with other Eastern nations of the Wabanaki Confederacy (Henderson, 1997: 80–1). However, Messamouet, a Mi'kmaw[5] scholar and prophet who had travelled to France and learned of how the Europeans conceptualized law and sovereignty, developed another option known as the "Beautiful Trail," which would involve the Mi'kmaq nation negotiating an alliance with the Holy See in Rome. . . .

By building an alliance with the Holy See, the Mi'kmaq nation sought recognition as a sovereign body among the European nations. In this way, Mi'kmaki could resist the authority of the French Crown. In 1610, Grand Chief Membertou initiated an alliance with the Holy See by negotiating a Concordat that recognized Mi'kmaki as an independent Catholic Republic. As a public treaty with the Holy See, the Concordat had the force of international law, canon law, and civil law. Its primary effect was to protect the Mi'kmaq from French authority "on the ground". . . . Under the Concordat and alliance, the Mawiomi maintained a theocracy which synthesized Catholic and Mi'kmaq spirituality and maintained Mi'kmaq independence from the French Crown.[6]

In 1648, the Treaty of Westphalia ended the Holy See's rule over European monarchies. The treaty's settlement of territorial claims placed some lands under the control of nation-states and others under the control of the Holy See: Mi'kmaki "reverted" to Mi'kmaq control and all protections ceased to exist.

Unfortunately for the Mi'kmaq, the French were not the only colonial power to invade their world. What the British sought was not furs and missions but land where they could build colonies for their surplus populations. . . . Nineteen out of twenty Indigenous people who came into contact with the British succumbed to disease. The British initiated a number of attacks against Indigenous villages, attacks which often escalated into full-scale wars. British slavers scoured the Atlantic coast for Indigenous people who were sold in slave markets all over the world. Indeed, they began raiding Mi'kmaq territory for slaves in the mid-1600s (Stannard, 1992: 238; Churchill, 1994: 34–5; Forbes, 1988: 54–8; Dickason, 1992: 108).

As the British encroached north from New England to Nova Scotia, the Mi'kmaq responded with open resistance. From the mid-1650s until the peace treaty of 1752 (which was reaffirmed in the treaty of 1761), they waged continuous warfare against the British, fighting land battles and capturing almost one hundred British ships. As the long war proceeded, and the Mi'kmaq were gradually weakened, the ascendant British developed policies to exterminate the Mi'kmaq. They used a variety of methods, including distributing poisoned food, trading blankets infected with diseases, and waging ongoing military assaults on civilian populations (Dickason, 1992: 159; Paul, 2000: 181–2). . . . The British introduced scalping policy as another method of extermination. For two decades, the British paid bounty for Mi'kmaq scalps and even imported a group of bounty hunters known as Goreham's Rangers from Massachusetts to depopulate the surviving Mi'kmaq nation (Paul, 2000: 207).

Those who survived this genocide were destitute, left with no food and without the necessary clothing to keep warm in a cold climate. Many were reduced to begging. Thousands died of starvation and exposure until limited poor relief was implemented on a local basis. Others eked out a bare existence selling handicrafts, cutting wood for whites, or working as prostitutes (which resulted in outbreaks of venereal disease). Those who struggled to acquire individual land plots were denied title; as a result, it was not uncommon for Mi'kmaw families to engage in the backbreaking labour of clearing and planting a patch of land, only to find that when they returned from fishing, hunting, or gathering excursions, white squatters had taken the land (Redmond, 1998: 116–17). When the British opened up the region for white settlement, they refused to set aside land for the Native peoples. . . .

By the early 1800s, the Mi'kmaq population had fallen from an estimated two hundred thousand to less than fifteen hundred people. Most whites were predicting that the Mi'kmaq would soon become extinct. During this period, Mi'kmaw leaders continuously petitioned London, finally managing to obtain a handful of small reserves. . . . The Mi'kmaq endured policies that tried to centralize and liquidate the few reserves that had been created, divide their bands, and dissolve their traditional governance. These policies aimed in every way to erase their existence.

Since the signing of the 1752 treaty, which brought an end to warfare, the Mi'kmaq have sought to resolve the ongoing land and resource theft, with little success. In 1973, the *Calder* case decision forced the Canadian government to recognize that it had some obligation to deal with land claims. . . .

In exploring Mi'kmaq resistance efforts— negotiating a Concordat with the Holy See, waging the longest anti-colonial war in North America, surviving policies designed to exterminate them— we see a picture of Native peoples as resourceful and capable of engaging a powerful enemy in armed conflict for a significant period of time. Perhaps even more important, we see Mi'kmaq people as actors on an international stage, engaging the European powers not only through warfare but through diplomacy, signing international treaties as a nation among nations. . . .

It is impossible to understand contemporary struggles for self-determination without this view of Native peoples as nations among other nations. Today, the spirit that enabled the Mi'kmaq to resist genocide is being manifested in the continuous struggles over the right to fish. . . . It is believed that Canada usurped lands accorded to the Mi'kmaq under the Concordat's international law. By re-establishing communication with the Holy See, the Mawiomi wish to recreate its partnership in ways that enhance the autonomy and spiritual uniqueness of the Mi'kmaq (Henderson, 1997: 104).

# Geopolitical Struggles between the Colonizers and Indigenous Resistance in the Great Lakes Region

The British entered the territory now known as Canada from two fronts: the East Coast region (primarily for settlement purposes) and Hudson's Bay (under the charter of the Hudson's Bay Company for the purpose of the fur trade). . . .

The struggle between Britain and France over the Great Lakes region had profound effects on the Iroquois and Ojibway peoples who lived there. The trade struggle between Europeans forced, first, one party, and then the other, to lower the prices of trade goods relative to the furs that were traded for them. Ultimately, when warfare broke out, the effect was devastating, as colonial battles fought in Native homelands destroyed these regions and drew Native peoples into battles, primarily to ensure that a "balance of power" resulted (which would ensure that both European powers remained deadlocked and that one power would not emerge victorious over another).[7]

In 1763, the warfare between France and Britain ended when France surrendered its territorial claims in North America. . . . Because it was important for Britain to reassert its formal adherence to the Doctrine of Discovery and to ensure that its claims to eastern North America would be respected by other European regimes, the British government consolidated its imperial position by structuring formal, constitutional relations with the Native nations in these territories. The Royal Proclamation of 1763 recognized Aboriginal title to all unceded lands and acknowledged a nation-to-nation relationship with Indigenous peoples which the Indian Department was in charge of conducting. Department agents could not command; they could only use the diplomatic tools of cajolery, coercion (where possible), and bribery (Milloy, 1983). The nation-to-nation relationship was maintained until the end of the War of 1812 when the post-war relationships between Britain and the American government became more amicable and made military alliances with Native nations unnecessary.

In the meantime, Britain's ascendancy in the Great Lakes region marked a disastrous turn for Native peoples. . . . It was also obvious to Indigenous people that one unchallenged European power was far more dangerous to deal with than a group of competing Europeans. During this desperate state of affairs, a number of Indigenous nations attempted to form broad-ranging alliances across many nations in an effort to eliminate the British presence from their territories, culminating in the Pontiac uprising of 1763.

Pontiac, an Odawa war chief, was inspired by the Delaware prophet Neolin. He wanted to build a broad-based multinational movement whose principles involved a return to the ways of the ancestors and a complete avoidance of Europeans and their trade goods. At least nineteen of the Indigenous nations most affected by the Europeans shared this vision. Their combined forces laid siege to Fort Detroit for five months, captured nine other British forts, and killed or captured two

thousand British. Within a few months, they had taken back most of the territory in the Great Lakes region from European control.

Between 1764 and 1766, peace negotiations took place between the British and the alliance. The British had no choice in the matter; the Pontiac uprising was the most serious Native resistance they had faced in the eighteenth century (Dickason, 1992: 182–4). As a consequence, the British were forced to adopt a far more respectful approach to Native peoples within the fur trade and to maintain far more beneficial trade terms. However, the dependency of many of the Indigenous nations on British trade goods and their different strategies in dealing with this dependency weakened the alliance and it could not be maintained over the long term.[8] This, unfortunately, coincided with the British plan to devise ways of removing the military threat that Native peoples clearly represented, without the cost of open warfare. The primary means they chose were disease and alcohol.

There is now evidence to suggest that the smallpox pandemic—which ravaged the Ojibway and a number of the Eastern nations including the Mingo, Delaware, Shawnee, and other Ohio River nations, and which killed at least one hundred thousand people—was deliberately started by the British (Churchill, 1994: 35). The earliest evidence of this deliberate policy is the written request of Sir Jeffrey Amherst to Colonel Henry Bouqet at Fort Pitt. In June 1763, Amherst instructed Bouqet to distribute blankets infected with smallpox as gifts to the Indians. On June 24, Captain Ecuyer of the Royal Americans noted in his journal, "We gave them two blankets and a handkerchief out of the smallpox hospital. I hope it will have the desired effect" (Wagner and Stearn, 1945: 44–5). . . .

The "chemical warfare" of alcohol was waged against the Ojibway in a highly deliberate manner. Major Gladwin articulated this policy clearly: "The free sale of rum will destroy them more effectively than fire and sword." The effects of widespread alcohol distribution were immediate.

In the Great Lakes region, chemical and germ warfare were used by the British as the primary means to acquire land and impose control. . . . The Pontiac uprising demonstrated the power of Indigenous nations organized in armed resistance to colonization. . . . These changes to Indigenous ways of life had long-term and highly significant effects on the possibilities of maintaining sovereignty and resistance to European expansion. The centuries-long fur trade changed the course of Indigenous history in Eastern Canada, as the considerable military power of the Indigenous nations was subverted by their need for trade goods to support their changing way of life.

# Ojibway Experiences of Colonization

## Immigration, Deception, and Loss of Land

As the fur trade spread further west, the British government consolidated its hold over the Great Lakes area by implementing settlement policies. At the end of the American Revolution, Loyalists poured into the territory that had become known as Upper Canada, bringing new epidemics of smallpox that decimated the Ojibway around Lake Ontario. . . .

Between 1781 and 1830, the Ojibway gradually ceded to the British most of the land north of what is now southern Ontario. The British knew that the Ojibway were aware of the warfare being committed against Native peoples in the United States, where uncontrolled, violent settlement and policies of removal were being implemented. Using this knowledge to their advantage, the British presented land treaties as statements of loyalty to the Crown and as guarantees that the lands would be protected from white settlement. Through the use of gifts and outright lies, to say nothing of improperly negotiated and conflicting boundaries, most of the land of southern Ontario was surrendered over a fifty-year period. The British used the following procedures to negotiate land treaties:

1. By the Proclamation of 1763, the rights of Indigenous peoples to the land were acknowledged.

2. The Indigenous peoples of each area were called to consider a surrender of lands, negotiated by traders or administrators that they already knew and trusted.

3. Only the chiefs or male representatives were asked to sign.[9]

4. The surrender was considered a test of loyalty.

5. The area ceded was deliberately kept vague.

6. Some compensation, in the form of gifts, was given.

7. In many cases, the land was left unsettled for a few years, until disease and alcohol had weakened potential resistance. When the settlers began to come in and the Native people complained, they were shown the documents they had signed and told there was no recourse (Schmalz, 1991: 123). . . .

## Settler Violence and Loss of Land

When the first two waves of land cessions were over in what is now southern Ontario, two million acres remained in the hands of Native peoples. Over the next fifty years, the British exerted continuous pressure on the Saugeen Ojibway, whose territories of the Bruce Peninsula and its watershed were still unceded. Eager to acquire their land, the British developed a new way of obeying the letter of the law while violating its spirit—they began to use the threat of settler violence to force land surrenders. The constant encroachment of armed, land-hungry settlers forced the Saugeen Ojibway to continuously retreat, negotiating small land surrenders, a piece at a time. Often the treaties were negotiated with individuals who had no authority within their communities to negotiate treaties; these treaties, therefore, were illegal. . . .

A large influx of settlers, primarily refugees from the Irish potato famine and from English industrial slums, put pressure on the colony for even greater tracts of land. Once again, armed squatters were allowed to invade and seize lands. . . .

The above discussion demonstrates how the British fur trade interests in Upper Canada were gradually supplanted by settlement policies, which allowed the Crown to use whatever means were at hand to consolidate its hold over former "Indian" territories. These policies resulted in the endless misery of relocation and land loss for the Ojibway people, of what is now southern and central Ontario, and left many unresolved claims for restitution of stolen lands. These claims include the efforts of the Caldwell Ojibway to obtain a reserve[10] after being forced off their land near Lake Erie during the first wave of land grabs in the early 1800s, and the monumental struggles around fishing rights waged by contemporary Saugeen Ojibway communities.[11]

## Moving North: Resource Plunder of Ojibway and Cree Territories

The consolidation of the land and resource base of what is now northern Ontario. . . . took place within the twentieth century.

Once the land base in southern Ontario was secure, business interests in the colony looked to the rich resources in the north. Within a few years, the vast timber forests were being cut, and the growing presence of mineral prospectors and mining operations in northern Ontario caused a number of Ojibway leaders to travel to Toronto to register complaints and demand payment from the revenues of mining leases. When there was no response to these or other entreaties, the Ojibway took matters into their own hands and forcibly closed two mining operations in the Michipicoten area. Soon troops, which were not called in to protect the Saugeen Ojibway from violent white settlers, were on the scene to quell the "rebellion," and government investigators began to respond to the issues that leaders were bringing to them (Dickason, 1992: 253). The Ojibway wanted treaties, but they demanded a new concession—that reserve territories be specified before the treaties were signed. After considerable discussion and many demands from the Ojibway leaders, the Robinson-Huron and Robinson-Superior Treaties were signed in 1850. These treaties ceded a land area twice the size of that which had already been given up in southern Ontario, set aside reserves (although much smaller than the Ojibway

had hoped for), and provided the bands with a lump-sum payment plus annual annuities of $4 per year per person. Most important, hunting and fishing rights to the entire treaty area were to be maintained.

With these treaties, the colony gained access to all the land around Lake Huron and Lake Superior, south of the northern watershed. All land north of this was considered Rupert's Land, the "property" of the Hudson's Bay Company. . . . Inherent in the concept of "Canada," then, was the notion of continuous expansion, a Canadian version of "manifest destiny," no less genocidal than the United States in its ultimate goals of supplanting Indigenous peoples and claiming their territory.

Under section 91(4) of the Constitution Act, 1867, the Canadian federal government was given constitutional responsibility for "Indians and Lands reserved for the Indians," while section 109 gave the provinces control over lands and resources within provincial boundaries, subject to an interest "other than that of the Province in the same" (Morrison, 1992: 4). . . .

In the late 1890s, the Liberal regime of Oliver Mowat, dominated by timber "barons" whose immense profits had been made through logging central Ontario and the Temagami region, was succeeded by the Conservative regime of James Whitney. Proponents of modern liberal capitalism, the Conservatives pushed aggressively ahead with northern development, focusing on railways, mining, and the pulp and paper industry (Hodgins and Benidickson, 1989: 88–9). Three northern railways were constructed to access timber, develop mineral resources, and access potential hydroelectric sites to power the resource industries. The railways opened up the territory to predators at an unprecedented rate. As a rule, if the presence of Cree or Ojibway people hindered development, the newly created Department of Indian Affairs relocated them away from the area.

It is important to understand the scale of the mineral wealth taken from the lands of the Ojibway and Cree in the past century, at great disruption to their lives and without any compensation. Since the early 1900s, the Cobalt silver mines brought in more than $184 million; Kirkland Lake gold mines produced $463 million; and Larder Lake produced $390 million (Longo, 1973: 66–107). Meanwhile, the Porcupine region, one of the greatest gold camps in the world, produced over $1 billion worth of gold and had the largest silver, lead, and zinc mines in the world (Guilbert and Park, Jr, 1986: 863).

Across northeastern Ontario, hydroelectric development was sought primarily for the new mining industry. In 1911, however, timber concessions for the pulp and paper industry were granted, mainly to friends of government ministers, on condition that hydroelectric dams be built to power them out of the industry's money. In many cases, pulp cutting and dam construction proceeded well before permits were granted to do so.[12]

## Reasserting a Silenced History

This chapter has introduced only a few examples of Indigenous writers, or non-Native historians working with Elders, who have recorded Indigenous nations' stories of their past. These stories

introduce new perspectives to what is considered "Canadian" history. . . .

Writing from the perspectives of the Indigenous nations enables specific communities to give a full and honest account of their struggles with colonizers intent on their removal and elimination as peoples, and to name the racism, land theft, and policies of genocide that characterize so much of Canada's relationships with the Indigenous nations. Even more important, Indigenous peoples are not cast as faceless, unreal "stick figures" lost in a ferment of European interests, but as the living subjects of their own histories. . . .

It perhaps goes without saying that the histories of Indigenous nations will decentre the histories of New France and Upper Canada as organizing themes to the histories of this land. Canadian historians who are currently considered the experts could work in conjunction with Indigenous peoples wanting to tell their stories of the land. But the works of the experts alone, which provide powerful and detailed histories of the Canadian settler state, do not represent the full picture. It is the voices of Indigenous peoples, long silenced, but now creating a new discourse, which will tell a fuller history.

## Notes

1. I have used a number of terms interchangeably to describe the subjects of this article. Generally, I use the term "Indigenous peoples," as it is the international term most commonly selected *by* Indigenous peoples to describe themselves. However, Indigenous peoples in Canada often use the term "Aboriginal" or "Native" to describe themselves; as a result, I have included these terms as well, particularly when focusing on the local context. Occasionally, the term "Indian" is included when popularly used by Native people (such as the term "American Indians").

2. Losing access to the European trade appears to have been devastating for many communities. In *The Ojibwa of Southern Ontario* (Toronto: University of Toronto Press, 1991), Peter S. Schmalz recounts how Captain St Pierre arrived at Madeline Island in 1718 to find an isolated community of Ojibway who had, over the past twenty-two years, lost access to the fur trade as a result of geographic isolation, war with the Iroquois, and the

deadly trading competition between the French and the English, which involved continuously cutting off each others' markets. After a century of growing dependence on European technology, the community no longer had the endurance to hunt without guns or the skills to make stone, bone, and wood tools and utensils to replace the metal ones they had become dependent on using. The women had lost many of the skills of treating skins (when they were able to obtain them) for clothing. St. Pierre found a ragged and starving community, desperate to enter into trade relationships again. It is not a matter, after all, simply of individuals "roughing it" and re-adapting to Indigenous forms of technology. Indigenous communities had to be able to live off the land on a scale that would keep whole communities viable.

3. Contemporary attacks on Aboriginal harvesting, as well as the distrust that many environmentalists apparently hold for Native communities' abilities to maintain ecological relationships with the environment, have only

been accelerated by the interest on the part of some historians in "debunking" notions of the viability of Aboriginal ecological relationships in the past. Calvin Martin, for example, has advanced theories that suggest Aboriginal peoples lost their respect for animals during the fur trade because of the breakdown of their spiritual framework, which was caused by illness contracted from Europeans.

4. The Doctrine of Discovery was the formal code of juridical standards in international law that had been created by papal edict to control the different interests of European powers in the different lands they were acquiring. For its primary tenets, see Ward Churchill, *Struggle for the Land: Indigenous Resistance to Genocide, Ecocide and Expropriation in Contemporary North America* (Toronto: Between the Lines, 1992), p. 36.

5. Mi'kmaq people generally wish to be referred to in the terms of their own language, rather than through the generic term "Micmac," which had been applied to them. My limited understanding of the Mi'kmaq language suggests to me that individuals and family groups are referred to as "Mi'kmaw," while the nation and its language is referred to as "Mi'kmaq." My apologies to those who are better language speakers, for whom my use of terminology may not be accurate enough.

6. The independence enjoyed by the Mi'kmaq under the Concordat did not sit well with the Jesuits who came to Acadia to minister to both Acadian colonists and Mi'kmaqs. The Mi'kmaq rejected the Jesuits' authoritarian ways, after which the Jesuits attended only to the Catholics of New France. Mi'kmaki continued a relatively anomalous independence from French missionaries and colonists for most of the period of French ascendancy in North America and indeed, for the most part considered themselves, and were considered as, allies with the French Crown in its escalating war with the British in North America.

7. Many of the Indigenous nations affected by this warfare appeared to have fought strategically to ensure that a balance of power between competing Europeans was maintained. It is significant that as the French and British became locked in a death struggle, the Ojibway appear to have signed a pact of non-aggression with the Iroquois. In general, as the extent of European interference in their affairs became crucial, many of the Great Lakes nations appear to have resisted fighting each other by the mid-eighteenth century. See Schmalz, *The Ojibwa of Southern Ontario*, p. 58.

8. Schmalz, *The Ojibwa of Southern Ontario*, has suggested that during the Pontiac uprising, the Ojibway and other nations were too divided by their dependence on European trade goods and by the inroads that alcohol was making in the communities to successfully rout the British from the Great Lakes region, as they might have been capable of doing in earlier years. Although driving the British out of the region was undoubtedly the wish of some of the Ojibway communities, there were other communities situated far away from encroaching British settlement, but equally dependent on European technology, that were less certain of the threat the British ultimately posed.

9. Excluding Native women from the process was central to its success. In eastern Canada, Native women's voices were in many cases considered extremely authoritative in matters of land use. Excluding them from the signing process made land theft that much easier, by allowing those who did not control the land to sign it over. See Kim Anderson, *A Recognition of Being: Reconstructing Native Womanhood* (Toronto: Sumach Press, 2001).

10. The traditional territory of the Caldwell band is Point Pelee, which is now a national park. The Caldwell band were involved in the War of 1812 as allies to the British Crown, where they were known as the Caldwell Rangers. After the war in 1815, the British Crown acknowledged their efforts and their loyal service and awarded them their traditional territory "for ever more." But it wasn't classified as a reserve, and meanwhile, British soldiers who retired after the war were awarded most of the land. By the 1860s the few remaining members of the Caldwell band that were still living on their traditional territories were beaten out of the new park by the RCMP with bullwhips. By the 1970s, the Caldwell band members dispersed throughout southern Ontario began to take part in ritual occupation of the park to protest their land claim. A settlement process is currently in effect (Anonymous Caldwell band member, interview with author, 1999).

11. After a series of struggles towards resolving historic land claims, the Chippewas of Nawash, one of two remaining Saugeen Ojibway bands, were recognized in 1992 as having a historic right to fish in their traditional waters. This decision led to three years of racist assaults by local whites and organized fishing interests, including the sinking of their fishing boats, the destruction of thousands of dollars of nets and other equipment, assaults on local Native people selling fish, the stabbing of two Native men in Owen Sound and the beating of two others. No charges were laid by the Owen Sound Police or the OPP for any of this violence until the band called for a federal inquiry into the attacks ("Nawash Calls for Fed Inquiry into Attacks," *Anishinabek News*, June 1996, p. 14).

Meanwhile, the Ontario Ministry of Natural Resources, in open defiance of the ruling recognizing the band's rights, declared a fishing free-for-all for two consecutive years, allowing anglers licence-free access to the waters around the Bruce Peninsula for specific weekends throughout the summer ("Fishing Free-for-all Condemned by Natives," *Anishinabek News*, July 1995, p. 1).

In 1996, despite considerable opposition, the band took over the fishery using an *Indian Act* regulation that severed their community from the jurisdiction of the provincial government (Roberta Avery, "Chippewas Take

Over Management of Fishery," *Windspeaker*, July 1996, p. 3). The other Saugeen Ojibway band on the peninsula, the Saugeen First Nation, announced the formation of the Saugeen Fishing Authority and claimed formal jurisdiction of the waters of their traditional territory. They demanded that sports fishermen and boaters would have to buy a licence from them to use their waters. The provincial government recognized the claims of neither bands, instead demanding they limit their catch and purchase licences from the provincial government in order to be able to fish at all (Roberta Avery, "Fishery in Jeopardy, Says University Researcher," *Windspeaker*, Aug. 1996, p. 16).

By 1997, a government study into fish stocks in Lake Huron revealed that certain fish stocks were severely impaired. While the report was supposed to be for the whole Lake Huron area, it in fact zeroed in on the Bruce Peninsula area a number of times, feeding the attitudes of non-Natives about Native mismanagement of the fishery (Rob McKinley, "Fight Over Fish Continues for Nawash," *Windspeaker*, Sept. 1997, p. 14). To add to the difficulties, in 1997, Atomic Energy of Canada announced their desire to bury 20,000 tonnes of nuclear waste in the Canadian Shield. This brought to the band's attention the extent to which the fishery was already affected by nuclear contamination from the Bruce Nuclear Power Development on Lake Huron, 30 km south of the reserve (Roberta Avery, "No Nuclear Waste on Indian Land," *Windspeaker*, April 1997, p. 4).

12. Howard Ferguson, then minister of Lands and Forests, had so consistently awarded timber and pulpwood concessions without advertisement, public tenders, or even formal agreements on price to individuals like Frank Anson who founded the powerful Abitibi Power and Paper Company, that he was found guilty in 1922 of violating the *Crown Timber Act*—one of the few whites to ever be prosecuted for disobeying federal legislation concerning Indigenous land. See Morrison, "Colonization Resource Extraction and Hydroelectric Development."

# References

Churchill, Ward. 1994. *Indians Are Us? Culture and Genocide in Native North America*. Toronto: Between the Lines.

Dickason, Olive. 1992. *Canada's First Nations*. Toronto: Oxford University Press.

Forbes, Jack D. 1988. *Black Africans and Native Americans: Color, Race and Caste in the Evolution of Red-Black Peoples*. Oxford: Basil Blackwell.

Guilbert, John M., and Charles F. Park, Jr. 1986. "Porcupine-Timmins Gold Deposits," in *The Geology of Ore Deposits*. New York: W.H. Freeman and Company.

Henderson, J.S.Y. 1997. *The Mi'kmaw Concordat*. Halifax, NS: Fernwood Publishing.

Hodgins, Bruce W., and Jamie Benidickson. 1989. *The Temagami Experience: Recreation, Resources and Aboriginal Rights in the Northern Ontario Wilderness*. Toronto: University of Toronto Press.

LaRocque, Emma. 1993. "Preface—or 'Here Are Our Voices—Who Will Hear?'," in Jeanne Perrault and Sylvia Vance, eds, *Writing the Circle: Native Women of Western Canada*. Edmonton: NeWest Publishers.

Longo, Roy M. 1973. *Historical Highlights in Canadian Mining*. Toronto: Pitt Publishing Co.

Milloy, John S. 1983. "The Early Indian Acts: Developmental Strategy and Constitutional Change," in I.A. Getty and A.S. Lussier, eds, *As Long as the Sun Shines and the Water Flows: A Reader in Canadian Native History*. Vancouver: University of British Columbia Press, 1983.

Morrison, James. 1992. "Colonization, Resource Extraction and Hydroelectric Development in the Moose River Basin: A Preliminary History of the Implications for Aboriginal People." Report prepared for the Moose River/James Bay Coalition, for presentation to the Environmental Assessment Board Hearings, Ontario Hydro Demand/Supply Plan, November.

Paul, Daniel N. 2000. *We Were Not the Savages: A Mi'kmaq Perspective on the Collision between European and Native American Civilizations*. Halifax: Fernwood Books.

Redmond, Theresa. 1998. "'We Cannot Work Without Food': Nova Scotia Indian Policy and Mi'kmaq Agriculture, 1783–1867," in David T. McNab, ed., *Earth, Water, Air and Fire: Studies in Canadian Ethnohistory*. Waterloo, ON: Wilfrid Laurier University Press.

Richardson, Boyce, ed. 1989. *Drumbeat: Anger and Renewal in Indian Country*. Toronto: Summerhill Press and the Assembly of First Nations.

Schmalz, Peter S. 1991. *The Ojibwa of Southern Ontario*. Toronto: University of Toronto Press.

Sioui, Georges E. 1999. *Huron Wendat: The Heritage of the Circle*. Vancouver: University of British Columbia Press.

Smith, Linda Tuhiwai. 1999. *Decolonizing Methodologies: Research and Indigenous Peoples*. London: Zed Books.

Stannard, David E. 1992. *American Holocaust: The Conquest of the New World*. Toronto: Oxford University Press.

Stevenson, Winona. 1999. "Colonialism and First Nations Women in Canada," in Enakshi Dua and Angela Robertson, eds, *Scratching the Surface: Canadian Anti-Racist Feminist Thought*. Toronto: The Women's Press.

Trigger, Bruce G. 1994. "The Original Iroquoians: Huron, Petun, and Neutral," in E.S. Rogers and D.B. Smith, eds, *Aboriginal Ontario: Historical Perspectives on the First Nations*. Toronto: Dundurn Press.

Wagner, E., and E. Stearn. 1945. *The Effects of Smallpox on the Destiny of the Amerindian*. Boston: Bruce Humphries.

# CHAPTER 6

# Indigenous Nationhood

*Chris Andersen*

The "nation" form, it seems, has become a near-ubiquitous source of collective self-understanding through which we perceive and act on the social world. So ubiquitous, in fact, that Ernest Gellner (1983) once remarked that we must have a nationalist allegiance as we have a nose and ears.[1] A second doyen of the nations and nationalism literature, Eric Hobsbawm (1990), suggested similarly that, were aliens to land on this planet following a nuclear war that wiped it clean of sentient beings but left untouched our libraries and archives, the last two centuries of human history would be incomprehensible without reference to the power of the nation and its associated nationalism.[2] If either view is correct, it isn't because it speaks to national origins outside the processes of modernity central to Western Europe: by definition, these were excluded.

Without suspending the nation form's link to modernity, we must understand it as a theory (and a claim) to political legitimacy and cultural unity, always already caught on the horns of two opposing sets of social forces, one centripetal and the other centrifugal.[3] Centripetally, the elemental power of *state* cultural projects acts as pivotal claims making that labours to reproduce the apparent naturalness of settler nations as culturally unified forms of individual and collective self-identification. In contrast, centrifugal forces of cultural difference perpetually undercut and thus belie such claims, producing what Homi Bhabha

(1990) has elsewhere described as its "deep ambivalence."[4] Pre-colonial Indigenous presence in particular shines a light on the conceptual and material fragility of settler nation-state claims to legitimacy in a manner unmatched by any other form of perceived difference.

Critical Indigenous studies scholars stand at the forefront of analyzing the relationship between Indigenous and settler claims to nationhood. In this context, two related uses of "nation" have gained currency: one that conceptually equates it with *tribe* and, in doing so, seeks to explore the distinctiveness of tribal histories; and another that differentiates between the substance and goals of Indigenous and settler nationalisms. This discussion has largely taken place in the context of previous literature about *non*-Indigenous nationhood, which has settled into two broad camps of arguments: those who stress a fundamental *continuity* and those who argue for a basic *discontinuity* between national and pre-national forms of sociation. While those in the continuity camp often position ethnicity as a central resource utilized in and by nationalist claims, others have explained nationalism and nations as hallmarks of modernity and of the associated development and expansion of industrial capitalism and, with it, the growth of the *nation-state* as a for(u)m of political legitimacy.[5] In this sense, nations and the state that sustains them act as teleological markers of progress over previous ethnic tribalism. And though such conceits complicate envisioning nationhood outside of a context of modernity, examples of pre-modern nations exist even within a European context.[6]

Whether or not one agrees with nationalism's necessary links to modernity, nation-states have

From *Métis: Race, Recognition, and the Struggle for Indigenous Peoplehood* (Vancouver: UBC Press, 2014). Reprinted with permission from *Métis* by Chris Andersen © University of British Columbia Press 2014. All rights reserved by the publisher.

become central to a serious contemporary discussions of nation, Indigenous, or otherwise—not simply (or even) for the reasons emphasized by Hobsbawm (1990), Gellner (1983), or Anderson (2006), but rather because modern states have become such authoritative sites of power that no sustained nation building can be envisioned that does not in some way position itself for or against the modern states material and symbolic authority.[7] As I discuss later, official state agents occupy a dominant position within Canada's larger colonial field, and any Indigenous "turning away" must continue to account for its presence, even if only to dismiss it as a political act.[8]

Of course, states have existed in one form or another for thousands of years prior to nation-states and, with varying levels of sophistication and efficiency, have coordinated a number of activities crucial to growth and maintenance of increasingly demarcated territorial spaces. While sociologist Max Weber (1978) famously defined states in terms of their ability to produce a monopoly over the legitimate use of force, over the past five centuries states have proven central to the coordination of economic and spiritual well-being as well.[9] Michel Foucault (1973) for example, has explored the (d)evolution of states from entities that reserve for themselves the "right to kill" to entities that labour to efficiently ensure a narrow range of freedoms within which subjects are asked to act responsibly ("the right to life").[10] Especially in the twentieth century, these intertwined government rationalities ("life" and "death") have manifested themselves in various public policy programs.

For our purposes, the cultural power of states thus lies not just in their claims to the monopolization of the legitimate means of physical violence but in their "symbolic violence" as well (a Bourdievian concept that bears a family resemblance to ideology). That is, states possess a singular ability to legitimize, as obvious or natural, what are in fact historical and thus ultimately arbitrary visions of the world. They possess a nearly unparalleled power to "make people see and believe, to get them to know and recognize, to impose the legitimate divisions of the social world and, thereby, to make and unmake groups."[11] For Bourdieu, if social reality is always produced through classification struggles, powerful categories like those ordained by state actors possess the power to construct social reality even as they seek ostensibly to describe it, and thus they cannot be as easily dismissed as we might think.

It is in this sense that Stuart Hall (1995) positions nations and national identities as the end result of particular claims to a cultural unity and homogeneity.[12] States are, to borrow Bbahha's (1990) term, powerful narrators of nation, and state-sanctioned discourses of nationalism deeply influence the ways we understand the social world and ourselves more generally.[13] They attempt to (re)produce sentiments and institutions of unity, homogeneity, and commonality in a number of ways (a common language, religion, education system, currency, and so on) but among the most powerful devices they use to produce legitimacy of policy rationalities are the two sites explored earlier: the courts and the census. These two fields are indicative of how official authority operates, and their associated legitimacy helps us to make sense of the comparative inability of the Métis Nation to make claims to Métis peoplehood, in these areas and in others.

Although it is tempting to think about "nationness" only in centripetal, archetypical moments (such as the Olympics, the FIFA World Cup, or, in Canada, the World Cup of Hockey), we should remind ourselves that "the nation" is not an ahistorical or a-contextual "thing" but, rather (the result of) an ongoing struggle between unequally, "symbolically armed" protagonists. Thus, the claims to popular political legitimacy or a common cultural heritage that underlie state-sanctioned nationalistic sentiment are just that: claims. Hall (1995) explains that far from representing an underlying unit, such claims in fact represent authoritative *attempts* to envision various differences (racial, gendered, class-based, hetero-normative, and so on) *as though* they constituted such a unity.[14] However, such claims are always scored and fissured by various internal points of strain, stress, and tension and therefore possess a discursive and material fragility otherwise unmarked by their own displays of power, spectacular or banal. Bhabha (1990) has expressed this national fragility in what he terms a "deep ambivalence," never more marked than when we catch it in the act of its composition.[15]

Indigenous nations now reside in the interiors of the territorial claims and thus amidst the cultural "pull" of our "captor nations."[16] Contemporary Indigenous articulations of nationhood thus ring a discordant note to the trumpeting of settler claims in that they offer contrasting memories of invasion, attempted conquest, and (re)settlement that belie the seemingly natural association between "nation" and "state."[17] This counter-narrative requires settler national narratives to be understood in terms of the physical and symbolic violence they enact to produce their legitimacy, and they ask us not only to think about prior claims to such territories but about the people-to-people negotiations through which territories were shared and collectivities governed.

In this spirit of discordance, Indigenous studies scholars and our progenitors have stripped the concept of nation of its teleological conceits to stake out a conceptual claim that, by definition, settler nationalism is enacted on territories owned by Indigenous nations. Many Indigenous studies practitioners have thus co-opted the term's narrower conceptions to demonstrate how thoroughly it characterizes the numerous and varied tribes in the pre-contact and pre-colonial world. If modernist discourse differentiates between tribal and national configurations by rendering the former as "other," Indigenous studies scholars have stressed in contrast that these others are and have always been nations.[18]

Indigenous studies nationhood scholarship is extensive and growing. Two broad trends offer discussions useful for my analysis. The first has turned on a straightforward substitution: "nation" for "tribe." Despite "whitestream" nationalism scholarship's attempts to situate the modern basis of nationhood as necessarily non-tribal, Indigenous Studies scholars have positioned "tribe" as possessing equal (though different) collective

historical and political consciousness, as well as a relationship to territory, one far more complex and relational than that of state-bounded Europe.[19] Along these lines, notions like self-determination and sovereignty have been wedded to a more specific focus on the nuances and complexities of individual nations, their histories, and their present configurations of power (on their own and/or in their relations with other nations, Indigenous, or otherwise).

The scholarly genealogy of "nation" is not much explored in Indigenous Studies, however—in a sense, the literature has simply adapted the former use of "tribe" to serve for "nation." In the humanities, for example, authors following on Simon Ortiz's (1981) seminal discussion have forwarded sophisticated discussions of "literary nationalism"[20] that emphasize the richness and distinctiveness of tribal/national literary traditions, both before and during colonialism.[21] These efforts have positioned national literature as an important aspect of "imagining community" and thus as a central symbolic stake in the Indigenous pursuit of the sovereignty usurped by settler nation-states. Similarly, more social scientific approaches have emphasized the concept of Indigenous nationhood as a marker of autonomy: Deloria and Lytle differentiate between nationhood and self-government (the former marking autonomy while the latter evidences subjection to Western forms of power), while Alfred (1995) positions nationhood as a distinctively formed culture and collectivity at war with nation-states.[22]

A second, related Indigenous Studies trend has attempted to rescue the "use value" of "nation" from the territorial and categorical conceits of its European contexts. The basic question that seems to motivate this rescue attempt is whether or not Indigenous nationhood requires the same sort of centralization and clear territorial boundaries that buttress European rhizomatic movement from nationhood to statehood. Anticipating by a number of years the discussions that would follow, Mohawk scholar Alfred (1995) argues, with respect to European-based theories of nationalism, that "[t]heorists have created a model of nationalism based upon a narrow view of one aspect of European history and applied it as the global standard."[23] Similarly, Mohawk scholar Simpson poses a foundational challenge to the over-valorization of the European-based nation model:

> "the nation" receives its analytical particularities in the process and the place that it is articulated through. In other words, if it is industrial England that defined those processes under discussion, "the nation" will be positioned and defined in just that context. Hence, the nation will exhibit the characteristics of industrialisation, of concomitant alienation from the means of production, and is understood as a form of social organization that is arrived at through the false consciousness of its people.[24]

Anderson's (2006) foundational logic of "nation" allows us purchase to think about the ways in which Indigenous society differed from the "pre-nation" societies of Europe.[25] For example, he argues that European nationalism emerged as a form of "deep, horizontal comradeship" in the face of the previous "divinely-ordained, hierarchical dynastic realm."[26] Of course, if we take Alfred (1995) and Simpson (2000) seriously (as we must), we might well ask: Why would we seek to impose a model of nationhood, constructed in the very specific material and symbolic circumstances of eighteenth-century, status-obsessed Europe, onto (Indigenous) societies without the "divinely-ordained, hierarchical dynastic realm" and already deeply steeped in the "horizontal comradeship" (in the case of Indigenous communities, through their complex kinship webs) that these new feelings of European "nation-ness" aspired to?

Along these lines, Cherokee Nation scholar Daniel Heath Justice (2006) argues that Indigenous nationhood—even pre-state forms—should not be conflated with the kinds of "whitestream" (Denis 1997) nationhood "dependent upon the erasure of kinship bonds in favour of a code of patriotism that places loyalty to the state above kinship obligations."[27] Less hierarchical in character, with power diffused across different (and

different kinds) of statuses, Indigenous nations turn on their ability to recognize "other sovereignties without that recognition implying a necessary need to consume, displace or become absorbed by those nations."[28] Similarly, Chippewa scholar Champagne refers to nations as "distinct cultural and political groups" but suggests that while Western understandings of nation and nationalism tend toward the secular, Indigenous understandings of nation and nationalism incorporate other-than-human beings.[29]

The two authors who most extensively position their constructions of Indigenous nationhood in relation to the previous genealogical frameworks of Western European thinking, however, include Mohawk scholar Audra Simpson (2000) and Ojibway/Dakota scholar Scott Lyons (2010).[30] Simpson (2000) situates her argument for Mohawk nationalism in light of both Gellner's 1983 "processes of modernity" and Anderson's 2006 "cognition and creation" as failing to account for the social and historical contexts within which Mohawk nationalism was produced. Noting a "well documented" nationhood that pre-dated contact with Western polities, Simpson (2000) offers a "bifurcated" Indigenous nationhood, forced to exist within the parameters of colonial/settler ones and, as such, one that necessarily "mix[es] parts, [drawing] from Iroquois teachings, from ancestral and immediate past, and from the neo-colonial present" —not, perhaps, in pursuit of statehood (the usual horizon of modernist national thinking) but, rather, in pursuit of an "abstraction—a principle, such as sovereignty, for moral victory or simply for *respect*" (emphasis in original).[31]

In contrast, and borrowing similarly from Gellner's (1983) and Smith's (1986) discussions of the relationship between nationhood and modernity, Lyons (2010) argues that while Native tribes may have historically possessed "a shared culture requiring protection" (a primary marker of nationhood), they lacked the "territorial, educational and legal aspects" of a nation.[32] Hence, markers like kinship culture—often associated with Indigenous nationalism—are, for Lyons, precisely why Indigenous societies are manifestly *not* nations but, rather, "ethnics" (people with a shared sense of culture but lacking a public culture and history, the *actual* bases of nationhood), Lyons (2010) argues that nationalism constitutes the political process through which ethnics become nations. In an Indigenous context, nations practise nationalism while ethnics (tribes) practice "cultural resistance." Thus, for Lyons, nationalism (Indigenous or otherwise) is always about the march to statehood: "[r]emember, it is one's aspiration for a state that produces nationalism, and it is nationalism that produces the nation."[33]

While Simpson (2000) and Lyons (2010) disagree on the origins and substance of Indigenous nationhood, their work shares in common a political rather than merely cultural orientation for Indigenous nationhood. This preference holds important consequences for understanding the relationship between modernist discourse and exclusive settler claims to nationalism and the original—and, from their standpoint, necessary—(dis)place(ment) of Indigenous collectivity within such a growing imaginary.

Recall our earlier discussion of Hall's (1995) positioning of "nation" as including both political and cultural elements. While settler nations and their associated states offer nationalism as legitimate claims to cultural unity, deep cultural fissures—the presence of "Others"—nevertheless traverse and thus destabilize such claims (just as they originally helped to stabilize these entities historically by serving as "exteriors"). The central importance of *difference* to colonial projects (institutionalized in racialized, gendered, and heteronormative hierarchies, to name but a few) was discussed earlier, but we should note here that while all political claims are cultural in the sense that they are embedded in specific meanings and social contexts, in settler nation-states, not all cultural claims are political. In fact, colonial nation-states' historical genealogies make it exceedingly clear that, especially in an Indigenous context, cultural claims (that is, claims to cultural difference) are often not political claims.[34] Indeed, modern nation-states and their institutions (such as the courts) often frame issues in terms of culture

precisely to avoid discussions about their political basis.[35]

Hence, and given what Simpson (2000) refers to as the "enframing power" of modern states, presenting the case for Indigenous nationhood in terms of cultural difference induces a Foucauldian "enunciative poverty" (120) that never simply distinguishes it from that of settler nationhood; it also *subordinates* it.[36] Justice explains that "[c]ulture alone is voyeuristic; it gives access without accountability, and it fetishizes the surface at the expense of deeper significance."[37] Similarly, Kristina Fagan (2004) argues that Aboriginal "cultures" are positioned as quaint and vaguely non-threatening by the dominant Canadian society: "they represent a non-challenging form of difference where Aboriginal peoples become yet another culture in the mosaic."[38]

What does it mean to speak of Indigenous nationhood in political rather than cultural terms? To pose the question slightly differently, what may be gained, if anything, by articulating Indigenous nationhood in terms of political rather than cultural difference? If by political difference we mean to again demonstrate how-we-are-different-from-settlers, then little differentiates it from cultural claims, however legitimate. However, Simpson's (2000) earlier discussion of Indigenous nationhood, which presents as its end point "the desire . . . for an abstraction—a principle, such as sovereignty, for moral victory or simply for *respect*" (emphasis in original), transports us to a very different analytical space.[39] What abstraction or principle might we aspire to in our assertion of our nationhood, if not to demonstrate our cultural or political difference?

In his discussion of Indigenous nationhood and sovereignty, Womack (1999) offers a compelling alternative. Rather than conceptualizing Indigenous nationhood in terms of difference, he suggests we do so in terms of our *separateness*.[40] Womack's argument is made in the specific context of literary canon, but it resonates more broadly. Arguing similarly in a Canadian context, Denis (1997) suggests that "it is not so much difference that matters, as separateness—and indeed wanting to self-govern expresses a will to be separate, autonomous, whether or not you want to do things differently than your neighbour" (82).[41] Emphasizing cultural difference (however legitimate it may be) denies us a historiography on equal footing with that of settler histories; conversely, rooting claims in political separateness cuts to the political core of what separates Indigenous nationalism from settler nationalism: our ability to envision a consciousness as Indigenous nations prior to the presence of settler nations.[42] Whether or not we operate in ways that appear similar to settler self-understandings is—or at least, should be—beside the point.

Hence, Womack's (and Denis's) notion of political "separateness" is a crucial corrective to a focus on difference. It offers a form of conceptual autonomy for the creative position-taking forced upon us by our resistance to and (yes) incorporation of colonial rationalities and intervention strategies. Likewise, it requires little demonstration of our difference from whitestream normativity as a basis for collective authenticity.[43] A focus on our cultural difference, by contrast, not only inhibits a complex recounting of the *intactness* of our history and our communities/nations in the face of the massive impact of settler nation-state intervention in the lives of Aboriginal community members but also reduces the likelihood of public recognition of our modernity.[44]

At least as a matter of logic, positioning Indigenous nationhood in terms of a respect for Indigenous immediacy or complexity carries less of this kind of conceptual baggage.[45] It encourages a proliferation of the "positions," "dispositions," and tensions through which Aboriginality is produced and practised, but it doesn't demand a demonstration of how our lived experiences differed/differ from those of the non-Aboriginal communities we live/d alongside. This is not to say, however, that "anything goes" when envisioning Indigenous nationhood—as with all forms of collective self-imagining, Indigenous nations will be haunted by the tendrils of history, culture, political consciousness, and the many colonial ironies within which we find ourselves situated as

contemporary (modern) Indigenous peoples. One of the most telling moments of the *Powley* case (an important 2003 Supreme Court of Canada Aboriginal rights case) comes in the form of an exchange, in the oral arguments, between two justices and an intervenor, about the extent to which Aboriginal rights can be allowed to change and how—or whether—the courts should or could protect Indigenous modernity.[46]

Whether we side with the continuity argument or the discontinuity argument, the idea of a nation/people is distinctive in international and Canadian literature as affording a right to *self-government* in a manner that does not adhere to "local" community governance. A vast literature has explored the myriad relations around the idea of Indigenous self-government: we need not reproduce it here.[47] The aspect of self-government most analytically important to this discussion of nationhood lies not in its ability to define citizenship codes or, for example, to sanction deviance—*internal* aspects, in other words. Rather, it speaks to the ability of Indigenous nations to enter into nation-to-nation relationships with other Indigenous nations and with colonial nation-states. In this context, RCAP defines an Aboriginal nation as "a sizeable body of Aboriginal people with a shared sense of national identity that constitutes the predominant population in a certain territory or collection of territories."[48] Its tautology notwithstanding, this definition is useful because it emphasizes the nation's relational character.

## The Relationality of Nationhood/ Peoplehood

Discussions of Indigenous nationhood often focus on its internal dimensions. This is a legitimate research strategy given that, for centuries, colonial powers have largely assumed that no such thing as Indigenous nationhood exists and that Indigenous culture and society is noteworthy only to mark its primitiveness or backwardness and, in that context, its eventual demise and disappearance. The little discussion on the *relationality* of Indigenous nationhood has thus concerned itself (again, legitimately) with de-naturalizing colonial attempts to dismantle it. Though Canadian section 3 jurisprudence and legislation has, with several exceptions, been content to recognize Indigeneity in terms of "community," I will lay out in more detail what I think makes nationhood/peoplehood a specific *kind* of community and, likewise, what separates it from the community-as-settlement discourses that largely shape juridical discussion around non-treaty based Aboriginal rights.[49]

The idea of peoplehood has become a mainstay of the international Indigenous literature, particularly that which is linked to the United Nations. Little of this literature focuses on what it is exactly that makes Indigenous peoples *peoples*, however. Instead, the focus has been on what makes us Indigenous. In this context, the UN includes several elements central to their working definition of Indigeneity:

- Self-identification as indigenous peoples at the individual level and accepted by the community as their member;
- Historical continuity with pre-colonial and/or pre-settler societies;
- Strong link to territories and surrounding natural resources;
- Distinct social, economic or political systems;
- Distinct language, culture and beliefs;
- Form non-dominant groups of society;
- Resolve to maintain and reproduce their ancestral environments and systems as distinctive peoples and communities.[50]

Indigeneity is usually defined in terms of contemporary self-identification as such, attachment to a pre-colonial (if not pre-contact) Indigenous and cultural distinctiveness that normally plays out through the establishment of our *difference*.

As a rule, "peoplehood" and "nationhood" are largely employed interchangeably. In the infamous *Re: Quebec Succession* case in which the Supreme Court of Canada was asked to address the issue of whether Quebec could legally secede, the Justices note that although the right of a people to self-determination is an anchor of international law, "the precise meaning of the term 'people' remains somewhat uncertain" (1998, para. 123). Only slightly more precisely, they argued that "a people" does not necessarily mean the same thing as the entire population of a state and that it possesses a distinctive language and culture (1998, para. 124).

In a similar way, current United Nations rapporteur and noted Indigenous scholar James Anaya (1996) defines peoplehood as "comprising distinct communities with a continuity of existence and identity that links them to communities, tribes or nations of their ancestral past," creating a conflation between "community" and "people."[51] Elsewhere, he uses "peoples" interchangeably with "group" and "population." And though at one point the RCAP (1996) explains that "nation" and "people" are overlapping (thus intimating a difference between them), they use them largely interchangeably.

The public documentation around peoplehood is not concerned so much with a distinction between peoplehood and nationhood but, rather, with differentiating these and allied concepts from more biological-cum-racial designations of Indigeneity. As RCAP explains, "The term Aboriginal peoples refers to organic political and cultural entities that stem historically from the original peoples of North America, not to collections of individuals united by so-called 'racial' characteristics. The term includes the Indian, Inuit and Métis peoples of Canada" (1996, vol. 2, ii).[53] The distinction between "local communities" and nations or peoples is a useful one: "We use terms such as a First Nation community and a Métis community to refer to a relatively small group of Aboriginal people residing in a single locality and forming part of a larger Aboriginal nation or people" (1996, vol. 2, ii).[54] The distinction asks us to imagine broader geographical spaces and more explicit political conversations about who owns that space and what may be undertaken in, on, or beneath it.

RCAP's definition of community proceeds roughly apace with Canadian section 35 case law that conflates community with settlement. Distinguishing between community-as-settlement and community-as-nation or people, however, is important for sorting through more and less racialized claims to Indigeneity. That is, claims to peoplehood speak to a "positive core" of Indigenous peoplehood, which in turn speaks to the kinds of historical political relationships that sustained Indigenous peoples' collective consciousness and identity.[55]

What does it mean to suggest that peoples are political rather than cultural? In a colonial country such as Canada, culture is pinned to Indigeneity in the form of cultural *difference* and, as we might suspect, in such contexts it is difficult to be both "different" and "not-different." A legion of legal jurisprudence and its commentary, for example, has grappled with the issue of which aspects of Indigeneity are protectable by a riddle the court most notoriously solved, in *R. v. Van der Peet* (1996), in terms of pre-*contact* community activities. This has subsequently been inched along to pre-colonial activities (in *Powley*) but nonetheless, the fundamental assumption lying at the heart of these discussions is that real Indigeneity *was* rather than *is*—the more modern we appear, the manifestly less Indigenous we must be. This truism, perhaps expressed most starkly in juridical logics, nonetheless lies at the heart of official Canadian discourses of Indigeneity more broadly.

One approach for situating Indigenous peoplehood politically—and perhaps offering hope for moving beyond this fixity—has been to focus on aspects of Canadian common law that emphasize historical *relationships*. Legal scholar Jeremy Webber defines Indigenous peoplehood in terms of the "intersocietal relationships" that arose during the early colonial period of North America.[56] He speaks in terms of *intersocietal norms* "that are fundamentally intercommunal, created not by the dictation of one society, but by the interaction of various societies through time."[57] Early interrelations between Indigenous peoples and settlers produced a diplomatic context that not only produced

more stable and predictable conduct (or, at least, expectations of such conduct) but also provided grounds for criticizing conduct that departed from those emerging norms.[58] Tully (2008) argues that although the kinds of relationships in which intersocietal norms were produced "were surrounded by a sea of strategic relations of pressure, force and fraud. . . . Aboriginal peoples and newcomer Canadians recognize[d] each other as equal, coexisting and self-governing nations and govern[ed] their relations with each other by negotiations, based on procedures of reciprocity and consent."[59]

Relationally based approaches offer an important corrective to colonial Aboriginal rights law that magnanimously seeks to find accommodation of Indigenous viewpoints within a colonial framework already thoroughly saturated with a colonial commonsense that incorrectly reads today's material and symbolic inequalities into historical configurations of power. Webber (1995a) cautions us to instead be attentive to the initially inchoate but increasingly stable "procedures, settled rules for the relations between colonists and indigenous peoples. They came to constitute a body of truly cross-cultural norms, born of the interaction between peoples and departing in significant ways from what either party would have required if it had been able to impose its own sense of justice."[60] While we should not use this to fashion a "Pollyanna" narrative of a history, free of conflict or turmoil, it equally requires us to give pause to the narratives like those fashioned by British Columbia Supreme Court Chief Justice Alan McEachern in delivering the decision on *Delgamuukw v. The Queen* in 1991—a narrative that, while widely admonished, displayed broad similarities to both historical and contemporaneous Aboriginal policy.[61]

Intersociality, or inter-normativity, is part of a broader discussion about how to properly characterize early interrelations between settlers and Indigenous peoples and about the fundamentally inter-societal character of Canadian common law. We may note with Slattery (2000) a major feature of the doctrine of Aboriginal rights important to a discussion of peoplehood: ancient custom. Like

Webber, Slattery explains the doctrine of Aboriginal rights as, in part, formed in light of the "inter-societal" law that governed early interactions between settlers and Indigenous peoples worked out in practice along the eastern seaboard of Indigenous territories now claimed by the United States and Canada, culminating formally in the *Royal Proclamation of 1763.*[62]

Much of the Canadian discussion around Indigenous "peoples" is juridically based, at least partly the result of including Aboriginal "peoples" in section 35 of the Constitution Act, 1982. Chartrand and Giokas (2002) argue that, in a juridical context, the "Métis people" must "be defined in light of the purposes of recognizing Aboriginal rights," a principle also enshrined in Canadian Aboriginal rights law (for example, *R. v. Sparrow* 1990).[63] Analogous to Webber's and Slattery's discussion, Chartrand and Giokas (2002) define peoplehood in terms of historical political relationships with the Crown (277) because they reflect an important part of the fiduciary doctrine that governs Canada's constitutional relationships with Aboriginal peoples.[64] We might well add to this, of course, evidence of relationships with other Indigenous peoples.

Chartrand and Giokas (2002) emphasize what they term a "positive core" of peoplehood. This is important for my argument because they are suggesting that throughout the twentieth century, official Canadian recognition practices have taken place in the shadow of a deep racialization in which two kinds of Indigenous individuals and communities exist: Status and non-Status Indians. The federal government in particular has staked a financial claim in establishing hard boundaries between these categories and likely cares little how Indigenous individuals actually self-identify. Thus, Chartrand and Giokas argue, a peoplehood-based discussion must begin with historical inquiry to identify collectives with a history of formal Crown–Indigenous relations and, for that matter, in formal Indigenous–Indigenous relations as well.[65]

The legal peoplehood debate has resulted in the valuable insight that peoplehood is at a fundamental level not only about internal practices of membership but about formal, externally oriented practices as well. As such, we should look for evidence of historical peoplehood in the formal interrelations *between* peoples (including but not limited to imperial powers) prior to the imposition of colonialism. This is a far cry from, for example, the kinds of recent claims that are rooted not in a pre-colonial claim to a positive core of peoplehood but, rather, in terms of a correction to the violation of the principles of natural justice that have severed descendants from their ancestors' historical Indigenous communities. It also requires us to think carefully about contemporary claims to Indigeneity based on links to historical fur trade communities, especially when these claims fail to work through the complexities of those relationships to their historical claim region's (other) Indigenous peoples.

# Notes

1. Ernest Gellner, *Nations and nationalism* (Ithaca: Cornell University Press, 1983).

2. Eric Hobsbawm, *Nations and nationalism since 1780: Programme, myth, reality* (Cambridge University Press, 1990).

3. Stuart Hall, "The question of cultural identity." In *Modernity: An introduction to modern societies*, edited by Stuart Hall, David Held, Don Hubert, and Kenneth Thompson, 595–634 (Cambridge: Polity Press, 1995).

4. Homi Bhabha, "Introduction: Narrating the nation." In *Nation and narration*, edited by Homi Bhabha, 1–7 (London: Routledge, 1990).

5. Most notably associated with Anthony Smith, *The ethnic origins of nations* (Oxford: Blackwell Press, 1986). See also Scott Lyons, *X-marks: Native signatures of assent* (Minneapolis: University of Minnesota Press, 2010) and Benedict Anderson, *Imagined communities: Reflections on the origins and spread of nationalism*, 3rd edition (London: Verso, 2006). Also, Gellner, *Nations and nationalism*; Hobsbawm, *Nations and nationalism since 1780.*

6. For an example of a beautiful discussion of pre-modern Czech nationalism, Derek Sayer, *The coasts of Bohemia: A Czech history* (Princeton, NJ: Princeton University Press, 1998).

7. Industrialization and elites' invention of traditions: the growth of a centralized, educated populace producing a common "high" culture: or print capitalism enacting the same, respectively.

8. Taiaiake Alfred, *Wasase: Indigenous pathways of action and freedom* (Peterborough, ON: Broadview Press, 2005); Glen Coulthard, "Subjects of empire: Indigenous peoples and the 'politics of recognition' in Canada." *Contemporary Political Theory* 6.4 (2007): 437–60.

9. For those interested in reading about these issues at an introductory level, see Richard Robbins, *Global programs amid the culture of capitalism* (Boston, MA: Pearson Education, 2011).

10. Michel Foucault, *History of sexuality. Volume 1, An introduction* (New York: Vintage Books, 1978).

11. Pierre Bourdieu, *Language and symbolic power.* Edited and introduced by John Thompson; translated by Gino Raymond and Matthew Adamson (Cambridge, MA: Harvard University Press, 1991), 221.

12. Hall, "The question of cultural identity," 614–615. See also, Anderson, *Imagined communities*; Gellner, *Nations and nationalism*; and Hobsbawm, *Nation and nationalism since 1780*, for a discussion of "nation" as common culture, including the perception of common roots and territory, along with their associated symbols.

13. Bhabha, "Introduction."

14. Hall, "The question of cultural identity."

15. Bhabha, "Introduction," 3.

16. Paul Chartrand, "'Terms of division': Problems of 'outside-naming' for Aboriginal people in Canada." *Journal of Indigenous studies* 2.2 (1991): 1–22.

17. Audra Simpson, "Paths toward a Mohawk Nation: Narratives of citizenship and nationhood in Kahnawake." In *Political theory and the rights of Indigenous peoples*, edited by Duncan Ivison, Paul Patton, and William Sanders, 113–136 (Cambridge, UK: Cambridge University Press. 2000), 116.

18. Lyons, *X-marks*.

19. Claude Denis, *We are not you: First Nations and Canadian Modernity* (Broadview Press, 1997).

20. Robert Warrior, *Tribal secrets: Recovering American Indian intellectual traditions* (Minneapolis: University of Minnesota Press, 1995); Jace Weaver, *That the people might live: Native American literatures and Native American community* (Minneapolis: University of Minnesota Press, 1997); Jace Weaver, Craig Womack, and Robert Warrior, *American Indian literary nationalism* (Minneapolis: University of Minnesota Press, 2006).

21. Simon Ortiz, "Towards a national Indian literature: Cultural authenticity in nationalism." *MELUS* 8.2 (1981): 7–12.

22. See Alfred, *Heeding* and Vine Deloria and Clifford Lytle, *The nations within: The past and future of American Indian sovereignty* (New York: Pantheon Books, 1984);

Deloria and Lytle emphasize Indigenous nationhood as a marker of autonomy (13).

23. Alfred, *Heeding*, 9.

24. Simpson, "Paths toward a Mohawk Nation," 118.

25. Anderson, *Imagined communities*.

26. Ibid., 7.

27. See Daniel Heath Justice, *Our fire survives the storm: A Cherokee literary history* (Minneapolis: University of Minnesota Press, 2006), 23; Denis, *We are not you*.

28. Justice, *Our fire*, 24.

29. Duane Champagne, "In search of theory and method in American Indian studies." *American Indian Quarterly* 31.3 (2007): 353.

30. Examples include Mohawk scholar Audra Simpson (2000) and Ojibway/Dakota scholar Scott Lyons (2010).

31. Simpson, "Path toward a Mohawk Nation," 118, 221.

32. Lyons, *X-marks*, 121.

33. Lyons argument is compelling only if one takes for granted Western European contexts for understanding nationhood as the only manner in which nationalism can be "located" analytically (132).

34. See Denis, *We are not you*; Kristina Fagan, "Tewatatha:wi: Aboriginal nationalism in Taiaiake Alfred's *Peace, power and righteousness: An Indigenous manifesto.*" *American Indian Quarterly* 28.1 (2004): 12–29; Daniel Heath Justice, "The necessity of nationhood: Affirming the sovereignty of Indigenous national literatures." In *Moveable margins: The shifting spaces in Canadian literature*, edited by Chelva Kanaganayakam. 143–59 (Toronto: Tsar Publications, 2005); Daniel Heath Justice, *Our fire survives the storm*.

35. See Chris Andersen, "Residual tensions of empire: Contemporary Métis communities and the Canadian judicial imagination." In *Reconfiguring Aboriginal-state relations, Canada: The state of the federation, 2003*, edited by Michael Murphy, 295–305 (Montreal and Kingston, McGill-Queen's University Press, 2005); Michael Asch, "The judicial conception of culture after *Delgamuukw and Van der Peet*." Review of Constitutional Studies 5.2 (2000): 119–37; Glen Coulthard, "Resisting culture: Seyla Benhabib's deliberate approach to the politics of recognition in colonial contexts." In *Realizing deliberative democracy*, edited by D. Kahane, D. Leydet, D. Weinstock, and M. Williams, 138–154 (Vancouver: UBC Press, 2009); Joyce Green, "The difference debate: reducing rights to cultural flavours." *Canadian Journal of Political Science* 31 (2005): 133–144: N. Kompridis, "Normativizing hybridity/neutralizing culture." *Political Theory* 33.3 (2005): 318–43; "The unsettled and unsettling claims of culture: A reply to Seyla Benhabib." *Political Theory* 34.3 (2006): 389–96; Jeremy Patzer, "Even when we're winning, are we losing? Métis rights in Canadian courts." In *Métis in Canada: History, Identity, Law, and Politics*, edited by Christopher Adams, Gregg Dahl, and Ian Peach, 307–336 (Edmonton: University of Alberta Press, 2013).

36. Michel Foucault, *The history of sexuality. Volume 1, An introduction* (New York: Vintage Books, 1978), 120; Jacques Derrida, *Positions*. Translated and annotated by Alan Bass (Chicago: University of Chicago Press, 1981), 41.

37. Justice, *Our fire survives the storm*, 151.

38. Fagan, "Tewatatha:wi," 12.

39. Simpson, "Paths toward a Mohawk Nation," 121.

40. See Craig S. Womack, *Red on Red: Native American literary separatism* (Minneapolis: University of Minnesota Press, 1999); Warrior, *Tribal secrets*.

41. Denis, *We are not you*, 82.

42. Simpson, "Paths toward a Mohawk Nation."

43. See also, Lyons, *X-marks*.

44. See also generally, Philip Deloria, *Indians in unexpected places* (Lawrence: University of Kansas Press, 2004).

45. See Sam Deloria, "Commentary on nation-building: The future of Indian nations." *Arizona State Law Journal* 34 (2002): 55–62. Deloria articulates this issue clearly "Nobody visits Liechtenstein periodically to make sure they are sufficiently poor and sufficiently culturally distinct from their neighbors to merit continued political existence. They're just around. So when we're waxing eloquent about . . . cultural sovereignty and all other kinds of sovereignty, be damned careful that we're not saying to this society, 'In exchange for a continued political existence, we promise to maintain some kind of cultural purity,' because you think it's going to be by our standards. Hell no . . . it's going to be by THEIR standards." 58–59 in Kim TallBear, "Genomic articulations of Indigeneity," *Social Studies of Science* 43.4 (2013): 515; also, Chris Andersen, "Critical Indigenous studies: From difference to density" *Cultural Studies Review* 15.2 (2009): 97–115; Brendan Hokowhitu, "Indigenous existentialism and the body." *Cultural Studies Review* 15.2 (2009): 101–18.

46. Oral arguments, 2003, *R. v. Powley*, Supreme Court of Canada (File No.: 28533), March 17th. Labrador Métis Nation Factum. 2003. *R. v. Powley*. Supreme Court of Canada File No.: 28533). Congress of Aboriginal Peoples Factum. 2002. *R. v. Powley*, Supreme Court of Canada (File No.: 28533); Métis Nation of Ontario (joint with Métis National Council) (2003) *R. v. Powley*, Supreme Court of Canada (File No.: 28533).

47. For a broad discussion of the major debates and conclusions in a Canadian context see Yale Belanger and David Newhouse, "Reconciling solitudes: A critical analysis of the self-government ideal." In *Aboriginal self-government in Canada: Current trends and issues*, edited by Yale Belanger, 1–19 (Saskatoon, SK: Purich Publishing, 2008).

48. Royal Commission on Aboriginal Peoples (RCAP), *Report of the Royal Commission on Aboriginal Peoples*. 5 volumes (Ottawa: Minister of Supply and Services. 1996, vol. 2, ii).

49. See Chris Andersen, "Settling for community? Juridical visions of historical Métis collectivity in and after

50. "Who are Indigenous peoples?" http://www.un.org/esa/socdev/unpfii/documents/5session_factsheetl.pdf.

51. James Anaya. *Indigenous peoples in international law* (New York: Oxford University Press, 1996), 3.

52. James Anaya, "The evolution of the concept of Indigenous peoples and its contemporary dimensions." In *Perspectives on the rights of minorities and Indigenous peoples in Africa*, edited by Solomon Dersso, 23–42 (Cape Town. South Africa: Pretoria University Law Press, 2010).

53. RCAP, *Report of the Royal Commission on Aboriginal Peoples*, ii.

54. Ibid.

55. See Paul Chartrand and John Giokas, "Defining 'the Métis people': The hard case of Canadian Aboriginal law." In *Who are Canada's Aboriginal peoples? Recognition, definition, and jurisdiction*, edited by Paul Chartrand, 268–304 (Saskatoon, SK: Purich Publishing. 2002).

56. Jeremy Webber, "The jurisprudence of regret: The search for standards of justice in Mabo." *Sydney Law Review* 17 (1995a): 5–28; Jeremy Webber, "Relations at force and relations of justice: The emergence of normative community between colonists and Aboriginal peoples." *Osgoode Law Journal* 33 (1995b): 623–60.

57. Webber, "Relations of force," 626.

58. Ibid., 628–29.

59. James Tully, *Public philosophy in a new key: Volume I* (Cambridge: Cambridge University Press, 2008), 226.

60. Webber, "The jurisprudence of regret," 75.

61. Janna Promislow, 2010. "'Thou wilt not die of hunger or I bring thee merchandise.' Consent, intersocietal normativity, and the exchange of food at York Factory, 1682–1763." In *Between consenting peoples: Political community and the meaning of consent*, edited by Jeremy Webber and Cohn Macleod, 77–114 (Vancouver: UBC Press. 2010).

62. Brian Slattery, "Making sense of Aboriginal rights." *Canadian Bar Review* 79 (2000): 198–200.

63. Chartrand and Giokas, "Defining 'the Métis people'," 277.

64. For a broader discussion of this issue and for a discussion on "intersocietal law" more generally, see J. Borrows, 2002, *Recovering Canada: The resurgence of Indigenous law* (Toronto: University of Toronto Press, 2002) and Brian Slattery, "Understanding Aboriginal rights." *Canadian Bar Review* 66 (1987): 727–783; 'Making sense of Aboriginal rights"; and "The generative structure of Aboriginal rights." In *Moving toward justice: Legal traditions and Aboriginal justice*, edited by John Whyte, 20–48 (Saskatoon, SK: Purich Publishing, 2008).

65. Chartrand and Giokas, "Defining 'the Métis people'," 272.

# Case Law

*Alberta (Aboriginal Affairs and Northern Development) v. Cunningham.* [2011] 2 SCR. 670

*Calder v. British Columbia (Attorney-General).* 1973. S.C.R. 313.

*Delgamuukw v. British Columbia,* [1991] 3 W.W.R. 97 (BCSC).

*Enge v. Mandeville et al.* 2013 NWTSC 33.

*Her Majesty in Right of Newfoundland and Labrador v. The Labrador Métis Nation.* 2007 NLCA 75.

*The Labrador Métis Nation v. Her Majesty in Right of Newfoundland and Labrador.* 2006 NLTD 119.

*Manitoba Métis Federation Inc., et al. v. Attorney General of Canada, et al.,* 2011, SCC case information, 33880.

*Manitoba Métis Federation Inc. v. Canada (Attorney General),* 2013 SCC 14.

*R. v. Castonguay,* 2006 NBCA 43 (CanLII).

*R. v. Castonguay,* [2003] I CNLR. (NBPCt).

*R. v. Daniels,* 2013 FC 6.

*R. v. Goodon,* 2008 MBPC 59 (CanLII).

*R. v. Hirsekorn,* 2013 ABCA 242.

*R. v. Hopper,* [2004] NBJ No. 107. (Prov. Ct.).

*R. v. Howse,* [2002] BCJ No. 379 (BCSC).

*R. v. Laviolette,* 2005 SKPC 70.

*R. v. Norton,* 2005 SKPC 46 (CanLII).

*R. v. Nunn,* 2003, unreported, Provincial Court of British Columbia. Court File No. 30689H (Penticton).

*R. v. Powley,* 2003 SCC 43.

*R. v. Sparrow,* 1990, C.N.L.R. 160 (SCC).

*R. v. Van der Peet,* [1996] 4 CNLR 177 (SCC).

*R. v. Willison,* [2006], BCJ No. 1505 (BCSC).

*R. v. Willison,* [2005], BCJ No. 924 (BCProvCt).

*Re Secession of Quebec,* [1998] 2 S.C.R. 217.

*R. v. Powley Files*

Trial transcripts, five volumes (transcription of original Ontario Court of Justice testimony).

Oral arguments, 2003. *R. v. Powley,* Supreme Court of Canada (File No.: 2853) March 17th.

Labrador Métis Nation Factum. 2003. *R. v. Powley,* Supreme Court of Canada (File No.: 28533).

Congress of Aboriginal Peoples Factum. 2002. *R. v. Powley,* Supreme Court of Canada (File No.: 28533).

Métis Nation of Ontario (joint with Métis National Council) (2003). *R. v. Powley,* Supreme Court of Canada (File No.: 28533).

# PART THREE

❖

# Additional Readings

Andersen, Chris. 2014. *Métis: Race, Recognition, and the Struggle for Indigenous Peoplehood.* Vancouver: UBC Press.

Dunbar-Ortiz, Roxanne. *An Indigenous Peoples' History of the United States.* Boston, MA: Beacon Press, 2014.

Goeman, Mishuana. *Mark My Words: Native Women Mapping Our Nations.* Minneapolis, MN: University of Minnesota Press, 2013.

Harris, Cole. *The Resettlement of British Columbia: Essays on Colonialism and Geographical Change.* Vancouver, BC: University of British Columbia Press, 1997.

Lyons, Scott Richard. *X-Marks: Native Signatures of Assent.* Minneapolis, MN: University of Minnesota Press, 2010.

Manuel, Arthur, and Grand Chief Ronald M. Derrickson. *Unsettling Canada: A National Wake-Up Call.* Toronto: Between the Lines Press, 2015.

Ramirez, Renya K. *Native Hubs: Culture, Community, and Belonging in Silicon Valley and Beyond.* Durham, NC: Duke University Press, 2007.

Simpson, Audra. *Mohawk Interruptus: Political Life across the Borders of Settler States.* Durham, NC: Duke University Press, 2014.

Simpson, Leanne. *Dancing on Our Turtle's Back: Stories of Nishnaabeg Re-Creation and a New Emergence.* Winnipeg: Arbiter Ring Publishing, 2011.

# Relevant Websites

**Library and Archives Canada Canadian Confederation website**

http://www.collectionscanada.gc.ca/confederation/index-e.html

*This website provides an overview and markedly unilateral narrative of individuals who played a part in the formation of Canada as a Settler nation state.*

**Transforming Relations: A Collaborative Collection**

https://transformingrelations.wordpress.com/category/land-struggles/

*This student-driven website based at Trent University provides an overview of ally engagements with lands and environmental justice movements of relevance to Indigenous nations including anti-fracking, pipeline development, and tar sands devastation.*

## Films

*Inuit Cree Reconciliation.* Dir. Zacherias Kunuk and Neil Diamond. Kingulliit Productions, 2013.

*Is the Crown at War with Us?* Dir. Alanis Obomsawin. National Film Board of Canada, 2002.

*Kanehsatake: 270 Years of Resistance.* Dir. Alanis Obomsawin. National Film Board of Canada, 1993.

*The Pass System.* Dir. Alex Williams. Tamarack Productions, 2015.

*Trick or Treaty?* Dir. Alanis Obomsawin. National Film Board of Canada, 2014.

*Two Worlds Colliding.* Dir. Tasha Hubbard. National Film Board of Canada, 2004.

*Wake Up!* Dir. Jessie Short. Jessie Short, 2015.

## Key Terms

Dispossession
Indigenous nationhood
Kinship
Métis
Nation-building

Peoplehood
Relationality
Settler violence
Urbanity/Indigeneity binarism

## Discussion Questions

1. What role do spatial understandings play in ongoing Settler colonialism, dispossession, and the disavowal of Indigenous identities?

2. What is meant by racialization? How did racialization impact Indigenous peoples and of what service is it to the ongoing history of Settler colonialism, lands theft, and dispossession?

3. What is the significance of Chris Andersen's peoplehood-based approach to historical inquiry? How does it address Settler–Indigenous/Indigenous–Indigenous relations, the "enframing power" of Settler States, and the contradictions inherent in European-based definitions of nationhood?

4. Bonita Lawrence writes that ". . . in order for Canada to have a viable national identity, the histories of Indigenous nations, in all their diversity and longevity, must be erased." What does she mean by this and what are the implications of this reality for *both* Indigenous and non-Indigenous peoples?

## Activities

Research the land on which your school, home, or community is built. To which Indigenous nation does it belong? What is the history of Settler colonialism or resistance against settlement on this land? Are there any historical grievances over this land? What are they? What are the central differences in these grievances?

Watch the 2002 National Film Board production *Is the Crown at War with Us?* (written and directed by Alanis Obomsawin). How might you analyze the actions of non-Indigenous fishermen with respect to race, space, and the law? Discuss the role of violence in upholding the boundaries of race and space under Settler colonialism. Where does this film and its history fit in relation to Lawrence's article on the history of Indigenous resistance in Eastern Canada?

Watch the 2006 television drama *One Dead Indian* (written by Hugh Graham and Andrew Wreggit, directed by Tim Southam). How might you analyze the actions of the provincial government and police with respect to racism, resistance, and the law? Where do their actions stand in relation to the findings and recommendations of the Ipperwash Inquiry? How did the inquiry process bring us closer to decolonizing relations between Indigenous peoples and majority Canadians? What needs to be done in both the short term and long term for these to be fully implemented?

# PART FOUR

❖

# Racialization, Heteropatriarchy, and Indigenous Identities

## Editor Introduction

Since 1850, the point at which the category "Indian" was established in law, Indian status has received increasing attention by courts of law, policy makers, and politicians in Canada. Much of the controversy has surrounded amendments to the *Indian Act*, specifically, the constitutionality of S. 12 of the 1951 Act and S. 6 of the 1985 legislation. Historically, these sections made invidious distinctions between male and female Indians in establishing the entitlement of persons to be registered as Indians. Until as recently as December 2010, following the historic case of *McIvor v. Canada* (see Cannon, this volume), as well as the passing of the *Gender Equity in Indian Registration Act*, these sections treated the children of men and women who married non-Indians differently and unequally under the law. Indian status embodied a long history of discrimination aimed at Indigenous communities, especially Indigenous women.

Not every Indigenous person is a status Indian. As a matter of historical fact, Indigenous peoples became Indians under a legal classification that did not distinguish between them, or for that matter, their multiplicity at early colonialism. People became Indians so that the State could delimit the occupation of certain lands to Indians alone. It was through the sorting out of lands that the idea of whiteness, and indeed race, became concretized in what is now called Canada. The category "Indian" is no more than a legal construction rooted in histories of lands appropriation and colonial domination. Prior to colonization, Indigenous peoples were not "Indians." They defined themselves as distinct peoples and nations with diverse kin-based, socio-economic, and political systems.

The very first act of colonial injustice is racialized injustice—literally, the process whereby Indigenous nations became status Indians for State and land administrative purposes. Broadly speaking, racialization refers to a set of practices, beliefs, ways of thinking, and State recognition processes (Coulthard, 2014), that have made Indianness compulsory. Governments have not addressed this matter in Canada. The injustice is one that even courts have been unable to reconcile despite progressive legal judgments like *McIvor v. Canada* and the *Gender Equity in Indian Registration Act* (2010). As Cannon (this volume) suggests, *McIvor* found the *Indian Act* to perpetuate sex discrimination, because it gave gives fewer rights to the descendants of female Indians based on sex and/or marriage to non-Indians. The court, however, said nothing about histories of racialization (ibid.).

The entitlement of persons to be acknowledged legally as Indians in North America is pertinent to any discussion of race, racialization, and colonial dominance. The criteria used to determine who is—and who is not—an Indian find their roots in early racist thinking about blood quantum and in colonial histories that did not recognize the linguistic and cultural differences between Indigenous groups. Indeed, until as recently as April 2016, following the historic case of *Daniels v. Canada* many people—specifically non-status and some Métis peoples—fell short of any legal acknowledgement by Canada as set out in legal criteria established so long ago for registration and enrolment as Indians. The removal of Indigenous people's ability to determine who belongs, as well as their own membership, must be addressed before histories of race and Settler colonialism can ever be reconciled. In this section, we provide a set of two articles written by Indigenous scholars on matters of racialization and identity.

Martin Cannon examines the case of *McIvor v. Canada*, a case that ultimately gave rise to Canada's *Gender Equity in Indian Registration Act* (2010) which currently restores federal recognition to the grandchildren of Indian women who were involuntarily enfranchised (i.e., legally assimilated) because of sexism and Indianness. Cannon illuminates how Canadian courts have told a "raceless story of sexism" when it comes to the *Indian Act* injustices brought forward by Indigenous women. At the level of common sense, the law has worked to entrench the category "Indian" by failing to address nationhood-based definitions of identity and belonging. Courts in particular also perpetuate a Eurocentric fiction that separates "woman" from "Indian" such that the historically colonizing and racialized processes whereby Indigenous women became Indians are left unaddressed. The effect has not only been to recuperate Settler sovereignty and theft of lands, it also disavows traditional ways of thinking about gender, identity, belonging, and peoplehood.

Indian policy not only worked to institutionalize a set of racialized understandings into law, it made heteronormative assumptions about the nature of identity and kinship organization. The colonizer's imperative to divide the world into strict male/female binaries, as Beverly Little Thunder (see first edition) argued, would have precluded the existence of "two-spirited wimmin." While one must take care to not describe the erotic and gendered diversity that existed prior to contact as homosexual (Cannon, 1998), in the words of the feminist poet and theorist Adrienne Rich, colonial policy would have worked to make European forms of heterosexuality compulsory. The impact of Christianity and residential schools further institutionalized homophobia and sexual shame within many nations and communities.

Despite colonizing efforts to dismantle the memory of gendered and erotic expression, both of them continue today. Chris Finley provides an overview of literature tracing anti-heteropatriarchal and Indigenous feminist writings that seek currently to engage and centre an anticolonial, nonheteronormative, and queer studies framework within Native studies. Her aim is to contemplate an intellectual, conceptual, and spiritual space for reimagining and rejuvenating a queer native body—indeed one that is intent on revitalizing the "sexy that never left" Native Studies or communities. Her work nuances the ways in which heteropatriarchy is being contested, opening "sex positive, and queer friendly discussions of sexuality in Native Studies and communities." She is less concerned with tracing the vested ways in which courts of law seek to impose heteronormative and Eurocentric ways of thinking about gender and sexuality than she is with matters of resistance and resurgence.

The writing we include by Indigenous scholars in this section suggests something in common; indeed, that configurations of sexism and racialization worked together concomitantly with heterosexism and heteronormativity to structure distinct kinds of discrimination for Indigenous women, nations, and two-spirited people. Even today, the law in Canada assumes that Indian status will be passed to children through opposite-sex marriage, throwing the constitutionality of the *Indian Act* into question where discrimination on the basis of sexual orientation is concerned. Racism, sexism, and heterosexism need to be challenged, but how can this be accomplished if discrimination is considered separate, unrelated historically, or only to involve one history of domination? We suggest the answer to this question starts with "recognizing how systems of discrimination have historically interlocked to place Indigenous men and women at a disadvantage relative to Settler populations, the State, the legal system, and to each other" (Cannon, forthcoming).

## CHAPTER 7

# Race Matters

## Sexism, Indigenous Sovereignty, and *McIvor*

*Martin J. Cannon*

## Introduction

In this article, I provide a critical reading of *McIvor*, a progressive case that challenges . . . sexism in the federal criteria for the recognition of Indianness. I argue that while *McIvor* had the potential to correct the history of sex discrimination in the *Indian Act* and to reconcile the matter of racialized injustice as it is realized through, and inseparable from, sexism, it ultimately failed.[1] . . . Canada's courts failed, not by refusing to hear the arguments about sex discrimination contained within the *Indian Act* but, rather, by refusing to address how racialized injustice grounded in "Indianness" is realized through sexism. . . . I argue that our sovereignty as nations is negated through Canada's ongoing refusal to address histories of racialized injustice exacted through sexism.

*Canadian Journal of Women and the Law* 26, 1 (2014): 23–50. Reprinted with permission from University of Toronto Press (www.utpjournals.com).

## Sex Matters: Defining the Interlocking Nature of Racialized Injustice

"Indianness" shapes the very opportunities and outcomes made available to us by Canada as a settler colony. The creation of Indianness was decidedly a part of a genocidal project aimed at both our physical and legal annihilation as peoples and nations.[2] In a very real material sense, the category "Indian" rests on a blood quantum logic that, as Kehaulani Kauanui points out, enacts, substantiates, and then disguises the appropriation of Indigenous lands.[3]

To be clear, the objective has never been to create more Indians in Canada but, rather, to eliminate us in order to acquire access to lands and territory.[4] This matter cuts deep to the heart of the colonial legacy and consciousness that has come to define Canada as a settler nation. Indeed, the logic of elimination was made clear as a *modus operandi* of Canadian policy and law as early as 1920, when Duncan Campbell Scott stood up in the new Dominion Parliament and proclaimed:

> I want to get rid of the Indian problem . . . after one hundred years, after being in close contact with civilization it is enervating to the individual or to a band to continue in a state of tutelage, when he or they are able to take their positions as British citizens or Canadian citizens, to support themselves, and stand alone . . . Our objective is to continue until there is not a single Indian in Canada that has not been absorbed into the body politic, and there is no Indian question, and no Indian Department.[5]

. . .

Canada is not unique in placing emphasis on the assimilation, acculturation, and elimination of Indigenous peoples. Indeed, scholars of settler colonialism have made this point abundantly clear in suggesting that racialized ways of thinking and acting are key to securing ongoing access to land and must therefore be institutionally reproduced every step of the way. . . .

The matter of federal recognition—meaning, literally, the making and then taking away of Indianness in what ought to be regarded as an act of forced citizenship—must therefore be understood as something greater than genocide. Thus, federal recognition is the structure (and not an event) aimed at the ongoing expropriation of lands and our legislative and physical extinction as Indians.

These matters of eliminating us as peoples are immediately discernable to us as status Indians. In fact, an eliminatory logic began wreaking havoc on our communities in the 1800s when the very idea of Indianness entered into legal parlance, imposing as it did citizenship boundaries on all of our nations and, then later, legislating some of us outside of them because of our mothers' gender and intermarriage. For many of us, the effects of colonial legislation are all too familiar because they have been so aimed at our elimination as peoples. These matters are not only palpable, but they are also known experientially

to us as the effect of legislation to create, and institutionalize, a hierarchical system of relations based on marriage, sexism, race, status, and rights. . . .

As *McIvor* makes clear, status Indians have come to know the logic of elimination through legal distinctions that influence and affect the material circumstances and entitlements afforded Indians as compared to non-Indians and, inseparably, because our (grand-) mothers are female. . . .

I suggest that there is no way to separate issues that affect us as status Indians and those that affect us because of our (grand-) mothers' gender and their choice to marry an unregistered or non-Indian person. The logic of elimination is realized through both the racialization of "Indianness" and sexism (that is, through the outward and deliberate targeting of women). As such, it is necessary to challenge the idea of Indianness as it has been, and continues to be, imposed upon our communities and then taken away in an effort to reduce our numbers and to undermine our sovereignty as nations.

The case of *McIvor*, like the case law in the four decades before it, makes it clear that the courts do not connect histories of sexism with racialization. . . . In *McIvor*, the Court outwardly acknowledged racialization and yet—in the process of doing the business of Indianness and in maintaining the colonial policy affecting it—left it as an unaddressed, if not unrecognizable, form of analogous discrimination facing status Indians in Canada. The truth of the matter is that neither courts nor Parliament view it as their responsibility to address matters of Indianness intended to colonize, assimilate, and divest our (grand-) mothers of sovereignty. . . .

The refusal by courts to address the matter of Indianness head on, let alone see it as a matter inseparable from sexism, has prevented justice for us as peoples. I argue that sexism needs to be seen by courts as a colonial apparatus of power effecting racialized injustice—that is, the legal assimilation of status Indians. . . .

## *McIvor*: Equality but for the Indianness of Our (Grand-) Mothers?

While *McIvor* is progressive case law within the range of status quo litigation and in the sense of having made it possible now for the (grand-) children of some women to register as status Indians, it is perhaps more rightly understood as being flawed from the start in not having ever moved us beyond Indianness, nor into reconciling the writing of race into Canadian law. . . .

Indianness is raised as a common sense, if not a taken-for-granted, category of legal difference and also, within the context and confines of something loosely referred to by the court in a total of twelve different paragraphs throughout the *McIvor* trial judgment, as "cultural identity." . . .

While it may be true that histories of racialization have required of us as nations and individuals to come to care about federal recognition as Indians, it is also true that Indianness, regardless of how meaningful it has become, is a colonial-inspired designation that has always been undesirable to us as sovereign nations. In fact, Bonita Lawrence has already written of this particular dimension of the *Indian Act*, highlighting in turn the complex, if not paradoxical, ways in which the category Indian operates when it comes to "cultural identity." While she does not deny that legal categories shape peoples' lives in terms of both belonging and identity, she also observes that they "set the terms that individuals and communities must utilize, even in resisting these categories."[6]

The trial court did nothing to address, disrupt, or reconcile the requirement that, in Canada, we are still being expected to appropriate and work within the confines of Indianness. Nor did it address the fact that it is perhaps preferable to have Canada restore jurisdiction over citizenship to Indigenous nations, instead of litigating the matter of Indianness as a cultural identity in Canadian courts of law. Indeed, the socio-legal and political contexts that have prevented our own

matrilineal, nationhood-based, and identification approaches to identity and citizenship—and, more importantly, the process of law that has kept them from being legally acknowledged—were quite simply absent altogether as well as non-negotiable in *McIvor* at trial. . . .

While worthy of recognition, in its judgment, the trial court stopped short of admitting any wrongdoing on behalf of Canada in creating and then imposing the category Indian. Furthermore, these matters of racialization were not seen as being in any way related to, or for that matter accomplished through, sexism. Nor did the trial court weigh in on the right of Parliament to determine the citizenry of Indigenous peoples through Indianness and other racialized ways of thinking and knowing.

In refusing to address these historical matters, the trial court left all questions of racialization untouched, demonstrating how, in the case law involving Indian status, the history of racialization can be at once acknowledged and then left unaddressed. The court seemed content in concluding that Indianness represents a significant cultural identity, never really moving us towards a discussion of jurisdiction. The effect was to render the discrimination facing Sharon McIvor and her son as one rooted only in sexism and not in the racialization of Indigenous peoples. The category Indian literally disappears below the surface in *McIvor*. It was as if McIvor herself was not an Indian, let alone litigating the inequality facing her male child—and, indeed, many other male children—because of sexism and Indianness.

## Sex Matters: Race, Citizenship, and Section 35 of the Canadian Constitution

The BC Court of Appeal later revisited, and simultaneously avoided, matters of Indianness, this time in contemplating McIvor in relation to section 28 and section 35 of the *Canadian Charter of Rights and Freedoms*. . . . In what amounted to a refusal on behalf of the court to deal directly with matters of racialization and to see them as being realized and indeed tied intimately to the history of sexism, the appeal court determined that it had neither the "reasoned argument" nor the "evidentiary foundation" before it to consider such questions. . . .

It is bewildering . . . that the court did not see McIvor and Grismer as both embodying (as Indians after all) a history that has made invidious distinctions between us as men and women—and, indeed, between us as men because of our mothers' gender and intermarriage. Neither distinction has served our interest as either Indigenous peoples or as Indians. Indeed, there is a legal argument embedded in *McIvor* in relation to section 35, but it cannot be addressed until courts start seeing Indian women as both Indian and women. Furthermore, the courts must acknowledge that Indian women have faced not only sexism in their own communities but also the racialized injustice that is Indianness. . . .

Had the BC Court of Appeal acknowledged this history in *McIvor*, it would have had to consider a set of equally urgent and critical questions related to jurisdiction, including the power that Canada unilaterally designated for itself under section 91 (24) of the *Constitution Act, 1867*, which was to claim jurisdiction and then legislate over what it called "Indians.". . .

At the level of status quo litigation, the Crown's duty to consult on matters of Indian status would invariably stem from the harm that has been done historically to Indigenous nations. The imposition itself was realized through sexism that has placed men in positions of power within our homes and communities. Both sets of arguments were presented at trial, although the BC Court of Appeal in *McIvor*—as if through a process of historical amnesia—considered neither of them substantively. . . .

[T]he court saw Sharon McIvor as speaking only as a woman and not as a person who had faced inequitable discrimination based on a system of legislative thinking that was developed, in the first colonial instance, to racialize us as peoples and then to legislate some but not all of us as children

outside of the registered Indian community on the basis of sex and intermarriage. McIvor herself, like so many other Indian women in Canada, was not only litigating a system that placed Indigenous men into positions of power where Indigenous women are concerned but was also litigating a system that made arbitrary distinctions between us based on Indianness and that, furthermore, appropriated our ability to exercise any legal jurisdiction over citizenship. . . .

A raceless story of sex discrimination prevents us from seeing the inequality of treatment that Indigenous women and their descendants—indeed, all status Indians—face as racialized peoples.[7] This way of thinking about discrimination does not, and will never, bring us any closer to acknowledging what the *Indian Act* actually did historically. The act installed, and then further consolidated, a way of thinking about ourselves and others (including the people we marry) as Indians in notably racialized terms. It failed to acknowledge what was required of Canada to assert physical control of a land base it claimed by discovery at first contact and onward into the colonial present.[8]. . .

When Indian women were made unequal to Indian men under the *Indian Act* because of sexism, they were also made unequal to settler women and their descendants under an imposed and legislatively sanctioned system of racialization. For a period of 135 years—from 1850 to 1985—some women acquired Indian status upon marriage to registered Indian men. It is, therefore, clearly a misnomer to describe the inequality facing Indigenous women as having only to do with sexism.

At the very least, the facts presented at trial ought to have made it unequivocally clear to the BC Court of Appeal that the *Indian Act* discriminates not only on the basis of sex but also on the basis of Indianness—that is to say, racialization. Even Ross J, in contemplating these matters, admitted to the court the full complexity of issues that were presented to her at trial with respect to Indian status and the matter of restoring equality for Indian women. In response to the defendant's claim that the plaintiffs did not have a viable claim under section 15 because the *Charter* cannot be applied retroactively to repair historical injustices, she reasoned:

> Strictly speaking, it is correct to say that the only way to give absolutely equal treatment to all persons would be to either grant status to spouses of Indian women who, prior to April 17, 1985, married persons who were not status Indians, or to take away the status of the women who married status Indians prior to April 17, 1985, and acquired status from their husbands. However, the plaintiffs do not seek any relief in relation to the non-Indian spouses of status Indians. That is, the plaintiffs do not seek equal treatment with respect to the non-Indian spouses of Indians, either in the form of granting or removing status. Rather, they seek treatment for Indian women and their children who claim Indian descent through them that is equal to that afforded to Indian men and their descendants. The defendants' submission overlooks the provisions of earlier versions of the *Indian Act* that granted registration status to the legitimate child of a male person who was registered or entitled to be registered as an Indian, for example, s. 11(d) of the *1951 Act*.[9]

The BC Court of Appeal would not return to this matter of "absolute equal treatment" as Ross J entertained it at trial. In fact, the court ultimately stumbled through this matter, deciding in the end—and, notably, on behalf of Grismer and McIvor—that their status in relation to non-Indian peoples, both current and historically, was not what either of them was asking the court to reconcile. In what amounted to a recolonizing move on behalf of the appeal court, *McIvor* did nothing to reconcile matters of citizenship injustice and jurisdictional infringements as both were realized through, and inseparable from, racialization and sexism.

What the appeal court needed to do in *McIvor* in order to secure justice for women such as McIvor, and, indeed, for status Indians in general, was to broaden the scope of sex discrimination to

include all women legally defined as "Indians." It did not. However, under such a redefinition, the results would have shed light on the racialization the *Indian Act* has institutionalized in Canada, not only between us as male and female Indians but also between settler and Indigenous women. The courts would have had to recognize that even on the basis of sex discrimination alone, not all Indian women were treated the same on account of the racialization that was realized through the legislative rules around marital status and intermarriage. It would also have had to recognize that Jacob Grismer, like so many other Indian men borne to out-marrying women before 17 April 1985, would have been—outside of a racialized way of thinking about identity, citizenship, and belonging in Canada—equal but for the race of his father.

*McIvor* worked, therefore, to recover a historic and notably ongoing refusal on behalf of courts and Parliament to address how all women, on account of both sex and race, were placed into unequal standing with one another. Even in scholarly literature, little is known of the process whereby women, over a period of 135 years, became Indians upon marriage to Indian men.[10] I suggest that these silences reveal the tendency to divorce matters of sexism from racialization in the precise ways I have discussed in this article. The tendency is to portray women as losing status as women only and not as Indians. Until the scope of anti-discrimination law is broadened to include all women legally defined as Indians, including those who acquired this definition under the *Indian Act* historically, we will not challenge colonial dominance, Indianness, or a way of thinking about identity, citizenship, and nationhood in state-based terms. We will furthermore disregard a series of urgent questions surrounding the matter of jurisdiction.

## Refusing Indianness and Resisting Re-Colonization

There is good reason, I have argued, to be skeptical that Canadian law can resolve colonial grievances or issues of substantive inequality related to

Indianness and Indigenous sovereignty. As Colin Samson has also argued, colonial law is not concerned with Indigenous sovereignty but, rather, focuses merely on the infringements of rights and the procedures that colonial governments must follow in order to legally extinguish "Aboriginal title."[11] It is through this process of when and how the rights of "Aboriginal peoples" can be infringed upon that the law accomplishes the ongoing usurpation of lands. Samson refers to this process of colonial law as none other than a "magical contrivance."[12] Samson draws attention to case law in an effort to demonstrate how Canada re-inscribes its sovereignty as a settler nation, and I have shown how *McIvor* is among the case law that serves this purpose.

It is essentially Indianness, and not nationhood, that is believed to define the political relationship of Canada with Indigenous peoples. The language of Indianness, or Aboriginal for that matter,[13] has been solidly written into section 35 of the constitutional law. Courts in general are steadfast in refusing to acknowledge Indigenous peoples as nations or, for that matter, anything beyond "Aboriginal title."[14] James Tully states that "the law incorporates Indigenous peoples into Canada [and the Canadian Constitution] and subjects them to the Canadian Constitution in the very act of recognizing their rights as rights within the Canadian constitution."[15] This tautological move protects Canadian sovereignty, as does foreclosing examinations of "Indianness" or "Aboriginal" in Canadian law. Canada's consideration, under section 15 of its *Canadian Charter of Rights and Freedoms*, of sex discriminatory inequality in the *Indian Act* enables Canada to avoid addressing its colonial existence.[16] . . .

Although we did not relinquish our sovereignty at contact nor our ability to determine and identify who it is that belongs to our nations as citizens, Canadian law has tended to disregard, if not actively work to supplant legislatively, these identities and practices. It has not questioned the myth of settler sovereignty in any way related to the distinct and marked historical processes surrounding the matter of outside naming at contact. Even the use and occupation of our traditional lands is reduced

to a legal matter involving "Aboriginal title," a designation created by the law itself to address what ought to be considered a re-colonizing move. . . .

In order to achieve true justice for Indigenous peoples, Canada must literally undertake the impossible under settler colonialism. It must acknowledge the identities that exist outside of the federal legislation it created to appropriate and dispossess us of lands. It must rejuvenate its own treaty and nation-to-nation agreements established at early colonialism and in partnership with Indigenous allies. It must acknowledge that the theft of lands was accomplished through the doctrine of Indianness. Furthermore, Canada must relinquish and move beyond the unilateral power it granted itself under section 91(24) of the *Constitution Act, 1867*, to claim jurisdiction and then legislate over what it called "Indians." . . .

Indeed, the invitation to litigate the *Indian Act* must be seen for what it is—a strategy on behalf of settler states to recover and re-inscribe the colonial dominance that is none other than Indianness in Canada.

The invitation to "equality," especially as relating to Indian status and the making of Indian status as more just and/or "fair" under the law, is an all too familiar colonial tactic that leaves in place the very idea of Indianness. It does absolutely nothing to alter, change, or repair the racialized and colonial assumptions inherent within the legislative designation itself. It does nothing to restore jurisdiction and the inherent right to self-definition or to return the ability to define Indigenous citizenship to its proper jurisdiction, which rests, since the first historical instance, with Indigenous nations.[17] Indigenous peoples' resurgences towards the restoration of jurisdiction and control over self-definition have been made clear and are particularly noteworthy in Canada, with some status organizations outwardly contesting the imposition of the Indian status designation.[18] In each case, the sovereignty of Indigenous peoples to determine their own citizenship has not been acknowledged, nor has Canada relinquished its legislative power where the inherent right to self-definition is concerned.

# Future Challenges and Concluding Thoughts: Reflections on the Way Forward

. . .

As a person impacted by the *Indian Act* and, more accurately, the sexism that is tied to our racialization as Indians, I suggest that it is not only women who have a story to tell about the history of sexism in Canada. Indeed, sexism does not simply impact upon women alone. *McIvor* demonstrates that men too have a story to tell about the idea of Indianness and how it is tied to our (grand-) mothers' statuses as Indians. We have come to know the logic of assimilation and elimination as one that has deliberately targeted us because our (grand-) mothers are female and also because our fathers are non-Indians. We have come to experience the complex and interlocking effects of both racialization and sex discrimination created in the first instance by colonial injustice and by the outward and explicit targeting of Indian women. . .

There is nothing that ought to grant us a monopoly over talking about the impact of sexism and patriarchy in our lives as men. It is significant, however, that in my nation—the Six Nations—we are matrilineal, meaning that we trace our ancestry through our (grand-) mothers and that many of us wish to retain a matrilineal way of thinking in our hearts and minds. The *Indian Act* has worked to reverse and denigrate this very idea of women's power

and thinking, but we have not forgotten that this is the way we belong as peoples, even if courts have refused to recognize it. Indeed, this knowledge provides, and will provide, the very basis upon which we will begin to imagine and (re-)create a new and different future, especially where matters of identity and citizenship are concerned. And this basis needs to be acknowledged by Canadian law as the way we have done our kinship business for centuries.

Canada needs to acknowledge who we are as Indigenous peoples and citizens outside of federal jurisdiction and colonial legislation. As an inseparable part of this process, we need to understand how it is that we belong outside of racialized ways of thinking. These ways of knowing our kin relations must be rejuvenated, first and foremost, as well as acknowledged legally and affirmed by courts. We also need to know, name, and talk pointedly about the complex vagaries of colonialism, sexism, and racialization, especially the way this history has placed us as men and women into unequal relation with one another as Indians. It is at this precise juncture of decolonization and legal transformation that men must come to understand, unequivocally, and speak more outwardly and openly about how it is that sexism has impacted on our lives as Indians. I hope to have shown that, in relation to the future of Indian status in Canada, we will need to dispense with "the raceless story of sexism" and an original fiction that separates "woman" and "Indian" in Eurocentric thought. It is time now, more than ever, to dispense with the category of Indianness in favour of nationhood.

# Notes

1. Martin J Cannon, "Sexism, Racism or Both?: A Closer Look at the Indian Act and the McIvor Case" (Fall 2007) 62 *New Socialist* at 22.

2. Martin J Cannon, "Revisiting Histories of Gender-Based Exclusion and the New Politics of Indian Identity" (Research paper submitted to the National Centre for First Nations Governance, 2008); Martin J Cannon and Lina Sunseri, eds, *Racism, Colonialism, and Indigeneity in Canada: A Reader* (Toronto: Oxford University Press, 2011) at 2; J Kehaulani Kauanui, *Hawaiian Blood: Colonialism and the Politics of Sovereignty and Indigeneity* (Dunham, NC: Duke University Press, 2008); Bonita Lawrence, *"Real"*

*Indians and Others: Mixed-Blood Urban Native Peoples and Indigenous Nationhood* (Vancouver, BC: UBC Press, 2004); Patrick Wolfe, "Settler Colonialism and the Elimination of the Native" (2006) 8:4 *Journal of Genocide Research* 387.

3. J. Kehaulani Kauanui, *Hawaiian Blood: Colonialism and the Politics of Sovereignty and Indigeneity* (Dunham, NC: Duke University Press, 2008) at 34–35.

4. Bonita Lawrence, "Rewriting Histories of the Land: Colonization and Indigenous Resistance in Eastern Canada" in Sherene H Razack, ed., *Race, Space, and the Law: Unmapping a White Settler Society* (Toronto: Between the Lines, 2002) at 21.

5.   Quoted in Darlene Johnston, "First Nations and Canadian Citizenship" in William Kaplan, ed., *Belonging: The Meaning and Future of Canadian Citizenship* (Montreal and Kingston: McGill-Queen's University Press, 1993) at 363.

6.   Bonita Lawrence, *"Real" Indians and Others: Mixed-Blood Urban Native Peoples and Indigenous Nationhood* (Vancouver, BC: UBC Press, 2004) at 230.

7.   Martin J Cannon, *(De)marginalizing the Intersection of 'Race' and Gender in First Nations Politics* (MA thesis, Department of Sociology, Queen's University, Kingston, 1995) at 1; Martin J Cannon, *Undoing Citizenship Injustice: Racism, Sexism, and Indian Status in Canada* (Toronto: University of Toronto Press, forthcoming 2013).

8.   Bonita Lawrence, "Rewriting Histories of the Land: Colonization and Indigenous Resistance in Eastern Canada" in Sherene H Razack, ed, *Race, Space, and the Law: Unmapping a White Settler Society* (Toronto: Between the Lines, 2002) at 4; Tracey Lindberg, "The Doctrine of Discovery in Canada" in Robert J Miller et al., eds, *Discovering Indigenous Lands: The Doctrine of Discovery in the English Colonies* (New York: Oxford University Press, 2010) at 89–125.

9.   *McIvor v The Registrar, Indian and Northern Affairs Canada*, 2007 BCSC 827 (Carol Ross J) [*McIvor* BCSC] at para 236.

10.  But see Katherine Ellinghaus, *Taking Assimilation to Heart: Marriages of White Women and Indigenous Men in the United States and Australia, 1887–1937* (Lincoln, NB: University of Nebraska Press, 2006).

11.  Colin Samson, "The Dispossession of the Innu and the Colonial Magic of Canadian Liberalism" (1999) 3:1 *Citizenship Studies* 5 at 19.

12.  Ibid. at 23.

13.  Taiaiake Alfred, *Wasáse: Indigenous Pathways of Action and Freedom* (Peterborough, ON: Broadview Press, 2005) at 23.

14.  James Tully, "The Struggles of Indigenous Peoples for and of Freedom" in Duncan Ivison, Paul Patton, and Will Sanders, eds, *Political Theory and the Rights of Indigenous Peoples* (Cambridge, UK: Cambridge University Press, 2000) at 45.

15.  Ibid.

16.  Patricia Monture, "Standing against Canadian Law: Naming Omissions of Race, Culture, and Gender" in Elizabeth Comack and Karen Busby, eds, *Locating Law: Race/Class/Gender/Sexuality Connections*, 2nd edition (Halifax: Fernwood Publishing, 2006) at 1.

17.  Martin J Cannon, "Revisiting Histories of Racialized Injustice and the New Politics of Indian Identity" (Keynote address delivered to the Anishinabek Nation, Garden River First Nation Conference, Garden River, ON, 21 April 2009) [unpublished] at 11.

18.  Michael Purvis, "Anishinabek Nation Will Decide Who Are Citizens," *Anishinabek News* (June 2008) at 11; Indigenous Bar Association (IBA), "Position Paper on Bill C-3: Gender Equity in Indian Registration Act" (Paper submitted to the Senate Committee on Human Rights, Ottawa, 6 December 2010) at 3; Senate of Canada, "Proceedings of the Standing Senate Committee on Human Rights," Issue 8 (2d) (final) Meeting on Bill C-3, An Act to Promote Gender Equity in Indian Registration by Responding to the Court of Appeal for British Columbia Decision in McIvor v. Canada (Registrar of Indian and Northern Affairs) (Ottawa: Senate of Canada, 6 December 2010) [*Senate Proceedings*] at 3.

# CHAPTER 8

# Decolonizing the Queer Native Body (and Recovering the Native Bull-Dyke)
## Bringing "Sexy Back" and Out of Native Studies' Closet

*Chris Finley*

> *Whence the Freudian endeavor (out of reaction no doubt to the great surge of racism that was contemporary with it) to ground sexuality in the law—the law of alliance, tabooed consanguinity, and the Sovereign Father, in short, to surround desire with all the trappings of the old order of power.*
>
> —Michel Foucault[1]

While gender is not a main theoretical framework in Native studies, discussions of gender occur more frequently than do those about sexuality. In Native studies, gender is not as scary a topic as sexuality, especially discussions of Native sexualities. This reaction should be reconsidered. An important analysis of colonial power for Native studies and Native nations can be found in Michel Foucault's theories of sexuality and biopower. He argues that the modern racial state comes into being by producing "sex" as a quality of bodies and populations, which get targeted for life or death as a method of enacting state power. He says that historically this "gave rise . . . to comprehensive measures, statistical assessments, and interventions aimed at the entire social body or at groups taken as a whole. Sex was a means of access to both the life of the body and the life of the species."[2] Scholars in Native studies increasingly argue that biopower defines the colonization of Native peoples when it makes sexuality, gender, and race key arenas of the power of the settler state.[3]

Histories of biopower deeply affected Native people's relationship to the body and sexuality. Natives, and lots of other folks, like sex but are terrified to discuss it. For many tribes, this shame around sex started in the boarding schools, and sexual shame has been passed down for generations. Throughout the imposition of colonialism in the United States, one of the methods Native communities have used to survive is adapting silence around sexuality. The silencing of sexuality in Native studies and Native communities especially applies to queer sexuality. While it does not differ from mainstream U.S. society, this attitude of silence has more intense consequences for Native peoples, because of the relationship of sexuality to colonial power. Sexuality is difficult terrain to approach in Native communities, since it brings up many ugly negative realities and colonial legacies of sexual violence. As Andrea

In Qwo-Li Driskill, ed., *Queer Indigenous Studies: Critical Interventions in Theory, Politics, and Literature* (Tucson, AZ: University of Arizona Press, 2011), 31–42. © 2011 The Arizona Board of Regents. Reprinted by permission of the University of Arizona Press.

Smith argues, sexual violence is both an ideological and a physical tool of U.S. colonialism.[4] Because of this reality, there is a high rate of sexual abuse in Native communities. Non-Native pedophiles target children in Native nations because there is little chance of perpetrators being brought to justice or caught by tribal police, since non-Natives on tribal lands are not bound to the same laws as Natives. Historically, and arguably in the present, Native women are targeted for medical sterilization. In some Native nations, tribal councils have adapted heterosexist marriage acts into their tribal government constitutions. All this proves that discussions of sexuality are happening in Native communities. Yet the relationship between colonial power and normalizing discourses of sexualities is not a part of these dialogues. Heterosexism and the structure of the nuclear family needs to be thought of as a colonial system of violence.

My goal here is to show how new and exciting work linking Native studies and queer studies can imagine more open, sex-positive, and queer-friendly discussions of sexuality in both Native communities and Native studies. This not only will benefit Native intellectualism but also will change the ways in which Native nationalisms are perceived and constructed by Native peoples, and perhaps non-Native peoples. How are queered Native bodies made into docile bodies open to subjugation by colonial and imperial powers? How does the queering of Native bodies affect Native sovereignty struggles? Can Native peoples decolonize themselves without taking colonial discourses of sexualities seriously? What might some of the results of a decolonizing revolutionary movement for Native people that challenged heteropatriarchy look like? How could a decolonizing movement that challenged biopower be constructed as a coalitional and community-building movement?

## Heteropatriarchy, Biopower, and Colonial Discourse: Not So Sexy

Imagining the future of sexuality in Native studies and Native nations produces many stimulating possibilities for decolonization. One place where sexuality is discussed explicitly is in queer studies, yet this field only rarely addresses Native peoples and Native issues. The debates over the civil rights of queer peoples form one of the main topics of discussion in queer studies. Thinking about sovereignty and colonialism in relation to theory in queer studies would shift conversations of citizenship and subjectivity to rethinking the validity of the U.S. nation state. Importantly, queer theory's critiques of heterosexism, subjectivity, and gender constructions would be very useful in the context of Native studies.

There are potential problems in intersecting queer studies with Native studies. For the most part, neither discipline has shown much interest in critically engaging the other.[5] It is my hope, along with other scholars in this collection, to change this relationship. I pursue that work here by: interrogating the queered colonial discourses that define Native people; critiquing the state for constructing Native people as nonheteronormative, since they do not conform to heteropatriarchy; and critiquing Native nation building that uses the U.S. nation state as a model. In Native studies, discussions of sexuality, gender, and colonialism have the possibility of exposing heteronormative discourses of colonial violence directed at Native communities. Heteropatriarchy and heteronormativity should be interpreted as logics of colonialism. Native studies should analyze race, gender, and sexuality as logics of colonial power without reducing them to separate identity-based models of analysis.... Heteropatriarchy disciplines and individualizes communally held beliefs by internalizing hierarchical gendered relationships and heteronormative attitudes toward sexuality. Colonialism needs heteropatriarchy to naturalize hierarchies and unequal gender relations. Without heteronormative ideas about sexuality and gender relationships, heteropatriarchy, and therefore colonialism, would fall apart. Yet heteropatriarchy has become so natural in many Native communities that it is internalized and institutionalized as if it were traditional. Heteropatriarchal practices in many Native communities are written into tribal law and tradition. This changes how Natives relate to one another. Native interpersonal and community relationships are affected by pressure to conform to the nuclear family and the hierarchies implicit in heteropatriarchy, which in turn, are internalized. The control of sexuality, for Native communities and Native studies, is an extension of internalized colonialism....

Colonialism disciplines both Native people and non-Native people through sexuality. The logics governing Native bodies are the same logics governing non-Native people. Yet the logic of colonialism gives the colonizers power, while Native people are more adversely affected by these colonizing logics. The colonizers may feel bad, stressed, and repressed by self-disciplining logics of normalizing sexuality, but Native people are systematically targeted for death and erasure by these same discourses. Rayna Green discusses the intersecting logics of race, gender, and sexuality in her work to show the unequal power relationship between the colonizer and the colonized.

Green's "The Pocahontas Perplex: The Image of Indian Women in American Culture" argues that colonial discourses represent Native women as sexually available for white men's pleasure.[6] These images of Native women equate the Native female body with the conquest of land in the "New World." In other words, the conflation of the "New World" with Native women's bodies presents Native women's heterosexual desire for white male settlers as justifying conquest and the settlement of the land by non-Natives. I would like to consider this sexualization, gendering, and racialization of the land by providing a queer reading. First, the land is heterosexualized within the heteropatriarchal order through the discovery, penetration, and ownership of the land by white men. Of course, this narrative erases the fact that Native peoples were living on and owning these lands. The conflation of Native women's bodies with racialized and sexualized narratives of the land constructs it as penetrable and open to ownership through heteropatriarchal domination. Becoming critically aware of the heterosexual construction of land while queering Native peoples would be a queer Indigenous studies approach to rethinking conquest, even as it would shift ideas of sovereignty, subjectivity, recognition, nationalism, and self-determination to include queer Indigenous readings of the land.

While I agree with Green's formulation, her focus on Native women's conflation with land erases the sexual desirability of Native men in the colonial matrix. Green states, "But the Indian woman is even more burdened by this narrow definition of a 'good Indian,' for it is she, not the males, whom white men desire sexually."[7] Here, I want to include Native men as well as Native women as having been sexualized, gendered, and racialized as penetrable within colonial and imperial discourses. In other words, it is not only Native women who are (hetero)sexually controlled by white heteropatriarchy, for Native men are feminized and queered when put in the care of a white heteropatriarchal nation state. Importantly, heteropatriarchy is effective whether Native women are read as queer or heterosexual, because "deviant" queer Native women need to be disciplined and controlled by colonial sexual and gendered "norms." Nevertheless, heteropatriarchy is more effective if Native women are read as heterosexual, since they can fit neatly as mothers and wives into its power hierarchies. All sexualization of Native peoples constructs them as incapable of self-governance without a heteropatriarchal influence that Native peoples do not "naturally" possess.

Under the disciplining logics of colonialism, Native women need to be heterosexualized to justify conquest. The "creation" story of the U.S. nation carefully includes a Native woman named Pocahontas who chooses her love for John Smith, and later John Rolfe, over the interests of her Native family. According to these colonial logics, Native women need to be managed, because they lack control over their sexuality and therefore their bodies. Native women embody the reproductive position of receiver of the fertile white colonial heteropatriarch and the mother of the U.S. nation. Under the logics of patriarchy and white supremacy, when a Native woman reproduces with a white man the child of this union becomes a white inheritor of the land. The child, although racially half Native, through white supremacy and patriarchy becomes white, since inheritance under patriarchy is passed on

through the father. Indigeneity, unlike blackness, is erased through miscegenation with whiteness, since colonizing logic stipulates that Native people need to disappear for the settlers to inherit the land. Then as soon as the Native mother gives birth, her indigeneity must disappear and die for her offspring to inherit the land and replace her body. For this whole narrative to work, the Native woman must be heterosexual and desire to have her body sexually and reproductively conquered through her love of the white man. Her body, and therefore her land, would now be owned and managed by the settler nation.

If the Native woman were read as queer, her heterosexual desire for white settlers to invade her nation would not be for the universal truth of love, since the sexual desire for white men would not exist. The narrative of universal love covering for imperial expansion and colonial violence would be exposed and destroyed. For this narrative to work, the Native woman *must* desire white heteropatriarchy through her desire of heteronormative sex and the love of white men. With a queer Native mother, the sex with the white settler may not have been consensual. In the absence of consent and the death of the mother sans the love story, conquest is revealed as a violent process with no regard for Native life. Colonialism naturalizes the heterosexual Native woman's desire for a white man to make conquest a universal love story.

In turn, in colonial narratives Native men must be queered as sexually unavailable object choices for Native women. While Native women are necessary for the imaginary origin story for the U.S. nation, Native men are not. In fact, Native men's presence in that story is erased. They must disappear to allow the white male heteropatriarch to rule over Native women without competition from Native men. For this to occur, Native men are constructed as nonheteronormative and unable to reproduce Native peoples. Native men are read as nonheteronormative because Native men do not correctly practice heteropatriarchy and govern Native women and children. Native gender norms and family structures, which vary from tribe to tribe, do not conform to Native men having control of the public space and the nuclear family or to caring for the land correctly. In other words, in a colonial reading, Native men "allow" matriarchal structures to govern society and extended families, while Native peoples do not make as much profit off the land as the settlers would. Native men are seen as sterile members of a dying race that needs a "genetically superior" white race to save it from the "unavoidable" extinction. Native men are constructed as nonheteronormative to justify the extinction of Native people. Since it is the father that gives the child the inheritance in patriarchy, white heteropatriarchy can slip in and "save" the Natives through the management of Native women and erasure of Native men.

Through the action of colonial discourses, the bodies of Native women and men are queered and racialized as disordered, unreproductive, and therefore nonheteronormative. By making Native bodies "disappear," the colonial logic of Native nonheteronormative sexualities justifies genocide and conquest as effects of biopower. On these terms, Native people are diseased, dying, and nonheteronormative, all of which threatens the survival of the heteronormative U.S. nation state. Native people are eliminated discursively or actually killed to save the heteronormative body politic from possible contamination by Native nonheteronormativity. Yet through death and disappearance, nonheteronormative Natives are transformed into heteronormative spirit/subjects in discourses told by the colonizer to appropriate the land and culture of Native peoples while building a heteropatriarchal nation.

## Nation-Building: Native Feminist Critiques and Decolonization as Foreplay for Sexy Native Nations

Taiaiake Alfred, a Mohawk Native, offers a decolonizing challenge to Native people. He does not center his construction of indigeneity in apolitical identity politics or solely on genealogy. Instead, he wants Native people to recreate the relations between themselves and their land base. He advocates fighting colonialism through regaining the

spiritual strength and integrity colonialism has stolen from Native communities (as well as the hope Native people have given away to colonialism). This is a beautiful conception of sovereignty and self-determination. Alfred writes:

> Wasáse, as I am speaking of it here, is symbolic of the social and cultural force alive among Onkwehonwe dedicated to altering the balance of political and economic power to recreate some social and physical space for freedom to re-emerge. Wasáse is an ethical and political vision, the real demonstration of our resolve to survive as Onkwehonwe and to do what we must to force the Settlers to acknowledge our existence and the integrity of our connection to the land.[8]

Alfred wants freedom for Native people that can come only from decolonizing Native communities. For him, this is a political project that involves Native communities *and* the colonizing settlers. Alfred does not discuss how colonialism impacts Native women specifically or how colonial discourses of sexuality dispossess Native people from the land and from capacity for governance. Yet his alternative construction of sovereignty can be used to include sexuality as part of politics and land management.

Jennifer Nez Denetdale is one of the few Native scholars overtly discussing the politics of sexuality, gender, and Native nationalisms in her work. Denetdale's work exposes homophobia as part of modern Native nation building. To critique masculinist discourses working within Navajo nationalism, Denetdale, along with other Native feminists, has found it necessary to critique traditionalism in Native communities. This is an important intervention, because Native peoples are often read as existing outside of homophobic discourse or as more accepting of trans and queer people in Native communities because of traditional Native ideas regarding gender and sexuality. Denetdale writes: "With the imposition of Western democratic principles, Navajo women find themselves confronted with new oppressions in the name of 'custom and tradition.'"[9] Here, tradition is invoked to justify heteropatriarchy and male leadership in the Navajo Nation (as in other Native nations) by discouraging or forbidding Native women from taking leadership roles, on account of this being constructed as untraditional. Ironically, as Denetdale points out, Navajo women are allowed to participate in the Navajo Nation beauty pageant but not to hold a position on the tribal council. Denetdale supports Native sovereignty, but she also believes Native traditions should be historicized so that traditions are not abused and used to support forms of oppression, such as antiblack racism and heteronormativity. She writes:

> While it is necessary for Native scholars to call upon the intellectual community to support and preserve Indigenous sovereignty, it is crucial that we also recognize how history has transformed traditions, and that we be critical about the ways tradition is claimed and for what purposes. In some cases, tradition has been used to disenfranchise women and to hold them to standards higher than those set for men. Tradition is not without a political context.[10]

Denetdale explains that traditionalism is used in Native communities to silence women and to disenfranchise them from possessing political power. She does not dismiss Navajo traditions when she asks critical questions about whether certain traditions emerge in a historical trajectory or how Navajo men benefit by defining traditionalism in a historical vacuum. Her critique denaturalizes heteropatriarchal traditionalism by placing it inside histories of heteropatriarchal discourse instead of outside of modern constructions of power.[11] Native nations should be self-critiquing of Native constructions of nationalisms.

Native nations' use of heteronormative citizenship standards also disallows nonheteronormative identity formations from belonging in Native nations. Denetdale discusses this matter further when she also takes on the Diné Marriage Act passed by the tribal council of the Navajo Nation, in her paper entitled, "Carving Navajo National Boundaries: Patriotism, Tradition, and the Dine Marriage Act of 2005."[12] Denetdale examines how the intersection of heteropatriarchy, militarism, and homophobia strengthened the Navajo Nation in the post-9/11 moment. She criticizes her tribe for participating in oppressive colonial nation building by trying to enforce heteronormative marriage practices on Diné people. This sort of homophobic nationalism is similar to the U.S. nation state's use of hyped-up homophobic nationalism and militarism in this time of war. Nationalism that is dependent on the exclusion of queer people has many consequences for Native communities. Denetdale tells how some Navajo youth left the Navajo Nation to move to urban areas and to find a queer community because of the backlash against nonheteronormative Navajos. This is a loss to the Navajo Nation. As Denetdale successfully argues, Native nations that mirror the U.S. nation state by relying on homophobia and heteropatriarchy to establish national belonging and exclusion are not ideal models to further Native sovereignty. She forcefully argues, "Critically examining the connections constructed between the traditional roles of Navajo warriors and present-day Navajo soldiering for the United States, as well as the connections made between family values and recent legislation like the Diné Marriage Act, are critical to our decolonization as Native peoples."[13] Denetdale, like many other Native scholars, advocates looking for a construction of sovereignty and Native nation building other than the model of the U.S. nation state. She does not want to reproduce the oppressive colonial methods that exclude queers, women, and black Natives. Instead, she, like Alfred, challenges us in Native studies to conceptualize a more harmonious construction of sovereignty and Native nationhood. Native people and Native studies need to understand how discourses of colonial power operate within our communities and within our selves through sexuality, so that we may work toward alternative forms of Native nationhood and sovereignty that do not rely on heteronormativity for membership.

Centering discourses of sexualities in Native studies engages gender, sexuality, and indigeneity as enmeshed categories of analysis, since examining gender is an important part of deconstructing sexualities and exposing colonial violence. . . . "In addition, this framework does not show the complex way in which Native women organizers position themselves with respect to other coalition partners."[14] I build my ideas upon the work of Indigenous feminist theorists whose ideas and articulations of indigeneity could transform other fields of study, such as white feminist and white queer theories. The scholarly work of Indigenous feminisms centers Native women and critiques white heteropatriarchy, colonialism, sexual violence, and the U.S. nation state model of nationalism. I want to take this a step further, as some Native feminists have done, and add the intersection of these power relations with sexuality to reveal colonizing logics and practices embedded in constructing Native peoples as hypersexual and nonheteronormative. It is time to bring "sexy back" to Native studies and quit pretending we are boring and pure and do not think or write about sex. We are alive, we are sexy, and some of us Natives are queer. Native nationalisms have the potential to be sexy (and are already sexualized), but to be sexy from a Native feminist perspective, they need to be decolonizing and critical of heteropatriarchy.

## Conclusion

[T]he silence in Native studies around issues of sexuality, even heterosexuality, does not benefit the work of decolonizing Native studies or articulating it as a project of freedom for Native people. Silence around Native sexuality benefits the colonizers and erases queer Native people from their communities.[15] Putting Native studies and queer studies in dialogue creates further possibilities to decolonize Native communities. Doing so will expose colonial violence in discursive practices that construct the Native body as hypersexualized, sexually disordered, and queer while presenting Native people as incapable of governance on Native land. Centering a queer studies framework within Native studies also calls Native communities to confront heteropatriarchal practices that have resulted from internalizing sexual colonization.

In response to Justin Timberlake's song "Sexy Back," the artist Prince stated, "Sexy never left."[16] The same can be said for Native studies and Native communities, because sex is always there, but Native sexualities are just beginning to be theorized. Sexuality discourses have to be considered as methods of colonization that require deconstruction to further decolonize Native studies and Native communities. Part of the decolonizing project is recovering the relationship to a land base and reimagining the queer Native body. What does this look like? We will have to imagine this and build this together. I want to imagine that Native peoples have a new bright future full of life and the spirits of our ancestors.

## Notes

1. Michel Foucault, *The History of Sexuality*, vol. 1, *An Introduction* (New York: Vintage Books, 1978), 150.
2. Michel Foucault, *The History of Sexuality*, vol. 1, *An Introduction* (New York: Vintage Books, 1978), 146.
3. See, for example: Andrea Smith, "Queer Theory and Native Studies: The Heteronormativity of Settler Colonialism" (this vol.).
4. Andrea Smith, *Conquest: Sexual Violence and American Indian Genocide* (Cambridge: South End Press, 2005).
5. This is changing rapidly and some Native studies scholars are engaging queer theory and queering indigeneity. See, for example: Daniel Heath Justice and James Cox, eds, "Queering Native Literature, Indigenizing Queer Theory," *SAIL: Studies in American Indian Literature*

20, 1 (2008); Daniel Heath Justice, Mark Rifkin, and Bethany Schneider, eds, "Sexuality, Nationality, Indigeneity: Rethinking the State at the Intersection of Native American and Queer Studies," *GLQ: A journal of Lesbian and Gay Studies* 16, 1–2 (2010).
6. Rayna Green, "The Pocahontas Perplex: The Image of Indian Women in American Culture," *Massachusetts Review* 16, 4 (1975).
7. Ibid., 703.
8. Taiaiake Alfred, *Wasáse* (Toronto: University of Toronto Press, 2005), 19.
9. Jennifer Nez Denetdale, "Chairmen, Presidents, and Princesses: The Navajo Nation, Gender, and the Politics of Tradition," *Wicazo Sa Review* 21, 1 (2006): 10.

10. Ibid., 20–1.

11. Traditionalism is seen as existing outside of discourse and existing before the invention of the law. By contextualizing tradition in history and heteropatriarchy, Denetdale disrupts the narrative of traditionalism as sacred and uncorrupted by modernity.

12. Jennifer Nez Denetdale, "Carving Navajo National Boundaries: Patriotism, Tradition, and the Dine Marriage Act of 2005," *American Quarterly* 60 (2008).

13. Ibid., 289.

14. Andrea Smith, *Native Americans and the Christian Right: The Gendered Politics of Unlikely Alliances* (Durham, NC: Duke University Press, 2008), 108.

15. Native people, who are racialized as being dead and gone, should be aware of the psychological damage erasure causes and be mindful not to do it to other people in our communities.

16. SFGate, "Prince Takes Swipe at Timberlake," 31 August 2006, http://www.sfgate.com/cgi-bin/blogs/dailydish/detail?blogid=7&entry_id=8455

# PART FOUR

❖

## Additional Readings

Andersen, Chris. *Métis: Race, Recognition, and the Struggle for Indigenous Peoplehood.* Vancouver, BC: University of British Columbia Press, 2014.

Anderson, Kim, and Rob Innes. *Indigenous Men and Masculinities: Legacies, Identities, Regeneration.* Winnipeg: University of Manitoba Press, 2015.

Cannon, Martin J. "The Regulation of First Nations Sexuality," *The Canadian Journal of Native Studies* 18, 1 (1998): 1–18.

Chacaby, Ma-Nee A. (with Mary Plummer). *A Two Spirit Journey: The Autobiography of a Lesbian Ojibwa-Cree Elder.* Manitoba: University of Manitoba Press, 2016.

Coulthard, Glen. *Red Skin, White Masks: Rejecting the Colonial Politics of Recognition.* Minneapolis, MN: University of Minnesota Press, 2014.

McKegney, Sam, ed. *Masculindians: Conversations about Indigenous Manhood.* Winnipeg: University of Manitoba Press, 2014.

Simpson, Audra. *Mohawk Interruptus: Political Life Across the Borders of Settler States.* Durham, NC: Duke University Press, 2014.

Yee, Jessica, ed. *Feminism for Real: Deconstructing the Academic Industrial Complex of Feminism.* Ottawa: Canadian Centre for Policy Alternatives, 2011.

## Relevant Websites

### He Inoa Mana (A Powerful Name)

https://www.youtube.com/watch?v=A5nQZ7_ApM4

*Hinaleimoana Wong-Kalu is a Kanaka Maoli cultural practitioner, educator, and transgendered woman who centres her Indigenous and Chinese roots through the lens of Indigeneity, history, relationships, kinship, responsibility, and sex/gender/cultural identity.*

### Lawrence Paul Yuxweluptun

http://lawrencepaulyuxweluptun.com/index.html

*Lawrence Paul Yuxweluptun is a Coast Salish artist whose vibrant and voluminous portfolio of sculpture, performance art, visual arts media, and surrealist inspired paintings explore critically topics of racism, Settler colonial policy, Indigenous lands, and the environment.*

### Métis National Council

http://www.metisnation.ca/

*The Métis National Council provides a political voice for a Métis Nation whose origins, land-based, and socio-political coordinates are rooted within an antifederalist, nationalist, and largely anticolonial history of Settler Canada.*

### Native Women's Association of Canada

http://www.nwac-hq.org

*The Native Women's Association of Canada (NWAC) provides media-based, archival, and community-based resources related to the health and wellness of Indigenous women and children, including events such as press releases, and historically, a voice for federally unrecognized and recognized women politically.*

# Films

*Drunktown's Finest.* Dir. Sydney Freeland. The Film Sales Company, 2014.

*First Stories—Two Spirited.* Dir. Sharon A. Desjarlais. National Film Board of Canada, 2007.

*Kuma Hina (A Place in the Middle).* Dir. Dean Harmer/ Joe Wilson. Dean Harmer, 2015.

*Onkwa-nistensera: Mothers of Our Nations.* Dir. Dawn Martin-Hill. Indigenous Health Research Development Program, 2006.

*Taniwha.* Dir. Mika Haka. Patangaroa Entertainment Ltd., 2015.

*Yuxweluptun: Man of Masks.* Dir. Dana Claxton. National Film Board of Canada, 1998.

# Key Terms

Racialization

Indian

*Indian Act*

Gender discrimination

Legal assimilation

Involuntary enfranchisement

Two-spirited

Compulsory heterosexuality

Heteronormativity

# Discussion Questions

1. How does the *Indian Act*, even following amendments in 1985, continue to regulate Indigenous identities and nationhood in Canada? How would you describe the nature of discrimination faced by Indigenous communities in contemporary times?

2. How have Indigenous women, in speaking out against unequal treatment within the *Indian Act* and other injustices, created awareness in Settler colonial societies? What are some examples?

3. What does it mean to suggest that the *Indian Act* "made heterosexuality compulsory" (Cannon, 1998)? What is it that links sexism and heteronormativity and how is it conterminous with Settler colonialism?

4. What is meant by "queer Indigenous studies" and what are the theoretical implications in terms of (re-)imagining; respectively, native studies and an identity that contests or even possibly rejects cis-gendered ways of thinking, heteropatriarchy, and white Settler colonialism?

# Activities

Invite an Indigenous activist to discuss the impact of colonial policy and the *Indian Act* on their identity and/or leadership.

Watch the 2008 National Film Board production *Club Native* (written and directed by Tracey Deer). How is the status Indian collective represented in the film? How are issues of racialization being addressed? How have definitions of Indianness become central to people's own self-identification? What is the difference between the racism institutionalized through federal legislation and the racism employed to resist further colonial encroachment? How are men impacted by histories of sexism and heteropatriarchy? What needs to happen before these voices are heard?

Watch the 2007 film *Two Spirits* (written and directed by Ruth Fertig). What factors contribute to Joey Criddle's experience in terms of gendered and erotic diversity? What is it that defines his aspirations as a two-spirited man and activist?

# PART FIVE

❖

# Gendered Violence

## Editor Introduction

Native Women's Association of Canada (2015) stated that "for years, communities have pointed to the high number of missing and murdered Aboriginal women and girls in Canada. As of March 31, 2010, Native Women's Association of Canada (NWAC) has gathered information about 582 cases from across the country. . . . Aboriginal women face life-threatening, gender-based violence, and disproportionately experience violent crimes because of hatred and racism . . . [they are] 3.5 times more likely to experience violence than non-Aboriginal women . . . [and] that homicides involving Aboriginal women are more likely to go unsolved."

Being Indigenous ourselves, reading/hearing such statistics affects us at a deep personal level, because the women that have been reported as missing and/or murdered are members of our communities; they are our relatives. When the Picktons' murder case captured the attention of the media and ordinary Canadians, we shared the following questions with our Indigenous relations: "How can this be? How is it possible that so many of our sisters have gone missing, or been killed? Why don't the police, the State, the media seem to care? Would they have cared if the women were middle-class white women? Why are Indigenous women the target of such tragic violence?" The objective of the readings in this part of the text is to analyze the gendered violence affecting Indigenous communities, examine some of its structural roots, and look at how Indigenous people have organized to respond to this alarming issue.

As both Olsen Harper and Blaney point out, the contemporary issue of gendered violence against Indigenous women is linked to a long history of colonial violence directed against Indigenous nations, but distinctly felt by women. Canadian colonial policies, laws, and social inequalities have been partly responsible for pushing "many Indigenous women and girls into precarious situations—ranging from inadequate housing to sex work—where there is a heightened risk of violence" (Amnesty International, 2014: 3; see also Bourgeois, 2015). Alongside colonial laws and policies, racist ideas about Indigenous women constructed by early Settlers have greatly contributed to the sexual violence. As Acoose (1995) has argued, Indigenous women were constructed as sexually promiscuous savages, easily available to European men, eventually making them vulnerable to sexual violent acts. The perpetrators of such violence were able to escape punishment, as Indigenous women were viewed as disposable, violable bodies. These sexist, demeaning, and racist stereotypes of Indigenous women have been used to justify past and persistent sexual and colonial violence, and are at the root of the current epidemic of the Missing and Murdered Indigenous Women in Canada.

Olsen Harper's reading covers the circumstances that led to the Sisters in Spirit initiative headed by Native Women's Association of Canada, and funded by the Government of

Canada. This initiative took "constructive and immediate action that would lessen future incidents and deal fairly, firmly, and absolutely with those found responsible." It established supportive networks for the families of the missing and murdered women, it documented the life stories of the women, and it drew attention to the issue of violence against Indigenous women both nationally and internationally. The Sisters in Spirit strongly believed that in order to eliminate the sexualized and racialized violence against Indigenous women, we need to first eradicate the negative racist attitudes that have birthed such violence.

In "Aboriginal Women's Action Network" (AWAN), Fay Blaney describes the important grassroots work done by Indigenous women in British Columbia to both raise awareness of the sexism and violence against Indigenous women, and help to end this. Founded in 1995, through workshops, support groups, vigils and lobbying, AWAN has given voice and support to Indigenous women who have survived acts of sexism and violence. Through their effort, AWAN has encountered resistance and a number of challenges, by either the police systems, the media, or some Indigenous organizations. From this, AWAN has learned that differences and divisions within Indigenous groups are inevitable, and must be worked through, not ignored. What remains at the heart of their work is a commitment to listen to the voices and interests of Indigenous women who have suffered at the hands of racist and patriarchal individuals and institutions, often in isolation and silence.

As Blaney concludes, "Finding our voices to articulate our realities, despite the contradiction, is our way to liberation. AWAN will continue to struggle against the top-down approach that has been imposed upon our communities and work towards achieving a collective model that affords Aboriginal women a place from which to speak."

A decade after the Amnesty International's report *Stolen Sisters* and the development of the Sisters in Spirit initiative, the numbers of Missing and Murdered Indigenous women had disturbingly increased, resulting in people and organizations across the country to repeatedly demand for the government to have an inquiry; however, it was not until the newly elected Liberal government came into power that this finally took place in 2015. This development signals some hope that finally the urgency of this problem is recognized and concrete action can take place. As former president of the NWAC Beverly Jacobs stated, in order for this inquiry to work, "it must be legitimate and led by those with credibility. It must contribute to the truth, reconciliation and accountability specifically related to having peaceful relations with Indigenous women" (Jacobs, 2014).

The report on the pre-inquiry engagement process the federal government undertook with various communities, organizations, and other stakeholders came out in May 2016, and the reported viewpoints and recommendations on how to proceed with the inquiry are similar to those pointed out by Jacobs. It was strongly recommended that the inquiry must be led by an Indigenous woman, and the majority of the commissioners be Indigenous and representative of diverse communities, cultures, organizations, and professionals with expertise in legal and justice matters. Respondents to the pre-inquiry survey and meetings stressed the importance that the inquiry be inclusive by facilitating and supporting the participation of female survivors of violence, their families, men, youth, elders, leaders, trans and two-spirit people, and "special effort should be made to reach out and support the poorest and most marginalized groups (e.g., the incarcerated, the homeless, sex workers, addicts and women fleeing domestic violence)" (Indigenous and Northern Affairs Canada, 2016).

The vulnerability, marginalization, and complex needs of Indigenous women in the sex work industry must be carefully examined as we move forward with the inquiry.

Firstly, as Bourgeois (2015) argues, we must recognize, and make accountable, the historical and ongoing complicity of the Canadian State in the human trafficking of Indigenous women and girls. Additionally, as Yee (2009) cautions us, we need to avoid taking a moralistic position against sex work, and always viewing sex work as inherently exploitative. Yes, sex work can be exploitative and violent, and we should question the degree of "choice" that some women or girls have in entering such activity when factoring in the level of poverty and other systemic inequities they have lived with (see Farley and Lynne, 2005; Aboriginal Women's Action Network, 2007). However, we also need to critically look at our role in further marginalizing and silencing the voices and diverse experiences of Indigenous sex workers. We agree with Yee—ultimately, we should truly listen to their voices, see them as individuals with agency, and work hard to become their allies in ensuring that they can conduct their work in an environment safe from sexualized and racialized violence.

# CHAPTER 9

# Aboriginal Women's Action Network

*Fay Blaney*

---

The oppression that Aboriginal women in Canada face on a daily basis has, until fairly recently, resulted in their lack of access to both formal and informal education and, therefore, to their very limited production of knowledge. This is one of the barriers that prevent many Aboriginal women from finding our voices and including our perspectives in the decolonization struggle. Plenty of non-Aboriginal researchers from a variety of disciplines have offered explanations for the marginal status of Aboriginal women. Yet despite these numerous scholarly accounts, the victimization of the majority of Aboriginal women and children, coupled with the normalized "cover up" and silencing, continues to encode our lives.

In Kim Anderson & Bonita Lawrence, eds, *Strong Women Stories: Native Vision and Community Survival* (pp. 156–170). Sumach Press. Reprinted by permission of Canadian Scholars' Press Inc.

The work of the Aboriginal Women's Action Network (AWAN) has taken the production of knowledge from a grassroots Aboriginal women's perspective as a starting point for ending our oppression. This chapter provides a brief history of AWAN and the many progressive actions its members have taken. The primary focus is on the women who have participated in AWAN's actions and projects.

AWAN is about Aboriginal women finding a voice. Through our activism, each of us has been exposed to new means and new opportunities to help us find our voices. AWAN women firmly believe that this process is key to our emancipation from the generations of suffering that Aboriginal women have endured. This chapter is dedicated to these women and to the women who are inspired to act as they read about these women. This is especially so for all of our daughters, our granddaughters and our great-granddaughters.

# Establishing the Aboriginal Women's Action Network (AWAN)

AWAN was founded in November 1995 in response to the firing of several women from various Aboriginal organizations in Vancouver. One woman was fired because of the questions she was asking about the organization's constitutional requirement to hold elections. Others were fired because they signed certification forms to unionize. Some of the firings took place to open up positions for family members or friends of the employer. What began as a weekly drop-in and support group for these women at the Vancouver Status of Women office became a network of women involved with social responsibility and political action.

Following our inception, we held a daylong visioning workshop to reflect on who we were and what we wanted to do. What was clear to us was the magnitude of the forces at work to silence Aboriginal women. Equally clear was our strength and conviction to resist that silencing. We came up with our logo[1] at that meeting, bringing our vision to life. We envisioned ourselves as salmon swimming upstream, against the flow of the river and with a determination to create new life and to renew hope for our future generations. Our logo is an image of the salmon in the circle of life, transforming into a woman.

As Aboriginal women, we continue to face a colonial system that is deeply patriarchal. Because of this, and because our own communities have been affected by generations of enforced patriarchy, AWAN has concentrated much of our attention and work on increasing our understanding of Aboriginal feminism.[2] While we struggle for our Aboriginal rights, we also work to make visible the "internal oppression" against women within our communities. For example, many of our women continue to be affected by their disenfranchisement as a result of section 12(1) (b)[3] of the Indian Act. Many of our modern-day political leaders and systems have adopted patriarchal ways. The Native Women's Association of Canada has identified these problems, stating that our matriarchal forms of government and matrilineal

ways have been forgotten or abandoned and that patriarchy is so ingrained in our communities that it is now seen as a "traditional trait."[4] Resisting this ingrained sexism is central to the work of the Aboriginal Women's Action Network.

AWAN women are mothers, grandmothers, aunties, educators, antiviolence workers, academics, students and others with full schedules. The range of socio-economic status, education and life experience among AWAN members is varied. Because some of us have been raised in our First Nations and Métis homelands, there is a strong connection to our cultures and communities. Some of our members are of mixed ancestry and/or have grown up displaced in urban centres and struggle to find a sense of culture and community. In addition to cultural identity issues, we have examined and reflected on same-sex issues with several of our two-spirited members. Our diversity has, at times, resulted in our near implosion. At the same time, however, it has created such an enriching worldview that we try to share this model with other Aboriginal and non-Aboriginal women's communities.[5] Part of that worldview involves teaching and learning from one another, and using collective and consensus-building processes. While this is a difficult path to follow, it has been invaluable in the sharing of skills, knowledge and motivation among AWAN women.

The skills and experiences that we have acquired as a result of our volunteer work in AWAN have been an integral part of finding our voice. Within our interactions and organizing efforts, we have learned such skills as researching, writing, interviewing and distributing press releases. AWAN members have worked through the challenges of negotiating with Aboriginal agencies and non-Aboriginal allies on issues that are important to us. We have written submissions and briefs to various government ministries. We have met with ministers and government committees at the federal and provincial levels, including the annual Justice Consultations of the Canadian Association of Sexual Assault Centres, the Status of Women Canada's Aboriginal Women's Roundtable, the (now defunct) BC Minister for Women's

Equality[6] and the Attorney General. Our members are frequently found in demonstrations against government policies or organizing against cuts that negatively impact Aboriginal women. Often, when our schedules permit, our members can be counted on to attend court hearings to support Aboriginal women in cases of violence or child apprehension.

AWAN members sit on various boards, committees and community organizations, including unions, anti-violence agencies, women's groups, Friendship Centres and anti-poverty groups. Since 1996, there have been four AWAN women on the executive of the National Action Committee on the Status of Women (NAC). Participation in the largest national women's organization has been key in our bid to identify our own Aboriginal form of feminism as it applies to our struggles. These mutually beneficial involvements have been extremely enriching as they have provided us with stronger strategies for creating a more feminist and just society. These strategies have permitted us to carry out antiracism work and to deliver our feminist and decolonization message to various cabinet ministers, social justice-seeking groups and the Aboriginal leadership. As well, these groups have offered immense support in such areas as networking, public relations, fundraising and in-kind donations.

Without this networking on a national level, we would be far less effective in dealing with the constant pressures and problems that besiege our communities. In one instance, a young woman approached us for support because her baby had been apprehended at birth. In a few short days, we managed to organize a lunchtime rally that brought out over two hundred people, including government officials. In addition, we uncovered the false allegations of medical professionals and social workers that this young mother was an active addict who had been "unco-operative during labour."[7] Similarly, we organized a vigil for Pamela George outside the Vancouver courthouse while the sentencing of the murderers was taking place in Regina.[8] And we worked collaboratively with NAC to bring Aboriginal women from the communities to the 2002 Annual General Meeting of the Assembly of First Nations (AFN) in Vancouver to Lobby on issues of importance to Aboriginal women. We also brought in speakers from Saskatchewan and Quebec who generated media attention on the issues of Bill C-31 and prison rights for Aboriginal women, and who helped us draft a fact sheet to circulate among AFN delegates.

# Ending the Silence around Violence Against Aboriginal Women

In the early 1990s, in the face of the large numbers of Aboriginal women who had died violent deaths in Vancouver's downtown eastside, family members began an annual march in their honour. It has become known as the Valentine's Day Memorial March. Without this event, all there would be to mark the violence that these Aboriginal women faced would be the ten-minute funerals that the Ministry of Social Services provides for them. Since we have become established as a network, AWAN has actively participated in this event. We find our voice through defending the interests of women in our families who are trapped in that lifestyle. For many of us, our own "inner child" knows intimately what that world is.

In March 2002, the remains of the bodies of fifteen women, the majority of them Aboriginal, were discovered on a pig farm in Port Coquitlam, BC, owned by Robert William Pickton. Pickton has been charged with fifteen counts of murder and is a suspect in the disappearance of fifty other women, mostly Aboriginal, who have been vanishing from the streets of downtown Vancouver since the 1970s.[9] Shortly after the story broke on the "Missing Women," AWAN put on a series of workshops and spiritual ceremonies for the Aboriginal women from the downtown eastside. Our primary objective was to create a safe space in which women could speak openly and freely—and speak they did!

As the same time that we were attempting to address the horror of the violence that we face, the Aboriginal Victim Services Program (operating under the umbrella of the Vancouver Police Department) openly opposed our series of workshops. This does not do much to increase our faith in the system. We had already heard about the discrimination of both the Aboriginal and non-Aboriginal policing systems from the women who participated in the "Journey for Justice" project. During this project, we held focus groups with women along the Fraser River on the subject of alternative justice and heard many stories about police misconduct and negligence, as described by these participants:

RCMP, Tribal police and other services have different judgments and beliefs about you. When children are apprehended, a lot of women are not allowed to express themselves if it doesn't conform to social workers. [For example,] if they are angry they get anger management, frustration around poverty is seen as a budgeting issue so they have to be silent and jump through hoops.

. . .

Police said I was drinking and partying because my abuser hit me over the head with a full bottle of beer so I smelled like a brewery—drunken Indian again.

. . .

My son was brutalized last week. They left their footprints on his back. I told my son they should have charged the officers. They bust all these people on the street and take all their money. I think the police take the drugs and alcohol themselves. My nephew was beaten last year real bad and it was terrible—he was just stumbling home because he didn't take the bus. They didn't get away with it; he got help from the UNN [United Native Nations]. It's still going on, my son getting it for nothing—it makes me so upset. It happened to a young woman, she had kids too and they pulled her pants down until she was naked in front of everyone at the bar.[10]

AWAN women saw the need for workshops that would allow the women to speak. If a huge number of participants is a measure of success, we did an outstanding job on this project.

The divisions among us are an ongoing reality as we organize around the violence we face. For example, each year during the Valentine's Day Memorial March, issues pertaining to class, race and gender are debated during the organizing of the event. Class issues come up when our right to participate in the organizing of a downtown eastside event is brought into question. This has to do with "turf wars" and issues of representation. We acknowledge that AWAN women do not meet the criteria of residing in the downtown eastside, but we feel we have a place because of our common history of colonialism.

In a different way, organizing for the march creates stress around race because we need to draw upon the leadership and spiritual practices of Aboriginal women while maintaining the active participation of non-Aboriginal women in the march. Race tensions can escalate. For example, during one meeting, a non-Aboriginal woman resorted to saying, "We bought this land fair and square." Our challenge is to continue bringing new Aboriginal women into a process in which they are subjected to these kinds of comments. And while the utterance of these words causes us to shudder, we are mindful of the insidious lateral violence that pits poor non-Aboriginal women against us.

There are additional tensions involved with the participation of Aboriginal men in organizing the Memorial March. The colonial process has had a very different impact on Aboriginal women than it has on Aboriginal men. Present-day systemic and institutionalized patriarchy ensures that the privileged male status in mainstream Canadian society is mirrored in Aboriginal communities. Men have considerable power in the political, economic and social spheres, and this enables violence against women and children. Many of us would argue that those masculine sites of power and influence are uncaring when it comes to violence and child apprehension in the lives of Aboriginal women, many of whom end up dead or disappeared in the mean streets of many urban centres across this country. Yet Aboriginal men continue to demand involvement on the organizing committee and have deliberately scheduled their own separate activities at the same time as the annual Memorial March.

Other divisions arose during our workshops to address the issue of the missing women. Some Aboriginal groups, as well as the media, were intent on conveying a single-minded message that the culprit responsible for the disappearances of these women had been apprehended, and that it was now in the competent hands of the police. Our view which we declared at a press conference, was that the police had mismanaged these cases for several years and they therefore had to be kept under close scrutiny. A Member of Parliament registered a complaint to the Police Complaints Commissioner on the handling of the "missing women" file, but the Commissioner chose to suppress this complaint. When the Commissioner came under pressure to resign, an Aboriginal leader from the downtown eastside came to his aid. This leader is quoted in the *Vancouver* Sun as stating that the Commissioner had acted appropriately despite his dismal record in cases involving Aboriginal people.[11] Such circumstances can clearly be described as "neo-colonial," when Aboriginal and non-Aboriginal authority figures collude against powerless Aboriginal people.

Another neo-colonial characteristic that we saw developing was the way the issue of the "missing women" was framed. The focus on the "families of the missing women" was detracting from a more critical aspect, namely, that this is an issue about "male violence against women." Having Aboriginal male relatives of the "missing women" as spokespersons is akin to having non-Aboriginal colonials delegated as our spokespersons. Nothing has changed for the women who continue to face the same reality in the downtown eastside, in spite of the police investigation into the crimes that are related to some of the missing women. In our workshops, women named instances of family members who had not even been declared missing and therefore were not under the purview of the police. Compounding this life-and-death situation are the harmful and misguided "deficit-reduction" policies of the provincial Liberal government towards social services, which are implemented at the expense of these women.

We acknowledge that these divisions of class, race, gender and ongoing colonialism that exist among us are not accidental and should not be glossed over. They are crucial to the manner in which Aboriginal women have been oppressed and silenced for so long. For this reason, how we do what we do is in many ways as important as the concrete things we have managed to accomplish.

## Grassroots Empowerment through Research

Through our organizing, we have learned that bringing about social change among severely oppressed people requires that we learn new ways of relating to one another. We know that many of us are familiar with the work of Brazilian educator Paulo Friere, and so we brought his methods of popular education into our AWAN work. Another educator, Rita Bouvier, also articulates critical pedagogy in the ways we apply it. She acknowledges the important role of each individual and the necessity for honest communication and co-operation in relationships, decision-making and conflict resolution. She writes, "Above all, community education development requires a willingness to accept change."[12]

Change is precisely what we aim for. We have come to recognize that there is an urgent need for a deeper level of analysis and goal setting to end sexism and neo-colonialism, both within Aboriginal communities and in the larger society. For this reason, we have adopted a form of "research for social change" known as participatory action research. This approach to our projects is our way of working towards attitudinal changes around sexism, racism and poor-bashing, as well as consciousness-raising around the concepts of patriarchy, colonialism, and misogyny. Central to this process is the privileging of the voices of Aboriginal women who are forced into the margins of Aboriginal and Canadian society. Feminist and Indigenous research methodologies, along with critical theory, have also been very informative in this process.[13]

A critical aspect of participatory action research is the equal value that is placed on process and end results. For example, as "insider" researchers, we break down the separations between our research subjects and ourselves. Outside researchers normally have goals and objectives that are external to the community, namely, the accumulation of knowledge for their own benefit. AWAN is able to identify our monalities as Aboriginal women, and hence, we can work together through social action and networking to improve conditions in all of our lives.

Like the women of Tobique, New Brunswick,[14] on the other side of the country, AWAN identified Bill C-31 and violence as the most pressing issues facing all Aboriginal women. Our organizing around the murders of Aboriginal women had already made it very clear to us that this was the level of violence we faced. During our work, however, the issue of Bill C-31 continued to come up. At one point, a young woman came to our meeting and shared her experiences of being denied her rights by her band. Her mother had been reinstated under Bill C-31, but the young woman had not grown up in her community. Each time this young woman tried to access education funding, she felt ignored. We knew of other situations in which students' funding was cut halfway through their school semester, without any explanation from chief and council and without any recourse being available to the students. Hence, we began working towards obtaining research funding for both of these issues. We began our Bill C-31 project in 1998 and completed it in December 1999. Our second project, "Aboriginal Women, Violence and the Law," overlapped with the Bill C-31 project, beginning in the summer of 1999 and concluding in 2001.

AWAN's goal for each of these projects was to prioritize inclusive decision-making. For the Bill C-31 project, we brought grassroots Aboriginal women together from all parts of the province to identify the research focus. These same women conducted interviews in their own communities. Although a different process was followed in the "Aboriginal Women, Violence and the Law" project, a great deal of effort was made to bring in women from the grassroots level to participate in the policy analysis process on alternative justice issues. At the same time that we AWAN women educated ourselves on federal and provincial anti-violence policies and legislation, we also invited other women to join us in a series of sixteen workshops. During the "Journey for Justice" project, we held focus groups along the Fraser River as a way of seeking out the voices of women on issues of alternative justice models. Once a draft report was prepared, focus group participants and other women were once again invited to a provincial symposium. The magnitude of each of these projects has been daunting, but we have placed the spot light on some very insightful and capable Aboriginal women who otherwise would not have been heard.

Our lived experience, as well as our political involvements, reinforce our belief in the importance of the work of these two projects. We recognize that while bands and Aboriginal agencies are funded for gender-specific programs and services to women, they lack a critical consciousness about and analysis of sexism. The result is internal oppression or "double jeopardy." This experience was identified by one of the participants in our Bill C-31 project:

> They are not willing to help females. In fact, [despite] all of the paperwork that I supplied, my Indian band pushed my brother's status through and totally ignored mine. In the end I had to get [the name of person] to give a little shove to hurry mine up because we ended up in the dead file.[15]

Our politicization leads us to conclude that the federal government is the author of the exclusion of women and children that resulted from section 12(1) (b). But it is evident that Aboriginal leaders collaborated in this exclusion, as another participant expressed it:

> I know I'm part of the band now, but at first, when they were first talking about this bill, [C-31] I remember being at a band meeting and some of my own people were saying that they didn't want these women to come back to the reserve, and that really hurt me. I went to school with these people.[16]

The confusion surrounding identity from section 12(1)(b) was not resolved with Bill C-31. The powers of this bill were shared between the federal government that controlled "status" and the band that controlled "membership." For some participants, this perpetuates the same problems:

> When I got married, I was told I wasn't an Indian anymore. I had no rights as an Indian. And that made me feel, well, who am I? I'm not a White person. So when Bill C-31 came along, it was ambiguous. I have mixed feelings about what my identity is.[17]

The personal crisis associated with identity confusion can be traced directly to systemic discrimination and internal oppression. This silences Aboriginal women and thereby increases their level of vulnerability.

While policies and legislation surrounding the "Aboriginal Women, Violence and the Law" project are different than the Bill C-31 issue, the similarity lies in women's marginalization and the struggle to gain voice in the decision-making process. Aboriginal women are at greatest risk of harm in each of these issues, and yet we are the least represented in positions of power and influence.

## Challenges, Considerations, and Lessons Learned

In our work, there have been many challenges and many lessons learned, but there are a few specific ones that stand out. The first has to do with our motivations for doing this work. We have had to ask ourselves, Are we only willing to work when there is pay, or are we willing to work as volunteers because of our belief in the need for profound social change? A second issue relates to our "insider" status during our research. Because we share the lived experiences of colonization with our research subjects, we also feel the pain that they describe and write about. The dilemma surrounding self-care constantly came to loggerheads with institutional requirements and deadlines. Another challenge has to do with the use of Aboriginal traditions for healing purposes, in the face of the colonized misogyny that we sometimes found within those philosophies and practices. And finally, we have had to deal with our subject positions relating to our Aboriginality. These are the issues we still struggle with and learn from.

Debates around work for pay have been ongoing in our group and elsewhere. The feminist movement has long fought for women's right to be remunerated for the work we perform. Yet we have had to ask whether we can afford to leave the work aside if there are no funds. Those who know Aboriginal collective ways have resisted putting a dollar sign on the struggle for liberation. Other comparable liberation struggles include those of the Palestinians and the Irish, many of whom willingly make sacrifices without asking for a per diem or an honorarium. There was conflict among us because some AWAN women had struggled long and hard to obtain funding for the work we wanted to do; however, limited finances meant that certain aspects of our projects went lacking unless they were taken on by volunteers or people who donated time to the cause. My conviction is that the non-profit societies can be a strategy for liberation, and that accepting state funding is sometimes what results in our demise.

The pinch between our collective worldview and modern-day individualism was another area of struggle for us. And yet, increasingly, we concluded that the issue of setting clear personal boundaries was a privilege that we could not afford. Those that argued for financial remuneration were the very same women who were critical of those of us who volunteered, due to our "lack of boundaries." We came to recognize that the concept of an "individual boundary" was clearly a Western concept that collided with our collective ways of being. The magnitude of the tasks before us in each of our research projects meant that many of us had to work without pay, with a level of devotion to the issues that merged the personal with the political. If we all shared the value of setting personal boundaries, as well as only working for pay, the work would not have gotten done. The reward had to go beyond those sets of values.

One of the many contradictions related to personal boundaries and healing relates to traditional values and belief systems. The best defence against assimilation is to sustain culture and tradition, but what are we to do when reinstated tradition is steeped in misogyny? Scholar Emma LaRocque describes this contradiction for Aboriginal women:

> We are being asked to confront some of our own traditions at a time when there seems to be a great need for a recall of traditions to help us retain our identities as Aboriginal people. But there is no choice—as women we must be circumspect in our recall of tradition. We must ask ourselves whether and to what extent tradition is liberating to us as women.[18]

The lesson we learned is that Aboriginal peoples cannot abandon our spiritual practices because of the contamination of imposed Christianity. Likewise, Aboriginal women cannot abandon our spiritual practices because of the contamination of imposed Aboriginal versions of patriarchy. We have adopted Shirley Bear, of Tobique, as our role model, and we emulate the feminist ceremonies she has developed.

Identity politics is also a big issue for us. We advocate for women who have been pushed out of our communities, whether through the child welfare system or Bill C-31. During our work together, as women coming from different locations, we have come to realize the need to be mindful of our own behaviour and practices. The Bill C-31 project showed us how Aboriginal people can discriminate against one another. For example, one of the participants said:

> The way I see it, Bill C-31 people are the stronger of the Nation. Many had to previously live off-reserve and they were not given the freebies that were given to status people, so they worked harder to become the more successful people. They had to work for what they had before 1985.[19]

This perspective of reserve life has been prevalent in non-Aboriginal Canada, and has evidently been taken up by some Aboriginal people. The reality is that we now have racism coming from within our communities. And we are divided by differences of appearance and experience, and by the varying levels of privilege and opportunity or discrimination that result. A Métis friend of mine has made a distinction among Aboriginal peoples by identifying "Aboriginal Peoples of Colour." At a moment in history when we are finally making gains in our social standing in Canadian society, there is a dramatic increase in the numbers of people claiming Aboriginal identity. How can we work together? In this era where racism factors into hiring practices—and privileges some Aboriginal people over others—this topic must be interrogated.

Ultimately, decolonization cannot be achieved with a top-down approach. Capitalist systems ravage our collective ways of being. And within that capitalist framework, collectivities rank low in priority. Capitalism sustains patriarchal models, and patriarchal models that uphold nuclear families also ravage our collective ways of being. As Aboriginal women, who simultaneously experience colonization and neo-colonialism, misogyny and poverty, our challenge in resisting each of these forms of oppression is great. Our political activism teaches us that one form of oppression is never the same as another form of oppression. Differences in forms of oppression result in different strategies, and often these strategies contradict each other. These contradictions wage war in our hearts and spirits. Finding our voices to articulate our realities, despite the contradictions, is our way to liberation. AWAN will continue to struggle against the top-down approach that has been imposed upon our communities and work towards achieving a collective model that affords Aboriginal women a place from which to speak.

# Notes

1. Our logo was designed by Clo Laurencelle.

2. Our understanding of feminism can be described as "a sociopolitical theory and practice that aims to free all women from male supremacy and exploitation or a social movement that stands in dialectical opposition to all misogynous ideologies." Taken from Roger Scruton, *Dictionary of Political Thought* (London: Macmillan, 1996).

3. Section 12 (1) (b) of the 1951 Indian Act removed Indian status from any Indian woman who married a non-Indian (by comparison, an Indian man who married a non-Indian was able to confer his status onto his wife). While similar legislation had existed in previous Indian Acts since 1869, section 12 (1) (b) effectively severed all connections between a woman and her band; one Supreme Court judge termed the 1951 legislation "statutory banishment."

4. As quoted in Sally Weaver, "First Nations Women," in Sandra Burt, Lorraine Cody and Lindsey Dorney eds., *Changing Patterns: Women in Canada* (Toronto: McClelland and Stewart, 1993).

5. This will be discussed more in the final section, "Challenges, Considerations, and Lessons Learned."

6. Liberal government policies merged this ministry with other ministries, including Aboriginal Affairs.

7. Anonymity of this woman prevents me from citing legal documents. But according to her grandmother whom she lived with, she had been clean and sober for two and a half years prior to the birth of her baby.

8. In 1995, Pamela George, a mother of two from Saskatchewan who worked occasionally as a prostitute to make ends meet, was raped and beaten to death by two young white middle-class men on break from university and who habituated "the stroll" for kicks. At the trial, where George's social standing as a prostitute was emphasized and where the murder was constantly downplayed as an out-of-character accident caused by drinking, the killers were convicted of manslaughter and were sentenced to six years in jail. Rob McKinley, "Pamela George Trust Fund," *Alberta Sweetgrass* (July 1997), 2. For further information on the Pamela George case, see Sherene Razack, "Gendered Racial Violence and Spatialized Justice: The Murder of Pamela George," in Sherene Razack, ed., *Race, Space and the Law: Unmapping a White Settler Society* (Toronto: Between the Lines, 2002), 121–156.

9. This is far from an isolated incident. Serial killers are suspected or have been convicted of the murders of Native women in other parts of British Columbia as well as Saskatchewan and Northern Ontario. One estimate is that over five hundred Aboriginal women have gone missing in the past fifteen years. Experts have clearly identified Aboriginal women as a marginalized group vulnerable to being preyed on by serial killers, and suggest that the numbers of missing women add up to an epidemic of violence against Native women that is encouraged by social attitudes and police indifference. See Paul Barnsley "Aboriginal Women at Risk: Disinterested Authorities Big Part of Problem," *Windspeaker* (December 2002), 3, 6.

10. Wendy Stewart, Audrey Huntley and Fay Blaney, "The Implications of Restorative Justice for Aboriginal Women and Children Survivors of Violence: A Comparative Overview of Five Communities in British Columbia" (Vancouver, 2001). Unpublished document in possession of the author.

11. Frank Paul, a Micmac man, died shortly after being released from custody. Police dropped him onto the street, knowing that his life was in danger. The Commissioner blocked this investigation too.

12. Angela Ward and Rita Bouvier, *Resting Lightly on Mother Earth: The Aboriginal Experience in Educational Settings* (Calgary: Detselig Enterprises, 2001), 57.

13. For feminist research, see Patricia Maguire, *Doing Participatory Research: A Feminist Approach* (Amherst, MA: University of Massachusetts, 1987): Shema Berger Gluck and Daphne Patti, *Women's Words: The Feminist Practice of Oral History* (New York Routledge, 1991); Sandra Burt and Lorraine Code, eds., *Changing Methods: Feminists Transforming Practice* (Peterborough, ON: Broadview Press, 1995). For Indigenous research, see Linda Tuhiwai Smith, *Decolonizing Methodologies: Research and Indigenous Peoples* (London: Zed Press, 1999). And for critical educational theory, see Paulo Friere, *Pedagogy of the Oppressed* (New York: Continuum Publishing, 1985), and bell hooks, *Teaching to Transgress: Education as the Practice of Freedom* (New York: Routledge, 1994).

14. Janet Silman, *Enough Is Enough: Aboriginal Women Speak Out* (Toronto: Women's Press, 1990).

15. Stewart, Huntley and Blaney, "The Implications of Restorative Justice for Aboriginal Women and Children Survivors of Violence," 41, 43.

16. Audrey Huntley and Fay Blaney, "Bill C-31: Its Impact, Implications and Recommendations for Change in British Columbia, Final Report" (Vancouver, 1999), 44. Unpublished report in possession of the author.

17. Ibid., 39.

18. Emma LaRocque, "The Colonization of a Native Woman Scholar," in Christine Miller and Patricia Marie Chuchryk, eds., *Women of the First Nations: Power, Wisdom and Strength* (Winnipeg: University of Manitoba Press, 1996), 14.

19. Huntley and Blaney, "Bill C-31," 46.

# CHAPTER 10

# Sisters in Spirit

*Anita Olsen Harper*

The traditional roles of women and men in pre-contact Aboriginal societies were balanced and stable; they allowed women safety and powerful places within those societies.[1] Within societies where men held political office, women were honoured and highly esteemed for their invaluable contribution to the survival of the whole nation, and for their places as mothers, grandmothers, wives, aunts, and sisters. The fact that many pre-contact Aboriginal societies were both matriarchal and matrilineal ensured women's authority and legitimate place.

In what is now southern Ontario, for example, Iroquoian clan mothers had a strong political voice; they were responsible for choosing and removing their leaders (*sachem*). They were autonomous and highly respected; while both women and men were considered equal, both exercised a great deal of personal autonomy within their societies. Other First Nations societies, even if they were patriarchal in structure, were similar to the Iroquoian in their recognition and placing of women in high standing. Hunting and gathering peoples considered their women essential and valued economic partners in the various work activities associated with each seasonal cycle. In these societies, women took on domestic roles that included food preparation, making of clothing, child care and socialization, as well as significant roles in essential livelihood activities such as tanning hides, winnowing rice, and preparing fish

nets and weirs. It was common understanding that any harm suffered by women would have a negative impact on the whole nation.

Among the Ojibwa, women were given the responsibility of directly relating to the earth and keeping up the fires of creation. They maintained the fires that were used for cooking and heating. In servicing the community's fires for ceremonial purposes, they were vigilant about ensuring that their attitudes were spiritually pure and honourable to the Creator and Mother Earth. Both the physical and spiritual activities were recognized and esteemed by community members for it was recognized that not all members could serve in the same capacity. Like the Iroquois, Ojibwa women were personally autonomous, appreciated, and treated as valued members in all aspects of community life.

The foundation of education in Ojibwa and Cree societies were based on women. Creation history begins with a woman descending from a hole in the sky; she needs to care for the earth and become its steward. As part of her work, the woman, who is known as Grandmother or Nokomis, taught the original people about the ways of keeping Mother Earth alive and well; this included instruction about its healing ways. Grandfather, or *Mishomis,* is honoured for the four directions and the ways of the sky. This is why the Ojibwa still honour Mother Earth and use sweet grass, the hair of Mother Earth, in most types of ceremonies.

At the heart of all traditional Aboriginal teaching was the expectation that people would treat one another with honour and respect in all circumstances, including wife–husband relationships. Consequently, there was very little family

In Gail Guthrie Valaskakis, Madeleine Dion Stout, and Eric Guimond, eds, *Restoring the Balance: First Nations Women, Community, and Culture* (Winnipeg: University of Manitoba Press, 2009), 175–200.

breakdown in most indigenous societies.[2] Within societies as a whole, the First Peoples held strongly to their beliefs that the Creator gave women special and sacred gifts of life-givers and caretakers, as mothers and wives, and that everything, including gender gifts and roles, was bestowed by the Creator.

The equality of men and women in pre-contact times was accepted as the voice of creation. Although their roles and responsibilities were different, men were not considered "better" or "more important" than women, or vice versa. The fulfillment of both roles together held a balance that was necessary for meeting both the physical livelihood and spiritual needs of the entire nation. These understandings were a continuing source of strength and peace for Aboriginal societies.

## . . . From Then to Now: The Roots of Sisters in Spirit

It is indeed intriguing to view the status of Aboriginal women today, in the new millennium. Have life conditions and circumstances improved over the years, and, if not, is there an explanation? Might we find a correlation to the legacy enforced by the *Indian Act*?

First, in looking at the area of health, ample research uncovers hard evidence of the poor health status of Aboriginal women in Canada and of social disparities in their lives compared with other Canadian women. Data from the Canadian Population Health Initiative state that Aboriginal people are the unhealthiest group in Canada[3] and that Aboriginal women experience a disproportionate burden of ill-health compared to other Canadian women. Incidence of diabetes among First Nations women, for example, is five times greater than among other Canadian women.[4]

HIV/AIDS is another area of major concern to Aboriginal women. Aboriginal people are dramatically overrepresented in HIV/AIDS figures: the percentage of AIDS cases in Canada represented by Aboriginal women (23.1 per cent) is almost three times that of their non-Aboriginal counterparts (8.2 per cent). The Canadian Aboriginal AIDS

Network states that "various social, economic and behavioural issues are believed to be influencing this health concern. In addition, Aboriginal women can experience a triple layer of marginalization, based on gender, race and HIV status." About 66 per cent of new HIV cases result from injection drug use in the overall Aboriginal population; for Aboriginal women, this risk factor is six times greater than for non-Aboriginal women.[5]

Poor economic prospects for Aboriginal women in Canada contribute to their high rates of HIV/AIDS. Native communities, and particularly Aboriginal women living on-reserve, are notorious for their high rates of unemployment and lack of economic opportunity. Unemployment rates of the female Aboriginal labour force (17 per cent) in 2001 are more than twice those of the female non-Aboriginal labour force (7 per cent).[6] Many, driven from their communities by divorce, separation, or other family-related reasons, enter into the sex trade in urban centres because it is the only way they can see of providing for themselves and their children. Long-term conditions of poverty and racism leave many of them with little option but to work the streets to "make ends meet." A 2005 study of prostitution in Vancouver revealed that 52 per cent of those prostitutes randomly interviewed were Aboriginal—a significant overrepresentation compared to the proportion of Aboriginal people (1.7 per cent) within the general Vancouver population. Similar proportions were found in British Columbia's capital city, Victoria.[7]

Aboriginal women recognize that the racism of everyday Canadian society and government institutions must come to a full halt in order for them to reach economic, social, gender, and racial parity. For example, regarding the widespread incidence of family violence within Aboriginal communities, many women are emphatic that the broader context of institutionalized violence against all Aboriginal people, regardless of gender, must first be addressed. This would include addressing all the failings within the justice and police systems that appear to target specifically Aboriginal people, and, in particular, Aboriginal women.

Violence against Aboriginal women is a problem of overwhelming proportion in Canada that, for the most part, remains ignored. Amnesty International's 2006 annual report for Canada states that "high levels of discrimination and violence against Indigenous women continued. Federal and provincial governments announced initiatives to address these problems, but officials failed to advance a comprehensive national strategy. Crucially, police responses to threats against Indigenous women's lives were inconsistent and often inadequate."[8] Topping Amnesty International's list of Canada's violations is the disproportionately high incidence of violence against Aboriginal women.

Many people think that revealing these findings is long overdue and that the Canadian consciousness is still suffering from collective (and selective) amnesia regarding Aboriginal women being subjected to such violence. Educators, students, Aboriginal women themselves, social work and health-care professionals have, over the decades, begun to talk about these issues in both formal and informal discussions. They see it as one way of cultivating positive change. Many tenaciously refuse to let these issues continue to be swept under the carpet and insist that the causes be identified, examined, and addressed. They continue to work at building a collective voice that asks, "How can we advocate for changes within Canadian society so it can no longer glibly tolerate, even foster, violence against Aboriginal women?"

## Sisters in Spirit: The Campaign Arises

. . . Unemployment on reserves had always been problematic, but the change from subsistence to wage-based economies encouraged women to leave their reserves to look for employment in urban centres. Because movement restrictions had been lifted, this was now easier to do. They also sought better life opportunities, through access to mainstream education. Communications were greatly improved, which led to the rise of public awareness on a number of issues. However, in spite

of these legal and social changes, racism against Aboriginal women was not abating and, instead, continued to plague them, especially those arriving in the cities.

The number of Aboriginal women who met harm along their life journeys, those who may have gone missing or may have been murdered during these years, is not known. One woman stated, when she was asked about missing or murdered Aboriginal women: "Aboriginal women are constantly being victimized. . . . Very little attention from police is given to missing Aboriginal women. There is a mindset among many non-Native agencies that Aboriginal people are nomadic and they are somewhere visiting, and not missing. This is not, and has not always been true."[9]

One case in particular drew national attention to the extent of violence faced by Aboriginal women in Canada: this was the racialized, sexualized murder of Helen Betty Osborne in The Pas, Manitoba. The most appalling aspect about this murder was that while Osborne was killed in 1971, a full sixteen years passed before her murderers were brought to trial. Also shocking was the fact that, during those years, the townspeople knew who her murderers were and did nothing to inform the police. Further, the RCMP investigation of the murder was bungled to the extent that the province established the Aboriginal Justice Inquiry. Racism against Aboriginal people, and against women in particular, inherent within the justice system and the town of The Pas was liberally mentioned in the findings of the inquiry.[10]

The media flurry[11] associated with the Osborne case, late as it was by more than a decade and a half, served a constructive purpose in raising public awareness about what many Aboriginal community members had already known for a long time: that violence, even the murder, of Aboriginal women is readily ignored by Canada's police and public. Several other high-profile serial murder cases involving Aboriginal women were to surface over the next few years.

The first began in the early 1990s when sex-trade workers in Vancouver's notorious Downtown Eastside began noticing that, for at least the past decade, many of their peers were simply vanishing and not heard from again. Their queries to police were largely futile; they believed that police were reluctant to act because most of the missing women were prostitutes, drug addicts, and/or Aboriginal. As the numbers of missing women kept rising, however, the media itself began to hear rumours, and the curiosity of those further outside the neighbourhood was piqued. In September 1998, a group of women, mainly Aboriginal, confronted the Vancouver police and demanded that action be taken. Reporters began to ask questions, and soon the public was aware that there was indeed some truth about missing women. In response, the joint Vancouver City Police/RCMP task force was initiated, but by this time more than seventy women were officially missing.[12] In early 2002, nineteen years after the first woman was reported missing, Robert William Pickton was arrested and later charged with twenty-seven counts of murder. It is believed that at least one-third of Pickton's victims were Aboriginal. This is the largest serial-killer investigation in Canadian history.

Another area in British Columbia is known as the "Highway of Tears" because of the large number of Aboriginal women who have gone missing or have been found murdered along this nearly 800-kilometre stretch of northern highway between Prince George and Prince Rupert. Known suspicious activity began in the mid-1990s, when three fifteen-year-old Aboriginal girls were found murdered in three separate instances. As the years went on, more and more young women travelling on that highway were later reported missing. The official count is now eleven and the unofficial count is three times that number. Only one of these young women was non-Aboriginal. The only entire family to have ever disappeared in Canada—an Aboriginal family—fell victim in this area.

During the past fifteen years, the bodies or remains of nine women have been found in rural communities near Edmonton, Alberta. Most of the victims were involved in prostitution or drugs, or both; many were Aboriginal. Project KARE was established by the RCMP in response to these murders, with the main focus on the more recent deaths. Almost all sex-trade workers in the Edmonton area cooperate with police in this initiative.

While these are not, by far, the only cases in Canada regarding missing and/or murdered Aboriginal women, it is important to note that media involvement helps concerned Aboriginal groups and individuals mobilize police and other authorities into concrete action. Far too often, police simply view prostitutes as unstable and disconnected from societal norms. By extension, this becomes a reason for ignoring extremely violent crimes against sex-trade workers, most of whom are Aboriginal.[13] As well as media, non-Aboriginal women's groups have given their voices as a conduit for the concerns of Aboriginal women because the voices of Aboriginal women by themselves are obviously insufficient and inadequate to draw the attention required. . . .

## Sisters in Spirit: From Campaign to Reality

Many non-Aboriginal organizations, particularly those involved in matters of social justice, are fully aware that Canada's justice system responds to violent crimes against Aboriginal women in a vastly different way than to crimes against non-Aboriginal women. The organizations that have helped the Native Women's Association of Canada (NWAC) in its push for the Sisters in Spirit campaign are mostly humanitarian, and include the Law Commission of Canada, Canadian Ecumenical Justice Initiatives (known as KAIROS),[14] Amnesty International, the Canadian Association of Elizabeth Fry Societies, and various groups within major churches.[15]

Amnesty International . . . began working closely with NWAC. It, too, is fully aware that police respond with detailed and ongoing investigations of missing persons reports on non-Aboriginal women, in contrast to those for Aboriginal women, which are too often treated lightly and not given proper credibility. Amnesty International was approached by NWAC president Brown, who, at the time, was in the process of pulling together a church-group coalition to advocate and lobby for research funding regarding missing and murdered Aboriginal women in Canada. She invited Amnesty International to be a part of this coalition as NWAC needed as many independent and credible voices as possible for support. By coincidence, Amnesty International was then launching a Violence Against Women campaign. To the advantage of both agencies, the objectives and the timing of those objectives extremely closely related.

As well, Amnesty International had just hired two researchers for a project that would tell the stories of the victims, as related by their close family members, and articulate the extent and circumstances of the violence that resulted in Aboriginal women being missing or murdered. The researchers were Giselle LaVallee and Beverley Jacobs (in September 2004 the latter became NWAC's next president). The resulting document was called the "Stolen Sisters" report, released in October 2004, and the national awareness it raised within Canada and widespread international responses were very encouraging. Ms. Jacobs presented an overview of the findings in 2005 to the United Nations Permanent Forum on Indigenous Issues in New York. Many say that "Stolen Sisters" was the main reason for the federal government's approval of NWAC's funding request for the Sisters in Spirit initiative.

The Sisters in Spirit campaign was also supported, both financially and otherwise, by the United, Anglican, Catholic, and other smaller churches. The campaign ran from March 2004 to March 2005 and worked towards several distinct objectives:

- to estimate the number of Aboriginal women who had died from violence, or suspected violence, and the number of missing Aboriginal women in Canada;
- to put a face on every name that appeared on the lists of missing or murdered Aboriginal women in the country;
- to document the life histories of all these Aboriginal women;

- to draw more media attention and foster public concern regarding missing Aboriginal women;
- to procure $10 million aimed at stopping violence against Aboriginal women and to raise awareness of the specific issues faced by Aboriginal women within Canadian society;
- to foster constructive action from all those who could make a difference in lowering the numbers of missing or murdered Aboriginal women, including police, medical officials, courts, and Aboriginal leaders; and
- to provide public education that would increase awareness of the underlying causes of violence against Aboriginal women.

## . . . Sisters in Spirit: Conducting the Activities

Because the driving motivation behind the Sisters in Spirit initiative is the eradication of the specific type of violence directed at Aboriginal women that leads to their disappearance or murder, its overall goal is to reduce the related risks while increasing the safety of all Aboriginal women in Canada. An anticipated side benefit is that gender equality will be improved; as well, the initiative expects that Aboriginal women will be able to participate more fully in the various segments of Canadian society so their economic, social, cultural, and political aspirations can be realized.

The foundation for achieving this overall goal is research. In this context, the research entails the methodical and systematic collection and evaluation of information on the topic of racialized, sexualized violence against Aboriginal women in Canada. This type of research is extremely valuable in bringing about social change. Interested Aboriginal community members, individual families, and friends will be actively involved by providing useful first-hand information about the background and most recent activities of the victim. These individuals will be providing the Sisters in Spirit research team with a better understanding of the victim's real-life issues and experiences. The results of this research, once analyzed and placed, will be used to educate others, affect public policy, promote community involvement, and, most importantly, make meaningful social change that will alleviate violence against Aboriginal women. The process itself gives authority to Aboriginal women's voices—voices that benefit all Aboriginal people, women and men, by contributing to positive social changes in Canada. This type of problem solving is accomplished through what the Sisters in Spirit initiative calls its community-based research plan.

Because it is so important to preserve and maintain the various cultures of the Aboriginal women involved, the entire research process is driven within a cultural framework that amalgamates cultural and ethical values. The Sisters in Spirit initiative has captured these under the headings of caring, sharing, trust, and strength.

. . . Regarding the policy agenda of the Sisters in Spirit initiative, the research team is working with participating families and the community to develop a strategy to initiate essential changes within various levels of government. A comprehensive strategic policy framework has been developed for use at both the national and international levels for discussion on indigenous women's human rights. The framework addresses the socio-economic, political, and legal status of indigenous women, and the underlying factors that contribute to racialized, sexualized violence against them.

There are several objectives in the Sisters in Spirit initiative. Primarily, the initiative aims to enhance public knowledge about the extent and global impacts of racialized, sexualized violence against Aboriginal women. In addition, it seeks to dispel popular myths and stereotypes about missing and murdered Aboriginal women by presenting the realities of racialized, sexualized violence, as derived from key informant interviews.[16] Also important to Sisters in Spirit is articulating the status of both Canadian and international laws as they relate to either supporting or suppressing the violation of indigenous women's human rights.

The following is a list of the benefits of the Sisters in Spirit initiative for Aboriginal families and communities:

- Sisters in Spirit will help mobilize the caring power of community;
- Sisters in Spirit will provide tools on its website to help all families of missing or murdered women navigate the justice and other systems effectively;
- The initiative's website will provide links to community organizations providing front-line service delivery in the area of violence against women, such as grieving support groups or victims' assistance;
- The Sisters in Spirit media strategy aims to reassure families that they are not forgotten and that their loved one is presented fairly, without stereotype or prejudice;
- Research will help to validate the experience of families of missing or murdered women, and help create much-needed networks that promote healing and wellness;
- The Sisters in Spirit initiative will target root causes, identify prevention strategies and risks, and assist in developing safety plans;
- In conjunction with other organizations, the Sisters in Spirit initiative will work to increase trust and inspire hope that violence against Aboriginal people, in particular, Aboriginal women, will end;
- The initiative will help families of missing and murdered women to have some peace of mind knowing that Sisters in Spirit is raising national awareness of their family member and the entire issue of racialized, sexualized violence against Aboriginal women;
- The Sisters in Spirit initiative will take into account the needs of the whole family and community, and friends.[17]

The Sisters in Spirit initiative is indebted to the participating families, for without their vision, strength, commitment, and efforts, it cannot move very far in achieving its stated objectives. Indeed, without them NWAC would not have been able to garner enough support to move the campaign into an actual initiative.

## The Resilience of Women

Oriented towards the positive, not the negative, Sisters in Spirit acknowledges the resilience of many survivors and close friends of missing or murdered women. Their perceptions as survivors are valuable to all women, even to those who do not experience such trauma in their lives. The ways in which these women deal with grief and their motivation in moving forward in their lives are stories of personal power and immense courage.

A death by murder is extremely difficult to acknowledge and accept, and so is the situation of a close relative or friend who simply disappears, never to be heard from again. In a single moment, everything taken for granted about that person no longer exists, and, instead, feelings of complete emptiness, anguish, shock, vulnerability, helplessness, and sometimes guilt engulf and overwhelm the survivors.[18] The violence associated with most murders must surely be one the worst feelings that survivors, especially parents, have to endure. Because the police and justice systems must be involved, the situation is exacerbated: the notorious relationship between Aboriginal people and police has well-entrenched roots in historical practices that compound and perpetuate the damaging experiences of Aboriginal people, including these kinds of experiences within the Canadian justice system. Circumstances related to a death can further complicate matters for the family. For example, coroners decide when a body is released for burial—this may take weeks, or even longer. During this time, family and friends have to wait for closure regarding the earthly remains of their loved one. Also, because of the public nature of murder, media may be involved and its participation may be intrusive, inconsiderate, marred by inaccurate and irrelevant reporting, incomplete, and biased.

Family members and friends dealing with murder are at risk of post-traumatic stress disorder[19] and need coping strategies to deal with their grief. Some, particularly parents, question their spiritual beliefs because of being unable to adequately account for such extreme loss.[20] Survivors need support. Almost anyone can be involved by listening non-judgmentally and with companionship.[21] One survivor stated that what was not helpful was impatience and irritation about what was perceived as a "lengthy grieving process"; in reality, families and friends never get over the murder of a loved one. While each person grieves in different ways, almost all experience feelings of loneliness and isolation, and find that talking about their loved one in a caring and trusting environment is very helpful to them.

Some women talk about their realization that they are also the victims of murder, by "giving in" to grief and not progressing with their own lives. They come to understand that keeping an eye on the future is vitally important and that they have to take conscious action to reflect their determination of moving ahead. One woman stated that she keeps focused by pursuing what she knows to be right, maintaining a positive attitude, having faith in God/the Creator, seeking and being sure to benefit from counselling, and fulfilling her own responsibility towards her other children and her friends.

There are elements in women's lives to describe the attributes of those who successfully cope with the stress and adversity that comes from the murder of a loved one. Some things to consider are[22]

- the family and community environments in which the survivor was raised, especially the extent to which significant nurturing and supportive qualities were present;
- the number, intensity, and duration of stressful or adverse circumstances that each woman faced, especially at an early age, and how she was able to deal with these; and
- each woman's internal characteristics, temperament, and internal locus of control or mastery.

# . . . Sisters in Spirit:
# One Woman's Account

The following is a narrative[23] from one mother whose worst nightmares were confirmed—her daughter's DNA was found at the infamous pig farm in Port Coquitlam, British Columbia. This mother had last heard from her daughter through a Christmas card in 1998. Years later, on 17 May 2002, a policeman knocked on her door and told her that the search was over—the remains of one woman were positively identified as that belonging to her missing daughter. This mother was asked what kept up her strength, day by day, and what kept her from giving up on life:

It is the spirit within that keeps me going. I myself did not grow up with my mother, and I know that my granddaughters have to grow up without theirs. I can relate to their pain at, say, Mother's Day—when I was in boarding school, making things for my mother such as a card with roses or other flowers on it, they were for my mom but she couldn't get them. . . . My stepmother was cold towards me, and when I'd come home for summers and after my dad went to work in the mornings (he maintained the roads), I would go up and spend most of my days up in the hills. I knew which berries to eat, like cranberries, raspberries, chokecherries, and saskatoons. There was spring water there that I would drink. Back then you could drink this water.

My grandchildren were in foster care already, before their mom died. In 1998, November 18, the last time I spoke with her, she had put them into temporary care, but I told her to wait until the 20th when my practicum was over and I could take care of them. This was in Vancouver. When I did call her on the 20th, their dad had already taken them to another city on the other side of the country. My grandchildren are now in a good foster home, and once a month I talk to them. The foster mom is now OK with me having their phone number, but at first she wasn't because she was afraid that I would give it out to the dad, as she is afraid of his violence. There was a lot of trust that had to be built, and that is still going on.

That is what helps me, that they would know I love them. In spite of them not having a mother, the next step is to have a grandmother, and that is me. They are starting to build up trust with me.

When I first found out what happened to my daughter, I took time off work in 2002 and went to a psychologist. She did help me, but the greatest psychologist was my sister. I had gone, in January 2003, to visit her and she was crying. When I asked her what was wrong, she said something like, "that SOB[24] not only took my niece, but he's taking my sister, too." This is when I woke up. I realized that he was taking me as a victim, too, and that I was letting him still be a perpetrator to my family.

This really helped me on my healing journey; my sister is my psychologist. I had to realize that he was taking my life, as well. At first, there was a point that I didn't want to live, I wasn't suicidal, but I didn't want to ever wake up because at night, I was flying in spirit. I would get up and feed myself and do some other things, but I really wanted to go back to where I'd go at nights. I would go back to where I came from, my power place, back in the hills, where the spring was, and the fresh water was running, and where the berries were food for me.

My daughter was there, too. She was so healthy, so alive.

In the process of seeing the psychologist, I trusted her enough to tell her about where I'd fly to at nights. She said that I needed to be reprogrammed and helped me with that even though I didn't want to do that; it was my time of joy. Now I don't do that anymore as an escape. Now, it just happens and I don't always go back to those hills.

I had befriended a local city policeman who understood my flights, and he promised that he would find an answer to me about my daughter, as the Vancouver police weren't doing too much. He warned me that I may not get the answer I wanted, but that I would get an answer. It was a short time later, on May 17, 2002, that I heard the knock on my door from a New Westminster RCMP officer with very bad news.

I am not going to let Pickton take my life. The victimization stops here. . . .

# Conclusion

As Canada's most rapidly growing female population,[25] Aboriginal females are still experiencing the difficult social conditions and deprived economic reality that has plagued them over the past several centuries. This continuing historic marginalization results in a shocking statistic related by the Toronto Metropolitan Action Committee on Violence Against Women and Children: "Up to 75% of survivors of sexual assaults in Aboriginal communities are young women under 18 years old. Fifty per cent of those are under 14 years old, and almost 25% are younger than 7 years old."[26] Violence against Aboriginal women only because they are Aboriginal (racialized violence) and because they are women (sexualized and/or genderized violence) has been ongoing in Canada for many generations. The *Indian Act* paved the way in formalizing the societal attitudes and behaviours that condone, accept, and perpetuate the marginalization of Aboriginal women and, ultimately, their victimization.

Many Aboriginal women become easy targets to dangerous, perverted, and violent men because their poverty forces them to live in unsafe situations with few viable options. These men, themselves products of Canadian society, are aware, whether on a conscious level or not, of Aboriginal women's vulnerability and of their lack of significant voice and value within society. They are also fully aware of the reticence of law enforcement agencies to take action when even very serious crimes are committed against Aboriginal women. Such violent men often vent against a specific social class or type, mostly on those they perceive to be the most defenceless.

It is in having to deal with adversity from the Canadian state and mainstream society, such as the unsolved murder of loved ones and the agonizingly slow draining of hope in cases of those missing, that Aboriginal women have come together. Their need for concrete answers and a strong desire for justice have resulted in common goals and understandings. They seek allies in the non-Aboriginal community who have already become aware that the type of thinking that normalizes violent activity against vulnerable populations, particularly against Aboriginal women, is still present in Canada. Recognizing that immediate action is needed, they also acknowledge that while attempts have been made through a myriad of policies and programs by various levels of government and different organizations, the actual outcomes for Aboriginal women are still vastly inadequate.

These are the circumstances into which Sisters in Spirit was born, originally as a campaign, then as a full initiative. Aboriginal people whose female family members went missing or were later found murdered began the process by networking and building camaraderie; others—most of whom did not share similar trauma in their lives—joined to show their support. Together, they built a collective resolve to take constructive and immediate action that would lessen future incidents and deal fairly, firmly, and absolutely with those found responsible. This group, perhaps loosely joined together in a formal sense, is woven together by a deep-seated understanding that effective strategies must target the cause of the problem, which is identified as really being the attitude of non-Aboriginal Canadians—a destructive and firmly entrenched attitude within mainstream Canada that allows and encourages the targeting of Aboriginal women for extreme violence and murder. Congruously, the same attitude permits Aboriginal women to drift away from society and its systems without notice—sometimes for great lengths of time, times in which despair and death may have actually overtaken them. Sisters in Spirit and its allies believe that the elimination of this condescending and pejorative attitude will eradicate sexualized, racialized violence, and indeed all types of violence against Aboriginal women.

Sisters in Spirit continues its work in helping to establish and maintain networks for surviving family members and friends: It has facilitated several circle-type gatherings in which participants meet and talk in a trusting and caring environment. Many family members and friends, once so isolated because of the racialized and sexualized violence that so deeply and permanently touched their lives, are finding ways to reach out to other survivors, to give and receive encouragement and hope. The network making up Sisters in Spirit, including those women who specifically work from NWAC, is finding creative ways and means of cultivating the internal resilience that rises above the suffering brought on by the murders and disappearances of their loved ones.

No doubt Sisters in Spirit will undergo transformations as it pursues its goals and as other groups or individuals become involved. Canada's Aboriginal community has been suffering from having its women go missing or found murdered for at least 180 years,[27] and those involved in Sisters in Spirit find that the time is ripe—indeed, long overdue—to rid the country of the bigotry and cultural bias that target Aboriginal people in general and Aboriginal women in particular.

# Notes

1. Judge M. Sinclair, foreword, in Anne McGillivray and Brenda Comaskey, eds, *Black Eyes All of the Time* (Toronto: University of Toronto Press, 1999).

2. Aboriginal Justice Implementation Commission, *Final Report* (Winnipeg: Government of Manitoba, 2001), ch. 13, "Revenue Generation."

3. Canadian Population Health Initiative, "Improving the Health of Canadians" (Ottawa: Canadian Institute for Health Information, 2004), http://www.cihi.ca.

4. Health Canada, "Diabetes among Aboriginal People (First Nations, Inuit and Métis) in Canada: The Evidence" (Ottawa: Health Canada, First Nations and Inuit Health Branch, 2000).

5. The estimated increase of HIV infections is 91 per cent (1430 to 2740) during the three years between 1996 and 1999 alone. On 8 March 2004, the Canadian Aboriginal AIDS Network issued a press release, "Aboriginal Women Continue to Face Major Challenges as International Women's Day Approaches," which included these figures.

6. Statistics Canada, *Women in Canada: A Gender-based Statistical Report*, 5th ed. Catalogue no. 89-503-XIE, p. 201.

7. Melissa Farley, Jacqueline Lynne, and Ann J. Cotton, "Prostitution in Vancouver: Violence and the Colonization of First Nations Women," *Transcultural Psychiatry* 42, 2 (June 2005): 242–71.

8. Amnesty International Canada, 2006 Annual Report, http://www.amnesty.ca/resource_centre/annual_report/Canada.php.

9. Anonymous contribution, Nova Scotia Native Women's Association, *Sisters in Spirit* Promotion/Consultation Session, Millbrook, NS, 7 February 2006.

10. Aboriginal Justice Inquiry of Manitoba, *The Deaths of Helen Betty Osborne and John Joseph Harper*, Volume 2 of *Report of the Aboriginal Justice Inquiry of Manitoba* (Winnipeg: Aboriginal Justice Inquiry of Manitoba, 1991).

11. These include Lisa Priest, *Conspiracy of Silence* (Toronto: McClelland and Stewart, 1989); Aboriginal Justice Inquiry of Manitoba, *Report of the Aboriginal Justice Inquiry* *of Manitoba* (Winnipeg: Government of Manitoba, 1991); *Conspiracy of Silence*, TV mini-series (Toronto: Canadian Broadcasting Corporation, 1991).

12. Officially, the issue of a large number of prostitutes missing from Vancouver's Downtown Eastside came to public attention in July 1999. This came in the form of a poster offering $100,000 from the Vancouver Police Department and the Attorney General of British Columbia for information leading to those person(s) involved. The American television program *America's Most Wanted* aired a segment on this shortly afterwards, but without results.

13. Farley, Lynne, and Cotton, "Prostitution in Vancouver," 256. In the city of Vancouver, the Aboriginal population is only 7 per cent of the overall population but 75 per cent of the prostitutes in the Downtown Eastside are Aboriginal.

14. KAIROS is a faith-based ecumenical movement for justice and peace; it consists of 100 communities spread across the country. Its Aboriginal component began in August 2001. See http://www.kairoscanada.org/e/index.asp.

15. These include eleven churches and church organizations, but is not limited to the Anglican, Catholic, United, Christian Reformed, Mennonite, Presbyterian, and the Religious Society of Friends (Quakers) Churches.

16. A "key informant" is anyone who is in a position to know the community as a whole or the specific portion that relates to this issue. This may be someone in a position of authority in government, justice, health care, and so on. The best way to derive information from these key informants is through a face-to-face interview.

17. These objectives are taken directly from the contribution agreement signed between Status of Women Canada and the Native Women's Association of Canada.

18. Amick Resnick Kirkpatrick, Fact Sheet (Medical University of South Carolina, National Crime Victims Research and Treatment Center).

19.  Martie P. Thompson and Paula J. Vardaman, "The Role of Religion in Coping with the Loss of a Family Member to Homicide," *Journal for the Scientific Study of Religion* 36, 1 (1997): 50.

20.  Ibid., 45.

21.  Jennifer Clegg, "Death, Disability, and Dogma," *Philosophy, Psychiatry, and Psychology* 10, 1 (2003): 69.

22.  Ester R. Shapiro, "Family Bereavement and Cultural Diversity: A Social Developmental Perspective," *Family Process* 35, 3 (September 1996): 317–22.

23.  Telephone conversation, 14 June 2006. Name of interviewee withheld by request.

24.  She is referring to Robert William Pickton, the accused in this case.

25.  "From 1996 to 2001, the number of Aboriginal females rose by 22% compared to the 4% growth rate among non-Aboriginal females. The female Aboriginal population is growing much more rapidly than the rest of the female population in Canada." Statistics Canada, *Women in Canada*, 183.

26.  METRAC (Metropolitan Action Committee on Violence Against Women and Children). Statistics Sheet: Sexual Assault, http://www.metrac.org/programs/info/prevent/stat_sex.htm (accessed 25 June 2006).

27.  An Algonquin artist, Janet Kaponoichin, depicts the true story of an Algonquin girl who was raped and murdered by British soldiers during the building of the Rideau Canal in 1827. This painting hangs in the Maniwaki Cultural Centre in Maniwaki, QC.

# PART FIVE

❖

## Additional Readings

Beads, Tina, with Rauna Kuokkanen. "Aboriginal Women Feminist Action on Violence Against Women," pp. 221–32 in Joyce Green, ed., *Making Space for Indigenous Feminism*. Black Point, NS: Fernwood Books, 2007.

Bourgeois, Robyn. "Colonial Exploitation: The Canadian State and the Trafficking of Indigenous Women and Girls in Canada," *UCLA Law Review* 62, 6 (2015): 1426–63.

Dean, Amber. *Remembering Vancouver's Disappeared Women: Settler Colonialism and the Difficulty of Inheritance*. Toronto: University of Toronto Press, 2015.

Hargreaves, Allison. *Violence against Indigenous Women: Literature, Activism, Resistance* Waterloo, ON: Wilfrid Laurier University Press, 2017.

Jacobs, Beverly. "Decolonizing the Violence against Indigenous Women" (Decolonization Blog). Available at: http://decolonization.wordpress.com/2013/02/13/decolonizing-the-violence-against-indigenous-women.

JJ. "We Speak for Ourselves: Anti-Colonial and Self-Determined Response to Young People Involved in the Sex Trade," pp. 74–81 in E. van der Meulen, E.M. Durisin, and V. Love, eds, *Selling Sex: Experience, Advocacy, and Research on Sex Work in Canada*. Vancouver: UBC Press, 2013.

Lavell-Harvard, D. Memee, and Jennifer Brant, eds. *Forever Loved: Exposing the Hidden Crisis of Missing and Murdered Indigenous Women and Girls in Canada*. Bradford, Ontario: Demeter Press, 2016.

Razack, S. "Gendered Racial Violence and Spatialized Justice: The Murder of Pamela George," *Canadian Journal of Law and Society* 15, 2 (2000): 91–130.

Smith, Ariel. "Indigenous Cinema and the Horrific Reality of Colonial Violence" (Decolonization Blog). Available at: https://decolonization.wordpress.com/2015/02/13/indigenous-cinema-and-the-horrific-reality-of-colonial-violence/

Yee, J. "Supporting Aboriginal Sex Workers' Struggles," *Canadian Dimension* 43, 91 (2009): 45–7.

## Relevant Websites

**Ariel Smith**

www.arielsmith.com

*Ariel Smith is an artist of mixed Nēhiyaw Iskwew and Jewish ancestry whose work uses a surrealist, expressionist, and horror genre aesthetic to expose and explore the history of gendered racial and colonial violence.*

**Government of Canada National Inquiry into Missing and Murdered Indigenous Women and Girls**

www.aadnc-aandc.gc.ca

*This is the official Federal Government of Canada's website that contains the launching of the Inquiry, and other relevant information on the MMIW.*

**I Am a Kind Man: Kizhaay Anishnaabe Niin**

www.iamakindman.ca

*I Am a Kind Man is an initiative by Indigenous men across Ontario to teach that violence against women is against traditional teachings and that men, together with women, have a communal responsibility to stop the abuse and violence.*

**Moose Hide Campaign**

www.moosehidecampaign.ca

*The Moose Hide Campaign is an effort by a group of Indigenous men to take a stand against violence against Indigenous women.*

**Native Women's Association of Canada**

www.nwac.ca

*This is the official website of the Native Women's Association of Canada. It contains the Sisters in Spirit Report and Fact Sheet on MMIW.*

**"There has been a war against Indigenous women since colonization" by Beverley Jacobs**

http://aptn.ca/news/2014/09/23/war-indigenous-women-since-colonization-former-nwac-president/

*Former President of the Native Women's Association of Canada speaks to APTN about the issues of gendered violence against Indigenous women.*

## Films

*Finding Dawn.* Dir. Christine Welsh. National Film Board of Canada. 2006.
*Missing: The Documentary.* Dir. Young Jibwe. Animikii Films. 2014. Available at: https://www.youtube.com/watch?v=sVQ4frDNDIk.

*How Do We Stop Aboriginal Women from Disappearing?* TEDx Talks by Beverly Jacobs. 2014. Available at: https://www.youtube.com/watch?v=8NtkmnJ2Q3w.

## Key Terms

Matrilineal societies
Sisters in Spirit
Gendered violence

Colonial violence
Aboriginal Women's Action Network

## Discussion Questions

1. Drawing from both Anita Olsen Harper and Fay Blaney's readings, discuss how violence against Indigenous women is similar to, and yet different from that of non-Indigenous women. Next, propose some strategies that could be used to properly address and eliminate such forms of violence.
2. What are some of the work and projects undertaken by the Aboriginal Women's Action Network? What are some of the challenges they faced, and lessons learned, through their work?
3. In her concluding paragraph, Fay Blaney states: "differences in forms of oppression result in different strategies,

and often these strategies contradict each other . . . Finding our voices to articulate our realities, despite the contradictions, is our way to liberation." What does she mean by this; how could Indigenous women have different experiences of sexual and colonial violence? Why is it important to acknowledge and respect such differences?
4. What were the circumstances into which Sisters in Spirit campaign started? What were its main objectives, strategies, and activities? How do you think the newly launched Missing and Murdered Indigenous Women and Girls Inquiry of the Canadian federal government could use its final report?

## Activities

Browse through the Missing and Murdered Indigenous Women and Girls National Inquiry website available online at http://www.aadnc-aandc.gc.ca. Answer the Discussion Questions on Designing the Inquiry posted on the website.

Visit the I Am a Kind Man and the Moose Hide Campaign websites listed above. Why and how are Indigenous men taking initiatives to respond to and eliminate gendered violence? Through their engagement, how you think they might be reconceptualizing Indigenous masculinities?

# PART SIX

❖

# Family, Belonging, and Displacement

## Editor Introduction

On 11 June 2008 Prime Minister Harper officially apologized on behalf of the Canadian State and ordinary Canadians to the survivors of the residential schooling system and Indigenous peoples, in general, for the many forms of abuse that happened in the schools and for other negative impacts inflicted on individuals, their families, and communities. This apology recognizes that the impacts of colonial policies, like residential schooling, are still ongoing in Indigenous communities. Contrary to what some might wish to believe, colonialism is not a thing of the past and a new path of reconciliation and healing must be taken. This section of the book examines the impact of racism, Settler colonialism, and displacement on familial relations and nationhood, in particular, the impact of these legacies on traditional ways of knowing, loving, caring, and nurturing.

As Ing (2006) has argued, through the separation of children from their families and communities, the State had hoped that the traditional cultures of Indigenous peoples would be forgotten, and assimilation to mainstream society would take place. In 2008, the House of Commons reported that this policy was racist because it deemed Indigenous cultures to be inferior to that of Eurocanadians. It reported the many violent forms of abuse that happened inside the walls of the schools, as well as the long-term impact on the bodies, minds, spirits, and hearts of the survivors and their families that is still being felt today.

Indigenous children were expected to suppress their sexuality, were punished for speaking their language and for maintaining bonds with their siblings, and suffered abuse from their teachers and schoolmates in residential schools. Children were left with feelings of shame about their Indigenous identity; they did not learn positive parenting skills, confusing love with violence and self-hate. When returning to their communities, they no longer possessed the love, confidence, self-esteem, cultural knowledge, and oftentimes, the language, to form positive relationships with their families. Many turned to negative coping behaviours to escape the internal turmoil, sometimes involving alcoholism and other addictions, as well as violence.

Following the apology in 2008, the Canadian federal government formed the Truth and Reconciliation Commission, led by Justice Murray Sinclair, in order for survivors of the residential schooling system to share their experiences, for all Canadians to learn of the history of that policy, so that healing and reconciliation might begin.

In December 2015, the Truth and Reconciliation Commission Report was released, detailing the history and legacy of the residential schooling system on both the children that attended those schools and their families (TRC, 2015). The report included 94 calls to action, some of which are specifically tied to child welfare: to reduce the number of Indigenous children in care; to develop culturally appropriate parenting programs for Indigenous families; to provide resources to Indigenous communities and organizations so that Indigenous families can stay together whenever possible; and to require that child welfare decision makers be trained on the impacts of residential schools system on children and caregivers (TRC, 2015).

Residential schools are not the only ways in which Indigenous peoples were forced to forgo their identities and to assimilate into mainstream society. By documenting her personal story, Shandra Spears shows how transracial adoptions, as frequently practised in Canada over many generations, displaced children from their Indigenous families and, in so doing, disconnected them from entire communities. This process links with the major theme of "disappearing" underscoring this anthology. As Spears writes: "In Canada, young Native people disappear into the dominant society through love, lies, and ideology—transracial adopting—disconnects them from nations, families." These "disappearances" embody an act of genocide: just like residential schools, the State had hoped to make "Indians" disappear through placing children into white families, impeding their ability to form strong Indigenous identities.

As Spears' narrative illustrates, the outcome was unjustly dramatic: many emerged angry, unable to formulate a positive sense of belonging either in white society or in the Indigenous community. The outcome of this history was a "fractured" identity, one characterized by "a collection of shutdowns and self-destructive behaviour." Just like the experience of residential schools, children were robbed through transracial adoption of their inherent right to Indigeneity and have had to struggle to recover and reclaim their identification.

Lynn Gehl's reading examines a policy that discriminates against many Indigenous people and children: the Aboriginal Affairs and Northern Development Canada's (now renamed Indigenous and Northern Affairs Canada) unstated paternity policy continues to deny Indian status registration to children whose father's signature does not appear on their birth certificate, as it assumes unknown and/or unstated paternity to mean a non-Indian man. As Gehl argues, this policy denies many children the ability to be legal Indians, members of their bands, and to have treaty rights. Furthermore, she points out, the policy "relies on a discourse. . . and practice that blames and targets mothers and their babies . . . sometimes . . . due to an abuse of power and sexual violence such as incest and rape, mothers may not obtain the father's signature on the child's birth registration form because they do not want the father to know about the child or have access to the child." Indeed, there might exist a myriad of complex and private reasons for not being able/willing to state a child's paternity. However, the current policy strives to regulate Indigenous women's choices and intimate lives, and in many cases, it further victimizes them, and continues to influence Indigenous familial arrangements and relations. At the end, this "legislative silence presently coded in the *Indian Act* was manipulatively crafted by sexist and racist patriarchs as a mechanism to then create discriminatory policy at the departmental level."

Despite the genocidal nature of residential schooling, transracial adoption, and other State policies, both authors speak of their own resilience and the courage of Indigenous people to survive the racist colonial attacks on Indigeneity. This is evident through efforts to recover both traditional gender and familiar relations, and to pass on these traditions to the younger generations, both by educating oneself in the history of residential schools, as well as through our family members who have experienced this history so that we can make sense of the lingering effects existing in our families and nations, and to find again our inner strength to heal and move forward. As Spears concludes, "the colonizer can try to hurt us, but can only succeed if we change who we are." In short, the work that we are doing today to both reclaim and resist past histories of racism and injustice suggest that Indigenous peoples are quite clearly "not disappearing."

# CHAPTER 11

# Strong Spirit, Fractured Identity
## An Ojibway Adoptee's Journey to Wholeness

*Shandra Spears*

Transracial adoption of Native children is more complex than anyone who has not lived through the experience can imagine. I have lived through it. Apart from the obvious disconnection from Native community and birth relatives, transracially adopted First Nations children face specific challenges, which we continue to face throughout the course of our adult lives. Mainstream society, when it acknowledges this issue at all, suggests that our trauma is a result of the abuse that we have experienced and that this abuse was inflicted by a few aberrant individuals. As with residential school survivors, this discourse can be stretched to say that many Native children did not experience violence first-hand and, therefore, have not experienced trauma.

By evaluating us as individual cases and by focusing primarily on our physical experience, the dominant society disconnects us from the larger aspects of politics and history. However, the removal of entire generations of Native children from our communities and families is a genocidal blow to our Nations, and we feel that violence in our bones. The myth of Native people as "conquered" implies that we were defeated in battle, but cultural warfare attacks the hearts and minds of vulnerable children. The myth of adopted Native children as "abandoned by troubled birth parents" denies the bonds of love between Native children and their families and communities and constructs white parents as heroic rescuers. . . .

In the context of colonization, the adoption of Native children by white families is an attempt to assimilate us into Canadian society. If Native children grow up as Canadians, we will presumably cease to be part of an "Indian problem." White adoptive parents are co-opted into this assimilation process by their urgent need to parent.

It is convenient to imagine that a parent's love can erase history and political conflict—but children grow up and conflict remains. Children are not "bridges between two worlds." Children cannot be programmed to become anyone but who they are. The attempt to mould Native children into an alien identity, out of laziness or self-interest, endangers our lives. Those of us who survive the experience often emerge angry at our loss and fiercely committed to our Native identity, once we rediscover it. The only way to have earned our loyalty in any permanent way would have been to meet our real cultural, spiritual, emotional, and physical needs with fairness and honesty. The possibility of finding accurate information about Native culture, which could lead parents to find culture-based support for Native children, is beyond the reach of the average Canadian, because this information is suppressed within dominant communication systems. In some totalitarian regimes, people disappear because death squads take them away. In Canada, young Native people disappear into the dominant society through love, lies, and ideology.

In Kim Anderson and Bonita Lawrence, eds, *Strong Women Stories: Native Vision and Community Survival* (Toronto: Sumach Press, 2003), 81–94. Reprinted by permission of Canadian Scholars' Press Inc.

# Challenging the Mythology of Adoption

My life story can be read from a couple of different ideological positions. One ideology states that colonization is a myth, that it no longer exists, that it wasn't bad for Indigenous people, and that it has had no lasting impact on our lives. This ideological position goes on to suggest that the Native way of life is unrealistic, backward and has little value, and that any child would be grateful for the chance to be raised by loving, white, middle-class parents and have access to good health care, education, and employment opportunities. Life on the reserve leads to life in prison or on the streets, so adoptive parents can give Native children a chance at a better life. If I understand my life according to this mythology, it was blessed and prosperous. This is one truth.

Another truth, from another ideological position, is that I was robbed of a political, historical, spiritual, linguistic, and cultural base which could have given me a great sense of self-esteem and strength. This position also acknowledges that a large proportion of Native people who ended up homeless, incarcerated, addicted, or psychologically scarred, were products of this "better life." Native people who remained connected to community and culture didn't come over to our house for dinner. I never heard my language spoken, and I was never given accurate information about my culture. I grew up within an ideology that said I did not exist, because Native people did not exist, except as mascots or objects of desire (Barthes, 1970). Through this process of symbolic annihilation (Tuchman, 1978), I ceased to exist as a Native person within my own mind.

I was already part white and lived surrounded by white colleagues and relatives. How much further could I step away from "Nativeness"—by marrying a white person and investing in a white, middle-class, Canadian way of life? Wouldn't that be simpler and less painful? How could my children return from that even greater distance? Love truly can conquer all. If I followed this process, it would use my own love relationships to turn me into a "death sentence" for my own descendants, at least in terms of being "practising" Ojibways. In my life, and in the history of my family, residential schooling and transracial adoption took me so far away from my language and culture that only a violent upheaval was able to bring me back. This is my story.

# The Story of My Survival

I was born in 1968 and was surrendered at birth for adoption. I lived in Toronto with two foster families before being adopted at five months of age. My older sister was very excited to have a new baby sister in the house. I had big brown eyes and auburn hair, and I'd already had the first of six surgeries to correct my club feet. My baby picture shows me sitting in my car seat on the sidewalk of my foster family's home with tiny casts on my legs on the day I was brought home from Toronto.

My first memory is of laughing. I was at the Hospital for Sick Children. I was eighteen months old, and I was about to have my ankle broken and reset with a pin. The surgeon was explaining that holes would have to be cut into the little boots attached to the brace I wore at night. I remember sitting on the counter in the blue light of the X-ray display, looking from the doctor to my parents, thinking that this was the funniest thing I'd ever heard. "Holes in my ankles; holes in my boots!" I thought it was hilarious.

Our family was playful, outdoorsy, and emotionally intense. We participated in a music society, the church, and Girl Guides. My sister and I took dance lessons and sang in the church choir. We had a little Pomeranian dog named Rusty. We camped almost every weekend, every summer, for most of my childhood. I loved it. When I was four years old, I learned that I was adopted. After many discussions, I came to understand that my other parents had been unable to take care of me, and that my Mom and Dad[1] were very happy that I was their little girl. I was adopted, and I had problems with my feet. My Dad's father had died. My Mom had health problems. My sister had allergies. Everyone in our family had her or his challenges.

My adoption story was that I was one-eighth Indian and that my grandfather had been an Indian chief. That made me an Indian princess. I had brown hair and brown eyes, and tanned well in the summertime. That was the extent of my Native identity.

Our home was also violent, and I became the family scapegoat. I experienced violence, shaming, and screaming. There were no cigarette burns and no rapes, and it didn't happen all the time. It was a pattern of domestic violence that had affected our extended family for several generations, so it did not begin as an attack on me as a Native child. But it was real. It happened—and it happened more to me than to my white sister. Conversations were dangerous and all members of the family were sensitized to signs of a fight. I couldn't negotiate my way through dangerous discussions very well, and I was a very sensitive child. Some Native adoptees say that they refused to cry when they were battered. I cried every time. I was always terrified of those experiences. . . .

The violence and fear didn't mean that I never had any fun. On the contrary, our family had family games, jokes, and traditions that were playful and imaginative. We could turn the smallest events into celebrations. We were voracious readers, and my earliest spiritual teachings came from the alternative worlds of fantasy and science-fiction novels. I loved my family and home. I didn't like feeling trapped and afraid.

I developed my sense of identity by internalizing everything around me. Having no Native women in my life, I had no way of knowing that I was a beautiful Native girl. I didn't even know that I was Native. There was no Native "mirror" that reflected my beauty; only a white mirror that reflected my difference. I compared myself to the girls around me, with their small waists and cute noses. I didn't look like them, but I had no reason to believe I was supposed to look any other way. Therefore, I "knew" that I was a white girl—an ugly white girl. I was a typical "ugly duckling." Having no one to tell me that I was worth protecting, I "knew" that I was worthless and bad.

At twelve years old, I started high school and discovered acting. I needed acceptance and affection, and I looked for those things outside the home, finding a place for myself with the artsy alternative crowd. I started to come out of my shell. By the end of high school, my days and nights were filled with arts activities, volunteering, part-time jobs, and going to night clubs. I came out of my shell at home as well. I stopped being silent and became openly hostile. The violence was escalating, and one parent was afraid of seriously injuring me. My parents called the Children's Aid Society to see if I could be placed in foster care. They were told that I would probably not find a foster home and could end up homeless. I stayed. I screamed and fought. I was sometimes kicked out, and sometimes I kicked myself out. I started keeping a running countdown on my bedroom door: "135 days until I can leave this house."

The violence stopped when I became physically large enough to fight back. No one in my family has hit me since my seventeenth birthday. Emotionally, however, I remained a scapegoat, and I acted out my role as a troublemaker. I smoked, drove when I was drunk, and engaged in other risky, self-destructive behaviours. I longed for affection from the young men who were most cruel to me and rejected those who treated me with respect. . . .

## From White to Native in Four "Easy" Years

The reunion with my birth mother was a positive experience, and we were very close for two years. She told me about my birth father, and that he was Ojibway. In that moment, I went from being "one-eighth Indian" to being Ojibway: the half-white daughter of an Ojibway man. This information had been falsified in my CAS file, where my birth father was listed as "one-quarter Indian." For the first time, I had a name for my Nation and names for my birth parents. I had the name of the reserve that he was from. These identifiers were very powerful for me. I also had images of people who looked like me. Almost overnight, like the ugly ducking, I decided I was quite good-looking! I started mentioning my Ojibway identity to random Native people; once, to a customer at K-Mart, and then to a student. This was a probing, hesitant process. I was checking to see whether they would laugh at me, because it was still obvious to me that I was the same white Shandra I had always been. But they encouraged me to continue searching for my Native relatives and even to apply for my Indian Status.

I felt like I had permission to continue. However, Ojibway identity was completely new to me. As a "one-eighth Indian," I lived in Canada as a white person and occasionally brought up the fact that I was "part-Indian." This meant that one of my ancestors had been Native but that I was not. If asked, I would say that I was proud to be part-Native, but it was a pride in something I had no direct experience with, like my artistic ability, or my post-punk music, or my family role as a rebel, it made me different, and I had learned to take pride in my uniqueness. I began to understand that I was an Ojibway person, but it still felt very unreal. I had no idea what to do with any of it. I wasn't really conscious of race, because I half-consciously believed that "race" referred only to "non-white" people. I started noticing the races of my friends and began talking to them about identity and culture.

My birth mother took me to events where I could meet other Native people and ask questions, and she took me to the first Toronto rally in support of the activists in Kahnesetake who had been attacked by provincial police. Before our relationship went sour, she gave me a lot of help in taking those first steps. By the end of the summer of 1990, I had had a crash course in activism. At first, I felt most comfortable with non-Native supporters. But then, I began to understand that Native activists would be maimed and killed while non-Native activists often faced less lethal consequences. That was a crucial moment, and it changed my sense of identity permanently.

Some Native women and men challenged my ethnicity in aggressive or insulting ways. I became very defensive about my fair skin, but didn't have enough confidence to really stand up for myself. Inside, part of me still felt like my Nativeness was a hoax, and I was seeing how far I could push it, but another part recognized that I had a right to pursue it and resented the discrimination I faced.

My life was full of "firsts." I worked in a Native organization for the first time and went to my first powwow. I lived with my first Native boyfriend. I was homeless and accessed a Native women's shelter for the first time. I learned to do beadwork and

went to cultural events. I made friends with Native people who were homeless or middle class; who were ex-cons, activists, healers, artists, executive directors, or entrepreneurs. My friends from high school and university were graduating, marrying, and moving on with their careers, while I was synthesizing a whole new sense of identity at every level of my body, mind, and spirit. I was angry about the loss of Native culture I had experienced as a child, and I was mourning the "white" direction that I was rejecting as an adult. This choice connected me to my new community and identity, and separated me from everything I had ever known. . . .

It had been four years since I met my birth mother, and I had immersed myself in the Toronto Native community without the legitimizing presence of an extended Native family. I was biracial, fair-skinned, non-status, urban, and culturally confused, and I had been raised by a white family, yet I had managed to make the identity shift. My reunion with my father's side of the family was my first trip to the reserve, and the family arranged for me to be instated as a band member. I was finally a Status Indian with a Native family. I even looked "more Native" when I returned, so that friends asked if I had dyed my hair. But my birth father, who had been homeless, was deceased. He had died in 1987, eighteen months before I began my search, and he had been left to die with no treatment in a hospital hallway. For the next six years, I wandered through the stages of a very confusing grief. Like so many other elements of my story, it felt unreal. How could I be grieving for someone I didn't know? Did I have a right to grieve? Eventually, it was through ceremony that I found some peace.

## Dressing Up Like an Indian

Ceremonies were very helpful to me, and I learned from excellent healers and traditional teachers. I learned to take on some responsibilities at our lodge. I learned my name and my clan and began to drum and sing. I explored the role of helper. I was learning to be respectful, and it felt good. My hair was very long and I kept it braided. I tried wearing skirts, as I had been taught to do. I even managed to find a way back to my teaching/leadership role, by teaching voice technique to Native women drummers. But I still felt I was out of my element.

The wild, expressive rebel that I had always been was being pushed aside for a long-haired, skirt-wearing woman working in social services between acting jobs. I wanted to be the irreverent, sarcastic, dynamic artist I had always been. I wore the uniform of a strong, traditional woman, but I still went home at night and felt crazy and self-destructive. I was invited to sing, but I couldn't speak the way I wanted to speak. I carried a journal around for those times when I wanted to say something that white or Native people in my life didn't accept or understand. I tried to be wild, expressive, proper, respectable, and rebellious all at once, but it was next to impossible. People could only accept a portion of me at a time. Lots of white friends dropped me completely, unable to cope with the changes I was going through.

I eventually split myself into different Shandras for each of these situations. One went home for weekends with the family, while another went to the lodge and sang, and yet another was an actor and martial artist. Switching from one reality to another gave me headaches, and triggered intense feelings of rage. I usually turned these rages on myself. There were times when I could barely recognize people I worked with every day, or forgot elements of traditional protocol because I was switched into "white" mode. Few people went from acting class, to martial arts class, to a traditional ceremony, to an all-night party; and then back to a nine-to-five office job all in one day. But I had done this all my life. I was a cultural chameleon, just as I had been growing up. I was feeling better and I had some of the answers I needed, but I was still pretending.

It can be very humiliating to be a Native adoptee within our community. Community members act as though our return to our community will solve all our problems. They think we should leave our childhood histories in the past and focus on behaving more like "real" Native people. After being constructed all our lives as "the problem," we return to our communities to face more of the same treatment. As recently as last year, a Native friend told me that she thinks I am brighter than most

adoptees and that's why I can understand our culture. That bigotry suggests that adoption equals stupidity. It seems unthinkable, but it exists.

Adoptees are called "lost birds." I don't feel like a lost bird! I am a strong, surviving Anishinaabe kwe who found my way back, alone, through a series of challenges, without any concrete or ideological support for my determination. That doesn't make me "lost." I understand the concept, though. What I call the "Adoptee Syndrome," a collection of shutdown and self-destructive behaviours, is very much like that of a bird who has fallen from the nest or a person who is so seriously ill that she or he can no longer eat.

## Healing the Fractures with Anger and Authenticity

How do I experience the Syndrome? It begins when situations restimulate my post-traumatic grief and rage. At this point, I either get what I need to relax the trigger or I stay triggered. For a while, I may continue to function, but I begin to lose some of my healthy habits. I eat proper meals and show up for work or appointments, but I stop using the prayers, meditation, or medicines that can help me. I dissociate, then shut down and go numb or feel overwhelmed by rage or panic. I reach out for help, but if the help isn't exactly what I need, I don't ask again. I beat up on myself. I start missing deadlines or I drop relationships. Sometimes, I get so "stuck" that I do nothing while my work, or my rent, is not taken care of. Thoughts of self-injury or suicide repeatedly enter my mind. I have to stay away from knives, subway ledges, and high balconies, because I feel the temptation to jump, or to cut.

Sometimes, I self-injure just enough to break out of the spin, although as a general rule I try not to. I become obsessed with negative, harmful people or situations. I become critical of others and of myself. Sometimes, I can't focus, or I run out of the room crying. Sometimes, my feelings boil over into physical gestures; I throw things. One such "release" cost me an expensive camera last year, because that was what was in my hand at the moment. This kind of trigger can last anywhere from a day to a year. I am using the present tense, because this is an ongoing obstacle. The fact that I can describe it, or even cope with it, does not mean that it goes away. . . .

The thing is that, even though I was an "instant Indian," I had knowledge and spiritual gifts the whole time, even as a child. "Real (Catholic/reserve) Indians" like to mock "urban Indians" who take up traditional spirituality. I was a prime target. I could even see their point! All they could see were assimilated Native people coming back, full of earnest longing and gobbling up teachings. But that "wannabe" image didn't matter to me. The more I learned, the more I discovered that I had had dreams and spiritual guidance helping me throughout my life. I discovered that my birth family had been spiritual and political leaders for generations before the boarding school/adoption disruption. I am not a pre-Colombian Ojibway woman. But neither are the "real Indians." We are all struggling through different aspects of the same genocidal program. . . .

## The Strong Spirit Knows What Is True

Back in 1991, at the abused women's shelter, a housemate gave me a strong teaching. She said that if I want to find my direction in life, I should go inside and find myself as a little kid and ask myself what I want to be. A few months later in ceremony, I had a chance to do just that. The ceremony brought us into connection with parts of ourselves.

I was reunited with myself at four years old. I was dancing and laughing inside one of those columns of light that I had seen as a young girl. I asked my four-year-old self, "Aren't you in pain? Don't your legs hurt? Aren't you afraid?" Four-year-old-me replied, "No, silly. I'm dancing!" A couple of years later, when I was named, Elder Waabishkamigizikwe named me "Laughter Woman." My first memory is of laughing. It is who I am.

Another grandmother taught me that people can try to hurt us, but they cannot change who we are. Or, as my Mother says, "Shandra, shit doesn't stick to you." I have an inner strength that bounces back from trouble, and I celebrate that. That ability to heal also exists within our families and communities and will lead us to solutions.

We can hold state and civic institutions responsible for their genocidal practices but that will not ultimately solve our distress. We are responsible for our own healing, and we are strong enough to achieve it. Native-child welfare organizations and open adoptions are creating better options for our children, and Native people are tackling problems in a variety of ways. Fortunately, we are not all one type of "Indian." Each of us has a different history, bringing different strengths to this cultural and political battlefield. In the polite Canadian culture war that seeks to break apart our strong families, we have an opportunity to discover our greatest strengths. The colonizer can try to hurt us, but can only succeed if we change who we are.

## Notes

1. The post-reunion life of an adoptee can be complicated for many reasons, including having two sets of parents. To clarify—my parents, who raised me, are called "Mom and Dad," while my birth parents are called "my birth parents," or are referred to by their first names. "Mom" and "Dad" have been capitalized throughout the essay to emphasize this distinction. I have been calling my parents Mom and Dad since I learned how to talk, and I have done so throughout this essay instead of using more clinical terms like "my adoptive parents." I prefer to express the normalcy and chaos of my adoption and post-reunion experience by using authentic language.

## References

Barthes, Roland. 1970. *Mythologies*. Paris: Seuil.

Tuchman, Gaye. 1978. "Introduction: The Symbolic Annihilation of Women by the Mass Media," in Gaye Tuchman,

Arlene Kaplan Daniels, and James Benét, eds, *Hearth and Home: Images of Women in the Mass Media*. New York: Oxford University Press.

# CHAPTER 12

# Protecting Indian Rights for Indian Babies
## Canada's "Unstated Paternity" Policy[1]

*Lynn Gehl, Gii-Zhigaate-Mnidoo-Kwe, Algonquin Anishinaabe*

Through Aboriginal Affairs and Northern Development Canada's (AANDC)[2] unstated paternity policy many Indigenous people and children are denied Indian status registration due to the lack of a father's signature on their birth certificates. I write this article for Indigenous community members, Indigenous women's organizations, and people caring for Indigenous women and their children to learn and draw from.

## History of the Sex Discrimination in the *Indian Act*

Eventually, through the imposition of colonial policy and laws, it was through the process of Indian status registration whereby Indigenous people became, and continue to be, entitled to their treaty rights. It is because of this relationship between Indian status registration and treaty rights that many people conflate "treaty" and "status" as in a "treaty status" Indian. Initially the legislative process of defining who was an Indian followed an Indigenous model, meaning being an Indian was more about community relationships and affiliation and thus broad and inclusive. Despite this inclusive beginning, through the application of an increasingly narrow definition of Indian status, the government of Canada began limiting the number of people entitled to Indian status, and through this process began

eliminating the federal government's treaty responsibilities established in 1764 during the *Treaty at Niagara* (Miller, 2004; Gehl, 2014). This process of narrowly defining and controlling who an Indian was, and is, is commonly referred to as eliminating the "Indian problem" (Scott qtd. in Troniak, 2011).

When it was determined that the process of enfranchising Indians and eliminating Indigenous treaty rights was proceeding at a snail's pace, Indian women and their children became the target of patriarchal and racist regime. Through a series of legislative acts dating back to the 1857 *Gradual Civilization Act*, Indian women and their children were enfranchised when their husband or father was enfranchised. It was through the 1869 *Gradual Enfranchisement Act* where Indian women, along with their children, who married non-Indian men (a.k.a. marrying out) were enfranchised, denied Indian status registration and thus their treaty rights (Miller, 2004). At this time, as per the European model of the world, women were considered chattel or appendages of their husbands and therefore if, and when, they married a non-Indian man they too became a non-Indian person (Gehl, 2006, 2013). Eventually, the process of eliminating status Indians through sex discrimination was codified in section 12(1)(b) of the 1951 *Indian Act* (Gilbert, 1996). Significant to this discussion is another form of sex discrimination first codified in the 1951 *Indian Act*: the double-mother clause. Essentially, through the double-mother clause a person was enfranchised at the age of 21 years if both their mother and paternal grandmother (two generations of

*First Peoples Child & Family Review* 8, 2 (2013): 54–73. http://journals.sfu.ca/fpcfr/index.php/FPCFR/issue/viewIssue/17/4. This is an edited version of original.

non-Indigenous mothers) were non-Indians prior to their marriage (Eberts, 2010).

With this loss of status, Indian women also lost their treaty rights, their right to live in their communities, their right to inherit property, and their right to be buried in the community cemetery. Further, through this sex discrimination "Aboriginal women have been denied opportunities to hold leadership positions within their communities and organizations and have been excluded from high-level negotiations among Aboriginal and Canadian political leaders" (McIvor, 2004: 108).

## Ogitchidaa Kwewag

As most know, many Indigenous women have worked tirelessly to eliminate section 12(1)(b) of the *Indian Act* and its intergenerational effects. I think it is appropriate to refer to these Indigenous women as Ogitchidaa Kwewag, an Indigenous term that best translates to a brave woman who is dedicated to the safety, security, and service of her family, community, and nation. On the national and international scale it is Mary Two-Axe Early, a Mohawk woman from Kahnawake, Quebec, who in 1966 began to speak publicly about the matter, where eventually she approached the Royal Commission on the Status of Women (Jamieson, 1978). It was in 1971 when now icon of Indigenous women's rights Jeannette Corbiere-Lavell, an Anishinaabe woman from Manitoulin Island, Ontario, took the matter of section 12(1)(b) to court arguing it violated the *Canadian Bill of Rights*. Yvonne Bedard, from Six Nations, Ontario, was also addressing the sex discrimination, and it was in 1973 when both their cases were heard together at the Supreme Court of Canada (SCC) level. Unfortunately, relying on a patriarchal line of reasoning, the SCC ruled that because Indian women who married non-Indian men "had equality of status with all other Canadian married females," there was no sex discrimination to resolve (McIvor, 2004: 113).[3]

Although this 1973 SCC decision was a setback, in 1981 Sandra Lovelace, a Maliseet woman from Tobique First Nation, New Brunswick, appealed to the United Nations Human Rights Committee (UNHRC) regarding section 12(1)(b). Because her marriage and loss of status registration occurred prior to the *International Covenant on Civil and Political Rights* the UNHRC declined to rule on the matter of sex discrimination. Nonetheless, the UNHRC did rule that the *Indian Act* violated section 27 of the International Covenant, which protected culture, religion, and language. Through this ruling it became evident that Indigenous women did have rights that international fora were willing to stand behind and protect (McIvor, 2004).[4]

Largely due to the actions of these Ogitchidaa Kwewag, combined with the patriation of Canada's *Constitution* in 1982 intact with the *Charter of Rights and Freedoms*, in particular section 15—the sex equality section—in 1985 the *Indian Act* was amended.[5] Through this amendment to the *Indian Act* many Indigenous women, involuntarily enfranchised for marrying non-Indian men, were re-instated as status Indians, and many of their children were *newly registered* as status Indians for the first time. Statistics Canada reports that by the end of 2002, more than 114,000 individuals gained Indian status registration through the 1985 amendment (O'Donnell and Wallace, 2012). Through this process, many re-instated women re-gained, whereas their newly registered children gained for the first time, First Nation band membership and entitlement to their treaty rights that were protected through the 1764 *Treaty at Niagara*. Indian status registration entitlement for the grandchildren of these reinstated Indian women, however, is another matter.

Although many think the 1985 amendment to the *Indian Act* was for the purpose of establishing equality between men and women, and foremost to achieve compliance with the equality provisions of the *Charter of Rights and Freedoms*, it in fact failed. Through the creation of the second-generation cut-off rule, the grandchildren of women once enfranchised for marrying out continued to be denied Indian status registration and consequently all that went with it such as band membership and their treaty rights. Succinctly, the second-generation cut-off rule is a process whereby after two successive generations of parenting with a non-Indian parent, either mother or father, the loss of status registration occurs.[6] While the second-generation cut-off rule applies to all births after 1985—the descendants of Indian men included—it was applied immediately in a retroactive way to the descendants of the re-instated Indian women one generation sooner. Through this discriminatory process, Corbiere-Lavell has stated, "Three of my five grandchildren do not have legal rights to be members of my community" (as cited in Keung, 2009: np).

To understand this legislative complexity is not a simple task. First, it is important to understand that because of the 1985 amendment, Indian status registration is now stratified into two main subsections: 6(1) and 6(2). While subsection 6(1) status, and its many paragraphs (subsubsections)—(a) (b) (c) (d) (e) and (f)[7]—allows a parent to pass on Indian status to his or her children in his or her own right, subsection 6(2) status does not. This means a 6(2) parent must parent with another status Indian in order to pass on Indian status registration to his or her children. For this very reason many people refer to 6(1) as a stronger form of status, and 6(2) as a weaker form. Certainly, this distinction is useful at conveying some of the legal complexity created in 1985.

Within the stronger form of Indian status registration, paragraph 6(1)(a) is the best form of status. When the *Indian Act* was amended, Indian men and all their descendants born prior to April 1985, the date of amendment, were all registered under paragraph 6(1)(a), whereas the Indian women who married out were only registered under paragraph 6(1)(c) and their children were only registered under the weaker form of status registration subsection 6(2). As a result of this difference in Indian status registration, and as suggested above, the grandchildren of Indian women became immediate targets of the second-generation cut-off rule. This of course means that the sex discrimination was not eliminated. Rather, through Bill C-31 the sex discrimination was passed on to the children and grandchildren of Indian women once enfranchised for marrying out (Eberts, 2010).[8] It

is precisely in this way that the 1985 amendment to the *Indian Act* through Bill C-31 was "failed remedial legislation" (Eberts, 2010: 28).

As most know by now Sharon McIvor and her son Jacob Grismer's situation is illustrative of the government of Canada's continued reluctance to resolve the sex discrimination. Through the 1985 amendment McIvor was designated as a 6(2) Indian, the weaker form of status registration which thus prevented her from passing on status to her children in her own right because the Indian status granted descends from her Indian women forbearers versus her Indian men forbearers (McIvor, 2004).[9] For 25 years, McIvor continued the important work of eliminating the sex discrimination that the children and grandchildren of Indian women once enfranchised continue to face (S. Day, 2011).[10]

An ally to Indigenous women, Mary Eberts, relying on her critical legal perspective, offers her comments and analysis on the McIvor decision. Eberts explains that Madam Justice Ross of the British Columbia Supreme Court agreed with McIvor's legal team that the comparator group for McIvor and her son Grismer was the Indian men who married non-Indian women and their children who on 17 April 1985, were registered as status Indians under 6(1)(a) of the *Indian Act*. Through applying this comparator group Ross J. ruled that the "preference for descent of status through the male line is discrimination on the basis of sex and marital status" (Eberts, 2010: 32). Ross J. ruled that 6(1)(a) must be equally applied to Indian men and their descendants and the Indian women once enfranchised and their descendants (Eberts, 2010). Alternatively stated, the children and grandchildren of both Indian men and the Indian women who married out should all be registered under 6(1)(a) of the *Indian Act*. This ruling was cause for celebration.

Unfortunately, through yet another questionable line reasoning the Court of Appeal narrowed the scope of Justice Ross' legal remedy by using a comparator group for Grismer thereby completely ignoring McIvor's situation of her inability to pass on status registration to her grandchildren. Yet it was McIvor, not her son, who brought the matter of sex discrimination to court. The new comparator group which Justice Harvey Groberman relied on was the grandchildren once enfranchised through the double-mother clause codified in section 12(1)(a)(iv) that came into effect on 4 September 1951. As discussed above, through the double-mother clause a person was enfranchised at the age of 21 years when both their mother and paternal grandmother were non-Indians prior to their marriage. This change means that McIvor's son is only entitled to 6(1)(c) and his children 6(2) status. In relying on this comparator group Groberman J.A. narrowed the scope, where as a result, and in line with Bill C-31, the legal remedy found in Bill C-3 fails to resolve all the sex discrimination. It is precisely for this reason that Eberts (2010) has argued the "Court of Appeal decision is a deep disappointment" and further "is, in fact, almost a case-book example of judicial activism producing bad law" (ibid., 39–40).

One can determine, through Justice Groberman's reasoning many caveats remain in the *Indian Act*'s current form. First, the grandchildren of Indian women once enfranchised, and born prior to 4 September 4, 1951—when the double-mother clause was first enacted—will continue to be denied Indian status registration, yet the grandchildren of Indian men in this same situation are registered. Second, grandchildren of Indian women born through common law relationships rather than the institution of marriage will continue to be denied status registration. Third, the female children (and their descendants) of Indian men who co-parented with non-status women in common law union will continue to be excluded, yet the male children (and their descendants) of Indian men who co-parented with non-status women in common law union have status. Fourth, the grandchildren of Indian women once enfranchised and now re-instated are only entitled to 6(2) status and therefore will not be able to pass on status to their children born prior to April 17, 1985, yet the grandchildren of Indian men are registered under 6(1)(a). Clearly, it is in these ways that matrilineal descendants remain targets of sex discrimination (McIvor and Brodsky, 2010).

Unfortunately, on 5 November 2009, the SCC refused to hear the appeal in the case of *McIvor v. Registrar, Indian and Northern Affairs Canada*. Although Brodsky and McIvor argued Bill C-3 as inadequate remedial legislation, in January 2011 it passed into law. Thus, despite the *Charter of Rights and Freedoms*, in particular section 15 which states women have the right to live free from racial and sex discrimination, like Lovelace before her, McIvor has been forced to pursue the elimination of the sex discrimination beyond the domestic arena. Shortly after Bill C-3 became law McIvor filed a complaint against Canada with the UNHRC (S. Day, 2011). In taking on this process McIvor herself has argued, "Canada needs to be held to account for its intransigence in refusing to completely eliminate sex discrimination from the *Indian Act* and for decades of delay" (as cited in Haesler, 2010: np). Similarly, the Director of the Women's Legal Education and Action Fund (LEAF), Joanna Birenbaum (2010), has argued that forcing Indigenous women such as McIvor "to endure the emotional and financial hardship of years and years of additional protracted litigation to remove the remaining areas of sex discrimination in the status provisions is unconscionable" (ibid., np). Notwithstanding these issues and arguments, it is estimated that as many as 45,000 grandchildren of Indian women once enfranchised for marrying out will gain the right to status registration through this more recent amendment (Day and Green, 2010; O'Donnell and Wallace, 2012). They will now also be more likely to be entitled to First Nation band membership and their treaty rights.

In sum, despite the efforts of Ogitchidaa Kwewag—Two-Axe Early, Corbiere-Lavell, Bedard, Lovelace, and more recently McIvor—the 156 year (as of 2013) history of the sex discrimination in the *Indian Act* continues. This is the case, regardless of the fact that Indigenous women have dedicated over fifty years to its elimination (Eberts, 2010: 42). Although living in a post-*Charter* era, for me and possibly many others, the equality outlined in section 15 of the *Canadian Charter of Rights and Freedoms* has no real practical value beyond that of a pitiful and meaningless fictional story. Through living, observing, and thinking about the process of remedial legislation—both in 1985 and 2011—I have come to realize that Canada manipulates legislative change as an opportunity to create new forms of sex discrimination rather than eliminate it. The next section of this article discusses yet another form of sex discrimination that has not received much attention: unknown and unstated paternity and the *Indian Act*.

# Unknown and Unstated Paternity and the *Indian Act*

## Traditional Knowledge

After assessing the needs of the Indians of Lower Canada, the 1845 Bagot Commission reported on child rearing practices stating, "an event of this nature [child of unknown or unstated paternity] does not cast a stigma upon the mother, nor upon the child, which is usually adopted into the tribe" (App. EEE, section 1, Indians of Canada East). Similarly, in his work on the Algonquin Nation of the Ottawa River, F.G. Speck observed it was the Chief's responsibility to take care of orphaned children (1915: 21). Further to this, Gordon Day has stated, "the basic unit of Algonquin society was the family: the father and mother, grandparents, children and adopted children" (1979: 3).

In my process of understanding the Indigenous family model, parenting, and community membership, I also turn to Anishinaabe governance laws, in particular the Clan System of Governance. Through clan teachings such as the need to keep our blood clean, men and women were encouraged to seek new genetic material from outsiders as the diversity assured the health and wellness of the people. In addition to this, it was common practice for Indigenous nations to adopt, kidnap, and assimilate young children when membership loss due to disease and war was great. In this way, parenting and community membership was not always reducible to the biological parents. Pamela D. Palmater (2011) arrives at a similar

realization of the limitations of blood as the criteria in determining identity and nationhood when she argues, "blood is not only unnecessary as an indicator of our identities; it is completely irrelevant" (ibid., 218). Rather, it is the social cultural aspect that determines who we are such as the deeply rooted connections to our nations that include family, larger community relations, and traditional territories, as well as the collective history, values, and beliefs that we share in common with one another (Palmater, 2011). Cannon (2008) concurs with this broader understanding of identity and belonging, offering there exists in Indigenous culture an "ancient context" that informs us of the importance of respecting women and the responsibilities they carry (ibid., 6).

# Legislative History

As the historical record, my family oral history, traditional governance practices, and sacred teachings inform, eventually the *Indian Act* began to impose European definitions and practices on who was and who was not an Indian child, even though the inclusion of all children regardless of paternity disclosure was once traditional Indigenous practice. In 1927, section 12 of the *Indian Act*, which remained in place until 4 September 1951, stated that "Any illegitimate child may, unless he has, with the consent of the band whereof the father or mother of such child is a member, shared in the distribution moneys of such band for a period exceeding two years, be, at any time, excluded from the membership thereof by the Superintendent General" (as cited in Gilbert, 1996: 34). This criterion was broad and inclusive in that all that was required was the sharing of band funds. From 4 September 1951, through 13 August 1956 the criteria of who was an Indian shifted slightly where the test was "the Registrar had to be *satisfied* that the father was not an Indian in order to omit adding a name to the register" (as paraphrased in Gilbert, 1996: 33, emphasis mine). The criteria shifted once again from 14 August 1956, through 16 April 1985, where section 12(2) stated that illegitimate children were automatically added to the Indian register whereby the band had twelve months to protest. This provision protected Indigenous mothers and their children. That said, if and when a protest was made and the Registrar determined that the father of the child was a non-Indian person then the child's name was removed from the official Indian register (Gilbert, 1996: 33). In summary, although regulated by legislation, and although the inclusive process was once narrowed, it was eventually re-expanded to include all children regardless of non-paternity disclosure unless a successful protest was made. This process of inclusion remained in place until 1985.

## Aboriginal Affairs' Unstated Paternity Policy Explained

Along with the issues that McIvor continues to pursue, today there is an additional form of sex discrimination of which few are aware. This sex discrimination is particularly disconcerting as it places many Indigenous children at risk of being denied their entitlement to Indian status registration and consequently First Nation band membership and treaty rights. This sex discrimination pertains to the Indigenous children whose father's signature is not on their birth certificate. Today, when a child is born and for some reason the father is unable to or does not sign the birth certificate AANDC assumes the father is a non-Indian person as defined by the *Indian Act*. This AANDC unstated paternity policy which I prefer to call "unknown and unstated paternity" is best thought of as the application of a negative presumption of paternity, and it occurs whether the parents are married or not. Succinctly, a father's signature must appear on a child's long form birth certificate as it is the long form birth certificate, and both parental signatures, that are relied upon in determining if a child is entitled to Indian status registration.

Interestingly, as with the sex discrimination that McIvor continues to challenge, this sex discrimination was created through the remedial action of the 1985 amendment to the *Indian Act*. What is really important here is that in actuality today the *Indian Act* is silent on this very matter of missing fathers' signatures. Regardless of this legislative

silence, through AANDC's unstated paternity policy these children are placed at risk for the denial of Indian status registration. More particularly, when administrating applications for status registration, this policy instructs the assumption of a non-Indian father to all applicants where a father's signature is lacking. Through this unfair negative assumption of paternity, when a mother is registered under section 6(1), the stronger form of Indian status, and a status Indian father does not sign the birth certificate the child is only registered under 6(2). While this child is entitled to Indian status registration, when a mother is registered under 6(2), the weaker form of Indian status, and a status Indian father does not sign the birth certificate the child is deemed a non-status person (Gehl, 2006, 2013).

What is really dubious about this policy assumption is that AANDC relies on a discourse—unstated paternity—and practice that blames and targets mothers and their babies. Clearly there is the need to understand the situation from the perspective of mothers.[11] My own reasoning informs me that sometimes, due to an abuse of power and sexual violence such as incest and rape, mothers may not obtain the father's signature on the child's birth registration form because they do not want the father to know about the child or have access to the child. Such situations may be best referred to as unreported and unnamed paternity. Again relying on my own reasoning sometimes a mother may record the father's name on the child's birth registration form, yet he refuses to sign the form because he needs to protect his standing in the community, and/or a marriage to another woman, and/or to avoid having to make child support payments, and/or the loss of his driver's license should he not make his child support payments. Such situations may be best referred to as unacknowledged and unestablished paternity.

Further, I have been told that in some situations mothers do record the father's name on the birth registration form, but because the father's signature is not obtained, an official of the government of Canada blanks-out his name. Alternately stated, an official removes the father's name from the birth form. Still further, I have also been told that in many situations the father may not be present during the birth of the child, such as when the mother is flown outside of her community to give birth as many communities are not equipped to fulfill this necessary area of health care. Moreover, once again my own reasoning informs me that sometimes the father dies prior to the birth of his child. Such situations may be best referred to as unrecognized paternity. What is more, a child may be conceived through the sexual violence of rape, gang rape, sexual slavery, or through prostitution where, as a result, the mother does not know who the father is and, possibly needless to say, could care less who he is as she has other matters to address. These latter situations may best be named unknown paternity.[12]

## Statistics and Figures

According to Stewart Clatworthy (2003) between 1985 and 1999 as many as 37,300 children of so-called unstated paternity were born to status Indian mothers registered under 6(1). During this same time period as many as 13,000 children of so-called unstated paternity were born to status Indian mothers registered under 6(2). Through AANDC's policy, these latter 13,000 children were immediately denied Indian status registration and, therefore, potentially band membership and treaty rights. Mann (2009) provides the percentage rates of so-called unstated paternity respective to age for section 6(1) mothers which, unsurprisingly, is higher for younger mothers. For example, mothers under the age of 15 years had a rate of 45 per cent. Mothers aged 15 to 19 had a rate of 30 per cent. Further, mothers aged 20 to 24 had a rate of 19 per cent, mothers aged 25 to 29 had a rate of 14 per cent, whereas mothers aged 30 to 34 had a rate of 12 per cent. Although these statistics represent rates for mothers registered under 6(1), it is not unreasonable to assume that similar rates also apply to mothers registered under 6(2).

## Administrative Remedies Offered and My Thoughts

According to Clatworthy (2003) 53 per cent of so-called unstated paternity cases are unintentional, while the remainder, 47 per cent are intentional.

Unintentional situations emerge due to compliance issues such as the father's signature not being achieved because of his absence during the birth, the dissolution of the relationship, and the inability to pay administrative charges for changes requested after amendment deadlines have passed. Intentional situations emerge because of unstable relationships, a father's denial of paternity, confidentiality concerns of the mother, child custody concerns, mothers afraid of losing Indian status registration or First Nation band membership, and an unwillingness to pay administrative fees for birth registration changes (Clatworthy, 2003: 16–18). Moving from this limiting framework Clatworthy offers a number of administrative remedies. These remedies include the development of a national policy; First Nation leadership development; the production of new resource materials for parents; education initiatives for parents; and the development of birth and status registration kits for parents (ibid., 19–22). For the most part these remedies emerge from an androcentric position.

Fiske and George (2006) critique Clatworthy for failing to explore in greater detail why Indigenous mothers might not disclose who the father is. They argue, paternity disclosure can at times place women in "jeopardy, perhaps endanger them, and at the very least cause social conflicts where a man either denies paternity or refuses to acknowledge it to state authorities" (Fiske and George, 2006: 4). Similarly, the Native Women's Association of Canada (NWAC) (2007) has noted, "Issues related to personal safety, violence, or abuse may provide a reason for a woman deciding to disassociate herself from a former partner or spouse" (ibid., 1). Adding, "mothers may wish to avoid custody or access claims on the part of the father: leaving the paternity unstated forms a partial protection against such actions by a biological father who may be unstable, abusive or engaged in unhealthy behaviours" (NWAC, 2007: 1). Mann (2009) adds intentional situations also emerge when a mother knows who a father is yet is unwilling to identify and name the father when the pregnancy is the result of abuse, incest, or rape (ibid., 33). Certainly Fiske and George, NWAC, and Mann are getting closer to the issues and reality that many Indigenous women are forced to endure in a sexist and racist patriarchal society.

Mann (2005) offers her own discussion of administrative remedies. In some ways they do pick up where Clatworthy left off. Mann suggests: access to travel funding for fathers when mothers have to leave the community to give birth, birth forms signed in the community prior to the mother leaving to give birth, increased administrative support in communities, and alternatives to notarization when there is the need to amend birth registration forms (ibid., 21). In offering this discussion of remedies, Mann admits that they will serve little in situations where a mother for some very legitimate reason cannot or will not disclose the name the father. Mann then proceeds to offer several recommendations: the use of affidavits or declarations as proof of paternity by either the mother or father, or at the very least allow for affidavits or declarations to identify who the father is when the child is the result of sexual violence such as incest or rape; provide necessary resources when affidavits or declarations are required; the need for educational initiatives for both men and women; conduct research to determine additional administrative remedies; and conduct research where key stakeholders such as First Nation women and First Nation representatives are included throughout the development of policy or legislative change (ibid., 26). In this way, Mann's analysis moves in the right direction extending Clatworthy's limitations. But there is more thinking and research required.

Certainly, administrative remedies are within AANDC's jurisdiction, and while these remedies offered by Clatworthy and Mann are on the right track—again, Mann more so—my own thinking informs me that they do not begin to consider and thus address situations where a father, for whatever reason, while accepting paternity refuses to officially acknowledge paternity and sign their child's birth certificate. For example, it is common knowledge that sometimes fathers go through a period of insecurity and jealously when their partner becomes pregnant. When I think about this state of being I view it as analogous to the postpartum depression–psychosis continuum that some mothers experience after childbirth. While this state of pathology has yet to be identified, named, and defined in the Diagnostic and Statistical Manual of Mental Disorders, and thus effectively addressed in our societal structures, many people know that it is during a woman's pregnancy when a father is more likely to become neglectful, abusive, and consequently likely to refuse to acknowledge paternity and sign a child's birth certificate.

Nor for that matter, and again drawing from my thinking, do these administrative remedies offered by Clatworthy and Mann address situations where a mother does not know who the father is due to situations of rape or gang rape by unknown perpetrators. While in some situations of sexualized violence a mother may know who the perpetrator is, in other situations she may not. Moreover, there may be more than one perpetrator. In addition, and this time drawing from my own experience of being denied Indian status, these administrative remedies offered do not address situations where an individual such as myself does not know who her grandfather was or is, and has no way of determining his identity. Like the Ogitchidaa Kwewag before me, I am forced to take the matter of an unknown paternity in my lineage, and consequently the denial of Indian status registration, through Canada's legal system.

That said, I think it is also important to understand that these remedies and recommendations offered by Clatworthy and Mann do not address situations where a non-Indigenous woman has a child with an Indian man yet for some reason is unable to attain the father's signature on their child's birth certificate. Certainly administrative remedies, whether at the policy level or legislative level, need to incorporate the realities of non-Indigenous mothers who have parented with Indian men. Further research is required, research that includes non-Indigenous mothers of Indigenous children as a stakeholder group.

As a measure of fairness, objectivity, and to assure this article is comprehensive, readers will find it interesting to know that AANDC (2012) offers three administrative remedies on this topic. First, AANDC recommends that applicants for Indian status have their birth certificate amended. Second, a statutory declaration signed by the applicant's mother and biological father should be provided. Third, in the event that a biological father is uncooperative, unavailable, or deceased, it is suggested that the applicant provide a statutory declaration from the biological father's family members that affirms what they believe. These remedies fail to address many of the issues discussed by Clatworthy, Mann, and myself and as such fail to crest the horizon of the issues.

## Summary and Conclusion

Despite decades of advocacy and litigation work by Indigenous women that eventually led to amendments to the *Indian Act*, under AANDC's current regime of determining Indian status registration, and as of 1985, a father must sign his baby's birth certificate for his Indian status registration to be factored into the child's eligibility. Otherwise, through an unstated paternity policy the Registrar of AANDC applies a negative assumption of paternity whereby the child may not be entitled to Indian status and consequently band membership, and their treaty rights. This assumption of non-Indian paternity is sex discrimination.

What is particularly disturbing about AANDC's unstated paternity policy is the way it targets Indigenous mothers and children. As I have discussed in this article, women sometimes conceive through an abuse of power such as in situations of incest, rape, gang rape, sexual slavery, and prostitution where as such the terms un-reported, unnamed, unacknowledged, un-established, unrecognized, and unknown paternity are more appropriate descriptors than the inadequate "unstated."

Through the creation of the 1985 AANDC unstated paternity policy it is now clear to me that the remedial legislation intended to eliminate the sex discrimination was little more than an opportunity for Canada to manipulate the legislative change process into an opportunity to create new and worse forms of sex discrimination. While many people may correctly argue additional research is required in remedying AANDC's unstated paternity policy, it is my contention that a well-defined research methodology alone will not resolve the issues faced by Indigenous women. It is my view that the legislative silence presently coded in the *Indian Act* was manipulatively crafted by sexist and racist patriarchs as a mechanism to then create discriminatory policy at the departmental level. AANDC's unstated paternity policy is a new low for the Canadian state that is "morally reprehensible" (McIvor, 2004: 133).

It is precisely this AANDC unstated paternity policy that is preventing me from Indian status registration and consequently First Nation band membership in my kokomis' (grandmother's) community, citizenship in the broader Anishinaabek citizenship endeavour, as well as access to my treaty rights such as health care. When AANDC denies me Indian status registration they deny me important aspects of my identity as an Indigenous person, and as a result my right to live minopimadiziwin (the good life) as an Algonquin Anishinaabekwe. It is precisely for this reason, as well as for young mothers and their babies, that I continue my effort.

## Notes

1. Originally published: Gehl, L. (2013). "Indian Rights for Indian Babies: Canada's 'Unstated Paternity' Policy," *First Peoples Child & Family Review* 8 (2): 55–73. http://journals.sfu.ca/fpcfr/index.php/FPCFR/issue/viewIssue/17/4. This is an edited version of the original.

2. Note that as of publication the department is no longer referred to as the AANDC but has instead been renamed as Indigenous and Northern Affairs Canada. This change was implemented in the days after Justin Trudeau's election as prime minister in 2015.

3. See also Monture Angus, 1999; S. Day, 2011.

4. See also Monture-Angus, 1999; Silman, 1987; Stevenson, 1999.

5. 17 April 2012 marked the thirtieth anniversary of the Charter of Rights and Freedoms. Possibly needless to say, I did not celebrate.

6. While many may argue that it was in 1985 when the enfranchisement process was removed from the Indian Act, I disagree. It is my contention that enfranchisement has a new form: the second-generation cut-off rule.

7. Outside of my discussion of 6(1)(a) and 6(1)(c) and how AANDC applies them to Indigenous women and men in an unequal manner, I do not discuss the other paragraphs (sub-subsections) of 6(1). This discussion is beyond the scope of this paper.

8. See also Gehl, 2006, 2013; Gilbert, 1996; McIvor, 2004.

9. See also Eberts, 2010.

10. See also Day and Green, 2010; Eberts, 2010; Haesler, 2010.

11. I need to qualify that many women conceived through the sexual violence that occurred during their Residential School and Day School experience. In these situations it is highly unlikely that the father's signature would be recorded on the birth registration form.

12. While thinking through all these situations we also need to keep in mind that while a mother, grandmother, or great-grandmother may know the father, this does not mean a child, a grandchild, or great-grandchild knows. Further, these categories—unstated, unreported, unnamed, unacknowledged, unestablished, unrecognized, and unknown paternity—also apply to the paternity of one's grandfather and/or great-grandfather.

# References

Aboriginal Affairs and Northern Development Canada. 2012. *Unstated paternity on birth certificate: Quick facts on documentation required.* 12 April. Retrieved from http://www.aadncaandc.gc.ca/eng/1334234251919

Bagot Commission Report. 1844-5. "Report on the Affairs of The Indians in Canada," *Journals of the Legislative Assembly of the Province of Canada.* App. EEE.

Bagot Commission Report. 1847. "Report on the Affairs of The Indians in Canada," *Journals of the Legislative Assembly of the Province of Canada.* App. T.

Birenbaum, J. 2010. *Women's Legal Education and Action Fund (LEAF) calls on the Conservative Government to withdraw its opposition to Amended Bill C-3* [News Release]. 5 May. Retrieved from http://www.leaf.ca/media/releases/Press_Release_May_5_2010_Bill_C-3.pdf

Cannon, M. J. 2008. *Revisiting histories of gender-based exclusion and the new politics of Indian identity.* Retrieved from http://fngovernance.org/ncfng_research/martin_cannon.pdf

Clatworthy, S. 2003. *Factors contributing to unstated paternity.* 20 January. Retrieved from http://dsp-psd.pwgsc.gc.ca/Collection/R2-255-2003E.pdf

Day, G. M. 1979. "The Indians of the Ottawa Valley," *Oracle* 30: 1–4.

Day, S. 2011. "153 years of sex discrimination is enough," *The Star.* 6 January. Retrieved from http://www.thestar.com/opinion/editorialopinion/article/916682—153-years-of-sexdiscrimination-is-enough

Day, S., and J. Green. 2010. "Sharon McIvor's fight for equality," *Herizons* 24 (1): 6–7.

Eberts, M. 2010. "McIvor: Justice delayed—again," *Indigenous Law Journal* 9 (1): 15–46.

Fiske, J., and E. George. 2006. *Seeking alternatives to Bill C–31: From cultural trauma to cultural revitalization through customary law.* Ottawa, ON: Status of Women Canada.

Gehl, L. 2014. *The Truth that Wampum Tells: My Debwewin on the Algonquin Land Claims Process.* Halifax and Winnipeg: Fernwood Publishing.

Gehl, L. 2006. "'The Queen and I': Discrimination against women in the Indian Act continues," pp. 162–71 in A. Medovarski and B. Cranney, eds, *Canadian woman studies: An introductory reader,* 2nd edn. Toronto, ON: Inanna Publications and Education Inc.

Gehl, L., with H. Ross. 2013. "Disenfranchised spirit: A theory and a model," *Pimatiziwin: A Journal of Aboriginal and Indigenous Community Health* 11 (1): 31–42.

Gilbert, L. 1996. *Entitlement to Indian Status and membership codes in Canada.* Scarborough, ON: Carswell Thomson Canada Ltd.

Haesler, N. 2010. "B.C. Aboriginal woman taking status battle to the UN: Sharon McIvor says Canada continues to discriminate under Indian Act," *Vancouver Sun.* 12 November. Retrieved from http://www.vancouversun.com/life/Aboriginal+woman+taking+status+battle/3817575/story.html

Jamieson, K. 1978. *Indian women and the law in Canada: Citizens minus.* Ottawa, ON: Minister of Supply and Services, Canada.

Keung, N. 2009. "'Status Indians' face threat of extinction: In some communities, last children with historic rights will be born as early as 2012," *The Toronto Star.* 10 May. Retrieved from http://www.thestar.com/news/canada/article/631974

Mann, M. M. 2009. "Disproportionate & unjustifiable: Teen First Nations mothers and unstated paternity policy," *Canadian Issues* (Winter): 31–6.

Mann, M. M. 2005. *Indian registration: Unrecognized and unstated paternity.* June. Ottawa, ON: Status of Women Canada. Retrieved from http://www.michellemann

.ca/articles/Indian%20Registration%20-%20Unrecognized%20and%20Unstated%20Paternity.pdf

McIvor, S. D. 2004. "Aboriginal women unmasked: Using equality litigation to Advance women's rights," *Canadian Journal of Women and the Law* 16 (1): 106–36.

McIvor, S., and G. Brodsky. 2010. *Equal registration status for Aboriginal women and their descendants: Sharon McIvor's comments on Bill C-3, An Act to promote gender equity in Indian registration by responding to the Court of Appeal for British Columbia decision in McIvor v. Canada (Registrar of Indian and Northern Affairs).* 13 April. Submission to the House of Commons Standing Committee on Aboriginal Affairs and Northern Development.

Miller, J.R. 2004. *Lethal legacy: Current Native controversies in Canada.* Toronto: McClelland & Stewart.

Monture-Angus, P. 1999. *Thunder in my soul: A Mohawk woman speaks.* Halifax, NS: Fernwood Publishing Company Ltd.

Native Women's Association of Canada. 2007. *Aboriginal women and unstated paternity: An issue paper.* 20–22

June. Retrieved from http://www.laa.gov.nl.ca/laa/naws/pdf/nwac-paternity.pdf

O'Donnell, V., and S. Wallace. 2012. *First Nations, Métis and Inuit women.* 24 February. Retrieved from http://www.statcan.gc.ca/pub/89-503-x/2010001/article/11442-eng.htm

Palmater, P. D. 2011. *Beyond blood: Rethinking Indigenous identity.* Saskatoon, SK: Purich Publishing Limiting.

Silman, J. 1987. *Enough is enough: Aboriginal women speak out.* Toronto, ON: The Women's Press.

Speck, F. G. 1915. *Family Hunting Territories and Social Life of Various Algonkian Bands of the Ottawa Valley.* Canada: Department of Mines, Geological Survey Memoir 70. Anthropological Series No. 8. 1–30.

Stevenson, W. 1999. "Colonialism and First Nations women in Canada," pp. 49–80 in E. Dua and A. Robertson, eds, *Scratching the surface: Canadian anti-racist feminist thought.* Toronto, ON: Women's Press.

Troniak, S. 2011. *Addressing the legacy of Residential Schools.* Retrieved from http://www.parl.gc.ca/Content/LOP/ResearchPublications/2011-76-e.pdf

# PART SIX

❖

## Additional Readings

Anderson, Kim. *A Recognition of Being: Reconstructing Native Womanhood*, 2nd edn. Toronto: Women's Press, 2016.

Castellano, Marlene Brant, Linda Archibald, and Mike DeGagné. *From Truth to Reconciliation: Transforming the Legacy of Residential Schools.* Ottawa: Aboriginal Healing Foundation, 2008.

Gehl, Lynn. "Unknown and Unstated Paternity and The *Indian Act*: Enough is Enough!" *Journal of the Motherhood Initiative for Research and Community Involvement* 3, 2 (2012): 188–99.

Ing, Rosalyn. "Canada's Indian Residential Schools and Their Impacts on Mothering," pp. 157–72 in Lavell-Harvard, Dawn Memee, and Jeanette Coribiere Lavell, eds, "*Until*

*Our Hearts Are on the Ground*": *Aboriginal Mothering, Oppression, Resistance, and Rebirth.* Bradford, ON: Demeter Press, 2006.

Lavell-Harvard, D. Memee, and Kim Anderson, eds. *Mothers of the Nations: Indigenous Mothering as Global Resistance, Reclaiming, and Recovery.* Bradford, ON: Demeter Press. 2014.

Nuttgens, S. "Stories of Aboriginal Transracial Adoption," *The Qualitative Report* 18, 2 (2013): 1–17.

Palmater, Pamela D. *Beyond Blood: Rethinking Indigenous Identity.* Saskatoon: Purich Publishing Limited, 2011.

Truth and Reconciliation Commission of Canada. *What We Have Learned: Principles of Truth and Reconciliation.* Ottawa: Government of Canada, 2015.

## Relevant Websites

**First Nations Child and Family Caring Society of Canada**

http://fncaringsociety.com

*This is the official website of the First Nations Child and Family Caring Society of Canada and it contains information, resources, and networks to assist Indigenous families.*

**Indigenous and Northern Affairs Canada, "Statement of Apology to former students of Indian residential schools"**

http://www.aadnc-aandc.gc.ca/eng/1100100015644/1100100015649

*This website contains the official apology given by the Canadian federal government to the survivors of the residential schooling system.*

# Films

*A Place Between: The Story of an Adoption.* Dir. Curtis Kalten-baugh. National Film Board of Canada, 2007.

*Club Native.* Dir. Tracey Deer. National Film Board of Canada with Rezolution Pictures, 2008.

*We Can't Make the Same Mistake Twice.* Dir. Alanis Obom-sawin. National Film Board of Canada, 2016.

*We Were Children.* Dir. Tim Wolochatiuk. National Film Board of Canada, 2012.

*3rd World Canada—The Movie.* Prod. and Dir. Andrée Caza-bon. Productions Cazabon, 2010.

*Birth of a Family.* Dir. Tasha Hubbard. National Film Board of Canada, 2016.

# Key Terms

Residential schooling
Transracial adoption
Fractured identity

Bill C-3
Bill C-31
Unknown and unstated paternity

# Discussion Questions

1. There is much evidence that residential schooling has had lasting intergenerational impacts on Indigenous communities. What are some of these impacts and how have communities enacted healing processes for survivors and their families?

2. Shandra Spears details her personal experience as an adoptee and the difficulties she encountered as a result from being removed from her Indigenous community. How do her experiences reflect the effects of Canadian colonialism? Does her narrative have a different effect than detailing the impacts of residential schooling through quantitative research and/or theoretical analysis?

3. Discuss how the sex discrimination codified in section 12(1)(b) of the *Indian Act* denied many Indigenous women their legal Indian status, and consequently created barriers on their familial and communal rights and responsibilities.

4. How is Canada's current Unstated Paternity Policy under the *Indian Act* still contravening the *Charter of Rights and Freedoms*? Why does Gehl argue that recent remedial legislative process fails to justly address systemic discrimination?

# Activities

Watch the documentary *Unrepentant: Kevin Annett and Canada's Genocide* (available online). Discuss the ongoing implications of residential schools on both Indigenous and non-Indigenous identities.

On 11 June 2008 the Government of Canada officially apologized for the residential school system. Watch the apology online and discuss your thoughts about it. Should Canada have apologized for residential schooling? Is saying "sorry" enough? What other concrete actions are needed for reconciliation and healing to begin, and to move forward? To prepare for this activity, read one or both of the following: (a) Sara Ahmed, "The Politics of Bad Feeling," *Australian Critical Race and Whiteness Studies Association Journal* 1 (2005): 72–85; (b) Megan Boler, "The Risk of Empathy: Interrogating Multiculturalism's Gaze," *Cultural Studies* 11, 2 (1997): 251–71.

# PART SEVEN

❖

# Indigenous Rights, Citizenship, and Nationalism

## Editor Introduction

On 13 September 2007 the United Nations adopted the Declaration on the Rights of Indigenous Peoples. The Declaration itself provided an overview of Indigenous peoples, including a framework for realizing a future of more just relations. States were urged to implement a series of steps to safeguard the rights of Indigenous nations. Moreover, and with great significance to the themes raised in this section of the anthology, the document acknowledged that "Indigenous peoples have suffered from historic injustices as a result of, inter alia, their colonization and dispossession of their lands, territories and resources." It recognized "the urgent need to respect and promote the inherent rights of Indigenous peoples which derive from their political, economic, and social structures and from their cultures, spiritual traditions, histories and philosophies, especially their rights to their lands, territories, and resources."

The Declaration was not legally binding on member States and does not signify a threat to their sovereignty. Nevertheless, Canada rejected this landmark document in September 2014 at the UN General Assembly. In choosing to reject the Declaration, the Conservative government at that time failed to acknowledge the distinct nature of equity claims and the historicity of Indigenous rights. On 12 November 2015, the newly appointed Indigenous and Northern Affairs Minister Carolyn Bennett announced that the Liberal government would implement the UN Declaration on the Rights of Indigenous Peoples. The move, she said, was to reflect the commitment that Prime Minister Justin Trudeau made when elected to build a better and healthier nation-to-nation relationships with Indigenous peoples, one whereby the State will fully consult and obtain consent from Indigenous peoples on any matters that directly affect them and their lands. This new direction is one full of promise and hope for Indigenous peoples, and many of our Indigenous relatives and friends have been saying that in fact, they are more "cautiously optimistic" that a future more positive relationship with the Canadian State can be built, and that respect for our inherent Indigenous rights might finally happen.

As both authors in this section point out, Indigenous rights are as unique as the peoples themselves. They are rooted in the inherent and never before extinguished rights of nations, as well as a colonial experience wherein people were dispossessed—and continue to be dispossessed—of lands. Indigenous peoples do not wish to integrate into mainstream structures, but rather wish to have their rights and nation-to-nation relationships affirmed. These demands derive from, and indeed shape, what it means to be Indigenous in the contemporary world.

Alfred and Corntassel (2005) suggest that contemporary Indigenous struggles are an affirmation of identity. The demand to have Indigenous rights affirmed is inherently decolonizing in nature. Remembering our ceremonies, traditions, laws, and autonomous nations is a journey of what they refer to as "self-conscious traditionalism." This type of traditionalism is a "reconstruction of traditional communities based on the original teachings and orienting values." Indigenous peoples are in a unique position relative to the Canadian political make-up. As Henderson (2002) writes, Indigenous peoples have a unique constitutional heritage enabling sui generis rights. Canada is "based on the foundation of shared sovereignty" (ibid., 419), since our ancestors agreed to a treaty relationship; he writes, "a relationship between nations . . . a belief in autonomous zones of power, freedom, and liberties" (ibid., 422). Although Canada has not respected our treaty rights, they are nonetheless real and binding to the parties originally promising to uphold them.

Bonita Lawrence's article brings attention to the fact that despite Indigenous peoples' inherent right to self-government and title to land, contemporary self-government and comprehensive claims policy negotiations are still constraining Indigenous peoples. Canada still unilaterally decides what constitutes Aboriginal culture and what can be discussed in a self-government negotiation process, and it still continues to not address questions of compensation of loss of lands and resources. What has transpired throughout "modern treaties" making, is that self-government is implied to merely apply to internal matters, to limit protection of only "pre-contact" cultures, and it definitely does not translate into a right of sovereignty in the international sense, hence further legitimizing the Canadian State's control over Indigenous peoples.

Given the power imbalances between the Canadian State and Indigenous nations, First Nations often feel pressured into accepting terms within a settlement claim that do not fairly address historical wrongs, and might even further damage them. As Lawrence points out, one of the most crucial concerns is that claims negotiations demand either a full extinguishment of title or modified rights. In either case, Crown sovereignty is maintained and what most often occurs is further loss of lands and resources. Lawrence's critiques are quite timely, as the Algonquins of Ontario are about to vote on a Proposed Agreement-in-Principle. Many Algonquin members are critical of the agreement and are encouraging all Algonquins to reject it. They highlight a few important components of the Agreement that would negatively impact their peoples: extinguishment of Algonquin Aboriginal title with no compensation for loss of lands and resources; only 1.3 per cent of their traditional lands will be transferred to the Algonquins; and the end of tax exemption by becoming a municipal type of government (Kebaowek First Nations, 2016). Lawrence's cautions indeed are evident in current self-government negotiations, and the latter do not come near to the promised nation-to-nation relationship that this country was to embark upon under the leadership of Prime Minister Justin Trudeau.

Indigenous rights of self-determination are ultimately tied to the ability to freely decide on matters of membership to each specific Indigenous nation. As Audra Simpson's article reveals, this is a very complicated task, and Indigenous nations, as they have always done, continue to imagine and construct alternative discourses of citizenship. In it, she addresses the complexities embedded in matters of citizenship, in particular the current challenges present in her community, the Kahnawake Mohawk nation. As with other nations, Canada imposed a definition of membership at Kahnawake through the *Indian Act*. Through the *Indian Act*, traditional ways of defining nationhood and national membership have been disrupted, especially patrilineal definitions of citizenship which robbed Mohawk women who "married out" of a right to be defined as Mohawk (Indian for that matter) and granted such rights to white women who "married in." In 1985 the State, in its attempt to redress gendered injustice granted "reserves" the right to define their own membership. Out of this history, Kahnawake passed a code of 50 per cent blood quantum as a criterion for membership to protect a small land base against those who are perceived to not have sufficient Mohawk blood.

Alongside band membership, other lived experiences of citizenship do exist in the community, such as those of Status Indians (who might or not have band membership) and "feeling" citizenship. All of these varied narratives and lived experiences of citizenship, Simpson reminds us, are collective experiences connecting all the people, (re)acting against the State's imposition, as well as against each other in the process. And they are living legacy of colonialism; as the Mohawk nation moves forward to a decolonizing future, "the challenge to the community is to harden these pieces of knowledge, these critiques and these possibilities into a membership policy that may accommodate the simultaneity of these experiences, these different trans-historic discourses (and people) so that these 'feeling citizenships' may then become *lived* citizenships for *all*."

After centuries of colonial transformations, it is difficult to remember Indigenous traditional systems of governance, and given the high levels of despair most Indigenous nations live under, it might be hard to resist the Canadian State's pressures in self-government and land claims negotiations. However, true warriors have always resisted colonial impositions and have insisted on the inherent rights to follow our own traditional ways of governing and be *equal* participants in a nation-to-nation relationship. We are waiting now to see if the current government will deliver on its promise made during the 2015 election that a new historical phase will begin wherein Indigenous rights will be respected and a nation-to-nation relationship formed.

# CHAPTER 13

# Aboriginal Title and the Comprehensive Claims Process

*Bonita Lawrence*

. . .

## Policy Framework

The inherent right to self-government policy and the comprehensive claims policy were both created by Ottawa in response to

In *Fractured Homeland: Federal Recognition and Algonquin Identity in Ontario* (Vancouver: University of British Columbia Press, 2012), 54–82. Reprinted with permission of the Publisher from *Fractured Homeland* by Bonita Lawrence © University of British Columbia Press 2012. All rights reserved by the Publisher.

constitutional changes and Supreme Court decisions that addressed Aboriginal rights and title. Both documents suggest that, within the implementation of these policies, everything is negotiable. Unfortunately, the reality is that the colonialist assumptions informing the Supreme Court decisions that constrain Aboriginal rights and title have moulded these policies as well. Both policies clearly articulate that Aboriginal laws and traditional jurisdictions cannot be part of negotiations relating to self-government or comprehensive claims, that Canada can unilaterally decide what constitutes an "integral" aspect of Aboriginal culture, that discussions on self-government will remain separate from those regarding territory (as if governance is not associated with territory), and above all, that questions of compensation will not be addressed. This last stipulation sidesteps any recognition that Canada's wealth has come (and continues to come) from appropriating Native peoples' lands and resources, and that Native poverty is therefore a direct result of Canada's wealth. Moreover, the Supreme Court decisions . . . limit what is possible to achieve by litigation, leaving Native people no other option but to negotiate with Ottawa, inevitably from a position of weakness.

When Aboriginal rights were first entrenched in the Constitution, many Native people believed that at least some aspects of their control over their own affairs would be "on the table" as part of asserting a right to self-government or making a claim based on Aboriginal title. But in 2002, when talks on a number of comprehensive claims were proceeding under this assumption, Ottawa walked away from several negotiating tables across the country, labelling them "unproductive." These tables—30 of approximately 170—dealt with various matters ranging from specific claims, to self-government negotiations, to comprehensive claims within the British Columbia treaty process. When interviewed by the CBC, then-Indian Affairs minister Robert Nault stated that he had discontinued negotiation with certain tables because Native leaders had made excessive demands. These included issues relating to Aboriginal jurisdiction and the right to enact certain laws and to resist having Ottawa delegate authority over all matters relating to self-government (Nahwegahbow, 2002: 2).

In an environment where the Supreme Court decisions regarding Aboriginal rights and title have essentially predetermined what is open to negotiation, it is perhaps not surprising that Aboriginal leaders who attempt to infuse Indigenous frameworks of understanding into Canadian processes are characterized as unreasonable and acting in bad faith. Nevertheless, it is important to explore the self-government and comprehensive claims policies in some detail, to understand these processes more clearly.

## The Inherent Right to Self-Government Policy

In 1995, the federal government released its Approach to Implementation of the Inherent Right and the Negotiation of Aboriginal Self-Government Policy. The document clearly states that recognition of inherent right is based on the view that the Aboriginal peoples of Canada have the right to govern themselves in relation to matters that are internal to their communities, integral to their unique cultures, identities, traditions, languages, and institutions, and with respect to their special relationship to their land and their resources (Canada, 1995). The language here is virtually identical to that of *Van der Peet, Pamajewon,* and *Delgamuukw* in that it limits self-government to purely internal matters and "culturalizes" Aboriginal rights, so that what is to be protected are not the existence, needs, and livelihoods of Aboriginal peoples, but their pre-contact cultures. The policy explicitly states that the inherent right of self-government does not include a right of sovereignty in the international sense and will not result in sovereign independent Aboriginal nations. Instead, the participation of Aboriginal peoples in the Canadian federation will be enhanced, and they and their governments will not exist in isolation, separate and apart from the rest of Canadian society. By suggesting that Aboriginal perspectives lead only to total independence from Canada, the policy ignores any notion that these perspectives should be part of the dialogue about *how* Indigenous people are to participate within Canada.

Negotiations relating to self-government are tripartite, involving the First Nation, Ottawa, and the relevant province or territory. The policy indicates that Aboriginal jurisdictions and authorities should work in harmony with those of other governments, which suggests that some "give" is expected from the provinces in the matter of jurisdiction. However, should an Aboriginal government's law conflict with any of the laws of the province or territory, it will be overridden by provincial or territorial law. Moreover, only matters considered internal to the group, integral to its distinct Aboriginal culture, and essential to its operation as a government can be part of self-government.

Although these limitations are extremely troubling, Aboriginal people are even more concerned about the financial aspects of the negotiations. The fact that no separate funds have been provided for implementation means that the considerable costs of transitioning to self-government must come from existing federal expenditures, which will depend on available resources. Second, although the policy suggests that self-government will ensure a stable source of funding for Aboriginal governments, there are no provisions to constitutionally protect transfer payments from Ottawa to First Nations in the manner in which provinces are constitutionally protected (McNeil, 2002: 32). This leaves First Nations in a very vulnerable position, particularly given Canada's history of significantly underfunding Aboriginal infrastructure and services relating to basic needs such as housing, clean water, sanitation, and accessible health care. . . .

As of September 2011, two BC bands (Sechelt and Westbank First Nations) had negotiated self-government agreements, and nine Yukon First Nations had negotiated a self-government agreement as part of their comprehensive claim (AAND, 2011). An examination of these agreements reveals that all generally adhere to a template, suggesting that the policy framework and process determined what was to be discussed. Notably, divisions between status and non-status Indians are maintained: Canada will continue to fund services for status Indians who come under self-government agreements but will not do the same for non-status or Metis groups, who must seek funding agreements

with their relevant provinces in order to obtain self-government. . . .

. . . The most problematic issue, . . . and one that applies equally to self-government and the comprehensive claims process, is identifying who has the right to self-government. The Royal Commission on Aboriginal Peoples carefully distinguished between Indigenous nations and local communities. It identified an Indigenous nation as a sizeable body of Indigenous people who share a sense of national identity and who constitute the predominant population in a territory or collection of territories. Local communities, on the other hand, are the smaller groupings of Indigenous people that are not themselves nations but are part of nations. The royal commission estimated that there are probably between fifty and eighty Indigenous nations in Canada and approximately a thousand local communities (RCAP, 1996b: 178–81).

McNeil (2002: 28) points out that due to the fragmenting effect of the Indian Act's band system, many Aboriginal communities are most comfortable dealing at the band level, or at most the tribal council level, and have little skill or experience in working at the nation level. Added to this actuality is the fact that treaties and provincial boundaries bisect Indigenous nations, dividing them into different jurisdictions, with the result that envisioning a reunited nation is difficult. McNeil suggests that this fundamental area needs significant research to address ways of overcoming these divisions.

## The Comprehensive Claims Policy

Federal policy assigns Aboriginal land claims to one of two broad categories. Comprehensive claims are based on the assertion of continuing Aboriginal rights and title that are not covered by a treaty or other legal vehicle. Specific claims arise from non-fulfillment of treaties or other legal obligations, or from the improper administration of lands or assets under the Indian Act or other formal agreement (Hurley, 2009: 1). Despite the stipulations of its own policy, Ottawa has agreed to negotiate a few comprehensive claims in areas governed by treaties. . . .

. . . All modern treaties, otherwise known as land claim agreements, are negotiated through the comprehensive claims policy, which came into existence in 1973 as a result of the *Calder* decision. Between 1973 and 2009, twenty-three comprehensive claims have been settled (Hurley, 2009: 1–2). However, to truly understand the comprehensive claims process, we must examine how a claim is negotiated.

### Negotiating a Comprehensive Claim

Before the negotiation process can begin, a First Nation is required to submit a statement of claim, which must include "a statement that the claimant group has not previously adhered to a treaty; a documented statement from the claimant group that it has traditionally used and occupied the territory in question and that this use and occupation continues; a description of the extent and location of such land use and occupancy, together with a map outlining the approximate boundaries; and, identification of the claimant group including the names of the bands, tribes or communities on whose behalf the claim is being made, the claimant's linguistic and cultural affiliation, and approximate population figures of the claimant group" (Canada, 1987).

The federal government funds the research stage of the process, and if the land claim is accepted, First Nations must annually secure loans or grants from Ottawa to finance their participation in the negotiations. Claims are accepted only if the Indian Affairs minister deems that they have a high probability of success. Once a claim is accepted, the minister appoints a senior federal negotiator, who receives his or her mandate from Ottawa.

The parties then enter into preliminary negotiations, outlining areas to be discussed. It is important to understand that the "Scope of Negotiations" in the comprehensive claims policy establishes very strict parameters concerning what can be put on the table, in terms of land rights,

waters, fisheries, subsurface royalties, and sacred sites. It rejects concepts such as co-management or sharing environmental management with First Nations. It also establishes fiscal caps and sets limits on royalties and revenue sharing—indeed, on most areas under discussion. Perhaps most importantly, it maintains the existing constitutional division of power between Ottawa and the provinces (ibid.). Clearly, control of the process is firmly in the hands of the federal government.

The first crucial issue to consider here is the power imbalance relating to funding. Because they are borrowing money from Ottawa, Native people who launch a claim are aware that during every day of the negotiations, their debt is mounting and that it will ultimately be deducted from the final settlement. Nor are these amounts trivial. According to an Indian Affairs estimate, the cost of negotiating a land claim can range from $15 to $50 million (INAC, 2003: 22). Once this amount has been deducted from the cash settlement, the actual monies received will be significantly reduced. Although Ottawa has forgiven some of these loans, the general rule is that they must be paid, and so the first "gun" held to the head of Indigenous people is the pressure to negotiate fast before the debt piles up. And since Ottawa controls funding, the possibility that funding may be withdrawn if agreements are not forthcoming represents an additional set of pressures.

Of course, the irony of these pressure tactics is that the poverty of Native communities, which makes them dependent on government loans for land claim negotiations, exists precisely because their wealth has been expropriated via the colonial process. In seeking title to the land, they are forced to borrow money from the very government that appropriated their land and resources in the first place. The funding issue highlights the fact that modern treaty negotiations are built upon a negation of the living reality of colonial history and the power it has granted Canada. For example, Canada continually denies that it should pay compensation for centuries of occupying people's land and usurping their resources. Its negotiators repeatedly insist that "history has been dealt with" via the apology to victims of residential schooling and the $350 million healing fund, and that the cash component of treaty settlements is an exchange of "value for value" (de Costa, 2002: 8). . . .

However, the biggest government pressure tactic is that untrammeled resource development continues while the treaty is being negotiated. For many Native people, the fact that clear cutting continues to devastate their homeland or that mines are being created on their territories while they sit in negotiations are powerful incentives to keep negotiations brief and accept whatever terms are offered.

The extinguishment of title is perhaps the most crucial concern for many Aboriginal people. Critics of the comprehensive claims process have suggested that the government should not seek to extinguish Aboriginal title: instead, it should specify which rights it is seeking from Native people to develop and use land and resources (Conseil Attikamek Montagnais et al., 1986). However, given the power imbalance that permeates the comprehensive claims policy, negotiations are grounded in either the full extinguishment of title or a specification of exactly what rights Aboriginal people will retain in the land.

The 1973 comprehensive claims policy contained what were referred to as "blanket extinguishment" provisions in that Indigenous people were to "cede, release and surrender" all Aboriginal rights and interests in and to the settlement area in exchange for the benefits provided by the settlement agreement. When Indigenous people's dissatisfaction regarding this requirement was obviously impeding the progress of claims, Canada adopted a new approach in 1986. This consisted of two alternatives—modified rights and non-asserted rights. In the former, which was first employed during the Nisga'a negotiations, Aboriginal rights are modified rather than extinguished, becoming solely the rights enshrined in the treaty. Under the latter, Aboriginal rights remain unextinguished, but Indigenous groups agree not to exercise them, confining themselves solely to the rights articulated and defined in the treaty. The 1986 policy allowed for the retention of

Aboriginal rights on land that Indigenous people will hold once their claim is settled, but only insofar as such rights are not inconsistent with the treaty. . . .

If comprehensive claims are really modern treaties, it is clear that at the heart of treaty making, past and present, lies the assumption of Crown sovereignty. Indeed, as Kent McNeil (2002) demonstrates, jurisprudence in this area is instructive. McNeil compares four Supreme Court cases—*Simon, Sioui, Sparrow,* and *Delgamuukw*—to reveal the inconsistencies in the establishment of sovereignty. The *Simon* case of 1985 considered the rights accrued under the 1752 Treaty of Peace and Friendship between the Mi'kmaq and Britain; *Sioui,* which dates from 1990, involved a 1760 treaty between the Hurons of Lorette and Britain. The court viewed the Mi'kmaq and the Hurons as "quasi-sovereign nations" who were treaty signatories with Britain, and it recognized a range of rights under the two treaties. By comparison, in *Sparrow* and *Delgamuukw,* the court saw the Musqueam, the Gitksan, and the Wet'suwet'en as having been subjugated simply because Britain had asserted sovereignty over British Columbia in 1846. McNeil highlights the contradictions here: According to the court, British sovereignty at the time of the two eighteenth-century treaties was not yet established in Eastern Canada, even though the British had been in the area for over a century. But in 1846, when a treaty between Britain and the United States established the forty-ninth parallel as the boundary between their respective western possessions, it conclusively proclaimed British sovereignty over the whole of British Columbia, even though the British had barely entered the west coast at this time. McNeil emphasizes the necessity of conducting research into how British sovereignty can supersede Indigenous jurisdiction—how it is that European settlement automatically confers Crown sovereignty, and indeed, how sovereignty can be asserted when no treaties are established with Indigenous people.

Although Crown sovereignty lies at the heart of the treaty relationship between Aboriginal people and the Crown, sacredness has been central to treaties between Aboriginal peoples themselves. According to the report of the Royal Commission on Aboriginal Peoples (RCAP, 1996a: 68–9), treaties were of the highest order of diplomatic relations across the continent and were maintained through the use of ceremony, replete with rituals, oratory, and specific protocols such as the exchange of wampum belts and smoking the sacred pipe, all of which were conscientiously observed by treaty partners. Indigenous terminology relating to treaties reveals an extraordinary attention to detail and to the various types of treaties. In the Ojibwa language, for example, there is a difference between *Chi-debahk-(in)-Nee-Gay-Win*, an open agreement with matters to be added to it, such as the Lake Huron Treaty of 1850, and *Bug-in-Ee-Gay*, which relates to "letting it go"—treaties requiring no further terms. However, treaties were always regarded as living entities to be renewed in ceremonies, which in turn renewed relationships. Nations cemented treaties with each other for purposes of trade, peace, neutrality, alliance, the use of territories and resources, and protection, resulting in far-reaching geopolitical alliances ranging from the Wendat Confederacy, which united four nations of similar dialects, to the Wabanaki Confederacy, the Iroquois Confederacy, and the Blackfoot Confederacy, each of which united diverse nations with many languages. Once formed, these confederacies were strengthened by the demands of the fur trade and became mechanisms for dealing with European colonists.

During the fur trade, Europeans entered into treaties according to Indigenous protocols, but this dynamic changed once Native people began to lose control of their territories. Particularly in Eastern Canada, the waning of the fur trade and its replacement with settlement policies, the drastic decline in Indigenous populations due to epidemics and warfare, and the growth of internecine divisions brought about by religious conversion and other destabilizing factors all contributed to this loss of power for Indigenous nations in their dealings with Europeans (Lawrence, 2002: 41). In this situation, it was all

too easy for Europeans to negotiate treaties that were ostensibly about peace and trade but were subsequently revealed to focus on land cession (ibid.). As a result, between 1781 and 1830, most of southern Ontario was surrendered to Europeans. Between 1814 until the census of 1851, the white population of what is now southern Ontario multiplied by a factor of ten, from 95,000 to 952,000 (Miller, 2009: 94). Given the attenuated power that Native peoples now commanded, the old alliances between themselves and Europeans were abandoned.

With Confederation and the increasing power of the Canadian state came an accelerated process of land acquisition treaties in Western Canada and the North, so that in less than fifty years, eleven numbered treaties had been signed, claiming all the land stretching from Lake Superior to the Rockies and north to the Arctic Ocean.

Lynn Gehl (2009: 5) has compared these historic treaties with the modern treaties of the comprehensive claims policy. She has discovered that, with the exception of the Nunavut settlement, the modern treaties involved First Nations obtaining self-government powers only at the level of a municipality.[1] In examining the numbered treaties, she also found that Treaties 1, 2, and 5 allocated 32 acres per person, whereas the other numbered treaties apportioned 120 acres per person. Under the terms of the Nisga'a Agreement, each individual received 80 acres.

And yet, this does not compare with the situation of the Lheidli T'enneh, a band near Prince George. With a traditional territory of 10,000 square kilometres, the band was offered 29 square kilometres, 7 of which were reserve lands that it already held. This band, whose land borders Treaty 8 territory, would have been entitled to 140 square kilometres had it signed that treaty a hundred years ago (de Costa, 2002: 4). In April 2007, it voted to reject the treaty that it had spent thirteen years and $1 billion negotiating with the federal and provincial governments. Only 47 percent of its 234 members voted in favour of the treaty. In general, it appears that modern treaties, at least those south of the sixtieth parallel, seek to leave Native people with less land than the historic treaties ever did.

In fact, more than any other aspect of Canadian policy, treaties grounded in European terms, both historically and in the modern era via the comprehensive claims policy, reveal the ongoing colonialism at the heart of Canadian society. It is not merely that Canada assumed sovereignty over the land with no clear basis under its own laws, it is also the hostile and mean-spirited attitude that Canada displays regarding any notion that it should now share the land in the traditional Aboriginal manner of negotiating treaties. Indeed, Canada appears determined to keep the door slammed shut on any possibility of real Native participation in activities on traditional lands. Ultimately, there is little difference between, on the one hand, historical treaty making and policies based on assimilation, and on the other, modern treaty making and policies based on containment and the notion that Native peoples will be domesticated through subordination to Canadian authority and therefore finally neutralized as sovereign entities.

Perhaps not surprisingly, the comprehensive claims policy has been challenged on a number of levels. For example, John Olthuis and Roger Townshend (1996), who voice many criticisms of the policy, assert that equity and compensation must be assessed according to the value of the assets on the date they are restored, not on the date in which they were improperly taken. . . .

## Rejecting the Politics of Recognition

A number of Aboriginal scholars have questioned the entire process of seeking recognition from settler governments. Glen Coulthard (2008: 188) notes that for the past thirty years, the self-determination efforts of Indigenous people in Canada have increasingly been cast in the language of "recognition." Coulthard applies the term "politics of recognition" to various recognition-based models of liberal pluralism that seek to reconcile Indigenous claims to nationhood with Crown sovereignty via the accommodation of Indigenous identities in some form of renewed relationship with the Canadian state. This may involve the delegation of land, capital, and political power from the state to Indigenous communities, generally through land claim agreements, economic development initiatives, and self-government packages. Coulthard argues that instead of establishing co-existence grounded on the ideal of mutuality, the politics of recognition in its contemporary form is reproducing the configurations of colonial power that Indigenous struggles for recognition sought to transcend in the first place.

In noting that our identities—as individuals and as groups—do not exist in isolation, Coulthard (ibid., 196) suggests that if our identities are shaped by recognition, they can also be distorted by misrecognition, so that distorting representations of Indigeneity serve to damage Aboriginal people and prevent them from flourishing. In an analysis based on the work of Frantz Fanon, Coulthard observes that the long-term stability of a colonial structure of dominance depends as much on the "internalization" of racist forms of asymmetrical and non-mutual modes of recognition as it does on brute force. According to Fanon, a colonial configuration of power must be attacked at two levels if one hopes to transform it; these are the objective level, where power is maintained through the appropriation of land and resources, and the subjective level, where ideological structures of dominance are ensconced in racist "recognition."

From this perspective, the politics of recognition can address colonial injustice only in reformist terms. The promotion of state redistribution schemes that grant certain "cultural rights" and economic concessions to Indigenous communities through land claims and self-government agreements fails to address the objective level of power that colonialist states have accrued via land and resource theft. The liberal recognition paradigm enables colonialist states to maintain power by "managing" land claims to their own benefit.

The second problem with the recognition paradigm relates to the subjective realm of power relations. Most recognition-based proposals rest on the problematic assumption that the flourishing of Indigenous peoples as distinct and self-determining is dependent on being recognized by the settler state. For Fanon, only resistance struggles—Coulthard calls them "transformative practices," such as struggles for cultural regeneration—are capable of enabling subjugated people to deconstruct the racist misrecognition that is so harmful.

When recognition is not accompanied by the transformative practice of cultural resistance, the fundamental self-transformation that comes with decolonization cannot occur. Under the politics of recognition, the colonized may receive constitutionally protected rights but cannot challenge the subjugation of their sovereign rights that is inherent in the process of delegating power. Indeed, those who engage in the politics of recognition must accept the infantilization and belittling of Indigenous societies that ensues when colonizers define the "integral" aspects of their "special cultures," delegating self-government that does not entail real Indigenous control and structuring land claims so as to permit no self-determination. In addition, Coulthard suggests that Indigenous people who work within the politics of recognition are in grave danger of adopting the limited and structurally contained terms of recognition as their own, so that in effect they identify with what he calls "white liberty" and "white justice."

As Coulthard (ibid., 195) points out,

Anybody familiar with the power dynamics that currently structure the Aboriginal rights movement in Canada should immediately see the applicability of Fanon's insights here. Indeed, one need not expend much effort at all to elicit the countless ways in which the liberal discourse of recognition has been limited and constrained by the state, politicians, corporations and the courts in ways that pose no fundamental challenge to the colonial relationship. With respect to the law, for example, over the last thirty years the Supreme Court of Canada has consistently refused to recognize Indigenous peoples' equal and self-determining status, based on the Court's adherence to legal precedent founded on the white supremacist myth that Indigenous societies were too primitive to bear fundamental political rights when they first encountered European powers. Thus, even though the Court has secured an unprecedented degree of recognition for certain "cultural" practices within the colonial state, it has nonetheless failed to challenge the racist origin of Canada's assumed authority over Indigenous peoples and their territories.

Coulthard's arguments reveal that, far from being liberatory, the politics of recognition is increasingly what Canada *needs* in order to absorb an Indigenous presence into its liberal democratic framework and to convince the world that it is *not* a colonial state. It seeks to demonstrate that "its" Indigenous peoples—tamed and domesticated—have become reconciled with the state and are happily co-existing within it, now that Canada protects its "special" cultures. For Indigenous people to step back from the politics of recognition—to refuse to be "reconciled" to Canada under such terms, and instead, to seek strength in their own traditions and their own land-based practices—may not challenge the brute force of colonial power, but it does delegitimize it.

Coulthard's reasoning is supported by Taiaiake Alfred (2005), who asserts that the large-scale "statist" solutions offered by Canada, such as land claim negotiations and self-government, merely provide a good living for those who represent their people in such contexts. At the same time, however, the great majority of Native people do not benefit from such practices, and indeed, are bearing the brunt of a racist society that denigrates their identities as Indigenous people and has done its best to erode and destroy Indigenous peoples' traditional frameworks of identity as ensconced in language and relationship to the land. The result is weakened and isolated people, too often consumed by addictions and tremendously unhealthy. Alfred suggests that a strategic focus on self-help for many Native people who are struggling with addiction and poor health is fundamentally necessary for decolonization, whereas those who are stronger and able to engage in critical resistance should concentrate on delegitimizing Canada's liberal democratic facade and reclaiming traditional practices on the land. . . .

## Notes

1. The Nunavut Agreement involved an entire territory where the Inuit were a majority population and therefore received some jurisdictions similar to provinces. For the terms of the agreement, see Government of Nunavut (1993).

## References

AAND. 2011. "Self Government." Aboriginal Affairs and Northern Development. http://www.aadnc-aandc.gc.ca/.

Alfred, Taiaiake. 2005. *Wasáse: Indigenous Pathways of Action and Freedom*. Toronto: Broadview Press.

Canada. 1987. *Comprehensive Claims Policy*. Ottawa: Minister of Supply and Services Canada.

———. 1995. "The Government of Canada's Approach to Implementation of the Inherent Right and the Negotiation of Aboriginal Self-Government Policy." Aboriginal Affairs and Northern Development Canada. http://www.aadnc-aandc.gc.ca/eng/.

Conseil Attikamek Montagnais, Council for Yukon Indians, Dene Nation, Métis Association of the N.W.T., Kaska-Dena, Labrador Inuit Association, Nishga Tribal Council, Taku River Tlingit, and Tungavik Federation of Nunavut. 1986. "Key Components of a New Federal Policy for Comprehensive Land Claims." 30 October. http://www.carc.org/.

Coulthard, Glen. 2008. "Beyond. Recognition: Indigenous Self-Determination as Prefigurative Practice," in L. Simpson, ed., pp. 187–204, *Lighting the Eighth Fire: The Liberation, Resurgence, and Protection of Indigenous Nations*. Winnipeg: Arbeiter Ring.

De Costa, Ravi. 2002. "Agreements and Referenda: Recent Developments in the British Columbia Treaty Process." Paper presented at "Negotiating Settlements: Indigenous Peoples, Settler States and the Significance of Treaties and Agreements," Institute for Postcolonial Studies, Melbourne, 29 August. http://www.atns.net.au/.

Gehl, Lynn. 2009. "Land Settlements Not Improving," *Anishinabek News*, July–August, 5.

Government of Nunavut. 1993. *Agreement between the Inuit of the Nunavut Settlement Area and Her Majesty the Queen in Right of Canada*. http://www.gov.nu,ca/hr/site/doc/nlca.pdf.

Hurley, Mary C. 2009. "Settling Comprehensive Land Claims," Parliamentary Information and Research Service, Library of Parliament, 21 September. http://www2.parl.gc.ca/Content/LOP/ResearchPublications/prhO9I6-e.pdf.

INAC (Indian and Northern Affairs Canada). 2003. *Resolving Aboriginal Claims: A Practical Guide to Canadian Experiences*. Ottawa: INAC.

Lawrence, Bonita. 2002, "Rewriting Histories of the Land, Colonization and Resistance in Eastern Canada," in Sherene Razack, ed., pp. 23–46, *Race, Space and the Law: Unmapping a White Settler Society*. Toronto: Between the Lines Press.

McNeil, Kent. 2002. "The Inherent Right of Self-Government: Emerging Directions for Legal Research." A Research Report prepared for the First Nations Governance Centre, Chilliwack, BC. November.

Miller, J.R. 2009. *Compact, Contract and Covenant: Aboriginal Treaty-Making in Canada*. Toronto: University of Toronto Press.

Olthuis, John, and H.W. Roger Townshend. 1996. "Is Canada's Thumb on the Scales? An Analysis of Canada's Comprehensive and Specific Claims Policies and Suggested Alternatives," in *Canada, for Seven Generations: An Information Legacy of the Royal Commission on Aboriginal Peoples*, 63 174–63877. Ottawa: Libraxus. CD-ROM.

RCAP (Royal Commission on Aboriginal Peoples). 1996a. Report of the Royal Commission on Aboriginal Peoples. Vol. 1, *Looking Forward, Looking Back*. Ottawa: Ministry of Supply and Services.

———. 1996b. Report of the Royal Commission on Aboriginal Peoples. Vol. 2, *Restructuring the Relationship*. Ottawa: Ministry of Supply and Services.

# CHAPTER 14

# The Gender of the Flint
## Mohawk Nationhood and Citizenship in the Face of Empire

*Audra Simpson*

. . .

## Narrating Territory and Rights

Even a dog could be buried in Kahnawà:ke, and we [the women who lost their Indian status upon out-marriage] could not! (Mary Two-Axe Early, ca. 1983)

The transition from property holder and status giver to a rank that is, upon death, beneath that of a dog requires a sudden and swift shift in power. . . . The utterance of Mary Two-Axe Early cited above tell us that notions of status and rights, and the complex of both that constitutes "political membership," must be tied up with something more than the power of the state. Why? Canada does not bury members in Kahnawà:ke; families do, and they do so in accordance with Mohawk Council of Kahnawà:ke (or traditional Longhouse) rules on membership and jurisdiction. Thus, the decision that allows dogs to be buried in the community and not women (who had lost their status) and *then* to cite this as a matter of injustice, references something deeper than the state. There is another story, another working even of *value* at play. There is evidence here of a local and Indigenous notion of "the utilitarian good" that is

historically driven and striving to be consensus based, attempting to recover and manage the vicissitudes of lawful and unlawful forms of dispossession that are borne by women today in various forms: dispossession of their rights as Indians, of their land, and of their lives. The agency exercised within the community, then, is an agency and instrumentality that work upon these notions "on the ground," notions that work in some relation to notions of territory.

. . . A traditional woman whom I interviewed from another Mohawk community answered my questions on Mohawk identity, nationhood, and territory in this way:[1]

Q: *Please give me some words to describe Mohawk people; how would you describe Mohawks to someone that does not know us?*

A: *Strong, peace loving, funny . . .*

Q: *Are these qualities the same for women as they are for men?*

A: *These qualities are more pronounced in women.*

Q: *Please tell me what nationhood is to you?*

A: *This is the disappearance of the boundaries between our reserves. In the ideal world, we would move through our traditional territory with no impediments, we would restore our relationship with the land as women. We would be free to do these things and not stay on the "ghettos" that they call reserves.*

In *Mohawk Interruptus: Political Life across the Borders of Settler States* (Durham, NC: Duke University Press, 2014), 147–76. Copyright © 2014, Duke University Press. All rights reserved. Republished by permission of the copyright holder. www.dukeupress.edu.

Territory is a large issue in her discourse on identity and nationhood and was throughout the course of the interview. She wanted to see the traditional territory of Mohawk people, which extends down from Kanehsatà:ke into the Ohio Valley, restored. In relation to this territory, she said, women are "the caregivers and own the territory, and the caregivers of the children and keep the communities going while the men are away." This is a neotraditional argument that takes the "traditional," precontact role of women and transposes it onto the contemporary. . . .

Here we are not yet finished with blood quantum or ideas about purity, as women still seem to carry the burden of this shift. Thus local membership options—such as matriliny, blood, and (in the case of one interlocutor in my data set) formal Canadian citizenship[2]—should also be viewed as adaptations, and somewhat sensible ones, to a colonial scene. Iroquois membership prior to the ascent of the settler state on the Canadian side of the international boundary line was about clan membership, and clan membership was transmitted through the woman's line. Particularly in light of the importance of women as clan bearers and as landowners in traditional Iroquois communities, blood quantum and the disregard for these *traditional* lines of descent—along with hooking ideas about nationhood to colonial forms of membership—seem especially problematic and self-defeating. If Iroquois women were the "mothers of the nation," then how could the nation continue without them in authoritative, structural positions of power?

. . . So how indeed could this "sudden and swift" shift in power occur? Land diminished rapidly; resources dwindled; being Indian mattered differently, and became hinged, perhaps, to a notion of decision making and loyalty to the community land base. Thus being Indian and having status became tied to notions of personal and individual responsibility. Women were told, "If you marry out, then you have to leave."[3] Interlocutors told me, "I always knew what would happen if I married out" (mind you, one woman in my data set purported to *not* know this). . . . These adaptations were tied as well to notions of territory that moved along with labour and travel beyond the confines of Kahnawà:ke. It is to this new "diasporic" space that disenfranchised women and their children, along with the shifting community of travellers and workers, would have to relocate. In this way, policy and cultural practice forced a new, gendered territorial imperative; this is especially the case if the women remain committed to the community and to their identities as Mohawks, transmitting this identity to their children. They may have had to leave the community proper, the bounded space of the reserve, but their activities in Chateauguay, Brooklyn, Ottawa, or elsewhere may have oriented them toward home or a re-created "home" away.

How does this predicament manifest itself in the present? This excerpt is from a woman who awaits recognition:

And so when we come out and we are [talking] about the things [that] are going on with the community, I am sure that the band council is not . . . going to Ottawa and telling the minister everything that he's doing to the people over there. You see, and yet he is saying "We are providing the services, we're doing everything that we're supposed to," but only to the few that they select. Now what about the rest of the population?

Now you've got people living off-reserve, because the community has rejected them—those people are not necessarily familiar with the daily activities that are going on in the community, so what they have done is basically removed themselves from having to deal with those situations on a daily basis. . . .

I mean life is hell there! I mean, it is not the best, I'll be the first to say it, living there; you gotta be damn tough to live there. And in order to survive there, you have to be really tough. Now some people might have gotten tired by it, and decided, "I'm gonna go live off the reserve where I won't have to deal and face those things on a daily basis, where somebody's telling me, 'Leave, you don't belong here,' facing the discrimination on a daily basis." Which is what we encounter.

I encounter it daily there; you never know what's going to happen from one moment to the next. I mean water and sewage is one thing, landfill is another, getting slapped in the face [when I got] my letter from the Education Centre . . . saying that they are not accepting me so that I can go ask and beg and plead to the Department to get it. . . . I never got rid of it—certificates of possession, with letters of rejection. . . .

I mean at every turn we are getting slapped in the face—every single turn—which should be normal things that we should be entitled to for the past seventeen years. And the federal government has been: "Well, sorry."

Now if anybody is going to . . . want us to trust them, they have to jump over a lot of loops to do that now, and hurdles, because there is no more trust. There is no trust in the councils, and there is no trust in the federal government because both have reneged on their responsibilities.

So, now we are sitting back, and this is why we are taking the position that we are taking, and this is why we are *angry*. I mean, I lived hell for *x* years, my whole entire life getting slapped in the face at every turn. I grew up in the city, them telling me "Go back to where you come from." I go to the town,[4] they tell me, "Go back to the city you don't belong here." Where the hell do you go? And then when you do decide to make your decision—your stance on where you are going—you still get slapped in the face daily. So life is not a bed of roses over there, but I choose to live there because it is my *right*.

I didn't get the land that I am living on by *buying* it; it was passed down from generation to generation within my family, and I am being told I am third generation, I am white, and I have no right. That is what I am being told, and yet I inherited that land; I never bought it; it has been passed down from generation to generation.

This narrative moves us through the historical spaces that one must simultaneously occupy to manage the question of rights and justice as a historically excluded woman of unambiguous Kahnawà:ke Mohawk descent. We can cull from her narrative that she is first constructed as a claimant upon the community as a non-status Indian (or in the eyes of some community members, as a non-Indian). As such, she is also being constructed as a claimant upon the resources of the community. Within her narrative, we can see that she experiences aggression from others in Kahnawà:ke, where she is told "to go back to the city." And the city, she makes clear, is also not a welcoming place for her. She wants to stay on the reserve in spite of this because it is her *right*. Now this notion of "right" that she is working with is an interesting one. It includes what she is owed by her Bill C-31 reinstatement of status and, as she makes clear toward the end of her narrative, to her position as a landowner. Her status as a landowner is owing to her descent from people who were property owners within the community. She is not directly invoking the notion of an Iroquois woman's role in pre-settler society as a caretaker of the land, but her argument is tied to the common-sense transparency embedded in the parentage of her right as a person descended from people who lived and owned land in the community. Thus it is her right to remain there. This for her is obvious; it is commonsense; and it is what she leaves us with, along with the dissent that greets her claim to this right within the community: "I am third generation, I am white, and I have no right."

. . . The following utterances will touch upon, in different ways, alternative conceptions of political membership in Kahnawà:ke and the larger body of the Mohawk nation (spread out across six different reserves in Ontario, Quebec, upstate New York, and urban areas). Consider now these propositions and how they shift and change as we move through different locales, from the reserve to the city.

## Clearing 1

When interviewed in *NOW* magazine, an alternative weekly in Toronto Ontario, Ida Goodleaf, a Kahnawà:ke Mohawk, offered her thoughts on the blood-quantum debate on the reserve. At the time of her interview in 1994, the debate over membership requirements in the community was in "full swing." The blood-quantum requirement of 50 percent was on the books, but was not ratified by the federal government. Consternation and conflict abounded within the community. The local and outside media sought to document and discuss the "racial" requirements for membership in the community and its implications. In response to her interviewer's questions, Ida Goodleaf said, perhaps defensively, "People have got to understand that this little postage stamp [the reserve]—I've got to fight for it. . . . I only want to keep my rights and what rightfully belongs to us, and anybody that is 50-percent Indian. If we had let that go [the land, the membership requirement], we would have already lost our rights" (quoted in Sero, 1994: 15).

This discourse is from the reserve. It clearly pronounces the reserve to be in a diminished state—"this little postage stamp"—and a site of protection, of a place that must, in her mind (and the minds of others), be protected against encroachment by those who do not have sufficient blood quantum. . . . The conditions of not belonging are determined by a degree of blood that is to approximate lineage and can be discerned by people in Kahnawà:ke. Blood quantum has always been a way of talking about lineage—descent from people who themselves were imagined to have 100 percent Mohawk blood, who were on the band list, and could be reckoned by others as Indians who were from and of that place. The rights that this woman speaks of would perhaps approximate collective rights, rights that belong to a group larger than herself, contrary to the model mapped out by the geographic and rights-based flux of the previous interlocutor who does not seem to belong anywhere, and yet has individual rights to property.

## Perception of Women's Roles

In 2002 I interviewed the Kahnawà:ke Mohawk who helped to draft the first blood-quantum requirement rules for the community. We were in Montreal, and when our meal had wound down I asked him, "What do you think of blood quantum? What is the legacy of C-31 in Kahnawà:ke? What about the role of our women in deciding membership?" He told me, "Look, I am 'hardline' on this issue, I believe that blood is part of identity. But I also believe that women are part of that too, they should be the decision makers; that is the way it was before white people got here, and that is the way it should be. Women should be in charge— they know what is going on in the community; the men have no idea—they are away all the time."

One sees how gendered even the exclusionary discourse can be, how tied it can be to ideas about "traditional" and actionable theories on gender (women simply are in charge) and the contemporary experience of that role of women in lives lived in the Longhouse structure of the past and transposed onto the life of the reserve today. "Men are away all the time" is a reference to the labour of ironwork, done almost exclusively by men, for the past century. It takes them down to New York City, almost always across the border to the United States. The conundrum, then, of gendered exclusion based on blood quantum is not addressed; there is no recognition that the descendants of women, and those women themselves who the Indian Act made white in the eyes of the state, are afflicted by exclusion. This man maintains a commitment to blood as the basis of recognition and rights, with shades of the more collectivist and territorially protectionist model of rights instanced by Ida Goodleaf in her *NOW* interview.

## The Forest

Eventually my research took me "away" from the reserve, the surrounding cities, and the suburbs, down to the "forest," to the place of men (it seems), to New York City. I found myself leaning against a bar in Greenwich Village, talking to the ironworkers who had just finished up a day of bolting and welding on the new student services building at New York University on West Fourth and La Guardia. I was interviewing a Mohawk man from Ahkwesáhsne.

"Hey, L, tell me, what is the ideal form of membership for us? What do you think makes someone a member of the community?"

He looks at me squarely in the eye, and doesn't answer. Instead he says, "Well, can I ask *you* something?"

"Sure . . . "

"When you look in the mirror, what do you see?"

"When I look in the mirror, what do I see?"

I repeat this out loud. The question hangs awkwardly and stubbornly between us. The silence between us is louder than the song by Kate Bush and Peter Gabriel that fills the bar. He pushes me,

"I asked you, Audra, when you look in the mirror, what do you see?"

My stupefied silence is audible, and somewhat embarrassing even now, when I replay it on my minidisc recorder. I finally answer him, I say,

"I see a nice person, L."

"Well, that is who we are, then—that is the answer to the question."

These utterances and narratives gathered and produced during fieldwork testify to the shifting content and positioning on the question of membership and citizenship *within* the political membership. Here we have different notions of rights, and what rights *should* be like, as well as the gendered valences of their form, their role, and the implications of this to contemporary territory.

The particular history of Indian women and territory in Canada factors into this analysis of territory and citizenship as the central subject of historical and legal exclusion, a subject whose (dangerous) Indigeneity was legally eliminated upon marriage to a non-Indian man. When she left her moral and "racial" community, she joined "civilization" through heterosexual practice. "Civilization" and citizenship (and geographic banishment from her family) was then achieved through the legal union with a non-Indian man. This completely counters Iroquois perceptions of gender roles (and thus a woman's access to institutional power) within communities where women are the carriers of the names, the owners of the land, the ones who appoint chiefs. These narratives pivot through the different ways in which these roles and responsibilities punctuate territory and how they mark it, but also how "rights" are subject to ongoing deliberation and debate.

The final narrative, a conversation I had with an ironworker in a bar, flips it all back into my face—gender roles, legal status, informal status—as he pushes me to define myself. I am struck now at how completely indifferent I was to gender and to responsibility, and defined myself in completely attributional terms that are not part of official discourse. "I see a smart person," "I see a funny person," "I see a person who is ethically challenged by these policies that are unfair." These transcendent qualities such as "nice" and "funny," when intertwined with a just genealogical configuration and authority to act on that configuration, may be the things that matter the most to the project of moving away from the choking grip that settler colonialism has on Indigenous governance and, consequently, membership and citizenship.

Yet there is no place in the formal political discussion for qualities; roles, history, and tradition are the terms of appeal. And it is no wonder; those were the very things that the Indian Act and its gendered imposition upon communities sought to change. During the course of my research, I attended as many community meetings on membership as I could. During one of these meetings, I witnessed a Kahnawà:ke woman stand up and read a prepared statement to the councillors, who are sometimes known as "elected chiefs." Here I paraphrase her letter: "Why is it that we as Mohawk women were important, that we owned the land, gave children their clans, and now we cannot even own land or build a house in this community?" This woman's mother is Mohawk and is from the community, and her father is non-Indian. Because she is not married to her Mohawk partner, she remains a "C-31" and off the band list, in spite of having grown up in the community, having a partner in the community, and having children with that Mohawk partner. What she reminds the community of in these moments and within a Mohawk Council of Kahnawà:ke meeting—what some traditional people would say is an authoritative space of Canada and of colonialism—is that "as women we had power; why do we not still have power? Why do we, as a Mohawk community, uphold non-Mohawk ways of recognizing descent?" And, further, "Why are women such as myself, who carry the clan with them, not recognized by this official, land-granting body of this community?"[5]

. . . . Membership is a social, historical, and, in the case of this study, *narrated* process that references personal and collective pasts while making itself over, parameters and boundaries and all, in a lived present. As a social, historical, and narrated process, gender is necessarily bound up in and speaks of and from the power that accrues to the settlement of space. Although membership is made over, the stories and practices in that remaking may reinterpret and subvert the metahistories (and fictions) of the state(s) in which one finds oneself; the narratives of membership may work to build a sense of nationhood not from the signs and symbols of the state, but rather from the words and interactions of the people—words and actions that are issued in the everyday moments of exchange. . . .

## Feeling Citizenship

There is a difference between what is prescribed and what actually should be, and that is being worked out in the day-to-day life of the community. This difference between "membership" and "citizenship" was made clear to me through the course of an interview with a man in his early twenties, "C". . . . He is a lifelong resident of the community, yet the situation regarding his own membership is difficult.

Q: *Are you a citizen of Canada?*

A: *I live and work, for the most part, within the territorial boundaries that Canada has unilaterally set. For the sake of ease, when crossing the border, or in discussion or signing any forms, for the sake of simplicity, and, as I said, ease, and to get things done with rather quickly, I will say I live in Canada. I will say I live in Canada, [that] I am a Canadian citizen, for simplicity's sake,*

*That is not how I feel, and when it could be avoided I never say that. But of course when I am crossing the border and they ask where I live, or if they say "what country" I will say "Canada" just to avoid any problems. Of course anywhere else I never say that—that is not how I feel. I am a Mohawk of Kahnawà:ke, not a Canadian citizen.*

Q: *What does that mean, to be a Mohawk from Kahnawà:ke, 'cause you said, "I will do this for the sake of ease." It is more like this citizenship of convenience.*

A: *Yes, "convenience."*

Q: *You know, it is like, "OK, don't give me a hard time, I was born . . ." Well, actually they were born in our territory, but now it looks like we were born in their territory.*

A: *We will say it was theirs, to avoid problems . . .*

Q: *So there is this citizenship of convenience, and then you also said, "This is not how I feel, but this is what I have to do, just in this situation," so what then is this other thing, the "feeling citizenship," is that a feeling citizenship?*

A: *Within Kahnawà:ke?*

Q: *Yeah, the idea, "I am a Mohawk from Kahnawà:ke?" is that your other citizenship? Is that your other . . .*

A: *That is my primary citizenship; that is my main citizenship. Canadian citizenship is sort of an ancillary citizenship, which I invoke to avoid hassle. I don't consider myself "Canadian." As I said, I am a Mohawk of Kahnawà:ke, and I feel that that is where my citizenship lies. If one would like to go even further, I could say, "I am a Mohawk of Kahnawà:ke of the Confederacy," although I see myself more limited to Kahnawà:ke. . . .*

Q: *Why is that?*

A: *I see no working, legitimate Confederacy to be a part of. It [would] be different if there was a true, governing, recognized body, but there is none that I am aware of, so I limit my citizenship to "Mohawk of Kahnawà:ke," perhaps a bit further the "Mohawk nation," but no Confederacy. In my eyes it's nonexistent.*

*Q: Would you be interested in that form of citizenship if it were possible, for us?*

*A: If it were possible, yes!*

*Q: If there were those operational—you are probably thinking about institutions? If we had our clans back up? If they were . . .*

*A: Not really, but a system of nations associated together for the betterment of all Aboriginals in that group. . . .*

*Q: Iroquois?*

*A: Iroquois. That I would agree to—I feel that in a way is what we should be; it isn't agreeing to anything new and extraordinary; it is just the way it should be. . . .*

*Q: There is this "citizenship of convenience," [but] your "primary citizenship," that "feeling citizenship"—what is the content of that citizenship for you? When you say you are a Mohawk of Kahnawà:ke, what does that mean to you?*

*A: That is where I associate with most, because that is where I've grown up; that's where my feeling and loyalty lie. I have . . . what is the word I can use? I have a bond with the community; that's the life that I know; that's the society, the setup, the whole setup to the society, the way life evolves and revolves around certain institutions in the community, is what I am used to, and that's how I feel that my citizenship lies there; that is the life that I know. . . .*

. . . . In spite of the rules of the state, in spite of the governance structure that attempts to implement them (or not implement them, or find an alternative to them), there are other workings of citizenship. . . . C's is in active and attached disaffiliation from the state—"for the sake of convenience,

I am a Canadian"—yet he was unrecognized by his primary space of self-articulation—the Mohawk Nation as instantiated by a tribal or band council governance system. Even so, he maintains a sense of himself as *still* belonging, and indeed he does belong to the community, in spite of the fact that they do not *legally* recognize him. He is distanced from the settler state as well. Here he elaborates further on the bite of that exclusion, the ways in which it cuts through, in some ways, his "feeling citizenship":

*Q: Tell me what you think our ideal form of . . . Are citizenship and membership the same thing?*

*A: From my understanding, and whomever I ask, I get these gray, cloudy answers in return, so I am not quite sure. I am a citizen of Kahnawà:ke, but I am not a member of Kahnawà:ke. I am not on this mysterious list that no one seems to have any information about.[6] So although I dearly love Kahnawà:ke, there are many positions I will never be able to hold until this membership issue is cleared up, so I don't know much about it, other than, I don't think it to be fair. There are those who leave the community, as I said—we all come back to Kahnawà:ke, but there are those who leave for twenty-five years and they come back and they're a member, and they will have all these opportunities that I won't, even though I've never left. I don't think that's fair. But I think there's a distinction—one could be a citizen without being a member.*

*Q: Interesting, and that citizenship is based on. . . . Let me push you on that then—how is that different; explain it to me?*

*A: Citizenship is—as I said—you live there; you grew up there; that is the life that you know. That is who you are. Membership is more of a legislative enactment designed to keep people from obtaining the various benefits that Aboriginals can receive. So I am a citizen; I live there; that is who I am; yet, I cannot be a member because of these laws, which I feel is unfair. If I had been there my whole life, I should have the same opportunity to run for Council that anyone else can. Yet I cannot.*

Q: *Do you think that's because of public sentiment, the Indian Act, is that because of . . .*

A: *I don't know what you know, or what others know—this is an area that I can't get straight answers from; no one seems to know.*

"No one seems to know" was laced through much of his discourse on C-31 and on his own predicament. However, people do seem to *know* the different forms of recognition that are at play in the exercising of rights, and that knowledge translates in the "feeling side" of recognition. I want to return us now to the community meeting that I discussed prior to this interview in order to compare the difference between my interlocutor's critical point on the difference between "citizenship" and "membership."

At the same meeting at which the woman read her letter to the community and to Council—a community member with an especially complicated membership, but with an official membership no less—stood up and made an impassioned speech about the perils of blood quantum and its similarity, in his mind, to Nazi policies on race purity. During his narrative, a woman sitting near him said loudly to the woman sitting next to her, "He shouldn't even be here" and then repeated herself, louder. When he reached the point in the trajectory of his argument about how Mohawk identity was about clan and language, not blood, she said even louder to no one in particular, "Then speak in Indian." This discursive challenge to his authority to speak on matters of culture was testament to the unfairness of the situation presented by these different cases. What I wish to suggest is that these *living, primary, feeling citizenships* may not be institutionally recognized, but are socially and politically recognized in the everyday life of the community, and people get called out on them—there is little room or toleration for an inconsistency in one's own situation and what is considered just—hailing at that moment, that which makes it unjust: the Indian Act, for example. One who has rights that another does not because of gender inequality and then pronounces on the "best way" in spite of his or her privilege will get pushed, discursively—will get reminded. The challenge to the community

is to harden these pieces of knowledge, these critiques and these possibilities into a membership policy that may accommodate the simultaneity of these experiences, these different trans-historic discourses (and people), so that these "feeling citizenships" may then become *lived* citizenships for *all*.

These feeling citizenships are narratively constructed, hinge upon sociality, and are tied in ways to the simultaneous topography of colonialism *and* Iroquoia—where certain women reside outside the boundaries of the community because they have to, and others remain in; where the forces of social, primary, "feeling" citizenships may work to enfold all into a narrative frame of collective experience. The narratives that connect these people deal heavily in the currency of "who we are, of who they are, of what rights we should have, of what we shall be in the future." They are a relentless process and practice, as Mohawks come up against the state and against each other, as they enfold each other into ambits of critique, refusal, care, and ambivalence in spite of forces that would have them completely banished.

I wish to argue here that the case of political membership is one that narrates "who we are" while archiving the living legacy of colonialism through recitation and reminder. These narratives are more, however, than colonial recitations of exclusion; they embed *desire* in ways that speak between the gulfs of the past and the present, whether this might be, as we have seen, for traditional modes of governance within the nation-state of Canada or the Mohawk nation (itself a member nation in the Iroquois Confederacy), for a limited form of self-government within the boundaries of the community, or for an abstraction such as justice. No matter what the final object of that desire may be, the narratives of citizenship in this study are laden with desires that want in some ways to affect the differentials of power that underwrite notions of nationhood and citizenship away from the politics of recognition and into other unfolding, undetermined possibilities. This desire is made from the intimacy, the knowledge, and the messiness of everyday life, and from the bonds of affection and disaffection that tie people into communities and communities into nations, even if they are unrecognizable or unrecognized.

# Notes

1.  A "traditional woman" would be defined as someone who self-consciously practices "tradition," and rejects the authority of the settler nation-state to define her or accord her rights. She does not vote in federal or provincial elections, she does not pay taxes, she uses a "red card" (with her clan, not her band number) to cross the US–Canadian border, she may refuse to use a provincially issued Medicare card to obtain health care. "Traditional" would entail a very adamant stance in terms of sovereignty, which is why much of the Iroquoianist literature on "culture" can exasperate contemporary ethnographers and ethnographic understandings of sovereignty. In 1997, way before I started formal fieldwork, I witnessed a "traditional" man refuse medical attention in a hospital in Chateauguay (the municipal suburb next the reserve) because he did not recognize the Province of Quebec or Canada.

2.  One man told me that his vision of community membership in Kahnawà:ke was predicated on recognition within the Longhouse; however, he had no problem personally with identifying as a Canadian, nor with concealing that he was Indian (as his mother had instructed) from kids that he played with in the Maritimes because they might beat him up if they knew. His willingness to "pass" as white in his youth was tied to fears surrounding the presence of the Ku Klux Klan and their violent attacks against visible minorities.

3.  I have been told this, and women I interviewed told me that they also were told this.

4.  People in Kahnawà:ke refer to the reserve community as "town."

5.  A good part of this meeting was devoted to land requests from community members who have to go before the community and Council to request land. They have to put themselves on the agenda, attend three meetings, and answer questions from people in attendance, if asked.

6.  He is referring to the locally controlled "band list."

# Reference

Sero, Peter. "Bloodlines Cross Mohawk Country," *Now* (6–12 October): 14–20.

# PART SEVEN

❖

# Additional Readings

Alfred, Taiaiake. *Wasáse: Indigenous Pathways of Action and Freedom.* Toronto: Broadview Press, 2005.

———. *Peace, Power, Righteousness: An Indigenous Manifesto.* Don Mills, ON: Oxford University Press, 1999.

Cobb, Daniel M. *Say We Are Nations: Documents of Politics and Protest in Indigenous America since 1887.* Chapel Hill, NC: University of North Carolina Press, 2015.

Dhillon, Jaskiran. *Prairie Rising: Indigenous Youth, Decolonization, and the Politics of Intervention.* Toronto: University of Toronto Press, 2017.

Gehl, Lynn. *The Truth That Wampum Tells: My Debwewin on the Algonquin Land Claims Process.* Halifax & Winnipeg: Fernwood Publishing, 2014.

Lawrence, Bonita. *Fractured Homeland: Federal Recognition and Algonquin Identity in Ontario.* Vancouver: University of British Columbia Press, 2012.

Palmater, Pamela D. *Indigenous Nationhood: Empowering Grassroots Citizens.* Halifax & Winnipeg: Fernwood Publishing, 2015.

———. *Beyond Blood: Rethinking Indigenous Identity.* Saskatoon: Purich Publishing, 2011.

Simpson, Audra. *Mohawk Interruptus: Political Life across the Borders of Settler States.* Durham: Duke University Press, 2014.

Sunseri, Lina. *Being Again of One Mind: Oneida Women and the Struggle for Decolonization.* Vancouver: University of British Columbia Press, 2011.

## Relevant Websites

### Defenders of the Land

http://www.defendersoftheland.org/

*The Defenders of the Land describe themselves as "a network of Indigenous communities and activists in land struggle across Canada, including Elders and youth, women and men." According to their website, the organization "was founded at a historic meeting in Winnipeg from November 12–14, 2008. Defenders is the only organization of its kind in the territory known as Canada—Indigenous-led, free of government or corporate funding, and dedicated to building a fundamental movement for Indigenous rights."*

### IGOV Indigenous Speaker Series. Dr. Audra Simpson talks on Mohawk Interruptus

https://www.youtube.com/watch?v=FWzXHqGfH3U

*Dr. Audra Simpson delivers a lecture at the IGOV on alternative discourses of Mohawk citizenship.*

### Indigenous Nationhood

http://www.indigenousnationhood.com

*According to their website, the Indigenous Nationhood is "dedicated to information about Indigenous peoples, communities, and Nations in Canada . . . meant to be a resource for everyone interested in the issues affecting Indigenous peoples in Canada."*

## Films

*Fractured Land.* Dir. Fiona Rayher and Damien Gillis. Crown-source funding, 2015.

*Kanehsatake: 270 Years of Resistance.* Dir. Alanis Obomsawin. National Film Board of Canada, 1993.

*Haida Gwaii: On the Edge of the World.* Dir. Charles Wilkinson. Shore Films Inc., 2015.

*Trick or Treaty.* Dir. Alanis Obomsawin. National Film Board of Canada, 2014.

## Key Terms

Self-government policy
Comprehensive claims policy
Status and non-status Indians
Historic/modern treaties

Politics of recognition
Nationhood/citizenship/membership
Feeling citizenship
Blood quantum

## Discussion Questions

1. What are the differences between nationhood, citizenship, and membership? What does Simpson mean by "feeling citizenship"? And, how does this "feeling citizenship" relate to the other three terms?

2. How has a blood-quantum criterion on membership to an Indigenous nation resulted in a gendered exclusion? How does such exclusion contrast to matrilineal/matrilocal traditional Indigenous governances?

3. Discuss how negotiations relating to the inherent right to self-government have not served very well the interests and goals of Indigenous Nations in Canada. What would be a better strategy for Indigenous peoples to undertake?

4. By referring to Glen Coulthard, what does Lawrence mean by the term "politics of recognition"? Why are both Coulthard and Lawrence critical of a politics of recognition? What do they propose as a better alternative?

## Activities

Watch the film *Sewatokwa'tsher'at: The Dish with One Spoon* (2008), directed by Dawn Martin-Hill. Discuss the notions of nation and nationalism as presented in the film: what do many white residents in Caledonia imagine Canadian nationalism to be? What kinds of Canadian national narratives inform these white residents' actions? How do you account for the discrepancy between representations of Six Nations' actions on the one hand as peaceful resistance against colonialism, and on the other hand, as terrorist? What role does race play in this discrepancy? How does the film show the connections between colonial concepts of race, entitlement, and land?

Watch the film *Trick or Treaty* (2014), directed by Alanis Obomsawin. Discuss how the development of modern treaties shown in the film highlight some of the arguments presented by Lawrence's reading.

# PART EIGHT

❖

# Decolonizing Indigenous Education

## Editor Introduction

On 11 June 2008, the Prime Minister of Canada and three other political leaders stood in the House of Commons and offered a public apology to former students of Indian residential schools. The nation watched and listened as the leaders spoke of religious orders that ran these institutions, the brutality that defined them, and, indeed, Canada itself who funded them. Surrounded by media and religious officials, Indigenous political leaders took turns responding to the apology, each of them recounting its impact on our families and nations. The event itself marked a turning point in Canadian history, one that cannot go unnoticed in the history of racism, education, and colonial reparations.

In Canada, the history of education is rooted in missionary schooling. Early schools were aimed at making all Canadians productive members of an emerging capitalist economy. For Indigenous peoples, this was a particularly violent and disruptive process, involving at times their forcible removal from homes and communities. Pedagogically, our ancestors were subjected to instruction premised on colonial superiority, in turn marking them inferior along with their knowledge and cultures. The history of racism and education is unmistakably linked and inseparable for Indigenous peoples. Ideologies of racism continue, furthermore, to shape modern educational contexts and structure a devastating series of outcomes.

A public apology does not, in itself, remedy years of colonial displacement, nor can it undo a century of cognitive, pedagogical, and linguistic supremacy that continues to shape the experience of schooling for us as nations. The modern face of racism no longer rests at the hands of Euro-Christian orders charged with the responsibility of "civilizing" Indian children. Instead, racism exists each time an Indigenous child is taught a history that neither describes nor reflects her experience as an Indigenous person; or conversely, is denied a vocabulary with which to describe and challenge histories of colonization that continue to shape his everyday life. It is precisely these kinds of practices that contribute to Indigenous peoples being pushed out of institutions of formal learning.

Despite ameliorative efforts, the systemic barriers facing Indigenous peoples in educational contexts appear endemic to Canadian society. The failure to acknowledge and understand these matters, structurally speaking, including the complexity of challenges that limit improvements to education and pedagogical change needs to be taken seriously. Indeed, a stage has been set for educational reform in Canada following recommendations made by the Truth and Reconciliation Commission in its final report released in June 2015. The

Commission issued 94 items in what it referred to as a "call to action," including recommendations to revitalize education by "building student capacity for intercultural understanding, empathy, and mutual respect" (2015: 331).

Calls to invigorate education with a focus on Settler–Indigenous relationships building and rejuvenation cannot be underestimated. Indeed, the idea echoes prior calls by the Association of Canadian Deans of Education who called for attention to "Non-Indigenous Learners and Indigeneity" (2010: 7) where educational reform is concerned, granting it precisely the same and equivalent status as "Culturally Responsive Pedagogies" (ibid., 6) and "Affirming and Revitalizing Indigenous Languages" (ibid., 7). The message to educators was clear in both 2010 and 2015: public education about the history of residential schools in Canada is necessarily based on pedagogical and programmatic efforts aimed at Settler decolonization and colonial reparations.

Given calls by both TRC and the ACDE that all Canadians take responsibility for colonial reparations, we explore in this section the role of public education in reconciling, and more importantly, disrupting colonial relations of power. We do not ask how non-Indigenous peoples—including educators—might work to acquire cultural competence or come to better understand Indigenous peoples customs, cultures, or languages. Rather, we are concerned with educational change and reform and indeed with critical and anticolonial perspectives that forgo a culturalist line. We ask in particular how non-Indigenous peoples might work to expose the violence engendered in privileged ways of knowing, including the advantages that accrue to individuals by virtue of race, Settler colonialism, gender, and social/economic capital.

As Cree/Métis scholar Verna St Denis outlines, culturally relevant education is only a partial solution to educational disparities and dropout rates, inadequate on its own for explaining or redressing the status quo of racism and structural inequality. She questions how the concept of culture itself—especially in educational anthropology—has come to both define and provide a solution to educational problems. The effect has been to ignore the impact of colonization in favour of celebrating—and working to revitalize—as much culture as possible. But there is reason to be skeptical of culture lending itself to any real or transformative change. As she suggests, a decolonizing education must be centered on cultural revitalization as well as antiracist and anticolonial pedagogy.

Martin Cannon is concerned with scholarly, activist, theoretical, and research-based frameworks that are centred on the creation, maintenance, and rejuvenation of Settler–Indigenous relationships building and learning. He asks how it is possible to engage privileged learners, especially white Settler, migrant, and migrant Indigenous populations to think about racism and colonial reparations. He asks how teacher education programs might be invigorated at this critical moment in time so that all Canadians are better able to consider, name, know about, and challenge an investment in colonial dominance and complicity. As Cannon suggests, there is an opportunity to transform teacher education so that all Canadians—teachers, and the children they teach in schools—come to realize and think more about Settler–Indigenous relations and alliances.

# CHAPTER 15

# Rethinking Culture Theory in Aboriginal Education

*Verna St Denis*

Will teaching Native culture remedy the many wounds of oppression? (Hermes, 2005: 23)

## Introduction

. . . When racialized conflict between Aboriginal and white Canadians erupts in a way that makes it clear that collective action is required, more often than not, what is recommended is not anti-racism education but cross-cultural awareness or race-relations training for the primarily "white" service providers, including police officers, social workers, and teachers. Usually the recommended cross-cultural awareness or race-relations training does not include a critical race theory analysis that might explore "how a regime of white supremacy and its subordination of people of color have been created and maintained" (Ladson-Billings, 1999: 14). Rather than acknowledging the need for a critical examination of how and why race matters in our society, it is often suggested that it is Aboriginal people and their culture that must be explained to and understood by those in position of racial dominance. A recent example is the Stonechild Inquiry that recommends race-relations training that will include "information about Aboriginal culture, history, societal and family structures" (Wright, 2004: 213).

In Cynthia Levine-Rasky, ed., *Canadian Perspectives on the Sociology of Education* (Toronto: Oxford University Press, 2009), 163–82. © Oxford University Press Canada 2009. Reprinted by permission of the publisher.

This chapter explores how the culture concept and the discipline of anthropology came to occupy such an important role in the conceptualizing and theorizing in the lives of Aboriginal people and especially in Aboriginal education. This knowledge is important because of the effects that the culture concept and discipline has had on the capacity for defining and suggesting solutions to Aboriginal educational problems. For example, in both explaining and seeking solutions to low achievement and high dropout rates for Aboriginal students, the call is usually made for "culturally relevant" education rather than the need for a critical race and class analysis. This chapter will suggest that a cultural framework of analysis is partial and inadequate on its own for explaining Aboriginal educational failures and that culturally based solutions can inadvertently contribute to further problems.

Current concepts of Aboriginal education and the sub-discipline of educational anthropology evolved during the same time period and are as related as are anthropologists and Indians in North America. As has been observed, the discipline of anthropology was "invented across the 'red/white' color line" (Michaelson, 1999: xvi). Both Aboriginal and American-Indian educators have acknowledged the predominance of the culture concept and anthropology in Aboriginal and American-Indian education. In a review of literature on American-Indian education, Deyhle and Swisher (1997: 117) observed that, "over the past 30 years, we found that the largest body of research was grounded in educational anthropology and sociology." Furthermore they state that this research "used the concept of culture as a framework for the analysis of schooling and the behaviour of Indian students, parents and their communities" (ibid.).

In the 1960s much of the educational anthropology literature suggested that racialized minority children failed in school because their cultural beliefs and practices predisposed them to failure, and they were, therefore, described as being "culturally deprived" or even "deviant" (McDermott, 1997). In the 1970s some adjustments were made to the cultural framework for analyzing educational failure, suggesting that it was not so much that some children were culturally deprived or culturally disadvantaged but that their way of life was merely "culturally different"—not better or worse than that valued by schools, but definitely different (McDermott, 1997). The subsequent educational interventions suggested that cultural differences needed to be celebrated rather than eradicated. This shift in emphasis was meant to advantage Aboriginal and American-Indian children whose culture would now be celebrated and observed through research that would focus on learning styles and acculturation processes.

This shift towards prescribing the celebration of cultural difference as a means to bring about educational equality provided a foundation for the growing focus on the importance and necessity of cultural and language revitalization for Aboriginal students. American-Indian educators and researchers Tippeconnic and Swisher note that, "beginning in the 1960s and into the 70s a revival of 'Indianness' in the classroom was now encouraged" (1992: 75). In a Canadian review of policy on Aboriginal education, Abele, Dittburner, and Graham also explain that between 1967 and 1982 Aboriginal education was increasingly regarded as a "means for the revitalization of Indian cultures and economies" (2000: 8).

As part of this cultural revitalization, the provision of culturally relevant education assumed great importance for improving the educational success of Aboriginal students, and the health and well-being of Aboriginal communities in general. This shift to regarding education as the means to revitalize Aboriginal culture and language is often attributed to processes of decolonization and, in Canada, to the policy outlined in "Indian Control of Indian Education" (National Indian Brotherhood, 1972). The idea that culture and language could be revitalized, and that Aboriginal people needed a "positive" cultural identity as a prerequisite to success in education and in life more generally, can also be understood to be derivative of anthropological concepts and theorizing.

In writing this chapter, I have been informed by my own experiences and professional knowledge as an Aboriginal teacher and educator. By the time I arrived on campus as a university student in the late 1970s, the move towards decolonizing education by Aboriginal people in Canada was already moving forward with the adoption of the policy position outlined in "Indian Control of Indian Education" (National Indian Brotherhood, 1972). With the recognition of this policy came the establishment of Indian cultural centres, Indian Teacher Education programs, cultural survival schools, and Indian and Native Studies departments across the country (Posluns, 2007). It was a very exciting time for us Aboriginal students since we could now pursue specialized studies in Aboriginal education and Native Studies.

In 1978 I enrolled in the Indian Teacher Education Program at the University of Saskatchewan. I was going to become an "Indian" teacher. I was younger than most students in the program at that time, and, although both my parents had spoken Cree, I myself was not fluent in Cree. Indian Teacher Education programs were at the forefront in calling for the cultural and language revitalization of Indian cultures, and Indian teachers were to play a significant role in this revitalization. In this educational context I sensed I was in trouble—I was well aware that my lack of fluency in my indigenous language placed me at a disadvantage. The analysis offered here in this chapter is one attempt to make sense of this "trouble."

I didn't realize back then the role that anthropological concepts and theory had in the formulations of Aboriginal education through notions like "cultural discontinuity," "cultural relevance," "cultural difference," and "acculturation/enculturation."

As a student and teacher of Aboriginal education and Native Studies, I never imagined that studying anthropology and its concepts would be useful in unravelling some of the ways in which we interpret the problems and solutions we have named and pursued in Aboriginal education.

Although I have now been involved in Aboriginal education for almost three decades, it is only in the past decade that I realized I needed to know more about anthropology. I had avoided learning about anthropology partly because anthropology and history were two mainstream disciplines that Native Studies and Aboriginal education had rallied against in the 1970s and 1980s. I regarded the discipline of anthropology, as some in the late 1960s referred to it, as the "child of colonialism" (Cough, in Caulfield 1969: 182) and therefore not worthy of attention. It was Rosaldo's *Culture and Truth: The Remaking of Social Analysis* (1989) that introduced me to a critique of classic notions in anthropology. Reading this book marked the beginning of my efforts to develop an understanding of how anthropologically informed social analysis has impacted the development of Aboriginal education. This chapter offers an analysis of how those of us in Aboriginal education have been historically and discursively constituted within and by anthropological theory and research.

I began to understand that the social and cultural analysis prevalent when I first enrolled in the Indian Teacher Education Program was informed not only by "Indian philosophy and worldview" but also by the social and cultural analysis practised by American anthropologists who combined psychology and anthropology through their focus on culture and personality and acculturation studies. The culture and personality movement and acculturation studies inspired psychologists and anthropologists who were interested in cross-cultural education, and who contributed to the development of educational anthropology. In turn, the social and cultural analysis offered by scholars of educational anthropology influenced the conceptualizing of Aboriginal/Indian education. As someone who

has been involved in Aboriginal/Indian education for almost 30 years, I find there is still much to learn about this legacy of anthropological ideas, concepts, problems, and solutions that helped to shape Indian education.

# European Philosophical and Intellectual Legacies

> Culture is . . . itself the illness to which it proposes a cure. (Eagleton, 2000: 31)

. . . Efforts to develop a history of the culture concept invariably requires attempts to make sense of the relationships between the varied usages of the concepts of "culture" and "civilization," and "Romanticism" and "Primitivism" within European thought and social practice. . . .

Both Romanticism and Primitivism have influenced our understanding of "culture" and "civilization" through articulations of self and Other. Scholarly writing about the history of the development of modern notions of culture is often situated within histories of Romanticism, if not Primitivism. Although Romanticism and Primitivism are two different social and intellectual developments, there is some overlap and similarities between these two schools of thought. And although neither Romanticism nor Primitivism has been consistently or constantly invoked in European imagination and fantasies of the Other, one of their recurring and enduring emphases is a valorization of the Other, as a way to critique and register dissatisfaction with European society (Stocking, 1986). . . .

Herder conceptualized "culture" as the "uniquely distinct" way of life, values, and beliefs of a people; culture was what distinguished one people from another (1774: 44f.). . . .

Herder's conceptualization of "culture" has lent itself to a belief in "cultural essentialism" and "cultural determinism" that is elaborated upon in Boasian anthropology. . . . It suggests an essential culture that is able to exist in the realm of the spiritual.

Herder also signalled language as important to the delineation of a nation, because within language dwells a people's "entire world of tradition, history, religion, principles of existence; its whole heart and soul" (Herder, in Malik, 1996: 78–9). This idea that the culture of a people is invoked through its language and stories is further developed in the efforts made in Aboriginal education to participate in cultural and language revitalization, as it was also an idea brewing within anthropological studies of culture and personality and acculturation.

Another of Herder's beliefs was in the "incommensurability of the values of different cultures and societies" (Malik, 1996: 78). . . .

This idea of the incommensurability of different cultures would eventually propel and motivate anthropology's interest in what makes people different. The idea would lend itself not only to an exaggeration of human difference but also a negative evaluation of these differences, making possible notions like folks who suffer, not from colonial oppression but, from "cultural incongruence," and "cultural discontinuity," both of which were seen as tangible threats to cultural self-preservation despite whatever cultural exchanges and accommodations have been made by cultural Others (Biolsi, 1997).

The idea of the "incommensurability" of cultures led anthropologists in search of "an Indian culture incommensurably alien from [their own]" (Biolsi, 1997: 140)—in other words, the search for the "real" Indian (Biolsi, 1997; Waldram, 2004). The belief in twentieth-century social analysis about the incommensurability of different cultures encourages a trivializing of the impact of colonial oppression by attributing the effects and the conditions of oppression to this very factor of incommensurability. In the example of Aboriginal people, effects of oppression are cast as "value conflicts" between white and Indian cultures, suggesting that inequality is inevitable, and merely an effect of different orientations to work, education, and family. When the affects of oppression are attributed to a "conflict of values" it is easy to see how the remedy then becomes cross-cultural awareness training or a "race"-relations program that does not disrupt the status quo of structural inequality while seemingly responding.

## Understanding American Anthropological Legacies

. . . Through concepts like "enculturation," this idea of a culture as a conditioning process became a central concept in educational anthropology, and suggested research into the "enculturation processes" of culturally different students, families, and communities. In addition, this idea that culture is a conditioning process implied that it is not people who create culture through the conditions of their everyday lives, but rather "culture" that creates people. It is as if culture is an object with its own agency divorced from people. This objectification of culture also suggests that culture is something to be "lost" and "found." It is as if people are no longer agents; culture happens to them. A notion like "cultural determinism" then becomes possible. Cultural determinism has been used to justify racism; hence the notion of "cultural racism" (Hall, 1982; Gilroy, 1990) that becomes another way to justify discrimination. . . .

This idea of culture as an entity outside of people provides a foundation for the belief in the potential for "cultural revitalization" and the very idea that culture can be retrieved. While the idea that culture resides deep inside one's "core" may be reassuring in the early stages of an engagement with cultural revitalization, when that "traditional" culture fails to appear or reveal itself, it can be very troubling. This failure of culture to appear becomes a very different kind of problem. It is a problem long familiar to those anthropologists who have been keenly interested in "authentic" and "real" Indians or the "primitive," and for whom evidence of "cultural change" would suggest otherwise, namely that culture is mutable.

Many have critiqued anthropologists' interest and fetishization of the most exotic and primitive Other (e.g., Biolsi, 1997; Caulfield, 1969; Deloria, 1969; Rosaldo, 1989). The implications for regarding cultural change as a threat and as a negative process continue to have repercussions for "Others" such as Aboriginal people. . . .

Not only was cultural change regarded as dangerous for the "primitive" Other, but "rapid" cultural change was regarded as even more detrimental. Culture was something primitive people "had," and it was understood that "primitive" people needed culture more than "civilized" people did. . . .

Educational anthropology would embrace the above ideas and to a large degree so would Aboriginal education. This conceptualization has resulted in that claim that it is "cultural discontinuity" between the school and the Aboriginal family and community and the inability of Aboriginal students to make adequate cultural adjustments that causes high levels of school failure for Aboriginal students despite evidence that racism and classism are equally, if not more compelling reasons for these levels of school failure (Ledlow, 1992). Culturally relevant education, rather than anti-oppressive education, has become a common-sense solution. As well, the idea that "primitives" learn less by instruction than by imitation led to research focusing on understanding different "learning styles" and with the effect of creating a new set of stereotypes about the nature of Aboriginal learning styles. . . .

This method of anthropological social analysis, exemplified by Benedict and Mead, compared and contrasted cultures as a whole and paved the way for cross-cultural comparisons that continue to remain popular in educational research. In particular, this method has been used as a way of explaining the low academic achievement of Aboriginal students. . . .

Acculturation studies . . . promoted ideas that the retention of "indigenous belief systems" was essential for Indians to adequately adjust to rapid social change (Waldram, 2004). Anthropologists were often not interested in documenting the creative and successful ways in which Indians were making cultural adaptations to their continually changing environments (Deloria, 1969). This was especially the case if anthropologists were particularly interested in finding the most

"incommensurable" and exotic Indian (Biolsi, 1997). Further advancing the belief that culture was a "cure," studies of acculturation, such as those conducted among the Hopi, claimed that "Personality disorders and social breakdown characterize Hopi communities that have lost their values and their ceremonies" (Thompson, 1946: 210, in Waldram, 2004: 37). This idea that Indian culture is "lost" and that Indians have lost their culture is a deceptively benign but very common way to refer to the effects of colonial and racial oppression on Aboriginal people. In acculturation studies, suggesting that "maintaining essential, internal cultural integrity" (Thompson, 1950, in Waldram, 2004: 35) is necessary for exploited and colonized people, has become a popular and common way to blame the victim of oppression.

The problem of inequality is now attributed to the Indian who does not have "cultural integrity" rather than the social, economic, and political context that does not recognize the human rights of Aboriginal people. Acculturation, and Culture and Personality studies, contributed to reducing the effects of colonial and racial oppression to a problem of an identity crisis. Restoring the Indian has become the imperative rather than ensuring social and political justice. The anthropological interest in a timeless and unchanging cultural Indian demeans Aboriginal and American-Indian Peoples who have had to constantly adjust to and live with the context of ongoing and normalized racism. . . . The idea that cultural adaptation is regarded as "broken" relegates Indians as interesting to the degree that they can serve as windows to the past, ignoring the effects of colonization by aiming to celebrate and recoup as much "traditional" culture as possible.

As many have stated, Boas and his many students "never showed any real interest in studying the situation of conquest and exploitation" (Caulfield, 1969: 184, italics in original). This failure by the anthropology of that time to explore the consequences and situation of exploitation continued to have repercussions for at least the early years in the development of Aboriginal education by and for Aboriginal people rather than examining the situation of conquest and exploitation, anthropologists like Benedict were more interested in bringing attention to "the desperate urgency of doing anthropological field work before the last precious and irretrievable memories of traditional American Indian cultures were carried to the grave" (Mead, 197: 3). . . . Here we have an anthropology that cared more about "Indian culture" than the people of that culture, yet another example of the belief in a culture as something outside and existing independently of its people.

This background knowledge of anthropology provides a basis to better understand the published conference proceedings of the first conference of educational anthropology. That conference helped initiate the field of Educational Anthropology, which has had its own set of implications for Aboriginal education.

## The Legacy of Educational Anthropology

. . . In 1954, the anthropologist George Spindler hosted a conference that brought together several educators and anthropologists; among them were anthropologists Margaret Mead, Alfred Kroeber, and Cora DuBois. Several papers were presented, along with remarks by formal discussants; conference proceedings were published in the book *Education and Anthropology* (Spindler, 1955a) and later republished in the edited collection, *Education and Culture: Anthropological Approaches* (Spindler, 1963). . . .

Some of the many concepts utilized in the papers and the discussions that followed included ones familiar to those who work in the area of Aboriginal education, including: cultural transmission; enculturation; acculturation; cultural awareness; bicultural, monocultural, and intercultural learners; cultural gap; and cultural discontinuity.

Conference participants acknowledged that the discipline of psychology made it possible to combine educational and anthropological interests (Frank, 1955). Participants agreed that

exploring cultural processes of socialization was one way in which anthropology could contribute to education. Socialization processes were understood to vary from culture to culture, and it was those "differences" that could form the basis of investigation in developing educational anthropology. Building on acculturation and personality studies in anthropology, educational anthropology would also explore processes of cultural change, cultural adaptation, and cultural continuity. Knowledge of socialization practices and processes could, in turn, help educators and schools assist culturally different students adjust to change. . . .

This idea that schools and education are the site for cultural continuity and cultural transmission has become accepted wisdom in Aboriginal education (see, e.g., Royal Commission on Aboriginal Peoples, 1996). Through the conceptual framework of educational anthropology, schools are increasingly instructed to become a place where "culturally relevant" education should occur so as to ensure cultural continuity and cultural transmission for the Aboriginal child. But in light of massive cultural change in regards to how Aboriginal people live, the task of providing culturally relevant education can prove to be perplexing and challenging for the well-intentioned Aboriginal teacher who asks, "what is it exactly that you want to be taught in the classroom, the parents say let's teach culture in a classroom, but they don't come out and say what they mean by culture" (Friesen and Orr, 1995: 22). In the context of ongoing cultural change, this line of questioning remains relevant, but it is also the legacy of an anthropology that was once intent on "reconstructing traditional culture" (Asad, in Stocking, 1991: 318).

By combining psychology and anthropology, the field of educational anthropology would pursue investigations that would seek to explain the impact of differences between the cultural values and beliefs of the culturally different child and the teacher. . . . It was proposed that this cultural knowledge could help teachers understand how "imitation, participation, communication, and informal methods" socialize members into one's culture, as well as how "cultural motivation incentives, values and school learning" are related (Quillen, 1955: 3).

Four decades later, this theorizing about difference has, more often than not, resulted in the production of stereotypes and classist and racist constructions of the culturally different child (Laroque, 1991; Razack, 1998). This anthropological orientation to understanding "difference" is now used to endorse the current demand that human service providers be "culturally competent" in their delivery of services. Without examining the impact of racism and classism, this requirement for cultural competency has the potential to repeat stereotypes of Aboriginal people rather than focusing on how racial dominance and poverty continue to detrimentally impact Aboriginal people (Razack, 1998; Schick and St Denis, 2005). . . .

There is no single straightforward trajectory to understanding how, when, and why the concept of culture, as opposed to the need for social and political justice, has come to occupy such a large role in articulating Aboriginal education. . . .

The politics of this articulation of culture as a concept associated with the Other, and the nation as a concept associated with the civilized person, has a long history, not only in anthropology but, in Western and European thinking, in general. It is not common for those in a position of racial dominance to risk relativizing their own way of life by describing it as a "culture": as Eagleton puts it, "One's own way of life is simply human; it is other people who are ethnic, idiosyncratic, culturally peculiar" (2000: 27). . . .

A review of literature reveals that teachers often have low expectations of Aboriginal and American-Indian students (Ambler, 1997; Delpit, 1995; Flail, 1993; Strong, 1998; Tirado, 2001; Wilson, 1991). Low expectations justify the lack of instruction and attention to Aboriginal students. Tirado (2001) found that teachers have a tendency to size up American-Indian students as underachievers; they don't expect the kids to do anything, so they don't teach them. Wilson found that "even before teachers knew the [Aboriginal]

students, they prejudged them. They could not have imagined that these students would ever be successful. Students were classified as unable to cope with a heavy academic load" (1991: 379). As a result, Aboriginal students are often placed disproportionately in vocational or special needs classes (Wilson, 1991). Rather than encouraging an examination of the ways in which class and racial bias impact educational processes, the legacy of the 1954 conference of anthropologists and educators has resulted in a large body of educational research primarily interested in "culture" as the explanatory concept for understanding how the culturally Other would or would not adjust to school. . . .

The idea that the cultural Other is not able to make cultural adjustments without a great deal of trauma is an idea that continues to have a negative effect on discussions of how to improve educational achievement for Aboriginal students. To a large extent these discussions tend to promote a stereotyped idea of the Aboriginal student as vulnerable and non-resilient and enables the avoidance of addressing the far more difficult questions of racism and classism in education. . . .

This idea of the Aboriginal cultural Other as unwilling and unable to adapt to changing social, economic, and political contexts is a long entrenched assumption that justifies oppression and inequality. For example, Sarah Carter (1986, 1996), a prairie Canadian historian, challenges the taken-for-granted assumption that Aboriginal people were unwilling and unable to adapt to a farming-based economy. Carter uncovers the extent to which white settlers and the Canadian government colluded to ensure that Aboriginal farmers failed at farming. The introduction of the pass and permit system prevented Aboriginal farmers from succeeding by limiting their ability to purchase farm machinery, limiting what produce they could grow, and limiting when and where they could sell their produce.

The All Hallows School in British Columbia, a boarding school attended by both Aboriginal and white girls between 1884 and 1920, described in the work of Barman (1986), provides another historical and educational example of unwarranted assumptions about Aboriginal people unwilling and unable to adapt to change. The establishment of the All Hallows School was a case in which Aboriginal parents welcomed change and the opportunity to adjust to a changing world by requesting that a school be established for their girls.

Because of inadequate financial resources, the All Hallows School could only function if white girls were allowed to attend alongside Indian girls. In the first years of the school, the Indian and white girls seemed content with their integrated schooling situation. Then a white parent protested about this integrated situation, so the effort was made to separate the white and Indian girls. But in his annual report, the bishop in charge of the school commented that the Indian girls were as intellectually capable as the white girls, claiming that at times the Indian girls had "the answers all respects being equal, and sometimes superior, to anything that could be expected from white children of the same age" (Barman, 1986: 117). Not only did the Indian girls achieve academically, but they also could from time to time serve as junior teachers, and their ability to learn the practices of another culture was demonstrated in two Indian girls, who alongside eight white girls passed the Royal Academy of Music exam.

These Indian girls did not seem to suffer any crisis due to the culture difference between the school and their home and community. When the Indian girls returned home for holidays and summer vacation, they often freely maintained contact with the teachers through letters. At least for one Indian girl, the only source of cultural conflict involved the dilemma of attending a potlatch even though it was "forbidden by law" (Barman, 1986: 118). In a letter to the sisters at the school, this student tried to persuade them that the potlatch is not something they should be afraid of because it is just "our way of praying" (Barman, 1986: 119).

Eventually the Indian and white girls were physically separated, although still offered equally challenging academic programs. But then the curriculum for the Indian girls shifted from a full academic program to one that included teaching them how to weave baskets. Finally, a shift in government policy lead to closing the school, a policy change justified by a larger concern that it was unwise to offer Indians an education that would allow them "to compete industrially with our people" (Minister of Indian Affairs, 1897, in Barman, 1986: 120). Throughout the proceeding decades, Aboriginal people continued to be denied the high-quality education for which First Nations treaty negotiators assumed they had signed on. The inability of an anthropology and, in turn, an educational anthropology to acknowledge the effects of "conquest and exploitation" of the cultural Other continues to reverberate.

As Biolsi (1997) explains, anthropologists such as those present at the time of that 1954 conference were typically not interested in Indians who accepted that change was inevitable. As a result, these examples of Indian farmers and the All Hallows School would not have drawn their attention. Not only were anthropologists not interested in Indians wanting to figure out how to adapt to the changing world around them, but anthropologists also typically maligned these Indians for not being "real" Indians (Biolsi, 1997; Waldram, 2004).

## Conclusion

> More powerful than their knowledge of cultural difference is their knowledge of the big picture—the context of socio-economic and cultural oppression of Native Americans. (Hermes, 2005: 21)

We started out a few decades ago in Aboriginal education believing that we could address the effects of racialization and colonization by affirming and validating the cultural traditions and heritage of Aboriginal peoples. There is increasing evidence that those efforts have limitations. As I have argued elsewhere, cultural revitalization encourages misdiagnoses of the problem (St Denis, 2004). It places far too much responsibility on the marginalized and oppressed to change yet again, and once again lets those in positions of dominance off the hook for being accountable for ongoing discrimination. It is to the advantage of the status quo to have Aboriginal people preoccupied with matters of authenticity. If cultural authenticity is the problem then we don't have to look at what is the immensely more difficult task of challenging the conscious and unconscious ways in which the ideology of white identity as superior is normalized and naturalized in our schools and nation, both in the past and in the present (Francis, 1997; Willinsky, 1998).

Instead of doing anti-racism education that explores why and how race matters, we can end up doing cross-cultural awareness training that often has the effect of encouraging the belief that the cultural difference of the Aboriginal "Other" is the problem. Offering cultural awareness workshops can also provide another opportunity for non-Aboriginals to resent and resist Aboriginal people. Offering cultural awareness education has become the mainstream thinking about proper solutions to educational and social inequality. In her research exploring the qualities of effective teachers of American Indians, Hermes, an American-Indian educator, found that "more powerful than [teachers'] knowledge of cultural difference is their knowledge of the big picture—the context of socioeconomic and cultural oppression of Native Americans" (2005: 21). We often hear that addressing racism or doing anti-racism education is too negative and that we need to focus on a more positive approach. However, that often means tinkering with the status quo. As Kaomea suggests, when schools offer benign lessons in Hawaiian arts, crafts, and values, this approach tends to erase Hawaiian suffering, hardship, and oppression. "It is time to tell more uncomfortable stories" (Kaomea, 2003: 23).

# References

Abele, F., C. Dittburner, and K.A. Graham. 2000. "Towards a Shared Understanding in the Policy Discussion about Aboriginal Education," pp. 3–24 in M.B. Castellano, L. Davis, and L. Lahache, eds, *Aboriginal Education: Fulfilling the Promise*. Vancouver and Toronto: University of British Columbia Press.

Ambler, M. 1997. "Without Racism: Indian Students Could Be Both Indian and Students," *Tribal College Journal* 8 (4): 8–11. Available at http://www.tribalcollegejournal.org/themag/backissues/spring97/spring97ee.html; accessed 8 October 2002.

Barman, J. 1986. "Separate and Unequal: Indian and White Girls at All Hallows School, 1884–1920," in J. Barman, Y. Hebert, and D. McCaskill, eds, *Indian Education in Canada*, Volume 1: The Legacy. Vancouver: University of British Columbia Press.

Biolsi, T. 1997. "The Anthropological Construction of 'Indians': Haviland Scudder Mekeel and the Search for the Primitive in Lakota Country," pp. 133–59 in Thomas Biolsi and L.J. Zimmerman, eds, *Indians and Anthropologists: Vine Deloria Jr. and the Critique of Anthropology*. Tucson: University of Arizona Press.

Carter, S. 1986. "'We Must Farm to Enable Us to Live': The Plains Cree and Agriculture to 1900," pp. 444–70 in R.B. Morrison and C.R. Wilson, eds, *Native Peoples: The Canadian Experience*. Toronto: McClelland and Stewart.

Carter, S. 1996. "First Nations Women in Prairie Canada in the Early Reserve Years, the 1870s to the 1920s: A Preliminary Inquiry," pp. 51–75 in C. Miller and P. Chuchryk, eds, *Women of the First Nations: Power, Wisdom, and Strength*. Winnipeg: University of Manitoba Press.

Caulfield, M.D. 1969. "Culture and Imperialism: Proposing a New Dialectic," pp. 182–212 in D. Hymes, ed., *Reinventing Anthropology*. New York: Pantheon Books.

Deloria, V., Jr. 1969/1988. *Custer Died for Your Sins: An Indian Manifesto*. Norman, OK: University of Oklahoma Press.

Delpit, L. 1995. *Educating Other People's Children: Cultural Conflict in the Classroom*. New York: New Press.

Deyhle, D. 1992. "Constructing Failure and Maintaining Cultural Identity: Navajo and Ute School Leavers," *Journal of American Indian Education* 31: 24–47.

Deyhle, D., and K. Swisher. 1997. "Research in American Indian and Alaska Native Education: From Assimilation to Self-determination," *Educational Review* 22: 113–94.

Eagleton, T. 2000. *The Idea of Culture*. Oxford: Blackwell Manifestos.

Francis, D. 1997. *National Dreams: Myth, Memory and Canadian History*. Vancouver: Arsenal Pulp Press.

Frank, L.K. 1955. "Preface," pp. vii–xi in G. Spindler, *Education and Anthropology*. Stanford: Stanford University Press.

Friesen, D.W., and J. Orr. 1995. "Northern Aboriginal Teachers' Voices." Unpublished manuscript, University of Regina, Saskatchewan.

Hall, J.L. 1993. "What Can We Expect from Minority Students?" *Contemporary Education* 64 (3): 180–2.

Herder, J.G. 1774/1967. *Another Philosophy of History Concerning the Development of Mankind. Translation of Auch eine Philosophie der Geschichte zur Bildung der Menschheit.* Frankfurt am Main: Suhrkamp.

Hermes, M. 2005. "Complicating Discontinuity: What about Poverty?" *Curriculum Inquiry* 35 (1): 9–26.

Kaomea, J. 2003. "Reading Erasures and Making the Familiar Strange: Defamiliarizing Methods for Research in Formerly Colonized and Historically Oppressed Communities," *Educational Researcher* 32 (2): 14–25.

Ladson-Billings, G. 1999. "Just What Is Critical Race Theory, and What's It Doing in a Nice Field Like Education?" pp. 7–30 in L. Parker, D. Deyhle, and S. Villenas, eds, *Race Is . . . Race Isn't: Critical Race Theory and Qualitative Studies in Education.* Boulder, CO: Westview Press.

Larocque, E. 1991. "Racism Runs through Canadian Society," pp. 73–6 in O. McKague, ed., *Racism in Canada.* Saskatoon: Fifth House.

Ledlow, S. 1992. "Is Cultural Discontinuity an Adequate Explanation for Dropping Out?" *Journal of American Indian Education* 31: 21–36.

McDermott, R.P. 1997. "Achieving School Failure, 1972–1997," pp. 110–35 in G. Spindler, ed., *Education and Cultural Process: Anthropological Approaches*, 3rd edn. Prospect Heights, IL: Waveland Press.

Malik, K. 1996. *The Meaning of Race: Race, History and Culture in Western Society.* New York: New York University Press.

Mead, M. 1974. Ruth Benedict: *A Humanist in Anthropology.* New York: Columbia University Press.

Michaelson, S. 1999. *The Limits of Multiculturalism: Interrogating the Origins of American Anthropology.* Minneapolis: University of Minnesota Press.

National Indian Brotherhood. 1972. "Indian Control of Indian Education." Ottawa: National Indian Brotherhood.

Posluns, M. 2007. *Speaking with Authority: The Emergence of the Vocabulary of First Nations' Self-Government.* New York: Routledge.

Quillen, J.I. 1955. "An Introduction to Anthropology and Education," pp. 1–4 in G. Spindler, *Education and Anthropology.* Stanford: Stanford University Press.

Razack, S. 1998. *Looking White People in the Eye: Race, Class and Gender in the Courtrooms and the Classrooms.* Toronto: University of Toronto Press.

Rosaldo, R. 1989. *Culture and Truth: The Remaking of Social Analysis.* Boston: Beacon Press.

Royal Commission on Aboriginal Peoples. 1996. *Report on the Royal Commission on Aboriginal Peoples.* 5 vols. Ottawa: Canada Communications Group.

Schick, C., and V. St Denis. 2005. "Troubling National Discourses in Anti-racist Curricular Planning," *Canadian Journal of Education* 28 (3): 295–317.

Spindler, G. 1955a. *Education and Anthropology.* Stanford: Stanford University Press.

———. 1955b. "Anthropology and Education: An Overview," pp. 5–22 in G. Spindler, *Education and Anthropology.* Stanford: Stanford University Press.

———. 1963. *Education and Culture: Anthropological Approaches.* New York: Holt, Rinehart and Winston.

St Denis, V. 2004. "Real Indians: Cultural Revitalization and Fundamentalism in Aboriginal Education," pp. 35–47 in C. Schick, J. Jaffe, and A. Watkinson, eds. *Contesting Fundamentalisms.* Halifax, NS: Fernwood.

Stocking, G.W., Jr. 1986. "Essays on Culture and Personality," pp. 3–12 in Stocking, ed., History of Anthropology Vol. 4. *Malinowski, Rivers, Benedict and Others: Essays on Culture and Personality.* Madison: University of Wisconsin Press.

Strong, W.C. 1998. "Low Expectations by Teachers within an Academic Context." Paper presented at the Annual Meeting of the American Educational Research Association San Diego, CA. (ERIC Document Research Service No. ED 420 62).

Tippeconnic, J.W., III, and K. Swisher. 1992. "American Indian Education," pp. 75–8 in M.C. Alkin, ed., *Encyclopedia of Education Research.* New York: MacMillan.

Tirado, M. 2001. "Left Behind: Are Public Schools Failing Indian Kids?" *American Indian Report* 17: 12–15. Available at Wilson Web. Accessed 9 October 2002.

Troulliet, M.R. 1991. "Anthropology and the Savage Slot: The Poetics and Politics of Otherness," pp. 17–44 in R.G. Fox, ed., *Recapturing Anthropology: Working in the Present.* Santa Fe, NM: School of American Press.

Waldram, J. 2004. *Revenge of the Windigo: The Construction of the Mind and Mental Health of North American Aboriginal Peoples.* Toronto: University of Toronto Press.

Willinsky, John. 1998. *Learning to Divide the World: Education at Empire's End.* Minneapolis: University of Minnesota Press.

Wilson, P. 1991. "Trauma of Sioux Indian High School Students," *Anthropology and Education Quarterly* 22: 367–83.

Wright, D.H. 2004. *Report of the Commission of Inquiry into Matters relating to the Death of Neil Stonechild.* Available at http://www.stonechildinquiry.ca/.

Zenter, H. 1973. *The Indian Identity Crisis: Inquires into the Problems and Prospects of Societal Development among Native Peoples.* Calgary: Strayer Publications.

# CHAPTER 16

# Changing the Subject in Teacher Education
## Centring Indigenous, Diasporic, and Settler Colonial Relations

*Martin J. Cannon*

---

. . .

## Introduction

[I]n Canada, it is routine to think about colonialism as having little, if anything, to do with non-Indigenous peoples. As such, it is typically Indigenous scholars, teachers, and populations who are left to explain the impact of colonization and residential schooling on our communities, and the history of oppressive legislation. As hooks observed, in analysis specific to the United States and Afro-Americans, "where [black] people are called upon to take primary responsibility for sharing experiences, ideas, and information [they are placed] once again in a service position, meeting the needs of whites" (1988: 47). While distinctions must be drawn between Indigenous peoples and ethnic/racial groups—in light of our history and sovereignty as nations (Cannon and Sunseri, 2011; Porter, 1999)—I believe hooks' message has as much currency within Indigenous contexts.

My intention is not to impart that the space we, as Indigenous peoples, have fought for in order to explain the impact of colonization on our lives is unimportant, nor that we should abandon it altogether. Instead, I propose that as long as we remain focused on racism and colonialism as an exclusively Indigenous struggle, we do very little in the way of encouraging non-Indigenous peoples to think about what it might mean to be an "ally" of Indigenous sovereignty and education. Moreover, we do little to . . . think about matters of

restitution, their own decolonization, and transforming their complicity in ongoing dispossession.

Others have raised the matter of having non-Indigenous peoples think carefully about their relationship with settler colonialism in Canada. . . . On 28 September 2010, the Honourable Justice Murray Sinclair, Chair of Canada's Truth and Reconciliation Commission (TRC), appeared before the Senate to update them on the TRC's progress since the 2008 Parliamentary apology (Government of Canada, 2010). He insisted:

> The residential schools have had such a dramatic impact upon Aboriginal people in Canada that sometimes people believe it is an Aboriginal problem. It is not an Aboriginal problem. It is a problem that all people in Canada need to think about and address. (ibid., 7–8)

It is incumbent upon us to take Justice Sinclair's assertion seriously. If the history of colonization is a problem facing all Canadians, then it is each and every Canadian who needs to acknowledge and understand how this is so. Canadians must come to know and understand the privilege of not having to know, name, or otherwise mark their own subjectivity and positionality relative to the ongoing project of settler colonialism. Indeed, I am suggesting that we need a wholesale rethinking of our departure points in educational, methodological, and activist-based contexts. We need to think of frameworks that start—not with Indigenous peoples—but with the identity-making processes, many of them racialized, that are specific to colonization and non-Indigenous Canadians.

*Cultural and Pedagogical Inquiry* 4, 2 (2013): 21–37.

What might these frameworks look like in practice? In developing possibilities, five preliminary questions come to mind, given my life as a Haudenosaunee person and my experience as a scholar:

1. Who do Canadian citizens know themselves to be, and how much of who they think they are depends on keeping racialized others, status Indians in particular, firmly in place?
2. How do we explain the need for certainty about Indigenous difference, and how much of this is tied to the dispossession of lands?
3. What are modern-day practices of difference-making, where are they located, and how do they operate in the contemporary world?
4. How do non-Indigenous peoples interact with our difference and alterity?
5. What sorts of material and symbolic work have gone into the dispossession of lands and spaces, including the urban spaces we occupy and have always occupied?

. . . Several Indigenous scholars have written about the matter of encouraging non-Indigenous peoples to contemplate settler colonialism (see Alfred, 2010; Dion, 2009; St Denis, 2009; St Denis and Schick, 2003; Unsettling Minnesota Collective, 2009). Their words bring to mind the story of a Kanienkehaka man who, when asked to recount his residential school experience for an Indian Affairs publication in 1965, responded astutely: ". . . when I was asked to do this paper I had some misgivings, for if I were to be honest, I must tell of things as they were; and really, this is not my story, but yours" (Milloy, 1999: xviii). My call for a different way of doing things—a changing of the subject, in educational, methodological, and everyday contexts—is, therefore, not new. What is new is that I am interested in what sorts of educational and/or equity-minded frameworks will bring about changes in the structural and interpersonal advantages that accrue to settlers as a result of colonialism. Furthermore, my focus is on what frameworks people can participate in as settlers—allies who want to be proactive—and how these might transform teacher education programs and priorities in Canada.

# Interrogating Binaries of Self/Other in Equity-focused and Indigenous Education

In *Braiding Histories*, Dion (2009), a Lenape scholar, asked teacher educators to think seriously about. . . . the bifurcation of self/Other that takes place in educational settings, where much of learning is structured by the way in which acquisition of information and attributes "presupposes a distance (or detachment) between the learner and [the] learned" (ibid., 183). These approaches do little to "support the self-interrogation [that is] necessary to address racism [and colonialism]" (ibid., 169). In effect, they do little to facilitate any real engagement with social change.

. . . With respect to anti-homophobia education, Schick (2004) explained that even if education about the Other is successful, "the approach cannot avoid rendering complex lives as something to be understood, creating voyeurs of . . . students and reinforcing a social and intellectual division of 'us' and 'them'" (ibid., 248). She called for an enabling pedagogy, centred on disrupting the self/Other binary, "to transform the process by which the Other is differentiated from and subordinated to the 'norm'" (ibid., 249). . . . Addressing colonial dominance must come to mean more than seeking to understand the lives of people who experience it (Srivastava and Francis, 2006; see also Ellsworth, 1997).

Schick and St Denis (2005) explored this set of possibilities and contradictions. The bifurcation of self/Other, they suggested, leads some teachers, students, and faculty to conclude that they are culturally neutral and, therefore, can be a helper to Indigenous peoples in defining their culture (see also Dion, 2009). As they stated:

> "The Other" [is frequently] positioned as an exotic spectacle that the dominant culture may appreciate and consume. As students like to say "I am fascinated by all the cultures." . . . The onus remains perpetually on Aboriginal teachers and students to explain [and] exhibit the markers by which they can be known as the other. (ibid., 309)

In short, focusing in on "the Other" does little to help non-Indigenous peoples to know, understand, and challenge their own investment in colonial dominance and self-identification. Therefore, Schick and St Denis called for a more systematic and far ranging pedagogy aimed at having non-Indigenous peoples think about the construction of the Other, and their own investment in that construction.

I would add the proviso that the objective must not be to dispense entirely with education about the Other. As Kumashiro (2000) noted, focusing on the Other may be important and strategically useful, especially where knowledge is "incomplete because of exclusion, invisibility, and silence, or distorted because of disparagement, denigration and marginalization" (ibid., 32). Indeed, some measure of reflexivity and self-examination is required to think critically about difference-making, or to provide, as Sefa Dei (2006) described, "a critical perspective that interrogates the nature of asymmetrical power relations, as well as the rationality of the power of dominance in society" (ibid., 8).

There is likely no one approach to anti-oppressive education that is "correct" and, in fact, many approaches compete with and at times contradict each other. As Kumashiro (2004) acknowledged, "No practice, in and of itself, is anti-oppressive. A practice can be anti-oppressive in one situation and quite oppressive in another. Or it can be simultaneously oppressive [and] anti-oppressive . . ." (ibid., 15). Kumashiro spoke of a reality that should come as no surprise if we have given thoughtful consideration to theories of anti-oppressive education. To build on his insight, no practice is anti-oppressive in and of itself because, for that to be possible, we would need to undermine our everyday lived subjectivity.

. . . If, as Razack (1998) took care to point out, "no one is off the hook since we can all claim to stand as oppressor and oppressed in relation to someone" (ibid., 47; see also Narayan, 1988), then it is incumbent upon us as educators to find ways to encourage people to engage with their privilege. And, as Hill Collins (2003) wrote, we need to do this

on both dominant and subordinate sides. I believe this is key to realizing the strategic frameworks for having all peoples—not just Indigenous peoples—participate in an anti-oppressive pedagogy.

It is noteworthy that much of the literature charting educational, pedagogical, and institutional shortcomings—and this is my major criticism—falls short of addressing the matter of reform, specifically the range of possibilities for having non-Indigenous peoples engage with histories of settler colonialism.

. . . But the most urgent challenge is in finding common ground. To find where this common ground lies, we need to . . . place developing literature concerned with the building of settler-Indigenous alliances into productive dialogue with educational literatures aimed at building anti-oppressive pedagogy.

## Finding/Troubling Common Ground in Anti-oppressive Pedagogy

. . . In . . . Khan et al. (2010) . . . , Smith spoke of working with privileged learners, and challenges this can pose in classroom and activist-centred contexts. She explained that it is often easier to start from a framework that assumes everyone a potential ally rather than an enemy. In clarifying what this means in practice, she stated:

> I find that when I talk about issues of racism . . . it is easier to talk about capitalism first. When everyone begins to see that they are not part of the five percent, it gives them the investment to start addressing the other privileges [because] addressing issues of class entails their own liberation too. This realization *enables everyone to see that the reason they need to deal with racism is not so that they can be nice to people of colour, but so that they can dismantle a larger system that oppresses them too.* (ibid., 42, emphasis mine)

. . . For Smith, the goal is finding common ground to address matters of privilege, and having people acknowledge the need to address privilege collectively, rather than individually (Khan et al., 2010). By having non-Indigenous peoples think about their access to class-based privilege, she invites them to envision a collective project to transform oppressive conditions and inequity—a world not characterized by unequal distribution of wealth, but where "everybody has privileges [and] skills [and] the power to make decisions" (ibid., 43), and where everybody is held accountable. Her praxis is consistent with Hill Collins (2003) who wrote that we are not in a position to realize "new ways of thought and action" until we understand "the multiple systems of oppression that frame our lives" (ibid., 332). The goal is neither to confess nor feel bad (Khan et al., 2010), but to foster a collective responsibility for our complicity in social inequality, and to work toward changing this.

. . . With respect to finding common ground, I start my course with a "step exercise" developed by Logan et al. (1991). The goal is to introduce the concept of privilege and oppression and its effects on all individuals, to foster a better sense about the complexity of individual identities, and to make transformative use of developing empathy.

By being assigned a pseudo identity, based on religious, ethnic, colonial, gender, sexual, social class, and ability differences, participants are encouraged to realize that privilege and oppression varies according to context and/or circumstances—mediating our everyday experience of racism, for example.

. . . More importantly, they realize that "there are very few pure victims or oppressors, and that each one of us derives varying amounts of penalty and privilege from the multiple systems of oppression that frame our lives" (Hill Collins, 2003: 332).

. . . In keeping with the focus on finding common ground, I incorporate matters of environmental sustainability into my teaching to illuminate how systems of oppression affect individual lives.

. . . I invite teacher candidates to see concerns about environmental sustainability as a problem we all share. Film and artistic media is useful in making this connection, particularly the film by Annie Leonard entitled *The Story of Stuff* (2007). This short video explores the excesses of consumerism, connecting environmental and social issues through basic Marxist concepts like production, distribution, consumption, and disposal. Leonard's message that "you cannot run a linear system on a finite planet," calls on viewers to create a just and sustainable world, and establishes Lyons' point that "we are all under the same law of the land, air, water, and spirit" (1989: 207).

These are some of many ways . . . the connection between consumerism and environmental destruction, including their intimate connections to colonization and capitalism, becomes clear. People begin to realize that the advantages accruing to them from colonialism will afford no relief from environmental devastation.

## Looking Forward and Hearing Back from Settlers about Colonialism

. . . While further research is needed to realize efforts to broaden and explore settler investments in anti-oppressive activism and pedagogy, the work of McCreary (2005) is one demonstration of what happens as individuals come to see their connection to histories of colonization, and develop a shared sense of commitment and thinking about actions that might reconcile these historic pasts (see also Freeman, 2000).

McCreary (2005) defined pedagogical strategies employed by the late Patricia Monture (see also Johnson, 2007), who would start her courses by asking those present to define their "treaty rights." McCreary reflected:

> Professor Patricia Monture asked us: who here has treaty rights? I did not raise my hand. Neither did any of the other white students.... Professor Monture pointed out that treaty rights ... possessed by whites and other settler nations are different than those possessed by First Nations, but each of us here possesses [them]. (ibid., 6–7)

As this excerpt suggests, a pedagogy that starts, not with Indigenous peoples, but with settlers, has the possibility of effecting important outcomes. Monture, a Kanienkahaka scholar, was committed to seeing those outcomes realized, and to teaching her students to think about treaty relations. For her Indigenous students, this meant keeping the spirit of nation-to-nation agreements on the minds of young people. For non-Indigenous peoples, it meant realizing themselves as beneficiaries, sometimes for the first time.... The importance of encouraging non-Indigenous peoples to engage with the question of treaty rights cannot be underestimated.

... Just as McCreary sought to recover the original spirit of relationships upon which Canada was established as a nation, I take the position that, in Canada, and in teacher education, we need to further cultivate and realize these sorts of endeavours.

... The idea of a decolonizing pedagogy aimed at fostering collaborative relationships, in working to find common ground with privileged learners, is entirely consistent with calls coming from literature concerned with apologies and "reconciliation" (see Alfred, 2009)....

My colleague and I (Cannon and Sunseri, 2011) suggested that ... it is necessary for Canadians to relinquish structural advantages acquired through colonialism and privilege. As Simon (forthcoming, 2012) emphasized, it will be of no use to only focus on Indigenous peoples, but will require "asking non-Aboriginal Canadians to work out where we 'fit in' to Aboriginal history, not just where Aboriginal history fits into the history of Canada" (ibid., para. 13).

And so we arrive back at the question of how to encourage privileged learners to take responsibility for histories of settler colonialism. Will it take place through the introduction of Indigenous world-views into teacher education curricula—or, through efforts to "Indigenize" the academy alone (Grande, 2011; St Denis, 2009)? Will it take place through the employment of "white complicity pedagogy" (Applebaum, 2010)? And, importantly, what does it mean to ask Canadians, especially new Canadians, to take responsibility for colonial injustice?

# Working across Our Differences to Engage New Canadians and Settlers of Colour

... Internationally, Indigenous-diasporic relationship building has received ample, and oftentimes discomforting, attention from Indigenous scholars. I refer here to Trask's (2000) "Settlers of Color and 'Immigrant' Hegemony: 'Locals' in Hawai'i," and Fujikane and Okamura's (2008) *Asian Settler Colonialism*, which charted the nature of White- and Asian-Settler colonialism in the context of Hawaii. In terms of putting forth similar discussions in scholarly and intellectual engagements in Canada, while we may not be as far advanced, it is important to note the contributions of Madden (2009), Lawrence and Dua (2005), and Lawrence and Amadahy (2009). The reality is that these conversations—including the one about the complicity of diaspora in the ongoing colonization of Indigenous peoples—have only started to play themselves out in Canadian scholarly literatures, and with notable gaps, in educational writings.

... Haig-Brown (2009) directly addressed the matter of building diasporic-Indigenous relationships. She charted a pedagogical set of interventions aimed at creating dialogue, including the use of a "decolonizing autobiography" (ibid., 12–15) that invited students to locate themselves in relation to the question: whose traditional land are you on? She described the importance of having students come to the realization that they do not only stand in relation to white peoples in Canada, but also in relation to Indigenous peoples and their lands....

Dion (2009) also ... pointed out, for diasporic populations in particular, disrupting the binary of self and Other can create unique opportunities as people engage with difference and the non-singularity of oppression. These were realized by a woman of colour who recognized that her own experience of colonialism was different than that of Indigenous peoples in Canada (ibid., 188). It is only in coming to understand these differences between us as colonized peoples that we might hope to lodge successful resistance against colonialism.

The work of Dion and Haig-Brown does not exhaust the theoretical range of educational literatures that address ways of engaging diasporic populations in thinking about Indigenous peoples and the history of settler colonialism.... What I have sought to do in identifying them is to suggest the need for further research and work in this area. Educational, classroom-based, and pedagogical literatures need to think about having non-Indigenous peoples, especially those who are new Canadians, locate and name their investment in colonial dominance, including how best to engage with questions of reform and restitution (Alfred, 2009; Day, 2010).

## Charting a New Path: Difference, Diaspora, and Indigenous Transnationalism

... How do we imagine and understand the relations between us as Indigenous peoples, both at home and globally? And, how do we envision relations between us in terms of citizenship, identity, belonging, and solidarity?

In Canada, it is unmistakable that even migrant Indigenous peoples are implicated—at least structurally speaking, and in terms of the nation-state—in the ongoing dispossession of our lands and nations (Lawrence and Amadahy, 2009; Lawrence and Dua, 2005). Much of this stems from institutionalized practices of citizenship that are premised on legacies of colonial power and white supremacy (Sefa Dei, 2011). Thobani (2007) observed how historically, and even today:

> The extension of citizenship rights to ... immigrants [has] resulted in their qualified integration into the political community [and] at the cost of fostering their complicity in the colonial domination of Aboriginal peoples. (ibid., 76)

As official state-based policy, multiculturalism works to further colonial injustice. Indeed,

"Canadian citizenship remains predicated upon the erasure of Aboriginal sovereignty" and will remain as such unless it "can be transformed in relation to the realization of Aboriginal sovereignty" (ibid., 250)....

Lawrence and Amadahy (2009) made a similar point with respect to citizenship in relation to Black–Indigenous relations. They suggested, "black people without known Indigenous heritage ... may have little allegiance to the Canadian settler state but have no option for their survival but to fight for increasing power within it" (ibid., 126; see also Madden, 2009). The literature reveals how difficult it is to realize citizenship outside of state-based terms.... Indigenous scholars in North America have been considering this matter for many years.

... [I]t is common for Indigenous scholars ... to refute state-based versions of sovereignty, and by extension, the structural limitations of Canadian citizenship (see also D'Arcangelis, 2010). The work of Monture (1999) is exemplary in this regard. As she wrote:

> Sovereignty (or self-determination) ... is not about "ownership" of territory.... We have a Mohawk word that better describes what we mean by sovereignty and that word is *tewathata:wi*. It best translates into "we carry ourselves".... What sovereignty is to me is ... the responsibility to carry ourselves collectively as nations, as clans, as families ... as [Mohawk citizens].... What must be understood then is that the ... request to have our sovereignty respected is really a request to be responsible. I do not know of anywhere else in history where a group of people has had to fight so hard just to be responsible. (ibid., 36, emphasis mine)

Monture insisted on realizing our agency as sovereign citizens outside of state-based taxonomies.... Schools in particular need to work at contemplating and realizing a way to inspire migrant Indigenous populations pedagogically, and in classrooms, to think differently about citizenship and to realize a new set of relationships....

The preference to think of our agency as sovereign citizens, outside of propertied notions of territory and occupied space, and in relational terms, is being addressed (see Mathur et al., 2011). . . . Adefarakan (2011) spoke of migrant Indigeneity, rejecting definitions of Indigeneity as sometimes co-opted by white settlers and their descendants that "anchor romantic amnesiac constructions of themselves as benevolent founders of Canada as a nation" (ibid., 40; see also Tuhiwai Smith, 1999). . . . Sefa Dei (2011) foregrounded similar thinking that Indigeneity be better theorized through "dialectical histories of materialism" and suggested the need "to understand holistically the limitations, possibilities, consequences, and the implications . . . of what constitutes settler, of the question of immigration, of how we come to experience/understand belonging" (ibid., 25). . . .

My point in drawing attention to this scholarship is . . . to acknowledge that much is being done already to build and foster such dialogue. To further this scholarship, teacher education programs and educators must find new ways of engaging Indigenous peoples (see Altamirano-Jiminéz, 2008). This process will undoubtedly reveal insights about the resilience of colonized peoples, the nature of colonial subjectivity, and perhaps more importantly an invigorated way of thinking about citizenship.

. . . Before it is possible to foster a collective responsibility for our complicity in social inequality, we need to think differently about privilege and oppression, seeing the myriad of ways in which we are at once invested. Oppression is both a shared experience and something that is experienced differently. As Sefa Dei and Asgharzadeh (2001) stated:

> Oppression should be looked at as a site encompassing varieties of differences, categories, and identities that differentiate individuals and communities from one another and at the same time connect them together through the experience of being oppressed, marginalized, and colonized. (ibid., 316)

How is education and academic scholarship bringing us closer to, or facilitating, these sorts of understandings? How is it placing the minds and voices of migrant Indigenous and Indigenous peoples in a diverse Canada together into new and productive dialogue? . . . Teacher education must seek to nurture, promote, and more actively understand the kinds of alliances that exist—and are yet to be built—between Indigenous peoples in Canada and migrant Indigenous peoples. . . .

But these are not the only things needed to build bridges. We need to create spaces, symposia, colloquia, and classrooms for exploring and developing critical connections, transformative pedagogies, and collaborations in both research and in practice. . . . It is in these very spaces that we will begin to chart out a new set of possibilities—and collaborations—aimed at the building of alliances, and at the rejuvenation of our historic, treaty-based, and nation-to-nation partnerships.

## Conclusion

It seems appropriate to conclude by asking: what does it mean to be an ally of Indigenous education? I want to re-state here that it starts, not in thinking about colonialism as an exclusively Indigenous problem or struggle, but rather, in recognizing that every non-Indigenous person has a stake in colonial dominance and reparations. It starts by thinking about, and working to disrupt, the binary of self/Other that keeps us from acknowledging our differences and connections, making us incapable of facilitating any real change or restitution for colonial grievances. Change must start by troubling, and teaching others to trouble, the interpersonal and institutional . . . the tendency to not name, know, or otherwise mark settler privilege.

In broader institutional terms, change means more than the mere incorporation of Indigenous culture and world-views into teacher education programs and other curricula. . . . In combating settler colonialism, we must challenge what we think we know about Indigenous peoples. Change takes place when we seek these kinds of self- (and Other-) interrogations.

# References

Adefarakan, T. 2011. "(Re)Conceptualizing 'indigenous' from anti-colonial and black feminist theoretical perspectives: Living and imagining indigeneity differently," pp. 34–52 in G. J. Sefa Dei, ed., *Indigenous Philosophies and Critical Education: A Reader*. New York: Peter Lang Publishing Inc.

Alfred, T. 2010. "What is radical imagination?: Indigenous struggles in Canada," *Affinities: A Journal of Radical Theory, Culture, and Action* 4 (2): 5–8.

Alfred, T. 2009. "Restitution is the real pathway to justice for indigenous peoples," pp. 178–9 in Aboriginal Healing Foundation Research Series, *Response, Responsibility, and Renewal: Canada's Truth and Reconciliation Journey*. Ottawa: Aboriginal Healing Foundation.

Applebaum, B. 2010. *Being White, Being Good: White Complicity, White Moral Responsibility, and Social Justice Pedagogy*. Lanham, Maryland: Lexington Books.

Cannon, M. J., and L. Sunseri, eds. 2011. *Racism, Colonialism, and Indigeneity in Canada: A Reader*. Toronto: Oxford University Press.

D'Arcangelis, C. 2010. "Exploring indigenous feminist relational sovereignty: Feminist conversations, non-colonizing solidarities, inclusive nations," *Atlantis: A Women's Studies Journal* 34 (2): 127–38.

Dion, S. D. 2009. *Braiding Histories: Learning from Aboriginal Peoples' Experiences and Perspectives*. Vancouver: University of British Columbia Press.

Ellsworth, E. 1997. *Teaching Positions: Difference, Pedagogy and the Power of Address*. New York: Teachers College Press.

Freeman, V. 2000. *Distant Relations: How My Ancestors Colonized North America*. Toronto: McClelland and Stewart.

Fujikane, C., and J. Y. Okamura, eds. 2008. *Asian Settler Colonialism: From Local Governance to the Habits of Everyday Life in Hawai'i*. Honolulu: University of Hawai'i Press.

Government of Canada. 2010. *Proceedings of the Standing Senate Committee on Aboriginal Peoples*. Issue #10 (September). Ottawa: Senate of Canada.

Grande, S. 2011. "Confessions of a full-time Indian," *Journal of Curriculum and Pedagogy* 8 (1): 40–3.

Haig-Brown, C. 2009. "Decolonizing diaspora: Whose traditional land are we on?" *Cultural and Pedagogical Inquiry* 1 (1): 4–21.

Hill Collins, P. 2003. "Toward a new vision: Race, class, and gender as categories of analysis and connection," pp. 331–48 in M. S. Kimmel and A. L. Ferber, eds, *Privilege: A Reader*. Colorado: Westview Press.

hooks, b. 1988. *Talking Back: Thinking Feminist, Thinking Black*. New York: South End Press.

Johnson, H. 2007. *Two Families: Treaties and Government*. Saskatoon: Purich Publishing.

Khan, S., D. Hugill, and T. McCreary. 2010. "Building unlikely alliances: An interview with Andrea Smith," *Upping the Anti: A Journal of Theory and Action* 10: 41–52.

Kumashiro, K. K. 2004. *Against Common Sense: Teaching and Learning toward Social Justice*. New York: Routledge.

Kumashiro, K. K. 2000. "Toward a theory of anti-oppressive education," *Review of Educational Research* 70 (1): 25–53.

Lawrence, B., and Z. Amadahy. 2009. "Indigenous peoples and black people in Canada: Settlers or allies?" pp. 105–36 in Arlo Kempf, ed., *Breaching the Colonial Contract*. Netherlands: Springer.

Lawrence, B., and E. Dua. 2005. "Decolonizing anti-racism," *Social Justice* 32 (4): 120–43.

Logan, J., S. Kershaw, K. Karban, S. Mills, J. Trotter, and M. Sinclair. 1991. *Confronting Prejudice: Lesbian and Gay Issues in Social Work Education*. England: Ashgate Publishing Ltd.

Lyons, O. (Jo ag quis ho). 1989. "Power of the good mind," pp. 199–208 in J. Bruchac, ed., *New Voices from the Longhouse: An Anthology of Contemporary Iroquois Writing*. New York: The Greenfield Review Press.

Madden, P. 2009. *African Nova-Scotian Mi'kmaw Relations*. Halifax: Fernwood Publishing.

Mathur, A., J. Dewar, and M. DeGagne. 2011. *Cultivating Canada: Reconciliation through the Lens of Cultural Diversity*. Ottawa: Aboriginal Healing Foundation.

McCreary, T. 2005. "Settler treaty rights," *Briarpatch* 34 (5): 6–9.

Milloy, J. 1999. *A National Crime: The Canadian Government and the Residential School System, 1879–1986*. Winnipeg: University of Manitoba Press.

Monture, P. 1999. *Journeying Forward: Dreaming First Nations' Independence*. Halifax: Fernwood Publishing.

Narayan, U. 1988. "Working together across difference: Some considerations on emotions and political practice," *Hypatia* 3 (2): 31–48.

Porter, R. B. 1999. "The demise of the Ongwehoweh and the rise of the Native Americans: Redressing the genocidal act of forcing American citizenship upon indigenous peoples," *Harvard Black Letter Law Journal* 15: 107–83.

Razack, S. H. 1998. *Looking White People in the Eye: Gender, Race, and Culture in Courtrooms and Classrooms*. Toronto: University of Toronto Press.

Schick, C. 2004. "Disrupting binaries of self and other: Anti-homophobic pedagogies for student teachers," pp. 243–54 in J. McNinch and M. Cronin, eds, *I Could Not Speak My Heart: Education and Social Justice for Gay and Lesbian Youth*. Regina: Canadian Plains Research Centre.

Schick, C., and V. St Denis. 2005. "Troubling national discourses in anti-racist curricular planning," *Canadian Journal of Education* 28 (3): 295–317.

Sefa Dei, G. J. 2011. "Revisiting the question of the 'indigenous'," pp. 21–33 in G. J. Sefa Dei, ed., *Indigenous Philosophies and Critical Education: A Reader*. New York: Peter Lang Publishing Inc.

Sefa Dei, G. J. 2006. "Introduction: Mapping the terrain—towards a new politics of resistance," pp. 1–23 in G. J. Sefa Dei and A. Kempf, eds, *Anti-colonialism and Education: The Politics of Resistance*. Boston, MA: Sense Publishers.

Sefa Dei, G. J. and A. Asgharzadeh. 2001. "The power of social theory: Towards an anti-colonial discursive framework," *Journal of Educational Thought* 35 (3): 297–323.

Simon, R. I. Forthcoming, 2012. "Towards a hopeful practice of worrying: The problematics of listening and the educative responsibilities of the IRSTRC," in P. Wakeham and J. Henderson, eds, *Reconciling Canada: Historical Injustices and the Contemporary Culture of Redress*. Toronto: University of Toronto Press.

Srivastava, S., and M. Francis. 2006. "The problem of 'authentic experience': Storytelling in anti-racist and anti-homophobic education," *Critical Sociology* 32 (2–3): 275–307.

St Denis, V. 2009. "Rethinking culture theory in Aboriginal education," pp. 163–82 in C. Levine-Rasky, ed., *Canadian Perspectives on the Sociology of Education*. Toronto: Oxford University Press.

The Story of Stuff Project. 2007. *The Story of Stuff*. Available at http://www.storyofstuff.com.

Thobani, S. 2007. *Exalted Subjects: Studies in the Making of Race and Nation in Canada*. Toronto: University of Toronto Press.

Trask, H. K. 2000. "Settlers of color and 'immigrant' hegemony: 'Locals' in Hawai'i," *Amerasia Journal* 26 (2): 1–24.

Unsettling Minnesota Collective. 2009. "Unsettling ourselves: Reflections and resources for deconstructing colonial mentality." Available at http://unsettlingminnesota.org.

# PART EIGHT

❖

## Additional Readings

Dei, George J. Sefa, and Meredith Lordan. *Anti-Colonial Theory and Decolonial Praxis*. New York: Peter Lang Publishing, 2016.

Dion, Susan D. *Braiding Histories: Learning from Aboriginal Peoples' Experiences and Perspectives*. Vancouver: UBC Press, 2009.

Grande, Sandy, ed. *Red Pedagogy: Native American Social and Political Thought, 10th Anniversary Edition*. New York: Rowman and Littlefield, 2015.

Jacobs, Beverley. "Response to Canada's Apology to Residential School Survivors," *Canadian Woman Studies* 26, 3–4 (2008): 223–5.

Land, Clare. *Decolonizing Solidarity: Dilemmas and Directions for Supporters of Indigenous Struggles*. London: Zed Books, 2015.

Simon, Roger I. "Towards a Hopeful Practice of Worrying: The Problematics of Listening and the Educative Responsibilities of Canada's Truth and Reconciliation Commission," pp. 129–42 in Jennifer Henderson and Pauline Wakeham, eds., *Reconciling Canada: Critical Perspectives on the Culture of Redress*. Toronto: University of Toronto Press, 2013.

Truth and Reconciliation Commission of Canada. *Honouring the Truth, Reconciling for the Future: Summary of the Final Report of the Truth and Reconciliation Commission of Canada*. Truth and Reconciliation Commission of Canada, 2015.

Tuck, Eve, and K. Wayne Yang. "Decolonization is not a metaphor," *Decolonization: Indigeneity, Education & Society*, 1, 1 (2012): 1–40.

## Relevant Websites

**Colours of Resistance Archive**

http://www.coloursofresistance.org

*This website was developed by the Colours of Resistance Network, a grassroots organization concerned with opposing global capitalism, and contains a number of useful articles and resources concerning antiracist and anticolonial engagements with Indigenous solidarity.*

**Leanne Simpson and Glen Coulthard on Dechinta Bush University, Indigenous land-based education and embodied resurgence**

https://decolonization.wordpress.com/2014/11/26/leanne-simpson-and-glen-coulthard-on-dechinta-bush-university-indigenous-land-based-education-and-embodied-resurgence/

*Leanne Simpson and Glen Coulthard discuss Dechinta Bush University in this audio interview providing a scholarly and participatory land-based pedagogy and practice that (re-)connects and (re-)embeds students in an anticolonial and land-centred way of knowing.*

**Transforming Relations: A Collaborative Collection**

https://transformingrelations.wordpress.com/?s=education

*This student-driven website, based at Trent University, provides an overview of ally engagements with Settler-colonialism and the numerous initiatives and resources available to and surrounding them.*

**Truth and Reconciliation Commission of Canada**

http://www.trc.ca/websites/trcinstitution/index.php?p=3

*This website provides information about the history of residential schools, the Truth and Reconciliation Commission of Canada, the programs available to individuals and communities affected by the legacy of residential schools, and final reports issued in summer 2015.*

# Films

*Cold Journey.* Dir. Martin Defalco. National Film Board of Canada, 1975.

*The Fallen Feather: Indian Industrial Residential Schools and Canadian Confederation.* Dir. Randy Bezeau. Kinetic Video, 2007.

*Hi-Ho Mastahey!* Dir. Alanis Obomsawin. National Film Board of Canada, 2013.

*Pelq'ilc (Coming Home).* Dir. Helen Haig-Brown and Celia Haig-Brown. V Tape, 2009.

*We Were Children.* Dir. Tim Wolochatiuk. National Film Board, 2012.

# Key Terms

Acculturation
Assimilation
Cultural revitalization
Cultural fundamentalism

Indigenous–Settler relations
Reconciliation
Restitution

# Discussion Questions

1. How did residential schools encourage the assimilation of Indigenous peoples and with what set of consequences? How do these strategies manifest themselves in contemporary contexts?

2. How does a focus on cultural education erase the systemic violence of Settler colonialism? What are the implications of turning dehumanization, disparities in educational attainment, and educational reform into a problem of culture, cultural incommensurability, or cultural misunderstanding?

3. What does Hill Collins (2003: 332) mean in stating: "there are very few pure victims or oppressors, and . . . each one of us derives varying amounts of penalty and privilege from the multiple systems of oppression that frame our lives"? How might education foster a collective responsibility for complicity in social inequality, privilege, and oppression?

4. How do anthropological notions of cultural difference manifest themselves in services delivery and educational contexts today? How does this tendency detract from conversations about racism and Settler colonialism?

# Activities

Rosemary Henze and Lauren Vanett (1993) suggest in their article "To Walk in Two Worlds—Or More?: Challenging a Common Metaphor of Native Education" that a two-world metaphor leaves the matter of culture both pre-determined and yet grossly under-defined. How does the film *Cold Journey* (NFB, 1975) produce a two-world metaphor, with what series of consequences, and as Henze and Vanett ask explicitly: "how do students who learn to walk in two worlds know when they have accomplished their task?" (ibid., 123) Are non-Indigenous students impacted by a two-world metaphor? How?

Read Roger Simon's "Toward a Hopeful Practice of Worrying" and Sara Ahmed's "The Politics of Bad Feeling" and organize a class discussion about the recommendations provided by the Truth and Reconciliation Commission of Canada in their report *Honouring the Truth, Reconciling for the Future.* What does the Commission say overall and with respect to public education about the history of residential schools? What recommendations would your class make for educational reform in Canada based on the TRC report? How might schools elicit empathy among Canadians that makes possible a restorative project, a claiming of responsibility for the colonial past, and a more just and equitable future?

# PART NINE

❖

# Violence and the Construction of Criminality

## Editor Introduction

In a democratic society like Canada, supposedly the law and the justice system are to treat all who live within its borders respectfully and equally. In fact, the image most people have of the law is that it is fair and objective. But, this presumes that the "subject of law is a universal, abstract person. . . . Indeed, law's claim to impartiality is derived from its commitment to the view that it does not deal with different types of people" (Comack, 2004: 23). Yet, there are *different* groups with particular race, gender, class, sexuality, abilities, and ethnicities that make distinct subjects of law. Additionally, despite the myth that Canadian law and the justice system have been/are just, fair, and respectful, the reality is that racism is quite present within the legal institutions and practices. A number of studies have shown that racial minorities and Indigenous peoples have experienced racist treatment from the justice system in various ways: by the police, the courts, the enactment of discriminatory laws, and policies (Henry and Tator, 2006: 130).

One only needs to remember that it was the *Indian Act*—a law made by non-Indigenous peoples without the consent or participation of those to whom it was directed—that allowed the establishment of reserves, dispossession of lands, removal of children from their families and their placement in residential schools, and the termination of "Indian status" to those women who married unregistered males. Evidently, Canadian law has not been an instrument of justice for Indigenous peoples; instead, it has been a tool of oppression and colonialism. In this section of the book, the authors provide a critical examination of the role of the Canadian justice system and laws in constructing and perpetuating colonial injustices and violent oppression against Indigenous peoples.

Both the irrelevance and inequities within the justice system towards Indigenous peoples are discussed by Monture-Okanee and Turpel who argue that "the criminal justice system is constructed with concepts that are not culturally relevant to an aboriginal person or to aboriginal communities. . . . [and this leads to question] whether, in the context of our experience to date, the criminal justice system can even be termed a 'justice' system for aboriginal peoples." The irrelevance of the system can be traced to the differing conceptualizations of law, conflict, and punishment between Indigenous and non-Indigenous worldviews. As one example, impartiality, an essential criterion of law within the Canadian system, is not deemed as important, if even possible, within Indigenous systems. Given the close-knit kinship nature of Indigenous communities, the person with the authority to solve conflicts ought to be one who is well-connected with the community and well-respected because of wisdom acquired through life experiences. Non-Indigenous professionals who see and are seen as detached, impartial persons of authority are not necessarily better equipped to deal with the complex issues faced by the communities. In fact, Monture-Okanee and Turpel show how child welfare workers removed children from their Indigenous families due to different conceptualizations of family, neglect, and a "best interest of the child" standard that did not serve Indigenous communities well.

Additionally, a major difference exists in how punishment is viewed and treated: while the Canadian system tends to punish those who have deviated from constructed social order by setting them into isolated institutions, from an Indigenous worldview such banishment is unusual. Indigenous societies emphasize restoration of balance and harmony between the "offender" and the community. As Monture-Okanee and Turpel explain, "this notion of restoring balance and harmony is the cultural equivalent of rehabilitation within aboriginal cultures." However, Indigenous values and practices have not been part of the Canadian system and, overall, Indigenous peoples have not been treated equitably by an alien legal and judicial system.

Indigenous peoples are culturally and historically *different* from the rest of Canadians and this difference, Monture-Okanee and Turpel argue, ought not to be dismissed in the pursuit of *equality*. An assimilationist approach to justice would deny Indigenous histories, worldviews, and unique rights as the original peoples of the land. This would not serve justice, but rather further strip them of their Indigeneity. What is needed, indeed, is to allow Indigenous nations to "design and control the criminal justice system inside their communities in accordance with the particular aboriginal history, language and social and cultural practices of that community . . . it will be our system and our law."

That the current justice system has failed Indigenous people is a point reiterated by Green in her examination of the Stonechild case and other similar unjust treatments by the system. The case of Neil Stonechild and that of many other men who had been taken by the police and left to freeze to death in Saskatoon is a clear example of racism within the justice system that has literally killed our peoples. A public inquiry into these events was opened in 2003 and, in 2004, Justice David Wright released his report. In it, he clearly criticized the whole Saskatoon police for the way they treated Mr Stonechild and the way in which they investigated (or not) the matter. However, Green criticizes the report itself for not directly naming racism as the main perpetrator of the injustice served in the Stonechild case and other similar cases. As Green maintains, these are exemplars of the racism in the political culture, a racism that is ultimately linked to colonialism: "The processes of colonialism provide the impulse for the racist ideology that is now encoded in social, political, economic, academic, and cultural institutions and practices, and which functions to maintain the status quo of the white dominance."

The Stonechild case provides us with the opportunity to reveal the racism that exists within the structures and to call for fundamental change to the white privilege it maintains. Unfortunately, the report failed to recognize the structural and systemic element of racism and only treated it as a consequence of a "chasm" between the different communities. As Green argues, this, though, would only see racism as caused by misunderstanding, rather than "by the disproportionate power and malice held by those in the dominant community, who also benefit from the subordinate status of Aboriginal people." Hence, what is required to ensure that such events do end, is to deconstruct racist ideologies and to dismantle the "relations of dominance and, consequently, with the race-coded privileges that accrue to, especially, white Canadians."

Similarly to their male counterparts, Indigenous women have been unjustly treated by Canadian white male-dominant society. Bodies of Indigenous women have been the target of male (often white) violence and State violent oppression in much higher numbers than those of non-Indigenous women. Amnesty International, together with the Native Women Association of Canada, has reported that hundreds of Indigenous women have been missing and/or murdered in Canada and neither outcry by society nor serious investigation by the police has taken place. Would the same occur if these were the bodies of affluent white females? Aren't the lives of our Indigenous sisters as worthwhile? Why is the violence against them not treated with the same seriousness and punishment?

These questions preoccupy and are examined by the authors in this anthology who argue that racism and colonialism are the underlying and often unmentioned factors that can partly explain both the violent acts and the lack of action by the justice system. Racist ideologies have helped to construct Indigenous female bodies as dangerous, promiscuous, dirty objects of male desires. Racism also helps to explain why their violation does not receive harsh punishment: often it is their perceived promiscuity and "risky" lifestyles that are the centre of media attentions, rather than the violent acts themselves. More recently, this issue of Missing and Murdered Indigenous Women of Canada has been at the forefront of media reports and movements of protest; many Indigenous and non-Indigenous groups, national and international ones, have demanded that the Canadian government take action to address the issue and for a national inquiry to be initiated by the government. The former Conservative government had refused to do so, stating that such an inquiry was not "high on our radar" (Harper, quoted in *CBC News*, 19 December 2014). Comments such as this highlight the lack of respect and justice towards Indigenous peoples that has existed within our political institutions. We are cautiously optimistic that the present Liberal government, under Prime Minister Justin Trudeau, has initiated an inquiry as it had promised during the election campaign. (See Part Five of this book for a fuller discussion of the Missing and Murdered Indigenous Women of Canada and the ongoing inquiry.)

# CHAPTER 17

# From *Stonechild* to Social Cohesion
## Antiracist Challenges for Saskatchewan

*Joyce Green*

The frozen body of Neil Stonechild, a seventeen-year-old Cree university student, was found on the outskirts of Saskatoon, on 29 November 1990. While his body bore cuts and marks that suggested he had been assaulted, the cause of death was determined to be freezing. He was last seen in the back of a police car by a friend, Jason Roy, to whom Stonechild was appealing for help. Denying Roy's account and attacking his credibility, the police officers in question also denied having Stonechild in police custody that night.

Neil Stonechild was not the first, nor the last, Aboriginal man to freeze to death in apparently similar circumstances. Indeed, the police practice

In *Canadian Journal of Political Science*, vol. 39, no. 1, 2006. Reprinted with permission from Cambridge University Press.

of taking Aboriginals out of town and leaving them even had its own moniker, "Starlight Tours," used by both the police service and the Aboriginal community.

Ten years after Stonechild's body was found, Darrel Night was taken out of town and left to his fate. Night survived, and later filed a complaint. Two police officers were subsequently charged and convicted of unlawful confinement for their actions in his case. That same winter, in February 2000, the frozen bodies of Lloyd Dustyhorn, Lawrence Wegner, and Darcy Dean Ironchild were also found, on separate occasions, in the same area. Within a few weeks, the RCMP was called in to investigate the matter, and in 2001 it produced a report. No charges were laid. The public inquiry looking into the circumstances surrounding Neil Stonechild's death, headed by Mr Justice David Wright, was not struck until September 2003. . . .

In October 2004, Mr Justice David Wright submitted the report of the Commission of Inquiry Into Matters Relating to the Death of Neil Stonechild (hereafter referred to as the Stonechild report), a provincial investigation. The report criticized the police investigation into Stonechild's death: "The deficiencies in the investigation go beyond incompetence or neglect. They were inexcusable" (Harding, 2004; Wright, 2004: 199). Moreover, Wright condemned not just the individual behaviour of those involved, but the command structure of the Saskatoon Police Force, writing that these deficiencies "would have been identified and remedied before the file was closed if the file had been properly supervised" (2004: 200). Wright concluded that the Saskatoon Police Service had conducted the investigation in a fashion that obfuscated the matter and, in particular, the role of officers on the force in the event. Wright found that Stonechild had been in the custody of the police on the night he was last seen alive, and that his frozen body bore injuries and marks likely caused by handcuffs. He found that the principal investigator on the case, Keith Jarvis, carried out a "superficial and totally inadequate investigation" of the death, and "dismissed important information" provided to him by members of the police.

Wright wrote: "The only reasonable inference that can be drawn is that Jarvis was not prepared to pursue the investigation because he was either aware of police involvement or suspected police involvement" (2004: 200).

Despite the Stonechild family's highly publicized concerns that racism was a factor in the quick closure of the file, the police chose not to investigate the officers implicated in the Stonechild death or to address racism in the Saskatchewan Police Service (Wright, 2004: 201–2). Wright found that in subsequent years, "the chiefs and deputy chiefs of police who successively headed the Saskatoon Police Service, rejected or ignored reports . . . that cast serious doubts on the conduct of the Stonechild investigation." Finally, he found that "[t]he self-protective and defensive attitudes exhibited by the senior levels of the police service continued . . . (and) were manifested by certain members of the Saskatoon Police Service during the Inquiry" (Wright, 2004: 212). Stonechild's family is now suing the Saskatoon Police Service for $30 million: for costs, exemplary, and punitive damages; for special damages, for behaviour characterized as trespass, assault and battery, deceit and conspiracy by police officers (CBC Radio One-Saskatchewan, 1 November 2005; Adam, 2005).

On 12 November 2004, Saskatoon Police Chief Russell fired Constables Larry Hartwig and Bradley Senger, announcing that they were "unsuitable for police service by reason of their conduct" (Harding, 2004: A6). Despite Wright's finding that Stonechild had been in police custody on the night he died, no charges were laid in connection with this. And what was the impugned conduct that cost the men their jobs with the Saskatoon Police Service? Not racism, not criminal negligence, and not manslaughter; instead, their failure was characterized as administrative. Chief Sabo said they had failed to properly report information and evidence about Stonechild being in their custody on 24 November 1990. The fired officers appealed the Sabo decision.[1]

More recently, Saskatoon Deputy Police Chief Dan Wiks was disciplined with a one-day unpaid suspension for giving inaccurate information to a Saskatoon *Star Phoenix* journalist. Wiks, in 2003, had told the reporter that "the police had no indication of officer involvement" in the Stonechild death, although he testified in 2004 to the Wright Inquiry that the Saskatoon police had, since 2000, known that the RCMP suspected constables Hartwig and Senger (Haight, 2005). The Saskatoon Police Force, under Chief Sabo's direction, appealed, seeking a more severe ruling. However, sources in the police force reported to the media that some officers disagreed with the decision to appeal, demonstrating that Chief Sabo faced some internal challenges to his approach and, possibly, to his policy direction on Aboriginal policing (CBC Radio One-Saskatchewan, 1 November 2005). Perhaps not co-incidentally, upon review in March 2006, Sabo's contract was not renewed and the chief, who had been recruited particularly to repair the police–Aboriginal relationship post-Stonechild, did not enjoy much support from the Saskatoon Police Force. However, obviously taking a different view, the Federation of Saskatchewan Indian Nations honoured Sabo at its winter legislative assembly, for "healing the rifts between police and the First Nations community" (CBC Radio One-Saskatchewan, 14 March 2006; Warick, 2006: A7).

Aboriginal activists and organizations have called the police force racist. Spokespersons for the police have denied the accusation, and defended the force's reputation and the claims of the individuals involved in the Stonechild matter. And yet, a number of factors suggest something is amiss: the pattern of denial and obfuscation around the Stonechild case, which ultimately led to the Wright inquiry; the high degree of public awareness regarding the "Starlight Tours"; and the anger toward and fear of cops in the sizeable Aboriginal community. In the white community[2] in Saskatoon, opinion was polarized between those supporting the police position and especially that of the officers involved, and those criticizing what appeared to be racism, apparent criminal behaviour on the part of some officers, and institutional practices violating human rights. . . .

Allegations of systemic racism are generally rejected by those who suggest that the way things are done, the status quo, is simply the product of social and intellectual consensus and is not laden with relations of dominance and subordination, nor the result of malicious intent. In order to challenge this, it is useful to employ the conceptual lens of Albert Memmi to Canadian colonial history. In Memmi's account, colonialism is tied to oppression, and is conditioned by "the oppressor's hatred for the oppressed" (1965: xxvii). This hatred is manufactured and perpetuated by sets of racist assumptions that form the ideological foundation for the systematic, bureaucratic and individual implementation of racist practices, while also constructing "self-absolution" of the racists (1965: xxvi). The consequence, racist ideology, both facilitates the maintenance of the economic potential and processes of colonialism, while simultaneously explaining its ineluctability and positive significance (1965: 82–83). . . .

Racism never happens in the absence of relations of privilege: "privilege is at the heart of the colonial relationship—and . . . is undoubtedly economic" (Memmi, 1965: xii; see also Cesaire, 1972: 10–11; van Dijk, 1993: 21–22). And what is the nature of this economic privilege? It derives from the obliteration of the political, cultural, and economic processes of the colonized, and their replacement by colonial models. This is done not to aid the "development" of the colonized, but rather to appropriate their land and resources for economic and political gain by the colonizers (Memmi, 1965: 3–18). And that, after all, is the primary motivation of most Canadians' ancestors in immigrating: there were opportunities, especially economic opportunities, and access to cheap or free land here, that were not available at home. "Colonization is, above all, economic and political exploitation" (Memmi, 1965: 149). . . .

Confronting and eradicating racism requires unmasking the white-preferential, male-preferential processes that facilitate access to power, privilege, education, influences employment, political positions, and so on. Because the effects of racism are unintended by individuals, and because most people in the dominant community are well intentioned and truly believe that their privilege is solely the result of their merit and diligence, the existence of intentional systemic patterns of discrimination and privilege is denied by most members of the settler population. This results in what Razack calls "the dominant group's refusal to examine its own complicity in oppressing others" (1998: 40). Thus, systemic racism is embedded in Canadian political culture, in the service, first, of colonialism and subsequently, in the maintenance of settler and white privilege. . . .

The systemic racism embedded in our political culture is inherited from the colonial relationships that have now been transmuted into the Canadian social context, where descendants of settler populations carry with them a preferential entry into social, political, and economic institutions; and who see themselves reflected in those institutions and in the dominant culture, in ways that Aboriginal populations do not. Further, the very fact of normativeness is a social asset to those who enjoy it. Finally, this asset is especially strongly correlated with white skin privilege, rather than with those racialized Canadians that our society labels "visible minorities." Ultimately, this phenomenon both perpetuates racist assumptions and processes, even as it is so normalized as to be invisible and non-controversial (Green, 2005). Yet, it is inescapably visible to those whose "race" constructs them as subordinate, and this realization is accompanied by anger at and resentment of those who benefit from race privilege while denying the existence and consequences of racism (for a good personal account of this see Fourhorns, 2005). . . .

Colonialism and its accompanying racism are practiced through "extreme discursive warfare" (Lawrence, 2004: 39). The trenches of this warfare lie in the media, in government bureaucracy and legislation, and in universities. The media write, speak, and produce for the "average reader," the normative working-class or middle-class white model, with its set of social assumptions about the world. The advertisers that underwrite the media pitch to this category. For the most part,

Aboriginal peoples do not exist for the media, except as practitioners of violence or political opposition, as marketing stereotypes, or as bearers of social pathologies. Virtually no real Aboriginal people write for or are portrayed in the media, especially the private media, for Aboriginal or settler consumption. (Doug Cuthand's occasional columns in the Regina and Saskatoon newspapers are so exceptional as to prove the rule.) The creators and enforcers of the laws and policies of the state are overwhelmingly non-Aboriginal, implementing regimes that are seldom directed at Aboriginal peoples and almost never with Aboriginal stakeholder or citizen participation. . . .

*Stonechild* provides us with a moment of opportunity, and is a call to arms for all who were appalled by this incident and who are committed to transformation of this damaging and sometimes deadly phenomenon. It is a moment when even those who have no race analysis, and no understanding of colonialism[3] are united with Aboriginal people in condemning the particular police actions that arguably led to the death of Neil Stonechild, and undeniably led to a set of institutionally sanctioned practices of police behaviour that frustrated the justice system. If we can trace the parameters of racism in political culture, it may be that the repugnance of those who reject police calumny and violence may also move them to reflect on our racist political culture, and how we are variously constructed within it. Then, we can move to strategies for building social solidarity, and for undermining race privilege as well as race discrimination.

*Stonechild* shows us that racism kills. The same lesson emerged from the Pamela George case, in which the young Saulteaux woman was assaulted and killed by two middle-class white men in Regina (Razack, 2002), and from the murders of Eva Taysup, Calinda Waterhen, Shelley Napope, and Mary Jane Serloin by a white man, John Crawford (Goulding, 2001). Racism maims, as demonstrated by the 2001 case of the 12-year-old Cree rape victim from the Melfort-Tisdale area, assaulted by three white adult males (Coolican, 2001; Prober, 2003; Buydens, 2005). Its pervasiveness limits opportunities and experience, depriving us all of human capital even as individuals' lives are marred. . . .

Razack argues that racism in Canada has a spatialized component. She suggests that the colonial society disciplines the colonized into particular and least valuable portions of communities. It is not only the bodies of people that are raced, but geographical space in communities, where whiteness constitutes a pass to all areas, but an exclusive pass to exclusively white areas; and where areas of predominantly Aboriginal occupation are coded as dangerous, degenerate spaces still available for white (and especially white male) tourism. It is in this white adventure into degenerate native space, Razack claims, that raced and gendered identities are enacted and confirmed—by the white agents, against the native ones. Thus, the Stroll in Regina, Saskatchewan, is worked predominantly by Aboriginal women, and white men can venture there for risky adventure, confirming the power relations between all as they act out their raced sexuality on Aboriginal bodies. However, the likelihood that the women would similarly enter the primarily white residential space of the murderers is slim. This spatialized relationship maintains the focus on the indigenous as needing to be controlled, for racism suggests they are ultimately not fit for civilized society (Razack, 2002). The Starlight Tours also fit with Razack's analysis, as they served to eject Aboriginal men from the primarily white urban society of Saskatoon.

Razack uses this analysis to illuminate the processes that played out in the murder of Pamela George. Her analytical framework can be applied to other situations to show similar or identical processes: the murdered women in Vancouver's notorious pig farm; the murdered sex workers in Edmonton and Saskatoon; the scores of missing Aboriginal women across the country. These cases show us the racial definition of space, into white space and Other space, and the racial conflation of Aboriginal with available and ultimately disposable women. In this way, the white public "knows" there is no need to be concerned about these issues, for it believes (it is taught) that these women

brought themselves into danger by "choosing their lifestyles." Consider the numbers of missing Aboriginal women whose cases are being documented and publicized by the Native Women's Association of Canada in its *Stolen Sisters* campaign. These women have been disregarded as objects for state concern and action because of the many factors in their lives that are a direct consequence of being Aboriginal: ultimately, they are ignored precisely because they are Aboriginal. . . .

In his book, *Just Another Indian*, Warren Goulding explores the context for the murders of four Aboriginal women by John Martin Crawford; the lack of media and state attention paid to the murders; Martin's eventual trial and conviction in Saskatoon, Saskatchewan; and the "lurid details of a triple sex murder." Goulding points out that, in contradistinction to the Paul Bernardo trial, the media didn't seem interested: the story had the ingredients of sex and violence, but it was about Aboriginal victims, not middle-class white girls. Racism played and plays a role; it was the in/significance of the Aboriginality of the victims to authorities, media and the white public that resulted in the lack of urgency around the case. Contrasting the response to the Crawford murders with those committed by Paul Bernardo and Karla Homolka, Goulding implies the middle-class whiteness of the latter rendered them subjects of empathy and interest. . . . The indifference of white media and the white public to the violence and misery that attend to many Aboriginal lives is a deeply racist position. . . .

While racism is most violently experienced by Aboriginal people, it also maims the humanity and civility of those who perpetuate it, deny it or ignore it. Racism injures the capacity of the body politic to work collaboratively toward common visions. It disables a common citizenship in a collective political project. In other words, the social cohesion that could sustain all of us is dependent on confronting and eliminating racism from Canada's social fabric.

This will be no easy task. Racism is the legitimating ideology of colonialism. Over decades, the racist assumptions that legitimate our politico-social order have been dignified by intellectuals, by policy, and by politics, until they have become part of what many understand as common sense. In families, in schools, and in popular culture, racism is reproduced intergenerationally and unconsciously by good people. This culture of white racism operates in ways that appear to be benign, unintentional, passive, or unknowing. It can only operate thusly because of its very normativeness, and because of the conventional consensus on the suspect nature of Aboriginal people. . . .

In his "final comments" section in the Stonechild Inquiry, Mr Justice Wright wrote: "As I reviewed the evidence in this Inquiry, I was reminded, again and again, of the chasm that separates Aboriginal and non-Aboriginal people in this city and province. *Our two communities do not know each other and do not seem to want to*" (2004: 208, emphasis added). He was troubled by the fact that "the Saskatoon Police Service's submissions regarding the improvements to the Service did not contain any reference at all to attempts to improve the Service's interaction with Aboriginals and other racial groups" (2004: 210). Apparently, then, the police force did not think it had a race/ism problem that needed to be fixed. The Stonechild matter was interpreted as an incident, decontextualized from the political and institutional culture of racism and the specifics of colonialism in Saskatchewan. Particular individuals could be faulted, but the system remained uninterrogated. Wright, whose report was in so many ways illuminative of the depth and pervasiveness of racism in the Saskatoon Police Force, was unable to grapple with its systemic and structural nature, and he concluded with the erroneous implication that the "chasm" is created by both communities, and is a matter of misunderstanding and of cultural differences, rather than systemic power relations with historical origins and contemporary practices. In concluding thusly, he invoked comforting myths of cultural difference to explain systemic racism—the myths of inalterable and incommensurate cultural essences that are mutually incomprehensible. While cultures assuredly have differences, some profound, these differences do not create the racism that leads to practices like Starlight Tours. . . .

Wright departed from the context for the institutional racism that led to the deaths of the frozen men by calling for greater "understanding" between the two communities. This suggests that the problem of racism is caused by misunderstandings, rather than by the disproportionate power and malice held by those in the dominant community, who also benefit from the subordinated status of Aboriginal people. Stonechild et al. did not die due to a misunderstanding. Indeed, on the same page that Wright turned to culturalist explanations, he also cited evidence from witnesses demonstrating the awareness and fear of white racism with which Aboriginal people live (2004: 209). Yet he seemed unable to clearly analyze the discrete notions of culture and racism, nor could he distinguish between them. Cultural awareness activities, such as having police officers participate in a smudge ceremony, are a good start, but on their own they will not bring about a shift in racist practices or institutions.

Racism in Canada is the malaise of colonialism. The continued structural racism sustains the "toxic gulf" between Aboriginal and settler communities that Wright identified but misunderstood, and its remedy will be found in positive strategies for decolonization. Wright misunderstood the toxic gulf because he saw it as personal and relational, and as being equally the responsibility of the dominant and Aboriginal communities. He did not conceptualize it as a logical consequence of the processes of colonialism. His even-handed condemnation of it, then, places an unfair portion of the blame on Aboriginal communities for the racism initiated by the dominant community's elites. This is not to suggest that there is no racism in Aboriginal communities—there is. But I argue that institutional racism on the order demonstrated by *Stonechild* is emblematic of relations of dominance and subordination, and the reactionary racism in Aboriginal communities is just that, not the legitimating ideology of dominance.[4] Destabilizing institutional and structural racism requires grappling with the relations of dominance and, consequently, with the race-coded privileges that accrue to especially white Canadians. White privilege is sustained by what Lawrence calls "[t]he intensely white supremacist nature of Canadian society, where power and privilege are organized along lines of skin colour" (2004: 175). The chasm is about unequal power relations, not moral equivalence. . . .

But a post-colonial Canada must have a place for the former holders of privilege. Unlike the British in India, the Belgians in Congo, and other instances of "elsewhere" decolonization, Canada is a settler society. The solution of withdrawing from the colony is not available to the vast majority of non-Aboriginal Canadians. Time has done its work of erasing boundaries and options, and creating rootedness and community. We must, in all our diversity, and much hybridity (Said, 1994) find ways to live together, to "bear with" each other in our stranger-hood (Hansen, 2004) and also in our commonalities. No collective public can be manufactured without some collective stake in a transformed future; no decolonization is probable in Canada without a beneficial future, both for the colonized, and those who are privileged by whiteness. And no profound transformation can occur without systemic, institutional, constitutional and, above all, cultural shifts.

Transforming any foundational intergenerational process is dicey. However, governments have on occasion taken the coercive apparatus and financing capacity of the state via government and initiated new directions in public policy, in acts of political will. This is what governments must do: provide a combination of ethical and pragmatic leadership in setting the conditions for and parameters of the Good Society for all of those to whom they are responsible. In the case of systemic, institutional and cultural racism, this is a challenge, as those who must take the lead on this are also those who, overwhelmingly, benefit from the relations of dominance and subordination that are the *raison d'être* of racism.

## Notes

1. The hearing into the matter concluded on 31 October 2005, though a decision was not then made (CBC Radio One-Saskatchewan, 31 October 2005).

2. I use the term "white" for two reasons. First, empirically, Saskatchewan's population is predominantly white, with the balance being almost entirely Aboriginal. Only a tiny percentage of Saskatchewan residents are "visible minorities," something less than four per cent. Second, "white" is intended to invoke the privileged component of a race-stratified society. Therefore, I also refer to "white racism," and have not taken up the ways in which non-white members of settler society may also be racist, or affected by racism.

3. Colonialism is an always exploitative relationship, in which the political, cultural, and economic autonomy of one society or nation is appropriated by another via coercion. It is legitimated by myths of superiority, inevitability, and racism, and it is enforced by the socio-political institutions of the colonizer. These myths and the practices of colonialism are transmitted intergenerationally through political culture.

4. Teun van Dijk writes: "Essential for racism is a relation of group power or dominance. (It is not) personal or individual, but social, cultural, political, or economic. . . . Given the definition of racism as a form of dominance, reverse racism or black racism in white-dominated societies is theoretically excluded in our framework" (1993: 21).

## References

Adam, Betty Ann. 2005. "Stonechild family sues for $30M," *Regina Leader-Post*, November 1.

Buydens, Norma. 2005. "The Melfort Rape and Children's Rights: Why *R v. Edmondson* Matters to All Canadian Kids," *Saskatchewan Notes* 4 (1) (January): 1–4.

Canadian Broadcasting Corporation (CBC). 2005a. "Girls in gangs: Disturbing reports from the inside," available at http://sask.cbc.ca/regional/servlet/View?filename=gangs-girls050321, 21 March.

CBC. 2005b. "They're young and often aboriginal—and they say they're waging a war," *Morning Edition*, available at http://sask.cbc.ca/regional/servlet/view?filename=favel030522, 21 March.

CBC. 2005c. "Re Saskatoon Police Service appeal of Dan Wicks' one-day suspension," *CBC Radio One*, 31 October.

CBC. 2005d. "Re Hartwig and Senger appeals for their jobs with the Saskatoon Police Service," *CBC Radio One*, 1 November.

CBC. 2006. "Re Federation of Saskatchewan Indian Nations honouring outgoing Saskatoon Police Chief Russell Sabo," *CBC Radio One*, 14 March.

Cataldo, Sabrina. 2004. "$750,000 donation to fund chair in police studies," University Relations, University of Regina communication, 1 December.

Cesaire, Aime. 1972. *Discourse on Colonialism*. New York and London: Monthly Review Press.

Comeau, Lisa. 2004. "The Purpose of Education in European Colonies: Mid-19th to Early 20th Century." Unpublished paper presented to SIDRU (Saskatchewan Instructional Development & Research Unit), University of Regina, 25 February.

Coolican, Lori. 2001. "Family wants look at accused," *Regina Leader-Post*, 16 October, A1, A2.

Dickerson, Mark, and Tom Flanagan. 1999. *An Introduction to Government and Politics: A Conceptual Approach*, 5th edn. Toronto: ITP Nelson.

Fourhorns, Charlene. 2005. "Education for Indians: The Colonial Experiment on Piapot's Kids," *Canadian Dimension* 39 (3): 42–4.

Goodale, Ralph. 2003. Speaking Notes for The Honourable Ralph Goodale, P.C., M.P., 8 November; available at http://www.ralphgoodale.ca/Speeches/speech-eginaAffordableHousing.html, retrieved 25 May 2004.

Green, Joyce. 2002. "Transforming at the Margins of the Academy," pp. 85–91 in Elena Hannah, Linda Paul, and Swani Vethamany-Globus, eds, *Women in the Canadian Academic Tundra: Challenging the Chill*. Kingston and Montreal: McGill-Queen's University Press.

Green, Joyce. 2005. "Self-determination, Citizenship, and Federalism: Indigenous and Canadian Palimpsest," pp. 329–52 in Michael Murphy, ed., *State of the Federation: Reconfiguring Aboriginal-State Relations*. Institute of Intergovernmental Relations, School of Policy Studies, Queen's University. Kingston and Montreal: McGill-Queen's University Press.

Goulding, Warren. 2001. *Just Another Indian: A Serial Killer and Canada's Indifference*. Calgary: Fifth House Limited.

Goulding, Warren. 2004. "Reconnecting with Human Rights." Notes for an address by Warren Goulding, Friday, 10 December, Regina, Saskatchewan. Unpublished, on file with the author.

Government of Saskatchewan. 2005. http://www.sask2005.ca/; http://www.cyr.gov.sk.ca/saskatchewans_centennial.html; http://www.gov.sk.ca/govinfo/news/premier speech.html?0085 (retrieved 22 May 2005).

Haight, Lana. 2005. "Wiks going back to work," *Regina Leader-Post*, 8 October.

Hansen, Phillip. 2004. "Hannah Arendt and Bearing with Strangers," *Contemporary Political Theory* 3 (1): 3–22.

Harding, Katherine. 2004. "Two police officers fired in Stonechild case," *Toronto Globe and Mail*, 13 November, A6.

Irlbacher-Fox, Stephanie. 2005. "Practical Implications of Philosophical Approaches Within Canada's Aboriginal Policy," Unpublished paper presented to the Canadian Political Science Association, University of Western Ontario, London, Ontario, June.

Jaccoud, Mylene, and Renee Brassard. 2003. "The Marginalization of Aboriginal Women in Montreal," pp. 131–45 in David Newhouse and Evelyn Peters, eds, *Not Strangers in These Parts: Urban Aboriginal Peoples*. Ottawa: Policy Research Initiative.

Kuokkanen, Rauna. 2005. "The Responsibility of the Academy: A Call for Doing Homework." Unpublished paper presented to the Canadian Political Science Association, University of Western Ontario, London, Ontario, June.

Lawrence, Bonita. 2004. *"Real" Indians and Others: Mixed-Blood Urban Native Peoples and Indigenous Nationhood*. Vancouver: UBC Press.

Memmi, Albert. 1965. *The Colonizer and the Colonized*. Boston: Beacon Press.

Razack, Sherene. 1998. *Looking White People in the Eye: Gender, Race, and Culture in Courtrooms and Classrooms*. Toronto: University of Toronto Press.

Razack, Sherene. 2002. "Gendered Racial Violence and Spatialized Justice: The Murder of Pamela George," pp. 121–56 in Sherene Razack, ed., *Race, Space, and the Law: Unmapping a White Settler Society*. Toronto: Between The Lines.

Prober, Rosalind. 2003. "What No Child Should Endure: *R. v Edmonston, Kindrat and Brown*," *Beyond Borders Newsletter* 3 (Fall): 1–2.

Said, Edward. 1994. *Culture and Imperialism*. New York: Vintage Books.

Saskatchewan Labour, Status of Women Office. 2003. "A Profile of Aboriginal Women in Saskatchewan." Unpublished, on file with the author.

Smith, Linda Tuhiwai. 1999. *Decolonizing Methodologies: Research and Indigenous Peoples*. London and New York: Zed Books.

van Dijk, Teun. 1993. *Elite Discourse and Racism*. Newbury Park: Sage.

Vipond, Mary. 2000. *The Mass Media in Canada*, 3rd ed. Toronto: James Lorimer and Company Ltd.

Warick, Jason. 2006. "Saskatoon police chief to be honoured," *Regina Leader-Post*, A7.

Woloski, Rosalie. 2005. "Re Donald Worme and systemic racism," *CBC Radio One*, Saskatoon, 21 June 2005. Script on file with the author.

Wright, David H., Mr Justice. 2004. *Report of the Commission of Inquiry Into Matters Relating to the Death of Neil Stonechild*. Regina: Government of Saskatchewan.

# CHAPTER 18

# Aboriginal Peoples and Canadian Criminal Law
## Rethinking Justice

*Patricia Monture-Okanee and Mary Ellen Turpel*

---

. . .

## I. Aboriginal Perspectives on Justice and the Criminal Code

### A. Introduction: Scope of the Reference

It is difficult to locate a matter as large and complex as criminal justice within a cultural perspective without first critically examining the presuppositions and structures of the Canadian criminal justice system as it is currently imagined. The Reference letter from the Minister of Justice requesting the Law Reform Commission of Canada to study the *Criminal Code*[1] and related statutes with a view to considering the extent to which they ensure that aboriginal[2] persons have *"equal access to justice, and are treated equitably and with respect"* requires the Law Reform Commission of Canada to reflect upon aboriginal perceptions on the notions of justice, equal access to justice, equitable treatment and, most of all, respect.

These concepts need to be carefully deconstructed in order to give content to the mandate for the Commission's work.[3] Moreover, a series of related concepts which frequently come to the fore in political discussions of aboriginal people and the criminal justice system, such as "alternative justice systems," "parallel justice systems," or "separate justice systems," should also be critically deconstructed and analyzed in light of the

Commission's mandate. This analysis must first recognize that none of these expressions are found in aboriginal languages—they are English expressions more or less rooted in legal discourse.[4] . . .

We would suggest to the Commission that the entire paradigm of the existing criminal justice system is one which needs to be looked at holistically in order to locate it in a context of Canadian cultural values and failings. By holistically we mean all aspects of the system, its institutions and its norms and also the broader jurisprudential goals of discipline, punishment and rehabilitation.[5]

The Canadian criminal justice system is completely alien to aboriginal peoples.[6] This is not a novel point and obviously the Minister's Reference is long overdue. Initial observations regarding the alien character of the criminal justice system can be made at this point to underscore the significance of holistic approaches to reform within the Canadian criminal justice system.

The criminal justice system is constructed with concepts that are not culturally relevant to an aboriginal person or to aboriginal communities. . . .

The notion of a written code or law is also foreign to aboriginal cultures.[7] This does not mean that aboriginal systems of law were not as "advanced" or "civilized" as European-based systems; these are racist stereotypes. It merely means that aboriginal law was conceptualized in different but equally valid ways. Laws were not written because law needs to be accessible to everyone. When an oral system is effective, the law is carried with each individual wherever he or she travels. Thus, a system in which laws are accessible only through

*University of British Columbia Law Review* (Special edition) 26 (1992): 239–77. Reprinted with permission.

lawyers and professionals seems very remote, un-approachable, and not connected to the kinship structure of aboriginal communities.

The Canadian criminal justice system is operated by a professionally trained class of prosecutors and defenders who decide the fate of an offender on terms that reflect their privilege and perspective. . . . If representatives of a particular population do not secure access to the professional legal class, their participation at this level is non-existent and they are excluded from the processes used to select decision-makers in the legal system. This is an example of systemic discrimination impacting on aboriginal peoples. . . .

Another "alien" norm of the Canadian criminal justice system, is the requirement that judges decide matters "impartially." This so-called "impartiality" is the basis for the institutional authority of criminal justice officials acting on behalf of the Canadian system. In aboriginal cultures, impartiality is not the essential ingredient when we think of relations of justice. Aboriginal communities are closely-knit kinship communities. Even those individuals who reside in urban settings commonly retain intimate connections with their communities.[8] These individuals also take their own values and understandings of how justice will operate with them when they come to the cities. The person with authority to resolve conflicts among aboriginal peoples in their communities must be someone known to them who can look at all aspects of a problem, not an unknown person set apart from the community in an "impartial" way. A "judge" from a non-aboriginal context is simply an outsider without authority.

Within aboriginal communities, the equivalent actor to the judge is the Elder. This is not to say that the Elder is the same thing as a judge or assumes that role. Elders are the most respected members of aboriginal communities. Elders are respected because they have accumulated life experiences and hold the wisdom of the community in their hearts and minds. Although it is a qualitatively different value, this respect for a person's knowledge of their culture and language, and for their wisdom, is the equivalent to respect for impartiality in European-based systems. . . .

Wisdom, knowledge, and the respect of an aboriginal community are gained through experience; therefore professionals who come into contact with aboriginal people are not necessarily viewed with respect simply by virtue of their professional qualifications. Aboriginal people hold no respect for "professionals," simply because they hold a professional title. Respect is earned through life experience and by demonstrating that you are a good member of your community, a good speaker of your language and a committed helper of your people.

Aboriginal mistrust of professionals has been validated by our experience with professional authorities. To raise but one example, one should consider the many child welfare cases where children have been removed from their family home. The professional social worker was deemed to know what was best for the aboriginal child, more so than the aboriginal parents and/or the aboriginal community. We now understand that this standard, the "best interest of the child," was bound by race, culture and class.[9] Professional authority based on a tide, especially when the professional is white, is understandably suspect within aboriginal communities. Too often it means disrespect for cultural practices and the imposition of alien values. . . .

The existing criminal justice system must be considered in light of other values it projects and the corresponding claims to justice which it hopes to sustain. For instance, the Canadian system is grounded in a belief in "correctional" punishment based on banishment to special institutions where the goals of retribution, deterrence and reform of the offender legitimize the punishment. Punishment is a concept which is not culturally relevant to aboriginal social experience.[10] Banishment is the most severe remedy available under aboriginal systems of justice. It means the end of social and cultural life with one's community. This is true for the individual who lives within his or her community as well as for the individual who lives in an urban area and is either directly connected to his or her community or understands what that connection is. Incarceration must be understood as banishment if the cultural perception of the aboriginal person facing a prison sentence (and their family as well as their community) is ever to be understood. If the goal of the social structure is to restore balance and harmony within the community, as it is for the aboriginal community, the act of pushing an "offender" outside the circle of social life is not seen as a solution. It is seen as counter-productive, creating further obstacles to the restoration of balance and harmony after an anti-social act.

From an aboriginal perspective, balance and harmony can be restored only through strengthening connections with one's community. This notion of restoring balance and harmony is the cultural equivalent of rehabilitation within aboriginal cultures. Through the kinship system (and/or the clan system of government) and through the involvement of the Elders, balance and harmony is restored for the offender, the victim and the community. Within the Canadian penal structure, the supervision of the offender after banishment is by a person from a specialized corrections bureaucracy who does not know the offender, the offender's family, or the offender's community. This person may even be biased against the offender in subtle or obvious ways.[11] The Canadian criminal justice system's notion of rehabilitation or corrections is fundamentally alien to aboriginal communities. . . .

We raise these preliminary cultural concerns because we have serious reservations about the extent to which aboriginal peoples have equal access to, or receive equitable treatment within, the existing criminal justice system. Meaningful participation and equitable treatment are pre-conditions to holding a sincere respect for any system, particularly a system of justice. However, aboriginal peoples' views of conflict and its resolution have absolutely no voice in the current order. We use the phrase "meaningful participation" as an alternative to the term "access," as it is a term which more accurately represents our view of the

situation. Aboriginal peoples have "access" to the criminal justice system which is all too generous. Our representation in the offender populations has been outrageously high.[12] We have serious reservations regarding whether, in the context of our experience to date, the criminal justice system can even be termed a "justice" system for aboriginal peoples.

The historical fact that the Canadian criminal justice system has absolutely failed to recognize and incorporate aboriginal cultures has important structural consequences. Aboriginal people do not need further access to the system which exists. What is needed is meaningful participation in the criminal justice system and less "access." By meaningful participation we suggest that aboriginal people must be encouraged to participate in the system by defining the meaning, institutions and standards of justice in their own communities. Also, all peoples must be partners in developing a criminal justice system outside aboriginal communities that can and does reflect aboriginal cultures. Thus far, aboriginal peoples have simply struggled to survive their experiences in an alien criminal justice system. To become meaningful participants would require an enormous shift in our experience and in conventional Canadian thinking about criminal justice. . . .

The search for justice within the criminal justice system has resulted only in systemic injustice for aboriginal peoples, either as victims of crime[13] or as accused persons.[14] How pervasive are these experiences? What courses of action represent ways out? We believe that the era of collecting data about the over-representation of aboriginal people in the criminal justice system must end. This gross over-representation is well documented and obvious. It is now time to begin to focus on meaningful change, to correct over-representation and to generate respect by implementing changes which allow aboriginal cultural practices to be recognized and supported. . . .

The Supreme Court of Canada has made it clear that the key to equality rights analysis is an examination of the larger context of discrimination. We must assess whether differential treatment has had an adverse impact upon certain groups in a manner contrary to that envisioned for a society that is pluralistic, free and democratic.[15] The Court is interested in correcting and ameliorating historic disadvantage and recognizes that this does not mean that all groups should be treated alike.[16] In fact, different treatment is often more appropriate.[17] Arguably, there is a built-in notion of respect for difference in this conception of equality.[18] However, if one looks both at the context for discrimination and at historical disadvantage and its impacts with relation to aboriginal peoples, it becomes apparent that something very different from similar treatment is required. . . .

It is not only the Ministry of Justice that recognizes and embraces the need for change of this nature. It is becoming more and more widely believed that aboriginal–Canadian relations can no longer be ignored. In discussing the aftermath of Kanasatake, Kanawake, Oka and the Mercier Bridge, the Canadian Human Rights Commission expressed deep concern over the current state of affairs:

> It is deeply regrettable that it has taken conflict and violence to bring about a realisation of the urgency of reform of aboriginal affairs. We believe that aboriginal and non-aboriginal Canadians alike see the present juncture as an opportunity to apply ourselves to the long-neglected national task of redesigning the aboriginal and non-aboriginal relationship in a spirit of collaboration and good faith. This process should get under way immediately and should tackle the fundamental questions in a thorough and innovative way.[19]

. . . In light of this, what do the terms "equal access," "equitable treatment" and "respect," mean to an aboriginal person? "Equal access" may, at first glance, be interpreted to require an analysis of equality in the access to the criminal justice system. However, because equality conjures up images of sameness or similar treatment (especially in the context of defining aboriginal rights), and is often tested merely by some form of data collection exercise, this interpretation is not completely helpful in this context. Equality is sometimes measured by how well aboriginal people can be integrated into the existing system.[20] Reliance on policies of integration and assimilation within the criminal justice system has doomed to failure many past efforts aimed at amelioration of our conditions. Further, assimilationist policies are antithetical to our desire for cultural survival—integration is not desired, rather the aboriginal goal is autonomy and respect for difference. Equal access framed in assimilationist terms could conceivably mean inequity when the position of aboriginal peoples is placed in historical, cultural, and linguistic perspective. For example, equal access for aboriginal and non-aboriginal people to a system of sentencing which is insensitive to the history and culture of aboriginal peoples does not take basic differences into consideration and contradicts the progressive notion of equitable treatment and respect. . . .

What must be remembered as we begin to face this new challenge together is that the shape of the answer is not singular. There is no single answer that will speak to the diversity of experience, geography and culture of aboriginal people and our communities. To give but one example, the problems and solutions will be different for aboriginal peoples living on reserves or Inuit or Métis communities, as compared to those living in urban centres. Any reasoned response must be tailored to answer both the internal dimension of criminal justice problems (i.e. for aboriginal communities) and the external dimension (i.e. for aboriginal individuals living away from their communities).[21]

An additional but related factor required for reform is an appreciation and sensitivity towards aboriginal political objectives. . . .

We see it as pivotal not only to understanding the sources of our discontent with the existing system, but also to providing direction for the "development of new approaches to, and new concepts of, the law in keeping with and responsive to the changing needs of Canadian society."[22] Eventually, and ideally at an early stage, changes in the criminal justice system will have to be placed before aboriginal peoples for their input and consent. Arguably, this requirement to seek input and gain the consent of aboriginal peoples is established by international human rights covenants.[23]

## B. Aboriginal Rights and Criminal Justice: Legal Premises

While we advocate a broad interpretation of the mandate placed before the Law Reform Commission, we also perceive political constraints on any study in this area dictated by what are, in our view, confused images of aboriginal peoples' experience and aspirations vis-a-vis criminal justice. The Minister of Justice has suggested on numerous occasions that "separate" justice systems or "alternative" justice systems are incompatible with the Rule of Law and are simply not open for discussion. . . . This position misconceives the aboriginal proposal as some kind of lawless zone which would be exempt from criminal sanctions. . . . Aboriginal rights are inherent and not contingent on Crown recognition. For example, the application of the *Criminal Code* may be seen, in the context of aboriginal rights recognized in s. 35 of Part II of the *Constitution Act, 1982*, as an infringement of long-standing justice practices by aboriginal peoples or of treaty guarantees. The basis of aboriginal rights has been accepted in numerous cases to be their inherency or the fact that certain rights or practices have been exercised for long periods of time. . . .

It is important to appreciate that aboriginal peoples are different keeping in mind all of the points we have outlined thus far. Aboriginal cultures are non-Anglo-European. We do not embrace a rigid separation of the religious or spiritual and the political. We have extended kinship networks. Our relations are premised on sets of responsibilities (instead of rights[24])

among individuals, the people collectively and toward land. Our cultures do not embrace discipline and punishment as organizing principles in the same fashion as Anglo-European peoples' do. Aboriginal peoples live with a basic connection to the natural order, which we see as the natural law.[25] This means that family connections, i.e. natural connections, are more important in controlling anti-social behaviour. The lessons offered by a family member, particularly if that person is an Elder, are more significant than any other type of correctional interaction. The personal, familial interaction is the consensual social fabric of aboriginal communities. It is this which makes aboriginal communities distinct culturally and politically from Canadian social institutions.

Aboriginal peoples are *different*. Also, aboriginal communities are *separate* geographically and socially from Canadian society. Our territories are frequently in remote areas and aboriginal people are more closely dependent upon the land for survival than Canadians who live, for the most part, on a narrow strip of territory hugging the United States border. Aboriginal peoples, given that we are both different and separate, simply cannot be considered as part of Canadian society for the purpose of designing a comprehensive criminal justice system. We are not necessarily culturally, linguistically or historically part of Canada or Canadian legal and political institutions. We are different and separate, set apart by our cultures, languages, distance and histories.

To suggest, then, that aboriginal peoples must be treated equitably and with respect by the criminal justice system means that we must be treated differently for the simple reason that we are different. This does not mean lesser treatment as we have so often been afforded. Especially insofar as criminal justice institutions reach *within* our communities, the criminal justice system can only work if premised on the notion that aboriginal peoples are different and separate. Therefore, aboriginal people must be allowed to design and control the criminal justice system inside their communities in accordance with the particular aboriginal history, language and social and cultural practices of that community. The justice system in aboriginal communities will, of necessity, be different than elsewhere (namely in non-aboriginal society) in Canada. It will not be a lesser system and it will not be Canadian law—it will be our system and our law. It will be the system required for the preservation of our peoples and the exigencies of our notion of justice based on principles of balance and harmony. . . .

## C. Aboriginal Political Goals and Criminal Justice

The development of new approaches to criminal justice responsive to the changing needs of Canadian society necessitates an examination of the aboriginal political agenda to discern the direction in which aboriginal peoples are heading and the implications of aboriginal political goals for the area of justice. The aboriginal political agenda can be capsulized around one key aspiration or motivation: self-determination. . . .

Aboriginal peoples, including Indian, Inuit and Métis, have unanimously articulated a desire for federal, provincial and territorial government recognition of their inherent right to "self-government." We use the term "self-determination" instead because it is broader and emphasizes the rights of peoples and not states to choose their form of governance. . . . Aboriginal people see the need for self-determination as the central and essential element to meaningful progress. It means officially recognizing aboriginal peoples' interest in jurisdictional authority and providing the resources necessary to sustain our communities and cultures. It is seen as the first step in ameliorating the grave social conditions under which many of us live our lives. Self-determination is our primary political agenda item for the very reason that control over our own lives, lands and community is the only way out of the widespread oppression we face. . . .

Self-determination means aboriginal design, control and management of institutions and programs. It also means control over fiscal arrangements. It obviously encompasses, at least from a community-based perspective, control over civil and criminal justice matters including dispute resolution structures. Within many reserve communities, this means the internal development and control over powers of criminal law.[26] For off-reserve or external matters, there is a desire for an increased aboriginal presence in the administration of criminal justice and a greater awareness of racism and the differential impact of norms and processes on aboriginal individuals. The extent and form of initiatives taken in urban and rural non-reserve areas will depend on the access and connection, including distance, to the internal mechanisms and structures which need to be developed within aboriginal reserve communities. . . .

Centuries of mistrust have been built upon the centuries of ill-founded approaches to aboriginal–Canadian relations. If we are to turn the tide and enter into a progressive relationship, then the historical mistrust must be resolved through genuine initiatives. Many aboriginal political leaders would suggest that anything short of recognition of self-determination in criminal justice matters is inconsistent with the goals of equal access, equitable treatment, and respect, as discussed above. If further mistrust and suspicion are to be avoided, the federal government must recognize that the aboriginal political agenda is genuine and legitimate. . . .

Aboriginal self-government will require a refashioning and, in many instances, a re-imagination of Canadian concepts of crime, punishment and victimization, and of our current, collective reactions to anti-social behaviour. . . . This is, in our view, the inevitable direction not only of aboriginal demands for self-determination, but of recent social science inquiry as well. Mere tinkering with criminal statutes, in a unilateral way by government, is antithetical to the movement for self-determination and contrary to the legitimacy it has gained in many circles including those of government.[27]

# Notes

1. R.S.C. 1985, c. C-46.

2. Although the authors have taken issue with this terminology in other contexts, in a desire not to confuse the issues, the expression adopted in Canadian constitutional documents, "aboriginal peoples," has been used throughout this manuscript. Section 35(2) of Part II of the *Constitution Act*, 1982, specifies that the expression "aboriginal peoples" includes the "Indian, Inuit and Métis." "Aboriginal peoples" refers collectively to the descendants of the First Peoples of the territory now known as Canada.

3. Here, we would like to echo a concern similar to that expressed by the Correctional Law Review in their report, "A Framework for the Correctional Law Review" (Working Paper No. 2, Part I, 1986) at 19. In that document, concern is expressed regarding the lack of a determined and express philosophical grounding of correctional policy and legislation which is perceived as necessary for a principled, integrated and workable system of justice.

4. We wish to recognize that this paper will be most accessible to those who have an academic background and/or legal training. The purpose of the paper is to educate the Law Reform Commission personnel, and it is therefore written in a language and style accessible to them. Consequently, and unfortunately, it will not be accessible to many aboriginal people; the very people who have inspired us to participate in this project. If we were writing for the aboriginal community our participation and expression would be very different.

5. The authors wish to emphasize that notions of discipline, punishment, and rehabilitation as they are understood within the Canadian criminal justice system are *not* necessarily the norms and values that have gained respect within traditional aboriginal justice practices.

6. One example of the total alienation of the criminal justice system, and in particular the structure of the court process was explained to the Marshall Commissioners by Bernie Francis, as cited in *The Mi'kmaq and Criminal Justice in Nova Scotia: A Research Study 1989, Volume 3 of the Report of the Royal Commission on the Donald Marshall Jr., Prosecution* (Halifax: Government of Nova Scotia, 1989) at 47:

   [M]any Micmacs translated the judge's question, "how do you plead: guilty or not guilty?" as "Are you being blamed?" Heard in this way, the natural response is to answer in the affirmative, which can then be interpreted by the court to mean "guilty."

   This comment does not capture the entire gravity of the situation. There is no word for "guilt" in most aboriginal languages. An accused, when standing in court, hearing, "are you being blamed"; only needs to look around at the formal and official surroundings, the court

personnel, and the police officers, to determine that in fact s/he is!

7. This does not mean that it would be impossible to codify aboriginal systems of law. That is a choice that may be necessitated by the technical society in which we live today. This choice should be left with each individual aboriginal community that chooses to participate in any process of reclaiming traditional relations of justice.

8. The Correctional Services of Canada indicated, in their *Final Report of the Task Force on Aboriginal Peoples in Federal Corrections* (Ottawa: Solicitor General, 1988), that at the time of admission to a federal institution 67.2 per cent of all Aboriginal offenders were residing in communities with a population of greater than 10,000 people. Urbanization is commonly cited as a causal factor specific to so-called "aboriginal criminality." The background to this statement must be explored before any automatic conclusions may be drawn. Aboriginal peoples are often transitory, moving frequently between cities and their communities. Those who come to the cities looking for work experience discrimination and often are forced by their unemployment to return to their reserves. But it is not an either/or proposition. The transitoriness of aboriginal persons also stands as evidence of a cultural focus on connection and community above materialistic values which would be actualized more readily away from the reserves. This is a factor which is not paralleled and therefore not usually relevant in the assessment of the crime patterns of non-aboriginal persons. The conclusion is that aboriginal persons who offend should not be treated differently based on where they were when the offence was committed. Even when residing in urban centres, many aboriginal people remain connected to the communities of their birth in highly significant ways. Interfering with this connection or severing it through the imposition of mainstream criminal sanctions which are not culturally sensitive can have life-long adverse impacts which go deep into the life and identity of an aboriginal person. Failure to consider the connectedness of aboriginal populations to a community is one quality which has made past "solutions" ineffective in redressing systemic discrimination within the criminal justice system.

9. For a discussion see P.A. Monture, "A Vicious Circle: Child Welfare and First Nations" (1989) 3 C.J.W.L. 1 at 12.

10. For a discussion see Monture, *supra*, note 15 at 4–7.

11. Detailed assessments of any component of the Canadian criminal justice system are beyond the scope of this report. Although numerous reports have been undertaken over the last five years with a view to reforming the system, none have included systematic and

rigorous analysis of its cultural implications. This work will only be necessary if agreement can be reached between government leaders, non-aboriginal and aboriginal, which supports the notion of a single justice system for all peoples. If we move in the direction of parallel or separate systems of justice, it will not be necessary to understand these complex cultural factors in their totality. Change can be based on the recognition that the old system was unjust without requiring such a detailed understanding of the content of that injustice.

12. For example the "Daubney Report," *Taking Responsibility: Report of the Standing Committee on Justice and the Solicitor General on its Review of Sentencing, Conditional Release and Related Aspects of Corrections* (Ottawa: House of Commons, 1988) at 211 indicates that while aboriginal people comprise two percent of the Canadian population we currently comprise 9.6 per cent of the federal inmate population. These figures are even greater in the west and the north, reaching 31 per cent in the prairie region.

See also, M. Jackson, *Locking Up Natives in Canada: A Report of the Canadian Bar Association Committee on Imprisonment and Release* (Ottawa: Canadian Bar Association, 1988) at 2–4. Jackson reveals that the situation for aboriginal women is more extreme: "A treaty Indian woman was 131 times more likely to be admitted" to a provincial correctional centre in Saskatchewan than a non-Native (at 3).

13. The most notorious case here is that of Helen Betty Osborne, one focus of the Aboriginal Justice Inquiry of Manitoba.

14. Donald Marshall, Jr's experience of discrimination as an aboriginal accused was a highly publicized and scrutinized example.

15. In *Andrews, supra,* note 7 at 171, Justice McIntyre notes: The promotion of equality entails the promotion of a society in which all are secure in the knowledge that they are recognized at law as human beings equally deserving of concern, respect, and consideration.

16. See *Andrews, ibid.* at 175; and *R. v. Turpin* [1989] 1 S.C.R. 1296 at 1325.

17. In *R. v. Big M Drug Mart* (1985) 18 D.L.R. (4th) 321 (S.C.C.) at 362, Justice Dickson states:
The equality necessary to support religious freedom does not require identical treatment of all religions. In fact, the interests of true equality may well require differentiation in treatment.

And in *Andrews, supra* note 7 at 164, Mr. Justice McIntyre comments:
It must be recognized . . . that every difference in treatment between individuals under the law will

not necessarily result in inequality and, as well, that identical treatment may frequently produce serious inequality.

18. Madam Justice Wilson has cautioned that:
[I]n these early days of interpreting s. 15, it would be unwise, if not foolhardy, to attempt to provide exhaustive definitions of phrases which by their nature are not susceptible of easy definition and which are intended to provide a framework for the "unremitting protection" of equality rights in the years to come.
*Turpin, supra* note 28 at 1326.

19. "A New Commitment: Statement of the Canadian Human Rights Commission on Federal Aboriginal Policy" (21 November 1990) at 2.

20. This is the lesson that should have been learned during the 1969 "White Paper on Indian Policy" experience which is documented in H. Cardinal, *The Unjust Society: The Tragedy of Canada's Indians* (Edmonton: M.G. Hurtig, 1969).

21. Aboriginal communities have, in fact, grown in major Canadian cities with a population of aboriginal people. The friendship centre movement has fostered the maintenance and development of these communities.

22. As provided in Minister's Reference letter of 8 June I 990, paragraph 2.

23. Particularly if a United Nations complaint currently before the United Nations Human Rights Committee against Canada is borne out. See *Mi'kmaq Tribal Society v. Canada,* CCPR/c/39/D/205/1986, released 21 August 1990.

24. P.A. Monture, "Reflecting on Flint Woman" in R. Devlin, ed., *Canadian Perspectives on Legal Theory* (Toronto: Emond Montgomery, 1990) 351 at 352–5.

25. For a discussion of what this means from an aboriginal perspective see O. Lyons, "Spirituality, Equality, and Natural Law," in L. Little Bear *et al.,* eds, *Pathways to Self-Determination: Canadian Indians and the Canadian State* (Toronto: University of Toronto Press, 1984) 5. Similar concepts are also discussed in T. Porter, "Traditions of the Constitution of the Six Nations" in L. Little Bear *et al.,* eds, *ibid.,* 11; Chief John Snow, "Identification and Definition of Our Treaty and Aboriginal Rights," in M. Boldt *et al.,* eds, *The Quest for Justice* (Toronto: University of Toronto Press, 1985).

26. This is too narrowly cast because traditional forms of dispute resolution focus on restoring the balance in the community. This means responding to offenders, victims and the community as a whole. Traditional justice, therefore, spans what Canadian law thinks of as criminal and civil jurisdictions.

27. Rt. Hon. B. Mulroney, *supra,* note 82.

❖

# Additional Readings

Amnesty International Report. *Stolen Sisters: A Human Rights Response to Discrimination and Violence against Indigenous Women in Canada*. Ottawa: Amnesty International, 2004.

Ash-Moccasin, Simon. "I was racially profiled, roughed up, & detained by police for being Indigenous," *Briar Patch Magazine*. 2014. http://briarpatchmagazine.com/blog/view/i-was-racially-profiled.

Chan, Wendy, and Kiran Mirchandani, eds. *Crimes of Colour; Racialization and the Criminal Justice System in Canada*. Peterborough, ON: Broadview Press, 2002.

Monchalin, Lisa. *The Colonial Problem: An Indigenous Perspective on Crime and Injustice in Canada*. Toronto: University of Toronto Press, 2016.

Murdocca, Carmela. *To Right Historical Wrongs: Race, Gender, and Sentencing in Canada*. Vancouver: University of British Columbia Press, 2014.

Native Women's Association of Canada. *Aboriginal Women and the Legal Justice System in Canada*. 2007. http://www.nwac-hq.org/en/documents/nwac-legal.pdf.

Reber, Susanne. *Starlight Tour: The Last, Lonely Night of Neil Stonechild*. Toronto: Random House Canada, 2005.

Simpson, Leanne. "Indict the System," *Briar Patch Magazine*. 2014. http://briarpatchmagazine.com/blog/view/indict-the-system.

Stanton, Kim. "Intransigent Injustice: Truth, Reconciliation and the Missing Women Inquiry in Canada," *Transitional Justice Review* Volume 1, Issue 2 (2013): Art. 4.

# Relevant Websites

### Native Women's Association of Canada (Sisters In Spirit)

http://www.nwac-hq.org/sisters-spirit-research-report-2010

*Sisters In Spirit is a research initiative conducted by the Native Women's Association of Canada. The 2010 report is a culmination of five years of research on murdered and missing Indigenous women in Canada and can be found at the following link.*

### Report of the Aboriginal Justice Inquiry of Manitoba

http://www.ajic.mb.ca/volume.html

*The Manitoba Government created the Public Inquiry into the Administration of Justice and Aboriginal People, commonly known as the Aboriginal Justice Inquiry. The Inquiry was created in response to the trial in November 1987 of two men for the 1971 murder of Helen Betty Osborne in The Pas. The Report can be found online on the Aboriginal Justice Inquiry's website.*

### Copwatch Vancouver

https://copwatchvancouver.wordpress.com/category/bc-native/

*Copwatch Vancouver is website that exposes interactions between the police and various communities in the Greater Vancouver area.*

### Cindy Gladue Murder Case

http://www.theglobeandmail.com/globe-debate/reduced-to-a-body-part/article23790508/

*This newspaper article reports on the tragic death of Cindy Gladue in a hotel room, and it highlights how her case is alarmingly similar to those of hundreds of Indigenous women in Canada.*

### Prime Minister Harper's comments on demands of inquiry on Missing and Murdered Indigenous Women

http://www.cbc.ca/news/aboriginal/stephen-harper-s-comments-on-missing-murdered-aboriginal-women-show-lack-of-respect-1.2879154

*This newspaper article reports on the response by former Prime Minister Stephen Harper to the demands of an inquiry on the missing and murdered Indigenous women in Canada, and the criticisms his response received by many individuals and Indigenous communities.*

# Films

*Circles*. Dir. Shanti Thakur. National Film Board of Canada, 1997.

*Finding Dawn*. Dir. Christine Welsh. National Film Board of Canada, 2006.

*Go Home, Baby Girl*. Dir. Audrey Huntley. CBC, 2005.

*Two Worlds Colliding*. Dir. Tasha Hubbard. National Film Board of Canada, 2004.

*TEDx Victoria Talk*. Sarah Hunt. https://www.academia.edu/5472574/In_Her_Name_Relationships_as_Law_at_TedX_Victoria.

# Key Terms

Social cohesion
Starlight Tours
Systemic racism
Sexual violence

Genocide
Systemic injustice
Meaningful participation
Self-determination

# Discussion Questions

1. Green asserts that sexual violence and colonialism are intimately interconnected. What does she mean by this and what are the implications? How are Indigenous women and/or men of colour constructed in the colonial imaginary and how do these constructions impel colonial/white heteropatriarchy?

2. Green insists that decolonization is vital to both colonizer and colonized: map the different components of this argument. How is dehumanization an essential part of colonialism? Why does Green argue it is necessary for Canada to deal with racism and colonialism? What are the ramifications if it does not?

3. How has the Canadian criminal justice system in reality resulted in systemic injustice towards Indigenous peoples? What steps need to be taken for true justice to take place?

4. Monture-Okanee and Turpel state that "Aboriginal people see the need for self-determination as the central and essential element to meaningful progress." How do they differentiate between self-determination and the other commonly known term, self-government?

# Activities

Read the Amnesty Internal Report about the Missing/Murdered Indigenous women and/or the Sisters in Spirit campaign (the latter can be found in the Native Women Association of Canada's website). How do colonialism, racism, sexism, and classism intersect in the events surrounding the lives and treatment of these Indigenous women? How did the police treat those cases? Are there any indications of systemic injustice?

Locate at least three cases of police's treatment of Indigenous peoples in your area. What were the main issues? How are these cases connected to the articles covered in this part of the anthology (e.g., Was a relationship of trust, co-operation, and respect existent or not? Could an argument be made that systemic racism played a part in the treatment of Indigenous people?)? What do you suggest could have been and/or should be done in order for a better relationship between the parties to occur?

Invite a local anticolonial activist to discuss about issues of hatred and violence against Indigenous peoples in your area and to strategize about ways in which to organize to bring public awareness and social change.

# PART TEN

❖

# Poverty, Economic Marginality, and Community Development

## Editor Introduction

On 22 January 2016 in La Loche, a small Dene community in northern Saskatchewan, a 17-year-old male shot and killed four people, and injured seven other community members. Aside from directly impacting the small community, this event shocked all Canada; however, we need to contextualize this tragedy, so to better understand its complex roots, and ultimately find proactive preventive strategies for the future.

La Loche is a community that has struggled for many years with poverty, unemployment, addictions, and alarmingly high numbers of youth suicides. As a member of La Loche told a CBC news reporter, "there is lack of everything . . . we don't have nothing." Agreeing with this community member, the Métis Nation president Clément Chartier added that such poor social conditions are linked to the loss of traditional economic systems since the 1960s, and the consequent long history of high unemployment rates, lack of social programs, and lack of other resources. This harsh reality has been felt particularly hard by the youth, who, feeling helpless about their future and having lost a strong cultural identity, have resorted to violence, either to others or to themselves. To grasp the severity of the existing conditions in remote northern Indigenous communities like La Loche, one only needs to learn that the average for suicide in La Loche was 61.1 per 100,000 according to a 2010 report. The event that took place in La Loche on 22 January 2016 must not be looked at in isolation from the social conditions that have surrounded the community for many decades. What happened on that day is strongly connected to a history of neglect and other colonial injustices that La Loche and many other Indigenous nations have endured.

The links between Indigenous peoples, poverty, and development policy have, in recent years, received attention by social researchers and analysts who have reported that "development itself has failed to provide answers to human suffering and disadvantage" (Eversole, McNeish, and Cimadamore, 2005: 1). Moreover, it has finally been internationally recognized that "[I]ndigenous peoples are nearly always disadvantaged relative to their non-[I]ndigenous counterparts. Their material standard of living is lower; their risk of disease and early death higher . . . there is a 'cost' to being Indigenous" (ibid., 2). Their socio-economic conditions have been described to belong to that of "Fourth World" communities, minority populations in their own lands, who suffer from a lack of political power, economic subjugation, and social and cultural stigmatization (Dick, 1985).

Rather than treating these conditions as outcomes of individual faults or bad personal choices we must recognize that poverty and economic marginalization are also linked to past and ongoing policy injustices, racist colonial attitudes, and discrimination. Legal and educational barriers routinely impact on the ability of Indigenous peoples to prosper. Indeed, as Cora Voyageur and Brian Calliou (2003: 121) explain, economic underdevelopment is not a "Native problem." They write: "the Canadian state's institutionalized and oppressive, economic and legal structures have played a key role in Aboriginal community underdevelopment, which has resulted in the increasing dependency of some Indigenous peoples on the state" (ibid.). They also observe that "the Canadian state, through its federal and provincial jurisdictions, often legislates access to land and resources that benefits corporate interests and is detrimental to Aboriginal peoples" (ibid., 125). A "blame-the-victim" ideology is therefore inadequate in analyzing current Indigenous economic conditions as it fails to recognize how racism and colonial attitudes and policies have significantly contributed to both the creation and the maintenance of those conditions.

Indigenous peoples' current economic conditions have been created by a combination of cultural barriers and systemic discrimination. Cultural barriers consist, for example, of the conflict between Indigenous values and Euro-Canadian ones, wherein Indigenous belief in collectivism and spiritual connection to the land clashes with the belief in individualism and treatment of land as a commodity. Racist ideologies have treated Indigenous values as inferior, hence justifying the devaluation of Indigenous peoples and their economies, and colonization. Their economic marginalization has been treated as a consequence of their outmoded value system and their unwillingness to let go of their "Indianness." Such racist ideologies disallow to closely examine any systemic barriers that have created and maintained Indigenous underdevelopment.

The points made above were reiterated in December 2009 at the Oneida of the Thames Longhouse, at their mid-winter ceremonies to honour Mother Earth and all her natural gifts. During the ceremonies, new members of the nation were welcomed and given traditional Oneida names. At the end of the first day of the ceremonies our spiritual elder gave us teachings about the ceremonies and also remarked that as the original peoples of the land we should resist assimilation and re-awaken our traditions and ways of governing. He reminded us of our responsibility to protect our lands and natural resources from some "development" projects that in actuality are threatening the climate, the waters, the trees, and the overall well-being of our nations. By resisting, we are not against all modern technological developments, or stating that we do not wish to participate in the economy or share the wealth created from our rich resources. But we do want sustainable economies that do not destroy the environment and Mother Earth; we must ensure that our present economies safeguard "all our relations" for the next seven generations. Our Haudenosaunee traditional teachings instruct us to keep the concept of "seven generations" in mind when making any decision. In actuality this means that any decision taken in the present must bear in mind the well-being of at least the next seven future generations (Lyons, 1989).

Indigenous peoples all over Turtle Island have not forgotten the responsibilities that our elder reminded us of. They have always been keenly aware of the negative impacts that both the Canadian State's laws and private corporations' activities have had on Indigenous territories and ways of life. They have always resisted against any threats on Mother Earth and all of its creations.

In the winter of 2012–2013 all of Canada saw evidence of such resistance when the Idle No More Movement, as Pamela Palmater discusses in this section of this book, "swept the country over the holidays, took most Canadians, including Prime Minister Stephen Harper and his Conservative government, by surprise." This movement was initiated by four women who wanted to bring to Canadians' attention the inevitable negative impacts that the then proposed Bill C-45 (which eventually came into effect) would have on the environment, and on Indigenous territories and rights.

The participants of the Idle No More movement effectively, with the use of social media and grassroots activism, brought to light the broader issues that have affected Indigenous peoples, such as dispossession of lands, disrespect of treaty rights, violence against Indigenous women, and the very poor socio-economic conditions under which most Indigenous communities live. When, during the period of the movement, Attawapiskat Chief Theresa Spence went on a hunger strike until the representatives of the Crown, including the Prime Minister, agreed to meet with First Nations leaders to discuss both Bill C-45 and the broader social issues that the Idle No More spoke about, Canada and the rest of the world could no longer be in denial or silent about the broken relationship between the Canadian State and Indigenous nations. As Palmater states in her article, "her strike is symbolic of what is happening to First Nations in Canada. For every day that Spence does not eat, she is slowly dying, and that is exactly what is happening to First Nations, who have lifespans up to 20 years shorter than average Canadians."

Other activists of Idle No More reminded those who were curious of the demands made by Indigenous peoples that "the political economy of Canada rests on claims of ownership to all lands and resources within our national borders . . . [and that] Indigenous labour and lands have shaped the political economy of Canada, right from the railroad development to current resources exploration and extractions" (Pasternak, 2014: 40–2). Acknowledging this would dispel the myth that "it is hard-earned tax dollars of Canadians that pays for housing, schools, and health services in First Nations" (Jay, 2014: 109). In reality, it is Indigenous peoples who have been subsidizing the rest of Canada, given that the Canadian economy has heavily relied on the natural and other resources drawn from Indigenous lands, most of which are unceded territories. The Idle No More movement has intended to make everyone aware of this reality, and has demanded, as Palmater states, "for Canada to negotiate the sharing our lands and resources, but the government must display good faith by withdrawing the legislation and restoring the funding to our communities. Something must be done to address the immediate crisis faced by the grassroots in this movement." It is time to end the continuing colonial relationship; none of us can remain idle, Indigenous peoples and allies alike.

Current socio-economic marginalization is deeply rooted in the history of colonization. Even homelessness is a by-product of economic marginalization. As Baskin (Chapter 20, this volume) suggests of her research with Indigenous youth in Toronto, homelessness is symptomatic of larger structural barriers resulting from Settler colonialism, including a lack of affordable housing, addictions, poverty, the intergenerational impact of residential schooling, racism, discrimination, cultural and geographical displacement, and domestic and community-based violence. Indigenous youth reported loneliness, isolation, abuse, and racism experienced under the child protection system as contributing to their time on the streets. As Baskin suggests, current policy and services delivery must do more to recognize and address the particularities of Indigenous family problems, most importantly their link with poverty. Support must be provided to extended family members in caring for children, so that they do not end up in foster and adoptive families.

We concur with Baskin, adding in tandem with her scholarly and activist analysis that we must regain control of our economies as Indigenous peoples in order to partake in a more equitable share of the wealth produced by natural resources in Canada, and to develop social policies and programs that are cognizant of the structural barriers we have faced as Indigenous peoples.

# CHAPTER 19

# Why Are We Idle No More?

*Pamela Palmater*

The Idle No More movement, which has swept the country over the holidays, took most Canadians, including Prime Minister Stephen Harper and his Conservative government, by surprise. That is not to say that Canadians have never seen a native protest before, as most of us recall Oka, Burnt Church, and Ipperwash. But most Canadians are not used to the kind of sustained, coordinated, national effort that we have seen in the last few weeks—at least not since 1969. 1969 was the last time the federal government put forward an assimilation plan for First Nations. It was defeated then by fierce native opposition, and it looks like Harper's aggressive legislative assimilation plan will be met with even fiercer resistance.

In order to understand what this movement is about, it is necessary to understand how our history is connected to the present-day situation of First Nations. While a great many injustices were inflicted upon the indigenous peoples in the name of colonization, indigenous peoples were never "conquered." The creation of Canada was only possible through the negotiation of treaties between the Crown and indigenous nations. While the wording of the treaties varies from the peace and friendship treaties in the east to the numbered treaties in the west, most are based on the core treaty promise that we would all live together peacefully and share the wealth of this land. The problem is that only one treaty partner has seen any prosperity.

The failure of Canada to share the lands and resources as promised in the treaties has placed First Nations at the bottom of all socio-economic indicators—health, lifespan, education levels and employment opportunities. While indigenous lands and resources are used to subsidize the wealth and prosperity of Canada as a state and the high-quality programs and services enjoyed by Canadians, First Nations have been subjected to purposeful, chronic underfunding of all their basic human services like water, sanitation, housing, and education. This has led to the many First Nations being subjected to multiple, overlapping crises like the housing crisis in Attawapiskat, the water crisis in Kashechewan, and the suicide crisis in Pikangikum.

Part of the problem is that federal "Indian" policy still has, as its main objective, to get rid of the "Indian problem." Instead of working toward the stated mandate of Indian Affairs "to improve the social well-being and economic prosperity of First Nations," Harper is trying, through an aggressive legislative agenda, to do what the White Paper failed to do—get rid of the Indian problem once and for all. The Conservatives don't even deny it—in fact Harper's speech last January at the Crown–First Nation Gathering focused on the unlocking of First Nations lands and the integration of First Nations into Canadian society for the "maximized benefit" of all Canadians. This suite of approximately 14 pieces of legislation was drafted, introduced, and debated without First Nation consent.

Idle No More is a coordinated, strategic movement, not led by any elected politician, national chief or paid executive director. It is a movement originally led by indigenous women and has been joined by grassroots First Nations leaders, Canadians, and now the world. It originally started as a way to oppose Bill C-45, the omnibus legislation impacting water rights and land rights under the

In Kino-nda-niimi Collective, eds, *The Winter We Danced* (Winnipeg: ARP Books, 2014), 37–40. Used by permission. Originally appeared in *The Ottawa Citizen*, 28 December 2012.

Indian Act; it grew to include all the legislation and the corresponding funding cuts to First Nations political organizations meant to silence our advocacy voice.

Our activities include a slow escalation from letters to MPs and ministers, to teach-ins, marches and flash mobs, to rallies, protests, and blockades. The concept was to give Canada every opportunity to come to the table in a meaningful way and address these long-outstanding issues, and escalation would only occur if Canada continued to ignore our voices. Sadly, Prime Minister Harper has decided to ignore the call for dialogue just as he has ignored the hunger-striking Attawapiskat Chief Theresa Spence.

Although Idle No More began before Chief Spence's hunger strike, and will continue after, her strike is symbolic of what is happening to First Nations in Canada. For every day that Spence does not eat, she is slowly dying, and that is exactly what is happening to First Nations, who have lifespans up to 20 years shorter than average Canadians.

Idle No More has a similar demand in that there is a need for Canada to negotiate the sharing of our lands and resources, but the government must display good faith first by withdrawing the legislation and restoring the funding to our communities. Something must be done to address the immediate crisis faced by the grassroots in this movement.

I am optimistic about the power of our peoples and know that in the end, we will be successful in getting this treaty relationship back on track. However, I am less confident about the Conservative government's willingness to sit down and work this out peacefully any time soon. Thus, I fully expect that this movement will continue to expand and increase in intensity. Canada has not yet seen everything this movement has to offer. It will continue to grow as we educate Canadians about the facts of our lived reality and the many ways in which we can all live here peacefully and share the wealth.

After all, First Nations, with our constitutionally protected aboriginal and treaty rights, are Canadians' last best hope to protect the lands, waters, plants, and animals from complete destruction—which doesn't just benefit our children, but the children of all Canadians.

## CHAPTER 20

# Aboriginal Youth Talk about Structural Determinants as the Causes of Their Homelessness

*Cyndy Baskin*

## Introduction

This article, which is based on a research project, explores the structural factors that may have led to the homelessness of Aboriginal youth

*First Peoples Child & Family Review* 3, 3 (2007): 31–42. Reprinted with permission from the author.

in an urban centre. It begins with definitions of homelessness, then examines the prevalence of homelessness for Aboriginal youth, and next turns to a brief discussion of colonization and the role of child welfare in this process. The article then reports on the findings of the project that was conducted with homeless Aboriginal youth in Toronto using a culture-based research methodology.

This research project was conducted by myself as the principal investigator and a youth who is currently attending university as the research assistant. I am of Mi'kmaq and Irish descent and a professor in a school of social work. The research assistant is a young, Ojibway woman with a social work degree who is now in law school. We are both active participants in Toronto's Aboriginal community and have many relatives who have been/are homeless youth and who have had involvement with child welfare.

Toronto was chosen as the site for this research project as both the principal investigator and research assistant reside there and have connections to several Aboriginal agencies that service youth. In addition, Toronto has a large Aboriginal population and represents many diverse Nations (Statistics Canada, 2003). The medicine wheel was selected as the research methodology for the project after consulting with Aboriginal youth workers and youth themselves. They confirmed that the majority of youth were familiar with the medicine wheel and it is a teaching tool used by many Nations such as the Cree and Ojibway.

While there does appear to be some overlap between Eurocentric models of structural determinants and those presented by Aboriginal scholars (DuHanmel, 2003; Thomas, 2003), such as education, income, and diet, this article proposes that to adequately address determinants faced by Aboriginal youth, a framework that is culturally appropriate and addresses colonization needs to be implemented. It further proposes that an arm of colonization, which is likely related to homelessness among youth, is their involvement in state institutional child welfare (Cauce and Morgan, 1994; Fall and Berg, 1996; Fitzgerald, 1995; Lindsey, et al., 2000; Maclean et al., 1999).

Current research on Aboriginal youth is minimal, especially in the area of homelessness. Available statistics do not illustrate the extent of the problem, although most advocates suggest that the rate of homelessness for this population is dramatically increasing (Abrahams, 2000; United Native

Nations Society, 2001). The purpose of this research project, then, was to explore with homeless Aboriginal youth the conditions under which they became homeless, how they may be assisted today, and what can be done to prevent homelessness from continuing in the future. The significance of this project is connected to the fact that Aboriginal youth are the fastest growing group in Canada while the non-Aboriginal population is aging (Hick, 2007; Hoglund, 2004; Statistics Canada, 2003). It asserts that it will become increasingly important to Canada's future, especially in terms of our workforce, to ensure that Aboriginal youth be healthy and productive members of society. This article contributes suggestions for change to social policies and direct practice focusing on control of child welfare by and with Aboriginal peoples.

## Definitions

Common definitions of homelessness include people that live on the street, stay in emergency shelters, spend more of their income on rent, or live in crowded conditions which keeps them at serious risk of becoming homeless (Golden, et al., 1999). The Toronto Disaster Relief Committee (1998) states that homelessness means simply not having secure housing. . . .

With particular attention to youth, homelessness is usually defined as those youth aged 15–24 who are not living with a family in a home, or not in the care of child protection agencies. Homeless youth are also described as those living "in an unsafe or temporary living environment" (Fitzgerald, 1995: 7). The Canadian Mortgage and Housing Corporation (2001) and Golden et al. (1999) describe homeless youth as those youth with no permanent address.

## Prevalence

Many sources state that there is no accurate data regarding homeless Aboriginal peoples, let alone Aboriginal youth (Golden et al., 1999; Layton, 2000; Native Counseling Service of Alberta, 2000; UNNS, 2001). In Layton's *Homelessness: The Making and*

*Unmaking of a Crisis* (2000), what statistics exist show that Aboriginal peoples in general do have a high rate of homelessness as compared to the rest of Canadian society. The NCSA states that "the Aboriginal homeless rate is at about 40 per cent Canada wide" (2000: 3). Golden et al. (1999), in their major report for the City of Toronto, reports that Aboriginal peoples make up 15 per cent of the homeless population in Toronto and that "many Aboriginal Canadian youth from reserves and urban communities end up on the streets of Toronto" (1999: 75). If this 15 per cent figure is correct, it means that Aboriginal peoples are overrepresented in the homeless population by more than a factor of three considering they make up only 4.4 per cent of the Canadian population (Statistics Canada, 2001).

It is also important to note that the rate of homelessness is usually derived from the number of people who use shelters. However, the UNNS (2001) indicates that shelter users do not represent the entire Aboriginal homeless population as many do not utilize the shelter system. Furthermore, the Aboriginal community is estimated to have a high rate of concealed homelessness and these numbers are not included in the official data. This category includes those in transition homes, jails and detox centres, and those who live in overcrowded, unstable, or inadequate housing. It also includes "couch surfing," which is when people stay at a friend or family members' dwelling for a short period of time, then move on to another person's home. Another category that often goes unnoticed is those who are at high risk of becoming homeless. This category includes many Aboriginal peoples who live in poor housing conditions and pay more than 25 per cent of their income for rental accommodations. Therefore, to completely capture the Aboriginal homeless population, all of these categories of homelessness must be included (UNNS, 2001). . . .

## Factors Associated with Homelessness

Within the literature, the most frequently cited cause of homelessness for all peoples in Canada is lack of affordable housing (Golden et al., 1999;

Hulchanski, 2004; Shapcott, 2001; TDRC, 1998). Some authors (UNNS, 2001; Weinreb et al., 1998) argue that personal factors, such as fetal alcohol spectrum disorder, addictions, poverty, poor health, and/or dysfunctional family relations are the cause of Aboriginal homelessness. Other literature states that socio-economic status and the lack of resources on reserves are also causes of homelessness (Beavis et al., 1997).

However, UNNS (2001) argues that even what appear to be personal factors are in fact the effects of structural barriers. UNNS (2001) states that the homelessness of Aboriginal peoples is rooted in "structural factors such as unemployment, low wages or lack of income, loss of housing, colonization, racism, discrimination (systemic or otherwise), patriarchy, cultural and geographic displacement, and the reserve system" (2001: 2). Other authors contend that the historical introduction of foreign systems such as education, justice, health, and child protection have left Aboriginal peoples in a "cycle of economic dependency, including high rates of poverty and unemployment" (Morrissette et al., 1993: 94).

Based on the literature outlined above, we assert that the factors associated with homelessness are connected to the omnipresent concept of colonization. Colonization did not only create the relationship between Aboriginal peoples and mainstream society—it is also experienced personally. Thus, we emphasize that the history of colonization and its current impacts explains, in large part, why some Aboriginal peoples are homeless in their own lands. We also believe that a framework which addresses the negative impacts of colonization on Aboriginal peoples and emphasizes our strengths needs to be developed. A Eurocentric lens fails to do this as it tends to frame Aboriginal peoples as social and economic disadvantages to the rest of Canadian society while negating our political power.

## Institutional Child Protection

The distinctive factor between homeless adults and homeless youth is that the latter are forced to leave home at an early age, before they have a chance to fully develop into healthy adults (Cauce and Morgan, 1994; Fitzgerald, 1995; Golden et al., 1999; MacLean et al., 1999). In general, many youth that are homeless come from the care of the child protection system such as adoptive homes, foster homes, or group homes (Cauce and Morgan, 1994; Fall and Berg, 1996; Fitzgerald, 1995; Lindsey et al., 2000; Maclean et al., 1999). According to one study, between 25 per cent and 50 per cent of homeless youth were previously in the care of foster homes (Lindsey et al., 2000). This may be connected to the fact that these systems are designed to care for young children (under 15), so youth encounter barriers to service because they are too old for children's services and not old enough for adult services. Therefore, they are often left with no choice but to live on the street (Fitzgerald, 1995).

The child protection system, historically a tool of colonization, continues to the present day (Anderson, 1998; Du Hamel, 2003; Hudson, 1997; McKenzie and Seidl, 1995; Report of the Aboriginal Justice Inquiry of Manitoba, 1998). Although there have been some Aboriginal child welfare agencies developed throughout Canada (Anderson, 1998; Hudson, 1997; McKenzie and Seidl, 1995), Aboriginal children are still over represented in the child protection system (Hudson, 1997; Mckenzie and Seidl, 1995; Thomas, 2003). This may be due to the restrictions placed on Aboriginal child welfare organizations. These organizations do have some control over the policies and procedures within their agencies; however, they are still usually required to comply with federal and provincial laws and policies. . . .

For anyone to take an institution such as child welfare, that has left a challenging legacy for many Aboriginal peoples, and turn it into something appropriate for Aboriginal communities is an enormous task. Yet it is obviously the goal of Aboriginal child protection services. As Hoglund (2004) advocates, both research and policies developed within an Aboriginal context by Aboriginal peoples is crucial because:

> Understanding how contextual mechanisms foster as well as challenge Native children's healthy social development is essential for generating informed, strengths-based research priorities and supporting Native sponsored policy and program development. . . . Researchers, educators, service providers, and policymakers need to look beyond Western European models of successful development to adequately understand favoured socialization and developmental processes within the sociocultural, historical, political, legal and socioeconomic contexts of Native children's lives and the families and communities in which Native children live. (Hoglund, 2004: 165, 168)

We stress that insider views are necessary in order to develop social policies that reflect Aboriginal worldviews and values. Thus, this research project explored the following questions with insiders—Aboriginal youth affected by homelessness:

- What is appropriate parenting within Aboriginal perspectives?
- What supports do Aboriginal parents, families, and communities need to raise children?
- How does prevention become a priority?
- How do we frame "neglect" within the realities of poverty?

## Aboriginal Youth Research Circles

In this research project with Aboriginal youth, which we (and an Aboriginal student research assistant) designed and conducted, one research circle took place at two youth programs within Toronto that service youth who are homeless or at risk of becoming so. A total of 24 youth participated. Basic information was obtained from the participants through a standard form that all of the youth filled out. Next, within the research circles, youth were invited to discuss specific areas about their past and current situations. They were free to decide for themselves which areas they wanted to contribute to. The research methodology was based on Aboriginal cultural protocols and integrated a tool known as the "Medicine Wheel". . . .

Sixteen youth had completed grades eight through eleven. This illustrates that many of the youth had a high incompletion rate for academic studies. This is especially significant considering that many of the participants were in their early twenties. One particular question on the information form was "what grade are you currently completing?" Six youth answered they were not completing any grade at the time and they had not completed grade twelve (needed for a high school diploma). This shows that in this group of Aboriginal youth in their early twenties, many have not completed high school and were not in the process of doing so. Of twenty-four youth, only three were currently completing a college education and none were attending university. This information demonstrates a great need for more comprehensive educational resources and greater access to education that addresses the worldviews and needs of Aboriginal youth.

## Eastern Direction: Looking Back

The first topic raised with the youth was "who they grew up with." It was suggested to them that they talk about who their family was/is, how they grew up, and what were their homes like before they moved on. Most of the youth stated that they grew up in the care of the Children's Aid Society (CAS), which included foster homes and group homes. More than half of all of the respondents mentioned having to relocate more than once. Those that stated they relocated said they moved to and from several different families and in some cases these homes or families were spread across the country. Four youth mentioned being in trouble with the law, were incarcerated, or always "getting into trouble." Seven youth mentioned living in a lone-parent female-headed family. Two of the youth lived with their mother, but later moved in with their father. One participant stated that he lived with his grandparents for a while. Only two youth stated that they lived in two-parent families—one of whom was later placed in the care of CAS. Hence, only one of the twenty-four participants had lived with both parents for a significant

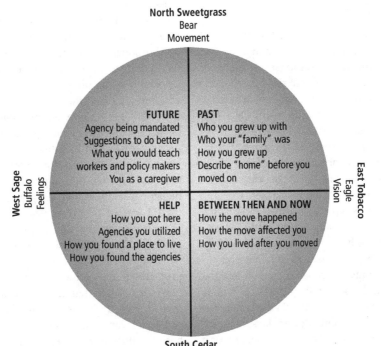

Figure 22.1 The Medicine Wheel

amount of time. Many of the participants had also moved back and forth between their biological families and foster care while growing up.

The predominant theme in the youths' profiles is that the majority were not living with their biological parents. The responses of the youth illustrates that many of them did not have what mainstream society considers as the "traditional" family. This in itself is not negative. What is negative is the fact that many of the youth were in the care of the state and placed in unstable homes meaning that they resided with families or in group homes where they experienced psychological, emotional, physical, sexual, and spiritual abuse, neglect, and acts of racism (e.g., one female youth was given the nickname of "squaw" in her foster home). Those who lived in one-parent families also lived with an element of instability. Many moved from home to home, both biological and otherwise, without consistency in their lives.

## Southern Direction: Between Then and Now

Youth were invited to talk about the move from their "homes" into homelessness and how they lived after this move. The responses of the youth were varied. Each had a different story to tell. Some came to Toronto with their caregivers or relatives to look for work or obtain an education. One youth was passing through Toronto, but experienced a crisis and was forced to stay. One stated that her adoptive parents were abusive which forced her to move out on her own. She stated that the street life was easier because she could make her own rules. Although this life was preferable in comparison to her home life, it was tough living on the streets. Resources were difficult to access because of her young age. One participant stated that she was "sick of group homes . . . too many rules" and that she was constantly moving from one group home to another. Two other participants explained how they lost their apartments due to lack of funds. Some of the youth that were in care, adopted, or in group homes stated that they lived in small towns and experienced a great deal of overt racism. They

had believed that they could escape this by moving to a multicultural city like Toronto. A few youth explained how they were just released from jail, and how they were often in and out of jail. Three youth stated that they came to Toronto for opportunities; they wanted to change their lives around.

The major theme in these stories illustrates that growing up in the care of, or being involved long term with, CAS—whether that be adoptive homes, foster homes, group homes, or moving between biological and foster families—is often a profoundly negative experience. When asked about the reasons for moving back and forth between biological and foster homes, youth explained that when a biological parent complied with the demands of child welfare, such as staying in counselling for a long enough time period or attending a substance abuse treatment program, they were able to go back to these parents. However, when the parent stopped complying by starting to drink again or getting back with an abusive partner, the child would once again go to a foster home.

In a number of ways, this response on the part of child welfare authorities can be linked to looking at Aboriginal parents only through a Euro-centric lens. Often when Aboriginal parents are placed in a position of complying with demands to get their children back into their care, intentionally or not, it is a set up for failure. For example, they may not be voluntarily participating in programs, these programs may not be relevant in terms of examining structural reasons for their situations or they may not be culturally applicable, there may not be enough emphasis on support of and resources for the parent or the values and worldviews of Western society are being applied to Aboriginal parents which skews assessments.

Few of the youth who participated in this project experienced a positive home life. Many participants felt that they were forced to leave their homes. This was explained as, for example, not being wanted any longer by adoptive parents because they were rebelling, getting into trouble or questioning the rules. Even though some expressed how difficult street life was, none of them regretted their decisions for this was better than what they left behind. Among other things, this demonstrates that interventions need to be implemented before youth feel forced to leave their homes.

# Western Direction: Help Along the Journey

The next area youth were asked to discuss was how they were able to receive help from social services agencies and how they were able to find a place to live once in Toronto. Some youth explained that they asked other Aboriginal peoples, they did not know, where they could stay for the night. Other youth stated that their friends or family members informed them of Aboriginal agencies in Toronto. One mentioned walking by a building that had an Aboriginal logo painted on the front, so he walked in. Four youth said that they were referred to an Aboriginal agency by mainstream organizations that service youth. Most of the participants agreed that they felt more comfortable at an Aboriginal agency. However, they also stated that it was good to get served by both Aboriginal and mainstream agencies. There were a few who expressed some dislike for certain Aboriginal organizations because of their experiences there regarding other peoples' behaviours such as intoxication and violence, but they still utilized them.

For the most part, the youth expressed a great sense of community amongst themselves, both within youth programs and on the streets. They spoke about helping each other out by sharing information about resources, agencies, and service providers within Toronto that were considered to be non-judgmental of them and some of their behaviours, such as substance using. Many youth talked about sticking together when on the streets for greater protection from both other people on the street and the police and letting others know about safe places to sleep. When they had something to share, whether that be money, alcohol, cigarettes, or food, they tended to share it with other youth. Some of them referred to each other as brothers and sisters even though they were not

related by blood. They also shared secrets, stories, emotions, and laughter.

# Northern Direction: Looking Towards the Future

The participants then explored what they would do to make the system better for future youth. They talked about what they would like to teach social workers and policy makers, especially with regards to the child protection system. To put this in context for themselves, the youth chose an Aboriginal child and family services agency becoming mandated as a child protection authority as an example to discuss what they would like social workers and policy makers to know. There were mixed feelings from the youth about the agency's change from offering voluntary services to taking on the responsibility of child protection. Many youth felt that bringing an Aboriginal perspective to child protection was vital. Others felt that it was a negative move because, in their opinions, the Aboriginal agency was too concerned with minor issues. One youth gave the example that "[a worker from the agency] stripped my kids because they had diaper rashes." Another young mother stated that the agency forced traditional ways on her, when she just wanted some emotional support. Another youth stated that other Aboriginal services were just as likely to involve child protection and related the example of an Aboriginal day care centre calling the Aboriginal child protection agency because her child had a "running nose." Some youth felt that the Aboriginal agency is "too quick to jump on rumours." Some of the participants who made these comments about the agency also expressed dislike for mainstream CAS, saying that they often felt like they were under "a microscope" and that they did not believe that child protection—either mainstream or Aboriginal—would be so cautious with older adults. Thus, they felt like they were being discriminated against specifically because they were Aboriginal youth.

Although some youth disagreed with Aboriginal family services agencies becoming mandated, their suggestions for change did express some common themes. One raised a great difficulty with child protection stating that children have to be protected, but at the same time, Aboriginal families have different needs that are often neglected by these services. Next, they talked about the importance of incorporating Aboriginal culture into the lives of youth, no matter who their families are. The majority of the youth agreed that even though Aboriginal family services becoming mandated is an empowering concept, it does not work if these services have to use the same legislation as mainstream CAS. Although mandated Aboriginal child welfare agencies employ Aboriginal peoples as workers to varying degrees and incorporate some practices such as involving extended families as care givers of children, they must follow the same legislation—the Child and Family Services Act in Ontario—as all other mandated child welfare authorities. This Act is not inclusive of Aboriginal values, particularly around collective responsibilities for raising children, nor does it acknowledge the impacts of colonization or the inherent strengths of Aboriginal peoples and communities. It does not make clear distinctions between neglect and poverty nor does it include aspects of prevention which is crucial to the well-being of the future of our children and youth. In keeping with these points, some youth spoke about how mainstream Canadian society decides what is acceptable child rearing for Aboriginal peoples and this is where the conflict lies. Other participants expressed that there is a need for more Aboriginal policy makers to change child welfare legislation or the cycle of oppression will continue. They explained that if this is not done, then it will simply mean "putting a brown face on it" [Aboriginal control of child welfare]. They further explained that this may "soften the blow" for some, but continue to oppress many.

The youths' suggestions about the need for more Aboriginal policy makers and changing child welfare legislation is brilliant. Since the current Child and Family Services Act does not address the sovereignty of Aboriginal peoples, what is necessary then is an Aboriginal Family and Child Services Act. Such an Act could address many of

the concerns that the youth raised in this research project. For example, it would be developed by Aboriginal peoples according to our definitions of family, child care, and parenting, This Act could clearly differentiate between poverty and neglect. It would reflect the values of Aboriginal peoples such as collective responsibility for children, communal sharing of resources and assisting families when they are struggling rather than taking their children away from them. Perhaps most importantly, an Aboriginal Family and Child Services Act would recognize the impacts of colonization upon all of us and focus our resources, both human and financial, on the well-being of everyone in our communities and on the prevention of further internalized oppression which leads to the harm of all.

The next major issue that youth discussed was the policies governing who is allowed to be a customary care (foster) or adoptive parent and how these need to be transformed to better fit the circumstances of Aboriginal peoples. First, youth concurred that permanency planning should be key, ensuring that workers try to keep children with family members. Another point was to have more customary care homes and adoptive families in reserve communities. Overall, the youth expressed their belief that there must be more Aboriginal families willing to adopt or care for children, and that the government needs to encourage and support this process through funding and legislation. Some of the examples they introduced were that some Aboriginal families may not have a lot of money, but that should not be a deciding factor in caring for children. They pointed out that many lower income families can do a good job of raising children. Furthermore, the youth took the stand that if being poor is such a concern, then the government should provide the necessary funds to foster families. They adamantly stated that, after all, the government is the reason why so many Aboriginal peoples are living in poverty in the first place. Moreover, these youth believe that preference should not be given to two parent families. Many Aboriginal families are headed by one parent who can raise children in a positive environment. Youth also stated that, if non-Aboriginal families are going to take in Aboriginal children, it needs to be mandatory that the children be connected to their cultures. They also believe that more effort needs to be put into keeping siblings together if families have to place their children into care. However, all of the youth were adamant that keeping families together must be of the greatest importance. One promising suggestion made to help keep families was that there could be a group of parents that can be used as an information resource for other parents who need it during times when they struggle with raising their children.

The participants also addressed the issue of child protection workers. They suggested that workers should be Aboriginal or, if not, have intensive training on issues affecting Aboriginal peoples. They stressed the need for greater consistency in training and education for helpers and how workers need to take into account what the client wants. They want workers to realize that everyone is different and what is "normal" for an Aboriginal family may not be "normal" for a mainstream one.

In conclusion, the theme for youth regarding the future was that for real positive change to occur, adding in a few cultural pieces is not enough, but rather legislation and social policies have to be completely changed to better suit the needs of Aboriginal families.

## Coming Full Circle: Analysis

The depth of analysis these young people demonstrate, both in terms of their knowledge and understanding of the reasons for their homelessness, and the critical lens from which they view the world is amazing. They are insightful and articulate. They call it the way they see it and no one is fooling them.

These youth were easily able to comprehend their life experiences, which were, for the most part, contact with child protection and separation from their biological families and home communities, within the realities of colonization and

oppression. A comment that stands out most perhaps is from a young man who said, "mostly we're taken away by child welfare because of poverty and this translates into neglect by them." For Aboriginal peoples, poverty is a direct result of colonization which destroyed the original economic basis of our communities. In contemporary society, breaking out of poverty is, in large part, dependent on acquiring formal education and employment. However, education has been historically genocidal and is currently alienating for many Aboriginal peoples so that 68.5 per cent of youth do not complete high school (Hick, 2007: RCAP, 1996). According to the RCAP report, both youth and parents are adamant that education does not prepare them for life in understanding themselves as Aboriginal peoples nor does it prepare them for life in the modern world. In fact, according to this report, youth stated they left school because they were made to feel ashamed of being Aboriginal, they experienced racism and there was no recognition of Aboriginal perspectives in history or respect for their cultures.

Certainly, low educational attainment affects peoples' future employment and income levels. However, according to the results of a study conducted by Kunz, Milan, and Schetagne (2000), Aboriginal peoples also have difficulty finding employment because of racism in the work place. They found that compared to white Canadians, Aboriginal peoples with university degrees are less likely to have managerial and professional jobs. In addition, they are over represented in the bottom 20 per cent and underrepresented in the top 20 per cent of income earners. Even with the same level of higher education, white Canadians are three times as likely as Aboriginal peoples to be in the top 20 per cent of income earners. These results are confirmed by Hick (2007) as well. Clearly, these studies reveal that even with university degrees, job opportunities are out of reach for many Aboriginal peoples.

Unlike the generation before them, this group of youth usually has a roof over their heads at night. But they do not have homes. Thanks to Aboriginal agencies that service youth, most of these young people are housed and have access to some health services. However, most struggle with poverty, have not completed high school, are transient, and, in the case of many female youth, are single mothers involved with child welfare who are often concerned that their children will be removed from them. This concern seems to come from a belief in the tendency for social service workers to "blame the victim" (Anderson, 1998; Hudson, 1997; Thomas, 2003). Even within Aboriginal child welfare agencies, internalized oppression has caused some Aboriginal peoples to believe the negative stereotypes about some members of their community and thus they treat them just as the dominant society does.

From a structural perspective, for the most part, Aboriginal child protection agencies continue to be mandated to operate within the framework of legislation and social policies not based on Aboriginal values and perspectives. Since these policies do not incorporate the distinct needs of Aboriginal peoples, a major focus needs to be creating legislation and policies that are compatible with Aboriginal worldviews, in general, while taking into consideration the great diversity of our Nations. In addition to this, the legislation and policies must also take into account past injustices and the effects they have on the health and behaviours of Aboriginal peoples today. To simply add in "culturally based practice" without any change to oppressive legislation is clearly detrimental for it changes little (Anderson, 1998; Hudson, 1997; RAJIM, 1998).

Furthermore, mainstream legal and political discourses regarding self-government, Aboriginal rights, and treaties are grounded in Western constructions of nationhood that originate from European history and cultures. Such discourses inevitably marginalize Aboriginal worldviews in the construction of nationhood in self-government and treaty negotiations. This approach, then, continues to entrench Eurocentric-Canadian structural power imbalances rather than creating positive economic, political, and social change for Aboriginal peoples. I emphasize that until constructs of nationhood can be examined from

both an Aboriginal and a Eurocentric lens equally, self-government that creates inclusive and sustainable Aboriginal communities is impossible.

The preliminary work from this research project also has many encouraging messages. These youth are greatly concerned about the next generation. When they spoke about their experiences and recommendations, they did not do so in ways that will necessarily benefit them, but rather because they hope to make contributions to the future of both their children and all Aboriginal children in general. These youth also view positive change as centering on re-structuring child welfare legislation and social policy. They identified that change simply by creating Aboriginal child protection agencies with Aboriginal workers is not enough.

Aboriginal child and family services agencies are to be commended for picking up the responsibility of child welfare and attempting to incorporate traditional knowledges into their work. However, many colonial legacies have been passed on to their shoulders, such as internalized oppression, family violence, poverty, and suicide, which they are expected to heal. They also must face unrealistic expectations placed upon them by both the Aboriginal communities they serve and mainstream society and governments (Hudson and Taylor-Henley, 1995; Bennett, Blackstock, and De La Ronde, 2005). Aboriginal peoples, including those who work in the area of child welfare, must re-claim the knowledge that prior to colonization, we lived as autonomous groups and our inherent right to self-determination—which included controlling the affairs affecting our families and children—was never abdicated despite the policies and actions forced upon us by Canadian governments (First Nations Child and Family Task Force, 1993; Association of Native Child and Family Services Agencies of Ontario, 2001; Bennett, Blackstock, and De La Ronde, 2005). Aboriginal responsibility and control must go beyond child welfare service delivery to the creation of legislation and policies that will restore traditional forms of government. This is crucial since present legislation and social policies related to child welfare

are based on Eurocentric values and worldviews, thereby making them an ongoing tool of colonization. Hence, as the youth raised, Aboriginal peoples must become policy makers in this area. Without significant changes to social policies, the major request to keep families together and concentrate heavily on prevention, which one youth described as "eliminating poverty," cannot possibly happen.

According to the voices of this group of youth, holistic good health rests largely on the value of supporting families through equitable access to resources to care for the well-being of their children. Such resources include inclusive education that is representative of Aboriginal youth, job opportunities based on merit and anti-colonial, anti-racist policies and legislation all of which aim to eliminate poverty caused by colonization.

# References

Abrahams, P. 2000. *The Toronto Report Card on Homelessness 2000*. Toronto: City of Toronto. Retrieved online 15 May 2004 from http://www.city.toronto.on.ca/homelessness/2000/index.htm.

Anderson, K. 1998. "A Canadian Child Welfare Agency for Urban Natives: The Clients Speak," *Child Welfare* 77: 441–61.

Association of Native Child and Family Services Agencies of Ontario. July 2001. *Pre-Mandated Native Child and Family Service Agencies: Issues and Recommendations*. Thunder Bay, ON: The Association.

Beavis, M., Klos, N., Carter, T., and Douchant, C. 1997. *Literature Review: Aboriginal Peoples and Homelessness*. Winnipeg: Institute of Urban Studies. Retrieved online 15 May 2004 from http://www.ginsler.com/documents/f_aborig.html.

Bennett, M., Blackstock, C., and De La Ronde, R. 2005. *A Literature Review and Annotated Bibliography on Aspects of Aboriginal Child Welfare in Canada*. Ottawa, ON: The First Nations Research Site of the Centre of Excellence for Child Welfare and the First Nations Child & Family Caring Society of Canada. Retrieved online 15 May 2004 from http://www.fncaringsociety.ca/docs/AboriginalCWLitReview_2ndEd.pdf.

Canadian Mortgage and Housing Corporation. 2001. *Environmental Scan on Youth Homelessness*. Ottawa: CMHC.

Castellano, M. 2002. *Aboriginal Family Trends: Extended Families, Nuclear Families, Families of the Heart*. Ottawa: The Vanier Institute of the Family.

Cauce, A., and Morgan, C.J. 1994. "Effectiveness of Intensive Case Management for Homeless Adolescents: Results of a Three Month Follow-up," *Journal of Emotional and Behavioural Disorders* 2: 219–27.

Du Hamel, P. 2003. "Aboriginal Youth: Risk and Resilience," *Native Social Work Journal* 5: 213–24.

Fall, K.A., and Berg, R.C. 1996. "Behavioural Characteristics and Treatment Strategies with Homeless Adolescents," *Individual Psychology* 52: 431–40.

First Nations Child and Family Task Force. November 1993. *Children First, Our Responsibility: Report of the First Nations Child and Family Task Force*. Winnipeg: Queen's Printer.

Fitzgerald, M.D. 1995. "Homeless Youth and the Child Welfare System: Implications for Policy and Service," *Child Welfare* 74: 717–31.

Golden, A., Currie, W.H., Greaves, E., and Latimer, E.J. 1999. *Taking Responsibility for Homelessness: An Action Plan for Toronto*. Toronto: City of Toronto.

Hick, S. 2007. *Social Welfare in Canada: Understanding Income Security*. Toronto: Thompson Educational Publishing Inc.

Hoglund, W.L. 2004. "Navigating Discrimination: The Interplay of Contexts on Native Children's Social Development," pp. 153–71 in C.A. Nelson and C.A. Nelson, eds, *Racism, eh? A Critical Inter-disciplinary Anthology of Race and Racism in Canada*. Concord, ON: Captus Press Inc.

Hudson, P. 1997. "First Nations Child and Family Services: Breaking the Silence," *Canadian Ethnic Studies* 29 (3): 161–73.

Hudson, P., and Taylor-Henley, S. 1992. *Interactions Between Social and Political Development in First Nations Communities*. Winnipeg: University of Manitoba, Faculty of Social Work.

Hulchanski, D. 2004. *Question and Answer: Homelessness in Canada*. Retrieved online 15 May 2004 from http://www.tdrc.net.

Kunz J.L, Milan A., and Schetagne S. 2000. *Unequal Access: A Canadian Profile of Race Differences in Education, Employment and Income*. Toronto: Canadian Race Relations Foundation.

Layton, Jack. 2000. *Homelessness: The Making and Unmaking of a Crisis*. Toronto: Penguin.

Lindsey, E.W., Kurtz P.D., Jarvis, S., Williams, N.R., and Nackerud, L. 2000. "How Runaway and Homeless Youth Navigate Troubled Waters: Personal Strengths and Resources," *Child and Adolescent Social Work Journal* 17: 115–40.

Maclean, M.G., Embry, L.E., and Cauce, A.M. 1999. "Homeless Adolescents Paths to Separation from Family: Comparison of Family Characteristics, Psychological Adjustment, and Victimization," *Journal of Community Psychology* 27: 179–87.

Mckenzie, B., and Seidl, E. 1995. "Child and Family Service Standards in First Nations: An Action Research Project," *Child Welfare* 74: 633–53.

Morrissette, V., McKenzie, B., and Morrissette, L. 1993. "Towards an Aboriginal Model of Social Work Practice," *Canadian Social Work Review* 10 (1): 91–108.

Native Counseling Services of Alberta [NCSA]. 2000. "Community Consultation on Homelessness Report." Edmonton: ncsa. Retrieved online 15 May 2004 from http://www .edmonton-omelessness.ca/aboriginal/consultation.doc.

Report of the Aboriginal Justice Inquiry of Manitoba. 1998. *The Justice System and Aboriginal People*. Winnipeg: Manitoba Government. Retrieved online 15 May 2004 from http://www.ajic.mb.ca/volumel/chapter14.html.

Royal Commission on Aboriginal Peoples. 1996. *Volume 1, Looking Forward, Looking Back*. Ottawa, ON: Canada Communication Group.

Shapcott, M. 2001. *Housing, Homelessness, Poverty and Free Trade in Canada*. Retrieved online 15 May 2004 from http://www.tdrc.net.

Statistics Canada. 2003. *2001 Census Analysis Series: Aboriginal Peoples of Canada, A Demographic Profile*. Retrieved online 15 May 2004 from http://www12.statcan .ca/english/census01/Products/Analytic/companion/ abor/pdf/96F0030XIE2001007.pdf.

Thomas, W. 2003. "The Social Determinants of Aboriginal Health: A Literature Review," *Native Social Work Journal* 5: 270–86.

Toronto Disaster Relief Committee [TDRC]. 1998. *State of Emergency Declaration*. Retrieved online 14 May 2004 from http://www.tdrc.net; "Resources" section.

United Native Nations Society [UNNS]. 2001. *Aboriginal Homelessness in British Columbia*. Retrieved online 15 May 2004 from http://www.urbancenter.utoronto.ca/pdfs/ elibrary/UNNS_Aboriginal_Homelessn.pdf.

# PART TEN

❖

## Additional Readings

Andrew, Paul, Tim Aubry, and Yale Belanger, eds. *Indigenous Homelessness: Perspectives from Canada, Australia, and New Zealand*. Winnipeg: University of Manitoba Press, 2016.

Blaser, Mario, Harvey A. Feit, and Glenn McRae, eds. *In the Way of Development: Indigenous People, Life Projects, and Globalization*. London & New York: Zed Books, 2004.

Bodley, John H. *Victims of Progress*. Lanham: Altamira Press, 2008.

Kenny, Carolyn, ed. *Living Indigenous Leadership: Native Narratives on Building Strong Communities*. Vancouver: University of British Columbia Press, 2012.

Loxley, John. *Aboriginal, Northern, and Community Economic Development: Papers and Retrospectives*. Winnipeg: Arbeiter Ring Publishing, 2010.

Simpson, Leanne, ed. *Lighting the Eighth Fire: The Liberation, Resurgence, and Protection of Indigenous Nations*. Winnipeg: Arbeiter Ring Publishing, 2008.

The Kino-nda-niimi Collective. *The Winter We Danced: Voices from the Past, the Future, and the Idle No More Movement*. Winnipeg: Arbeiter Ring Publishing, 2014.

Voyageur, Cora, and Brian Calliou. "Aboriginal Economic Development and the Struggle for Self-Government," pp. 121–44 in Les Samuelson and Wayne Anthony, eds, *Power and Resistance: Critical Thinking about Canadian Social Issues*, 3rd edn. Halifax: Fernwood Publishing, 2003.

Westra, Laura. *Environmental Justice and the Rights of Indigenous Peoples: International and Domestic Legal Perspectives*. London: Earthscan, 2008.

## Relevant Websites

### Assembly of First Nations (Policy Areas)

http://www.afn.ca/article.asp?id=23

*The Assembly of First Nations (AFN) website provides a number of Fact Sheets with respect to First Nations and has a section on policy, including a discussion of economic partnerships.*

### Idle No More

http://www.idlenomore.ca

*The website includes the vision statement of the Idle No More Movement, updates on events across the country, and relevant resources.*

# Films

*Beating the Streets*. Dir. Lorna Thomas. National Film Board of Canada, 1998.

*Flooding Job's Garden*. Dir. Boyce Richardson. Prod. Tamarack Productions, 1991.

*No Address*. Dir. Alanis Obomsawin. National Film Board of Canada, 1988.

*The People of the Kattawapiskak River*. Dir. Alanis Obomsawin. National Film Board of Canada, 2012.

*We Can't Make the Same Mistake Twice*. Dir. Alanis Obomsawin. National Film Board of Canada, 2016.

# Key Terms

Homelessness
Structural determinants
Poverty
Eurocentric models

Idle No More Movement
Bill C-45
Chief Theresa Spence

# Discussion Questions

1. How have histories of Settler colonialism, including Eurocentric models of child welfare, influenced the Indigenous youth involved in Cindy Baskin's homelessness research project?

2. How might an Aboriginal Family and Child Services Act, as proposed by Baskin, work to remedy the marginalization experienced by Indigenous youth? How might internalized oppression be prevented?

3. Discuss the significance of the Idle No More movement both in bringing awareness of the historic injustices towards Indigenous nations in Canada, and in mobilizing a strong resistance to Settler colonialism.

4. What was the symbolic significance of Chief Theresa Spence's hunger strike? How was her individual act linked to the poor socio-economic conditions experienced by Indigenous peoples across Canada? How did it influence the Idle No More movement?

# Activities

Invite a local community worker in a social services sector to speak about issues of poverty, homelessness of Indigenous youth in the area, and how the community agency is working to address these.

Locate a recent news item that highlights the economic and social conditions of Indigenous peoples in cities. What are the main issues? Does the article link these conditions with a colonial context at all? What proposals, if any, are offered as possible solutions, and how do these reflect those offered by the authors of this part of the book?

# PART ELEVEN

❖

# Health

## Editor Introduction

On 19 September 2008, Brian Lloyd Sinclair wheeled himself into an emergency room at Winnipeg's Health Sciences Centre. After waiting 34 hours for medical attention, he later died. Requiring only routine care to remove a blocked catheter, an inquiry later revealed that no one seemed to know what to do with Mr Sinclair, or even what he was doing there (Provincial Court of Manitoba, 2014). Among the possibilities: he was sleeping (ibid., 70–1); waiting for another assessment (ibid., 71–2); possibly another bed (ibid., 72–3). The inquiry also concluded that he was believed intoxicated—a drunk seeking shelter and warmth (ibid., 74–8). Brian Sinclair was not intoxicated. Much to the horror and protest of selected onlookers—at times even vomiting on himself—he died alone in a wheelchair. He escaped the attention of medical personnel.

The story of Brian Sinclair would seem atypical were it not for the suspicion of alcoholism, a pattern that is common in Settler–Indigenous encounters today. In fact, the story of Mr Sinclair is entirely consistent with a scholarly literature suggesting already that intoxication—or even suspected drunkenness—recurrently precedes Indigenous deaths in custody (Razack, 2015). It is furthermore consistent with an interview-based literature documenting the experience of Indigenous peoples in search of health care services (Browne and Fiske, 2009; Fiske and Browne, 2006). Alcohol, it is argued, works to discredit Indigenous peoples in health care contexts (ibid., Razack, 2015: 116). It fuels a deadly and racist perception that people struggling (or perceived to be struggling) with addictions are unworthy of care—a phenomenon that left an Anishinabe man dying in a wheelchair for 34 hours.

Indigenous peoples do not always die due to a negligence rooted in suspected alcoholism. Jordan River Anderson—a Cree boy with a complex medical condition requiring special services—died as an outcome of governments trying to decide on who would pay the bills (Blackstock, 2009). Anderson required an immediate determination, later dying in hospital because provincial governments have viewed health care for Indians as a federal responsibility. Some of us die in Canada because governments cannot decide on jurisdiction, while others die due to racial profiling. In either case, the deaths are preventable and are but two sides of the same coin. They both involve a societal and legislative history that places Settlers into positions of power and privilege over Indigenous health and well-being. These matters of life and death are not new.

The marking of Indigenous peoples as diseased, addicted, and unworthy of care—along with the deaths attached to them—are deeply historical. Kelm (1998) wrote of the discursive construction of Indigenous peoples as sick and vulnerable, arguing that it has worked under Settler colonialism to construct a population of peoples believed incapable of governing themselves. Razack (2015: 45) argues, furthermore, that the presence and/ or mere suspicion of addictions and alcohol use—along with the inquiries that follow and indeed document them—is constitutive of a material and symbolic violence required for an ongoing project of Settler colonialism to ensue. "Marked as surplus . . ." she writes, "Indigenous people [sic] are considered by settler society as the waste or excess that must be expelled" (ibid., 24).

Sick, damaged, and addicted populations are incapable of governing themselves, a conceptual if not ideological formulation that must be shown repeatedly if Settler colonialism is to lay ongoing claim to stolen lands (Kelm, 1998; Razack, 2015). Thus, when men like Brian Sinclair die in hospital, and a subsequent order of inquiry never moves beyond sorting out if whether or not he was drunk or an alcoholic, the privilege of never having to know, name, or mark Settler investments in white normalcy and difference making persists. Unfortunately, a dearth of inquiry focuses on difference making in health care services delivery. Typically, and instead, we are invited into a conversation about how to better procedures, offer a more compassionate or humanitarian response—especially to alcohol use (Razack, 2015: 103)—if not engage in cultural sensitivity training.

The invitation to cultural competence and/or sensitivity training places individuals—including health service providers—into positions of power and superiority (Jeffery and Nelson, 2009). Indigenous peoples are there to be helped, tolerated, if not better understood and culturally managed as different and deficit. Under the formulation, Settlers are never asked to name, transform, and/or remedy systemic inequities, or a process of identity making that is rooted in Indigenous inferiority. They do not need to know their own culture, institutions, or to realize and nuance Settler complicity and responsibility. Rather, and in re-enacting a historical process of Settler entitlement, the objective is to steer Indigenous peoples away from an inherent ill health and poverty and toward civility, or remove them—violently if necessary—from Settler spaces of belonging (Razack, 2002, 2015).

Cultural competence and sensitivity training ought to be looked upon with a great deal of skepticism if we consider that much of education and even literacy today—including that which is offered up pedagogically and institutionally—is based on coming to better understand a (different) culture. Polaschek (1998) wrote of New Zealand—now some 17 years ago—that health practitioners would be better off actively focusing on access to education and affordable housing versus that of cultural difference. Culturally safe services are not only informed and delivered through cultural sensitivity training. They require the participation of non-Indigenous peoples in terms of demarcating racism, colonialism, and a Settler entitlement to lands. Cultural safety requires a changing of the subject in education (Cannon, 2014; Dion, 2009; St Denis and Schick, 2003).

The authors included in this section are concerned with culturalist solutions to problems involving racism and colonialism in the context of health care services delivery. It is important to draw a distinction between culturalist and anti-colonial approaches to health care services delivery. Janet Smylie and Billy Allan argue, for example, that cultural sensitivity training actively prevents health care practitioners from dealing effectively with issues of racism, and from producing scholarly epidemiological research illuminating the social determinants of health. They argue that Indigenous peoples are impacted by poverty, poor water quality, stress, and identity related issues, and that this impacts health and health outcomes. The focus of research, they suggest, ought to be on health outcomes, and on remedying disparate and negative health indicators.

Brascoupé and Waters interrogate the expectations held of health care professionals today using cultural safety as a yardstick. The authors borrow the concept of cultural safety in part from

New Zealand–based scholarship, pointing toward the limitations of the literature in Canada. They suggest that the responsibility of Settler populations beyond a concept of self-reflexivity and healing has not yet been determined. They also note that the concept of cultural safety is intended to prompt Settlers to ask critical questions about their own entitlement to lands, belonging, and a further dismantling of a Settler colonial project. Combined, the articles call for decolonizing solidarities, reform, and Settler–Indigenous relationships building and rejuvenation as this relates to combating racism, colonialism, and disparities in health care practice and policy.

## CHAPTER 21

# Cultural Safety

## Exploring the Applicability of the Concept of Cultural Safety to Aboriginal Health and Community Wellness

*Simon Brascoupé and Catherine Waters*

## Introduction

### 1. Introduction and Definition

This paper describes and analyzes the concept of cultural safety as it pertains to Aboriginal policy and assesses its usefulness as a means of designing and developing government policy and service delivery. It seeks to draw together a range of literature sources to assess the applicability of cultural safety in a Canadian context.

The concept of cultural safety evolved as Aboriginal people and organizations adopted the term to define new approaches to healthcare and community healing . . . the concept is used to express an approach to healthcare that recognizes the contemporary conditions of Aboriginal people which result from their post-contact history. . . .

To be able to introduce cultural safety into policy and delivery, policy-makers must understand what cultural safety fundamentally means, the difference it makes to policy development and delivery, and where cultural safety lies conceptually and in practice in relation to previous considerations of cultural difference.

This paper seeks to clarify and deepen the definition of cultural safety, and explore practical strategies, approaches and lessons learned that address the key drivers of risk and crisis in First Nation communities. . . .

Finally, this paper addresses the relevance of programs and services to the values, traditions, beliefs, and practices of Aboriginal people. The issue of culture and the degree to which it can and should be part of policy design and implementation are complex, but increasingly it is recognized and accepted that policy cannot be effective if it does not acknowledge and take some account of the cultural context in which it is applied. . . .

*International Journal of Indigenous Health* 5, 2 (2009): 6–41. Reprinted with permission by the authors.

## 2. Literature Search

The literature search includes academic literature, focused both on health and indigenous cultures, grey literature and the Internet.... An Internet search included national and international literature available on the Internet (the Google search identified 6,860,000 citations for "cultural safety;" 455,000 citations for "cultural safety in health care," and 273,000 citations for "cultural safety Canada") presented a comprehensive review of relevant academic and professional research.

## 3. Cultural Competence and Cultural Safety Evidence Base

The evidence base for cultural competence and cultural safety is being examined from the perspective of quantitative, qualitative and traditional research methods....

In a major study of the cultural competence evidence-base in health care, the National Center for Cultural Competence found some promising studies supporting health outcomes and patient satisfaction (Goode et al., 2006)....

The challenge is to extend the understanding of the role of *cultural competence* in health-care delivery to the concept of *cultural safety*, by distinguishing between these concepts and understanding what difference cultural safety brings to policy outcomes.... Cultural safety and cultural competence are key concepts that have practical meaning for Indigenous people. They form the basis for effective patient-centred care and the professional advocacy role of the general practitioner (Nguyen, 2008).... In Canada, there are a few studies by scholars (Smye and Browne, 2002) that explore how Aboriginal peoples experience cultural safety, to deepen the understanding of the effectiveness of cultural safety tools and interventions in nursing practice. Other researchers, like Jessica Ball (2007a), ask "How safe did the service recipient experience a service encounter in terms of being respected and assisted in having their cultural location, values, and preferences taken into account in the service encounter?" (Ball, 2007a: 1),

explicitly linking service delivery to cultural respect and awareness....

Finally, no cultural competency and safety research was found that focused explicitly on communities at risk or in crisis....

This paper begins to map out the link between cultural safety and communities at risk or in crisis. Further research and work is needed to demonstrate how cultural safety theory contributes to community development strategies in supporting communities at risk and in crisis....

# Cultural Safety and Power

Throughout the literature, there is considerable reference to the concept and practice of *cultural competence*. This appears to represent a high-water mark of cultural understanding demonstrated by health-care professionals and, as the literature reveals, is taught and measured as a function of knowledge and understanding of Aboriginal culture by practitioners....

Elsewhere, the literature reveals a different understanding of cultural safety.... This conceptualization of cultural safety represents a more radical, politicized understanding of cultural consideration, effectively rejecting the more limited culturally competent approach for one based not on knowledge but rather on power....

## 1. The Culture Continuum or Paradigm Shift?

... Cultural safety is not just a process of improving program delivery; it is also part of the outcome.

Scholar Jessica Ball (2007a) supports this view of cultural safety as an outcome, but views cultural safety as a departure from cultural competence, rather than an extension of it. In essence, she sees a link between cultural sensitivity and cultural competence, but not between these concepts and cultural safety. She stresses that, while the responsibility for cultural competence lies with the service provider, cultural safety turns this on its head, transferring the responsibility (and the power) of determining how successful the experience was to the service recipient. . . .

Ball goes on to describe five principles necessary for cultural safety:

- **Protocols**—respect for cultural forms of engagement.
- **Personal knowledge**—understanding one's own cultural identity and sharing information about oneself to create a sense of equity and trust.
- **Process**—engaging in mutual learning, checking on cultural safety of the service recipient.
- **Positive purpose**—ensuring the process yields the right outcome for the service recipient according to that recipient's values, preferences and lifestyle.
- **Partnerships**—promoting collaborative practice. (adapted from Ball, 2007b: 1)

## 2. Multiculturalism and Cultural Blindness

. . . Multiculturalism can be seen, not as a "celebration of diversity," but a means of making culture and race invisible, by blurring and ultimately ignoring important differences between people into a meaningless notion of diversity. Verma St Denis, a Canadian scholar examining race and education, particularly as it pertains to Aboriginal students, argues that the danger of the "multi-culturalism myth" is that it creates an ideology of "racelessness," making race invisible when it should be acknowledged and understood, and reinforcing Whiteness as the standard of what is normal. With colleague, Carol Schick, St Denis examines racial attitudes in education in the Canadian prairie provinces, observing that the invisibility of White privilege which is accepted sub-consciously as the norm has the effect of marginalizing Aboriginal people and other racial minorities, and causing the "inferiorization" of Aboriginal people for their apparent failure to meet White measures of success and achievement (Schick and St Denis, 2005; St Denis, 2007).

York University scholar Susan Dion takes the same view of race relations in education as St

Denis, underlining the need for carefully designed curricula to trace the history of the "colonial encounter" between Aboriginal and non-aboriginal people and understand 20th century issues in the light of this history. . . .

Dion, St Denis and McIntosh all relate their studies of interracial relations primarily to the field of education and curriculum-design. . . . Most interestingly, in contrast to the cultural competence model of transcultural relationships, these scholars all point to the need for White people, and White professionals in particular, to understand themselves and their own race and culture, rather than learning about their clients' races and cultures. This element of self-knowledge is integral to cultural safety and any possible redefinition of power relations.

## 3. Transculturalism and Cultural Safety

. . . Transcultural nursing, expounded in the writing of Leininger (1991, 1998) is, according to Ramsden, based on the traditional western approach to health care, represented by the non-Aboriginal nurse. Transcultural nursing focuses on the knowledge and understanding of Aboriginal culture of the Canadian nurse; it therefore uses as its starting point the norms of the nurse and, in this sense, represents an approach based on cultural competence, rather than cultural safety. Transcultural nursing appears to fit the model of race relations criticized by St Denis and McIntosh, where the White professional establishes the context in which the service encounter will take place. In transcultural nursing, the power to define the norm and the onus for action to understand and know about another culture fall to the nurse (Ramsden, 2002: 112–14). . . .

Ultimately, the deficiency of cultural competence is that it is, as both a concept and as a practice, too one-sided and focuses on the knowledge and training of the service provider. This focus reinforces inherent power positions and reduces the role of Aboriginal patients to one of passive receivers of culturally competent behaviours. This is not to say that cultural competence does not play a crucial part in a successful interaction, but it cannot on its own create an equal relationship.

The transformation of the relationship cannot be effected through more culture training and greater knowledge by the service provider.... Both parties require the capacity to play their part in successful engagements; this capacity depends on the knowledge, understanding and confidence of both, as well as their self-knowledge and cultural self-awareness....

At the individual, institutional and government levels, the parties need to view cultural safety as neither an extension to cultural competence on the cultural continuum, nor as a paradigm shift, but as a navigation model to transform cross-cultural relationships.

## 4. Social Determinants of Health

... The environment in which people live has a profound effect on their health difficulties. These are known as the social determinants of health (SDOH), including poverty, unemployment, poor education, bad nutrition, poor housing, and unclean water....

The focus of the literature that explicitly explores cultural safety is limited to a narrow area of healthcare delivery, specifically nursing. But to limit the discussion to nursing and health care delivery ignores the many issues, such as education, economic opportunity, and lifestyle issues (such as nutrition, smoking, and alcohol and drug consumption) that are integral to the area of health care delivery.

Although the academic and professional literature concentrates almost exclusively on a narrow range of health care delivery, it is clear that cultural safety must extend beyond health if its full implications are to be realized....

In order to explore the full meaning of cultural safety and its possible application to different areas of social policy, we now analyze a number of specific policy areas which make up the context and environment for Aboriginal health and wellness.

# Application to Policy Areas

... In this section, we examine some areas of public policy where the literature on cultural safety examines the relevance of the concept to produce ... practical outcomes: health and the social determinants of health, education, and self-determination. In addition, in a subsequent section, the relevance of cultural safety is considered in the context of the criminal justice system....

## 1. Health

To understand health as a policy area, it is necessary to consider the wider definition employed by the World Health Organization (WHO) and further supported by the WHO's Commission on Social Determinants of Health (SDOH). WHO reports that the most common definition of health for the last fifty years is "a complete state of physical, mental and social well-being and not merely the absence of disease or infirmity" (Ustun and Jakob, 2005, quoted in Stout, 2008: 3[sic])....

Health policy regarding Aboriginal people which reflects the prescription of cultural safety could provide the policies to improve health outcomes, the institutional structures for on-going partnership and shared responsibility, and the symbolism of enlightened governance....

## 2. Education

... Possibly the single most important social issue for inclusion within the cultural safety model is education, particularly at the secondary and post-secondary levels....

Culturally safe teaching practices have also been the subject of considerable study, though the actual term "cultural safety" has not been transferred from the health literature. Scholar Pamela Toulouse draws on growing research when she argues that Aboriginal students' self-esteem is a key factor in success in school. She lists a number of factors that contribute to the academic success of Aboriginal students:

- Educators who have high expectations and truly care for Aboriginal students.
- Classroom environments that honour who they are and where they come from.
- Teaching practices that reflect Aboriginal learning styles (differentiated instruction and evaluation).
- Schools with strong partnerships with Aboriginal communities. (Toulouse, 2008: 1–2)

As in the health arena, the success of the bicultural educational encounter between teacher and student must be a two-way exchange, based on an equal partnership. The teacher's skills and knowledge must allow for the student to feel respected and understood. The student must feel safe in order to enter into their part of the encounter.

## 3. Self-determination

. . . Used in the context of health care, the term "self-determination" . . . encompasses a variety of forms which allow Aboriginal people to regain control at some level. At the same time, it may be a matter of practicality for Aboriginal people to take advantage of those forms of self-determination which can be negotiated and agreed quickly. . . .

These could include: a strong political voice through Aboriginal organizations; inspirational community leadership and role models; the reinterpretation of historical events; use of Aboriginal languages; the formation of intertribal and international networks; recognition and respect for traditional knowledge; the establishment of Aboriginal schools, colleges, community centres, clinics, treatment centres, and cultural and spiritual institutions; the use of cultural symbols and ceremony in the community and in wider Canadian society; a greater role for Elders; the use of consensual decision-making; the use of

traditional healing and justice; and negotiated treaties and agreements granting greater governance powers to First Nations. Finally, the literature on cultural safety in health care implies that self-determination exists also in the form of individual confidence and self-esteem, personal choices about treatment, an equal exchange of information with health care professionals, and a feeling of trust. . . .

The aspects of this form of self-determination, focusing on spirituality, tradition, respect, and community are in keeping with the concept of cultural safety. The cultural safety model of Aboriginal power does not advocate separateness of the Aboriginal community. . . . This is consistent with Ramsden's conception of cultural safety as, by definition, bicultural (Ramsden, 2004 [sic]; Coup, 1996) . . . ; it was a way of defining a two-way relationship.

## Personal and Community Healing

. . . First Nations are developing institutions and curricula to build the capacity in their youth. However, one of the legacies of colonialism is social and economic conditions that often preclude full participation in their community and . . . put communities at risk and potentially in crisis unless healing can take place. In this section we look at the subject of healing from three perspectives: the concept of healing in general, community healing, and indigenous knowledge and law.

### 1. Healing

The Aboriginal healing movement is based on a traditional community-based shared counselling process which includes physical, emotional, mental, and spiritual healing. It traditionally involves Elders bringing together the people involved in a dispute or harmful incident to talk, listen and learn from each other and to agree on a solution. . . .

While there are variations in the way First Nations depict the medicine wheel, generally the healing path of the medicine wheel includes a:

- Talking Lodge.
- Listening and Teaching Lodge.
- Healing Path Lodge.
- Healing Lodge . . .

Healing is . . . a society-wide exercise, whereby Aboriginal and non-Aboriginal peoples come to terms with the past and redefine the future. In this way, the healing relationship is depicted in the same way as the cultural safety model and is consistent with the writings of St Denis and McIntosh regarding the need for mutual understanding and also self-knowledge and understanding . . .

## 2. Community Healing

The literature on cultural safety is curiously silent on the issue of communities in crisis. The cultural safety of nurses' interaction with Aboriginal patients is defined in individual terms, with the feelings of the individual patient determining the success of the interaction. But the application of cultural safety to the wellness of a community is not considered . . .

Aboriginal communities face different challenges depending on their history and resources. It is possible to imagine other questions that could be asked in different circumstances, such as questions about the state of housing, the existence of employment opportunities, and the condition of the family. In the literature on Aboriginal communities and economic development are descriptions of communities who have healed from crisis to create a vibrant healthy life for their residents . . .

## 3. Indigenous knowledge and law

Indigenous knowledge is "a complete knowledge system with its own epistemology, philosophy and scientific and logical validity . . . which can only be understood by means of pedagogy traditionally employed by the people themselves" (Battiste and Henderson, 2000: 41[sic]). . . .

Indigenous knowledge allows Aboriginal people to express themselves in languages and terms which reinforce their social, spiritual, political, and cultural identity. While indigenous knowledge can be of practical use to individuals and families, in the context of cultural safety, its significance is in the recognition of and respect shown by service providers for traditional ways of doing things. . . .

Indigenous knowledge and laws strengthen Aboriginal people in claiming the respect and equality in relation to figures of authority in Canadian society, including nurses, teachers, social workers, judges, and others. . . .

It is evident that Aboriginal people can draw on the strength of their indigenous knowledge and cultures. However . . . there is the opportunity for enrichment for non-Aboriginal society as well in terms of mutual respect and understanding. In the Truth and Reconciliation Report, Anne Salmond comments: " . . . the process of opening Western knowledge to traditional rationalities has hardly yet begun" (Bielawski, 2004: 1[sic]).

# Conclusion

The concept of cultural safety . . . remains confined largely to academic studies and government reports, and little hard evidence appears to have been applied to professional practice. It seems that the practicalities of cultural safety as an *outcome* rather than a *concept* have yet to be realized. . . .

[A]s several writers have discussed, the concept of cultural safety carries an explicit political component. This derives from the express transfer of power in a culturally safe exchange from the professional to the Aboriginal client, where the success of the exchange is judged by the Aboriginal person, and not the professional. Expressing cultural safety in terms of power explicitly challenges the existing power structures within institutions and wider society and can appear threatening. . . .

The differences between the concept of cultural safety versus cultural competence and transcultural practice are profound. . . .

Cultural competence (and the linked concepts of cultural sensitivity and transcultural practice) is based on the *process* of building an effective service delivery interaction with Aboriginal clients, rather than the *outcome* of the success of the interaction. However knowledgeable or sensitive the professional is, this does not in itself ensure the effectiveness of the interaction. . . .

While it is desirable that professionals be knowledgeable of Aboriginal cultures, this criterion is inadequate to ensure that the *outcome* of the interaction with Aboriginal clients is culturally safe. . . .

[F]or cultural safety to become entrenched in professional practice in health and other policy areas, including education at all levels, justice, and social work, cultural safety has to be practiced not just by individuals but also by institutions. . . .

Since the literature on cultural safety focuses strongly on the individual level of Aboriginal people interacting with health care professionals, it is largely silent on the issues of community wellness and communities at risk and in crisis. . . . However, moving from the issue of power to culture, it is possible to see links that could be explored in literature in the future.

# References

Ball, J. 2007a. *Creating Cultural Safety in Speech-language and Audiology Services.* PowerPoint Presentation: Presented at the Annual Conference of the BC Association of Speech-Language Pathologists and Audiologists, Whistler, BC, 25 October 2007.

Ball, J. 2007b. "Supporting Aboriginal Children's Development," *Early Childhood Development Intercultural Partnerships,* University of Victoria, retrieved Nov. 2008, www.ecdip.org/capacity/.

Coup, A. 1996. "Cultural Safety and Culturally Congruent Care," *Nursing Praxis in New Zealand* 11 (1); 4–11.

Dion, S. 2007. "Disrupting Molded Images: Identities, Responsibilities and Relationships—Teachers and Indigenous Subject Material," *Teaching Education* 18 (4): 329–42.

Goode, T. D., M.C. Dunne, and S.M. Bronheim. 2006. "The Evidence Base for Cultural and Linguistic Competency in Health Care," *The Commonwealth Fund* 37, http://www.commonwealthfund.org/ publications/publications_show.htm?doc_id=413821.

Leininger, M. 1991. "Transcultural Nursing: The Study and Practice Field," *Imprint.*

Leininger, M. 1998. "Leininger's Theory of Nursing: Cultural Care Diversity and Universality," *Nursing and Health Care* 1: 152–60.

McIntosh, P. 1988. *White Privilege: Unpacking the Invisible Knapsack.* Wellesley College Center for Research on Women.

McIntosh P. 1998. "White Privilege, Color and Crime: A Personal Account," in C. R. Mann and M. S. Zatz, eds, *Images of Color, Images of Crime: Readings.* Los Angeles: Roxbury Publishing Company.

Nguyen H.T. 2008. "Patient Centred Care—Cultural Safety in Indigenous Health," *Australian Family Physician* 37 (12): 990–4.

Ramsden, I. 2002. *Cultural Safety and Nursing Education in Aotearoa and Te Waipounamu.* Wellington: Victoria University, http://culturalsafety.massey.ac.nz/RAMSDEN%20THESIS.pdf.

St Denis, V. 2007. "Aboriginal Education and Anti-Racist Education: Building Alliance across Cultural and Racial Identity," *Canadian Journal of Education* 30 (4): 1068–92.

St Denis, V., and C. Schick. 2005. "Troubling National Discourses in Anti-Racist Curricular Planning," *Canadian Journal of Education* 28 (3): 295–317.

Smye, V. and A.J. Brown. 2002. "Cultural Safety and the Analysis of Health Policy Affecting Aboriginal People," *Nurse Researcher* 9 (3): 42–56.

Stout, M. D., and B. Downey. 2006. "Nursing, Indigenous Peoples and Cultural Safety: So what? Now what?" *Contemporary Nursing,* International Council of Nurses, http://www.contemporarynurse.com/archives/vol/22/issue/2/article/749/nursing-indigenouspeoples-and-cultural-safety.

Toulouse, P.R. 2008. *Integrating Aboriginal Teaching and Values into the Classroom.* Government of Ontario, Literacy and Numeracy Secretariat, www.edu.gov.on.ca/eng/literacynumeracy/inspire/ research/Toulouse.pdf.

World Health Organization. (2008). Final Report—Closing the Gap in a Generation: Health Equity through Action on the Social Determinants of Health. Commission on Social Determinants of Health.

CHAPTER 22

# The Role of Racism in the Health and Well-being of Indigenous Peoples in Canada

*Billie Allan and Janet Smylie*

## . . . Scope and Purpose of the Review

. . . This paper explores the role of racism in the health and well-being of Indigenous peoples in Canada. It provides an overview of the historical and contemporary contexts of racism which have and continue to negatively shape the life choices and chances of Indigenous peoples in this country, and then examines the ways in which racism fundamentally contributes to the alarming disparities in health between Indigenous and non-Indigenous peoples. Indigenous peoples experience the worst health outcomes of any population group in Canada (Royal College of Physicians and Surgeons of Canada, 2013), underscoring the urgency and importance of understanding and addressing racism as a determinant of Indigenous health. . . .

[T]his paper is composed of three key sections. First, we examine racism and colonization as root determinants of Indigenous/non-Indigenous health inequities. We draw on Indigenous approaches to the social determinants of health and focus on describing specific colonial policies and how these policies have historically shaped and continue to shape Indigenous health determinants, outcomes and access to care. Second, we review the literature documenting and describing Indigenous peoples' experiences of racism in Canada and the links to health,

well-being, and access to health care. Third, we review responses and interventions aimed at addressing the impacts of racism at the individual, community, health services, and policy levels. We conclude with emerging ideas and recommendations for moving forward that we hope will contribute to broader discussions and collaborative action. . . .

## Methods

### Telling Our Own Stories

. . . The rippling effects of the trauma and rupture caused by colonial policies have served to reinforce or seemingly legitimize racist stereotypes about Indigenous peoples.

Stereotypes of the "drunken Indian" or the hyper-sexualized "squaw,"[1] the casting of Indigenous parents as perpetual "bad mothers" (Kline, 1993) or "deadbeat dads" (Ball, 2010; Bell and George, 2006), or media portrayals of Indigenous leadership as corrupt and/or inept, all serve to justify acts of belittlement, exclusion, maltreatment, or violence at the interpersonal, societal and systemic levels. . . . Stereotypes are examples of the ways in which the dominant stories in Canadian society of who we as Indigenous peoples are and how we are, are told about us and not by us.

. . . [I]n preparing this paper, we attempted as much as possible avoid the perpetuation of deficit-based stereotyping of Indigenous peoples. Rather, we set out to support the telling of our own stories as Indigenous people about our experiences

The Wellesley Institute, 2015. Reprinted with permission.

of racism and the impact of racism on our health and well-being. To accomplish this we have used a mixed methods approach. First, we have included narratives shared by our Counsel of Indigenous Grandparents with the aim of grounding our paper in their knowledge and experience and to prevent our discussion of the reality of racism in the lives of Indigenous peoples from being reduced to an intellectual exercise. . . . Second, in contextualizing our discussion of the role of racism in Indigenous health in Canada, we utilize a critical Indigenous lens to examine colonial policies and practices and their impacts on Indigenous health and well-being (Smylie, Kaplan-Myrth, and McShane, 2009). . . .

Finally, keeping in mind that the indexed published literature systematically prioritizes non-Indigenous voices and perspectives (Smylie, 2014), we draw on the results of a systematic search of multiple databases of published literature using search terms designed to identify publications re-garding Indigenous populations in Canada that addressed the interface of racism/discrimination and health/health care. . . .

## Racism, Colonization, and The Roots of Indigenous Health Inequities

. . . Despite the fact that race is a socially con-structed category with no biological basis, it has been used for hundreds of years to argue for and promote hierarchies of supposed superiority and civility among "races" of people (Reading, 2013). . . .

### Telling Another Story: Indigenous Understandings of Social Determinants of Health

Social determinants of health approaches seek to understand not only the causes of health inequi-ties, but the causes of the causes (Rose, as cited in Marmot, 2005), such as access to income security, employment, education, food, and shelter (Smylie, 2009). The social determinants of health mark

an important departure from strictly biomedical and health behaviour paradigms (Raphael, 2009), which can further stereotype and pathologize marginalized people by inferring that the health inequities they face are a matter of personal choice or poor genetics. . . .

The authors identify a range of proximal determinants including physical environments (including housing and infrastructure), health behaviours, education, employment, income, and food security. . . .

The authors emphasize the importance of accounting for the historic and ongoing impacts of colonization in public health strategies and communications with Aboriginal peoples, as well as the need for more detailed explanations for why particular groups are identified as at-risk. Moreover, they recommend increased specificity in identifying priority groups by attributes that increase risk (e.g., lower socioeconomic status, overcrowded housing) as opposed to ethnic-ity to decrease experiences stigmatization and discrimination.

Indigenous approaches to the social deter-minants of health also offer a significant contri-bution to health knowledge in centering holistic perspectives of health which may include con-sideration of the four aspects of self (body, heart, mind, spirit); the lifecycle; the importance of under-standing our past, in the present for our future (Greenwood and de Leeuw, 2012; Loppie, Reading, and Wien, 2009; Smylie, 2009); and the understand-ing of ourselves in relationship to the land and our natural environment (Blakney, 2009 [sic]). . . .

## Canadian Policies and The Institutionalization of Racism Against Indigenous Peoples

. . . Racist beliefs about Indigenous peoples un-derlie the historical and ongoing overrepresenta-tion of Indigenous children in the care of child welfare agencies. Indigenous children were his-torically removed from the care of their families and communities to residential schools, a system of institutionalized education and care that lasted well over 100 years[2] and aimed to assimilate Indigenous children into European and Christian cultural norms, beliefs and practices. . . .

As concerns about poor conditions and widespread abuses surfaced, support for residential schools began to wane in the late 1940s and into the 1950s. This gave way to a new wave of assimilationist practice taken up by child welfare agencies and the social workers they employed. Beginning in the 1950s and peaking in the 1960s, there was an enormous influx of Indigenous children taken into the care of child welfare agencies which is now known as the Sixties Scoop (Sinclair, 2004). . . . The removal of children from their homes and the impact of cross-cultural adoption not only had damaging effects on the identity and well-being of adoptees, but on the families from whom they were taken (Carriere, 2005; Sinclair, 2007; Alston-O'Connor, 2010).

Overrepresentation of Indigenous children in child welfare is not a vestige of the past, but in fact remains an urgent and ongoing challenge facing Indigenous communities across Canada. . . .

## The Gendered Impact of Colonial Racism: Indigenous Women's Health and Well-Being

Indigenous women in Canada carry a disproportionate burden of ill-health and disease, including higher rates of hypertension, heart disease, diabetes, cervical and gallbladder cancer, HIV/AIDS, substance abuse, mental illness, and suicide (Bourassa, McKay-McNabb, and Hampton, 2005; Dion Stout et al., 2001; Gatali and Archibald, 2003; Ghosh and Gomes, 2012; Grace, 2003; Kirmayer et al., 2007). . . .

The epidemic of violence against Indigenous women profoundly threatens our health and subsequently that of our families. Aboriginal women experience higher rates than non-Aboriginal women of both spousal and non-spousal violence, and report more severe forms of violence including being sexually assaulted, choked, beaten, or threatened with a knife or gun (Mathyssen, 2011; Statistics Canada, 2013). . . .

Indeed . . . the Society of Obstetricians and Gynaecologists of Canada recently released a newly revised set of clinical practice guidelines for health professionals working with First Nations, Inuit, and Métis highlights which notes [sic] in its clinical tips that some women may choose to terminate their pregnancy in fear that if carried to term their child would be apprehended by the child welfare system (ibid., S31; Wilson et al., 2013). Addressing the alarming health disparities and barriers to health care experienced by Indigenous women and supporting our right to reproductive justice foundationally requires understanding the historical and contemporary racist policies and practices that shape our lives, health care access, health, and well-being.

## What We Know about the Magnitude of Racism Experienced by Indigenous Peoples in Canada and Its Impacts on Health, Well-Being and Access to Health Services

In Canada, there is a range of survey data documenting the experiences of racial discrimination of Indigenous people (e.g., Regional Health Survey (RHS), Aboriginal Peoples Survey (APS), Urban Aboriginal Peoples Study (UAPS), Toronto Aboriginal Research Project (TARP), and the Our Health Counts (OHC) study) and a small but growing body of research focused on delineating the relationship between racism and Indigenous health and health care access. In this section, we provide a brief overview of existing information documenting the burden of racism experienced by Indigenous peoples followed by a synopsis of what is known about the impacts of racism on Indigenous health and well-being. . . .

### A Snapshot of Available Information Regarding Indigenous Peoples' Experiences of Racism in Canada

The Urban Aboriginal Peoples Study (UAPS) drew on an income stratified convenience sample of

Aboriginal people across 11 Canadian cities. Non-Aboriginal participants from these cities were also interviewed regarding their attitudes and knowledge about Indigenous people in Canada. Of the Aboriginal participants, 43 per cent reported poor treatment as a result of racism and discrimination, and 18 per cent reported negative experiences of racism and discrimination resulting in shame, lower self-esteem or self-confidence, or the hiding of one's Aboriginal identity (Environics, 2010). . . .

At the provincial level in Ontario, the Urban Aboriginal Task Force (UATF) used a mixed-methods approach involving a convenience sample survey, key informant interviews, life histories, focus groups, and plenary discussions to engage Aboriginal peoples across five Ontario cities. In this study 78 per cent of participants identified racism as a problem for urban Aboriginal peoples (McCaskill and FitzMaurice, 2007). The UATF Final Report describes the racism faced by Aboriginal peoples in urban areas as widespread and systemic, impacting access to housing and employment, interactions with police and school systems, and treatment in public spaces like restaurants, shopping malls and buses (McCaskill and FitzMaurice, 2007). . . .

The First Nations Regional Longitudinal Health Survey (RHS) is a national health survey developed by and for on-reserve First Nations and uses a population based sampling method. In the 2002–2003 RHS 39 per cent of participants reported experiencing racism, with experiences of racism more likely to be reported by those with a completed high school education, those employed for 15 hours or more a week, and those with a disability (First Nations Centre, 2005). Findings in the 2008–2009 study indicated a slight reduction in reported racism (33 per cent); reported racism data was not stratified by education, employment, or disability in the RHS 2008–2009 National Report (FNIGC, 2012). . . .

Racism has undeniably had a negative impact on Indigenous identity (McCaskill and FitzMaurice, 2007), with one of the most painful outcomes reflected in the racism experienced among Indigenous peoples which is sometimes referred to as intra-group racism, internal racism, or lateral violence.

## Understanding the Impacts of Racism and Discrimination on Indigenous Health and Well-Being

At present, the data addressing racial discrimination against Indigenous peoples in Canada and its effects on health is limited and piecemeal, utilizing cross-sectional samples that cannot address issues such as exposure and lag time (e.g., examining exposure to discrimination and the development of chronic diseases that develop over time) (Williams and Mohammed, 2009). . . .

In addition to the CCHS based on the 2006 census sample, there have been multiple studies examining the experiences of urban Indigenous people (Currie et al., 2012b; Environics, 2010; McCaskill and FitzMaurice, 2007; McCaskill, FitzMaurice, and Cidro, 2011; Smylie et al., 2011). . . .

Despite the limitations described above, the body of research knowledge addressing the relationship between racism and Indigenous health and health care access in Canada is slowly but steadily growing. . . .

The studies of Currie et al. (2012a, 2012b) and Bombay et al. (2010) highlight the need for research that addresses the complex relationship between racism, trauma, Indigenous identity, and Indigenous health. . . . Understanding the impact of historic, collective, and intergenerational trauma in the lives of Indigenous peoples is a necessary precondition to improving health care access and service delivery. Moreover, it is foundational to informing anti-racist efforts addressing the pathologizing and dehumanizing stereotypes that have fueled the marginalization and poor treatment of Indigenous peoples in Canadian society, and to advancing awareness of how these stereotypes are reinforced by the ongoing social exclusion and inequities faced by Indigenous communities subsequent to these traumas, including poverty, unemployment, homelessness, and poor health. . . .

# Race-Based Policies, Racism, and Access to Health Care

In the preceding sections of the paper we have described the historical policy context and the current state of knowledge regarding the burden of racism in the lives of Indigenous peoples in Canada. In the following sections, we turn our attention to the ways in which racism appears in Indigenous-specific health policies and within the interactions between Indigenous peoples and the Canadian health care system.

## State-Imposed Indigenous Identity and Access to Health Care

. . . In the context of contemporary Indigenous health, Canada's race-based legislation has normalized the uneven distribution of health funding, resources and services according to state-constructed Indigenous identities, such that only status First Nations and Inuit peoples are entitled to the NIHB program and to the Indigenous health services and support provided through the federal government via the First Nations and Inuit Health Branch. Métis and non-status First Nations lack access to these services and resources while facing the same determinants of health that have created egregious disparities in health in comparison to non-Indigenous people, such as lack of access to secure, affordable, or adequate housing, increased rates of unemployment and underemployment, food insecurity, poverty, and disproportionate rates of incarceration and child welfare apprehension (Greenwood and de Leeuw, 2012; Loppie and Wien, 2009; Smylie, 2009; Smylie and Adomako, 2009; Statistics Canada, 2008).

The NIHB program provides coverage for status Indians and Inuit people registered with a recognized Inuit Land Claim organization to access a range of medical goods and services. This includes dental and vision care, prescription medications, specified medical supplies, equipment and transportation, short-term crisis intervention, and mental health programming (Health Canada, n.d.). However, simply being eligible for NIHB does not necessarily ensure access since some services require on-reserve residency in order to receive funding for or access the service or program, and the roster of approved services and medications is constantly changing (Haworth-Brockman et al., 2009; Mother of Red Nations, 2006). Moreover, the delivery of NIHB also poses challenges to equitable access to health services in comparison to non-Indigenous people, particularly in northern and remote communities. . . .

## Racism in the Health Care Experience

In addition to the uneven access to health services and resources created through the NIHB and other race-based policies, experiences, and anticipation of racist treatment by health care providers also acts as a barrier to accessing needed health services for Indigenous peoples (Kurtz et al., 2008; Tang and Browne, 2008; Browne et al, 2011). Qualitative studies documenting the health care experiences of Aboriginal peoples highlight anticipated and actual poor treatment. For example, in examining the experiences of Aboriginal and non-Aboriginal persons accessing an inner-city emergency department, Browne et al. (2011) found that Aboriginal participants described anticipating that being identified as Aboriginal and poor might result in a lack of credibility and/or negatively influence their chances of receiving help. This was such a common experience that participants actively strategized on how to manage negative responses from health care providers in advance of accessing care in the emergency department. . . .

## Fatal Racism: The Death of Brian Lloyd Sinclair

Grandmother Madeleine Keteskwew Dion Stout of the Well Living House Grandparents Counsel asked that our paper include the story Brian Sinclair's tragic and unnecessary death at the Winnipeg Health Sciences Centre. . . .

Brian Sinclair was a 45-year-old Indigenous man who died after a 34 hour wait in the emergency room of the Winnipeg Health Sciences Centre in

2008. He was referred to the ER by a community physician for a bladder infection, which the Chief Medical Examiner of Manitoba has suggested would have required approximately a half hour of care to clear his blocked catheter and to prescribe antibiotic treatment (Puxley, 2014a). Instead, Mr Sinclair died slowly and unnecessarily of bladder infection in the waiting room of the ER without ever receiving treatment, despite vomiting several times on himself, and despite pleas from other ER visitors for nurses and security guards to attend to him (Puxley, 2013a, 2013b). Mr Sinclair's body was already cold and stiff, demonstrating the onset of rigour mortis by the time staff responded and attempted to resuscitate him (Puxley, 2014 [sic]).

Mr Sinclair was a double amputee, having lost his legs to frostbite after being found frozen to the steps of a church in 2007. He suffered a cognitive impairment from previous substance use and had endured homelessness, although he had housing at the time of his death. The Sinclair family, their legal counsel, and local Indigenous leaders asked the provincial inquest into the matter to strongly consider the ways in which Mr Sinclair's race, disability, and class resulted in his lack of treatment and subsequently his death (Puxley, 2014a). In fact, several staff testified they had assumed Mr Sinclair was in the ER simply to warm up, watch TV, or sleep off intoxication, while others have reported that they never saw Mr Sinclair despite the fact that his wheelchair partially blocked the same part of an aisle of the ER for more than 24 hours (Puxley, 2013a, 2014a, 2014b). During inquest testimony, hospital staff and the Chief Medical Officer of Manitoba, Dr Thambirajah Balachandra, vehemently denied the role of racism in Mr Sinclair's death, with Dr Balachandra blithely suggesting that even Snow White would have received the same treatment as Mr Sinclair under the circumstances ("Brian Sinclair dead for hours," 2013). Racism, the refusal of care and poor treatment of Indigenous peoples in the Canadian health care system are well documented in health research. For Mr Sinclair, the impact of racism proved fatal. On 18 February 2014, the family of Mr Sinclair withdrew from the provincial inquest because

its failure to examine and address the role of systemic racism in his death and in the treatment of Indigenous peoples in health care settings more broadly (Sinclair, 2014). . . .

## Racism versus Culture: Implications for Access to Health Care

We argue here for consideration of how Indigenous peoples' experiences of racism in health care systems are mischaracterized as and/or reduced to matters of "cultural difference" that are best addressed through cultural sensitivity or cultural competence approaches as opposed to anti-racism. The critique of a reliance on culture as a way to diffuse or avoid addressing racism in Canada is not new (Browne and Varcoe, 2006; Fiske and Browne, 2006; Henry, Tator, Mattis and Rees, 2000 [sic]). However, it is central to advancing understanding of and responses to Indigenous peoples' experiences of racism since Indigenous peoples have become synonymous with "culture" in the Canadian consciousness (personal communication, Grandmother Madeleine Dion Stout, 2014).

Browne and Varcoe (2006) assert that culture-focused approaches to working with Indigenous peoples (i.e., cultural sensitivity, cultural competence) require a critical analysis of how we understand culture in the first place, in order to account for the impact and influence of racism, colonialism, and our historical and contemporary contexts. This is necessary to understand and respond to the ways in which Indigenous peoples endure a disproportionate burden of ill-health and experience poorer access to social and economic determinants of health and health care that have been structurally created and maintained through historical and ongoing racism (Browne and Varcoe, 2006). Moreover, it is important to draw attention to how models such as cultural sensitivity or cultural competence maintain a focus on interactions between service users and health care providers, downloading matters of racism (under the guise of "cultural difference") to the individual and interpersonal levels and failing to address the role of systemic, institutional, and organizational racism in shaping the encounters between service users and health care providers. Cultural safety, a more recent and Indigenous model of health care, directly addresses the role and impact of racism in Indigenous inequities in health care access and health outcomes and attends to power dynamics in the interactions between health care provider and service user. . . .

# Racism, Health and Health Care: Responses and Interventions

The published Indigenous-specific literature on interventions aimed at addressing racism within the context of Indigenous health and health care is very scant. . . .

Our systematic literature search for articles, which focused on racism and discrimination against Indigenous people and health or health care in Canada (but did not include "disparities" more generally) identified only descriptive literature, with not a single indexed article describing or evaluating an intervention specifically focused on addressing racism within the context of Indigenous health or health care. We did, however, locate published literature describing initiatives designed to train health care professionals to improve their "cultural competence" or their ability to provide "culturally secure" care (Saylor, 2012). . . .

## What Do We Know about the Impacts of Racism on Health Services and Interventions to Address These Impacts with Respect to Indigenous Peoples in Canada?

In this section, we provide an overview of multiple examples of responses and interventions (including policy recommendations) aimed at addressing racism (including colonial policy and practice) and the impacts of racism on the health and health care of Aboriginal peoples in Canada. . . . We first acknowledge the strong individual, family and community strategies and resiliencies that are employed by Indigenous people. We then examine health care service and deliver responses; health

professional and training responses (including cultural safety training); national, provincial/territorial level interventions both specific to Aboriginal health and/or health care and impacting Aboriginal health. . . .

## Health Care Service and Delivery Responses

### Community-directed Indigenous services and programs specific to health

At the level of health care service and delivery, there has been a variety of developments aimed at increasing access to health care for Indigenous peoples and mitigating the impact of racism they experience in attempting to manage their health and well-being in the Canadian health care system. The emergence in recent decades of health services and programs directed by the Indigenous communities that they are designed to serve is of fundamental importance to improving the health inequities faced by Indigenous peoples in Canada. . . . For example, the Community Health Representatives (known as CHRs) and the National Native Alcohol and Drugs Addictions Program (NNADAP) have been managed by First Nations since inception (ibid.), and presently, a large majority of First Nations communities are administering and managing their own health services according to one of several federal contribution agreement funding models (Health Canada, 2012a). . . . Transfer of program and service plans that adequately ensure for escalating future costs have been notoriously difficult for First Nations to negotiate with the federal government. Below, we describe four key examples of community-directed health systems, organizations and services.

### First Nations Health Authority (FNHA)

The establishment and implementation of the First Nations Health Authority (FNHA) in British Columbia has broken new ground in the efforts of First Nations communities to control their health services. . . . Guided by principles of respect, discipline, transparency, and culture, the overarching goal of the FNHA is to achieve better health outcomes for all First Nations in BC. . . .

### Indigenous Midwifery: Inuulitsivik Health Centre

The initiation of the maternity program at the Inuulitsivik Health Centre in Puvirnituq, Quebec also represents an important landmark example of Indigenous community controlled health services. . . .

### Urban Indigenous Health Centres: Anishnawbe Health Toronto

In the urban context, the establishment of multiple urban Indigenous health centres represents Indigenous community-controlled health services, the large majority of which are run by Indigenous boards of directors and offer both traditional healing and medical services (Association of Ontario Health Centres, n.d.). . . .

### Indigenous Youth Leadership in Health and Well-being: Native Youth Sexual Health Network

The Native Youth Sexual Health Network (NYSHN) is an Indigenous for youth, by youth organization serving Indigenous youth across Canada and the US, emphasizing empowerment, cultural safety, reproductive justice, sex positivity, and healthy sexuality (NYSHN, n.d.). . . .

### Community-directed Indigenous Services and Programs that Generally Impact Health

There are thousands of community-directed Indigenous services and programs across the domains of housing, education, employment, language, and culture that impact health more generally. . . .

In Vancouver, British Columbia, the Aboriginal Mother Centre Society (AMCS) provides a transformational housing program for Aboriginal women and their children who are at risk of homelessness or child welfare intervention (AMCS, 2012). . . . Given the devastating impact of invasive child welfare intervention in Indigenous communities described in this paper, the AMCS represents an innovative model of service aimed at preventing or mitigating the involvement of child welfare authorities in the lives of Aboriginal

women and their families and supporting their overall well-being and success. . . .

### Community Level Health and Health Impacting Services and Programs (Not Indigenous-specific or Indigenous-directed)

There are many important non-Indigenous specific community level health and health impacting services and programs that are making important inroads with respect to Indigenous access to health care. . . . Some of these mainstream centres, such as the Queen West Community Health Centre[3] in Toronto, also offer Indigenous-specific programming to meet the needs of Indigenous community members living in their catchment. . . .

### Mainstream Health Institution Level Efforts to Improve Access to Health Care

Within some mainstream institutions, efforts to improve access and service for Indigenous clients has included the development of Indigenous-specific programs or services (e.g., the Aboriginal Services of Centre for Addictions and Mental Health (CAMH) based in Toronto, Ontario; the First Nations Health Programs based in the Whitehorse Hospital), or the employment of Indigenous staff in specialized roles such as Aboriginal patient navigator (APN) or Aboriginal patient liaison (APL) intended to improve access to and outcomes of health care by serving as a bridge between Indigenous patients and the health care system. . . .

## Health Professional Education and Training Responses

Since 2000, there has been a steady emergence of policy statements and guidelines for medical professional and medical training organizations in Canada towards identifying and developing the competencies needed by health professionals in order to optimize the care that they provide to Indigenous individuals and communities, followed by the development of educational guidelines, curricula and training programs for medical and nursing professionals and trainees. . . .

## National, Provincial, or Territorial Level Policy Responses Specific to Health and Impacting Health

In addition to federal policies regarding transferring the control of First Nations health services to First Nations communities and the First Nations Health Authority, there are several other sets of policies and policy recommendations aimed at increasing Indigenous governance and management of Indigenous health services. . . . At the national level both the Royal Commission on Aboriginal Peoples (1996) and the Kelowna Accord (2005 [sic]) deliberations advocated for fundamental shifts in the governance and management of Indigenous health services from the federal government to Indigenous communities (First Ministers and National Aboriginal Leaders, 2005; RCAP, 1996). . . . There has been some tracking of impacts of the implementation of policy recommendations although in most cases, the track record is not encouraging. For example, in 2006 the Assembly of First Nations published a ten-year report card examining the implementation of the recommendations of the 1996 Royal Commission on Aboriginal Peoples, giving the federal government a failing grade on 37 of the 62 recommendations included in their report card. . . .

## What Do We Know about the Impacts of Racism on Health Services and Interventions to Address These Impacts More Generally?

. . . Implicit bias refers to attitudes and stereotypes that occur unconsciously and inform our thinking, beliefs and behaviours (Staats, 2014 [sic]). . . .

There is an emerging body of research examining the role of health care provider implicit bias in racialized health disparities; this literature is overwhelmingly based in the US context and most heavily focused on contrasting service providers' perceptions and treatment of Black vs. white patients as Black people experience some of the most egregious and persistent health disparities among all marginalized people in the US. . . .

# Looking and Moving Forward

## Count Us In: Transforming the Conversation about Racism and Health in Canada

. . . Given that much of the existing research on racism and health has been led by scholars in countries with colonial histories similar to Canada (i.e., the US, Australia and New Zealand) in which Indigenous health disparities are strikingly similar to those of Indigenous peoples in Canada, there is much that can be learned in drawing from this work to adapt existing or establish new research instruments, approaches to policymaking, programming, service provision, and anti-racism interventions. . . .

Moving the conversation of race and health forward in Canada requires engaging in a decolonizing approach to anti-racism that centres colonization in discussions and knowledge production about race and racism, fundamentally acknowledging the historic and ongoing colonization of Indigenous peoples (Lawrence and Dua, 2005). This is necessary to ensure that Indigenous peoples are no longer left out of or sidestepped in conversations of racism and health. . . .

## Count Us In: Improving Indigenous Health Data Collection in Order to Address Racism as a Driver of Indigenous Health Disparities

. . . The need for meaningful data is critical to understanding and addressing the role of racism in creating and sustaining the health disparities experienced by Indigenous people in Canada. This echoes the work of scholars from Australia and New Zealand who are at the forefront of advancing knowledge addressing the impact of racism on Indigenous health (Paradies et al., 2008) and their call for research in four key areas: 1) the prevalence and experience of racism experienced by Indigenous peoples across the life course; 2) the impact of racism on Indigenous health across the life course; 3) the development of measures to assess systemic racism against Indigenous peoples; and 4) identifying best practices in addressing systemic racism against Indigenous peoples (ibid.16). We especially argue for concerted effort to develop or adapt effective interventions addressing attitudinal/interpersonal and systemic racism towards Indigenous peoples, and to undertake bold and brave evaluation of existing anti-racism strategies and interventions.

## Telling Another Story

We end where we began: we as Indigenous peoples must be the authors of our own stories. It is necessary to interrupting the racism that reduces our humanity, erases our histories, discounts our health knowledge and practices, and attributes our health disparities and social ills to individual and collective deficits instead of hundreds of years of violence, marginalization, and exclusion. The stories shared here describe the ways in which racism has shaped the lives of generations of Indigenous peoples and contributed towards our contemporary health disparities. It is time for stories of change: change in how we imagine, develop, implement, and evaluate health policies, services and education, change in how we talk about racism and history in this country. This is fundamental to shifting what is imagined and understood about our histories, our ways of knowing and being, our present and our future, and to ensuring the health and well-being of our peoples for this generation and generations to come. . . .

## Notes

1. The stereotype of the "squaw" portrays Indigenous women as dirty, uncivilized, savage, lazy, and hypersexual; this stereotype has been linked to efforts to undermine the roles and responsibilities of Indigenous women during the early stages of colonization and to justifying the historical and ongoing physical and sexual violence experienced by Indigenous women (Anderson, 2004; Gilchrist, 2010; Larocque, 1994).

2. The last residential school in Canada closed in 1996 on Gordon's First Nation in Saskatchewan. It was also the longest running residential school in Canada operating for 107 years (George Gordon First Nation, 2014).

3. Queen West Community Health Centre, part of the Central Toronto Community Health Centres, offers an Aboriginal diabetes program.

## References

Aboriginal Mother Centre Society (AMCS). 2012. *About the Aboriginal Mother Centre Society*, http://www.aboriginalmothercentre.ca.

Alston-O'Connor, E. 2010. "The sixties scoop: Implications for social workers and social work education," *Critical Social Work* 11 (1): 53–61.

Association of Ontario Health Centres. n.d. *Aboriginal health access centres*, http:// aohc.org/aboriginal-health-access-centres.

Ball, J. 2010. "Indigenous fathers' involvement in reconstituting 'circles of care'," *American Journal of Community Psychology* 45 (1–2): 124–38.

Bell, J., and R. George. 2006. "Policies and practices affecting Aboriginal fathers' involvement with their children," pp. 123–44 in J. White, S. Wingert, D. Beavon, and P. Maxim, eds, *Aboriginal Policy Research: Moving Forward, Making a Difference*, Vol. 111. Toronto, ON: Thompson Educational Publishing, Inc.

Blakney, S.L. 2010. Connections to the Land: The Politics of Health and Well-being in Arviat Nunavut. (Doctoral dissertation). University of Manitoba, Winnipeg, Manitoba.

Bourassa, C., K. McKay-McNabb, and M. Hampton. 2005. "Racism, sexism and colonialism: The impact on the health of Aboriginal women in Canada," *Canadian Woman Studies* 24 (1): 55–8.

Browne, A.J., and C. Varcoe. 2006. "Critical cultural perspectives and health care involving Aboriginal peoples," *Contemporary Nurse* 22 (2): 155–67.

Browne, A., V. Smye, P. Rodney, S. Tang, B. Mussell, and J. O'Neil. 2011. "Access to primary care from the perspective of Aboriginal patients at an urban emergency department," *Qualitative Health Research* 21 (3): 333–48.

Carriere, J. 2005. "Connectedness and health for First Nation adoptees," *Paediatrics and Child Health* 10 (9): 545–8.

Currie, C.L., T.C. Wild, D.P. Schopflocher, L. Laing, and P. Veugelers. 2012a. "Racial discrimination experienced by Aboriginal university students in Canada," *Canadian Journal of Psychiatry* 57 (10): 617–25.

Currie, C.L., T.C. Wild, D.P. Schopflocher, L. Laing, P. Veugelers, and B. Parlee. 2012b. "Racial discrimination, post-traumatic stress, and gambling problems among urban Aboriginal adults in Canada," *Journal of Gambling Studies* 29: 393–415.

Dion Stout, M., G.D. Kipling, and R. Stout. 2001. *Aboriginal women's health research synthesis project: Final report*. Ottawa, ON: Canadian Women's Health Network.

Environics Institute. 2010. *Urban Aboriginal Peoples Study: Main Report*. Toronto, ON: Author.

First Ministers and National Aboriginal Leaders. 2005. *First ministers and national Aboriginal leaders strengthening relationships and closing the gap*. [Press release]. http://www.health.gov.sk.ca/aboriginal-first-ministers-meeting.

First Nations Centre. 2005. *First Nations Regional Longitudinal Health Survey (RHS) 2002/03: Results for adults, youth and children living in First Nations Communities*. Ottawa, ON: Author.

First Nations Information Governance Centre (FNIGC). 2012. *First Nations Regional Health Survey (RHS) 2008/10: National report on adults, youth and children living in First Nations communities*. Ottawa, ON: FNIGC.

Fiske, J., and A.J. Browne. 2006. "Aboriginal citizen, discredited medical subject: Paradoxical constructions of Aboriginal women's subjectivity in Canadian health care policies," *Policy Sciences* 39 (1): 91–111.

Gatali, M., and C. Archibald. 2003. "Women and HIV," in M. DesMeules and D. Stewart, eds, *Women's Health Surveillance Report: A Multidimensional Look at the Health of Canadian Women*. Ottawa: Canadian Institute for Health Information. http://secure.cihi.ca/cihiweb/products/WHSR_Chap_26_e.pdf.

Ghosh, H., and J. Gomes. 2012. "Type 2 Diabetes among Aboriginal Peoples in Canada: A focus on direct and associated risk factors," *Pimatisiwin* 9 (2): 245–75.

Grace, S.L. 2003. "A review of Aboriginal women's physical and mental health status in Ontario (Commentary)," *Canadian Journal of Public Health* 94 (3): 173–5.

Greenwood, M., and S. de Leeuw. 2012. "Social determinants of health and the future well-being of Aboriginal children in Canada," *Paediatrics and Child Health* 17 (7): 381–4.

Haworth-Brockman, M., K. Bent, and J. Havelock. 2009. "Health research, entitlements and health services for First Nations and Métis women in Manitoba and Saskatchewan," *Journal of Aboriginal Health* 4 (2): 17–23.

Health Canada. 2012a. *First Nations & Inuit Health: Contribution Agreements*. http://www.hc-sc.gc.ca/fniah-spnia/finance/agree-accord/index-eng.php.

Health Canada. n.d. *First Nations Inuit and Aboriginal Health: Non-Insured Health Benefits for First Nations and Inuit*. http://www.hc-sc.gc.ca/fniah-spnia/nihb-ssna/index-eng.php.

Kirmayer, L.J., G.M. Brass, T. Holton, K. Paul, C. Simpson, and C. Tait. 2007. *Suicide among Aboriginal people in Canada*. Ottawa, ON: Aboriginal Healing Foundation.

Kline, M. 1993. "Complicating the ideology of motherhood: Child welfare law and First Nations women," *Queen's Law Journal* 18 (2): 306–42.

Kurtz, D.L.M., J.C. Nyberg, S. Van Den Tillaart, B. Mills, and Okanagan Urban Aboriginal Health Research Collective (OUAHRC). 2008. "Silencing of voice: An act of structural violence: Urban Aboriginal women speak out about their experiences with health care," *Journal of Aboriginal Health* 4 (1): 53–63.

Lawrence, B., and E. Dua. 2005. "Decolonizing anti-racism," *Social Justice: A Journal of Crime, Conflict and World Order* 32 (4): 120–43.

Loppie Reading, C., and F. Wien. 2009. *Health inequalities and social determinants of Aboriginal peoples' health*. Prince George, BC: National Collaborating Centre for Aboriginal Health.

Marmot, M. 2005. "Social determinants of health inequities," *The Lancet* 365: 1099–104.

Mathyssen, I. 2011. *Ending violence against Aboriginal women and girls: Empowerment—A new beginning: Report of the Standing Committee on the Status of Women*. Ottawa: Standing Committee on the Status of Women.

McCaskill, D., K. Fitzmaurice. 2007. *Urban Aboriginal Task Force, Final Report*. Commissioned by the Ontario Federation of Indian Friendship Centres, Ontario Metis and Aboriginal Association and Ontario Native Women's Association. http://ofifc.agiledudes.com/sites/default/files/docs/UATFOntarioFinalReport.pdf.

McCaskill, D., K. Fitzmaurice, and J. Cidro. 2011. *Toronto Aboriginal Research Project, Final Report*. Toronto, ON: Toronto Aboriginal Support Services Council.

Mother of Red Nations: Women's Council of Manitoba. 2006. *Twenty years and ticking: Aboriginal women, human rights and Bill C-31*. Winnipeg, MB: Author. http://morn.cimnet.ca/cim/dbf/morn_billc31_complete.pdf?im_id=5088&si_id=92.

Native Youth Sexual Health Network. n.d. Areas of work. Retrieved from: http://www.nativeyouthsexualhealth.com/areasofwork.html.

Paradies, Y., R. Harris, and I. Anderson. 2008. *The impact of racism on Indigenous health in Australia and Aotearoa: Towards a research agenda (Discussion Paper No. 4)*. Darwin, Australia: Cooperative Research Centre for Aboriginal Health.

Puxley, C. 2013a. "Woman tells inquest she tried to get nurses to check on man in Winnipeg ER," *Maclean's*, 24 October. http://www.macleans.ca/general/woman-tells-inquest-she-tried-to-get-nurses-to-check-on-man-in-winnipeg-er/.

Puxley, C. 2013b. "Woman in ER where man died after lengthy wait says it was obvious he needed help," *Maclean's*, 30 October. http://www.macleans.ca/general/woman-in-er-where-man-died-after-lengthy-wait-says-it-was-obvious-he-needed-help/.

Puxley, C. 2014a. "Brian Sinclair inquest to look at hospital backlogs; man died after 34- hour ER wait," *CTV News*, 5 January. http://www.ctvnews.ca/canada/brian-sinclair-inquest-to-look-at-hospital-backlogs-man-died-after-34-hour-er-wait-1.1618464

Puxley, C. 2014b. "Nurse tells inquest it didn't seem urgent to check on man in Winnipeg ER," *Maclean's*, 6 January. http://www.macleans.ca/general/nurse-tells-inquiry-it-didnt-seem-urgent-to-check-on-man-in-winnipeg-er/.

Raphael, D. 2009. "Social determinants of health: An overview of key issues and themes," pp. 2–19, in D. Raphael, ed., *Social determinants of health: Canadian perspectives*, 2nd edn. Toronto, ON: Canadian Scholars' Press Inc.

Reading, C. 2013. *Understanding Racism*. Prince George, BC: National Collaborating Centre for Aboriginal Health.

Reading, J., and E. Nowgesic. 2002. "Improving the health of future generations: The Canadian institutes of health research institute of Aboriginal peoples' health," *American Journal of Public Health* 92 (9): 1396–400.

Royal College of Physicians and Surgeons of Canada. 2013. *Indigenous health values and principles statement.* http://www.royalcollege.ca/portal/page/portal/rc/common/documents/policy/indigenous_health_values_principles_report_e.pdf.

Royal Commission on Aboriginal Peoples (RCAP). 1996. *Report of the Royal Commission on Aboriginal Peoples. Ottawa, ON: Indian and Northern Affairs Canada.* http://www.collectionscanada.gc.ca/webarchives/20071124130216/http://www.ainc-inac.gc.ca/ch/rcap/sg/ sgm10_e.html.

Saylor, K. 2012. "Development of a curriculum on the health of Aboriginal children in Canada," *Paediatric Child Health* 17 (7): 365–7.

Sinclair, R. 2004. "Aboriginal social work education in Canada: Decolonizing pedagogy for the seventh generation," *First Peoples Child & Family Review* 1 (1): 49–61.

Sinclair, R. 2007. "Identity lost and found: Lessons from the sixties scoop," *First Peoples Child and Family Review* 3 (1): 65–82.

Sinclair, Robert. 18 February 2014. *Statement of Robert Sinclair re: withdrawal of Sinclair Family from Phase 2 of the Brian Sinclair inquest.* https://dl.dropboxusercontent.com/u/8827767/Withdrawal/2014–02-18%20Statement%20of%20Robert%20Sinclair%20FINAL.pdf.

Smylie J., M. Firestone, L. Cochran, C. Prince, S. Maracle, M. Morley, S. Mayo, T. Spiller, and B. McPherson. 2011. *Our Health Counts Urban Aboriginal Health Database Research Project—Community Report First Nations Adults and Children, City of Hamilton*. Hamilton, ON: De Dwa Da Dehs Nye's Aboriginal Health Centre.

Smylie, J. 2009. "Chapter 19: The health of Aboriginal peoples," pp. 280–304 in D. Raphael, ed., *Social determinants of health: Canadian perspectives*, 2nd edn. Toronto, ON: Canadian Scholars' Press Inc.

Smylie, J. 2014. "Indigenous Child Well-being in Canada," pp. i–j in A. C. Michalos, ed., *Encyclopedia of Quality of Life and Well-being Research*. Dordrecht, Netherlands: Springer.

Smylie, J., N. Kaplan-Myrth, and K. McShane. 2009. "Indigenous knowledge translation: Baseline findings in a qualitative study of the pathways of health knowledge in three indigenous communities in Canada," *Health Promotion Practice* 10 (3): 436–46.

Smylie, J., and P. Adomako. 2009. *Indigenous Children's Health Report: Health Assessment in Action*. Toronto: St. Michael's Hospital.

Smylie, J., M. Firestone, L. Cochran, C. Prince, S. Maracle, M. Morley, S. Mayo, T. Spiller, and B. McPherson. 2011. *Our Health Counts Urban Aboriginal Health Database Research Project—Community Report First Nations Adults and Children, City of Hamilton*. Hamilton: De Dwa Da Dehs Ney's Aboriginal Health Centre.

Staats, C. 2013. *State of the Science: Implicit Bias Review 2014.* Columbus, OH: The Kirwan Institute for the Study of Race and Ethnicity. http://kirwaninstitute.osu.edu/docs/SOTS-Implicit_ Bias.pdf.

Statistics Canada. 2008. *Aboriginal Peoples in Canada in 2006: Inuit, Métis, and First Nations, 2006 Census*. Ottawa: Ministry of Industry, Catalogue number 7-558-XIE. http://www12.statcan.ca/census-recensement/2006/as-sa/97-558/pdf/97-558-XIE2006001.pdf.

Statistics Canada. 2013. *Measuring violence against women.* Ottawa, ON: Author. http://www.statcan.gc.ca/pub/85-002-x/2013001/article/11766-eng.pdf.

Tang, S., and A.J. Browne. 2008. "'Race' matter: Racialization and egalitarian discourses involving Aboriginal people in the Canadian health care context," *Ethnicity & Health* 13 (2): 109–27.

Wilson, D., S. de la Ronde, S. Brascoupé, A.N. Apale, L. Barney, B. Guthrie, O. Horn, R. Johnson, D. Rattray, and N. Robinson. 2013. "Health Professionals Working With First Nations, Inuit, and Métis Consensus Guideline," *Journal of Obstetrics & Gynaecology Canada* 35 (6) Suppl 2: S1–S52.

# PART ELEVEN

❖

## Additional Readings

Baskin, Cindy. *Strong Helpers' Teachings: The Value of Indigenous Knowledges in the Helping Professions*, 2nd Edition. Toronto: Canadian Scholars Press, 2016.

Browne, Annette J., and Colleen Varcoe. "Critical Cultural Perspectives and Health Care Involving Aboriginal Peoples," *Contemporary Nurse* 22, 2 (2006): 155–67.

Browne, Annette J., and Jo-Ann Fiske. "First Nations Women's Encounters with Mainstream Health Care Services," *Western Journal of Nursing Research* 23, 2 (2001): 126–47.

Greenwood, Margo, Sarah de Leeuw, Nicole Marie Lindsay, and Charlotte Reading, eds. *Determinants of Indigenous Peoples' Health in Canada: Beyond the Social*. Toronto: Canadian Scholars' Press Inc., 2015.

Jeffery, Donna, and Jennifer J. Nelson. "The More Things Change . . . : The Endurance of 'Culturalism' in Social Work and Healthcare," pp. 91–110 in Carol Schick and James McNinch, eds, *"I Thought Pocahontas Was a Movie":*

*Perspectives on Race/Culture Binaries in Education and Service Professions*. Regina: Canadian Plains Research Center Press, 2009.

Kelm, Mary-Ellen. *Colonizing Bodies: Aboriginal Health and Healing in British Columbia, 1900–50*. Vancouver: University of British Columbia Press, 1998.

Menzies, Robert, and Ted Palys. "Turbulent Spirits: Aboriginal Patients in the British Columbia Psychiatric System, 1879–1950," pp. 149–75 in James E. Moran and David Wright, eds, *Mental Health and Canadian Society: Historical Perspectives*. Montreal: McGill-Queen's University Press, 2006.

Pon, Gordon. "Cultural Competency as New Racism: An Ontology of Forgetting," *Journal of Progressive Human Services* 20, 9 (2009): 59–71.

Razack, Sherene H. *Dying From Improvement: Inquests and Inquiries into Indigenous Deaths in Custody*. Toronto: University of Toronto Press, 2015.

## Relevant Websites

**Aboriginal Healing Foundation**

http://www.ahf.ca

*An archived website providing information about funded research related to residential schools, AHF publications, press releases, and speeches related to Indigenous peoples' health, healing, and wellness.*

**National Aboriginal Health Organization**

http://www.naho.ca

*This website contains a vast and comprehensive number of resources spanning from fact sheets to multimedia items to career-based resources and numerous health related publications including a link the Journal of Aboriginal Health.*

**National Collaborating Centre for Aboriginal Health**

http://www.nccah-ccnsa.ca/en/

*This website was established in 2005 to support health equity through knowledge translation and exchange and contains a newsletter, events calendar, video resources, and publications related to social determinants literature and child and family health.*

**Native Youth Sexual Health Network**

http://www.nativeyouthsexualhealth.com

*This website provides information about safer sex, sexuality, harm reduction, and reproductive health, and contains numerous outreach resources, press releases, memes, and publications including a Two-Spirit Resource Directory.*

## Films

*A Healing Journey: Aboriginal Children's Environmental Health.* NAHO, 2003.

*Jidwá:doh, Let's Become Again.* Dir. Dawn Martin-Hill, 2005.

*My Legacy.* Dir. Helen Haig Brown. Vtape, 2014.

*Young Lakota.* Dir. Marion Lipschutz and Rose Rosenblatt. Incite Pictures/Cine Qua Non, 2013.

# Key Terms

Cultural competence
Cultural sensitivity
Culturalism
Cultural safety

Healing and wellness
Historical trauma
Multiculturalism
Social determinants of health

# Discussion Questions

1. What is meant by the terms "cultural safety" and "culturalism"? What similarities exist between them, and how are they different? What exists as an alternative to these approaches? How are the alternatives generative of (and informed by) anticolonial thinking? How would you define an anticolonial approach to health care services delivery?

2. What has it meant to belong in Canada? Who is in charge of defining how we belong in Canada, and what sorts of alternatives exist? What would it mean to position oneself differently and in relation to belonging, the land, and Indigenous sovereignty? How might the alternatives ensure a restorative approach to health care and well-being in Canadian society?

3. How is it possible to die in health care contexts or custody if you are suspected of alcohol use? What would it mean to challenge one's own, and others' complicity in the structural relations of colonial power and racism that is fuelled by stereotypical depictions of diseased, damaged or "drunken Indians"? How does one interrupt a structural relation of power that effects Indigenous dispossession and that is constitutive of white Settler identity and belonging?

4. What is meant by the term "health"? How does the term differ from "well-being"? What would it mean to re-define health care from a perspective that ensures the inter-relational and sovereign well-being of Indigenous peoples and Settler populations? How might this re-articulation look toward original principles involving treaty and nation-to-nation agreements and understandings?

# Activities

Your class has been asked to prepare a list of recommendations related to non-Indigenous peoples who work in health care services delivery with Indigenous populations. What do you recommend and why? What is unique about your approach? How is it critical of other approaches to health care services delivery?

Helen Haig Brown depicts a portrayal of love, renewal, and intergenerational healing in her film *My Legacy*. Why is her message important, and what series of questions involving resiliency, health, and well-being are being raised?

# PART TWELVE

❖

# Resistance

## Editor Introduction

In late fall 2012 and winter 2013 Canada's news was filled with images of flash mob dances, rallies, blockades, teach-ins, and interviews of Indigenous people all over Turtle Island: what came to be known as the Idle No More Movement (INM). This movement was initiated by four women (three Indigenous and one non-Indigenous) who were concerned about the impacts of the proposed federal government's Bill C-45 on the environment and on Indigenous communities. Through the use of Facebook and other social media these women initiated a dialogue about the threats to the environments, and the lack of meaningful consultation with Indigenous communities whose rights were to be mostly affected by the changes proposed in the Bill. These brave women inspired people all over the country and worldwide to "not be idle" about such political events. They encouraged all to become more informed about the historical relationship between Indigenous peoples and mainstream society, and about how the newly proposed laws would threaten our environment.

In the height of the movement, the chief of Attawapiskat, Theresa Spence, began a fast to bring attention to the conditions of her community and demanded that the Prime Minister and the Governor General (as the representative of the Crown) meet with her and other Chiefs to discuss the many issues faced by Indigenous communities, such as poverty, gendered violence, cultural loss, and environmental degradation. For months, her demands were largely ignored by the Prime Minister, but the INM gained more momentum and visibility, and saw many groups, both Indigenous and not, joining at the events occurring across the globe. Their words, drums, and songs could no longer be ignored, and Prime Minister Stephen Harper agreed to meet with Chiefs on 11 January 2013, but without the presence of the Governor General. Chief Spence and others refused to participate at that meeting because they felt that the Governor General's absence would lessen the significance and concrete result of a meeting. Chief Spence ended the hunger strike on 24 January 2013.

The INM was a significant moment in our Canadian history; however, we must remember that Indigenous peoples have never been idle against the ongoing colonialism and have always resisted the dispossession, discrimination, and threat to our inherent Indigenous self-determination. Hence, INM should "be remembered—alongside the maelstrom of treaty-making, political waves like the Red Power Movement and the 1969–1970 mobilization against the White Paper, and resistance movements at Oka, Gustefson's Lake, Ipperwash, Burnt Church, Goose Bay, Kanostaton, and so on. . . . most Indigenous peoples have never been idle in their efforts to protect what is meaningful to our communities—nor will we ever be" (The Kino-nda-niimi Collective, 2014: 21). This long history of resistance represents a true commitment to the principles embedded in the original treaty/nation-to-nation relationship that our ancestors entered with the first Settlers and later the State, such as the Two-Row Wampum that has been discussed at various points in this book. Indigenous nations have been faithful to this sacred relationship, and when the other party has strayed from its original intent, our people have acted to protect and nurture it, reminding others that we are meant to share the resources of this land and to act in a just and equitable way with each other. Hence, when such relationship has been disrespected, as was the case with Bill C-45, Indigenous people have been ready to even risk their own lives in order to reawaken the true intent of the wampums. Indigenous peoples have always been vocal about following the just principles of a nation-to-nation relationship and have asked that everyone act responsibly and follow those principles in their daily lives.

INM has to be seen as a continuation of that commitment to a nation-to-nation relationship and a call to act responsibly towards *all our relations*, including our lands, waters, and all animals. The movement differed a bit from other acts of resistance: it was a bottom-up informal one, initiated and led by women, and it used social media, arts, round dances, and other culturally specific means to address important issues. It also was effective in drawing support from many non-Indigenous peoples, including environmentalists, youth, labour activists, and some politicians. It spread all over the globe, reaching Indigenous communities as far as New Zealand and Australia, who could identify similar experiences of historical grievances against Settler States as their Canadian counterparts. INM awakened all, Indigenous and non-Indigenous, to act responsibly and remember that treaties and original wampums are living documents from which our daily actions must flourish. The solidarity shown by many individuals gave us some hope for the future: that a just equitable relationship wherein Indigenous inherent self-determination is respected might be possible.

The authors of this section give illustrations of everyday acts of self-determination and resistance to colonialism, and in each case, Indigenous people are simply acting upon their responsibility to their lands, their people, and all creation. In doing so, they are demanding a structural change to the current systemic inequities, and a shift towards a true shared power, a lived nation-to-nation relationship. Corntassel and Bryce's article shows us that environmental destruction has made it difficult for Indigenous nations to practice sustainable self-determination. However, Indigenous peoples have not been sitting idly; for example, the Lekwungen communities are trying to revitalize and protect their traditional kwetlal food system from the effects of colonial developments, and the "Water Walkers" movement in Wikiwemikong Unceded First Nation in Ontario, Canada is resisting against the environmental pollution to our lakes and traditional waters. In both these cases, one can see that Indigenous peoples are asserting their inherent rights to sustainable self-determination, and fulfilling their responsibility to maintain a sacred traditional holistic relationship with their territories and all relations. Such assertive acts move us away from a politics of recognition that limits Indigenous peoples' self-determination.

A politics of recognition is a rights-based strategy that largely depends on the State's recognition and accommodation of Indigenous self-determination. But, as Coulthard (2014) argues, "the politics of recognition in its contemporary liberal form promotes to reproduce the very configurations of colonialist, racist, patriarchal state power that Indigenous peoples' demands for recognition have historically sought to transcend" (ibid., 3). This is because, in the current structurally unequal relationship, the colonial Canadian State still controls the definition of "Indigenous self-determination" and "Indigenous rights" and frames both the discourse of politics of recognition and any practical consequence of it. Ultimately, such a strategy has not significantly transformed the relationship between the State and Indigenous nations, especially when any Indigenous claims are viewed as a threat to Canadian "interest" or "sovereignty." Rather than wishing for such recognition by the State, Indigenous peoples, Coulthard maintains, ought to assert cultural practices of critical individual and collective self-recognition, empower themselves, and "practice decolonial, gender-emancipatory, and economically nonexploitative alternative structures of law and sovereign authority grounded on a critical refashioning of the best of Indigenous legal and political traditions" (ibid., 179). Acts taken by the Water Walkers and Lekwungen communities are examples of such types of decolonial self-recognition.

Simpson's article also illustrates an example of decolonial self-determining act: Chief Spence's fasting was a very culturally significant political act, as was the broader INM movement. Chief Spence willingly decided to refuse to eat so that attention to her peoples' condition would reach the mainstream society and the Canadian State. Her self-determining act reminded all Canadians that her people have been "fasting" for centuries, due to the ongoing colonial conditions in Turtle Island. She asserted her self-determination by staying firm and brave, despite the heavy criticisms and racism she faced, and she stood strong in her demands for a meeting with the State and the Crown's representative. Her act inspired many Indigenous peoples all over Turtle Island who prayed for her, and sang at the flash mob dances in her honour. As Simpson points out, she reminded each of us that we all have a specific position in this nation-to-nation relationship, and from that place comes great humility and responsibility to do what each of us can to re-light the fire of the original treaties and wampums. We each must continually resist colonialism and work toward restoring a real, well-balanced, and equitable relationship with all our relations.

# CHAPTER 23

# Fish Broth and Fasting

*Leanne Betasamosake Simpson*

---

A year ago, after the community of Attawapiskat had been dragged through the racist lens of the media for more than a month, I began to write about the situation. I wrote two pieces. One that was published in *Briarpatch* magazine that was political, and one that was a spoken word piece using the music of Cree cellist Cris Derksen. I am not from Attawapiskat and I've never been there. I wrote because I felt a strong sense of solidarity with the community because like most Indigenous Peoples, I have personal connections and history that links me to all of the same issues. I felt a sense of responsibility to speak out not only on the way

the issues were playing out in the media, but on the response of Canadian society. I feel the same way again this year. I am not going to correct all of the slander designed to discredit Chief Spence and her hunger strike—my friends and colleagues have already done a fantastic job of that. Check out the work of Chelsea Vowel and Alanis Obomsawin's *The People of the Kattawpiskat River* if you haven't. The past few weeks have been an intense time to be Anishinaabeg. There is a lot to write about and to process. I felt overwhelmingly proud on #J11 with tens of thousands of us in the streets worldwide, with the majority of our Indian Act Chiefs standing with us in those streets. I also felt the depths of betrayal on that day. But it was during the local #J11 actions in my community

In Kino-nda-niimi Collective, eds, *The Winter We Danced* (Winnipeg: ARP Books, 2014), pp. 154–7. Used by permission.

that I started to think a lot about fish broth. Fish broth and Anishinaabeg governance.

*Fish broth has been cast by the mainstream media as "the cheat."* Upon learning Chief Spence was drinking tea and fish broth coverage shifted from framing her action as a "hunger strike" to a "liquid diet," as if 32 days without food is easy. As if a liquid diet doesn't take a substantial physical, mental, and emotional toll or substantial physical, mental, and emotional strength to accomplish. Of course this characterization comes from a place of enormous unchecked privilege and a position of wealth. It comes from not having to fight for one's physical survival because of the weight of crushing poverty. It comes from always having other options. This is not where Indigenous Peoples come from. My Ancestors survived many long winters on fish broth because there was nothing else to eat—not because the environment was harsh, but because the land loss and colonial policy were so fierce that they were forced into an imposed poverty that often left fish broth as the only sustenance.

*Fish broth.* It carries cultural meaning for Anishinaabeg. It symbolizes hardship and sacrifice. It symbolizes the strength of our Ancestors. It means survival. Fish broth sustained us through the hardest of circumstances, with the parallel understanding that it can't sustain one forever. We exist today because of fish broth. It connects us to the water and to the fish who gave up its life so we could sustain ourselves. Chief Spence is eating fish broth because metaphorically, colonialism has kept Indigenous Peoples on a fish broth diet for generations upon generations. This is utterly lost on mainstream Canada, as media continues to call Ogichidaakwe Spence's fast a "liquid diet" while the right-wing media refers to it as much worse. Not *Chief* Spence, but *Ogichidaakwe* Spence—a holy woman, a woman that would do anything for her family and community, the one that goes over and makes things happen, a warrior, a leader because Ogichidaakwe Spence isn't just on a hunger strike. She is fasting and this also has cultural meaning for Anishinaabeg. She is in ceremony. We do not "dial back" our ceremonies.

We do not undertake this kind of ceremony without much forethought and preparation. We do not ask or demand that people stop the fast before they have accomplished whatever it is they set out to accomplish, which in her case is substantial change in the relationship between the Canadian state and Indigenous nations. We do not critique the faster. We do not bandwagon or verbally attack the faster. We do not criticize because we feel she's become the (unwilling) leader of the movement. We do not assume that she is being ill advised. We do not tell her to "save face." We support. We pray. We offer semaa. We take care of the sacred fire. We sing each night at dusk. We take care of all the other things that need to be taken care of, and we live up to our responsibilities in light of the faster. We protect the faster. We do these things because we know that through her physical sacrifice she is closer to the Spiritual world than we are. We do these things because she is sacrificing for us and because it is the kind, compassionate thing to do.

We do these things because it is our job to respect her self-determination as an Anishinaabekwe—this is the most basic building block of Anishinaabeg sovereignty and governance. "We respect her sovereignty over her body and her mind. We do not act like we know better than her." Fasting as a ceremony is difficult. It is challenging to willingly weaken one's body physically, and the mental and emotional strength required for fasting is perhaps more difficult than the physical. So when we fast, we ask our friends and family to support us and to act as our helpers. There is an assumption of reciprocity—the faster is doing without, in this case to make things better for all Indigenous Peoples, and in return, the community around her carries the responsibility of supporting her. A few days ago I posted these two sentences on Twitter: "I support @ChiefTheresa in her decision to continue her hunger strike. The only person that can decide otherwise is Chief Spence." Within minutes, trolls were commenting on my feed with commentary on Chief Spence's body image, diet jokes, calls for "no more special treatment for Natives," and calls to end her hunger strike. One person called her a "cunt."

I understand we need to be positive, I do. We also need to continue telling the truth. The racism, sexism, and disrespect that has been heaped on

Ogichidaakwe Spence in the past weeks have been done so in part because it is acceptable to treat Indigenous women this way. These comments take place in a context where we have nearly 1000 missing and murdered Indigenous women. Where we still have places named "squaw." Where Indigenous women have been the deliberate target of gendered colonial violence for 400 years. Where the people who have been seriously hurt and injured by the backlash against Idle No More have been women. Where Ogichidaakwe Spence's voice has not been heard. Ogichidaakwe Spence challenges Canadians because no one in Canada wants to believe this situation is bad enough that someone would willingly give up their life.

Ogichidaakwe Spence challenges me, because I am not on day 32 of a fast. I did not put my life on the line, and that forces me to continually look myself in the mirror and ask if I am doing everything I can. This is her gift to me. Idle No More as a movement is now much bigger than the hunger strikers and Bill C-45, but it is still important to acknowledge their sacrifice, influence, and leadership. I want my grandchildren to be able to live in Mississauga Anishinaabeg territory as Mississauga Anishinaabeg—hunting, fishing, collecting medicines, doing ceremony, telling stories, speaking our language, governing themselves using our political traditions, and whatever else that might mean to them, unharassed. *That's not a dream palace—that is what our treaties guaranteed.*

We now have hundreds of leaders from different Indigenous nations emerging all over Mikinakong (the Place of the Turtle). We now have hundreds of eloquent spokespeople, seasoned organizers, writers, thinkers, and artists acting on their own ideas in any way and every way possible. This is the beauty of our movement. Chi'Miigwech Theresa Spence, Raymond Robinson, Emil Bell, and Jean Sock for your vision, your sacrifice, and your commitment to making us better. Chi'Miigwech to everyone who has been up late at night worrying about what to do next and then who gets up the next morning and acts. I am hopeful and inspired and look forward to our new, collective emergence as a healthy and strong Anishinaabeg nation.

# CHAPTER 24

# Practicing Sustainable Self-Determination
## Indigenous Approaches to Cultural Restoration and Revitalization

*Jeff Corntassel and Cheryl Bryce*

Today there are approximately 370 million indigenous people living in over 70 states throughout the world, constituting five per cent of the global population. Eighty per cent of all biodiversity on the planet thrives in the twenty-two per cent of global territories home to indigenous peoples.[1] Increasingly, researchers recognize that the same forces that threaten biodiversity also threaten indigenous peoples' longstanding relationships with their homelands and the health and well-being of native communities. Ongoing environmental destruction

*Brown J. World Aff.* 18 (2011): 151. Reprinted with permission.

jeopardizes the sustainable relationships indigenous nations have practiced for thousands of years, including land-based and water-based cultural practices such as gathering medicines, hunting, fishing, and farming. . . .

As a result of colonial encroachment onto their homelands, being indigenous today means engaging in a struggle to reclaim and regenerate one's relational, place-based existence by challenging the ongoing, destructive forces of colonization.[2] According to Mohawk scholar Taiaiake Alfred, "colonialism is best conceptualized as an irresistible outcome of a multigenerational and multifaceted process of forced dispossession and attempted acculturation—a disconnection from land, culture, and community—that has resulted in political chaos and social discord within First Nations communities and the collective dependency of First Nations upon the state."[3] These forces of disconnection further distance indigenous peoples from their spiritual, cultural, and physical relationships with the natural world and serve to destroy the confidence and well-being of indigenous peoples.

When addressing contemporary colonialism and cultural harm, it is important to understand that the indigenous rights discourse has limits and can only take struggles for land reclamation and justice so far. Indigenous mobilization around rights-based strategies premised on state recognition of indigenous self-determination—which entails unconditional freedom to live one's relational, place-based existence, and practice healthy relationships—has serious shortcomings in terms of redressing cultural harms and loss. According to Dene political theorist Glen Coulthard, "the politics of recognition [for indigenous peoples] in its contemporary form promises to reproduce the very configurations of colonial power that Indigenous peoples' demands for recognition have historically sought to transcend."[4] It follows that indigenous self-determination is something that is asserted and acted upon, not negotiated or offered freely by the state. Based on Coulthard's description of the politics of recognition, it is clear that the rights discourse has certain limitations in relation to indigenous struggles for

self-determination. Rights are state constructions that do not necessarily reflect inherent indigenous responsibilities to their homelands. Rather, rights are conditional in that the state can withdraw them at any time or selectively enforce them. Additionally, the rights discourse compartmentalizes indigenous self-determination by separating questions of governance and community well-being from homelands and relationships to the natural world. Consequently, a right to indigenous self-determination is often reduced to self-governance, when this is only one of several layers of indigenous self-determining authority. Finally, by embedding themselves within the state-centric rights discourse, indigenous peoples risk mimicking state functions rather than honoring their own sustainable, spiritual relationships with their homelands. In this context, indigenous self-determination can be rearticulated as part of a sustainable, community-based process rather than solely as narrowly constructed political or legal entitlements.

As the above discussion indicates, when approaches to indigenous cultural revitalization and self-determination are discussed solely in terms of strategies, rights, and theories, they overlook the everyday practices of resurgence and decolonization. Indigenous resurgence is about reconnecting with homelands, cultural practices, and communities, and is centred on reclaiming, restoring, and regenerating homeland relationships. Another dimension centres upon decolonization, which transforms indigenous struggles for freedom from performance to everyday local practice.[5] This entails moving away from the performativity of a rights discourse geared toward state affirmation and approval toward a daily existence conditioned by place-based cultural practices. What, then, does a process of sustainable self-determination look like in practice as indigenous peoples move from rights to practicing their everyday responsibilities? This article examines indigenous communities in Lekwungen (Songhees First Nation in Victoria, British Columbia, Canada) as they work to overcome cultural loss by reclaiming their homelands and distinct cultural practices.[6] First, however, concepts of culture and sustainability are further developed in terms of their applicability to international law.

# Cultural Harm and Community Resurgence

Indigenous peoples in urban areas often find ways to maintain their links to families, communities, and homelands by going "home" for ceremonies and/or practicing their ceremonial life in the cities. . . . Whether on their homelands or maintaining homeland connections through regular visits and other land-based/water-based cultural practices, indigenous peoples defy the standard reservation/off-reservation dichotomies.

One example of community resurgence in action is the "Water Walkers" movement in Wikiwemikong Unceded First Nation in Ontario, Canada. The movement began in the winter of 2002 in response to mounting threats of environmental pollution to community lakes and traditional waters. According to one of the leaders of this movement, Josephine Mandamin, they asked themselves, "What can we do to bring out, to tell people of our responsibilities as women, as keepers of life and the water, to respect our bodies as Nishnaabe-kwewag, as women?"[7] They decided as a group to undertake a spiritual walk around the entire perimeter of Lake Superior with buckets of water to raise awareness of the need to protect water. According to Josephine, "This journey with the pail of water that we carry is our way of Walking the Talk. [. . .] Our great grandchildren and the next generation will be able to say, yes, our grandmothers and grandfathers kept this water for us!"[8] When examining indigenous community resurgence, questions of sustainability and subsistence become key starting points for assessing cultural harm, and, ultimately, for the restoration of cultural practices. In a comprehensive United Nations study examining indigenous peoples and their natural resource rights, Special Rapporteur Erica-Irene Daes found that "few if any limitations on indigenous resource rights are appropriate, because the indigenous ownership of the resources is associated with the most important

and fundamental of human rights: the rights to life, food, shelter, the right to self-determination, and the right to exist as a people."[9]

Given that their future survival depends on it, indigenous communities adamantly assert an inherent right to subsistence living. For indigenous peoples, subsistence living involves everyday cultural, spiritual, and social interactions grounded in reciprocal relationships that sustain communities for generations. Cree activist Ted Moses discusses how self-determination and a right to subsistence are interrelated in this regard: "We may not be denied our own means of subsistence. [. . .] We may not be denied the wherewithal for life itself— food, shelter, clothing, land, water and the freedom to pursue a way of life. There are no exceptions to this rule."[10]

How does the most comprehensive indigenous rights instrument in effect today—the 2007 UN Declaration on the Rights of Indigenous Peoples— protect indigenous rights to subsistence and sustainable self-determination within Canada? While it initially voted against adoption of the Declaration (along with Australia, New Zealand, and the United States), Canada has since reversed course due to political pressure from First Nations and formally endorsed the Declaration in 2010.[11] When providing the details of its endorsement, the Canadian government emphasized that the Declaration is a "non-legally binding document that does not reflect customary international law nor change Canadian laws."[12] Notwithstanding this interpretation, some international legal scholars contend that the Declaration has political and legal force because it is grounded in universally upheld principles of self-determination. . . .

Drafted by indigenous activists, scholars, and state delegates over the past three decades, the Declaration is comprised of 46 articles that mirror several international customary norms already in place.[13] The main articles of interest here are those which outline the rights of indigenous peoples to restorative justice, including redress for any action which has the aim or effect of depriving them of their ability to live as indigenous peoples, such as their means of subsistence (Article 20); access to health and traditional medicines (Article 24); or the right to maintain and strengthen their distinctive spiritual relationship with their traditionally owned or otherwise-used and occupied lands, territories, waters, coastal seas, and other resources (Article 25).[14]

Despite the potential for existing international legal institutions and standards to hold signatories accountable, as of this writing no global forum has yet held Canada accountable for its denial of indigenous cultural practices and everyday subsistence. In this regard, Article 46, Part 1 of the UN Declaration on the Rights of Indigenous Peoples is revealing: "Nothing in this Declaration may be interpreted as implying for any State, people, group or person any right to engage in any activity or to perform any act contrary to the Charter of the United Nations or construed as authorizing or encouraging any action which would dismember or impair, totally or in part, the territorial integrity or political unity of sovereign and independent States." While indigenous peoples do not tend to seek secession from the state, the restoration of their cultural practices is often portrayed as a threat to the territorial integrity of the countries in which they reside, and thus, a threat to state sovereignty. The politics of recognition highlight the shortcomings of pursuing rights-based strategies for indigenous peoples desiring decolonization and restoration of their relationships to the natural world. . . .

. . . How, then, do subsistence and sustainability fit into a discussion of cultural practice and continuity in indigenous communities? For indigenous peoples, sustainability is upheld by honoring longstanding, reciprocal relationships with the natural world, as well as by transmitting knowledge and everyday cultural practices to future generations. . . . An indigenous notion of sustainability involves upholding one's responsibilities to the land and natural world and giving back more than one takes, rather than simply residing on the land. It follows that indigenous *sustainable self-determination* is both an individual and community-driven process where "evolving indigenous livelihoods, food security, community

governance, relationships to homelands and the natural world, and ceremonial life can be practiced today locally and regionally, thus enabling the transmission of these traditions and practices to future generations."[15]

Whether living in rural or urban areas, indigenous peoples are finding new pathways to resurgence and cultural continuity in order to strengthen their nations amidst ongoing colonialism and legacies of cultural harm. Rights have limits when addressing issues of cultural harm, and new indigenous movements, such as the Water Walkers, are emerging to protect indigenous lands, cultures, and communities. Terms such as *subsistence* and *sustainability* are being redefined by indigenous peoples to express their complex relationships with their homelands. Resurgence ultimately entails community reclamation, restoration, and regeneration of local cultural practices, and the Lekwungen people have begun a movement to fight for their unique way of life.

## Kwetlal and Community Resurgence

. . . One example of everyday practices of resurgence in action comes from British Columbia, Canada. The Lekwungen ancestral homelands are also known as Victoria (Metulia) and Greater Victoria in British Columbia, Canada. Diverse ecosystems, such as the Garry Oak Ecosystem (GOE), which is known for the *kwetlal* (*camas*, a starchy bulb that has been a staple food and trade item for indigenous peoples in the region for generations), have thrived on Lekwungen territories for centuries. The GOE remains vital to the kwetlal food and trade system, and Lekwungen communities were known worldwide as the place to trade for kwetlal. . . . Additionally, the University of Victoria is located in the one area where kwetlal was celebrated, harvested, pit cooked, and traded with people up and down the coast.

Lekwungen women have been the backbone of the kwetlal food system by managing it for centuries and, through their connections to kwetlal and management of their traditional homelands, have sustained their communities. This important role was passed down from mothers to daughters. Cheryl Bryce and her family have been managing their traditional Lekwungen territories for several generations, and Bryce continues to harvest kwetlal on parklands and private property despite threats to her and her family's well-being from settlers attempting to deny her access to Lekwungen homelands.[16] The struggles of Bryce and her family highlight how these foods systems have been greatly impacted by settler colonial encroachment that continues today.

In 1844, James Douglas decided to settle the new Hudson Bay Fort in Metulia (downtown Victoria) because of the beautiful kwetlal food system, and Fort Victoria became the first "box store," so to speak, in the Lekwungen ancestral homelands. Initially, the Lekwungen people maintained relations with the alien settler economy as a secondary form of trade. However, Fort Victoria was developed in the centre of the Lekwungen ancestral lands and its impacts were directly aimed at destroying the combined strength of the culture, people, and land. As a result, this trading system deteriorated over time, and led to the decline of the kwetlal food systems. Today, the kwetlal food system comprises less than five per cent of its original yield over 150 years ago.

Given that 95 per cent of the ancestors' land base for this food system is not available today, the current state of the indigenous food system is evidence of colonial development, pollution, and cultural suppression and oppression, which has led to cultural loss and the destruction of roles and responsibilities within the Lekwungen community. For example, the Lekwungen people have seven major families each with food resources, roles, and an area of land. However, as a result of colonial encroachment, gender roles relating to traditional land management and harvesting have been disrupted and fishing and planting areas governed by particular families have been encroached upon by settler populations. Additionally, local environmental conservation efforts have focused on the revitalization of the GOE,

rather than on addressing the reality of indigenous food systems and community sustainability in the region.

Today, the work continues among the women with inherent family rights to the kwetlal food system. It will take generations of Lekwungen peoples acting in solidarity to reinstate cultural food systems such as kwetlal. Cultural revitalization starts with protecting the land, reinstating traditional roles, and practicing everyday acts of resurgence. Harvesting, pit cooking, and trading continue today despite the colonial disruption. However, Lekwungen homelands, roles, and nationhood remain threatened as they have been since the first contact with settlers. After all, Lekwungen homelands remain at the centre of ongoing colonial expansion. Cheryl Bryce is a Lekwungen woman visibly reinstating her role among both Lekwungen and settlers. It was around 1999 when Bryce realized she needed to educate and develop a working network toward reinstating kwetlal food systems. As a child, Bryce remembers going to parks in Lekwungen ancestral lands early in the morning with her grandmother Edna George née Norris and, upon encountering settlers, being told that they did not have the right to harvest in "Victoria parks." Within Victoria and throughout Canada, acts of community resurgence are criminalized when it comes to regenerating one's cultural practices on original indigenous homelands, which are often considered private properties or public parklands. As an adult Bryce continues to encounter this type of ignorance coupled with threats of physical force. These experiences and her concern with the decline of the food system led Bryce to raise awareness and build networks of like-minded indigenous and settler peoples.

Bryce took the struggle for cultural restoration beyond her family and invited indigenous peoples and settlers to partake in public events such as kwetlal pit cooks and invasive plant species removal and to engage in creative awareness-building campaigns. The goals of the "Community Tool Shed" founded by Bryce focus on education and the reinstatement of indigenous food systems such as kwetlal. There is a strong educational component to this work, because Bryce has developed maps of Victoria with traditional place names and has also spoken to several school groups and residents about the history of the region, as well as their obligations to the kwetlal food systems in Lekwungen territories.[17] In order to protect the remaining five per cent of kwetlal yields and reinstate kwetlal food systems, it will take generations working at removing invasive plant species (such as Scotch Broom), pollution concerns, and colonial development.... Bryce's efforts to revitalize kwetlal food systems, as well as to regenerate community roles and responsibilities, are critical to the future survival and resurgence of Lekwungen peoples. As the Lekwungen example points out, communities must assert sustainable self-determination rather than negotiate for it. Ultimately, a community's cultural continuity is premised on direct actions to protect these sacred relationships.

## Conclusion

When discussing questions of indigenous community sustainability, the previous research and an in-depth look at community resurgence on Lekwungen homelands make it clear that the revitalization of land-based and water-based cultural practices is premised on enacting indigenous community responsibilities, which "entails sparking a spiritual revolution rather than seeking state-based solutions that are disconnected from indigenous community relationships."[18] Processes of reclamation, restoration, and regeneration take on a renewed urgency given the high stakes of dispossession and disconnection from indigenous territories.

The pursuit of self-determination should be reconceived as a responsibility-based movement centred on a sustainable self-determination process, not as a narrowly constructed, state-driven rights discourse. Overall, one sees that grassroots efforts like those referenced above do not rely heavily on rights as much as they do on community responsibilities to protect traditional homelands and food systems. By resisting colonial authority and demarcating their homelands via place-naming and traditional management practices, these everyday acts of resurgence have promoted the regeneration of sustainable food systems in communities and are transmitting these teachings and values to future generations.

We also have to remember that change happens in small increments—*one warrior at a time*. As Cheryl Bryce's actions in Lekwungen demonstrate, "Measurable change on levels beyond the individual will emanate from the start made by physical and psychological transformations in people generated through direct, guided experiences in small, personal groups and, one-on-one mentoring."[19] In her role as a mentor, Bryce brings indigenous children to pull invasive species and learn more about native plants. Passing on this experiential knowledge to younger generations is crucial to the survival of indigenous communities. Additionally, the Community Tool Shed is a place where both indigenous and non-indigenous people can come together under a common goal of protecting the land from invasive species so that native plants will flourish once again. All of these grassroots efforts begin to create awareness of these local struggles and the urgency to protect indigenous homelands.

There is also an educational component to this struggle. Bryce creates teachable moments in order to convey the history and contemporary struggles of the indigenous peoples in the region. For example, she makes bouquets out of cut-outs of kwetlal (camas) flowers, along with cedar and other native plants, and brings them to Parliament in order to remind people of the local battles being waged over the land. Bryce uses symbolism to urge people to practice healthier relationships so that the land itself can also heal.

By understanding the overlapping and simultaneous processes of reclamation, restoration, and regeneration, one begins to better understand how to implement meaningful and substantive community decolonization practices. Future generations will map their own pathways to community regeneration, ideally on their own terms. By moving from performance to everyday cultural practices, indigenous peoples will be recognized by future generations for how they defended and protected their homelands.

# Notes

1. United Nations Development Programme, *Human Development Report 2011* (New York: Palgrave Macmillan, 2011), 54.

2. The United Nations has not adopted an official definition of indigenous peoples, but working definitions, such as the one developed by the United Nations Working Group on Indigenous Populations in 1986, offer some generally accepted guidelines for self-identifying Indigenous peoples and nations:

   • Self-identification as indigenous peoples at the individual level and accepted by the community as their member;

   • Historical continuity with pre-colonial and/or pre-settler societies;

   • Strong link to territories and surrounding natural resources;

   • Distinct social, economic, or political systems;

   • Distinct language, culture, and beliefs;

   • Form non-dominant groups of society; and,

   • Resolve to maintain and reproduce their ancestral environments and systems as distinctive peoples and communities.

   For more on the complexities of defining 370 million indigenous peoples around the world, see: Jeff Corntassel, "Who is Indigenous? 'Peoplehood' and Ethnonationalist Approaches to Rearticulating Indigenous Identity," *Nationalism & Ethnic Politics* 9, no. 1 (2003): 75–100.

3. Taiaiake Alfred, "Colonialism and State Dependency," *Journal of Aboriginal Health* 5 (2009): 52.

4. Glen S. Coulthard, "Subjects of Empire: Indigenous Peoples and the 'Politics of Recognition' in Canada," *Contemporary Political Theory* 3 (2007): 1–29.

5. Kahikina de Silva, "Pathways to Decolonization" class session, Indigenous Governance Program course IGOV 595: *Reclaiming Ćelaṉen: Land, Water, Governance* (University of Victoria: July 19, 2011). This quote is used with Kahikina's written permission.

6. For the purposes of this article, cultural practices comprise the everyday activities of indigenous peoples in relation to their homelands. Additionally, it is understood that indigenous peoples who live outside their territories continue to practice their cultures, though they express their deep relationships and connections to place in different ways on a daily basis. For example, while over 50 per cent of indigenous peoples in Canada live in urban areas, there is a multidirectional flow between urban and rural communities.

7. Renée Elizabeth Mzinegiizhigo-kwe Bédard, "Keepers of the Water: Nishnaabe-kwewag Speaking for the Water," in *Lighting the Eighth Fire,* Leanne Simpson, ed. (Winnipeg: Arbeiter Ring Publishing, 2008), 103.

8. Ibid., 104.

9. Erica-Irene A. Daes, *Final Report on Indigenous Peoples' Permanent Sovereignty Over Natural Resources,* July 13, 2004, UN Doc. E/CN.4/Sub.2/2004/30.

10. Ted Moses, "The Right of Self-Determination and its Significance to the Survival of Indigenous Peoples," in *Operationalizing the Right of Indigenous Peoples to Self-Determination,* ed. Pekka Aikio and Martin Scheinin (Tuku/Abo: Institute for Human Rights, Abo Akademi University, 2000), 161.

11. Australia, New Zealand, and the United States have also reversed their 2007 positions on the Declaration and formally endorsed UNDRIP.

12. S. James Anaya, "The Right of Indigenous Peoples to Self-Determination in the Post Declaration Era," in *Indian and Northern Affairs Canada,* "Canada's Statement of Support on the United Nations Declaration on the Rights of Indigenous Peoples," November 12, 2010.

13. The Universal Periodic Review (UPR) process, which is a new inter-state mechanism of the Human Rights Council, may also be an important mechanism for mainstreaming the provisions of the Declaration into existing human rights law and establishing human rights obligations for states under review. See: Luis Rodriguez-Pinero, "'Where Appropriate:' Monitoring/ Implementing of Indigenous Peoples' Rights Under the Declaration," in *Making the Declaration Work: The United Nations Declaration on the Rights of Indigenous Peoples,* ed. Claire Charters and Rodolfo Stavenhagen (Copenhagen: International Working Group on Indigenous Affairs, 2009), 321–22.

14. Other relevant articles in UNDRIP include Article 8, 11, 21, 28, 29, 31, 32, and 40.

15. World Commission on Environment and Development, *Report of the World Commission on Environment and Development,* A/ RES/42/187; posted by UN Department of Economic and Social Affairs (DESA), December 11, 1987, http://www.un.org/documents/ga/res/42/ares42-187.htm; United Nations Development Programme, *Human Development Report 2011* (New York: Palgrave Macmillan, 2011),, 119.

16. Briony Penn, "Restoring Camas and Culture to Lekwungen and Victoria: An interview with Lekwungen Cheryl Bryce," *Focus Magazine,* June 2006, http://www.firstnations.de/media/06-1-1-camas.pdf.

17. For example, see: Cheryl Bryce and Brenda Sam, "Lekwungen People: The Traditional Territory of the Songhees and Esquimalt People" (pamphlet), 1997, http://bcheritage.ca/salish/ph2/map/lekwungen.htm.

18. Jeff Corntassel, "Toward Sustainable Self-Determination," 124.

19. Alfred, "Colonialism and State Dependency," 56.

# PART TWELVE

❖

## Additional Readings

Belanger, Yale D., and P. Whitney Lackenbauer. *Blockades or Breakthroughs? Aboriginal Peoples Confront the Canadian State.* Montreal & Kingston: McGill-Queen's University Press, 2015.

Bowles, Paul, and Henry Veltmeyer, eds. *The Answer Is Still No: Voices of Pipeline Resistance.* Halifax: Fernwood Publishing, 2014.

Coulthard, Glen Sean. *Red Skin White Masks: Rejecting the Colonial Politics of Recognition.* Minneapolis & London: University of Minnesota Press, 2014.

The Kin-nda-niimi Collective. *The Winter We Danced: Voices from the Past, the Future, and the Idle No More Movement.* Winnipeg: ARP Books, 2014.

Lyons, Scott Richard. *X-Marks: Native Signatures of Assent.* Minneapolis: University of Minnesota Press, 2010.

Manuel, Arthur. *Unsettling Canada: A National Wake-up Call.* Toronto: Between the Lines, 2015.

McGregor, D. "Anishnaabe-Kwe, Traditional Knowledge, and Water Protection," in *Canadian Woman Studies* 26 (3/4), 2008.

Simpson, Audra. *Mohawk Interruptus: Political Life across the Borders of Settler States.* Durham, NC: Duke University Press, 2014.

Simpson, Leanne, ed. *Lighting the Eighth Fire: The Liberation, Resurgence, and Protection of Indigenous Nations.* Winnipeg: Arbeiter Ring Publishing, 2008.

## Relevant Websites

**Sisters host Toxic Tours of their home in Canada's Chemical Valley**

http://anishinabeknews.ca/2015/01/07/sisters-host-toxic-tours-of-their-home-in-canadas-chemical-valley

*Two Aamjiwnaang sisters are hosting toxic tours of Canada's Chemical Valley, which includes 63 petrochemical plants located adjacent to their home community.*

**Divided No More**

http://dividednomore.ca

*A blog inspired by the Idle No More Movement hosting writings on Indigenous issues.* -

**Transforming Relations: A Collaborative Collection**

http://transformingrelations.wordpress.com/

*This website contains a section on social movements and one on resistance.*

**Honor Earth**

http://www.honorearth.org

*A website created to bring awareness and support for Indigenous environmental issues.*

**Decolonization Wordpress**

https://decolonization.wordpress.com

*A blog associated with the journal* Decolonization, Indigeneity, Education & Society

**Idle No More**

http://www.idlenomore.ca

*This is the official website of the Idle No More Movement.*

## Films

*Kanehsatake: 270 Years of Resistance.* Dir. Alanis Obomsawin. National Film Board of Canada, 1993.

*Is the Crown at War with Us?* Dir. Alanis Obomsawin. National Film Board of Canada, 2002.

*Sewatokwa'tshera't = The Dish with One Spoon.* Dir. Dawn Martin-Hill. Haudenosaunee Confederacy, 2007.

*Six Miles Deep.* Dir. Sara Roque. National Film Board of Canada, 2010.

*Tar Sands Healing Walk.* htttps://www.youtube.com/watch?v=OeFBW5R7xXM

*The People of the Kattawapiskat River.* Dir. Alanis Obomsawin. National Film Board of Canada, 2012.

*Trick or Treaty?* Dir. Alanis Obomsawin. National Film Board of Canada, 2014.

# Key Terms

Gendered colonial violence
Ogichidaakwe (i.e., Holy Woman)
Land-based cultural practices

Indigenous sustainable self-determination
Politics of recognition
Community resurgence

# Discussion Questions

1. What is sustainable self-determination? What contemporary examples of it, aside from those discussed by Corntassel and Bryce, can you think of?
2. Why does Leanne Betasamosake Simpson believe it was important to support and show solidarity to Chief Teresa Spence?
3. What did the Idle No More Movement stand for, and against? Do you believe it was effective in its goals?

4. Explain what Corntassel and Bryce mean by "moving from performance to everyday cultural practices, Indigenous peoples will be recognized by future generations for how they defended and protected their homelands" (ibid., 161). Next, describe what this means to you, personally.

# Activities

Watch *Unis'tot'en Action Camp—Speaking Tour by Deep Green Resistance*, available on YouTube. Discuss some of the main points brought up in the video, and why it is important for environmentalists to support Indigenous sovereignty.

Invite an Indigenous representative of a local Indigenous community or organization to speak to the class about contemporary issues faced by the Indigenous community in the area, and how the community has been organizing to address such issues. Next, discuss how non-Indigenous people can best support Indigenous communities in asserting their inherent self-determination.

Cheryl Bryce uses symbolism, such as the bouquets of camas flowers and invasive species cutouts presented in politically significant situations, to "urge people to practice healthier relationships so the land itself can also heal" (ibid., 161). Brainstorm symbolic and artistic expressions that you and your fellow community members could use to express desires to live in ways that demonstrate respect for the health of the Earth and for the health of *all* community members.

# Conclusion

In concluding this second edition, we recognize that there have been significant developments in Canadian politics, in particular, since our first edition in 2011. On 19 October 2015, after some nine years of leadership under the rule of Steven Harper, Canadians elected a new liberal government. Prime Minister–elect Justin Trudeau, on election night, reiterated a promise made throughout his campaign. He called for a "renewed nation-to-nation relationship with Indigenous peoples" in Canada. In his own words, he told Canadians that a relationship "that respects rights and honours treaties must be the basis of how we work to close the gap and walk forward together" (*Macleans*, 20 October 2015).

Shortly after election night, Trudeau appointed as Minister of Justice Jody Wilson-Raybould, Canada's first Indigenous federal Justice Minister. He renamed Indian Affairs Canada as the Department of Indigenous and Northern Affairs Canada. In the weeks that followed, Indigenous Affairs Minister Carolyn Bennett promised to not fight a noteworthy child welfare ruling, brought together Status of Women Canada and other ministries, and called for an inquiry into Missing and Murdered Indigenous Women. Later, Bennett promised to mobilize the 94 calls to action by the Truth and Reconciliation Commission. Canada has since promised furthermore to remove its "objector status" as a nation and implement the terms of the United Nations Declaration of the Rights of Indigenous Peoples.

After some nine years of zero movement under conservative rule, the future path looks promising and encouraging, especially given recent talks to challenge and change fundamental laws of the land, including Canada's *Indian Act*. Justice Minister Jody Wilson-Raybould has promised to "complete the unfinished business of Confederation and replace the *Indian Act* with a reconciliation framework that would outlast the life of this [Trudeau] administration" (*APTN News*, 13 April 2016). At the heart of these changes, Wilson-Raybould's proposal holds promise in ushering in a stronger and more appropriate political model that moves beyond the current *Indian Act* structure of governance (ibid.).

On a moral if not legal basis, these sorts of changes are overdue and furthermore necessary to realize in part the promises for a "renewed relationship" made throughout the Trudeau campaign. Promises to address the gap between the social conditions of Indigenous and Settler populations will also require some attention as also promised. It has become apparent that this gap remains alarmingly disparate, in particular issues involving poverty, suicide, and housing conditions, quite often in northern and remote communities where recent news of La Loche and Attawapiskat has created public attention (*CBC News*, 8 May 2016).

At a recent public engagement in Saskatoon, Prime Minister Trudeau fielded questions from Indigenous youth about social and economic conditions experienced by some Indigenous peoples. One resounding question asked: "How do you, Justin, with all your politicians and representatives plan to right the wrongs of the past 22 elected prime ministers?" (*CBC News*, 27 April 2016). The young woman asking the question demanded some explanation as to why some Indigenous communities continue to live under "Third World conditions" (ibid.). In response to the question, Trudeau pointed toward a recent $8.4 billion promise to improve the lives of Indigenous peoples, albeit clarifying that: "It's a good start, but this is going to take many more years and many more billions of dollars to fix a relationship that has been broken for centuries—as you point out" (ibid.). In contrast to past relationships that have existed between governments, Trudeau's commitment to change them is both encouraging and promising.

In writing this anthology, we are conscious of the enormous complexity of issues facing governments and Indigenous nations committed to changing vast social inequalities. For example, we have hoped to show that it will not be easy through politics alone to change things like poverty, health, and gender violence—issues that have been systemic throughout much of history. We also recognize that a colonial politics of recognition whereby Indigenous peoples are invited into a particular discursive framework continues to be formulated by a Canadian colonial state and has not served Indigenous peoples well. A colonial politics of recognition has been carefully detailed and outlined by Indigenous scholars concerned with Settler colonial state formations (Alfred, 2005; Coulthard, 2014; Turner, 2006). In summary, we also hope this second edition of the textbook will spur readers to further contemplate and reflect on some of the major conclusions we first introduced in the first volume of this textbook, including:

1. That neither Settler colonialism, racism, nor Indigenous peoples are disappearing into the twenty-first century. Despite promising political engagements, interpersonal apathy and everyday racism persists;

2. That the options available for repairing the mistrust and disavowal structuring modern colonial consciousness have already been set out in early historical and nation-to-nation-based agreements, and that a shift has taken place at least politically by Canada's current federal government to recognize these principles;

3. That poverty and economic marginalization continue as obstacles as evident and reported in current news events, requiring us to revisit colonial legacies, and—in the first historical instance—the dispossession of lands before fully understanding, repairing, and eradicating them;

4. That Indigenous peoples continue to face serious disparities in educational attainments and health despite ameliorative efforts, the nature of which require us to consider histories of difference-making, antiracist and anticolonial pedagogies and health care approaches, along with—and sometimes even before—strategies aimed at cultural awareness and revitalization;

5. That neither institutionalized racism nor Settler colonialism are disappearing, especially as this has been directed toward Indigenous women, men, and nations through the *Indian Act*, even despite recent amendments and a Supreme Court ruling that now recognizes Métis and non-status peoples as "Indians";

6. That Settler colonial, racialized, and gendered violence (e.g., opposition and backlash to Idle No More, Missing and Murdered Indigenous Women, Stonechild Inquiry, Ipperwash, Caledonia, Burnt Church, and Gustafsen Lake) continues to take place in Canada embodying, in itself, the ongoing physical—and symbolic—removal of Indigenous peoples from their lands into the twenty-first century; and

7. That our resistance and resilience as peoples is not disappearing as is evidenced by the Idle No More movement, the occupation of Indian Affairs in response to reports of suicides at Attawapiskat, and the contributions we continue to make in reformulating academia (see Mihesuah, 1998), the arts, sports, and legal reform in Canada.

Dismantling colonial dominance requires breaking with cycles of oppression founded in the first instance upon histories of racism and sex discrimination. As we have shown,

Settler colonialism may seem altogether unrelated to other systems of oppression like racism, sexism, social class exploitation, and even heteronormativity. But Indigenous scholars have nuanced how these systems work together simultaneously to structure distinct kinds of discrimination for Indigenous nations, women, and to a lesser extent in published literature, two-spirited individuals (see Chacaby, 2016). Racialization, sexism, and heteronormativity have quite simply intersected historically to place Indigenous men and women at a disadvantage relative to the state, the justice system, and to each other. As Cannon (forthcoming) writes, "we cannot hope to be free of colonial dominance until the sexism directed at our (grand-) mothers is seen—in the first instance of Settler colonialism—as belonging to us all collectively as 'Indians' and as working contrary to the well-being of all Indigenous persons, including men." We suggest that any meaningful discussions about racism and Indigeneity in Canada need to take these complex interrelationships into account, as they profoundly shape and structure the experiences of Indigenous peoples.

Colonial injustice is racialized injustice. In the first instance, the *Indian Act* set into motion a way of thinking about identity, governance, and nationhood in racialized terms. It also made compulsory a racialized order of *Indian Act* governance on Crown lands reserved for Indians. As Indigenous scholars, we believe it is incumbent upon us to revisit these early historical precedents, especially because much of our lives is shaped by them. On the one hand, we agree with scholars who insist that we refuse at every turn the invitation to citizenship (Henderson, 2002), a colonial politics of recognition (Coulthard, 2014), and who reject the fashioning of sovereignty grievances under the guise of racial minority status (Porter, 1999). At the same time, we cannot help but be concerned by a racialized construct of Indianness, largely because it is so fundamentally tied to colonialism in the first instance. For better or worse, Indianness shapes the everyday experience of Indigenous peoples in Canada, but it does not prevent us from naming and then employing a politics of self-recognition and the revitalization of Indigenous governance, cultural, and identity practices (Coulthard, 2014).

Racism cannot fully be understood, nor reconciled, so long as Indigenous peoples are administered as Indians under federal legislation. The word "Indian" is a race-based concept but, as John Raulston Saul (2009: 8) makes clear, it does not belong to Indigenous peoples, nor is it one that is desirable to us, or that rightfully defines our nation-to-nation-based relationships. "If today's land claims [*sic*], treaty rights, and membership in particular seem to be dependent on definitions of race," writes Saul, "that is entirely the outcome of a European-imposed approach, one that had nothing to do with the Aboriginal idea of expandable and inclusive circles of people" (ibid.). Saul points to histories of dominance through which Indigenous lands were deemed *terra nullius*—empty or unoccupied—and to nation-to-nation-based relationships and identities becoming racialized. He draws attention to the origins of Canadian nation state wherein racialized categories of difference became entrenched in law, economics, and politics.

Canada's earliest categories of racial difference are contained in the *Indian Act* (RSC, 1985). This piece of federal legislation remains with us today, and has come to define the relationship between Indigenous nations and Canada, in effect rendering all prior treaty and nation-to-nation agreements with our peoples null and void. We appreciate that current relationships may have become shaped by monetary wealth and its unequal distribution, but we also recognize the spirit of our initial nation-to-nation agreements. Our original agreements were about responsibilities and how to best live amongst one another. We think these prior arrangements set an important historical precedent, and we encourage the current liberal government to rejuvenate and realize a relationship based on original treaty and nation-to-nation principles. Indigenous peoples must be truly self-determining, not only self-governing, and to share in the significant royalties that are derived from the land.

The *Indian Act* needs to be challenged and was recently challenged on the basis of blatant sex discrimination in what is known as the *McIvor* case. Although it is now possible as an outcome to this case for the grandchildren of Indian women to be federally recognized as Indians we also feel that someone should raise the matter of racialization, or racialized injustice as a constitutional challenge (Cannon, this volume); and relatedly, to deal with the matter of unknown and unstated paternity (Gehl, this volume). As mentioned in the Introduction of this anthology: the very first act of colonial injustice in Canada is racialized injustice. It is none other than the process through which Indigenous peoples became Indians for state administrative purposes and for the sake of dispossessing us of the lands that are required for capitalist expansion and exploitation. We have meant to draw attention in this anthology to racialized injustice as the earliest form of colonial dominance in Canada, a matter that can no longer go unnoticed or unchallenged in the law (ibid.).

We have hoped to show that racialized thinking represents a double-edged sword for Indigenous peoples. While we might wish to avoid its usage, Indianness shapes the opportunities and outcomes made available to us by the colonizer. It is also tied to a genocidal project that legally requires our total disappearance as nations. In a material sense, the category Indian rests on a blood quantum logic that, as Kauanui (2008: 34–5) points out, enacts, substantiates, and then disguises the further appropriation of lands. In order to justify the appropriation of Indigenous territories, the colonizer has always to mark the bodies of Indigenous peoples as Indians through policy-making and other symbolic, highly gendered practices of difference making. Blood quantum logic effects the denigration of our genealogical connection to territory or place. It is premised on our dilution, reducing our nations in turn to racial minorities instead of sovereign nations.

However paradoxical it may seem, we cannot help but reconcile histories of racism and racialization in Canada without engaging in precisely the same racialized discourses that produced them. As Anishinabek scholar Dale Turner writes: "It is no secret that for Aboriginal peoples to participate effectively in Canadian legal and political cultures they must engage the normative [liberalist] discourses of the state" (2006: 81). It is furthermore paradoxical that a department concerned with the administration of Indians has become known under a Trudeau administration as Indigenous and Northern Affairs. A name change will mean nothing if it does not challenge the status quo, work in itself toward the devolution of an Indian bureaucracy that stems from the *Indian Act,* or the invitation we face at every turn to deal with Canada as "unequal participants" or as Indians (Coulthard, 2014).

Our colleagues suggest to us that the socio-legal and political contexts that prevent Indigenous nationhood, as well as identification approaches to identity and citizenship, require our intense scrutiny and unwavering political will. Histories of racialization require us as nations to posit Indianness—and at once resist it—in a dual-gestured, combative force against colonial and racialized injustice. This will not be an easy process, as Lawrence (2004: 239) explains:

> It is one thing to recognize that *Indian Act* categories are artificial—or even that they have been internalized—as if these divisions can be overcome simply by denying their importance. Legal categories, however, shape peoples' lives. They set the terms that individuals must utilize, even in resisting these categories.

Despite what is believed in some circles, Indigenous peoples are not at all disappearing. Between 2006 and 2011, the "Aboriginal ancestry population" grew by 20.1 per cent compared with 5.2 per cent for the non-Aboriginal population (Statistics Canada, 2011: 4). Today, some of us are registered as status Indians, while others go federally unrecognized and without reserve lands. More recently, some Métis and non-status individuals are able to register as Indians as an outcome to a 2016 Supreme Court ruling (*Daniels v. Canada, Indian and Northern Development*, 2016). Still others blend effortlessly into decidedly urban, multicultural milieu, invisible to many Canadians as Indigenous peoples because of a politics of authenticity structuring the representation of our everyday lives. Indeed, Indigenous peoples are quite literally rendered invisible and unintelligible, not simply by our own choice or determination, but rather by a highly racialized and structured way of thinking about Indianness as if we were a static or unchanging essence, untouched by modern conveniences or even privileges based on social class, education, and skin colour.

In writing this anthology, we have hoped to show how racism pervades the everyday reality of Indigenous people, from criminal justice to the availability of clean and safe drinking water in reserve communities like Kashechewan Cree Nation (*Globe and Mail*, 28 October 2005), and also issues involving poverty and housing at Attawapiskat that are contributing, and indeed, leading to reports of suicide (*CBC News*, 12 April 2016; *CBC News*, 8 May 2016). These realities cannot be represented as stemming alone from what John Steckley (2003: 58–63) and Métis scholar Emma LaRocque (1993: 212) have referred to as a "social problems" or "victim blaming" approach to Indigenous disparities. The reality is that systemic and economic inequalities require real solutions, and we cannot only become visible to Canadians when, and only when, we fit into a social problems category of analysis. These perceptions play themselves out in both the living rooms and classrooms of Canada. More often than not, "statistical outliers," including stories of Indigenous successes, receive limited public attention, or they are rendered invisible or inauthentic.

The tendency to represent Indigenous peoples in these ways concerns us greatly. As we have shown, it is true that Indigenous peoples and majority Canadians experience enormous disparities in education, income, health, and well-being. The statistics have been well documented and—in a somewhat peculiar way—are called rapidly to mind by many individuals in our classrooms. But when issues affecting all Canadians like poverty, racial profiling, suicide, or the availability of clean and safe drinking water become a convenient means of showcasing social problems among Indians, it forces us as the original peoples to contemplate the purpose being served. We are encouraged by recent efforts toward critical reflection and possibly even reconciliation and the resolution of Indigenous disparities that are rooted in social and economic inequality. We also believe these practices of representation must be reconciled, especially as the construction of racialized subjects is—and has been—so fundamental to reproducing racism under contemporary colonialism.

As nations of individuals, Indigenous peoples are determined to maintain our presence and livelihood. Many of us work tirelessly in communities to address the social issues we are currently facing. Collectively, we have resisted, survived, dealt with, and indeed envisioned a way forward, often in the face of adversity. We continue to make steadfast contributions to the arts, sports, academia, and legal reform in Canada. Our communities offer programs that are culturally specific and appropriate, many of them seeking to reclaim and revitalize the language, traditions, and teachings of our people. These successes demonstrate our perseverance and our resistance to colonialism. They are indicative of a widespread resilience and resurgence taking place in our nations to maintain our Indigenous ways of knowing, our stories, and our ways of being. We believe this resurgence is key to securing Settler colonial reparations and to combating racism.

Guswentah, or Two Row Wampum, is exemplary of the kinds of continuity and resurgence we are meaning to highlight. We believe this agreement and other nation-to-nation agreements hold an original set of instructions that are key to showing how Indigenous and Settler populations might secure redress for contemporary injustices like colonialism, heteropatriarchy and racism. The principles embodied in nation-to-nation agreements delineate original partnerships, the maintenance of separate jurisdictions, and a clear commitment to self-determination. Not only do these principles remind us of the unbroken assertion of sovereignty (Mitchell, 1989), they are furthermore useful for revisiting, and rethinking, matters of governance, land grievances, citizenship, criminal justice, education, economics, and the family. In each of these areas, we have witnessed the greatest intrusion of colonial dominance and racism. Settler colonialism has sought to undo the sovereignty of our nations.

Combating Settler colonial racism in Canada does not at all require a reinvention of the proverbial wheel. Instead, it requires a return to original principles and partnerships. In doing so, we start by acknowledging that Indigenous territories cannot be reduced to Indian reserves, governance to *Indian Act* band councils, or citizenship to Indian status. Reserves, Indian status, and band council governments embody the very kinds of infringement that were, in the very first instance, motivated by racialized thinking. Each of them was an affront to Indigenous jurisdiction and sovereignty. We have shown in this anthology that Indigenous scholars each share in this understanding, albeit differently, and that reconciliation requires the restoration of sovereignty and jurisdiction. Whether it is in calls for Indian control of Indian education, the dismantling of the *Indian Act* (*APTN News*, 13 April 2016), or even the right to determine our own citizens, reparations start with revisiting principles of autonomy and governance contained in historic arrangements.

In our view, recent calls by the Truth and Reconciliation Commission to engage Settler Canadians in a conversation about shared responsibility, mutual respect, reciprocity, and obligation represent positive steps in a healthier and more equitable future on Turtle Island. Murray Sinclair's reminder that the history of residential schools is a Canadian problem and not simply one facing Indigenous peoples points to the reality that solutions to a Settler colonial past will ultimately befall on all Canadians as well as governments to repair. His call is not dissimilar to Indigenous leaders who, in responding to the government of Canada's apology asked similar questions, in particular: "Words must turn into action, . . . What is it that this government is going to do in the future to help our people?" (Jacobs, 2008: 224).

While we in no way wish to denigrate the apology offered to residential school survivors in June 2008, we are asking how Settler populations in particular might start to engage with the 94 calls to action issued by the TRC in summer 2015 (TRC, 2015). These calls to action include matters involving child welfare, education, language and culture, health, and justice. The matter of justice is in particular significant. Sinclair calls on federal, provincial, and territorial governments to have law schools make a course on Aboriginal people and the law mandatory in Canada. This is significant in light also of the Canadian Deans of Education *Accord on Indigenous Education* (2010) to centre non-Indigenous learners, teachers and calls by administrators in particular to address issues related to the "Non-Indigenous Learner and Indigeneity," and the "build[ing of] student capacity for intercultural understanding, empathy, and mutual respect."

It is incumbent on Canada to look to the lessons learned in other countries that have already sought to reconcile the colonial past where the non-Indigenous learner is concerned. An apology is only restorative, when, as Sara Ahmed (2005: 76) has written of the Australian context, "the shamed other can 'show' that its failure to measure up to a social ideal is temporary." Roger Simon (2013: 136) echoed this call by Ahmed by "asking non-Aboriginal Canadians to work out where they 'fit in' to Aboriginal history, not just where Aboriginal history fits into the history of Canada." How will TRC calls result in educational reform and invite critical Settler engagements in colonial reparations? A few of these calls in particular interest us as Indigenous scholars, especially calls to engage non-white populations in anti-colonial activism.

In seeking to reconcile colonial pasts, specifically histories of Settler colonialism, racialization, and residential schools, it is necessary for Canadians to relinquish structural advantages acquired through both colonialism and privilege. Canadians cannot simply be asked to "feel good about feeling bad," or as Roger Simon (2013: 133) explains:

> [T]he act of acknowledging victimhood [cannot be] reduced to an affective transaction in which one both recognizes and "feels for" the pain of others, a situation in which there is no need to ask difficult questions that might implicate one's psychic, social and economic investments in the conditions and institutions responsible for the genesis and prolongation of that pain.

Having said that, what does it mean to ask Canadians, especially new Canadians, to take responsibility for colonial injustice in the way that Simon is suggesting? Finding answers to that question needs to be taken seriously. Indeed, a burgeoning scholarship has emerged since our first edition exploring the scholarly, intellectual, and everyday relationships that exist between Indigenous peoples and non-white Settler populations (Amadahy and Lawrence, 2009; Dhamoon, 2015; Lawrence and Dua, 2005; Phung, 2011; Sehdev, 2011; Wallia, 2012). The matter of new Canadians being asked to take responsibility for racialized injustice when they are often fleeing violent, racist situations themselves is on the minds, and in the actions, of some of those in charge of pursuing colonial reparations. At a recent occupation of the Department of Indigenous and Northern Affairs Canada, Black Lives Matter joined in solidarity with Indigenous activists to occupy federal offices (*CBC News*, 13 April 2016). Furthermore, migrant peoples have been outwardly speaking about what it means to belong as a non-white Settler in a colonizing Canada (Dhamoon, ibid.; Wallia, ibid.).

What sets of challenges and limitations surround the building of anticolonial coalitions between migrant and often racialized communities and Indigenous peoples in both theory and in practice? This question requires ongoing scholarly research and analysis (Amadahy, 2008; see also Land, 2015). Our hope is that recent outcomes will lead to the founding of new partnerships. At best, the building of coalitions in particular stands to open new fields of scholarly research and decolonizing inquiry. We view the following as a set of gestures and activities aimed at critical coalitions building, a process which is sure to open fruitful, decolonizing avenues of research and exploration.

1. Idle No More is a grassroots activist political movement comprised of Indigenous peoples and their non-Indigenous allies initiated in December 2012 to draw attention to Settler colonial, legislative, and treaty rights violations in the Canadian and international contexts. We view the spirit and aspirations of Idle No More as both productive

and important in that it worked to challenge Bill C-45—one of several omnibus bills brought forward by a Stephen Harper government—to disavow nation-to-nation and treaty relationships in Canada. Idle No More worked also to create and further Settler–Indigenous relationship-building and rejuvenation in the Canadian context.

2. The National Inquiry into Missing and Murdered Indigenous Women and Girls (NIMMIW) is a particularly encouraging development since it was initiated in December 2015 following a campaign promise made by the current Trudeau government to address an historic issue of colonial violence that has been neglected for over 50 years. The NIMMIW is significant in that it has brought together Indigenous and non-Indigenous groups in solidarity; and after many years without voice, has finally included the families of missing women in the planning and design stages of the inquiry. We view the involvement of families in the inquiry process as one that is important and respectful of Indigenous nations and communities.

3. Harsha Wallia (2012, 2013) has written of border imperialism and the ways in which non-white and migrant Indigenous peoples are invited into a particular version of citizenship and belonging that is inherently state based and colonizing. Similar to Sunera Thobani (2007: 175) who argues that "state sponsored multiculturalism compels [migrants] to negotiate and comprehend their identities on very narrow grounds . . . foreclosing the possibility of alliances," Wallia invites similar questions with respect to challenging white dominance and global corporate capitalism. We view these discussions as especially productive in drawing attention to the solidification of Settler sovereignty through the law and borders in ways also described—albeit differently—by Audra Simpson (2008). We are interested in work that explores the confluence of Settler colonialism and border imperialism. These works and activism hold significant theoretical purchase where the formidable task of contesting white supremacy, building non-white–Indigenous alliances, and working across differences in everyday practice is concerned;

4. On 13 April 2016, Black Lives Matter joined in solidarity with Indigenous activists to occupy the federal offices of the Department of Indigenous and Northern Affairs Canada in Toronto, Canada. The goal of protests was to draw attention to the living conditions leading young people to take their lives by suicide at Attawapiskat First Nation, and to demand that adequate action be taken to address the matter that has been without a solution since Teresa Spence's hunger strike in December 2012. We think the building of coalitions between racialized and Indigenous communities such as Black Lives Matter holds enormous potential where shedding light on white supremacy and our collective experience of Settler colonialism is concerned. In fact, we believe that talking about our differences stands to transform the very way in which we view notions of privilege and disadvantage both theoretically and in practice, offering a much more nuanced and sophisticated understanding about the confluence of race, gender, Settler colonial, and class-based inequality;

5. A "Refugee" (quoted in Amadahy, 2008: 27–8, emphasis added) writes:

> I didn't come here as a settler, I came here as a refugee. That makes a great difference and *we can only know about that if we talk about it*. You can't say many of the racialized people here are privileged but they still don't know anything about Aboriginal history or people. I see myself as having a role there.

We recognize the complexity of privilege and disadvantage as this is experienced in relation to other people. We also recognize the significant developments since our first edition textbook with respect to the conversations taking place between non-white Settlers and Indigenous peoples. Having said that, we feel some of the most valuable kinds of insight and teaching will continue to stem from our relationships with each other. These kinds of complexity still need to be addressed in Canada, especially following the recent Truth and Reconciliation Commission which called for the restoration and renewal of respectful relationships.

At worst, working across differences may result in "postures of innocence" (Amadahy and Lawrence, 2009: 105; Fellows and Razack, 1998; Land, 2015), making it difficult or even impossible to develop a new vision of mutual responsibility and coexistence. In reconciling histories of racism and colonial injustice, we feel it will be important to avoid thinking hierarchically about the oppressions between us. This point is made eloquently by Patricia Hill Collins (2003: 332) who writes:

> Once we realize that there are very few pure victims or oppressors, and that each one of us derives . . . penalty and privilege from the multiple systems of oppression that frame our lives, then we will be in a position to see the need for new ways of thought and action . . . [without which we remain] locked in a dangerous dance of competing for attention, resources, and theoretical supremacy.

In contemplating the future of self-determination and colonial reparations, one thing is for certain: racist beliefs and practices continue in Canada despite the last five years of ameliorative efforts to curb their effects. In writing the second edition of this anthology, we have hoped to show how this continues to be so. However, we believe that much can be gained by working across differences, rejuvenating original partnerships and agreements, and endeavouring collectively with all Canadians to combat racism. In the words of the Lakota Chief Sitting Bull: "Let us put our minds together and see what kind of life we can make for our children." These are words that require our tenacity and spirit. The time is now. We cannot afford not to.

# Glossary

**Aboriginal community development** A holistic community development model rooted in traditional Aboriginal values of sharing and community with the ultimate goal of restoring healing and decolonizing Aboriginal communities (Silver et al., 2006: 133).

**Aboriginal Women's Action Network** A grassroots Indigenous organization founded in 1995 in Vancouver, British Columbia, aimed at ending sexist discrimination and violence against Indigenous women in Canada.

**Aboriginalism** "[T]he ideology and identity of assimilation, in which Onkewehonwe are manipulated by colonial myths into a submissive position and are told that by emulating white people they can gain acceptance and possibly even fulfillment within mainstream" (Alfred, 2005: 23).

**Acculturation** "[P]henomena which result when groups of individuals having different cultures come into continuous first-hand contact, with subsequent changes in the original patterns of either or both groups" (Linton, 1940: 463–4).

**Antiracism** A field of theoretical and historical study, as well as a set of ideas that inform activist practice. The "anti" in antiracism signifies a commitment to undo and identify racist ideas that form the root of white supremacist and Eurocentric knowledge systems. Unlike "non-racism," antiracism theory and practice encourages the undoing of racist ideas in our own minds and ways of understanding the world (van Dijk, 1993).

**Assimilation** Defined by Davis Jackson (2002: 74) as "the loss, by an individual, of the markers that served to distinguish him or her as a member of one social group, and the acquisition of traits that allow that person to blend in with, and succeed in, a different social group."

**Authenticity** A state of being authentic, real, and genuine. Colonial powers have used concepts of authenticity to quantify "Indianness," through, for example, blood quantum. To be recognized as a "real Indian" and therefore to hold Indian status, individuals must fit the qualifications created by the colonizer.

**Banking concept** A term used by Paulo Friere to refer to a pedagogical style, approach, and/or educational framework that "views the students' minds as 'containers' to be filled by teachers [knowledge] thus allowing [for] the imposition of one worldview over another, sometimes with a velvet glove" (Battiste, 1986: 37)

**Binarism** A way of thinking and/or knowledge that creates, justifies, and reinforces the idea that phenomena in the world exist in binary either/or opposites. Examples of binary thinking include the creation of Evil versus Good, White versus Black, Female versus Male, etc.

**Bill C-3** *The Gender Equity in Indian Registration Act*, popularly known as Bill C-3, came into effect in 31 January 2011 and entitled eligible grandchildren of women who lost status as a result of marrying non-status Indian men to be registered as status Indians.

**Bill C-31** Bill C-31, *An Act to Amend the Indian Act* became law on 28 June 1985 promising to end over 34 years of blatant sex discrimination directed toward Indigenous women and their male and female children under s.12(1)(b) of the prior *Indian Act* of 1951 (Cannon, 2007).

**Bill C-45** An omnibus bill passed through the Canadian Senate on December 14, 2012. It made many changes to several Canadian laws, including removal of protection for waterways, and it infringed on treaty and Indigenous rights. In the fall of 2012, the announcement of the Bill inspired the formation of the Idle No More movement, bringing together Indigenous and non-Indigenous allies to stand up against the Bill and show solidarity with Indigenous peoples.

**Blood quantum** Descent-based criteria for determining eligibility to membership to a band/nation. The percentage of blood quantum required in order to establish one's Indigeneity, and hence eligibility, varies from band to band (Palmater, 2011).

**Cartesian dualism** Renee Descartes, a seventeenth-century philosopher, understood the mind as non-physical. Cartesian dualism is often called the mind/body split, whereby the mind is understood as separate from the body. This dualism constructs a binary or sense of separateness between the mind and body.

**Chief Theresa Spence** The former Chief of the Attawapiskat First Nation in Canada. During her tenure, she became a prominent figure by bringing awareness of the housing and infrastructure crises in her community. Additionally, during the Idle No More movement, she participated in a hunger strike to raise concern about Indigenous issues, and the negative impacts of Bill C-45 on the environment and on Indigenous nations.

**Cognitive assimilation** The tendency in education to devalue—either by force or implicit curricular measures—Indigenous traditions and replace them with Western educational modes and methods (see Battiste, 1986).

**Colonial imaginary** A set of ideas that makes up the colonial narrative. This narrative or imaginary establishes how the colonizer imagines the world and sees own self in it. The colonial imaginary has key racial tropes and root ideas that make sense of and justify the colonial project.

**Colonial violence** In a Canadian context, violence against Indigenous peoples, and women in particular, is "not the result of individual criminal acts (although the acts are indeed criminal and often deeply disturbing) but rather a reflection and function of the longstanding disregard for the lives of the original occupants of the territory, which has served the colonial project since contact" (Lavell-Harvard and Brant, 2016: 3).

**Colonialism** Defined by Henry and Tator (2006, 348) as: "(1) A process by which a foreign power dominates and exploits an indigenous group by appropriating its land and extracting the wealth from it while using the group as cheap labour. (2) A specific era of European expansion into overseas territories between the sixteenth and twentieth centuries during which European states planted settlements in distant territories and achieved economic, military, political, and cultural hegemony in much of Asia, Africa, and the Americas."

**Colonization** A process of conquest whereby one nation establishes a colony on another nation's territory with the intent of taking power, land, and resources. European colonialism dates from the fifteenth century onwards, and involved the brutal establishment of European sovereignty on stolen non-European territory. Colonialism is not only about material accumulation but requires the production of ideologies that justify the theft and violent practices at its root (Said, 1979; 1994).

**Community resurgence** A term referring to Indigenous cultural revitalization and self-determination. As a decolonizing approach, it reconnects Indigenous peoples with their homelands, cultural practices, and restores relationships with their homelands (Corntassel and Bryce, Chapter 24, this volume).

**Comprehensive claims policy** A Canadian federal policy on Indigenous land claims "based on the assertion of continuing Aboriginal rights and title that are not covered by a treaty or other legal vehicle" (Lawrence, Chapter 13, this volume). As Pasternak (2017: 5) writes: "the Comprehensive Land Claims Policy requires negotiating groups to cede their Aboriginal title and the majority of their territory to the Crown in exchange for 'certainty' about their rights." The CCP requires the "extinguishment of all aboriginal rights and title as a part of a claim settlement" (ibid., 142).

**Compulsory heterosexuality** A term first developed by lesbian feminist poet Adrienne Rich (2003). The term defines the phenomenon of making heterosexuality compulsory—something that is required and enforced through threat of violence, whether ontological, psychological, physical, or emotional, and through everyday taken-for-granted relations and state practices.

**Cultural competence** The endeavour, typically by service providers (police, courts, health care providers, social workers, teachers, etc.) to acquire knowledge about, or better understand Indigenous peoples' customs cultures and languages (Cannon, forthcoming). Under a current regime of cultural competence, settler populations are not expected to know about, transform, and/or remedy systemic inequities, to realize and nuance their own complicity and responsibility within hierarchies of settler colonial power, or reconcile a process of identity making that is rooted in the perception of Indigenous inferiority and settler superiority (ibid.). "Cultural competence" can be understood as a settler re-enactment of lands appropriation, entitlement, and futurity (ibid.), where the objective is to learn as much as possible about Indigenous peoples leading to "a superficial reading of differences that makes power relations invisible" (Jeffery and Nelson, 2009: 98; also see Razack, 1998).

**Cultural fundamentalism** St Denis (2004: 36) suggests that "cultural revitalization and restoration" has achieved "fundamentalist status" in having become "the primary goal of those involved in promoting Aboriginal education." Cultural fundamentalism, St Denis (ibid.) writes: "encourages Aboriginal people to assert their authenticity and to accept cultural nationalism and cultural pride as solutions to systemic inequality; ironically, this helps keep racial domination intact."

**Cultural revitalization** A movement in education and/or policy that "calls for the celebration, affirmation, and revitalization of Indian cultures and peoples" (St Denis, 2004: 35). St Denis outlines the way in which an "adherence to cultural revitalization encourages the valorization of cultural authenticity and cultural purity among aboriginal people [helping] to produce the notion and the structure of a cultural hierarchy" (ibid., 37).

**Cultural Safety** Originally "a concept used to express an approach to healthcare that recognizes the contemporary conditions of Aboriginal people which result from their post-contact history" (Brascoupé and Waters, Chapter 27, this volume; see also Polascheck, 1998). Examples of these conditions include social determinants of health such as poverty, poor water quality, stress, and identity-related issues. Culturally safe services delivery requires the participation of non-Indigenous peoples in terms of knowing about, interrogating, and actively dismantling negative health indicators and outcomes, including histories of racism, settler colonialism, and a Settler entitlement to lands.

**Cultural sensitivity** An approach to remedying and/or undertaking services delivery that creates a Self/Other binary where Indigenous peoples are thought there to be helped, tolerated, if not better understood and culturally managed as different and deficit instead of calling on service providers to question their own entitlement to lands and belonging, the meaning of culturally safe services provision, and to work in activist ways to improve disparate and negative social and economic conditions.

**Culturalism** A concept frequently employed in the context of social life and services delivery "to represent the attribution of minority groups' cultural backgrounds characteristic—including behaviours, traditions, problems, barriers—to their cultural backgrounds" (Jeffery and Nelson, 2009: 92). Jeffery and Nelson (ibid.) define culturalism as "a particular form of essentialism whereby the so-called essential characteristics of a group are attributed to the groups' cultural characteristics, performances and forms of knowledge." As Nelson (2009: 27) writes, culturalism typically "provides ways for professionals to engage with racial difference that do not require a systematic rethinking of institutionalized racism."

**Dead Indians** The "stereotypes and clichés that North America has conjured up out of experience and out of its collective imaginings and fears" that are intent on disappearing both "Live" and "Legal" Indians (Thomas King, 2012: 53).

**Decolonization** A process of struggle whereby colonized nations and peoples reject colonial authority and (re)establish freedom, recognized self-determining governing systems, and self-determined existence on their territories.

**Dehumanization** A process through which a person or group of people is rendered as less than human. Dehumanization is often the first step in legitimizing and systemizing violence against particular bodies. Dehumanization can be a singular individual act, but in the case of Canadian colonialism there is a political, social, legal, and institutional system of dehumanization.

**Democratic racism** "[A]n ideology in which two conflicting set of values are made congruent with each other. Commitments to democratic principles such as justice, equality, and fairness conflict but coexist with attitudes and behaviours that include negative feelings about minority groups, differential treatment, and discrimination against them" (Henry and Tator, 2006: 22).

**Dispossession** "[T]he forcible and relentless ... theft of [Indigenous] territories, and the implementation of legislation and policies designed to effect their total disappearance as peoples ..." (Lawrence, 2002: 23–4).

**Enculturation** The process through which an individual learns and is taught cultural competency.

**Eurocentric models** A reference to Eurocentric bias, which is a view that takes the West/Europe as the normative or universal standard for measuring, understanding, and describing the world.

**Eurocentrism** A product of "Europe's ascent to global dominance, the imperatives of commercial expansionism are advanced in language proclaiming that the outcome of history is inevitable, even as it frequently ascribes to very local and specific historical circumstances and unwarranted authority derive from false claims of universality" (Hall, 2003: 71).

**Feeling citizenship** In the context of membership to her Mohawk nation, Audra Simpson (Chapter 14, this volume) distinguishes "feeling citizenship" from alternative conceptions of identity that rooted in and stem from laws established by the state. Feeling citizenship refers to "an affective sense of being Mohawk of Kanawà:ke, in spite of the lack of recognition that some might unjustly experience" (ibid.).

**Fourth World** A term that is used to refer to some 350 million Indigenous peoples in the world, and also to the "unifying nature of Indigenous action in the struggles against colonialism throughout the world" (Alfred and Corntassel, 2005: 610).

**Fractured identity** Refers to identity outcomes effected by trans-racial adoption and/or the expectations placed on Indigenous peoples to think of their identities and experience in dichotomous, "either/or" terms.

**Gdoo-naaganinaa** A precolonial treaty known as "Our Dish" between Nishnaabeg and Haudenosaunee Confederacies; a symbol and protocol of diplomatic, ecological, and sovereign relationships (Simpson, 2008).

**Gender discrimination** This term refers broadly to the systematized inequitable treatment of a person or group of persons based on gender. Gender discrimination was systematized and institutionalized in the *Indian Act* through years of "blatant sex discrimination toward Aboriginal women under section 12(1)(b)" (Cannon, 2007: 35).

**Gendered colonial violence** Violence against Indigenous women must be understood through an intersectional analysis of gender, race, sexuality, and colonialism. "In a nation founded on the suffering and violent oppression of Indigenous peoples generally and the targeting of Indigenous women specifically, it is not surprisingly that racist and sexist beliefs coalesce and harden, which continues to encourage the persecution of our women and to justify a lack of response or concern" (Lavell-Harvard and Grant, 2016: 5).

**Gendered violence** Any act of violence directed at a woman due to her gender that can result in physical, sexual, or psychological harm or suffering (United Nations, 1993).

**Genocide** Genocide refers to the physical or cultural erasure/elimination/extermination of a people by another group of people. Andrea Smith (2006: 68) writes that "[The logic of genocide] holds that indigenous people must disappear. In fact, they must always be disappearing in order to allow non-indigenous peoples rightful claim over this land."

**Healing and wellness** Wellness refers to the "interconnectivity and relational supports, which enable each person to live a good life, following and applying [Indigenous] laws. ... When there is an imbalance in a person's life, healing is required" (Tagalik, 2015: 30). Million (2013: 105) suggests that healing is a "prerequisite to [Indigenous] self-determination" requiring colonial reparations and social-structural transformation. She writes furthermore: "The space of our medicalized diagnosis as victims of trauma is not a site wherein self-determination is practiced or defined ... The site and projects that define and manage our trauma must be seen in light of biopower, and what it produces ... In order to heal what is imagined as past aggression must be reconciled; this view pictures the state as presently humane and benefic" (ibid., 150, 156).

**Heteronormativity** A concept defined as "the notion that heterosexuality is the only 'natural' orientation" (Schick, 2004: 249).

**Historic/modern treaties** Lawrence (Chapter 3, this volume) distinguishes between historic and modern treaties. The former are agreements between Indigenous nations and the Crown entered into during the eighteenth century wherein "the question of title has never been addressed." The latter "otherwise known as land claims agreements, are negotiated through the comprehensive claims policy which came into existence in 1973 as a result of the *Calder* decision."

**Historical trauma** The "cumulative wounds inflicted on First Nations people over their lifetime and across generations, and which often resulted in debilitating social, psychological, and physical conditions" (Valaskakis, Dion Stout, and Guimond, 2009: 4).

**Homelessness** A reference to individuals that live on the street, stay in emergency shelters, or who have otherwise unsafe or unstable housing. Homelessness often affects "those who have suffered from the effects of colonization and whose social, economic, and political conditions have placed them in a disadvantaged position" (Baskin, 2007: 32).

**Idle No More** An ongoing movement that started in 2012 by four women, as a response to Bill C-45 of the Conservative federal government. It united Indigenous and non-Indigenous groups worldwide to bring awareness to the systemic injustices suffered by Indigenous nations of Canada.

**Imperialism** The domination of another land and people through economic and political control established by violent or coercive force. Edward Said writes: "(n)either imperialism nor colonialism is a simple act of accumulation and acquisition. Both are supported and perhaps even impelled by impressive ideological formations that include notions that certain territories and people *require* and beseech domination" (1994: 9).

**Indian** The label "Indian" has been an external descriptor, meaningless to the Indigenous peoples of the Americas prior to colonization. As a common identity, it was imposed on Indigenous populations when Settler governments in North America usurped the right to define Indigenous citizenship, reducing the members of hundreds of extremely different nations, ethnicities, and language to a common raced identity as "Indian" (Lawrence, 2002: 23).

**Indian Act** Defined by Henry, Tator, Mattis, and Rees (1998: 130) as "the legislation that has intruded on the lives and cultures of status Indians more than any other law. Though amended repeatedly, the act's fundamental provisions have scarcely changed. They give the state powers that range from defining how one is born or naturalized into 'Indian' status to administering the estate of an Aboriginal person after death . . . the act [sic] gave Parliament control over Indian political structures, landholding patterns, and resource and economic development. It covered almost every important aspect of the daily lives of Aboriginal peoples on reserve. The overall effect was to subject Aboriginal people to the almost unfettered rule of federal bureaucrats. The act [sic] imposed non-Aboriginal forms on traditional governance, land-holding practices, and cultural practices."

**Indigenous knowledge** Indigenous knowledge includes systems of thought, ways of being, ways of knowing, and ways of thinking that are held and developed by Indigenous nations and peoples. There is not one Indigenous knowledge system, but often, Indigenous systems of knowledge hold key similarities rooted philosophical ideas and understandings about humanity and the world.

**Indigenous nationhood** A constructed sense of community that predates Settler colonialism. Indigenous nationhood contains a shared language, culture, territory, and principles of kinship relations and political organization (Sunseri, 2011: 36–43).

**Indigenous sustainable self-determination** Refers to "both an individual and community-driven process where evolving indigenous livelihood, food security, community governance, relationships to homelands and the natural world, and ceremonial life can be practiced today" (Corntassel and Bryce, Chapter 24, this volume).

**Indigenous-Settler relations** Refers in general to the relationships (historic and contemporary, present and absent) held between Settler and Indigenous populations, including white Settlers, and sometimes, "appellants facing a political order that is already constituted" (Veracini, 2010: 3) or those described by Wallia (2013: 126, emphasis in original) as: "Indigenous to their own lands, but often displaced due to Orientalist crusading and corporate plundering . . . thrown into capitalism's pool of labor and, in a cruel twist, violently inserted into the political economy of genocide: *stolen labor on stolen land.*"

**Institutional racism** "[R]acial discrimination that derives from individuals carrying out the dictates of others who are prejudiced or of a prejudiced society" (Henry and Tator, 2006: 352).

**Institutionalized patriarchy** Refers to "male dominance in personal, political, cultural, and social life, and to patriarchal families where the law of the father prevails" (Code, 2000: 378).

**Intergenerational impacts** Refers to the present-day trauma experienced by individuals whose parents, grandparents, or ancestors attended residential schools (Ing, 2006: 157).

**Involuntary enfranchisement** A process through which Indigenous peoples lose *Indian Act* status through involuntary activities. Involuntary enfranchisement continues today for the grand-children of women who married non-Indians before 1985 because, unlike the grand-children of men, they do not choose do become non-Indians under section 6(2) of the *Indian Act* (Cannon, 2007: 39).

**Kinship** Refers in general to the means through which people become linked together socially, whether through the mother's line (as with matrilineal societies), the father's line (as with patrilineal societies), clan-based systems of social organization structured by matrilineal or patrilineal descent; and sometimes, through the division of labour in society itself.

**Land-based cultural practices** Refers to Indigenous practices of self-determination which (re) establish "longstanding, reciprocal relationships with the natural world, as well as by transmitting knowledge and everyday cultural practices to future generations" (Corntassel and Bryce, Chapter 24, this volume).

**Legal assimilation** Legal assimilation is the word that is used to describe the act of losing legal status of *Indian Act* status in Canada (Cannon, 2007: 38).

**Matrilocal/matrilineal societies** Refers to kinship organization and residence patterns organized through the female line of descent. Women in the vast majority of matrilineal and matrilocal societies hold economic and political power unknown in patriarchal societies.

**Matrimonial real property** Refers to "the house or land that a couple occupies or benefits from while they are married or living in a common-law relationship" (Bastien, 2008: 90). Until only recently, "provincial laws regarding matrimonial real property have generally been found not to be applicable on First Nation lands through a number of Supreme Court decisions" (Anishinabek Nation, 2007: 4).

**Meaningful participation** "Meaningful participation and equitable treatment are pre-conditions to holding a sincere respect for any system, particularly a system of justice. . . . By meaningful participation we suggest that aboriginal people must be encouraged to participate in the system by defining the meaning, institutions and standards of justice in their own communities. Also, all peoples must be partners in developing a criminal justice system outside Aboriginal communities that can and does reflect Aboriginal cultures" (Monture-Okanee and Turpel, 1992: 249).

**Métis** A Nation or People with specific roots and histories rooted in kinship-based forms of nationalism, peoplehood, and precolonial relationships in Canada (Andersen, 2014: 91)

**Multiculturalism** Defined by Henry and Tator (2006: 351) as "an ideology that holds that racial, cultural, religious, and linguistic diversity is an integral, beneficial, and necessary part of Canadian society and identity. It is an official policy operating in various social institutions and levels of government, including the federal government." As Porter (1999: 158) suggests, multiculturalism would have us believe that Indigenous peoples ought to be represented and/or dealt with as a component of ethnic diversity—as racialized groups—but never as sovereign Indigenous nations. As a model of education, multiculturalism "is centered on unifying all peoples in the nation-state" (Grande, 2004: 47). Within this model of education, there is very little room to call attention to matters of lands appropriation and dispossession, a truly decolonizing education, or to centre a conversation about Indigenous nationhood and futurity (Cannon, forthcoming). The effect is also to create the impression that Indigenous peoples are "of culture not mind" (Cote-Meek, 2010).

**Nationhood/citizenship/membership** Audra Simpson (2014: 27) defines nationhood as "both a traditional and contemporary form of political organization . . . Nationhood is a construct . . . that is a cultural and political "right" and a "good", and a matter of principle rather than procedure." Furthermore, Simpson distinguishes between citizenship and membership to an Indigenous nation, in particular her Mohawk nation. Membership is an institutional and legal recognition to an Indigenous nation by enlistment to a band. Citizenship is "socially and politically recognized in the everyday life of the community" (Simpson, Chapter 14, this volume).

**Nation-building** The process of building and maintaining a nation. It can refer to Indigenous nation-building processes following from colonialism, or to the process of colonial nation-building. According to Lawrence (2002), nation-building is central to the maintenance of Settler colonialism. As mythology, it refers to the way in which "Canada maintains its posture of being 'innocent' of racism and genocide" (ibid., 26).

**Native Economic Development** A revitalization of Aboriginal communities in which Aboriginal peoples regain control over their lives, territories, and resources (Voyageur and Calliou, 2003).

**Ogichidaakwe (i.e., Holy Woman)** Leanne Betasamosake Simpson refers to Chief Theresa Spence as Ogicidaakwe—"a holy woman, a woman that would do anything for her family and community, the one that goes over and make things happen, a warrior, a leader" (Simpson, Chapter 23, this volume).

**Peoplehood** A term referring to Indigenous peoples who find their origins and ethnogenesis not in histories of racialization, but in a distinct constellation of land-based, historical, and pre-colonial relationships. Andersen (Chapter 6, this volume) describes a peoplehood way of thinking about identity, nationhood, and events at once tied to and embodied in the land. He writes of Métis peoplehood: "I'm Métis because I belong (and claim allegiance) to a set of Métis memories, territories, and leaders who challenged and continue to challenge colonial authorities' unitary claims to land and society" (2011: 165).

**Politics of recognition** A liberal pluralist rights-based strategy premised on Canadian state's recognition of self-determination that does not reflect inherent Indigenous rights and responsibilities to their homelands, or Indigenous cultural practices (Coulthard, 2014).

**Racial profiling** Racial profiling "occurs when law enforcement or security officials, consciously or unconsciously, subject individuals at any location to heightened scrutiny based solely or in part on race, ethnicity, Aboriginality, place of origin, ancestry, or religion or on stereotypes associated with any of these factors rather than objectively reasonable grounds to suspect that the individual is implicated in criminal activity" (Tanovich, 2006: 13)

**Racialization** The process by which people are formed into a racial category, and through which racism is justified by representations of these groups. "Sociologists refer to this process, whereby a heterogeneous, linguistically diverse population is singled out for different (and often unequal) treatment in Canada, as racialization" (Li, 1990: 7).

**Racism** "[T]he assumptions, attitudes, beliefs, and behaviours of individuals as well as the institutional policies, process, and practices that flow from those understandings" (Henry and Tator, 2006: 5).

**Reconciliation** Defined in the Canadian context by Coulthard (2014) as threefold: (1) "the diversity of individual or collective practices that Indigenous people undertake to re-establish a positive "relation to self" in situations where this relation has been damaged or distorted by some form of symbolic or structural violence" (ibid., 106–7); (2) "the act of restoring estranged or damaged social and political relationships" (ibid., 107), and (3) "rendering *consistent* Indigenous assertions of nationhood with the state's unilateral assertion of sovereignty over Native people's lands and populations" (ibid., *emphasis added*).

**Relationality** A term referring in general to the exchanges taking place historically and at present between Settler–Indigenous and Indigenous–Indigenous populations that relinquishes an exclusively judicial or colonial-based policy way of thinking about these relationships (Andersen, Chapter 6, this volume)

**Representation** The way in which a person, place, or thing is commonly represented by another.

**Residential schooling** A colonial system of schooling enforced on Indigenous nations aimed at effecting cultural genocide and assimilation on children, many of whom were forcibly removed and abducted from their families and communities. The residential school experience is characterized by forced removal from families; systemic and ritualized physical and sexual assault; spiritual, psychological, and emotional abuse; and malnutrition, inhumane living conditions, death, and murder.

**Restitution** Refers to "the return of Indigenous lands and resources and power to determine their uses" (Joseph, 2008: 212). As Joseph (ibid., 218) writes: "Restitution assumes the continuing co-existence of the harmed and the perpetrator of the harm, although with an altered balance of power. Restitution involves the restoration of what was taken to right the imbalance caused by injustice."

**Resurgence** "Regeneration of power gives us the strength to continue to fight; restoring connection to each other gives us the social support that is crucial to human fulfillment; reconnection to our own memory roots us in a culture; and reconnection to spirit gives us a strong and whole mind. These are the elements of resurgence" (Alfred, 2005: 256).

**Romanticism** The representation of noble, innocent, and idealized "Indians." Often romantic colonial images have "Indians" disappearing through their innocence.

**Royal Commission on Aboriginal Peoples** (RCAP) "The Royal Commission on Aboriginal Peoples was the largest and most expensive public inquiry under-taken in Canadian history. . . . The commission interviewed Aboriginal from across the country . . . as with most inquiries, the RCAP Report . . . condensed hundreds upon hundreds of interviews and [was condensed] into five converted volumes . . . [wherein] the more radical Aboriginal views [e.g., assertions of sovereignty] were marginalized in favour of more moderate ones" (Andersen and Denis, 2003: 379).

**Self-determination** The right of all peoples to determine their own destiny. "International and human rights norms contained in many instruments to which Canada is a signatory clearly provide for the protection of group rights and also underscore the right of all peoples to self-determination. Self-determination means that peoples must determine their own destiny" (Monture-Okanee and Turpel, 1992: 255).

**Self-government** Self-government is based on an *a priori* concept of governance as defined through Canadian federal policy and the Department of Indian and Northern Development. It is often understood to stand in lesser and inferior relation to self-determination, which refers in general to an inherent set of rights given to Indigenous peoples by the Creator.

**Sequential literacy** Refers to the ability to read, understand, and write a sequential phonetic script of written letters. European languages are written in this manner (see Battiste, 1986).

**Settler violence** A specific form of violence, often genocidal in nature, that occurs in ongoing colonial contexts. It refers to the systemized ideological, political, social, symbolic, spiritual, military, and state violence enacted with impunity by Settlers on Indigenous nations and individuals.

**Sexual violence** Violence that is of a sexual or sexualized nature. It can include "individual" acts of violence as well as systemic forms of violence enacted through political, state, and social institutions, practices, and policies. As Andrea Smith (2005: 8) writes, "sexual violence is not simply a tool of patriarchy but also a tool of colonialism and racism."

**Silenced history** Histories that are silenced in official records and in the dominant telling of history. Silenced histories are those histories that are marginalized and erased through various power systems that control the production and dissemination of knowledge. Bonita Lawrence insists that "in order for Canada to have a viable national identity, the histories of Indigenous nations, in all their diversity and longevity, must be erased. Furthermore, in order to maintain Canadians' self-image as a fundamentally 'decent' people innocent of any wrong-doing, the historical record of how land was acquired—the forcible and relentless dispossession of Indigenous peoples, the theft of their territories, and the implementation of legislation and policies designed to effect their total disappearance as peoples—must also be erased" (Lawrence, 2002: 23).

**Sisters in Spirit** A research initiative conducted by the Native Women's Association of Canada on the case of the Missing and Murdered Indigenous Women of Canada.

**Social Cohesion** Refers to "a common citizenship in a collective political project" (Green, Chapter 17, this volume). As Green (ibid.) argues, in Canada, racism limits the possibility of achieving the said project.

**Social determinants of health** Environmental factors linked to Settler colonialism such as poverty, unemployment, educational and housing disparities, unclean water, and nutritional concerns, which all have a profound effect on health (Brascoupé and Waters, 2009: 17).

**Squaw Drudge/Indian Princess binary** A binary classification finding its roots in the patriarchal Victorian virgin/whore dichotomy. Colonial imperatives—fuelled by racist ideology—intensified the binary racializing the sexuality of Aboriginal women.

**Starlight Tours** The "practice of [police] taking Indigenous people out of town and leaving them, sometimes to freeze to death. This practice is also used against non-Native homeless people" (Green, 2007: 507).

**Status and non-status Indians** Individuals of Indigenous heritage are categorized as either status or non-status Indians in a process that is commonly understood as federal recognition. As Lawrence (2012) states: "in Canada, historically, there is only one means of recognition of Indianness—to be registered as a status Indian within the meaning of the Indian Act" (2012: 8). Furthermore, "*Individuals* are non-status for a variety of reasons. Either their ancestors once held Indian status but lost it due to certain regulations under the Indian Act, or they never acquired it because their ancestors for various reasons were left off the list of band members developed by Indian agents" (ibid.).

**Stereotype** Representations created by a dominant group to typecast and classify the "Other." These stereotypical representations, whether "positive" or "negative," are used to justify objectification, control, and oppression by the dominant group (for example, "Native people are lazy"). This hyper-disseminated stereotype works to justify the systematic impoverishment of Indigenous nations by blaming Indigenous people for the economic conditions created by the colonizer.

**Structural determinants** Factors that arise from or are affected by social and political structures (e.g., colonization, Eurocentrism).

**Structural racism** "[I]nequalities rooted in the system-wide operation of a society that exclude[s] substantial numbers of members of particular groups from significant participation in major social institutions" (Henry and Tator, 2006: 352).

**Symbolic literacy** Refers to the ability to read, understand, and write a system of language that uses symbols rather than sequential phonetic scripts (see Battiste, 1986).

**Systemic injustice** A context whereby injustice is systematized and institutionalized for a group of people. In the case of Canada, a colonial white Settler state, Monture-Okanee and Turpel indicate that "the overall perspective of an Aboriginal person toward Canadian legal institutions is one of being surrounded by injustice without knowing where justice lies" (1992: 250).

**Systemic racism** While racism is often equated with abhorrent individual prejudice or ignorance, systemic racism is a form of power that controls power relations between dominant and oppressed racial groups. In the case of Canadian colonialism, the manufacturing of the racial group "Indian," occurred alongside the creation of racist political, social, and economic systems used to maintain white Settler dominance and the control of lands.

**The Other** The theoretical term used to refer to the creation of an us/them binary, where normality is understood in the "us" and the abnormality, sub-humanity, or inferiority is understood as belonging to "them"—the Other.

**Transracial Native adoption** The adoption of Indigenous children into non-Indigenous families. Shandra Spears (2003: 81–2) writes: "[T]he removal of entire generations of Native children from our communities and families is a genocidal blow to our Nations, and we feel that violence in our bones."

**Treaty** An agreement made between international actors, between sovereign and self-determining Indigenous Nations, that becomes a *sui generis* part of international law (Henderson, 2002).

**Two-spirited** A pan-Indigenous term that identifies Indigenous people who do not fit into Western binaries of sex, gender, and/or sexuality.

**Ukwehuwé** In the Onyota'a:ka language (Oneida, People of the Standing Stone) a word used to refer to "original people"; the "first people" or "real people" (also see Hill, 2017: 290).

**Unknown and unstated paternity** The current Indigenous Affairs and Northern Development Canada's policy in regard to eligibility to Indian Status, whereby the Registrar of Indigenous Affairs denies Indian Status registration to those who lack a father's signature on their birth certificate (Gehl, 2013).

**Urbanity/Indigeneity binarism** The tendency to view Indigenous peoples as either urban- or reserve-based and, in binary fashion, the imaging of both spheres as separate and distinct, with "reservation Indians depicted as the 'real' Natives and urban Indians depicted as hopelessly assimilated and alienated from their cultures" (Smith, 2008: 204; also see Ramirez, 2007).

**White Settler society** A white Settler society is one that is established through processes of colonialism and genocide effected by Europeans on non-European soil (Razack, 2002: 2–3). "Settler states in the Americas are founded on, and maintained through, policies of direct extermination, displacement, or assimilation" (Lawrence and Dua, 2005: 123).

# Bibliography

Aboriginal Women's Action Network. 2007. *Statement Opposing Legalized Prostitution and Total Decriminalization of Prostitution* . 6 December.

Acoose, Janice. 1995. *Iskwewak-Kah'Ki Yaw Ni Wahkomakanak: Neither Indian Princesses nor Easy Squaws.* Toronto: Women's Press.

Alfred, Taiaiake (Gerald). 2005. *Wasáse: Indigenous Pathways of Action and Freedom.* Peterborough: Broadview Press.

———. 1999. *Peace, Power, Righteousness: An Indigenous Manifesto.* Toronto: Oxford University Press.

———. 1995. *Heeding the Voices of Our Ancestors: Kahnawake Mohawk Politics and the Rise of Native Nationalism.* Toronto: Oxford University Press.

Alfred, Taiaiake, and Jeff Corntassel. 2005. "Being Indigenous: Resurgences Against Contemporary Colonialism," *Government and Opposition* 40 (4): 597–614.

Ahmed, Sara. 2005. "The Politics of Bad Feeling," *Australian Critical Race and Whiteness Studies Association Journal* 1: 72–85.

Amadahy, Zainab. 2008. "Listen, Take Direction and Stick Around: A Roundtable on Relationship-Building in Indigenous Solidarity Work," *Briarpatch* June/July: 24–9.

Amadahy, Zainab, and Bonita Lawrence. 2009. "Indigenous Peoples and Black People in Canada: Settlers or Allies?" pp. 105–36 in Arlo Kempf, ed., *Breaching the Colonial Contract: Anti-Colonialism in the US and Canada.* New York: Springer.

Amnesty International. 2014. *Violence against Indigenous Women and Girls in Canada: A Summary of Amnesty International's Concerns and Call to Action.* Available at www.amnesty.ca

Andersen, Chris. 2011. "'I'm Métis, What's Your Excuse?': On the Optics and the Ethics of Misrecognition of Métis in Canada," *Aboriginal Policy Studies* 1 (2): 161–5.

Andersen, Chris. 2014. *Métis: Race, Recognition, and the Struggle for Indigenous Peoplehood.* Vancouver: UBC Press.

Andersen, Chris, and Claude Denis. 2003. "Urban Native Communities and the Nation: Before and After the Royal Commission on Aboriginal Peoples," *Canadian Review of Sociology and Anthropology* 40 (4): 373–90.

Anderson, Kim. 2000. *A Recognition of Being: Reconstructing Native Womanhood.* Toronto: Second Story Press.

Anishinabek Nation. 2007. *Matrimonial Real Property Regional Consultations.* March.

APTN News. 2016. "During suicide debate Justice Minister says it's time for First Nations to shed Indian Act 'shackles'," *APTN News*, 13 April. Available at http://aptn.ca/news/2016/04/13/during-first-nation-suicide-debate-justice-minister-says-its-time-for-first-nations-to-shed-indian-act-shackles/

Association of Canadian Deans of Education. 2010. *Accord on Indigenous Education.* Association of Canadian Deans of Education. Available at http://www.csse-scee.ca/docs/acde/acde_accord_indigenousresearch_en.pdf

Baskin, Cyndy. 2007. "Aboriginal Youth Talk about Structural Determinants as the Cause of Their Homelessness," *First Peoples Child & Family Review* 3 (3): 31–42.

Bastien, Elizabeth. 2008. "Matrimonial Real Property Solutions," *Canadian Woman Studies* 26 (3 & 4): 90–3.

Battiste, Marie. 1986. "Micmac Literacy and Cognitive Assimilation," pp. 23–44 in Jean Barman, Yvonne Hébert, and Don McCaskill, eds, *Indian Education in Canada: Volume 1: The Legacy.* Vancouver: UBC Press.

Blackstock, Cindy. 2007. "Residential Schools: Did They Really Close or Just Morph into Child Welfare?" *Indigenous Law Journal* 6 (1): 71–8.

———. 2008. "Reconciliation Means Not Saying Sorry Twice: Lessons from Child Welfare in Canada," pp. 163–75 in Marlene Brant Castellano, Linda Archibald, and Mike DeGagné, eds, *From Truth to Reconciliation: Transforming the Legacy of Residential Schools.* Ottawa: Aboriginal Healing Foundation.

Blaney, Fay. 2003. "Aboriginal Women's Action Network," pp. 156–70 in Kim Anderson and Bonita Lawrence, eds., *Strong Women Stories: Native Vision and Community Survival.* Toronto: Sumach Press.

Borrows, John. 1997. "Wampum at Niagara: The Royal Proclamation, Canadian Legal History, and Self-Government," pp. 155–72 in Michael Asch, ed., *Aboriginal and Treaty Rights in Canada: Essays on Law, Equality, and Respect for Difference.* Vancouver: UBC Press.

Bourgeois, Robyn. 2015. "Colonial Exploitation: The Canadian State and the Trafficking of Indigenous Women and Girls in Canada," *UCLA Law Review* 62 (6): 1426–63.

Brascoupé, Simon, and Catherine Waters. 2009. "Cultural Safety: Exploring the Applicability of the Concept of Cultural Safety to Aboriginal Health and Community Wellness," *International Journal of Indigenous Health* 5 (2): 6–41.

Browne, Annette J., and Jo-Ann Fiske. 2001. "First Nations Women's Encounters with Main Stream Health Care Services," *Western Journal of Nursing Research* 23 (2): 126–47.

Canada. 2010. *Gender Equity in Indian Registration Act.* Ottawa: Public Works and Government Services Canada.

Cannon, Martin J. forthcoming. *(Re-)storying Indigenous Masculinity and Indian Act Patriarchy: An Interlocking Approach.* Vancouver: University of British Columbia Press.

———. 2014. "Race Matters: Sexism, Indigenous Sovereignty, and McIvor," *Canadian Journal of Women and the Law* 26 (1): 23–50.

———. 2012. "Changing the Subject in Teacher Education: Centering Indigenous, Diasporic, and Settler Colonial Relations," *Cultural and Pedagogical Inquiry* 4 (2): 21–37.

———. 2008. "Revisiting Histories of Gender-Based Exclusion and the New Politics of Indian Identity." A Research Paper for the National Centre for First Nations Governance.

———. 2007. "Revisiting Histories of Legal Assimilation, Racialized Injustice, and the Future of Indian Status in Canada," pp. 35–48 in Jerry White, Erik Anderson, Wendy Cornet, and Dan Beavon, eds, *Aboriginal Policy Research: Moving Forward, Making a Difference, Volume V*. Toronto: Thompson Educational Publishing.

———. 1998. "The Regulation of First Nations Sexuality," *Canadian Journal of Native Studies* 18 (1): 1–18.

———. 1995. "Demarginalizing the Intersection of 'Race' and Gender in First Nations Politics." Unpublished MA thesis, Queen's University.

Carter, Sarah. 1997. *Capturing Women: The Manipulation of Cultural Imagery in Canada's Prairie West*. McGill-Queen's University Press.

CBC News. 2016a. "First Nations leaders call for action from Justin Trudeau on Attawapiskat suicide crisis," *CBC News*, 8 May. Available at http://www.cbc.ca/news/canada/sudbury/first-nation-leaders-seek-action-1.3571709

CBC News. 2016b. "Justin Trudeau takes pointed questions from Indigenous youth," *CBC News*, 27 April. Available at http://www.cbc.ca/news/politics/justin-trudeau-indigenous-youth-pointed-questions-1.3555042

CBC News. 2016c. "Idle No More, Black Lives Matter protesters demand action on Attawapiskat suicide crisis," *CBC News*, 13 April. Available at http://www.cbc.ca/news/canada/toronto/protesters-occupy-indigenous-northern-affairs-office-1.3533662

CBC News. 2016d. "Desperation in Attawapiskat, where First Nation leaders fear for the worst," *CBC News*, 12 April. Available at http://www.cbc.ca/news/canada/sudbury/attawapiskat-suicide-emergency-going-forward-1.3531531

CBC News. 2014. "Stephen Harper's comments on missing, murdered aboriginal women show 'lack of respect'," *CBC News*, 19 December. Available at http://www.cbc.ca/news/indigenous/stephen-harper-s-comments-on-missing-murdered-aboriginal-women-show-lack-of-respect-1.2879154

Chaat Smith, Paul. 2009. *Everything You Know about Indians Is Wrong*. Minneapolis, MN: University of Minnesota Press.

Chacaby, Ma-Nee, and Mary Louisa Plummer. 2016. *A Two-Spirit Journey: The Autobiography of a Lesbian Ojibwa-Cree Elder*. Winnipeg: University of Manitoba Press.

Code, Lorraine. 2000. *Encyclopedia of Feminist Theories*. New York: Routledge.

Collins, Patricia Hill. 2003. "Toward a New Vision," pp. 331–48 in Michael S. Kimmell and Abby L. Ferber, eds, *Privilege: A Reader*. Boulder, CO: Westview Press.

Comack, Elizabeth, and Gillian Balfour. 2004. *The Power to Criminalize: Violence, Inequality and the Law*. Halifax: Fernwood Publishing.

Cornet, Wendy. 2003. "Aboriginality: Legal Foundations, Past Trends, Future Prospects," pp. 121–47 in Joseph Eliot Magnet and Dwight A. Dorey, eds, *Aboriginal Rights Litigation*. LexisNexis Butterworths.

Cote-Meek, Sheila. 2010. Exploring the Impact of Ongoing Colonial Violence on Aboriginal Students in the Postsecondary Classroom. PhD Dissertation, University of Toronto.

Coulthard, Glen Sean. 2014. *Red Skin, White Masks: Rejecting the Colonial Politics of Recognition*. Minneapolis: University of Minnesota Press.

Davis Jackson, Deborah. 2002. *Our Elders Lived It: American Indian Identity in the City*. DeKalb, IL: Northern Illinois University Press.

Deer, Sarah. 2015. *The Beginning and End of Rape: Confronting Sexual Violence in Native America*. Minneapolis: University of Minnesota Press.

Dhamoon, Rita. 2015. "A Feminist Approach to Decolonizing Anti-Racism: Rethinking Transnationalism, Intersectionality, and Settler Colonialism," *Feral Feminisms: Complicities, Connections and Struggles: Critical Transnational Feminist Analysis of Settler Colonialism* 4 (Summer): 20–37.

Dion, Susan D. 2009. *Braiding Histories: Learning from Aboriginal Peoples' Experiences and Perspectives*. Vancouver: University of British Columbia Press.

Doxtator, Deborah. 1996. "What Happened to the Iroquois Clans?: A Study of Clans in Three Nineteenth Century Rotinonhsyonni Communities." Unpublished PhD dissertation, University of Western Ontario.

Dyck, Noel. 1985. *Indigenous People and the Nation-State: Fourth World Politics in Canada, Australia and Norway*. St. John's NF: Memorial University of Newfoundland.

Eversole, Robyn, John-Andrew McNeish, and Alberto D. Cimadamore, eds. 2005. *Indigenous Peoples and Poverty: An International Perspective*. London/NY: Zed Books.

Farley, M., and J. Lynne. 2005. "Prostitution of Indigenous women: Sex Inequality and the Colonization of Canada's First Nations Women," *Fourth World Journal* 6 (1): 1–29.

Fellows, Mary Louise, and Sherene Razack. 1998. "The Race to Innocence: Confronting Hierarchical Relations among Women," *Journal of Gender, Race and Justice* 1 (2): 335–52.

Fiske, Jo-Anne, and Annette Browne. 2006. "Aboriginal Citizen, Discredited Medical Subject: Paradoxical Constructions of Subjectivity in Health Care Policies," *Policy Sciences* 39 (1): 91–111.

Fleras, Augie. 2009. "'Playing the Aboriginal Card': Race or Rights?" pp. 75–8 in Maria Wallis and Augie Fleras, eds, *The Politics of Race in Canada: Readings in Historical Perspectives, Contemporary Realities, and Future Possibilities*. Toronto: Oxford University Press.

Gehl, Lynn. 2014. *The Truth That Wampum Tells: My Debwewin on the Algonquin Land Claims Process*. Halifax: Fernwood Publishing.

Grande, Sandy. 2004. *Red Pedagogy: Native American Social and Political Thought*. New York: Rowman and Littlefield Publishers, Inc.

Green, Joyce, ed. 2007. *Making Space for Indigenous Feminism*. Halifax, NS: Fernwood Publishing/Zed Books.

———. 2006. "From *Stonechild* to Social Cohesion," *Canadian Journal of Political Science* 39 (1): 507–27.

Grossman, Zoltan. 2005. "Unlikely Alliances: Treaty Conflicts and Environmental Cooperation between Native American and Rural White Communities," *American Indian Culture and Research Journal* 29 (4): 21–43.

Haig-Brown, Celia. 2009. "Decolonizing Diaspora: Whose Traditional Land Are We On?," *Cultural and Pedagogical Inquiry* 1 (1): 4–21.

Hall, Anthony J. 2003. *The American Empire and The Fourth World: The Bowl with One Spoon*. Montreal: McGill-Queen's University Press.

Harris, Cheryl I. 1993. "Whiteness as Property," *Harvard Law Review* 106 (8): 1707–91.

Haudenosaunee Confederacy. 1983. "Statement of the Haudenosaunee Concerning the Constitutional Framework and International Position of the Haudenosaunee Confederacy," in *House of Commons Minutes of Proceedings and Evidence of the Special Committee on Indian Self-Government*, Issue # 31, Appendix 36. Ottawa: Queen's Printer.

Henderson, James (Sákéj) Youngblood. 2002. "Sui Generis and Treaty Citizenship," *Citizenship Studies* 6 (4): 415–40.

Henry, Frances, and Carol Tator. 2006. *The Colour of Democracy; Racism in Canadian Society*, 3rd edn. Toronto: Thomson Nelson Canada.

Henry, Frances, Carol Tator, Winston Mattis, and Tim Rees. 1998. *The Colour of Democracy: Racism in Canadian Society*, 2nd edn. Toronto: Thomson Nelson Canada.

Henze, Rosemary C., and Lauren Vanett. 1993. "To Walk in Two Worlds—Or More? Challenging a Common Metaphor of Native Education," *Anthropology and Education Quarterly* 24 (2): 116–34.

Hill, Susan M. 2008. "'Travelling Down the River of Life Together in Peace and Friendship Forever': Haudenosaunee Land Ethics and Treaty Arrangements as the Basis for Restructuring the Relationship with the British Crown," pp. 23–45 in Leanne Simpson ed., *Lighting the Eighth Fire: The Liberation, Resurgence, and Protection of Indigenous Nations*. Winnipeg: Arbeiter Ring Publishing.

Hill, Susan M. 2017. *The Clay We Are Made Of: Haudenosaunee Land Tenure on the Grand River*. Winnipeg: University of Manitoba Press.

Indigenous and Northern Affairs of Canada. 2016. *Full Summary of What We Heard: Final Report of the Pre-inquiry Engagement Process*. Available at www.aadnc-aandc.gc.ca

Ing, Rosalyn. 2006. "Canada's Indian Residential Schools and Their Impacts on Mothering," pp. 157–72 in D. Memee Lavell-Harvard and Jeanette Corbiere Lavell, eds, *"Until Our Hearts Are on the Ground": Aboriginal Mothering, Oppression, Resistance and Rebirth*. Toronto: Demeter Press.

Jacobs, Beverley. 2014. "There has been a war against Indigenous women since colonization: Former NWAC president," *APTN National News*, 23 September.

———. 2008. "Response to Canada's Apology to Residential School Survivors," *Canadian Woman Studies* 26 (3 & 4): 223–5.

Jay, Dru Oia. 2014. "What If Natives Stop Subsidizing Canada?" pp. 108–112 in The Kino-nda-niimi Collective, eds, *The Winter We Danced: Voices from the Past, the Future, and the Idle No More Movement*. Winnipeg: Arbeiter Ring Publishing.

Jeffery, Donna, and Jennifer J. Nelson. 2009. "The More Things Change . . . : The Endurance of 'Culturalism' in Social Work and Healthcare," pp. 91–110 in Carol Schick and James McNinch, eds, *"I Thought Pochahontas Was a Movie" Perspectives on Race/Culture Binaries in Education and Service Professions*. Regina: Canadian Plains Research Centre Press.

Johnston, Darlene M. 1986. "The Quest of the Six Nations Confederacy for Self-Determination," *University of Toronto Faculty Law Review* 44 (1): 1–32.

Joseph, Robert Andrew. 2008. "A Jade Door: Reconciliatory Justice as a Way Forward Citing New Zealand Experience," pp. 207-27 in Marlene Brant Castellano, Linda Archibald, and Mike DeGagné, eds, *From Truth to Reconciliation: Transforming the Legacy of Residential Schools*. Ottawa: Aboriginal Healing Foundation.

Kappo, Tanya. 2014. "Stephen Harper's comments on missing, murdered aboriginal women show lack of respect," *CBC News*. Available at http://www.cbc.ca/news

Kauanui, J. Kehaulani. 2008. *Hawaiian Blood: Colonialism and the Politics of Sovereignty and Indigeneity*. Durham, NC: Duke University Press.

Kebaowek First Nations. 2016. "Urgent Message to Pikwakanagan Anishinabe." Available at www.medium.com

Kelm, Mary-Ellen. 1998. *Colonizing Bodies: Aboriginal Health and Healing in British Columbia, 1900–50*. Vancouver: University of British Columbia Press.

King, Thomas. 2012. *The Inconvenient Indian: A Curious Account of Native People in North America*. Toronto: Doubleday Canada.

Kruchak, Matthew. 2016. "Saskatchewan school shooting: La Loche faces uphill battle with hope." Available at http://www.cbc.ca/news/canada/saskatoon/la-loche-saskatchewan-shooting-recovery-1.3421251

Land, Clare. 2015. *Decolonizing Solidarity: Dilemmas and Directions for Supporters of Indigenous Struggles*. New York: Zed Books.

LaRocque, Emma. 1993. "Three Conventional Approaches to Native People in Society and in Literature," in Brett Balon and Peter Resch, eds, *Survival of the Imagination: The Mary Donaldson Memorial Lectures*. Regina, SK: Coteau Books.

Lavell-Harvard, Memee, and Jennifer Brant, eds. 2016. *Forever Loved: Exposing the Hidden Crisis of Missing and Murdered Indigenous Women and Girls in Canada*. Bradford, ON: Demeter Press.

Lawrence, Bonita. 2004. *"Real" Indians and Others: Mixed-Blood Urban Native Peoples and Indigenous Nationhood*. Vancouver: UBC Press.

———. 2003. "Gender, Race, and Regulation of Native Identity in Canada and the United States: An Overview," *Hypatia* 18 (2): 3–31.

———. 2002. "Rewriting Histories of the Land: Colonization and Indigenous Resistance in Eastern Canada," in S. Razack, ed., *Race, Space, and the Law: Unmapping a White Settler Society*. Toronto: Between the Lines.

Lawrence, Bonita. 2012. *Fractured Homeland: Federal Recognition and Algonquin Identity in Ontario*. Vancouver: UBC Press.

Lawrence, Bonita, and Zainab Amadahy. 2009. "Indigenous Peoples and Black People in Canada: Settlers or Allies?" pp. 105–36 in Arlo Kempf, ed., *Breaching the Colonial Contract: Anticolonialism in the U.S. and Canada*. Netherlands: Springer.

Lawrence, Bonita, and Ena Dua. 2005. "Decolonizing Anti-racism," *Social Justice* 32 (5): 120–43.

Li, Peter. 1990. *Race and Ethnic Relations in Canada*. Toronto: Oxford University Press.

Linton, Ralph. 1940. *Acculturation in Seven American Indian Tribes*. New York: Appleton-Century.

Little Thunder, Beverly. 1997. "I Am a Lakota Womyn," pp. 203–10 in Sue-Ellen Jacobs, Wesley Thomas, Sabine Lang, eds, *Two-Spirit People: Native American Gender Identity, Sexuality, and Spirituality*. Champaign, IL: University of Illinois Press.

Lyons, Oren. 1989. "Power of the Good Mind," pp. 199–208 in Joseph Bruchac, ed., *New Voices from the Longhouse: An Anthology of Contemporary Iroquois Writing*. New York: The Greenfield Review Press.

Mackey, Eva. 2016. *Unsettled Expectations: Uncertainty, Land and Settler Decolonization*. Halifax: Fernwood Publishing.

*Macleans*. 2015. "Justin Trudeau, for the record: 'We beat fear with hope,'" *Macleans*, 20 October. Available at http://www.macleans.ca/politics/ottawa/justin-trudeau-for-the-record-we-beat-fear-with-hope/

Madden, Paula. 2009. *African Nova Scotian–Mi'kmaw Relations*. Halifax: Fernwood Publishing.

Magnet, Joseph Eliot. 2003. "Who Are the Aboriginal People of Canada?" pp. 23–92 in Joseph Eliot Magnet and Dwight A. Dorey, eds, *Aboriginal Rights Litigation*. LexisNexis Butterworths.

Martin, J. Forthcoming. "Teaching and Learning Reparative Education in Settler Colonial and Post TRC Canada" in Abigail B. Bakan, George Sefa Dei, and John P. Portelli, eds, *Social Justice Education in the 21st Century: Places, Bodies, Approaches, and Practices of Resistance*.

Martinot, Steve. 2003. *The Rule of Racialization: Class, Identity, Governance*. Philadelphia: Temple University Press.

Mihesuah, Devon A., ed. 1998. *Natives and Academics: Research and Writing about American Indians*. Lincoln, NE: University of Nebraska Press.

Million, Dian. 2013. *Therapeutic Nations: Healing in an Age of Indigenous Human Rights*. Phoenix, AZ: University of Arizona Press.

*McIvor v. Canada* (Registrar, Indian and Northern Affairs). 2007. BCSC 827.

Mitchell, Grand Chief Michael. 1989. "Akwesasne: An Unbroken Assertion of Sovereignty," pp. 105–36 in Boyce Richardson, ed., *Drum Beat: Anger and Renewal in Indian Country*. Ottawa: Summerhill Press/The Assembly of First Nations.

Montour, Martha, 1987. "Iroquois Women's Rights with Respect to Matrimonial Property on Indian Reserves," *Canadian Native Law Reporter* 4: 1–10.

Monture, Patricia. 2008. "Women's Words: Power, Identity, and Indigenous Sovereignty," *Canadian Woman Studies* 26 (3 & 4): 154–9.

———. 1999. *Journeying Forward: Dreaming First Nations Independence*. Halifax, NS: Fernwood Publishing.

———. 1995. *Thunder in My Soul: A Mohawk Woman Speaks*. Halifax, NS: Fernwood Publishing.

Monture-Okanee, Patricia, and Mary Ellen Turpel. 1992. "Aboriginal Peoples and Canadian Criminal Law: Rethinking Justice," *University of British Columbia Law Review* (Special Edition) 26: 239–77.

Native Women's Association of Canada. 2015. *Fact Sheet: Violence Against Aboriginal Women*. Available at www.nwac.ca/wp-content/uploads/2015/Fact_Sheet_Violence_Against_Aboriginal_Women.pdf

Nelson, Jennifer J. 2009. "Lost in Translation: Anti-racism and the Perils of Knowledge," pp. 15-32 in Carol Schick and James McNinch, eds, *"I Thought Pocahontas Was A Movie" Perspectives on Race/Culture Binaries in Education and Service Professions*. Regina: Canadian Plains Research Centre Press.

Palmater, Pamela D. 2011. *Beyond Blood: Rethinking Indigenous Identity*. Saskatoon: Purich Publishing.

Pasternak, Shiri. 2014. "Occupy(ed) Canada: The Political Economy of Indigenous Dispossession," pp. 44–51 in The Kino-nda-niimi Collective, eds, *The Winter We Danced: Voices from the Past, the Future, and the Idle No More Movement*. Winnipeg: Arbeiter Ring Publishing.

Pasternak, Shiri. 2017. *Grounded Authority: The Algonquins of Barriere Lake Against the State*. Minneapolis MN: University of Minnesota Press.

Phung, Malissa. 2011. "Are People of Colour Settlers Too?" pp. 291-8 in Ashok Mathur, Jonathan Dewar, and Mike DeGagné, eds, *Cultivating Canada: Reconciliation through the Lens of Cultural Diversity*. Ottawa: Aboriginal Healing Foundation Research Series.

Polaschek, N.R. 1998. "Cultural Safety: A New Concept in Nursing People of Different Ethnicities," *Journal of Advanced Nursing* 27 (3): 452–7.

Porter, Robert B. 1999. "The Demise of the Ongwehoweh and the Rise of the Native Americans: Redressing the Genocidal Act of Forcing American Citizenship upon Indigenous Peoples," *Harvard Black Letter Law Journal* 15: 107–83.

Posluns, M. 2007. *Speaking with Authority: The Emergence of the Vocabulary of First Nations' Self-Government*. New York: Routledge.

Provincial Court of Manitoba. 12 December 2014. *In the Provincial Court of Manitoba in the Matter of The Fatalities Inquiries Act and in the matter of Brian Lloyd Sinclair, Deceased*.

*R. v. Kapp*. 2008. SCC 41.

Ramirez, Renya. 2007. *Native Hubs: Culture, Community, and Belonging in Silicon Valley and Beyond.* Durham, NC: Duke University Press.

Razack, Sherene H. 1998. *Looking White People in the Eye: Gender, Race, and Culture in Courtrooms and Classrooms.* Toronto: University of Toronto Press.

Razack, Sherene H. 2015. *Dying from Improvement: Inquests and Inquiries into Indigenous Deaths in Custody.* Toronto: University of Toronto Press.

——. 2002. "Gendered Racial Violence and Spatialized Justice: The Murder of Pamela George," pp. 121–56 in Sherene H. Razack, ed., *Race, Space and the Law: Unmapping a White Settler Society.* Toronto: Between the Lines Press.

——., ed. 2002. *Race, Space and the Law: Unmapping a White Settler Society.* Toronto: Between the Lines Press.

Rich, Adrienne. 2003. "Compulsory Heterosexuality and Lesbian Existence," in Henry Abelove, Michele Aina Barale, and David Halperin, eds, *The Lesbian and Gay Studies Reader.* New York: Routledge.

Said, Edward W. 1994. *Culture and Imperialism*, 1st Vintage Books edn. New York: Vintage Books.

——. 1979. *Orientalism.* New York: Vintage Books.

Schick, Carol. 2004. "Disrupting Binaries of Self and Other: Anti-Homophobic Pedagogies for Student Teachers," pp. 243–54 in James McNinch and Mary Cronin, eds, *I Could Not Speak My Heart: Education and Social Justice For Gay and Lesbian Youth.* Regina, SK: Canadian Plains Research Centre/University of Regina.

Schick, Carol, and Verna St Denis. 2005. "Troubling National Discourses in Anti-racist Curricular Planning," *Canadian Journal of Education* 28 (3): 295–317.

Saul, John Ralston. 2008. *A Fair Country: Telling Truths about Canada.* Toronto: Penguin Canada.

Sehdev, Robinder Kaur. 2011. "People of Colour in Treaty," pp. 264–74 in Ashok Mathur, Jonathan Dewar, and Mike DeGagné, eds, *Cultivating Canada: Reconciliation through the Lens of Cultural Diversity.* Ottawa: Aboriginal Healing Foundation Research Series.

Sharma, Nandita, and Cynthia Wright. 2008–9. "Decolonizing Resistance, Challenging Colonial States," *Social Justice* 35 (3): 120–38.

Silman, Janet. 1987. *Enough Is Enough: Aboriginal Women Speak Out.* Toronto: Women's Press.

Silver, Jim, Parvin Ghorayshi, Joan Hay, and Darlene Klyne. 2006. "Sharing, Community, and Decolonization: Urban Aboriginal Community Development," pp. 133–173 in Parvin Ghorayshi, Peter Gorzan, Joan Hay, Cyril Keeper, Darlene Klyne, Michael MacKenzie, Jim Silver, and Freeman Simard, eds, *In Their Own Voices: Building Urban Aboriginal Communities.* Halifax: Fernwood Publishing.

Simon, Roger. 2013. "Towards a Hopeful Practice of Worrying: The Problematics of Listening and the Educative Responsibilities of Canada's Truth and Reconciliation Commission," pp. 129–42 in Pauline Wakeham and Jennifer Henderson, eds, *Reconciling Canada: Critical Perspectives on the Culture of Redress.* Toronto: University of Toronto Press.

Simpson, Audra. 2014. *Mohawk Interruptus: Political Life Across the Borders of Settler States.* Durham, NC: Duke University Press.

——. 2008. "Subjects of Sovereignty: Indigeneity, the Revenue Rule, and Juridics of Failed Consent," *Law and Contemporary Problems* 71: 191–216.

——. 1998. "The Empire Laughs Back: Tradition, Power, and Play in the Work of Shelley Niro and Ryan Rice," pp. 48–54 in Doris I. Stambrau, Alexandra V. Roth, and Sylvia S. Kasprycki, eds, *IroquoisArt: Visual Expressions of Contemporary Native American Artists.* Altenstadt, DE: European Review of Native American Studies.

Sinclair, Murray. 2009. "Truth and Reconciliation: They Came for the Children." University of Toronto, Faculty of Law, 11 December.

Smith, Andrea. 2008. *Native Americans and the Christian Right: The Gendered Politics of Unlikely Alliances.* Durham, NC: Duke University Press.

——. 2006. "Heteropatriarchy and the Three Pillars of White Supremacy," pp. 66–73 in *Color of Violence: The Incite! Anthology. Incite!: Women of Color against Violence.* Cambridge, MA: South End Press.

——. 2005. *Conquest: Sexual Violence and American Indian Genocide.* Cambridge, MA: South End Press.

Smith, Joanna. 2015. "Canada will implement UN Declaration on Rights of Indigenous Peoples, Carolyn Bennett says," *Toronto Star.* Available at http:// https://www.thestar.com/news/canada/2015/11/12/canada-will-implement-un-declaration-on-rights-of-indigenous-peoples-carolyn-bennett-says.html

Sorenson, John. 2003. "Indians Shouldn't Have Any Special Rights," in Judith C. Blackwell, Murray E. G. Smith, and John Sorenson, eds, *Culture of Prejudice: Arguments in Critical Social Science.* Peterborough, ON: Broadview Press.

Spears, Shandra. 2003. "Strong Spirit, Fractured Identity: An Ojibway Adoptee's Journey to Wholeness," pp. 81–94 in Kim Anderson and Bonita Lawrence, eds, *Strong Women Stories: Native Vision and Community Survival.* Toronto: Sumach Press.

Statistics Canada. 2011. *Aboriginal Peoples in Canada: First Nations People, Metis and Inuit (National Household Survey).* Statistics Canada. Available at https://www12.statcan.gc.ca/nhs-enm/2011/as-sa/99-011-x/99-011-x2011001-eng.cfm

St Denis, Verna. 2004. "Real Indians: Cultural Revitalization and Fundamentalism in Aboriginal Education," pp. 35–47 in Carol Schick, JoAnn Jaffe, and Aisla M. Watkinson, eds, *Contesting Fundamentalisms.* Halifax, NS: Fernwood Publishing.

St Denis, Verna, and Carol Schick. 2003. "What Makes Anti-racist Pedagogy in Teacher Education Difficult? Three Popular Ideological Assumptions," *The Alberta Journal of Educational Research* 49 (1): 55–69.

Steckley, John. 2003. *Aboriginal Voices and the Politics of Representation in Canadian Introductory Sociology Textbooks.* Toronto: Canadian Scholars Press.

Stevenson, Winona. 1999. "Colonialism and First Nations Women in Canada," pp. 49–80 in Enakshi Dua and Angela Robertson, eds, *Scratching the Surface: Canadian Anti-racist Feminist Thought*. Toronto: Women's Press.

Sunseri, Lina. 2011. *Being Again of One Mind: Oneida Women and the Struggle for Decolonization*. Vancouver: UBC Press.

———. 2005. "Indigenous Voice Matters: Claiming Our Space through Decolonising Research," *Junctures* 9: 93–106.

———. 2000. "Moving Beyond the Feminism versus the Nationalism Dichotomy: An Anti-colonial Feminist Perspective on Aboriginal Liberation Struggles," *Canadian Woman Studies* 20 (2): 143–8.

Supreme Court of Canada. 14 April 2016. *Daniels v. Canada (Indian Affairs and Northern Development)*. Supreme Court of Canada. Available at https://scc-csc.lexum.com/scc-csc/scc-csc/en/item/15858/index.do

Tagalik, Shirley. 2015. "Inuit Knowledge Systems, Elders, and Determinants of Health," pp. 25–32 in Margo Greenwood, Sarah de Leeuw, Nicole Marie Lindsay, and Charlotte Readings, eds, *Determinants of Indigenous Peoples' Health in Canada: Beyond the Social*. Toronto: Canadian Scholars' Press Inc.

Tanovich, David M. 2006. *The Colour of Justice: Policing Race in Canada*. Toronto: Irwin Law.

The Kino-nda-niimi Collective, eds. 2014. *The Winter We Danced: Voices from the Past, the Future, and the Idle No More Movement*. Winnipeg: Arbeiter Ring Publishing.

Thobani, Sunera. 2007. *Exalted Subjects: Studies in the Making of Race and Nation in Canada*. Toronto: University of Toronto Press.

Tobias, John L. 1983. "Protection, Civilization, Assimilation: An Outline History of Canada's Indian Policy," pp. 39–55 in Ian A.L. Getty and Antoine S. Lussier, eds, *As Long as the Sun Shines and Water Flows: A Reader in Canadian Native Studies*. Vancouver: UBC Press.

Truth and Reconciliation Commission of Canada. 2015. *Honouring the Truth, Reconciling for the Future: Summary of the Final Report of the Truth and Reconciliation Commission of Canada*.

Turner, Dale. 2006. *This Is Not a Peace Pipe: Towards a Critical Indigenous Philosophy*. Toronto: University of Toronto Press.

United Nations. 2007. *United Nations Declaration on the Rights of Indigenous Peoples*. Available at http://www.un.org/esa/socdev/unpfi/en/declaration.html

———.1993. *United Nations Declaration on the Elimination of Violence against Women*. Available at http://www.un.org/documents/ga/res/48/a48r104.htm

Valaskakis, Gail Guthrie, Madeleine Dion Stout, and Eric Guimond, eds. 2009. *Restoring the Balance: First Nations Women, Community, and Culture*. Winnipeg: University of Manitoba Press.

van Dijk, Teun A. 1993. *Elite Discourse and Racism*. New York: Sage Publications.

Varanine, Lorenzo. 2010. *Settler Colonialism: A Theoretical Overview*. New York: Palgrave Macmillan.

Venne, Sharon Helen. 1981. *Indian Acts and Amendments 1868–1975: An Indexed Collection*. Saskatoon, SK: University of Saskatchewan, Native Law Centre.

Voyageur, Cora, and Brian Calliou. 2003. "Aboriginal Economic Development and the Struggle for Self-Government," pp. 121–44 in Les Samuelson and Wayne Anthony, eds, *Power and Resistance: Critical Thinking about Canadian Social Issues*, Third Edition. Halifax: Fernwood Publishing.

Wallia, Harsha. 2013. *Undoing Border Imperialism*. Oakland, CA: AK Press and the Institute for Anarchist Studies.

———. 2012. "Decolonizing Together: Moving Beyond a Politics of Solidarity toward a Practice of Decolonization," *Briarpatch* Jan/Feb: 27–30.

Wallis, Maria, and Augie Fleras, eds. 2009. *The Politics of Race in Canada: Readings in Historical Perspectives, Contemporary Realities, and Future Possibilities*. Toronto: Oxford University Press.

Weis, L., A. Proweller, and C. Centrie. 1997. "Re-Examining 'A Moment in History': Loss of Privilege inside White Working-Class Masculinity in the 1990s," pp. 210–28 in M. Fine, L. Weis, L.C. Powell, and L.M. Wong, eds, *Off White: Readings on Race, Power, and Society*. New York: Routledge.

Wente, Margaret. 2008. "What Dick Pound said was really dumb—and also true," *The Globe and Mail* 25 October: A21.

———. 2005. "Crisis in Kashechewan," *The Globe and Mail* 28 October: A1.

Williams, Paul, and Curtis Nelson. 1995. *Kaswantha*. Ottawa: Royal Commission on Aboriginal Peoples [paper no. 88a].

Wolfe, Patrick. 2006. "Settler Colonialism and the Elimination of the Native," *Journal of Genocide Research* 8 (4): 387–409.

Wotherspoon, Terry L., and Vic Satzewich. 1993. *First Nations: Race, Class and Gender Relations*. Toronto: Nelson.